A COMPANI
THE CLASSICAL TRADITION

M000202571

BLACKWELL COMPANIONS TO THE ANCIENT WORLD

This series provides sophisticated and authoritative overviews of periods of ancient history, genres of classical literature, and the most important themes in ancient culture. Each volume comprises between twenty-five and forty concise essays written by individual scholars within their area of specialization. The essays are written in a clear, provocative, and lively manner, designed for an international audience of scholars, students, and general readers.

A COMPANION TO THE CLASSICAL TRADITION

Edited by

Craig W. Kallendorf

Advisory Editors

Ward Briggs

Julia Gaisser

Charles Martindale

A John Wiley & Sons, Ltd., Publication

This paperback edition first published 2010
© 2010 Blackwell Publishing Ltd

Edition history: Blackwell Publishing Ltd (hardback, 2007)

Blackwell Publishing was acquired by John Wiley & Sons in February 2007. Blackwell's publishing program
has been merged with Wiley's global Scientific, Technical, and Medical business to form Wiley-Blackwell.

Registered Office
John Wiley & Sons Ltd, The Atrium, Southern Gate, Chichester, West Sussex, PO19 8SQ,
United Kingdom

Editorial Offices
350 Main Street, Malden, MA 02148-5020, USA
9600 Garsington Road, Oxford, OX4 2DQ, UK
The Atrium, Southern Gate, Chichester, West Sussex, PO19 8SQ, UK

For details of our global editorial offices, for customer services, and for information about how to apply for
permission to reuse the copyright material in this book please see our website at www.wiley.com/wiley-
blackwell.

The right of Craig W. Kallendorf to be identified as the author of the editorial material in this work has been
asserted in accordance with the UK Copyright, Designs and Patents Act 1988.

All rights reserved. No part of this publication may be reproduced, stored in a retrieval system, or
transmitted, in any form or by any means, electronic, mechanical, photocopying, recording or otherwise,
except as permitted by the UK Copyright, Designs and Patents Act 1988, without the prior permission of
the publisher.

Wiley also publishes its books in a variety of electronic formats. Some content that appears in print may not
be available in electronic books.

Designations used by companies to distinguish their products are often claimed as trademarks. All brand
names and product names used in this book are trade names, service marks, trademarks or registered
trademarks of their respective owners. The publisher is not associated with any product or vendor
mentioned in this book. This publication is designed to provide accurate and authoritative information in
regard to the subject matter covered. It is sold on the understanding that the publisher is not engaged in
rendering professional services. If professional advice or other expert assistance is required, the services of a
competent professional should be sought.

Library of Congress Cataloging-in-Publication Data

A Companion to the Classical tradition / edited by Craig W. Kallendorf.
    p. cm. — (Blackwell companions to the ancient world)
   Includes bibliographical references and index.
    ISBN: 978-1-4051-2294-8 (hardcover : alk. paper) ISBN: 978-1-4443-3416-6 (pbk.: alk. paper)
1. Classical philology—study and teaching—History. 2. Civilization, Classical—Study and
teaching—History. 3. Classical education—History. I. Kallendorf, Craig.
Pa51.C66 2007
480.071— dc22

                                            2006016369

A catalogue record for this book is available from the British Library.

Set in 10/12.5pt Galliard by SPi Publisher Services, Pondicherry, India.
Printed in Singapore

1   2010

Contents

Figures

Maps

Notes on Contributors

Jerzy Axer, Professor Ordinarius at Warsaw University, is founder and director of the Centre for Studies on the Classical Tradition in Poland and East-Central Europe. His interests include classical and Neo-Latin studies, the texts of historical sources (sixteenth–nineteenth centuries), and theatrical studies; his main research focuses on the reception of the classical tradition in Polish and European culture (sixteenth–twentieth centuries). His publications include *M. T. Ciceronis oratio pro Q. Roscio Comoedo* (Leipzig, 1976), *Filolog w teatrze* (Warsaw, 1991), *Españoles y polacos en la corte de Carlos V* (Madrid, 1994, with A. Fontán), and *Łacina jako język elit* (*Latin as the Language of the Elites*), as co-author and editor (Warsaw, 2004).

Alastair J. L. Blanshard is Lecturer at the University of Sydney, Australia. He has published a number of articles in the fields of gender, sexuality, and the classical tradition. He is the author of *Hercules: A Heroic Life* (London, 2005) and is one of the founders of the Australasian Classical Reception Studies Network (ACRSN).

Ward Briggs is Carolina Distinguished Professor of Classics and Louise Fry Scudder Professor of Humanities at the University of South Carolina. He has published widely on the history of American classical scholarship and is at work on a biography of the American classicist Basil L. Gildersleeve.

William J. Dominik is Professor of Classics at the University of Otago, New Zealand. He is the author or editor of a number of books, including (with Jon Hall) *The Blackwell Companion to Roman Rhetoric* (Oxford, 2006), and is a contributor to *The Blackwell Companion to Ancient Epic* (Oxford, 2005). He has also published numerous chapters and articles on Roman literature and other topics and is the founding editor of the journal *Scholia*.

Katie Fleming is Lecturer in the School of English and Drama, Queen Mary College, University of London. Her research interests lie in the classical tradition, particularly in the intellectual and political thought of the twentieth century. She has published articles on the relationship between the politics of reception and the feminist appropriation of Antigone, and the use and abuse of the past.

Philip Ford studied French and Latin at King's College, Cambridge, before embarking on a PhD there on the neo-Latin poetry of George Buchanan under the supervision of Ian McFarlane. After a research fellowship at Girton College, Cambridge, his first teaching post, at the University of Aberdeen, was in seventeenth-century French literature. Since 1982, he has taught in the Cambridge University French Department, where he is now Professor of French and Neo-Latin Literature, as well as holding a fellowship at Clare College. His research, funded for two years by a British Academy Research Readership, is on the reception of Homer in Renaissance France.

Karl Galinsky is Floyd Cailloux Centennial Professor of Classics and University Distinguished Teaching Professor at the University of Texas at Austin. He is the author of numerous books and articles and has received awards both for his research and teaching.

Bruce Graver is Professor of English at Providence College. He edited Wordsworth's *Translations of Chaucer and Virgil* for the Cornell Wordsworth series (1998), and coedited *Lyrical Ballads: An Electronic Scholarly Edition* for Cambridge University Press at Romantic Circles (www.rc.umd.edu/editions/LB/). He has published numerous articles on Romantic classicism and the history of classical scholarship in the late eighteenth and early nineteenth centuries.

Lorna Hardwick teaches in the department of Classical Studies at the Open University, UK, where she is Professor of Classical Studies and Director of the Reception of Classical Texts Research Project (www2.open.ac.uk/Classical Studies/GreekPlays). Recent publications include *Translating Words, Translating Cultures* (London, 2000) and *New Surveys in the Classics: Reception Studies* (Oxford, 2003). She is working on a monograph analyzing the relationship between modern classical receptions and cultural change.

Kenneth Haynes teaches in the Department of Comparative Literature at Brown University. His most recent books are *English Literature and Ancient Languages* (Oxford, 2003) and *The Oxford History of Literary Translation in English*, vol. 4: *1790–1900* (Oxford, 2005), which he coedited with Peter France. He is preparing an annotated translation of selected philosophical works by Johann Georg Hamann, to appear in the Cambridge Texts in the History of Philosophy.

Richard Jenkyns is Professor of the Classical Tradition at the University of Oxford; he has been a Fellow of Lady Margaret Hall since 1981 and was previously a Fellow of All Souls. His books are *The Victorians and Ancient Greece* (Cambridge, Mass., 1980), *Three Classical Poets* (Cambridge, Mass., 1982), *Dignity and Decadence: Victorian Art and the Classical Inheritance* (Cambridge, Mass., 1991), *Classical Epic: Homer and Virgil* (London, 1992), *The Legacy of Rome*, as editor (Oxford, 1992), *Virgil's Experience* (Oxford, 1998), *Westminster Abbey* (Cambridge, Mass., 2004), and *A Fine Brush on Ivory: An Appreciation of Jane Austen* (Oxford, 2004).

Craig W. Kallendorf is Professor of Classics and English at Texas A&M University. A specialist in the reception of the Roman poet Virgil, his books include *Virgil and the Myth of Venice: Books and Readers in Renaissance Italy* (Oxford, 1999), *Humanist Educational Treatises*, as editor and translator (Cambridge, Mass., 2002), and *The Other Virgil: Pessimistic Readings of the Aeneid in Early Modern Culture* (Oxford, 2007). He is working on a bibliography of the early printed editions of Virgil.

Thomas Kaminski teaches in the English Department at Loyola University in Chicago. He is the author of *The Early Career of Samuel Johnson* (New York, 1987) as well as of a number of articles on the development of English neoclassicism.

Andrew Laird is Professor of Classical Literature in the Department of Classics and Ancient History at the University of Warwick. He has held visiting positions at Princeton University, the University of Cincinnati, and the Institute for Research in the Humanities at the University of Wisconsin. His publications include *Powers of Expression, Expressions of Power* (Oxford, 1999), *A Companion to the Prologue of Apuleius' Metamorphoses* (Oxford, 2001), *Ancient Literary Criticism* (Oxford, 2006), and *The Epic of America: An Introduction to Rafael Landívar and the Rusticatio Mexicana* (London, 2006).

Gail Levin is Distinguished Professor of Art History, American Studies, and Women's Studies at Baruch College and the Graduate Center of the City University of New York. She is the author of numerous books and articles, including *Edward Hopper: A Catalogue Raisonné* (New York, 1995), *Edward Hopper: An Intimate Biography* (New York, 1995), *Aaron Copland's America* (New York, 2000), and *Becoming Judy Chicago: A Biography* (in press). Her writing has often been translated and has been published in more than a dozen countries. Her scholarship has been supported by grants from Fulbright, National Endowment for the

Humanities, Andrew Mellon Foundation, American Council of Learned Societies, Pollock-Krasner/Stony Brook Foundation, Harvard University, Yale University, and Brandeis University, among others.

Luisa López Grigera was born in La Coruña, Spain, and studied at the Universidad Nacional de Buenos Aires and at the Universidad Complutense in Madrid, where she received her doctorate in romance philology. Catedrática at the Universidad de Deusto (Bilbao, Spain) and Professor at the University of Michigan, she specializes in Spanish literature of the Middle Ages and of the Golden Age, with a particular interest in the evolution of rhetoric in the fifteenth through seventeenth centuries. She has published many books and articles in these areas.

David Marsh studied classics and comparative literature at Yale and Harvard, and is Professor of Italian at Rutgers, The State University of New Jersey. He is the author of *The Quattrocento Dialogue: Classical Tradition and Humanist Innovation* (Cambridge, Mass., 1980) and *Lucian and the Latins: Humor and Humanism in the Early Renaissance* (Ann Arbor, Mich., 1998). He has translated Leon Battista Alberti's *Dinner Pieces* (Binghamton, N.Y., 1987), Giambattista Vico's *New Science* (London, 1999), and Paolo Zellini's *Brief History of Infinity* (London, 2004). His recent editions of humanist Latin texts include Francesco Petrarca's *Invectives* (Cambridge, Mass., 2003) and the anthology *Renaissance Fables: Aesopic Prose by Leon Battista Alberti, Bartolomeo Scala, Leonardo da Vinci, and Bernardino Baldi* (Tempe, Ariz., 2004).

Charles Martindale, Professor of Latin at the University of Bristol, has written extensively on the reception of classical poetry. In addition to the theoretical study *Redeeming the Text: Latin Poetry and the Hermeneutics of Reception* (Cambridge, 1993), he has edited or coedited collections on the receptions of Virgil, Horace, and Ovid, as well as *Shakespeare and the Classics* (Cambridge, 2004). His most recent book is *Latin Poetry and the Judgement of Taste: An Essay in Aesthetics* (Oxford, 2005).

Volker Riedel studied Latin and German at the Humboldt University in Berlin and was Professor of Classical Philology (Latin) at the Friedrich Schiller University from 1987 to 2009. A specialist in classical reception, Roman literature of the first centuries BC and AD, and German literature of the eighteenth and twentieth centuries, he is the author of many publications in these areas and has recently edited *Prinzipat und Kultur im 1. und 2. Jahrhundert* (Bonn, 1995), *Der Neue Pauly* (coeditor, 18 vols., Stuttgart and Weimar, 1996–2003), and *Die Freiheit und die Künste* (Stendal, 2001).

Ingrid D. Rowland is Visiting Professor of Architecture at the University of Notre Dame in Rome. Her most recent books include *The Ecstatic Journey: Athanasius Kircher in Baroque Rome* (Chicago, 2000), *The Correspondence of Agostino Chigi (1466–1520) in Cod. Chigi R.V.c.* (Vatican City, 2001), *The Scarith of Scornello: A Tale of Renaissance Forgery* (Chicago, 2004), and *From Heaven to Arcadia: The Sacred and the Profane in the Renaissance* (New York, 2005).

Minna Skafte Jensen was Assistant Professor of Greek and Latin, Copenhagen University, from 1969 until 1993 and Professor of Greek and Latin, University of Southern Denmark, from 1993 until 2003. A member of the Danish, Norwegian, and Belgian Academies of Sciences and Letters, she is the author of *The Homeric Question and the Oral-Formulaic*

Theory (Copenhagen 1980) and the editor of *A History of Nordic Neo-Latin Literature* (Odense 1995). *Friendship and Poetry: Studies in Danish Neo-Latin Literature*, ed. M. Pade, K. Skovgaard-Petersen, & P. Zeeberg (Copenhagen, 2004), was prepared in her honor.

Fabio Stok teaches Latin literature at the University of Rome, Tor Vergata. He has published extensively on classical Latin authors (e.g., Cicero, Virgil, Ovid) and their reception. He specializes in particular in textual criticism and in ancient medicine, ethnography, and the biographies of Virgil (he has published the critical editions of the *Vita Vergili* of Suetonius-Donatus and of other medieval and Renaissance lives). Professor Stok is also one of the editors of Niccolò Perotti's *Cornu copiae* (8 vols., Sassoferrato, 1989–2001), and he is working at present on several other humanist and neo-Latin authors.

Christopher Stray is Honorary Research Fellow in the Department of History and Classics, Swansea University. He works on the history and sociology of classics teaching and learning, and also on the history of universities, on textbooks, and on family languages. His *Classics Transformed: Schools, Universities, and Society in England 1830–1960* was published by Oxford University Press in 1998. He is editing a collection of essays on Gilbert Murray, to be published by the same press in 2007. Other projects include an edited reprint of Charles Bristed's 1852 book *Five Years in an English University* (Exeter, 2007) and an edited selection of the letters of Richard Jebb.

Gilbert Tournoy is Professor of Classical, Medieval, and Neo-Latin and, since 1998, Director of the Seminarium Philologiae Humanisticae at the Catholic

University of Leuven. He is editor of *Humanistica Lovaniensia* and past president of the International Association for Neo-Latin Studies (1997–2000). He is the author or editor of 15 books, including two essay collections in honor of his longtime colleague Jozef IJsewijn and the catalogues to several important exhibitions on humanism in the Low Countries, especially relating to Juan Luis Vives and Justus Lipsius.

Norman Vance is Professor of English at the University of Sussex. He has published widely on Victorian and Irish topics. His books include *The Victorians and Ancient Rome* (Oxford, 1997), *Irish Literature, a Social History* (2nd edn., Oxford, 1999), and *Irish Literature since 1800* (London, 2002), and he is editing the nineteenth-century volume of the *Oxford History of Classical Reception in English Literature*. He is a Fellow of the English Association and Chair of its Higher Education Committee.

Jan M. Ziolkowski is Harvard University's Arthur Kingsley Porter Professor of Medieval Latin. His books include monographs, anthologies, editions, translations, and collected essays. Three are in press: *Fairy Tales from before Fairy Tales: The Medieval Latin Past of Wonderful Lies* (Ann Arbor, Mich.), *Nota Bene: Reading Classics* and *Writing Songs in the Early Middle Ages* (Turnhout, Belgium), and, with Michael C. J. Putnam, *The Virgilian Tradition to 1500* (New Haven). A National Merit Scholar in college, he held a Marshall in graduate school. Earlier a recipient of Guggenheim and ACLS fellowships, he was at the Netherlands Institute for Advanced Study in 2005–6.

Introduction

Craig W. Kallendorf

The chapters that follow are designed to provide a guide to the study of the impact of the classics on postclassical culture, broadly defined. Each author has been asked to make his or her chapter comprehensible to nonspecialists, from advanced under-graduates and postgraduate students to general readers and professors in other fields. The goal has been to provide as much basic information as possible in one volume along with guidance on how a reader might pursue points of interest elsewhere, but also to convey what is new and exciting about a field that is currently experiencing a real "renaissance" in scholarship and teaching.

To use this book most profitably, one should have some idea of what the classical tradition has been understood to mean. There is, of course, no one moment when antiquity can be said to have ended, and as institutions, values, and cultures moved gradually away from Greece and Rome, it took many years – centuries, actually – for people to see that they were living in a fundamentally different society. This difference was self-consciously articulated in a decisive way in the fourteenth century by Petrarch, whose polemical call for a revival of antiquity led him to define the Middle Ages as the period between ancient Greece and Rome, now seen as definitively past, and a present that could be influenced by the best that had been said and done in that past. For the next several centuries, as the chapters in this volume show, the literature, art, and social structures of antiquity were handed down to successive generations, to be transformed and absorbed into new institutions and cultures.

The idea that the classics could be "handed down" derives from the etymology of the word "tradition," which comes from the Latin *tradere*, meaning "hand down, bequeath." While this is what was understood to be happening for several centuries, however, the idea of a "classical tradition" and a phrase to describe it are actually, as Jan Ziolkowski points out, a modern notion. For many scholars, the seminal studies are the ones by Gilbert Highet (1949) and R. R. Bolgar (1954), which convey their fundamental approach in their titles (*The Classical Tradition* and *The Classical Heritage and Its Beneficiaries*, respectively) and trace in great detail this handing down of material from the past to the present. If someone wants to know which classical authors Milton knew, for example, a great deal of valuable information can still be found there. Since the 1950s, however, a good many more data have emerged. To take but one example, recent work in book history has led to the discovery of a large number of copies of Greek and Latin texts that were owned and annotated by later authors, helping us to see firsthand how they read and understood the classics. Highet knew that Montaigne had read Lucretius, but the recent discovery of his annotated copy allows us to trace Lucretius' role in the development of the *Essays* in ways that were simply not possible until now (Screech 1998).

While there have been significant changes recently in what is known about the classical heritage, the need for this *Companion to the Classical Tradition* has been driven as much, if not more by the changes in *how* we know what we know in this area. The last decades of the twentieth century saw the impact of the "theory revolution" in most areas of the humanities, and this field is no exception. As Charles Martindale shows, a key innovation derives from the development of reception theory, especially as practiced since the 1960s at the University of Constance by such critics as Hans Robert Jauss and Wolfgang Iser. To quote Martindale (ch. 20), reception "operates with a different temporality" from the passive handing down of classical material from the past to the present: it involves "the *active* participation of readers (including readers who are themselves creative artists) in a two-way process, backwards as well as forwards, in which the present and the past are in dialogue with each other." This has profound consequences for how Greece and Rome are under-stood by later ages. Traditional classical philology aims to recover the meanings that ancient texts had in their original contexts. If, however, the reader is an active participant in the making of meaning, then it will be very difficult, indeed perhaps impossible, to recover the original meaning of any text. If interpretation is not simply grounded in original meaning, the different readings of a classical text over time become not misreadings, but the only readings we have, ours being simply the last in the chain of receptions. From this perspective, the chain of receptions moves from the margins to the center, as it has been doing in the works of an increasing number of scholars over the last several decades.

The chapters that follow reflect this shift in perspective in each of the three major sections of the book. After an essay on the role of the classics in education that serves as the first essay in the volume, the next seven chapters trace the transformations of the classical tradition chronologically, from the Middle Ages to the modern period. The period labels are in many ways conventional enough, but the understanding of how classical material was handled in different times is often not. Petrarch's period-ization, for example, rests on the assumption that he could see the past as it had actually been, while those who had lived in the generations before him could not. This assumption remained unchallenged for hundreds of years, with the result that medieval classicism has been approached even by many modern scholars as narrow, primitive, and often simply wrong. By resting in the principles of reception theory, however, Jan Ziolkowski is able to show how "[m]edieval perspectives on classical texts and their contents are increasingly respected by medievalists and classicists alike, rather than being dismissed for having at best interfered with and at worst corrupted a grand legacy" (ch. 2). Another period in which the role of the classics has been thoroughly reevaluated is the romantic. As Bruce Graver shows, "Highet resisted yoking the terms 'Romantic' and 'classical,' as if to do so would be an act of violence on both words" (ch. 6). Yet even here, when the emphasis on originality, nature, and emotion has seemed to offer little reason to highlight the classics, Greece and Rome remained very much alive. Keats's classicism was different from Dryden's, but both meditated deeply on the remnants of antiquity and created great art from those meditations. What emerges from the chapters in this section is that readers of different times have appropriated different fragments of antiquity: as Kenneth Haynes puts it, the "orientation toward an ever more remote antiquity – from Hellenistic sculpture to the marbles of classical Athens to preclassical Greek figures – parallels a broad feature of the classical tradition in western Europe since the Renaissance, where in successive periods the dominant focus of attention moved from the Rome of seventeenth-century classicism to the Athens of nineteenth-century Hellenism to the preclassical Greece of the modernists" (ch. 8).

If the reader participates in shaping the understanding of antiquity, it becomes important to take into account readers on the margins of scholarship on the classical tradition as well as readers in the center. The second section does this by surveying the geographical presence of the classical heritage. The length and level of detail in the treatments of Italy (David Marsh, ch. 14) and Germany (Volker Riedel, ch. 12), for example, confirm the importance of Greece and Rome in two countries whose creative engagement with the classical past has long been known. A quick look at Highet's table of contents, however, suggests that much remained to be done when he was writing. When his book appeared it was severely taken to task for virtually ignoring Spain, an omission corrected by Luisa López Grigera's chapter (ch. 13) in this volume. Rather surprisingly for someone writing at Columbia University, Highet also gave short shrift to the United States – the impact of the classics on the Founding Fathers is limited to a two-page addendum to the discussion of the French Revolution – a picture that is filled out by Ward Briggs's chapter (ch. 19) here. Virtually nothing has been available in any western language on the classical tradition in central and eastern Europe; Jerzy Axer (ch. 10) corrects this oversight by exploring system-atically what it meant to interact with the classical past on the borders of what had been the classical world. Moving further afield, Andrew Laird's chapter on Latin America (ch. 15) and William Dominik's on Africa (ch. 9) show that the classical tradition was alive and well outside Europe and North America.

In the classics, as in other areas, scholarship has taken some novel turns since, say, the 1980s, and the chapters in the final section suggest some of the transformations of the classical tradition that have taken place even since the publication of *The Legacy of Greece: A New Appraisal* (Finley 1981) and *The Legacy of Rome: A New Appraisal* (Jenkyns 1992). Alastair Blanshard, for example, shows how our ideas of what "mas-culine" and "feminine" mean go back to antiquity (ch. 22), and Lorna Hardwick illustrates some of the ways in which the classics have continued to provide cultural capital even after countries that were colonized by Europe achieved their independence (ch. 21). Christopher Stray's chapter suggests that by all rights, classical themes should be difficult to find in contemporary art, since Greek and Latin no longer play the central role they once did in western education (ch. 1), but Gail Levin shows that, rather surprisingly, this is simply not the case (ch. 25). Indeed, as Karl Galinsky explains, the fascination with antiquity continues to inspire film and television production into the twenty-first century (ch. 26).

Each contributor was asked to write a coherent narrative on his or her subject and given the freedom initially to develop it as she or he saw fit. In the absence of a template, somewhat different approaches emerged – a quick glance at the chapters on the classical tradition in various countries, for example, shows that most are developed chronologically, but a couple unfold more thematically, while some of the period chapters give greater emphasis to belles-lettres, some to art, and some to broader social and political forces. These differences are instructive, suggesting that as a concept, the classical tradition has not always been interpreted in precisely the same way. Some overlap is theoretically possible – Lope de Vega, for example, could potentially play as great a role in a chapter on the classical tradition in the Iberian peninsula as in one on the Baroque – but in fact the chapters as the authors have developed them present relatively few cases in which the same material is treated at length in more than one place. Readers interested in where, precisely, the treatment of a particular person or subject has ended up are referred to the index.

This, then, is the classical tradition as we find it in 2007, robust, widely dispersed in time and place, and continuing to be transformed anew as it is appropriated by new generations. I would like to thank each of our contributors both for their hard work and for rearranging their schedules so that the volume could be finished on time. My student assistants, Robert Scott Garbacz and Joe Salvaggio, got more than they bargained for when they agreed to help, and I am grateful to them; the bibliography in particular is largely their work. Ward Briggs, Julia Gaisser, and Charles Martindale, the advisory board for the volume, provided invaluable assistance, helping to define the scope and nature of the project and providing expert commentary and advice on each of the chapters. Finally, I would like to thank Al Bertrand at Blackwell for asking me to do this project in the first place; Sophie Gibson, Angela Cohen, and Janey Fisher for putting up with all of us along the way; and Eldo Barkhuizen for a truly superb copy-editing job.

CHAPTER ONE

Education

Christopher Stray

Tradition! Tradition! Tradition!
Tradition! Tradition! Tradition!

Aleichem, *The Fiddler on the Roof*

1   Greek and Latin at School

Thus sings Tevye the milkman in *The Fiddler on the Roof*, the 1964 musical based on Sholem Aleichem's stories of a Jewish family in Tsarist Russia. But what is "tradition"? For the men, it means the duty of supporting a family, and in return the right to "have the final say at home"; for the women, the duty of keeping "a proper home, . . . a kosher home" and to "run the home, so Papa's free to read the holy books." The asymmetric gender division is familiar, but what may be less obvious is the assertion of fixity: this is the way (Jewish) things have been and will be. Yet as the leader of another religious communion has recently reminded us, "When people set out to prove that nothing has changed, you can normally be sure that something quite serious *has*" (Williams 2005: 4). *Traditio* is a handing on, and this is always a two-way process, since we cannot assume that learning or reception is passive, though teaching or transmission can hardly not be active (Whitfield 1971; Stray 2001: 207–11). Yet handing on can be, and often is, a highly routine, even ritualized activity, in which neither teacher/transmitter nor learner/receiver questions, or even thinks about, the process in which both are involved. To learn Latin, in many countries and periods, has been, at least for some social groups, simply the ordinary thing to do. Parents have not, under these circumstances, wondered whether this was right, or better or worse than alternatives. Alternatives simply did not occur to them.

This was often the situation within what Waquet calls the "empire" of Latin, by which she means that the language operated as a pervasive symbol of intellectual and social power (Waquet 2001). This imperial situation was gradually eroded in Europe in the eighteenth and nineteenth centuries, as challenges were mounted by the growth of new scientific knowledge and by the emergence of vernacular literatures in the nation-states that flourished especially in the nineteenth century (Gellner 1983). The universal accessibility of Latin, within delimited social circles, had made it superior to the local languages and dialects of nations and regions. Romantic nationalism, however, valorized the vernaculars, and commitment to the individual rather than the universal became a virtue rather than a vice.[1] The slow but inexorable decline of Latin as a language of scholarly communication was mirrored in the statistics of book production, where vernacular publishing can be seen to have equaled and then outstripped Latin publishing in the course of the eighteenth century (Martin 1996: 25–7).

In the following century, Latin, having lost an empire, retained a kingdom (Waquet 2001): it still possessed a powerful social cachet, but was no longer the default means of scholarly or scientific communication. A significant process of the transition from "imperial" to "royal" status was the ideology of mental discipline, renamed by twentieth-century psychologists the transfer of training (Kolesnik 1962). This presented Latin as a subject of study superior to all others, in that mastering it would facilitate the mastery of other subjects. Psychologists and teachers alike had ideological axes to grind, and the debate on transfer of training was never likely to be settled through rational discussion. In 1934, a scientifically trained British headmaster was quoted in a Latin textbook as follows: "If I were in a runaway motorcar, and the driver had to dodge a dog, put his foot on the right one of three pedals and show presence of mind in handling the steering wheel, the prayer I should put up would be: I hope this fellow has learnt Latin" (Lyne 1934: 10–11). The same witness is quoted as explaining that

> The study of the classics . . . deals with an expression of human experience which is once for all finished and unchangeable. All rules are definite, and all exceptions established in the known literature. The result is that the mind acquires both a precision and flexibility which the study of no language or science which is still in the course of development can give. (Lyne 1934: 10)

Two aspects of this defense of classics are noteworthy. First, the conception of classics as something complete and finished. The ancient world is dead: all that is left is to learn its lessons. The contrast posited here is that referred to by the nineteenth-century polymath William Whewell as that between "permanent" and "progressive" knowledge. The former included geometry, Latin, and Greek; the latter, chemistry, geology, and philology (Whewell 1838: 5–10). Whewell's point was that knowledge that changes is unsuitable as a basis for education: stability and certainty were needed in the education of youth. The second aspect to notice is that, as the reference to "rules" and "exceptions" makes clear, the writer is concerned not with "classics" but only with language – and, as his peroration shows, with Latin. The "presence of mind" he admires, the crucial link between a history of learning and its deployment in a challenging situation, is the presence of a mind that acquires certainty from grammatical rules and flexibility from "established exceptions."

This neatly formulated combination of discipline and flexibility aptly summarizes the requirements classics must meet if it is to operate as an adequate resource in making sense of human life. It needs to possess permanent and universal value so as to be proof against the corroding effects of change (the emergence of new social and cultural formations) and relativity (e.g., the challenge of other sources of meaning – natural science, vernacular languages). Yet it must be flexible enough to adapt to new circumstances and to a wide variety of cases. The conception of classics as centered on literature, and that in turn as centered on language, seen largely in grammatical terms, is curiously limited, but in some historical periods it has been very widespread. Its attraction has surely lain in the notion of rules, not exceptions: in the terms used by the source quoted above, in "precision," not "flexibility." If, however, we look beyond the kingdom of Latin, we find another area of classics that has often been seen as providing the flexibility Latin lacks: Greek. Latin's older sister glories in its flexibility, its more relaxed grammatical and syntactic structure under-cutting to some extent the Latinate opposition of rule and exceptions. With two languages in play, we are presented with a bipolar conception of classics. These twin poles have generally been seen as sources of culture (Greek) and discipline (Latin), and defenses of classics and its teaching vary according as they privilege the one or the other (Stray 1998: 8–11).

There are other ways of conceiving of classics, however, that bring with them yet more patterns of inclusion and exclusion. The contrasts discussed above center on language, and the teaching and learning of language has constituted a central thread in the classical tradition. Yet the ancients did more than speak and write in Latin and Greek: they built, traded, fought, and prayed, walked, and sailed. The tendency, dominant in the nineteenth century and persistent even in the twentieth, to refer to "the classics" as a subject of study conflated the study of the ancient world with the study of its literature. "The classics" were the ancient authors. The disappearance of the definite article has weakened this link: that it still survives, however, can be seen by the use of the phrase "classics and ancient history" in the titles of some university departments. ("The Classics" is now rarely found, though examples survive at Harvard University and the University of Illinois.)[2]

The history of the teaching and learning of classics can to some extent be told in terms of the contrasts and issues mentioned above. In classical Greece, the shared consciousness of Greekness was underpinned by the learning of the Homeric poems, despite internal political and ethnic divisions (e.g., Dorian vs. Ionian). Homer was the first European "classic," but later writers also became canonized by the scholars of Alexandria as they compared texts and annotated manuscripts. The conquests of Alexander led to the formalization of grammatical rules in the teaching of Greek to non-Greek speakers, following the analyses of the fifth-century sophists. Recent work based on papyri has extended our knowledge in this area, but the evidence is patchy and the specialists disagree on its interpretation (Morgan 1998; Cribiore 2005). It was not long before the non-Greeks learning the language included conquerors rather than conquered, and the Romans learned Greek while often despising its native speakers. The captured Greeks who taught grammar in Rome began a long tradition of such teaching, though the social status of *grammatici* later rose. Both grammar and rhetoric became central to the education of high-status Roman boys, and this continuing social imperative led to a fossilization of the pedagogic tradition under the empire (Kaster 1988; Atherton 1998).

The later career of grammar is complicated, and this is no place to trace its history through the speculative theories of the Middle Ages and the new learning of the Renaissance (Law 2003) to the flowering of comparative philology in the nineteenth century (Davies 1998). What does need to be stressed is the link between the formal structure of grammar and the discipline imposed by teachers on pupils. (As the word *disciplina* itself suggests, the pedagogic scene is the prime example of discipline: learning goes with orderliness.) An important aspect of the mental discipline / transfer of training tradition of justifying classics was the centrality of formal grammar. From the standpoint of the twenty-first century, we can see that this tradition, usually maintained as a set of unexamined assumptions, gave way in the 1960s to an antigrammar (and antidiscipline) tradition that is still similarly maintained (Mulroy 2003). The lower depths of a grammar-based teaching tradition in which continuing links between classics and social status meant the subject was both embedded and in effect uncriticizable can be glimpsed in Geoffrey Willans's stories of Nigel Molesworth (Willans and Searle 1958). Here the text and the powerfully sardonic drawings of Ronald Searle show a world where pupils do not expect Latin to make sense and teachers are often not competent to explain it: as a result, the pupils make their own, subversive sense both of what they are supposed to learn and of their own situation (Stray 1994).

The world of Molesworth is one where classics is compulsory; the corollaries are not only that many pupils cannot cope, but that the supply of adequate teachers is insufficient. The paradigms of the grammar book symbolize and underpin a peda-gogical relationship of hierarchical rule, but they also encapsulate formal rules that enable pupils to discover gaps in the teacher's knowledge. Avoidance, ambiguity, and subversion characterize both ends of the classroom. The fierce reaction against this embedded world of rote learning in the 1960s led initially to Latin courses that avoided formal grammatical labels, as in the Cambridge Schools Latin Course (Forrest 1996). In many schools, the new course presented difficulties for teachers who had been brought up to believe that classics was Latin, Latin was grammar, and grammar symbolized discipline (Stray 1998: 293–7).

This brings us back to the question of change, an inescapable and constant element of tradition, however large the image of tradition as total fixity may loom in culture and curriculum wars (Carnochan 1993). As the above example suggests, unless change in schooling is carefully managed, it can lead to confusion and, for some individuals, tragedy. The history of classical education in Europe includes long periods in which relatively stable systems of teaching and learning were established and maintained. From the Middle Ages to the seventeenth century, the persistence of Latin as a spoken language played an important part in this. Schools either encour-aged or forced pupils to converse in Latin, and this interacted with a curriculum that was dominated by Latin grammar and then literature to embed the pupil in a Latinate world of experience. He (it was mostly he) did not so much study a distant world as inhabit a modern version of it, and the mastery of the language was part of a kind of puberty rite (Ong 1959). Those boys who went on to university continued to use

Latin in oral disputations with teachers and other students, the characteristic mode of testing that was still vigorous in the eighteenth century, though in Cambridge particularly it was increasingly subordinated to written examinations (Chang 2004; Stray 2005). This world of familiar Latinity is reflected in the *Orbis sensualium pictus* (The world of experience in pictures) of Jan Comenius, an illustrated dictionary of everyday experience in Latin and German that has some claim to be the first book written for children (Comenius 1658). It begins with the teacher–pupil relationship, its first page depicting these two figures, Magister and Puer. At the end of the nineteenth century, W. H. D. Rouse, despairing of the by-then traditional rote learning of grammar in British schools, attempted to return to the world of oral Latin (and Greek) by advocating the use of a direct method of teaching. In his school, classics was taught through conversation in Latin and Greek, but the wider movement eventually failed, largely because the method demanded so much of the teacher – a mastery both of classical vocabulary and of the skills to deploy it in the classroom (Stray 1992). A similar movement in the US was led by Gonzalez Lodge of Columbia University.

Many attempts at the reform of classical teaching have failed because of the massive inertia built into systems of schooling. This is particularly the case when teachers are not professionally trained to teach, and especially when they spend their careers in a single institution. The extreme case in Britain can be seen in Eton College, the leading public (independent) school. In the nineteenth century its scholars went to King's College, Cambridge, a linked foundation, and often returned to Eton to teach. This was a closed system in which traditions of teaching were perpetuated: the Latin and Greek grammars used had been written for Eton, and change or substitution was seen as disloyal. The more general phenomenon is reflected in the comment of the lexicographer and textbook writer William Smith to his publisher John Murray in 1850: "I need not tell you of the difficulty of getting new grammars introduced into schools" (Smith 1850). The history of classical teaching is littered with examples of inspired teachers who undermined contemporary assumptions but had little influence outside their own classrooms. A few spread the word through publishing: an example is D'Arcy Thompson Sr. (1829–1902: Irwin 2004), whose *Day Dreams of a Schoolmaster* (Thompson 1864) recorded his attempts to teach classics in Edinburgh without rote learning or corporal punishment. His book was much reprinted as an inspirational guide to teachers, but significantly, without the chapters on the details of classics teaching. A good example of a successful attempt at change is the success of Mason Gray's *Latin for Today*, a course developed in the US in the 1920s which, very unusually, crossed the Atlantic to become a market leader in Britain in the following decade (Stray 1998: 278). This course attempted to provide a systematic alternative to the standard grammar/translation approach, basing itself instead on the cultivation of reading skills, grammar being learned en passant. *Latin for Today* was adapted for the British market in the 1930s by an experienced teacher, Cuthbert McEvoy. The rarity of such cross-national transfers is striking: the Latin grammars of Benjamin Kennedy (1804–89), dominant in Britain by the 1870s, never gained US editions because of differences of terminology (e.g., Kennedy used the "new" order of cases inspired by comparative philology: nom-voc-acc-gen-dat-abl [Allen and Brink 1980; Stray 1996]).

2   From University to Adulthood

So far I have been discussing classical teaching and learning in schools, but of course this is not its only site. Since the twelfth century, classics has also been taught in universities, usually, but not always, at a higher level than in schools. The prohibition on teaching Greek in schools enacted in the Scottish Book of Discipline (1560) led to its being taught at an elementary level in the universities. Talented scholars like the Cambridge classicist Richard Jebb (1841–1905) and his Oxonian successor Gilbert Murray (1866–1957), attracted to the chair of Greek at Glasgow by the high salary, found they had to teach the rudiments to classes of over a hundred, with ages ranging from 15 to 30. This is a useful reminder that the neat succession of educational stages we are used to today is a recent phenomenon. Modern educational systems are the creations of the nation-state, dating from the early nineteenth century in France and Germany, the end of that century in Britain. Education in classical Greece lacked our modern apparatus of dedicated buildings, educational stages, and common syllabuses. The ideas of "curriculum" and "class" emerged only in the sixteenth century. They can be linked to Calvinist ideas of schooling and to the *modus et ordo Parisiensis*, a system that combined the subdivision of schools into classes with individual teaching (Hamilton 1989). All these ideas came out of religious concerns for the gaining and retention of faith, and had to do with *disciplina*, a system of controlled learning.

Since its origins in Paris in the twelfth century, the university has come to be taken for granted as a part of the life of nation-states. Yet it has taken on many different forms, as has the classics that has been taught in it. In the seventeenth and eighteenth centuries, many European universities were confessional institutions in which classical learning was deeply entangled with the exposition and defense of Christian theology. The French Revolution marked a watershed, leading as it did to the destruction of some universities and the founding of others in new molds (Brockliss 1997; Anderson 2004). In some institutions, classical learning was frowned on as a symbol of the old (clerical, pre-revolutionary) order; in others it emerged under new, secular but spiritual auspices. Most notably, in the new University of Berlin the ideology of *Altertumswissenschaft*, the systematic study of the classical world as an integrated whole, promulgated by Friedrich Wolf, was enthusiastically expounded, an emphasis that spread to other German universities (Grafton 1983). The movement was based on the tenets of romantic Hellenism, and Greek was placed firmly above Latin in the linguistic pantheon. The contrast with France was striking: here, in a former Roman province, Latin was revered as the ancestor of French, and the ancient world was seen as the beginning of a continuous link, rather than as a lost world to be regained.

Within *Altertumswissenschaft* there were differences of emphasis, most famously celebrated by the disputes between Gottfried Hermann and August Boeckh and their pupils. Hermann rooted his scholarship firmly in the linguistic details of texts, while Boeckh argued for a wider vision of cultural and social history (Most 1997). What they shared was a crucial pedagogical tool, the seminar, developed originally for clerical training but now transformed into a training device for advanced work in classics. Here the professor taught his students, encouraging them to offer the results of their own research for criticism by himself and by fellow-students (Anderson 2004: 104–6). By the end of the nineteenth century, the seminar system had percolated down to the undergraduate level in both Europe and the US. It offered an alternative to the dominating monologue of the all-powerful professor, but in practice this semidivine figure often used the seminar as a source of loyal disciples. The seminar was hardly known in Britain, and its importation into Oxford in the 1930s, most notably by Eduard Fraenkel, created a culture shock of some local magnitude. Fraenkel's classical seminar, in which Oxford dignitaries were treated like any other pupils, was described as "a circle of rabbits addressed by a stoat" (Horsfall 1990: 63).

The pedagogic burrow that Fraenkel invaded was based on a long tradition of one-to-one tutorial teaching (in James Garfield's American evocation, "sitting with Mark Hopkins on a log") in which knowledge was imparted within a close personal relationship, a typical procedure being for the pupil to read out an essay on which the tutor then commented. This tradition was closely bound up with Greats (*Literae Humaniores*), the Oxford classical course founded in the nineteenth century that focused almost entirely on ancient history and on ancient and modern philosophy. The pedagogical relationship was an intimate one, and indeed Hellenism and homosexuality often went together (Dowling 1994). In Oxford, more than anywhere else, ancient culture and contemporary personal identity were fused to create a recognizable social style. In Cambridge, the central university loomed larger, the power of college tutors was curtailed, and teaching outside lectures was conducted in "supervisions" that typically lacked the more intense overtones of the Oxford tutorial. The typical classical graduate of Cambridge had lower and more circumscribed horizons than his Oxonian counterpart, his watchword being caution and thoroughness rather than a high-flying ambition (Stray 2001).

Nineteenth-century Oxford and Cambridge both offered examples of a bizarre mismatch between secondary and higher education. The schoolboys who came to Oxford after years of intense training in grammar, translation, and composition in Latin and Greek found more of the same (Honour Moderations), but then encountered Greats, for whose history and philosophy they were hardly prepared. Many scored highly in "Mods" and then collapsed to poor degrees, or failed, in Greats. In Cambridge, these schoolboys entered a university in which there was until 1824 no final examination in classics, and where that examination could until 1857 only be entered by those with high scores in the mathematical honors examination. In the first half of the century at least, almost nothing except classics was taught at the public (independent) schools. A pupil would often be introduced to Latin at age 6, and to Greek soon afterwards, at a junior school. The curriculum was dominated by repeated and repetitious learning of grammar, and this continued in the secondary school. There a few standard authors (Homer, Horace, and Vergil, usually) would be read, and read again in the following year – a practice common in antiquity (Cribiore 2001: 241). Exercises in verse composition were set, at first as "nonsense," the meter being all-important, the meaning of words disregarded. This was followed by "sense," in which meaning became a criterion. The centrality of this in some schools is illustrated by the naming of two classes at Eton: Sense and Nonsense (Clarke 1959: 74–97). The years of practice in turning Latin and Greek into English and vice versa produced large numbers of men who found it easy to tackle such tasks every day, while walking, on a train journey, in a boring committee meeting. The modern equivalents might be doodling or doing crossword puzzles, but this was in a mundane way a method of keeping in touch with the classical literature that had dominated these men's days at school and, in some cases, university. In much smaller numbers, the system produced virtuoso composers who were revered by their contemporaries; some of them produced remarkable Latin and Greek verses, while their English poetry was jejune (Silk 2005). An outstanding example was Richard Jebb's translation of Robert Browning's "Abt Vogler" into Pindaric verse – difficult English into difficult Greek (Jebb 1907: 2–15). This tradition was very different from the German, and may have contributed to the American tendency to avoid British practice in favour of the German tradition.

The image of the ambulatory (by no means pedestrian) composer reminds us that learning does not have to happen in schools or universities. Extramural learning has been made easier since the invention of printing, although the earliest books were expensive, and classical textbooks were typically owned by masters, not pupils. It was not long, however, before books were produced for autodidactic reading: the teacher and the learner were the same person. A mass reading audience in the nineteenth century was catered for by cheap books produced on newly invented steam presses, and later on stereotyping reduced the costs of printing even further. Lithography, an invention of the 1790s that spread rapidly in Europe and the Americas, enabled teachers to write short-run textbooks for their own classes. Composing on to stone or via transfer paper, they could incorporate Greek as easily as English (Stray 2002, 2006). The working-class autodidacts of the nineteenth century had a wide variety of books to choose from, including Latin lessons in instalments and classical texts with interlinear translations. Such books were the ancestors of the "Teach Yourself" series of the twentieth century. Cheap books were also accessible to school children, but this was a matter for regret, even alarm, among teachers. Cribs ("ponies," "trots") were widely available and much used, though usually forbidden, in schools. Plain texts were preferred by teachers, or, failing them, school editions with notes at the back rather than on the same page as the text. When Richard Jebb's great Sophocles edition began to appear in 1883, with its facing translation and notes in English, one critic commented that "When Professor Jebb has finished his Sophocles, we shall have to banish the plays from our schools."

The experience of teaching and learning is typically absorbed into mature adult engagement with the world, often in an entirely unconscious way; but on occasion a gifted writer observes, remembers, or imagines, and we catch a glimpse of the experience in a heightened form. Rudyard Kipling's Stalky stories are by no means a simple reflection of his time at Westward Ho! (1878–82), but they do use his memories as an armature for meditations on classics, patriotism, and imperialism, especially through the teaching and learning of Horace (Kipling 1899; Medcalf 1993; Gaisser 1994; Kenney 2006). Fifty years later, in the Caribbean colony of St. Lucia, Derek Walcott learnt Latin at school and then stayed on to teach it. The uneasy weight of the classical legacy is reflected in his poem "A Latin Primer": "the bronze dusk of imperial palms /[curling] their fronds into questions /over Latin exams." The pupil became a teacher, and "I taught Love's basic Latin /*Amo, amas, amat*...The discipline I preached /made me a hypocrite; /Their lithe black bodies, beached, /would die in dialect" (Walcott 1988: 21–4; Greenwood 2005: 81–2). The Latin primer has served other writers as an organizing focus for meditations on learning classics. In Willans and Searle's *Down with Skool*, Benjamin Kennedy is drawn by Searle as a game hunter, leading those exotic beasts the gerund and gerundive into captivity. The bars of their cages mirror the rigid lines of the tabulated pages of the primer, images of order and control. Several decades later, the poet Carol Rumens wrote "A Latin primer: for Kelsey" for her daughter, who was about to start learning Latin (Rumens 1987: 36). The course being used was the Cambridge Latin Course, set in a vividly recalled Pompeii just before the eruption of Vesuvius. Rumens begins by announcing

> Today, a new slave,
> you must fetch and carry, obeying
> plump nouns, obstreperous verbs
> whose endings vacillate
> like the moods of tyrants

but ends by hoping that her daughter will walk "the bright streets of grammar / where poets lark and sigh." If the first lines recall the exotic beasts imagined by Searle, the last lines hint at the world of Roman civilization to which Latin gives access, and the nuances of human experience (larking, sighing) that the pupil may one day be able to understand. Here Rumens had in mind the similarity of the primer's tabulations to the grid pattern of Roman towns: the reality of the pedagogic tool, and that of the historical reality to be recalled.

3   Conclusions

I began with Aleichem's Jewish milkman and his cry of "Tradition." Tevye kept in touch with his tradition by reading "the holy books." The same is true of the classical tradition, often seen as at least semisacred: the books are read and the reader is kept in touch with a pure fount of value, a precious source of guidance in a changing and challenging world. (We should remember, too, that classical and Hebrew learning have been not just parallel, but interacting formations [Grafton 1991: 214–43]). Machiavelli famously declared that he changed into "royal and curial robes" before entering his study, where he communed with the ancients by reading their texts. This is surely learning without a teacher – though Machiavelli claimed that the ancient writers "out of their humanity answer me" (Stray 1998: 72). We have already seen a variety of permutations of teaching and learning, a variety that stretches well beyond the contemporary norm of teacher and pupils in a formal educational setting. Some activities, in turn, belong to both formal and informal learning – for example, reading (Fischer 2003). The cultural genres discussed in later chapters all offer opportunities for learning about the Greeks and Romans, though in very different and sometimes curious ways. A history of Greece based on the scripts of Hollywood movies would surely need to come with editorial warnings and extensive annotation. Yet in a way, it is unfair to single out film, when it is so clear that academic writing is pervaded and indeed inspired by personal, gender, class, nationalist, and other agendas. Such agendas are an inevitable part of the study of the past, but we can also learn from each other, and from the evidence we interrogate. In that sense, the ancients may still answer us, as they did Machiavelli.

FURTHER READING

For ancient education, the classic account of Marrou (1956) has recently been joined, though not superseded, by Too (2001). For the Middle Ages and Renaissance, see Black (2001). A stimulating and in parts controversial analysis is given by Grafton and Jardine (1986). The role of Latin is explored across several centuries by Waquet (2001). For the US, a crisp analysis is given by Winterer (2002). Classical education in Britain was dealt with by Clarke (1959); a wider range of contexts is considered by Stray (1998). The pupil's eye view is explored in Stray (1994). For classics at Oxford, see the chapters by Jenkyns and Murray in Brock and Curthoys (1998–2000); for Cambridge, see Stray (2002b). A stimulating collection of essays on classical and other scholarship is Humphreys (1997).

NOTES

1 The exemplary language of this romantic particularism was Greek: as Trapp called it, "the patron saint" of the vernaculars (Trapp 1971).
2 The modern use of "classics" may date from the bureaucratization of knowledge in the new University of London examinations of the late 1830s, in which a wide range of subjects was included. "Classics" here became just one subject among many.

PART I

Periods

CHAPTER TWO

Middle Ages

Jan M. Ziolkowski

1   The Classics and the Middle Ages

The very etymology of "classics" attests to a relationship with classism and perhaps even with class struggle. Early Romans were reportedly subsumed into five classes by their sixth king, Servius Tullius (conventionally dated 578–35 BC). A citizen of the highest class qualified as *classicus*, while any of the four lower ones fell *infra classem* (approximately the same as our "below the grade"). In literary-critical terminology the adjective was also attached to authors whose style characterized them as being truly authoritative: Aulus Gellius (second century AD) sets off the *classicus adsiduus- que aliquis scriptor* (any classical or authoritative writer) against any *proletarius* writer (*Attic Nights* 19.8.15, quoting Cornelius Fronto, also second century). Finally, in scholastic parlance the noun *classis* had been used to denote a class of pupils at the latest since Quintilian (first century AD). By transference *classicus* was employed a few centuries later by Magnus Felix Ennodius (sixth century AD) to describe a pupil who belonged to a class in school (*Dictio* 9.16). Thus the ancient Romans had already laid the groundwork for the blurring between the classic as "top class" literature and the classic as a standard text in school classes that still holds true nowadays. All these usages fell into disuse during the Middle Ages, when nothing more was needed to bring home the *gravitas* (majesty) of a major writer than to describe him with the word *auctor*: in intellectual contexts, authority derived from being (or citing and quoting) an author (Ascoli 2000; Minnis and Scott 1991). "Classic" was not revived until the early sixteenth century, when it became an epithet for ancient authors that referred particularly to their high quality.

Over the past half millennium the connection with education has often been para- mount, since as applied to literary texts, classics have often earned and retained their status from having been assigned in classes. At the same time, it would be mistaken to regard the classics as inherently or solely scholastic. Many of the texts secured their places in the schools after having demonstrated qualities that had made them appealing to other reaches of society. Those other strata have comprehended not only the upper crust that had been *classicus* from the outset but also lower social ranks.

Whereas the concept of the classic has an ancient pedigree, "the classical tradition" is a modern notion (Bolgar 1954; Highet 1949). It may be linked to conservativism, not so much of an overtly political as of a cultural brand, since tradition is what is handed down from one generation to the next. Those who work with (and within) the classical tradition have had a vested interest in its continuation or reinstatement. Initially the impetus for the study of the classical tradition was to appreciate how antiquity, especially ancient texts, shaped later times, in this case the Middle Ages. Over the last quarter century the fairly rigid and constrictive dynamic of "source and influence" has been enriched and complicated as the notion of reception has achieved favor (Holub 1984). Whatever bondage was latent in the metaphor of a "chain of influence" has been sundered, and now reception studies aim not merely to track how the classics outlasted the Middle Ages so as to be renewed in the Renaissance, but rather to appreciate how medieval people responded to them and adapted them. Medieval perspectives on classical texts and their contents are increasingly respected, by medievalists and classicists alike, rather than being dismissed for having at best interfered with and at worst corrupted a grand legacy.

Today, when the word "classics" pertains to texts written in Greek and Latin, it designates with deceptive straightforwardness "the literature of ancient Greece and Rome." Understood most ecumenically, "classical literature" would bridge two languages and extend over at least a dozen centuries, from the *Iliad* and *Odyssey* ascribed to Homer, a hazy but oft-invoked figure of the eighth century BC, through the famous writings associated with fifth-century Athenians such as Plato and Thucydides, to the masterpieces of late Republican and Augustan Rome by Vergil, Horace, and others in the first century BC, and down even to Augustine and other Latin-speakers and -writers in the Empire of the fourth and fifth centuries AD. (The preceding is, of course, only a very partial roll call, making no effort to comprehend much of Greek literature and naming only a handful of authors.) A narrower definition would exclude the total of seven centuries at the early and late ends of the spectrum and would be restricted to the stretch from fifth-century Athens to late Republican and Augustan Rome.

If classical antiquity covers a long expanse, so, too, do late antiquity and the Middle Ages. According to the perspective that the Renaissance promoted, the Middle Ages commenced when antiquity faded, and they drew to a close when antiquity was reborn in the Renaissance. This perspective has the obvious effect of making the Middle Ages at least implicitly anticlassical, and it sidesteps the question of chronology. What should be done about dating? Rather than seeking dates relating to decisive military, political, economic, or religious vicissitudes that mark beginning and ending points, we may consider the combined late-antique and medieval period as diverging from the strictly classical on the one hand and the early modern and beyond on the other in its principal means for recording writing (Ullman 1963). Whereas antiquity favored the papyrus roll or scroll and modernity the printed book, the millennium from roughly four hundred to fourteen hundred AD was bound up (and the verb is meant both literally and figuratively here) with the manuscript codex, an object that bears a superficial resemblance to the printed book but that is made by hand (hence the word form "manuscript").

In the Middle Ages codexes generally consisted of parchment rather than paper or papyrus leaves. Parchment is the hide of an animal such as a calf or sheep that has been treated to render it suitable as a writing surface (Reed 1975). The durability of parchment accounts in no small part for the survival of most classical Latin texts, which would not have come down to us had they not been copied in this form first in late antiquity and then recopied in the ninth century and later in monastic scriptoria. Had transmission depended largely on papyrus, the prolonged social and cultural disruptions in the middle centuries of the first Christian millennium would have conspired with the northward thrust of the Latin Church to jeopardize the continued existence of many texts. There would not have been enough writing material, and what could be found would not have lasted long in damp climates, as opposed to the drier weather of lands surrounding the Mediterranean. Finally, as a medium the roll suffers more wear from frequent consultation than does the codex.

2   Authors and Authority

The classics in the Middle Ages may have been recorded on a different medium from what had been used before or is used today, but were they exactly contiguous with the classics now, or did such a category even exist then? If the term "classics" relates powerfully to the Middle Ages, it is because in no era have the classics (or at least a shifting subset of them) and education been bundled together more tightly (Riché 1976, 1989; Orme 1973). The paradox is that in the Middle Ages the classics were not defined as such. In fact, it may be anachronistic to impose a schema of "classical" and "nonclassical" upon the medieval period. Schoolmasters and exegetes, the medieval equivalents of modern-day literary historians, did not differentiate texts as classical and postclassical, but rather as pagan or Christian; prose, metrical, or rhythmic; and so forth.

For people in the Middle Ages, authors who are now labeled "postclassical" or at best "late antique" sometimes stood on a comparable if not equal footing with Horace, Statius, or Vergil in the frequency with which they were written out in scriptoria and in the intensity with which they were perused in the curriculum (Munk Olsen 1991). Medieval scholars found a rough parity among the different authors whose texts had already been enshrined in the curriculum for more than half a millennium. Alongside the great authors of ancient pagan Rome came writers of late antiquity, including poets and Christians, such as Prudentius (348–ca. 405), Martianus Capella (fifth century), Boethius (ca. 480–524), Priscian (ca. 500), and the poets of the so-called Bible epics, Juvencus (fourth century), Sedulius (fifth century), and Arator (sixth century); all of them were *auctores* (authors) whose words were replete with *auctoritas* (authority) (Glauche 1970).

The acceptance of pagan authors from antiquity alongside Christian authors from late antiquity by no means occurred automatically or easily. Not unexpectedly, many early Christians felt ambivalent about the amount of attention they lavished upon the classics.

Both Jerome (ca. 350–420) and Augustine (354–430) give voice famously to regrets about time squandered on pagan authors (Hagendahl 1958, 1967; MacCormack 1998b). Jerome tells (*Epistle* 22) of having dreamed that God, after calling him a Ciceronian rather than a Christian, had the saint whipped, while Augustine in the *Confessions* (1.13) rues having wasted his hours and energies on Dido in Vergil's *Aeneid*. But elsewhere the two deploy images drawn from the Bible that helped to justify retaining the pagan classics as the basis of education. Jerome, on the basis of Deuteronomy 21:11–12, envisaged pagan learning as a female slave whose services could benefit Christianity, but only after she had pared her nails and trimmed her locks (*Epistle* 21.13). Augustine justified the acquisition of pagan learning by citing the episode in Exodus 3:22 and 12:35–6, in which the Israelites plundered the gold of the Egyptians (*On Christian Doctrine* 2.40.60–1).

As Jerome's image makes apparent, for Christians to appropriate texts by pagan authors required accommodations, and these adjustments could take multifarious forms. One was to make the pagan author a Christian, even if an unwitting one. This was the effect of the nearly ubiquitous interpretation that expounded Vergil's fourth (and so-called "Messianic") Eclogue as foretelling the birth of Christ (Benko 1980). Dante Alighieri (1265–1321) maintains (*Purgatorio* 22.73) that reading this very poem (together with the *Aeneid*) by Vergil caused Statius (ca. 45–96) to be saved (Martinez 1995). But obviously it would not have been feasible to make all pagans retroactively Christian.

Another strategy entailed replacing pagan classics by reassembling their elements in forms that better suited Christian beliefs and aesthetics. Medieval churches sometimes incorporated architectural components, such as columns, from pagan temples, as reliquaries did small craft objects from antiquity, such as engraved gems, cameos, and coins. The most extreme literary parallel to such reutilization in architecture and art was the cento, a type of poetry that was constructed entirely or mainly of lines and phrases quoted from earlier poems. The main quarry for such reuse was the oeuvre of Vergil, which was centoized (to give two extreme examples) by Proba (flourished ca. 385–7), a female poet who in her *Vergilian Cento on the Praises of Christ* gave a condensed account of the life of Christ and its biblical background (Clark and Hatch 1981; Green 1995), as well as by Ausonius (ca. 310 – ca. 394), who in his narrated quite explicitly the activities of a wedding night (O'Daly 2004).

A third approach to the classics was to find veiled behind their literal surface a background of allegorical meaning. The metaphor of the veil is deliberate, since especially in the twelfth century these allegorizing interpretations sometimes touched upon long-established hermeneutic constructs like *integumentum* (covering) and *involucrum* (wrapping) (Dronke 1974). The *Aeneid* underwent such allegorization repeatedly (Jones 1986), notably at the hands of Fulgentius (mid- or late-sixth century) and Bernardus Silvestris or pseudo-Bernardus Silvestris (twelfth century), both of them predecessors of Cristoforo Landino (1424–92). Nor was Ovid's *Metamorphoses* exempted from this process, which was taken to its heights in the anonymous *Ovide moralisé* (Ovid moralized, after 1309), not only the first complete translation but also an exposition of the poem according to multiple interpretative levels, and in the *Ovidius moralizatus* (Ovid moralized), Book 15 of the *Reductorium morale* (Bringing back to the moral) of Pierre Bersuire (died 1362), also known as Petrus Berchorius (Hexter 1989). Greco-Roman myth attracted indefatigable scrutiny from mythographers, many of whom coaxed from the stories meanings that made them more consonant with Christianity – or, to be more precise, with a Neoplatonism that was itself in greater harmony with Christianity (Chance 2000).

The educational system that developed in the Middle Ages out of its ancient Roman forebear emphasized imitation of models (Ziolkowski 2001). Many medieval authors (particularly but not solely those who wrote in Latin) followed, sometimes consciously, at other times unconsciously, the vocabulary and style of ancient authors. In the ninth century, Einhard modeled his *Life of Charlemagne* (dated variously between 817 and 833) after Suetonius (Innes 1997). In the tenth, Hrotsvitha of Gandersheim (ca. 935–75) set out to supplant the comedies of Terence, with all their moral shortcomings, by creating imitations that dealt with Christian saints. In the twelfth, Aelred of Rievaulx (ca. 1110–67) wrote a dialogue *On Spiritual Friendship* that was a Christian (and even more a Cistercian) response to Cicero's *On Friendship* (Hyatte 1994).

Besides the shift from paganism to Christianity, a further factor of the utmost relevance in understanding the classical tradition in the Middle Ages is that of language (Ziolkowski 1991). Even in antiquity a command of literary Latin was a skill that had to be won through effort, with formal study being a *sine qua non*. The need for schooling only grew, since in western Europe the literate forms of Latin and the spoken ones related to it drew apart from each other decisively in late antiquity and the early Middle Ages, from the sixth through the eighth centuries. Although Latin ceased to be a mother tongue, it lived on in the Middle Ages as both the written language of record par excellence and the spoken language of religion, learning, and high culture. Its unifying force was so potent that the entire region of Latin Christendom was designated not Europe but rather *omnis Latinitas* (all Latinity; Hexter 1987). This overarching Latinity was acquired through a basic education that emphasized Latin texts, many of them ancient. These classics, whether ancient or not, were without exception read in Latin. They looked nothing like their equivalents today. For one thing, poems were packaged differently, with special introductions (known as *accessus ad auctores* [introductions to the authors]), metrical commentaries, commentaries of other sorts, and so forth (Minnis and Scott 1991). For another, lines that are now regarded as authentic were sometimes missing or arranged differently, or lines that are rejected were included (Clogan 1968).

It warrants special mention that medieval manuscripts teem with texts that were falsely attributed to classical authors (Lehmann 1927). Thus Vergil's *Aeneid* opened with verses that do not grace the pages of standard editions today. The 13 poems of the so-called *Appendix Vergiliana* were believed unreservedly to have been composed by Vergil, and occasional other poems, such as a *Conflictus veris et hiemis* (Debate of spring and winter) and a death lament for Emperor Henry III, were now and again taken to be works of Vergil as well. And the number of pseudepigrapha wrongly credited to Vergil pales beside the number eventually foisted upon Ovid. In the author-centered world of the Latin Middle Ages, there was good reason to present texts as the creations of established *auctores*.

As for the other half of the classics as they are now conceived, whatever Greek prose and poetry survived, it did so almost exclusively in Latin translations, such as the "Latin Homer" (as was known a poor Latinization of the *Iliad*) and (until the twelfth century) the bits of Aristotle that Boethius had put into Latin before his execution. Intrepid souls managed to acquire knowledge of Greek, but such individualists stand apart as having been unusual (Berschin 1988). Even when Greek texts began to be translated into Latin in greater volume in the twelfth century, often the base text for the work was an Arabic version that had already existed. Thus the earliest form of Aristotle's *Poetics* to be Latinized contains Latin versions of Arabic poetry that had been substituted earlier in its transmission for the passages of ancient Greek verse in the original. The names of a few major Greek authors were common knowledge among the educated, so that Hesiod, Pindar, and Apollonius were not forgotten, but their works were available in neither the original Greek nor Latin translation. When Dante enumerates the illustrious poets (*Inferno* 4.83 and 88–90) who for a while stride alongside Vergil and him in limbo, he names Homer, Horace, Ovid, and Lucan. Even in the case of a poet as great and as well read as Dante, such lists do not always signify that the poet had a direct acquaintance with the authors in question. A lesser writer than the poet of the *Divine Comedy* might well include in a catalogue authors whose works were familiar to him only through excerpts.

3   Shifting Canons

Even if we cast aside worries about when the classical period began and ended, and even if we exclude from consideration most Greek literature, what remains is not a static hierarchy but instead a canon of authors that shifts from time to time and place to place (Glauche 1970). Although many of the same texts would have been rated as classics by any medieval author, whether a late eighth-century or early ninth-century intellectual affiliated with Charlemagne or a twelfth-century master or student in Paris, others grew or diminished in fame. Thus Lucretius was copied amply in the Carolingian period, but afterward ceased to be copied and read. Quintilian became more familiar later in the Middle Ages. Last but not least, certain authors who have become familiar today, if not household words, were unknown or nearly so, such as Catullus and Apuleius.

To gauge the fluctuations in the relative importance of classical authors during the Middle Ages, one may consult tabulations of manuscripts with their works from the ninth, tenth, eleventh, and twelfth centuries (Munk Olsen 1991). Statistics may not lie, but they can and do mislead, since sometimes a drop in copying indicates that a text was read less often, whereas in other instances it means only that enough manuscripts from preceding centuries still circulated to meet demand; parchment is durable, and codices did not demand replacement at the pace we would expect from our experiences of printed books, especially paperbacks.

The resultant century-by-century listing lends loose support to the well-worn division of the Middle Ages into three stages, a Vergilian age (*aetas Vergiliana*) in the eighth and ninth centuries that yielded first to a Horatian age (*aetas Horatiana*) in the tenth and eleventh and subsequently to an Ovidian age (*aetas Ovidiana*) in the twelfth and thirteenth. (We owe this tripartite formulation, which continues to hold value so long as it is not exaggerated, to Ludwig Traube [1861–1907], often honored as the founder of medieval Latin philology [Hexter 1986].) In literary history, these stages would match three cultural renewals in the Middle Ages that have been singled out, not without debate and dissent, as renaissances; namely, the Carolingian, Ottonian, and Twelfth-Century Renaissances. The last-mentioned was named first and remains the most widely mentioned and studied (Haskins 1927; Benson and Constable 1982).

One of the starkest differences between printed books and manuscript codices is that whereas the former may achieve much of their power through being very similar or even identical across print runs, the latter are each individual objects, *sui generis*. A token of the prestige that medieval culture attached to manuscripts may be found in numbers. More codices are extant from the Middle Ages than are cathedrals, rose windows, suits of armor, or almost any of the other tokens that we might think would survive in particular abundance. Not all of these manuscripts are deluxe objects – far from it! Many received heavy use, which can be detected not only in the wear and tear but even more significantly (for our purposes) in the encrustation that the folios promoted or endured, as schoolmasters, students, and other readers inserted inter-linear and marginal glosses (in Latin or vernacular languages) to explain words and phrases, continuous or excerpted commentary to interpret the text (for representa-tions of such techniques transposed into modern type, see Coulson 1991), scansion marks to make evident the workings of the meter, construe marks to elucidate the sequence in which words would be ordered in the spoken language (Draak 1957), and even neumes (a form of musical notation).

To expand upon the last observation, a fascinating feature of classical manuscripts from the early Middle Ages that has been recognized only recently is how many contain neumes (Ziolkowski forthcoming b). Neumes have been located for nearly two dozen of Horace's *Odes* as well as for one section of the *Carmen saeculare* (Song of the ages or Secular hymn) and for parts of two *Epodes*; for more than a dozen passages in six books of Lucan's *Civil War* (alternatively, and less properly, known as the *Pharsalia*); for eight in seven books of Statius' *Thebaid* and one in his *Achilleid*; for four in two of Terence's comedies; and for two in two of Vergil's *Eclogues*, two in the *Georgics*, and more than two dozen in ten books of the *Aeneid*. To shift from mere numbers to statistics, it has been calculated that approximately 21 percent of all Statius manuscripts from the tenth through the twelfth century contain neumes, 15 percent of all Horace manuscripts, and between 7 and 11 percent of Lucan, Terence, and Vergil manuscripts (Riou 1991: 103). The authors whose texts are neumed, such as Statius, Vergil, Lucan, and Horace, are precisely those poets whose texts were copied most energetically in the tenth and eleventh centuries. By the twelfth century, the balance of interest tipped heavily to the advantage of Ovid, for whom no neuming has been discovered in the classical manu-scripts.

Many of the passages that received neumation were direct address and especially laments. The most arresting of these scenes soon became the topics of newly com-posed medieval Latin poems, as well as of adaptations in the vernacular languages.

The twelfth century saw in Old French the three "romances of antiquity," all linked to the court of Henry II and Eleanor of Aquitaine and all accommodating ancient pagan matter to the cultural values and social structures of their times. The anonymous *Romance of Thebes*, anonymous *Romance of Enéas*, and *Romance of Troy* by Benoît de Sainte-Maure were based on Statius' *Thebaid*, Vergil's *Aeneid*, and the late-antique prose of Dares and Dictys, respectively. They paved the way for the later Arthurian romances of Chrétien de Troyes, as well as for the equivalents to the "romances of antiquity" in other literary traditions, such as the German (or Dutch) *Eneit* by the author generally known as Heinrich von Veldeke (before 1150 – ca. 1190). Heinrich and later vernacular poets could draw upon both their Old French predecessors and Latin texts; Jacob von Maerlant (ca. 1230 – ca. 1300), a prolific Middle Dutch poet, provides avatars of such fusion in his *Deeds of Alexander* and *History of Troy*; and in English, Chaucer was only one of several poets who were also inspired by the romances as well as their Latin progenitors (Nolan 1992).

Whenever classicism has held sway for long enough, a reaction sets in. This pattern of dominance and resistance, which can be seen in the *querelle des anciens et des modernes* (quarrel of the ancients and moderns) or in Classicism and Romanticism, had at least one memorable expression in the Middle Ages, in the twelfth century (Martin 1982). The classicizers among Medieval Latin authors showed their colors most clearly in their handling of the dactylic hexameter, which in the medieval period was the classical meter par excellence (Norberg 2004). They practiced elision, a fusion of syllables required under carefully defined circumstances; avoided a break (after the first syllable of the penultimate foot in hexameters, unless it was a monosyllable); and refrained from internal and end rhyming. The opposing camp of "modern" Latin poets shunned elision, allowed a caesura to fall after the first syllable in the fifth foot, and evidenced a predilection for rhyme.

4   Learned and Popular Traditions

The sharpest antagonisms run not between classicism and its alternatives in the learned tradition, but rather between classicism in Latin and other forms in the spoken languages. The classical tradition, passed down through reading and writing and constituted by texts responding to earlier texts, stands at least implicitly in contrast to the oral tradition, transmitted from mouth to ear and back again in unending loops. Yet although the classical tradition goes together with book learning and the oral tradition with folklore, the traditions were not partitioned altogether from each other during the Middle Ages (Ziolkowski forthcoming a). Formerly the two were envisaged hierarchically, with the learned above and the popular below. According to this model, elements of the higher form sometimes seeped down to the lower, to become *gesunkenes Kulturgut* (sunken cultural materials); less often, there was talk of movement in the opposite direction, *gehobenes Kulturgut* (elevated cultural materials). Now the tendency is to acknowledge the interpenetration of folklore and learned lore, official and popular culture, and orality and literacy, and not to privilege the one over the other (Bakhtin 1968; Burke 1978; Ong 1982).

Legends proliferated around major personages and authors of classical antiquity, permeating not only Latin manuscripts but also vernacular literature and decorative arts associated with secular audiences and settings. Thus the truly popular cluster of heroes known as the Nine Worthies comprised three classical pagans, three biblical Jews, and three Christians; the first threesome was made up of Hector, Alexander the Great, and Julius Caesar (Gerritsen and van Melle 1998). Hector was one of many characters from Trojan legend who belonged to the broadest culture of the Middle Ages. So exalted was the prestige of the story that many royal and noble families traced their lineage back to the post-bellum Trojan diaspora: Britain was purportedly founded by one Brutus, the name of the Norse god Thor was alleged to have originally been Tror (from Troy), and so forth (MacDougall 1982: 7–27; Waswo 1995). Just as Rome had the Trojan-born Aeneas, so northern European nations devised Trojan originators for their own dynasties.

For all the glamor of the Trojan legend, the so-called romance of Alexander the Great (356–323 BC) seems to have seized the imagination of even more people during the Middle Ages (Cary 1956). Its accounts of his global conquests as well as his adventures among the marvelous races of the East, in space, and in the depths of the ocean stimulated treatment by artists not only in manuscript illuminations but also in mosaics, stone sculptures, woodcarvings, ivories, and tapestries.

The historical Alexander had Aristotle as his teacher. Their relationship inspired a legend that speaks volumes about the interplay between folklore and learned lore in the Middle Ages. According to the legend, Alexander became romantically involved with a beautiful young woman named Phyllis (Smith 1995). When Aristotle endeavored to have Alexander break off the liaison so that his charge could devote more time to his studies, Phyllis arranged for the philosopher to see her as she sang and performed her coiffure. Smitten, Aristotle became infatuated to the point where he agreed to allow her to ride him piggy-back.

Another exemplum that cautioned against the wiles of women, in particular against the readiness of women to exploit their sexual power by abasing learned men, had Vergil as its protagonist (Putnam and Ziolkowski forthcoming). Unlike that of Aristotle and Phyllis, it lacks even the most tenuous tie to any biographical facts. Rather, it pays tribute to Vergil in his guise as necromancer, a role that was awarded to him only in the Middle Ages, as an understandable (if not logical) extension of the universal knowledge that had been attributed to him already in antiquity. In the tale of Vergil in the basket, the great Roman poet pursued the emperor's daughter in the hope of an assignation. After he refused repeatedly to take no for an answer, the young woman agreed to meet. The agreement was that he would enter one night into a large basket and that she would draw it up so that he could share a rendezvous with her in the tower where she had her chamber. All went according to plan until he had been pulled halfway up the tower, at which juncture the emperor's daughter left the poet stranded. Once day broke, a crowd gathered and ridiculed him. The humiliation has its counterpoint in the tale of Vergil's revenge. After being made a laughingstock, Vergil summoned his magical powers and extinguished all the fires in Rome. Eventually he let it be realized that the only way for the fires to be rekindled was by lighting torches and tapers at one of the most intimate orifices on the body of the woman who had spurned him. Like the legend of Aristotle and Phyllis, the two about Vergil received artistic treatment in various media.

The exempla about Aristotle and Vergil in the representational arts were not conditioned by any ancient treatments of them, but in many other ways Roman art and architecture exercised influences upon the Middle Ages that should not be overshadowed by Roman texts. The early medieval style that is termed Romanesque has an ambiguous name that was coined to describe an architecture (in vogue from the tenth through the thirteenth centuries, roughly) that stands in the same relation to ancient Roman institutional architecture as the Romance languages do to Latin. Alongside this indirect but pervasive afterlife of ancient architecture, many regions of Latin Christendom contained direct evidence of the Roman empire in the ruins of ancient monuments that served as quarries and also as reminders of a grandeur of building scale and technique that went unsurpassed until the Gothic cathedrals. Responses to this aspect of the classical tradition may be detected in texts as unlike each other as the Old English poem from the Exeter Book, *The Ruin* (thought to have been inspired by the remains of Roman Bath), and the two Rome elegies of Hildebert of Lavardin (1056–1133), one of which marvels at the greatness of what Rome must once have been, the other of which professes that Rome's function as the seat of Christianity elevated the city more than any manmade edifices ever did (Witke 1990; Czapla 1998). Loosely related would be travel guides to Rome that scrutinized its antiquities, such as the twelfth- or thirteenth-century *Marvels of Rome*, conventionally attributed to "Master Gregorius" (or to a canon named Benedict) (Osborne 1987; Kinney 1990).

5   Culture Wars

Many medieval authors who have been identified here wrote in the twelfth century, a circumstance that is no coincidence. The long twelfth century witnessed extensive "culture wars," in which authors of new Latin texts had to vie for recognition as never before in an ever-more-crowded market. One aspect of the competition was with the past: if they hoped to have their compositions become fixtures in the curriculum, they had to oust the old standbys of earlier poets that were already entrenched there. Thus was born the friction between *antiqui et moderni* (the ancients and the moderns), a *querelle des anciens et des modernes* centuries before the phrase existed (Gössmann 1974; Zimmermann and Vuillemin-Diem 1974). The relationship of the twelfth-century poets with antiquity marked a departure from preceding centuries, since it was characterized by a rivalry with the past. Much has been made, rightly, of the twelfth-century image of the "modern" author and scholar as a dwarf standing on the shoulder of a giant (and "modern" deserves quotation marks, since the adjective came into its own in Latin precisely during this century) (Merton 1965). By this same pygmaean measure, Walter of Châtillon (ca. 1135 – ca. 1179) invoked Vergil with apparent deference in the prologue to his great *Alexandreis*. But simultaneously Walter evidenced pride at having had the audacity to deal with lofty material, the epic of Alexander the Great, that no classical poet had dared to essay. A different, but equally elaborate, expression of the same uneasy emulation of bygone works comes to the fore in the *Courtiers' Trifles* of Walter Map (ca. 1140–1209). After he has interpolated his (in)famously misogamous "Dissuasion of Valerius to the Philosopher Rufinus, that he should not take a Wife," he inveighs at length against the popularity it had enjoyed when it had circulated pseudonymously, since it would never have won renown had it been published under the name of its modern-day author, without the patina of pseudo-antiquity:

> My only offence is, that I am alive; it is, however, one which I have no intention of correcting – by dying. I changed our names for those of dead men in the title, for I knew that would be popular: had I not done so, my book, like myself, would have been thrown aside. . . . Every century has disliked its own modernity; every age, from the first onwards, has preferred the previous one to itself. (Map 1983: 312–13)

Another part of the competition that twelfth-century poets had to face was with their contemporaries, since rivalries about style and content burned intensely. A case in point is the blistering contempt that Alan of Lille voices in his *Anticlaudianus* for the *Alexandreis* of Walter of Châtillon as well as for the equally classicizing treatment of *The Trojan War* by Joseph of Exeter (died ca. 1210). Although Alan bandies about the names of Ennius and Maevius as bywords for his two rivals, these particular ancient poets were to him no more than that – names. More germane than tracing the poems and commentaries from which he would have been familiar with the reputations of these two ancient poets is to grasp what divided Alan on the one hand and Walter and Joseph on the other. Whereas Alan wrote a philosophical-allegorical epic with near complete avoidance of elision, Walter and Joseph produced classicizing epics with heavy use of the same technique. Despite the rifts among the three poets, all of them gauged shrewdly their audiences and markets and earned outstanding and abiding places in it: within a short span of their appearance, the *Alexandreis*, *Trojan War*, and *Anticlaudianus* each had been explicated in a commentary or gloss, one solid mark that a text had passed the hurdle into the schools.

The library catalogues and reading lists of the eleventh and twelfth centuries furnish data to document the burgeoning interest in the poetry of Ovid, satires of Horace, Persius, and Juvenal, and prose of Cicero. The growth in the cultivation of the Latin classics was such that the twelfth century has been justly recognized for its distinctive humanism (Southern 1995–2000). The respect and appetite for Ovid in particular led to the generation of a substantial pseudo-Ovidian corpus, not to mention many attempts to foster appreciation and acceptance of genuine Ovidian texts through glosses, commentaries, and the cullings of extracts or "flowers" that are known as *florilegia* (Coulson and Roy 2000).

The exaltation of such suspect authors as Ovid provoked a backlash from moralists who viewed secular learning with distrust or outright contempt; but the gravest threat to the revered school authors, the *auctores* whose words and concepts endued their users with *auctoritas* (authority), came from the spreading fascination with dialectical methods of analysis. Whereas Chartres and especially Orléans were associated with literary studies and the classics, Paris became the center for training in dialectic (Ferruolo 1985). In the thirteenth century a French poet, Henri d'Andeli, cast the rivalries as *The Battle of the Seven [Liberal] Arts*, in which Orléans and the proponents of classical literature suffer defeat at the hands of Paris and the dialecticians (Ziolkowski 1985).

The skirmishes over grammar and dialectic, over knowledge through reading canonical texts or intelligence through learning methods of reasoning, and over the relative weight to be accorded ancient and modern authors were waged fervently in the schools and universities. Whereas in the age of Charlemagne and his successors most formal education had been restricted to monasteries and monastic schools, by the end of the tenth century the cathedral schools had become a force to be reckoned with; from the mid-eleventh through the mid-twelfth centuries they expanded greatly (Jaeger 1994). In comparison with monasteries, cathedral chapters allowed their members a rule that was looser and a life that was far less constrained by the burdens of religious duties. Yet whether young men were destined for ecclesiastical service or lay careers, all of them were still supposed to be clerics, functionally literate in Latin although native speakers of at least one vernacular dialect.

At the very latest by the beginning of the thirteenth century, the earliest universities had become well established in France, Italy, and England. Education had progressed from being groups of boys under the tutelage of a single teacher to crowds of young men who studied with an assortment of masters (Le Goff 1993). The exuberance manifested itself not only in the vast and varied products of Latin literary culture, but also in the rapid refinement of the Romance vernaculars. This refinement was accompanied by a newfound confidence in the worthiness of vernacular cultures as well as languages. According to Chrétien de Troyes (second half of the twelfth century) in his *Cligés* (lines 28–42), medieval France had inherited the distinction in chivalry and learning that in earlier times had been possessed by Greece and Rome (Freeman 1979). Chrétien's outlook can be construed as the secular, vernacular equivalent to Hildebert's views in his two elegies on Rome: although the magnificence that had been pagan had largely crumbled into ruins, the glory that was the Christian *Urbs* (city) prospered as never before. More generally, the distinctively twelfth-century optimism of combining reverence for the past with recognition of the advantages of the present comes to life memorably in the previously mentioned cliché of "dwarfs standing on the shoulders of giants": however deficient twelfth-century men found their own aptitudes in comparison with those of their intellectual and cultural forebears, they cherished a belief that nonetheless their perspectives surpassed those of their predecessors. As the beneficiaries of the university and other institutions that the twelfth century created without the benefit of Athens and Rome, we should perhaps credit them with even greater powers of perception than they allowed themselves.

The relationship of the twelfth century, as of the ninth and tenth centuries before it, to ancient Greco-Roman culture went beyond mere revival. At least since the Renaissance many scholars have been indoctrinated to accept classical antiquity as the preeminent model of culture and have tended therefore to perceive the Middle Ages as a cycle of cultural collapses and classicizing renewals that are sometimes termed renaissances or renascences. Yet the classics were hardly the only wellspring of energy and discontent among the literate in the twelfth century, who grappled with a past that rested equally firmly on Christianity – on the Bible and patristic writings, not to mention medieval additions to the already-sizable sea of Christian literature. Furthermore, the classics were never imitated as closely in the twelfth century as they were to be in the Renaissance: the classicizing of John of Salisbury (ca. 1115–80), if classicizing it can be called, is a far cry from that of Petrarch (Martin 1984). However much we admire the humanism that comes to the fore occasionally in his *Metalogicon*, *Policraticus*, and verse works, however much we are impressed by John's admiration of Vergil, Ovid, Seneca, and Cicero, we must not be misled into mistaking twelfth-century humanism for the later humanism *tout court*. At the same time, we must fight the impulse to judge the one by the other and especially the temptation to criticize the Middle Ages for falling short of the Renaissance. John of Salisbury was no Petrarch, it is true, but by the same token Petrarch was no John. Rather than pitting the one against the other, we would do well to esteem each in his own way – and to see that there were more than passing likenesses in two poets who rested their hopes for fame on Latin hexameter epics about, respectively, Alexander the Great and Scipio Africanus.

FURTHER READING

Two dated overviews of the classical tradition, Highet (1949) and Bolgar (1954), remain useful, with the latter being more detailed and reliable for the Middle Ages. (Other volumes edited by Bolgar contain essays on medieval topics.) Curtius (1953) offers a monumental synthesis. On the textual traditions of individual authors, see Reynolds (1983); on textual traditions more generally, see Reynolds and Wilson (1991). Details on manuscripts are in Munk Olsen (1982–9), with findings distilled in Munk Olsen (1991). Valuable bibliographies can also be found in Munk Olsen and Leonardi (1995), and Munk Olsen and Friis-Jensen (1997). Author-by-author listings may be found in the "Fortleben" section of the annual bibliography *Medioevo Latino*. On commentaries and translations, see Kristeller et al. (1960–). Paradigmatic books have been devoted to the reception of individual authors. Vergil: Comparetti (1997) and Baswell (1995), with a massive anthology of materials by Putnam and Ziolkowski (forthcoming). Ovid: Hexter (1986) (for citation and analysis of Traube's three *aetates* [ages], see pp. 2–3). Horace: Reynolds (1996).

CHAPTER THREE

Renaissance

Craig W. Kallendorf

1 What's in a Name? (Part 1)

The Renaissance is unusual, in that unlike many other periods (e.g., the Baroque), its name can be traced back to one particular individual and his cultural agenda. In the centuries beforehand, annalists and chroniclers wrote universal history in which the flow of time was divided either according to a principle articulated by Jerome, whose commentary on Daniel's prophecy about the statue (Daniel 2:31 ff. and 7:1 ff.) led to a succession of four world monarchies, or to one articulated by Augustine, which relied on six ages (*City of God* 22). The decisive intervention into the system was the birth of Christ, which replaced the darkness of condemnation with the light of salvation. As Theodor Mommsen showed over 60 years ago, this approach was first challenged in a decisive way by Petrarch (1304–74). When he began planning his *De viris illustribus* (On illustrious men) in 1337/8, he intended to "bring together the illustrious men of all countries and of all times" (*Familiares* 8.3), just as the annalists and chroniclers before him had done. Five years later, however, he had decided to restrict his attention to the centuries from the Roman Republic to the first hundred years of the Empire. During the years in which his plans changed, Petrarch had gone to Rome to be crowned poet laureate in a ceremony that was believed to revive one from antiquity, and he had taken the time to think more about what the ruins around him might mean. From this point on, he conceived of the time from the end of the Roman Empire to his own day as an era of darkness: that is, the metaphor had been transferred from a fundamentally religious context, in which light represents revealed truth, to a fundamentally secular one, in which light represents the truth that people create through culture. The light shone brightly in antiquity but was extinguished afterward; now, "when the darkness has been dispersed," those who return to the ancients "can come again in the former pure radiance" (*Africa* 9.456–7). Or, to use the other metaphor that became popular with Petrarch and his descendants, antiquity was in the process of being born again, in a renaissance (Mommsen 1942: 226–42; Ullman 1973).

This process was generally seen in the generations that followed Petrarch to be relatively uncomplicated. In a famous letter to his friend Francesco Vettori (dated December 10, 1513), Niccolò Macchiavelli (1469–1527) describes how, after a difficult day spent amidst the toils and tribulations of daily life, he would return home, retreat into his study, and "step inside the venerable courts of the ancients . . . where I am unashamed to converse with them and to question them about the motives of their actions, and they, out of their human kindness, answer me. . . . I absorb myself into them completely" (Atkinson and Sices 1996: 262–5). Macchiavelli makes two assumptions that are important here. First, the texts of the classical authors offered unimpeded access to their values and their culture: the reader can "become completely part of them." And second, the classics were to be encountered in private, away from the distractions of daily life that keep the reader from a clear vision of the best that human beings once were, and could be again. As with Petrarch, the encounter was moved from the monastic cell to the scholar's study, from a primarily religious to a primarily secular space.

In the following generations this scheme was refined. But it was Petrarch who presented himself as "situated as if at the boundary of two peoples, looking at one and the same time both forward and back" (*Rerum memorandarum* [Memorable matters] 1.2). Antiquity had been reborn.

2 Acceptance

The Renaissance account of its own origins did not go uncontested – the scholastic thought against which the classical revival defined itself did not simply disappear, especially in northern Europe – but it came to prevail in its own day and was accepted with very little criticism for several hundred years afterward. The major historians of the nineteenth century were still emphasizing many of the same themes as Petrarch: *The Renaissance* of Jules Michelet (1798–1874) stressed the revival of classical antiquity, *The Revival of Classical Antiquity* of Georg Voigt (1827–91) makes its emphasis clear in the title, and even the synthesis that suggests that there could have been a Renaissance without the revival of antiquity, *The Civilization of the Renaissance in Italy* of Jakob Burckhardt (1818–97), admits that the classics guided the new modern individual to his or her full potential (Burckhardt 1958: 1:175; Coroleu 2004: 3–15). And indeed, the claim that the classics were reborn in the Renaissance still seems to explain many things that happened from the fourteenth through the sixteenth centuries.

By the middle of the fifteenth century, for example, Italian education at the pre-university level had been taken over by a new kind of teacher, the humanist school-master, who taught grammar, rhetoric, history, poetry, and moral philosophy, drawing on the classics for his texts. In *A Program of Teaching and Learning* (1459), Battista Guarino (1435–1505) tells us which authors his father, the famous teacher Guarino da Verona (1374–1460), taught: Valerius Maximus and Justin in history; Vergil, then Lucan, Statius, Ovid's *Metamorphoses*, Seneca's tragedies, Plautus, and Terence among the poets; Cicero for rhetoric, with Quintilian as a supporting text; and Cicero,

Aristotle's *Ethics,* and Plato in moral philosophy (Kallendorf 2002: 260–309). Less talented teachers with less talented students might limit the curriculum, which could end up being restricted largely to Cicero in prose and Vergil in poetry, but in theory at least more classical authors were read with greater historical sensitivity in the Renaissance than in the Middle Ages (Waquet 2001: 7–40). What is more, Greek, which had largely disappeared in western Europe during the Middle Ages, was again taught regularly, at least to the best students.

Scholarly and literary activity at the higher levels gave further credence to the claim that antiquity had been revived. During the preceding centuries Cicero's *De oratore* (On the orator), *Orator,* and *Brutus,* the complete text of Quintilian, and Statius' *Sylvae* had for all practical purposes dropped from sight (Reynolds 1983: 102–9, 332–4, 398–9). Humanist scholars set out in conscious pursuit of these and other texts; what they found is chronicled elsewhere in this volume. These discoveries in turn stimulated new literary efforts like the love poetry of Joannes Secundus (1511–36) and the silvas of Angelo Poliziano (1454–94) and Francisco de Quevedo (1580–1645).

A similar development might be observed in art and architecture. Roman columns were often incorporated into Romanesque churches that, in spite of what their name suggests, were built with a decidedly unclassical style and proportion. In dialogue with Vitruvius, however, Leon Battista Alberti (1404–72) wrote an influential treatise, *On the Art of Building,* then disseminated a new style that was clearly classical in inspiration, as seen in the Church of San Francesco in Rimini, San Sebastiano and Sant'Andrea in Mantua, and the Rucellai Palace, Santa Maria Novella, and the tribune of Santissima Annunziata in Florence (Grafton 2000: 261–330). To be sure, Mars and Jupiter had not died in the Middle Ages. But on the bell tower of the Florentine cathedral they took medieval form: as a knight and a monk, respectively. When Rosso Fiorentino depicts Mars with Venus in a drawing that appears to have been presented to Francis I, however, and Giulio Romano depicts Jupiter with Olympias in the Palazzo Te in Mantua, the medieval trappings are gone (Bull 2005: 157–9, 370).

This can only have come about because the Renaissance artist was conscious of historical distance in a way that his medieval predecessor was not. In other words, Mars could be seen as a knight only if the artist saw continuity between past and present. Once it became apparent, however, that classical antiquity no longer existed and that a thousand years separated the people of the fourteenth century from it, a conscious effort had to be made to reconstruct what had been lost. As Eugenio Garin has stressed, this can also be done through words: philology provided a tool for the study of language, and through an imaginative reconstruction of the past, the correct meaning of texts could be recovered (Garin 1965: xx–xxii). When Machiavelli spoke with the ancients, he used his philological skill to close the distance between himself and them.

Once this distance had been closed, the humanist scholar or artist could even, if he wanted, return from "the ancient courts of ancient men" with books and objects he had made himself, but present them as genuine. A protégé of Michelangelo Buonarotti (1475–1564), Francisco de Hollanda, for example, notes that the famous statue of *Bacchus* "was a work that Michelangelo had completed a long time ago for the purpose of fooling the Romans and the pope with its antique style" (Barkan 1999: 201–2).

In 1498, approximately two years after Michelangelo had finished his *Bacchus*, the Dominican Annius of Viterbo (1432–1502) published his *Commentaries on Various Authors Discussing Antiquities*. The book purports to be a history of the world in which Annius' commentary connects his sources, some of which are genuine (e.g., Archilochus) and some not (e.g., Metasthenes) (Grafton 1991: 76–103). More outrageous yet was the forgery of Curzio Inghirami (1614–55), who used his position as a member of one of Tuscany's powerful families to perpetrate a scandal that would ultimately attract the attention of the pope. Curzio indulged his country-men's eagerness to have proof of their heritage by forging a host of documents in Latin and Etruscan (the pre-Latin language of north-central Italy) and hiding them in scarith, small containers made of hair and mud. After "finding" the scarith, Curzio published the documents in a book, *Fragments of Etruscan Antiquities* (1636) (Rowland 2004). The same philological methods that allowed one scholar to manu-facture nonexistent records from the past allowed others to expose them, with the give-and-take that arose around Renaissance forgeries showing the extent to which the past had indeed come alive again.

Fake statues and fake histories seem far removed from daily life, and indeed, Petrarch and his immediate followers – even the honest ones – preferred the study to the forum. A number of modern scholars have noted that some later humanists endorsed the active over the contemplative life (e.g., Garin 1965: xix), and when we look at the philosophical dialogues of the period, it appears that there is some truth in this observation. Rudolf Pfeiffer's *History of Classical Scholarship from 1300 to 1850* (1976), however, locates the classical tradition in men like Niccolò Niccoli (1364–1437), Poggio Bracciolini (1380–1459), and Lorenzo Valla (1407–57), then in their successors across the Alps – scholars rather than businessmen or politicians. And Gilbert Highet's influential *The Classical Tradition* (1971) is tellingly subtitled *Greek and Roman Influences on Western Literature*. Again, we see Machiavelli retreating into his study. The classical tradition had been reborn, but it was a hothouse plant, one that flourished far from the everyday world.

3 Ideological Critique

While the claim that the classics had been reborn in the Renaissance explains a number of important phenomena about the period, it also leaves the modern obser-ver more than a little uneasy. Some classical texts were taught throughout the Middle Ages, and the poetry of Dante Alighieri (1265–1321) and the illustrated manuscripts of the *Ovide moralisé* (Ovid moralized) make it difficult – indeed impossible – still to argue that the classics ever died during the thousand years after the fall of the Roman empire. What is more, a closer look at the so-called rebirth itself raises more ques-tions. For example, let us return once more to Machiavelli in conversation with the ancients. The process as he describes it seems easy and natural enough: he asks them questions and they answer. They, however, were speaking ancient Greek and classical Latin, languages that no one in sixteenth-century Europe learned without a great deal of time and effort. Why does Machiavelli pass over in silence the philological effort that is necessary to "enter into the courts of ancient men"? What kinds of people can make this effort, and why would they choose to do so, presenting themselves as disinterested scholars in timeless colloquy with the "great truths"? For the remainder of this chapter, I shall query the interests in which a seemingly disinterested metaphor rests, in an attempt to unmask the ideology of rebirth and to incorporate into the discussion what is occluded when we simply accept at face value what Petrarch and his followers wrote about themselves.

Let us begin with the idea that it was Petrarch who first found himself "situated as if at the boundary of two peoples, looking at one and the same time both forward and back." It was indeed Petrarch who attained an international reputation for reviving the cult of antiquity, but he was not the first priest of the new religion. In fact he was preceded by a number of "prehumanists," the most prominent of whom lived and worked in Padua. The founder of this movement was Lovato Lovati (1241–1309), a lawyer whose passion for classical literature led him to a brilliant exposition of the meters in Seneca's tragedies, a role in the rediscovery of lost material from Livy, and a guiding place in the construction of a tomb for Antenor, the mythical founder of the city. Albertino Mussato in turn wrote the first secular tragedy since the fall of the Roman empire, *Ecerinis*, for which a grateful Padua revived an ancient ceremony and gave him a laurel crown for his poetic achievement. Giovanni Mansionario (died 1337), who lived and worked within sight of the chapter library in Verona where the poems of Catullus had been preserved, first established the existence of two Plinys, not one, then wrote a history in whose margins he copied out Roman coins and drew pictures of Roman circuses, demonstrating clear antiquarian interests (Weiss 1973: 16–29).

If the classics had never really died, and if a more modern approach to them had precursors as well, what, exactly, did Petrarch do? One answer might be that he systematized what went before him, using his prodigious intellect in one area of classical studies after another, setting new standards for what could be achieved. A better answer might stress his personal role in popularizing the veneration of antiquity. Almost 150 years ago Jakob Burckhardt argued that the inward develop-ment of the individual that characterized the Renaissance ("man became a spiritual *individual*, and recognized himself as such") was accompanied by an outward sign, the passion for being famous (Burckhardt 1958: 1:143–62). This passion had its roots in antiquity – Cicero comes to mind immediately – and Petrarch took great pains to fashion himself into a celebrity: like Cicero he made public his supposedly private letters, carefully reworked to present himself in the best possible light; like Mussato, he, too, arranged to be crowned poet laureate, going so far as to encour-age a competition for which city would have the honor of hosting the ceremony; and he even composed a letter to posterity in an effort to have the last word on how he would be viewed after his death (Wilkins 1961: 24–9, 87–8, 252–62). This is an early example of what Stephen Greenblatt would call "self-fashioning," an increased self-consciousness that human identity could be manipulated in a way that tends to efface the difference between life and art (Greenblatt 1980: 1–4). The ascent of Mt. Ventoux that generated one of Petrarch's most famous letters, modern schol-arship tells us, may never have taken place (Baron 1966: 196–202), but in a sense it doesn't matter: the letter served as a vehicle for Petrarch to present himself to the world in a certain way, not as an historical record. In what way did Petrarch want himself to be seen? As the man who revived antiquity, of course. There may be some simplification and exaggeration here, but there would be many more examples to come in which details were glossed over and achievements overstated by those who wanted to be famous.

One of those later examples is provided by Desiderius Erasmus (ca. 1476–1536), who exploited one of the great inventions of the Renaissance, printing, to advance his career and to shape the image he left to later ages. The invention of printing with movable type by Johann Gutenberg (ca. 1398–1468) in the middle of the fifteenth century had an enormous impact on classical scholarship, for hundreds of copies of a text could then be produced in the same amount of time that it had taken medieval scribes to produce one (Eisenstein 1979: 163–302). Erasmus saw quickly the potential of the new medium and traveled to Venice to see his collection of adages through one of the best classical presses of his day, that of Aldus Manutius (ca. 1449–1515). In Erasmus' hands, however, the printed book became an object of self-promotion, with the author regularly breaking lengthy works into smaller parts that could each be dedicated to a different potential patron. Erasmus' own letters were carefully shaped to present his actions and motivations in a favorable light, and second and third editions were meticulously prepared to enhance his reputation as scholar and man of letters (Jardine 1993: 3–26). Printing offered Erasmus a tool that Petrarch did not have, but both men pursued fame as revivers of antiquity.

On a more fundamental level, the idea that the classics were born again in the Renaissance turns out to be problematic in several ways. Petrarch and his followers tended to stress what they wanted to have happen, that the ideas, values, and language of the past were being recreated in the same way in the present. "Born again," however, is a term that is also used by evangelical American Protestants in a different context, where the emphasis is on re-creation as a new creation, fundamentally different from the old one. To what extent, then, does the classical tradition in the Renaissance mark something different from its ancient original?

In the first place, *the* classical tradition is something of a misnomer: classical tradition*s* would be more accurate. For example, one classical tradition associated the empires and kingdoms of the Renaissance with the empires and kingdoms of the classical world from which it was claimed that they descended. The funeral catafalque of Philip II (1527–98) in Seville, for example, contains an inscription taken from the *Aeneid*: *Imperium sine fine dedi* (I have given an empire without end, *Aeneid* 1.279). The message here is clear: the endless empire passed from Rome to Spain, ratified by the reference to Vergil's prophetic vision (Tanner 1993: 204). Ironically Philip's great enemy Elizabeth I of England anchored her power in the same text. As Elissa, she invited comparison to Dido, who was also known by this name; what is more, the famous *Siena Sieve* portrait uses scenes from *Aeneid* 4 to invite the viewer to focus on the role of the monarch, who had to separate out good from evil, as the sieve separated wheat from chaff. At a time when Elizabeth was the subject of an unpopular suit by the Duke d'Alençon, she had to discern the difference between a virtuous love, represented by the non-Vergilian Dido who remained true to her first husband Sychaeus, and a love intertwined with vice, represented by the fallen queen of

Aeneid 4 (Gallagher 1991: 123–40). The problem here is that the governments of antiquity also included nonmonarchical forms, as did the later polities that traced their origins to antiquity. Thus early Renaissance Florence, for example, defined itself in reference to classical republicanism. Under attack by Giangaleazzo Visconti, the tyrant of Milan at the beginning of the fourteenth century, Leonardo Bruni (1370–1444) and his friends crafted an ideology of civic activism that rested in a renewed appreciation of Cicero, the great defender of the dying Roman Republic (Baron 1966: 3–98). Here we have two different classical traditions.

In philosophy we can find several more. It is sometimes still said that the Middle Ages were Aristotelian and the Renaissance Platonic, but this is a generalization that is rife with exceptions: Platonism had an earlier revival during the Middle Ages, and Aristotelian scholasticism continued strongly into the Renaissance as well. It is true, however, that Plato was more influential in the Renaissance than he had been in the preceding centuries. Only the *Timaeus* and parts of the *Parmenides* had been known in the Middle Ages, but beginning in the Renaissance a number of humanists supplied translations of parts of the corpus, until Marsilio Ficino (1433–99) trans-lated Plato's complete works (1484), then added a commentary (1496). Renaissance philosophy also absorbed the interpretive tradition around Plato, first with Ficino's translation of and commentary on Plotinus' *Enneads* (1492), then with *Against Plato's Slanderer* (1469) of Cardinal Bessarion (ca. 1403–72), which introduced western readers to the Byzantine debates on the relative merits of Plato and Aristotle (Hankins 1990). Platonism resonated through the literature (e.g, *The Courtier* of Baldesar Castiglione [1478–1529]) and art (e.g., the *Birth of Venus* of Sandro Botticelli [1445–1510]) of the Renaissance; the trouble is, so did other ancient philosophies like Stoicism. The major figure here is a Fleming, Justus Lipsius (1547–1606), who edited Seneca's works and developed a modern version of ancient Stoicism. This in turn was passed on to the painter Peter Paul Rubens (1577–1640), who used Stoic philosophy and allegory in many paintings, including *The Four Philosophers* (Morford 1991). Other philosophical systems made less progress in the Renaissance, but Epicureanism appeared in Lorenzo Valla's *On Pleasure* (1431) (Lorch 1985: 1–211) and skepticism in the essays of Michel Montaigne (1533–92). In philosophy, as in history, there is more than one classical tradition.

Once it has been decided which classical tradition is to be reborn, other problems presented themselves. To begin with, identifying the remains of the past could be surprisingly difficult, such that mistakes were often made. For example, the humanists of the Renaissance found the style of handwriting they inherited distasteful and, beginning with Petrarch, initiated a reform. Coluccio Salutati (1331–1406), the scholarly chancellor of Florence, called the new style *littera antiqua* (ancient letter), which suggests that in handwriting as well as other areas, the ancient style was being reborn. The problem, however, is that the old manuscripts the humanists were imitating were in fact not ancient, but Carolingian, from the ninth to the twelfth centuries. In other words, in the effort to return to antiquity, the progressive thinkers of the Renaissance accidentally exchanged one set of medieval models for another. What is more, the humanists were drawn to Carolingian manuscripts not only because they were old, but because they contain important texts of many important classical authors, like Terence, Caesar, and Cicero. This is because Carolingian culture also marks a renaissance, an earlier rebirth of antiquity. Just as we should speak more properly of classical tradition*s*, we should also speak of Renaissance*s*, of which the one initiated by Petrarch is simply the most profound (Ullman 1963: 105–17, 137–44).

Identifying the remains of the past was problematic in other ways as well. Ancient statues, for example, rarely come with name tags. Take the pair of heroic figures with rearing horses that stood on the Quirinal hill in Rome during the Renaissance. They do have an inscription, rendered as "the work of Phidias" and "the work of Praxiteles," which led Petrarch to suggest that they might have been carved by the ancient Greek sculptors with these names. By the middle of the sixteenth century some observers thought that both statues might well represent Alexander and his horse Bucephalus, but by the 1590s other observers were suggesting the man-eating horses of Diomedes that Hercules had tamed. Some 50 years later the consensus settled on the twin horsemen Castor and Pollux, and scholars concluded that, notwithstanding the inscription, the statues had probably not been carved by Phidias and Praxiteles themselves (Bull 2005: 7–8). To put this in Machiavellian terms, a succession of observers were asking questions of the ancients, but sometimes the answers came with the opacity of the sibylline oracle.

Another problem is connected to the fact that the remains of the past are often incomplete: manuscripts like that of Petronius' *Satyricon* are missing pages, and ancient sculpture is almost always broken. At times artists of the Renaissance attempted to restore the fragments of ancient statues, but this was dangerous, since the restoration made permanent an identification that was still open to question and revision. Some statues, like the *Torso Belvedere*, however, were never restored, and they in turn raise other issues. This statue consists of part of a large body, extending from shoulder to knee, which is dramatically rotated at the waist. In its unrestored state it served as a model repeatedly for Michelangelo, beginning with an *Ignudo* in the Sistine Chapel frescoes, then in the recumbent *Day* and the projected *River Gods* for the Medici tombs, then (distantly) with the *Victory* in the Palazzo Vecchio, and finally in two key figures of the *Last Judgment*, the judging Christ and the flayed Bartholomew who is holding his own skin (Barkan 1999: 191–200). This example, along with such depictions of antique-strewn ruins as *The Tempest* of Giovanni Bellini (died 1516), suggests that the Renaissance had developed the capacity to respond to antiquity in its fragmentary state, a civilization that was sufficiently Other at times that it could not, or should not, be completely restored and recreated.

When the remnants of the ancient world needed restoration, the process, again, was not as straightforward as Macchiavelli suggests. This comes through most clearly when the remnants are textual. The process of restoration was philological, but scholars of the Renaissance debated how, exactly, it should proceed. There were two basic ways of restoring a text in the Renaissance: *emendatio ope codicum*, in which sections of textual witnesses were selectively compared; and *emendatio ope ingenii* or *coniecturae*, in which the editor used his talents and knowledge to make conjectures independently of manuscript authority. Conjectural emendation tended to prevail, but there was debate over when and to what extent it should be used. Angelo Poliziano, for example, was the first to develop a procedure for identifying where manuscripts came from, for dating them and relating them to one another, for citing them clearly and for describing them; he gave primary authority to readings found in the old manuscripts, secondary authority to support that could be gleaned from other ancient writers, and tertiary credence to the sense of the text, which could provide a controlled form of conjectural emendation. Poliziano came close to modern practices in several key areas, but in his day, he was the exception rather than the rule. Other editors made other advances – Desiderius Erasmus, for example, devised the principle of the harder reading (*difficilior lectio*), the idea that more difficult variants were more likely to be correct because scribes were more likely to change an unfamiliar phrase into a familiar one than vice versa (D'Amico 1988: 8–38) – but it is important to note that consensus on how to prepare a text was not reached until the nineteenth century. In other words, the ancients continued to say different things to different people in the Renaissance, depending on the principles being used to recover their words.

Even if this problem had been solved in the Renaissance, it would still have been difficult for antiquity to have been reborn in precisely the same way as it had once arisen. To stay with textual matters, what happened when a writer sat down to recreate antiquity? The process used is generally called "imitation," but as Thomas Greene has persuasively demonstrated, there are several ways in which imitation can unfold. Greene calls the simplest imitative strategy "reproductive" or "sacramental": it takes place when a later poem follows its classical subtext with religious fidelity, as when Petrarch reproduces the dream of Scipio from Cicero's *De republica* (On the republic) in Books 1 and 2 of his *Africa*. When allusions, echoes, phrases, and images from many authors stand together in a new poem, the imitation is "eclectic" or "exploitative," as when Petrarch alludes to Cicero and Horace along with Saint Matthew, Saint Augustine, and Dante in his "Triumph of Eternity." Imitation becomes "heuristic" when it distances itself from its subtext at the same time as it advertises its derivation from it: a Petrarchan example would be sonnet 90 from the *Canzoniere*, whose repeated echoes of *Aeneid* 1 are as obvious as the gaps in language, sensibility, and cultural context. Heuristic imitation shades into "dialectical" when the text becomes the site of a struggle between two worlds whose conflict cannot be easily resolved, a good example being Petrarch's *Secretum* (Secret), in which the engagement with Augustine's *Confessions* remains unresolved because the classical pursuit of fame is fundamentally incompatible with a Christian value scheme. Ironically, a modern reader at least would probably conclude that the literary quality of the imitation is inversely proportional to its degree of fidelity to its model. In other words, sacramental recopying of great literature is unlikely to produce more great literature (who has read Petrarch's *Africa*?), while the interplay of values in dialectical and heuristic imitation can produce aesthetic excitement of the highest order, as we see when Erasmus' *Praise of Folly* draws from Lucian while at the same time introducing Christian values that are, in the final analysis, incompatible with ancient satire (Greene 1982: 28–53).

The examples of Petrarch's *Secretum* and Erasmus' *Praise of Folly* raise the most fundamental complication to the rebirth of antiquity in the Renaissance: the classical tradition and Christianity are two very different things, and the men and women of the Renaissance were in no position to cast off the latter in pursuit of a pure revival of the former. Nineteenth-century historians like Burckhardt liked to stress what they saw as the fundamentally secular character of the Renaissance (Burckhardt 1958: 2:444–83), but modern scholarship has reminded us that there were few, if any, real atheists in the fifteenth century. Sometimes, to be sure, reborn antiquity blended seamlessly into Christian values. The catafalque of Philip II with the quotation from the *Aeneid*, for example, also contained another inscription: *His vincimus armis* (we conquer with these arms), which contemporary observers explained as an allusion to the emperor Constantine, who adopted the motto *In hoc signo vinces* (in this sign you will conquer) after he had his famous vision of the cross and set out to unite the empire in Christ (Tanner 1993: 204). Indeed the Escorial, the combination palace, church, crypt, library, monastery, hospital, and alms house that Philip II built for himself, illustrates well this syncretism. The pagan gods share space with Christian images in the library and in the royal reception hall; and on Jacopo da Trezzo's medal struck to commemorate the foundation of the Escorial in 1563, the yoke recalls the scales of justice associated with Augustus' apotheosis while earth's globe is inscribed with the cross. The complex as a whole may well have been designed to evoke Augustus' combined temple-palace on the Palatine, which was known from the description in Suetonius, and the church in the Escorial enshrined the Eucharist, which Spanish courtiers referred to as the "true Palladium of the Hapsburg gens." The complex was dedicated to Saint Lawrence, whose martyrdom by grilling was given its definitive treatment by Prudentius (born 348), for whom the story demonstrates the inextricable intertwining of Christian faith and Roman political sovereignty (Tanner 1993: 162–82).

Examples like this, however, the visual equivalent of sacramental and eclectic imitation, tend to obscure the tensions between two value systems whose interaction is often more heuristic and dialectical. For one thing, viewing antiquity through the prism of Christianity played an important role in determining which classical traditions would be reborn. In his fourth Eclogue, for example, Vergil wrote the following lines:

> Now hath the last age come, foretold by the Sibyl of Cumae;
> Mightily now upriseth a new millennial epoch.
> Justice the maid comes back, and the ancient glory of Saturn;
> New is the seed of man sent down from heavenly places.
> Smile on the new-born Babe, for a new earth greets his appearing;
> Smile, O pure Lucina; the iron age is departing.
> Cometh the age of gold …
>   (*Eclogue* 4.4–10) (Royds 1918: 74–83)

Modern classical scholars agree that these lines have nothing to do with Christ, but scholars of the Renaissance were less sure: Cristoforo Landino (1424–98) saw pagan and Christian theology as two parallel streams, but the debate that began in the time of Petrarch about whether certain virtuous pagans could have received a partial Christian revelation was still going on at the end of the fifteenth century (Kallendorf 1999b: 95–124). In any event, the fourth eclogue ensured that Vergil took a central place in Renaissance education along with Cicero, whose humanistic values were also considered broadly compatible with Christianity. Lucretius, however, whose atomism led to uncomfortable conclusions about the absurdity of religion and the mortality of the soul, remained marginal, as did Petronius, whose characters engage in sexual escapades that the church could hardly condone. In other words, the classical traditions that were clearly incompatible with Christianity were not reborn, but were almost stillborn in the Renaissance.

Indeed Petrarch himself, the father of antiquity's rebirth, actually remained conflicted about what he was doing throughout his career. In *De otio religioso* (On religious leisure) Petrarch uses the familiar opposition between *negotium* (business) and *otium* (leisure) to contrast the peaceful contemplation of the religious life to the endless, and ultimately meaningless, activity of worldly affairs. Addressed to the monks of the Carthusian monastery at Montrieux to which his brother Gherardo belonged, the treatise examines the actions of Aeneas from this perspective and finds them wanting:

> How much more correctly does that heavenly father [say] to us than Aeneas in Virgil [says] to his son, "From me, my son, learn virtue and true labor" [*Aeneid* 12.435]. What virtue, I ask, O son of Anchises? The betrayal of your country . . . ? [S]acrifices carried out with the bloody slaughter of friendly demons? Christ, however, our true father and lord and master and God, teaches through his law not that we learn from him virtues like these, which are not to be imitated, but that we be gentle and humble in heart, which is especially appropriate to a human being. (Petrarca 1975: 1:740)

First a traitor, then a worshipper of false gods, Aeneas is ultimately culpable for not being *pius*, here understood as "gentle and humble in heart" (Kallendorf 1999a: 394–5). In this passage Petrarch found Augustan culture to be different from the Christian culture of his own day, and the "otherness" of antiquity is acknowledged at the same time as its values are called into question.

Sometimes the clash was more dramatic than this. Pomponio Leto (1427–98), for example, was the foremost humanist of fifteenth-century Rome. He and his friends formed a loose-knit Roman Academy, which gathered periodically to eat, drink, and discuss classical texts. One of the scholars in Leto's circle ran afoul of Pope Paul II, who felt an antipathy at very least to certain kinds of ancient poetry if not to classical learning in general. Paul responded by accusing the members of the academy of neopaganism, hostility toward religion, and heresy, with sodomy and republicanism thrown in for good measure, then had them arrested, imprisoned, and tortured. After Sixtus IV became Pope, the academy was reformed as a religious association and its members (including Leto) went on to successful curial careers, but the incident illustrates well the tensions inherent in the Christian humanism of the Renaissance. These tensions emerged again in the Counter-Reformation, when classical texts that were perceived to challenge Christian morality ended up on the Index, the list of books that Catholics could read only in expurgated form, or not at all.

This incident also illustrates the final problem with Machiavelli's account of the rebirth of antiquity, the idea that one retreats from the press of daily life to converse with the ancients. As Leto discovered, one could set up a private club to read Latin poetry, but at the end of the day the members of the club had to return to the world outside. What is more, what was discussed within the club was not ideologically neutral. Reading Latin poetry in the shadow of the republican forum led naturally enough to a yearning for the days when Rome enjoyed the freedoms of a republican political system, and while there is little evidence that this ever got beyond talk in the Roman Academy, Pope Paul II was hardly in a position to forget that his predecessor Eugenius IV had been expelled by the city government of Rome in the name of a revived Roman republic (D'Amico 1983: 91–7). One can yearn for freedom from the constraints of daily life, but as Michel Foucault has so eloquently demonstrated, there is no vantage point outside the systems of power in which people find themselves implicated.

That is not to say, however, that the classical tradition is inherently either conservative or subversive. As we have already seen, Philip II appropriated the imagery of Augustus first in support of his bid to become Holy Roman Emperor, then as a way to project his power in the Escorial complex. With the "discovery" of the "new" world, Europeans projected their power westward in a rewriting of Aeneas' journey from Troy to Rome. But during the same time that Philip was casting himself as a new Augustus, however, the poet Alonso de Ercilla (1533–94) made his bid to become the new Vergil, writing a poem on the Spanish conquest of Chile, *La Araucana*, which is clearly intended to serve as a new *Aeneid*. In this poem the failure of the Spanish invaders to adhere to the ideals they profess is contrasted repeatedly to the virtues of the indigenous inhabitants of South America. In the end Ercilla's subversive tendencies are contained – the author is, after all, a Spaniard – but the Vergilian subtext clearly provides a dissident strain (Kallendorf 2003: 394–414).

Once we begin asking how, consciously or not, Renaissance people appropriated the classics outside the study as well as inside it, we can get a picture of cultural history and its defining metaphors in which seemingly disinterested activities like writing the history of classical scholarship mark interventions into the larger world. It is by no means apparent, for example, why anyone would have invested time and money to learn Latin at a time when it was not anyone's native language. The intuitive answer would be that in some way, the investment should pay off, and this proves to have been the case in the Renaissance. Throughout this period Latin was the one language that every educated person spoke, since it formed the basis for the curriculum in the schools. If, therefore, one wanted a career in the church, or in government, or in education, one had to learn Latin. In addition, Latin served as a class marker: a gentleman, by definition, was someone who had the leisure and resources to learn a difficult second language that did not have the immediate utility that farming or printing or sewing did (Waquet 2001: 173–229).

In the end, then, the classics were reborn in the Renaissance, not as the radical recreation of a tradition that had never completely died, not through a straightforward process of simple reappropriation, and not in isolation from the political, economic, and social events of the world in which they were reinserted, but as a part of the mental equipment of an era, a part of the way in which Renaissance people made sense of the world around them. This is true even in respect to the most revolutionary event of the day, the "discovery" of the "new" world. Thus according to Christopher Columbus (1451–1506), there were pearls in the new world, but they were formed just like the ones in the old world, as described by Pliny; and Vasco de Quiroga saw the Indians as characters in Lucian's *Saturnales*, simple and good in their primitive state (Todorov 1984: 17, 197).

4   What's in a Name? (Part 2)

If it has proved worth the effort to interrogate the idea of rebirth as the defining metaphor of the Renaissance and to ask what interests were being occluded in the use of the term, it should be instructive as well to ask briefly what we are doing when we use Petrarch's term today. "Renaissance" does reflect the worldview of the people it purports to describe, but not all of them, equally. The idea that culture demands the revival of antiquity began among the rich and powerful, along with the scholars and educators whose livelihood depended on them, and the idea stayed centered there. It certainly drifted down to the masses, in a diluted form, now and again: when Philip II traveled through the Low Countries in an effort to secure the title of Holy Roman Emperor, the classicizing triumphal monuments that were erected along the way were designed to be viewed by everyone (Tanner 1993: 133–9). And when Francesco de' Medici and Joanna of Austria married in 1565, the program ended in a procession of chariots on which the pagan gods who were supposed to be attending the wedding could be seen. Unfortunately the common people were thoroughly confused (Bull 2005: 44), and therein lies the point: even when classical culture drifted down to the masses, it generally failed to form a meaningful part of their lives. So when we use the term "Renaissance" today, we are approaching the period with a bias toward the rich and powerful people whose self-understanding rests disproportionately in the metaphor that was chosen by the scholars whose interests were allied with theirs.

There is another possibility. Instead of trying to write a linear cultural history that emphasizes the continuities with the past and fosters the interests of the rich and powerful, we could concentrate on the fissures and gaps that have been raised in the preceding discussion. At its best and most creative, the reborn culture was in dialectical debate with the past, probing and questioning rather than simply reproducing the cultural achievements of antiquity. A strategy like this links *The Praise of Folly* with T. S. Eliot's *The Waste Land* as well as with Lucian's satires. Indeed, as we have seen, the remnants of the past often remained fragmentary, which seems (at least sometimes) not to have bothered their later viewers, a point in turn that links Michelangelo with Picasso. In other words, the culture that Petrarch initiated has links with modernity as well, so that "early modern" has emerged in recent years as a term to challenge "Renaissance" and the values it projects.

In an essay in a book entitled *Companion to the Classical Tradition*, I am not going to propose that we abandon the latter term in favor of the former one. But I do think that when we use the term "Renaissance," we should do so with an awareness of the issues that are raised when we refer to the same period as "early modern." As we do this, we should end up with a richer, deeper understanding of the impact of classical antiquity on Petrarch and the people who followed him, until a new metaphor, baroque, was required to signal a new aesthetic sensibility for a new period.

FURTHER READING

Surprisingly there is not a single survey of the classical tradition in the Renaissance that offers full geographical, chronological, and disciplinary coverage; older, more factually based treatments of the Renaissance as part of a larger survey may be found in Highet (1949) and Bolgar (1954), and Grafton (1992) offers an essay similar to this one that covers some of the same ground in a different way. On education, see Grafton and Jardine (1986) and Waquet (2001), with Grendler (1989) and Kallendorf (2002) providing good supplementary material for Italy. The intellectual underpinnings of the study of the classics in the Renaissance can be tracked in Kraye (1996), with the standard history of classical scholarship remaining Pfeiffer (1976). Wilkins (1961) offers a good orientation to Petrarch, and Jardine (1993) to Erasmus. Much has been written about how the texts of Greek and Roman authors were treated by scholars in the Renaissance; D'Amico (1988) and Grafton (1991) offer a good introduction. Reynolds (1983) and Reynolds and Wilson (1991) provide concise information on the transmission of classical authors to the Renaissance, Wilson (1992) offers a good introduction to Greek studies in western Europe, and Kristeller et al. (1960–) offers invaluable catalogues of the commentaries to classical authors written by Renaissance scholars and teachers. Exemplary studies of the impact of individual classical authors in the Renaissance may be found in Gaisser (1993), Hankins (1990), and Kallendorf (1989, 1999b), although the works of the two latter authors are restricted to Italy. For the archaeological evidence, the older study of Weiss (1973) has been updated by Schnapp (1996) and Barkan (1999). Bull (2005) offers an excellent, thought-provoking analysis of the role of classical mythology in Renaissance art. The role of the classics in Renaissance religious thought can be traced through Trinkaus (1970). Grafton (1992) and Lupher (2003) offer useful orientations to the way in which the classics shaped the understanding of the "new" world in the "old."

CHAPTER FOUR

Baroque

Ingrid D. Rowland

1 Introduction

The Portuguese word "barrocco" originally applied to misshapen pearls. To the eyes of eighteenth-century neoclassicists, the same kinds of deformity seemed to mar every aspect of the seventeenth century, from its religious extremism to its opulent art, elaborate rhetoric, and fledgling science, and thus an adjective describing a jewel came to describe a whole era. Baroque art, especially, carries an additional close association with Catholicism: in southern Europe, but also in Latin America and Asian outposts like Goa, Macao, and Beijing, where Jesuit missionaries created dense, genuinely global networks of communication from the late sixteenth century onward – and discovered, in their travels, that the classical tradition of Greece and Rome had reached Asia already in antiquity. The same age whose dogmatism condemned Galileo Galilei to silence and house arrest (in 1633) was also, therefore, an age of unprecedented openness to foreign cultures.

Both Galileo and the Jesuit missionaries opened European eyes to a world of infinitely greater complexity than that described by ancient authors. There were continents beyond Europe, Asia, and Africa, and by the sixteenth century philosophers and mathematicians had called into question the very structure of the universe as Aristotle and Ptolemy had described it: the fifteenth-century cardinal Nicholas of Cusa (1401–64) and the sixteenth-century heretic Giordano Bruno (1548–1600) both argued that the universe was infinite, composed of an infinite number of "worlds" – that is, planetary systems. Western Christianity had split definitively into Catholic and Protestant, on the level of congregations, cities, and states. Former neighbors turned against one another with a vicious enthusiasm that may have been the most unsettling aspect of an unsettling age. It is no accident that Baroque art and music are so concerned with movement, with testing boundaries, with investigating limits of every kind, and it was no accident that in the same seventeenth century Newton and Leibniz, in two different ways and in two different places, would begin to explore the mathematics of motion and limits to arrive at the calculus (1684–7).

In this age dominated by political, religious, and cosmological uncertainty, the classical tradition provided Europeans (and their overseas correspondents) with a common language, Latin, and an overriding sense of cultural continuity. But then the classical tradition itself, from Periclean Athens to Ptolemaic Alexandria to imperial Rome, originated in cosmopolitan cities, always incorporating elements from a variety of ages and civilizations into a shared civic culture. Furthermore, the qualities that enabled the works of ancient authors to survive so many previous centuries still held for the seventeenth. The religious wars of Baroque Europe might have claimed different pretexts than the Peloponnesian War, but human behavior hewed recognizably to the same patterns traced by Thucydides. Homer, Vergil, Tacitus, and Marcus Aurelius still wrote convincingly about life, no matter the details of their own religion or cosmology and the profoundly different beliefs of their readers. For yet another century, Vitruvius continued to dispense his advice about architecture and education, and for yet another century he continued to make sense.

At the same time, the seventeenth-century exploration of the classical tradition took its own distinctive directions, especially when investigating the tradition's concrete reality: by seeking out the sites of ancient cities, by collecting ancient artifacts, by finding clues to the ancient world preserved in contemporary customs. In an age when every aspect of Christian doctrine was coming under question, the first centuries of Christian history, indivisible from the history of the Roman Empire, provided a sure foundation on which to base the Church, especially the Church of Rome.

2   Rome

To Roman Catholics of the sixteenth and seventeenth centuries, the adjective "Roman" had a meaning that was literally physical. For them, the Christian gospel was completely rooted in classical history: indeed, the Nicene Creed specifies that Jesus was "crucified under Pontius Pilate" – that is, in Roman-occupied Judaea during the reign of Tiberius. Artists from the first days of Christianity often tried to show biblical figures in togas and matrons' *stolae*; scholars since the fifteenth century had subjected early Christianity to the same kinds of investigations they directed toward the ancient Romans, Etruscans, and Greeks. The connection of actual places with classical and sacred history, both in Europe and in the Holy Land, reinforced the natural associations between classical and Christian culture. This association was nowhere more powerful than in Rome itself, where the institution of the papacy traced its history back to the tradition that St. Peter had been crucified in the Circus of the emperor Nero in AD 64. A no-less-venerable tradition traced the presence and martyrdom of St. Paul to the capital city, to the same year and the same notorious emperor. Long after it had ceased to be a political capital of any consequence, Rome continued to attract pilgrims, who associated its ancient ruins automatically with tales of the saints and apostles. It is not surprising, then, to find that every aspect of Baroque art, thought, and spirituality is pervaded by an awareness of the classical world.

The distinctive qualities of Baroque art drew their inspiration from a religious event that drew out over nearly a generation: the Council of Trent, convened in 1545 by Pope Paul III (reigned 1534–49), but concluded only in 1563. Its eventual decrees for reforming every aspect of the Catholic Church included strict guidelines for religious art and architecture, beginning with the form of churches themselves. The traditional basilica with central nave and side aisles, a design borrowed from the ancient Romans at the very beginning of Christianity, was now to be replaced by buildings that emphasized a single, unified place of worship. Side aisles were transformed into side chapels, and the freestanding high altar was pushed to the very back of the church so that clergy and congregation visibly shared the same space. The supreme model for all churches, as it neared completion in the late sixteenth century, was St. Peter's Basilica, its interior articulated by Corinthian pilasters modeled directly on those of the Pantheon and crowned by a tall, immense, coffered dome that immediately became – and remains – the dominant feature of the Roman skyline. The Council also decreed that painting and sculpture should convey clear, simple messages rather than the riddling imagery so favored by Renaissance artists, in works like Donatello's *David*, Botticelli's *Primavera*, Raphael's *School of Athens*, or even Michelangelo's intricate Sistine Chapel ceiling. Nothing, however, prevented making these new, easily understandable works of art as visually ravishing as anything that had gone before. Thus Federico Barocci (ca. 1535–1612), the favorite painter of the austere St. Philip Neri, specialized in blushing flesh and furry animals – cats, sheep, dogs – whose incredible softness has invited surreptitious touches ever since, much to the detriment of the paintings' surfaces. The realism of Baroque painters has often been contrasted with the classical tradition that inspired earlier generations, but in fact classicism and realism worked together to bring ancient Bible stories vividly home to modern viewers. The most dramatically innovative painter of the Baroque period, Caravaggio (Michelangelo Merisi da Caravaggio, 1571–1610), mixed classical references with real-life characters as cleverly and as pervasively as his "classical" rival, Annibale Carracci (1560–1609), whose own low-life paintings, like *The Bean Eater* (Galleria Colonna, Rome), are as grubbily persuasive as Caravaggio's. Thus Caravaggio's *Deposition from the Cross*, now in the Vatican Museum, recreates the poses of figures from an ancient Roman marble sarcophagus depicting the death of Meleager. But rather than mourning the dead Greek hero, Caravaggio's men and women, dressed like contemporary Italians, lament the dead Christ (who, in an explicit nod to a specific local Christian tradition, is wrapped in the Turin Shroud). Caravaggio's powerful mixture of biblical history, classical form, and contemporary detail shows the extent to which the classical tradition, which in a large sense included Hebrew, pagan, and local Christian culture, pervaded every aspect of religious life by the end of the sixteenth century.

The greatest Baroque sculptor, Gianlorenzo Bernini (1598–1680), studied his ancient models as intently as had his Renaissance predecessors, Donatello or Michelangelo, and as with these Renaissance sculptors, the skill of the ancients challenged him to the point that he transformed his own medium. Bernini's facility at carving marble was, like Michelangelo's, unrivaled in his day, and that very skill drove him to compete with the ancients for ingenuity of pose, variety of texture, and the quality that both ancient and modern critics praised above all others in works of art: likeness to life. The Apollo in his *Apollo and Daphne* (1622–5) is evidently the same *Apollo* from the Vatican Belvedere, but set into panting pursuit of the nymph whose limbs are turning into sculpted marble branches, one of them – characteristically of Bernini – rudely poking Apollo where it is most likely to hurt. The complexity of the composition and its meticulous details (some added in stucco) come as close as carved marble has ever come to pulsing life, and by carving the Apollo Belvedere on the run, Bernini suggests, in effect, that he is kicking the classical tradition of sculpture into new motion. Created for a cardinal, Scipione Borghese, Bernini's *tour de force* retells a classical myth with the conceptual simplicity and sumptuous visual detail that sums up the essence of Baroque art. Furthermore, like any seventeenth-century churchman, clever Cardinal Scipione would have been able to offer the statue's viewers any number of Christian lessons to be learned from the sun god's futile pursuit of his nymph, and her transformation into the symbol of poetry and music; classical myths had been "moralized" to Christian purpose ever since the Middle Ages. Bernini was more than a masterful sculptor of classical myths: his portrayals of religious ecstasy, his *Saint Teresa in Ecstasy* (1647–52; church of Santa Maria della Vittoria, Rome) and his *Blessed Ludovica Albertoni* (1674; church of San Francesco a Ripa, Rome), both housed in chapels of his own design, exploit not only his skill as a sculptor but also as an architect. Following the lead of ancient Roman architects, he set these figures beneath specially designed windows, exploiting the symbolic and visual force of natural light to convey the idea of divine illumination.

The most innovative Baroque architect, Francesco Borromini (1599–1667), was in many ways the most dedicated student of Rome's monuments, not only those of the ancients, but also the works of Early Christian and medieval builders. He pored over the principles that had guided earlier architects in their placement and decoration of architectural elements, the detailing that enabled them to achieve the qualities of harmony, order, and proportion. And then he changed it all around, making up new forms of columns, changing squares to triangles, egg-and-dart moldings to flying cherub's heads, circles to ovals. At the same time, he infused his newly invented forms with an energy that was essentially based on modern mathematics. Ancient architects created their designs with ruler and compass; Borromini's curves, infinitely more dynamic and instantly recognizable, are formed by a compass with a moving center; similar investigations of motion would lead shortly afterward to the simultaneous invention of the calculus by Newton and Leibniz. Borromini invested his architectural detailing with all the richness of sculpture; his palm fronds and cherub wings literally stroke the pediments that contain them, and his sculpted fruits are ripe to bursting. His buildings are as sensuous as the painting and sculpture created by his contemporaries. Like these other works of art, moreover, Borromini's architecture conveys strong, clear messages, not only architectural messages about load and support, horizontals and verticals, but also Christian messages about divine illumination. There is no architect in the seventeenth century who was more expert at bathing an enclosed space in light, a skill he refined by observing the example of the ancient Romans in spaces like the Baths of Diocletian.

The energetic motion contained in Baroque artworks often visibly bursts its boundaries: painted ceilings literally leak out of their architectural frames, sculptures squirm or fly free of pediments and pedestals, façades twist and pop in and out. The lines between the arts may be erased entirely, and it is not surprising, therefore, to discover that many Baroque artists excelled in more than one skill: Bernini painted and put on plays in addition to his work as sculptor and architect, and many of his works are glorious mixtures of media. Pietro da Cortona (1596–1669) was an extraordinary painter as well as an architect of rare inventiveness; Borromini's detailing, as noted, already often qualifies as sculpture. Metalwork, embroidery, and inlaid marble often rounded out the visual impact of Baroque design, and many of the spaces were specifically designed for music. Always, however, the example of the ancients served as an inspiration: the rotating ceiling of Nero's Golden House, sprinkling guests with perfume; the ingenious mingling of stucco, painting, and architecture in ancient Roman ruins like the Golden House and the tombs of the Appian Way; the mosaics of the catacombs and basilicas of Christians who were still full-fledged ancient Romans.

3   Egyptians and Etruscans

Increasingly, too, Baroque artists had begun to understand the differences between ancient Roman, Etruscan, and Egyptian art, and to exploit those differences to deliberate effect. Ever since the fifteenth century, both Etruria and Egypt had figured as symbols of the most ancient strains of ancient wisdom, their high levels of civilization attested by ancient Greek and Roman authors, and, in the case of Egypt, by the Bible (where Moses is described as "learned in all the wisdom of the Egyptians"). In the fifteenth century, a series of problematic texts embroidered, and greatly complicated, the picture. First a series of Greek dialogues attributed to "Thrice-great Hermes," Hermes Trismegistus, seemed to suggest that the Egyptians had anticipated crucial elements of Christian theology at the very dawn of classical history. Then a series of late-fifteenth-century forgeries by the Dominican friar Annius of Viterbo (1432?–1502) added a layer of pseudo-ancient and pseudo-biblical evidence to round out the story: the first Etruscan had been none other than the biblical patriarch Noah. By the early seventeenth century, the Hermetic dialogues had been identified as post- rather than pre-Christian and the forgeries of Annius of Viterbo had been largely discredited, but no scholarly attack could possibly have dispelled the aura of wisdom and mystery that surrounded the Egyptians and Etruscans, not when their artifacts came forth from the earth inscribed in strange, incomprehensible scripts, carved, molded, and cast in shapes of odd, compelling beauty.

Rome in particular was a treasure house of Egyptian art: Roman emperors had imported more than 50 obelisks, some stripped from Egyptian temples and some made to order. The area around Piazza Venezia, the site of an ancient temple to Isis and Serapis, yielded up prizes ranging from a bronze table-top inlaid with silver figures and hieroglyphic inscriptions (an entirely Roman artifact with Roman pseudohieroglyphs, now in the Egyptian Museum in Turin) to marble statues in Hellenistic style (including the cult statues of Isis and Serapis, several images of the rivers Nile and Tiber, and a little, life-sized cat) to Egyptian images in basalt (lions, baboons, scribes, and a table leg). The Roman emperor Hadrian had been obsessed with Egypt, and his villa at Tivoli, just outside Rome, provided its own trove of Egyptian and Egyptian-revival sculpture; so did the ruins of the huge sanctuary of Fortune at Palestrina outside Rome, where a mosaic showing the Nile coursing from the African desert into Alexandria was discovered in the mid-seventeenth century. A painter with the historical interests of Nicolas Poussin (1594–1665) could not resist setting paintings like *The Finding of Moses* in a landscape dominated by the Egyptian buildings he saw in the Palestrina Mosaic (although nothing could prepare a European artist for the idea of the Egyptian desert – Poussin paints his obelisks and Nilometers amid the lush vegetation of the Roman countryside). To orient pilgrims on their journey through the streets of Rome, Pope Sixtus V (reigned 1585–90) reerected an impressive number of the city's toppled obelisks, duly baptizing them and topping each with a cross (along with a star and mountains drawn from his own coat of arms) to symbolize the victory of Christianity over ancient "superstition." In an amazing feat of technological bravado, the pope's favorite architect, Domenico Fontana (1543–1607), moved the massive Vatican obelisk from the side of St. Peter's basilica to the open space in front, employing 144 horse-drawn cranes to perform the feat. The bronze ball on top, rumored to contain the ashes of Julius Caesar, proved disappointingly empty – not every local legend was based on truth.

The most impressive Egyptian-revival monument of the seventeenth century, and perhaps the richest in symbolism, is the *Fountain of the Four Rivers* (1651) in Rome's Piazza Navona, commissioned by Pope Innocent X (reigned 1644–55) in the late 1640s, and designed by Gianlorenzo Bernini with the help of the German Jesuit who claimed to be able to read Egyptian hieroglyphics, Father Athanasius Kircher (1602–80). Originally intended as an attraction for pilgrims to Rome in the Jubilee Year of 1650, the fountain was finally completed in 1651, an Egyptian obelisk set above a travertine cavern that gushes water beneath the colossal figures of river gods representing the great rivers of four continents: the Nile, Danube, Ganges, and Argentina's Rio de la Plata. As Father Kircher explained in a companion volume to the glorious fountain, the Egyptian obelisk, surmounted by the Cross and symbols from the pope's coat of arms, symbolizes the eternal "truths of religion and laws of nature," anticipated by the ancient Egyptians and realized in full by contemporary Christianity. The travertine understructure represents the world in all its change and uncertainty, where the only sure foundation is that provided by God through the Church. For Kircher, who nurtured passionate interests in magnetism and geology as well as Egyptology, there is no conflict between science and religion, or between science and the classical tradition, or between the classical tradition and religion: they are all paths that lead to God, and he presents the fountain, still one of Rome's most compelling tourist attractions, as a joyous testimony to religious faith.

A little over a decade later, Bernini and Kircher joined forces again, for Pope Innocent's successor, Alexander VII, to design a pedestal for yet another obelisk, discovered in the gardens of the Dominican convent at Santa Maria Sopra Minerva. The bearer of this little spire, after Bernini had run through a delightful series of preliminary sketches (including a struggling Hercules who staggers with the obelisk alarmingly off kilter), is an elephant who expresses the wisdom of the ages in a knowing smirk, turning his fat tail towards the Dominicans' front door (Roman legend has it that the elephant is protesting the condemnation of Galileo, which happened inside this very convent; it certainly seems more than possible that Kircher and Bernini, both notorious pranksters, are having a joke on the Dominicans with the collusion of their friend, Pope Alexander VII, who notably favored Kircher's Jesuit order).

Because Etruscan culture was so thoroughly absorbed by ancient Rome, it was difficult for later artists to recognize, let alone establish for themselves, a recognizably Etruscan style in art. Vitruvius' description of "Etruscan design" (*Tuscanicae dispositiones*) in his *Ten Books on Architecture* provided one of the few clues to how Etruscan temples might have looked, with four simple, unfluted columns widely spaced across the facade, and Tuscan artists like Baldassare Peruzzi (1481–1536) and Giuliano da Sangallo (1445–1516) used this form to convey the idea of Etruscan heritage in commissions for Tuscan patrons (Peruzzi in a painting of the *Presentation of the Virgin* for the Sienese banker Filippo Sergardi in Santa Maria della Pace, Rome, and Sangallo for the façade of the Villa Medici at Poggio a Caiano). Sixteenth-century architectural theorists, including Raphael (1483–1520) and Jacopo Barozzi da Vignola (1507–73), grouped classical columns into five canonical "orders," enshrining unfluted columns with simple capitals and bases as the Tuscan Order; thereafter Tuscan columns became the most evident indicators of Etruscan style. At the very beginning of the sixteenth century the architect Donato Bramante (1444–1514), inspired by the forged Etruscan histories of Annius of Viterbo, employed a distinctive combination of Doric entablature, Tuscan columns, and rustication to create buildings that reflected the supposed Etruscan origins of the papacy, as in an elegant round church marking an alternative site for St. Peter's crucifixion, the "Tempietto" (Little Temple) of San Pietro in Montorio (1502). Bramante repeated this same combination in his designs for St. Peter's Basilica and the Vatican Palace, so that it became standard for the buildings commissioned by later sixteenth-century popes, from Paul III to Sixtus V (and also for the architecture of the Escorial in Spain – for Annius of Viterbo had also involved the Spanish monarchy in his Etrusco-Egyptian fantasies). When Gianlorenzo Bernini designed his dramatic oval colonnade for the piazza of St. Peter's in the mid-seventeenth century, he continued to use Tuscan columns – his patron, Pope Alexander VII, was a native of Siena who prided himself on Etruscan ancestry – but topped them with an Ionic dentil frieze to match the friezes that adorned both the interior and exterior of the church itself.

4   The Baroque outside Rome

The realities of seventeenth-century politics led other European powers to challenge Rome's claim to ownership of the classical tradition, and, by extension, of cultural supremacy. The most insistent challenge of the seventeenth century came from France, for Paris, unlike Rome, ranked as one of the largest cities in the world and the French monarchy nurtured ambitions on a comparable scale. A close relationship developed between the Florentine Pope Urban VIII Barberini (1622–44) and the French court, resulting in a series of lavish classical publications, sponsored by the papacy, adorned with title pages by the greatest engravers of the day, and issued by the French Royal Press, including works of Vergil, Horace, Theocritus – and the poetry of Urban himself. But France also emphasized its distinctive heritage, from the Gauls to Charlemagne, taking pride in the way that the French language had evolved from Latin, and the way in which French scholars and French universities had upheld the classical heritage. With the encouragement of King Louis XIII (reigned 1610–43), the powerful Cardinal Richelieu rebuilt the Sorbonne (1626–9) and founded the Académie de France (1635) to ensure that French intellectual life, and the French language, challenged Latin and Latin-based culture as the basis of international exchange. After the death of Pope Urban VIII in 1644, the young King Louis XIV (reigned 1643–1715) adopted the late pope's Egyptian-inspired solar imagery to become the Sun King par excellence. For this same long-lived monarch, the physician and architect Claude Perrault (1613–88) produced an illustrated translation of Vitruvius in 1673, and an *Ordonnance des cinq espèces des colonnes selon la méthode des anciens* (Order of the five types of columns according to the method of the ancients) in 1683, implicitly transforming the French king into a new Augustus and identifying France, not Rome, as the place where the classical tradition in architecture continued to grow and thrive with the greatest vigor. When Perrault defeated no less than Gian Lorenzo Bernini for a commission to design a new wing at the Louvre, the transfer of the classical mantle to France was seen as complete, at least in French eyes.

But France was not the only European country to claim its place in the classical tradition, or to use Baroque art and architecture to cement that claim. Belgians, Swedes, Germans, Spaniards, Portuguese, and Hungarians all scoured ancient Greek and Latin authors to find connections between their forbears and the cultures of Greece and Rome, and commissioned works of art to promote those connections. The haunting picture by Rembrandt (1606–69) of *The Oath of Claudius Civilis* (1661), now in the National Museum of Stockholm, provides a telling example: commissioned by the City Council of Amsterdam to adorn the City Hall, it shows a scene recounted by Tacitus: in AD 69, Claudius Julius Civilis, the one-eyed king of the ancient Batavians, swore with his comrades to overthrow Roman rule. The Batavians had inhabited the Low Countries in ancient Roman times; Rembrandt's huge, dramatic painting not only celebrated local antiquity and local independence, but also made pointed reference to recent history: Spain had ruled all the Low Countries into the late sixteenth century, and Flanders well into the seventeenth. It was not hard to recognize Catholic Spain in imperial Rome, or Protestant Amsterdam in the Batavians. Unfortunately, the subject was not classical enough for Amsterdam's regents (the Batavians look like a rough, unrefined crew): they ordered Rembrandt to remove the "pagan" work, and he slashed it to pieces – the canvas in Stockholm is a fragment.

In Spain itself, Diego Velázquez (1599–1660), court painter to Philip IV, more safely cast contemporary political figures (possibly including Pope Urban VIII) as classical gods in *The Forge of Vulcan* of 1630 (now in Madrid's Museo del Prado). Peter Paul Rubens (1577–1640), a diplomat and scholar as well as a consummate painter, used classical gods to denounce the brutality of the battles between Catholics and Protestants in the Thirty Years War (1618–48). He painted *Allegory on the Blessings of Peace* (1629; National Gallery, London) on a diplomatic mission to King Charles I of England. As he attempted, successfully, to convince Charles to exchange ambassadors with Spain, he made an equally fervent plea in paint: Peace, a ripe Rubens nude, squirts milk from her breast into the mouth of baby Plutus, the embodiment of wealth (the pairing of Peace and the child Plutus, as Rubens well knew from the *Natural History* of Pliny the Elder, went back to a famous statue by the Athenian sculptor Cephistodotus, father of Praxiteles). Just in front of Peace, a satyr looks hungrily at the fruit tumbling from a cornucopia, while one of the leopards of Dionysus bats at a trailing grapevine like a huge, playful kitten. Just behind this sexy scene, a rather stolid-looking Mars, flanked by the fury Allecto, still tries to rush into battle, but he is blocked by a shield borne on the strong arm of Minerva, her blazing armor fully a match for his in brilliance. Peace, Rubens implies, brings abundance. Peace is the intelligent choice. In 1630, Charles I and Philip IV of Spain signed a treaty.

The peace that Rubens helped to foster would not last; his painted protest against resumption of hostilities, *The Consequences of War* (1637–8; Galleria Palatina, Pitti Palace, Florence), composed on a forceful diagonal sweep that moves from lower left to upper right, centers on a contest between Venus and Allecto, each pulling on an arm of a Mars run amok, bloodied sword at the ready. Beautiful as she is, Venus has lost the contest to the dark hag Allecto; Mars pulls away from his mistress as he and his demonic troops, egged on by the screaming Fury, trample women and children underfoot. Rubens's agitated brushwork adds an electric charge to the sense of chaos and over-whelming ugliness. Just as in ancient times, when Aristophanes could cast contemporary politicians as gods, heroes, or Paphlagonian slaves, classical myths provided Baroque authors and artists with ways of telling stories, rendering opinions, and recommending action without explicitly naming names. The ancients' freedom in showing the human body allowed Baroque painters and sculptors a similar freedom for their art; Velázquez' voluptuous *Venus with a Mirror* (now in the National Gallery, London), Rubens's plump, rosy *Three Graces* and *Andromeda*, along with Guido Reni's (1575–1642) endless legions of gasping, snowy-breasted *Lucretia*s and *Cleopatra*s, were heroically nude rather than shamefully naked, as was Bernini's big, smiling *Allegory of Truth Revealed by Time* (1645–52), who holds the blazing sun of enlightenment in her hand, burning the consciences of liars but not her own dimpled hand.

5 Scholarship

The learned conceits of Baroque art called for learned artists: Borromini eventually owned a thousand books, Bernini four hundred; Rubens studied with the classical scholar Justus Lipsius (1547–1606). In addition, artists and scholars often worked together to devise allegories, mythological representations, historical scenes, and frontispieces. Printed books opened a whole new range of options for engravers, many of whom developed a specific ability to reproduce designs created by other artists – or by authors, whose clumsy sketches a good book engraver could somehow turn into beautiful illustrations. Gianlorenzo Bernini's sometime collaborator, the Jesuit scholar Athanasius Kircher, published a monumental series of folio picture books on subjects ranging from ancient Egypt to magnetism, geology, China, music, and optics, each volume more lavishly illustrated than the last. For many of these works, Kircher's own forceful but clumsy drawings provided the basis for exquisitely polished illustrations that issued from the studios of professional engravers in Rome and Amsterdam.

Although Baroque artists regarded the artists of classical antiquity as the supreme masters of style, they also noted the profound differences between that style and the styles of medieval, Byzantine, and Asian art: a pair of engraved illustrations in one of Father Athanasius Kircher's books, *China illustrata* (China illustrated), depicts an Asian statue in the style of a Chinese ink drawing and then, on the facing page, shows the same work in Western style with cross-hatched shading. With similar care, artists in Baroque Rome copied early Christian paintings and mosaics for the "paper museum" of the wealthy antiquarian Cassiano dal Pozzo (1588–1657), who collected drawings of the objects he could not amass for himself. Although recognizable as seventeenth-century work, these copies for the "paper museum" make an evident effort to reproduce style along with subject matter. Dal Pozzo also commissioned a series of paintings from Nicolas Poussin of *The Seven Sacraments* (ca. 1637–42; Belvoir Castle, Grantham); these large, impressive works combined Church history with archaeological investigation to show the traditional Catholic ceremonies as if they were taking place in Early Christian times and in real locales around Rome.

Cassiano dal Pozzo's combined interest in classical antiquity, nature, and exotic civilizations was typical of his time: in Florence, the Grand Dukes of Tuscany collected Aztec and Olmec figurines and carved elephant tusks alongside ancient Roman cameos. Athanasius Kircher's famous museum in the Jesuit College of Rome contained Roman and Etruscan statues, skeletons, a stuffed armadillo (which still exists), a statue carved from a meteorite in the fourteenth century, dinosaur teeth, and a series of Egyptian amulets that he may well have produced himself. For the seventeenth century was also a century of outrageous forgeries. The most notorious may have been the pseudo-Etruscan documents "discovered" in 1634 by the young Tuscan nobleman Curzio Inghirami (1614–55) and definitively condemned as fake in 1640 by the Greek-Italian scholar Leone Allacci (1586–1669), but the temptation to create or embroider a classical heritage proved irresistible in every corner of Europe: as the Dutch identified themselves with the Batavians, in Sweden, the physician Olof Rudbeck (1630–1702) gathered archaeological evidence and citations from classical authors to prove that the real site of lost Atlantis had been his own town of Uppsala. Some scholars contentedly embellished the ancient histories of their adopted homes: thus a Scotsman, Thomas Dempster (1579–1625), and a Frenchman, Guillaume Postel (1510–81), both concentrated their considerable ingenuity on further embellishing the history of the Etruscans. Amid this remarkable population of forged documents and embroidered histories, one genuine text stands out: in 1625, near Xi'an, China, the Jesuit Alvaro Semedo (1585–1658) discovered a 9-foot-tall monument inscribed in Syriac and Chinese that commemorated the introduction of Christianity ("the Luminous Religion") in the year 781. This stele, called the "Nestorian stone" after a common, if inaccurate, name for the easternmost branch of the Church (now known as the Assyrian Church of the East), provided seventeenth-century scholars with a genuine, concrete clue to the real immensity of the ancient classical world and the Christian cultures that had descended from it. Indeed, between archaeological exploration and travelers' tales, the physical realities of the classical world seemed to become ever more tangible in the seventeenth century; the past was proving as exciting a source for new discoveries as nature itself.

For many scholars, the discoveries of the seventeenth century, whether about the classical past, the peoples of the world, or the structure of the universe, served only to reinforce their religious faith (Athanasius Kircher's books are filled with praises of God), but the same kinds of questioning that led to the Protestant Reformation also led some seventeenth-century thinkers into deep skepticism, a stance that had its own impeccable classical roots. As the contours of the ancient world became better known, so did its differences from the modern world, and these differences may have been most apparent in the field of natural philosophy. To be sure, an ancient philosopher, Aristarchus, had already proposed a sun-centered world system, and even the idea of an infinitely large universe could find support among ancient authors, but nothing in antiquity could quite anticipate the discoveries of the telescope and the microscope. The very success of the humanist movement's concentration on the testing and scrutiny of ancient texts had led scholars and thinkers to a more general emphasis on empirical investigation, of texts, of traditions, of cultures, of the phenomena of nature, and the sense of perpetual movement that characterized the Baroque view of the world could make human institutions seem temporary, culture-bound, rooted in provisional rather than absolute truths. Beset by this sense of general unrest, the seventeenth century gave rise both to libertines and to Inquisitors, to Voltaire and to Robert Bellarmine, the Jesuit cardinal who himself believed that space was a liquid rather than Aristotle's crystalline spheres, but who condemned the philosopher Giordano Bruno, who proclaimed the infinity of the universe, to burn at the stake for heresy in 1600. More than at any time in the history of the classical tradition, perhaps, the Baroque era put the very nature of that tradition to the test.

6   Music

Baroque music, like Baroque art and Baroque scholarship, took the classical tradition in unexpected new directions during the seventeenth century. Ancient poets, both Greek and Latin, had described their activity explicitly as singing: thus Homer began his *Iliad* by asking the Muse to "sing the wrath of Achilles," and Vergil his *Aeneid* by claiming to "sing" of "arms and the man." Propertius claimed that the poet was a "priest" who "sings sacred things" (*sacra canit vates*). Hence when groups like the Camerata of Florence or individuals like the composer Claudio Monteverdi (1567– 1643) resolved to recreate ancient Greek tragedy at the very beginning of the seventeenth century, they assumed that dramatic poetry, too, was sung. Monteverdi's *Orfeo* of 1607 introduced solo arias and half-spoken recitatives amid passages of choral music to present the story of Orpheus and Eurydice to the Duke of Mantua and his court – but rather than recreating Greek tragedy as he had intended, Monteverdi had invented something entirely new: opera.

With his ravishing orchestral writing and his arias' masterful use of harmony and dissonance to convey emotional states (all based on his idiosyncratic understanding of the ancient Greek musical modes), Monteverdi proved irresistible to Baroque audiences; so did opera, and arias, which became increasingly ornamental to match the visual opulence of most performances. Composers like Giulio Caccini of Rome (ca. 1545–1618) used vocal acrobatics as well as chromatic passages to express the throes of love, rage, joy, and despair, writing for women singers as well as men and castrati. The Roman painter Andrea Sacchi (1599–1661) produced a particularly mordant portrait of the famous castrato Marcantonio Pasqualini (1614–91; the portrait, dated 1641, is in the Metropolitan Museum of Art), who entered the Sistine Chapel choir in 1630 and made his solo debut two years later: the short, dark singer, in elaborate formal dress – including some striking red socks – stands next to a tall, blonde, stark naked Apollo (modeled, as usual, on the Apollo Belvedere) who flaunts his own intact manhood; the finial on the castrato's portable pipe organ shows another of Apollo's victims, Daphne, turning into a tree. Behind Apollo, his onetime rival in music, the satyr Marsyas, lies bound and ready to be flayed in punishment for daring to challenge Apollo to a contest between his pipes and Apollo's lyre; the beautiful god will go to any lengths to enforce the purity, and superiority, of his art, which in the 1640s implied the kind of solo singing at which Pasqualini excelled. This image of the castrato must have been popular, for Sacchi painted another version, although this time with Apollo clothed in a strategically fluttering drape.

In the religious sphere, the Council of Trent had made recommendations for music as well as art, urging Catholic composers, like Catholic artists, to emphasize clarity – their Protestant competitors had found a formidable weapon in the rousing hymns of Martin Luther and Hans Sachs. Under this pressure to communicate, the elaborate polyphonic church music of the fifteenth and sixteenth centuries gave way in the mid-sixteenth century to the pointed simplicity of composers like Giovanni di Pierluigi da Palestrina (ca. 1526–94), whose ability to invent limpid polyphonic masses effectively saved the medium from extinction. Baroque composers continued to emphasize clarity, but enriched their music with elaborate ornamentation. Gregorio Allegri's (1582–1652) *Miserere* (1638), written for Pope Urban VIII, combined the repetitive litany of Psalm 51 with a stratospheric soprano line to create a haunting, ethereal effect without sacrificing the intelligibility of a single word in the sacred text. Opera's combination of solo and choral singing worked as memorably for Bible stories and saints' lives as for ancient myth: Stefano Landi's (ca. 1586–1609) *Il Sant'Alessio* (Saint Alexis, 1634), with stage sets by the versatile Pietro da Cortona, was an early, and successful, example, entirely modeled on Baroque ideas of ancient drama. True Religion descends on a cloud like a classical deus ex machina, and St. Alexis, scored for a castrato, produces the same vocal fireworks that any mythological hero might, although his heroic achievement was to live in Christian poverty under the stairs in his family home, unrecognized even by his parents.

In music, as in the arts, the developments of the Baroque era demonstrate not only the power of the classical tradition, but also, pointedly, its infinite flexibility;

antiquity's most careful students, like Borromini, Monteverdi, or Isaac Newton, sometimes became its most radical reinterpreters. Ironically, even in empirical science, the area where the ancients proved most fallible as models for their seventeenth-century followers, classical principles continued to guide intellectual endeavor, and guide it still: contemporary scientists, no less than Aristotle or Galileo, prize "elegant" solutions, "robust" proofs, and a harmonious universe. Like Baroque artists, they have found their greatest freedom in discipline.

FURTHER READING

Excellent overviews of the Baroque period, especially in Rome, can be found in Haskell (1980) and Magnuson (1981), which concentrate on social as well as artistic life; for more strictly artistic information, see Wittkower (1999). For life inside a Baroque palazzo, Waddy (1990) and Scott (1991) provide information on everything from hygiene to etiquette and patronage. Two remarkable views of Baroque architecture are provided from two different perspectives by Connors: the use of façades to communicate social relationships in Connors (1989), and the connection between Baroque architecture and the gentleman's hobby of turning on the lathe (Connors 1990).

For Caravaggio, see Langdon (2000). For Bernini, see Magnuson (1981) and Marder (1998). For Borromini, Blunt (2005) is eminently readable, if opinionated; for the competition between Bernini and Borromini, see Morrissey (2005). Montagu (1993) provides a witty introduction to Baroque sculpture. For Rubens, several recent exhibition catalogues provide excellent illustrations and essays: Brejon de Lavergnée et al. (2004), Logan and Plomp (2005), Piotrovsky et al. (2005). For Velázquez, see Brown (1986); and look for the catalogue of an exhibition at the National Gallery, London, from October 2006.

For the intellectual setting of Baroque Italy and an introduction to the "Paper Museum" of Cassiano dal Pozzo, see Freedberg (2003); see also Miller (2000). The articles in Findlen (2004) provide a look at the wide interests of Athanasius Kircher. For Egypt in Rome, see Curran (2004). For Etruscan themes, the forgeries of Curzio Inghirami and forgery in general, see Rowland (2004). For the "Nestorian Stone," see Hsia (2004) in Findlen (2004). For Olof Rudbeck's Swedish Atlantis, King (2005) is a vivid storyteller.

Hammond (1994) provides a vivid picture of Baroque music and its performance; see also Murata (1997). Stefano Landi's *Il Sant'Alessio* has been recorded by Les Arts Florissants (Landi 1996), but hear also his *Homo fugit velut umbra* (Man is as fleeting as a shadow) (Landi 2003), performed by the phenomenal Marco Beasley.

CHAPTER FIVE

Neoclassicism

Thomas Kaminski

1 Introduction

Of all the periods of literary history, the one that spans the years 1660 to 1800 is most commonly identified with the classical tradition. The chief literary movement in France at this time is termed "classicism" and its English cousin "neoclassicism" – and with good reason. The writers of the age consciously adopted the genres and conventions of ancient literature and applied ideas and techniques derived from the classics to their own literary practice. These authors, though, were not simple, backward-looking admirers of ancient glory; they were in fact intent on creating the most compelling works of art in the most up-to-date style. Paradoxical though it may seem, to learn from the past and to renovate its forms was for these artists the height of sophistication; indeed, the neoclassical style was the true modern style.

The development of neoclassicism was a gradual process that can be traced back to early seventeenth-century France. François de Malherbe, disapproving of various kinds of Renaissance exuberance, sought to "reform" French verse by tightening its structure. There was in fact nothing inherently "classical" in Malherbe's reforms, but by mid-century they had become established guides to poetic technique, and the disciples of Malherbe had come to see in them a parallel to the refined poetic style that Vergil and Horace had introduced in the age of Augustus.

The parallel was not wholly without basis. In his satires and epistles, Horace had offered a desultory history of Roman literature. The early Italians, he tells us, had written a primitive sort of verse, the Saturnian (*Epistles* 2.1.158). Then Ennius introduced Greek prosody, and the long road towards literary sophistication began. Progress, though, was slow. Lucilius' verse was muddy (*Satires* 1.4.7–13), and Plautus was inelegant and crude (*Ars poetica* 270–4). It was not until the modern age (the age of Augustus) that Roman poetry achieved perfection of form. This version of literary history, clearly tendentious and often unfair, is the founding myth of neoclassicism. French and English authors of the late seventeenth century used it as a template to redraw the histories of their own national literatures. In *L'Art poétique* (The art of poetry, 1674) Nicolas Boileau tells a similar story: Villon and Marot had established the basic verse forms; Ronsard then tried to bring order to art, but through pride and pedantry had failed. Finally Malherbe came ("Enfin Malherbe vint," line 131) to teach Frenchmen how to write. A tour of Dryden's criticism finds the same myth of literary progress being worked out on English soil. In the *Defence of the Epilogue to the Second Part of the Conquest of Granada* (1672), Dryden surveys the playwrights of the previous age, including Shakespeare and Ben Jonson, and finds them wanting. Like Horace's Plautus, they were brilliant but crude. The current age, Dryden argues, demands a new literature befitting its greater refinement.

In all three versions of this story, literary progress is directly tied to a certain kind of societal progress, a move away from the crudity of earlier times and towards refinement and sophistication. Such a movement had been under way in aristocratic circles in France throughout the seventeenth century, beginning in the *précieux* culture of the Parisian salons and culminating in the elegance and splendor of the court of Louis XIV. Charles II had spent the Interregnum in France and brought back to England many of the same prejudices that had characterized French society; and although the English still boasted of their greater native vigor, they nevertheless emulated the elegance of their French neighbors. Neither court, it bears saying, displayed an exemplary level of morals, but in manners each appeared to surpass its predecessors. The poets flattered both Louis and Charles as the new Augustus, and they began to wonder aloud whether they were not living in a new Augustan age. In England, the literature resulting from this interplay between aesthetic and social forces came to be called "polite letters" – a polished form of writing that appealed to a cultured and discriminating audience – and it is by this name that neoclassicism was known in its own day. (To a later age of critics, the movement was often called "Augustanism.")

Finally, by the middle of the seventeenth century, a consensus had formed among French authors concerning a true "classical" style. The principles of this new doctrine were on the whole derived from Aristotle and Horace, but they showed the influence of Malherbe as well. The new style was one of restraint and careful craftsmanship; it relied on the imagination, but kept it under tight rein. Exuberance was its enemy. And since the seventeenth century was a century of intellectual systems, critics like René Rapin and Dominic Bouhours reduced classical theory to a coherent set of principles.

2   Classical Doctrine and the "Rules of Art"

The new classical doctrine had five major elements: (1) that imitation was the basis for artistic creation, (2) that "rules" existed to guide the artist, (3) that genius must submit to the yoke of "art," (4) that propriety was required in all aspects of a work, and (5) that art must teach as well as delight. From this simple enumeration of principles one can already spy out "reason" lurking in the shadows, but the principles were often developed in subtle ways that encouraged creativity as much as they frowned on excess.

We can begin with imitation. In the *Poetics* Aristotle tells us that art imitates nature, but how is this accomplished? The artistic culture of the Romans, on which the French critics based so many of their judgments, was both conservative and pragmatic. For them the literary tradition had already answered most of the difficult questions. A wise poet learns from the experience of his predecessors. As a result imitation takes on a new meaning: the best way to capture nature is to imitate existing works that accomplished this goal. In his *Essay on Criticism* (1711) Alexander Pope offers his own fantastic literary history to illustrate the idea for his contemporaries:

> When first young Maro [Vergil] in his boundless mind
> A work t'outlast immortal Rome design'd,
> Perhaps he seem'd above the critick's law,
> And but from Nature's fountains scorn'd to draw:
> But when t'examine ev'ry part he came,
> Nature and Homer were, he found, the same.
>
> (lines 130–5)

That is, Vergil discovered that he could best imitate nature by imitating Homer. The doctrine of imitation, then, was a sort of literary short cut, a means of exploiting the achievements of one's predecessors and engaging one's readers on familiar terrain.

The idea that there are "rules" governing artistic creation flows directly from the concept of imitation. For most genres the rules were little more than the successful practices of former writers. The precept that an epic should begin *in medias res* (in the middle of the story), for example, could have no basis in logic; it was merely a successful practice that resulted in a more satisfying narrative. Alexander Pope again offers a contemporary expression of the principle:

> Those Rules of old discover'd, not devis'd,
> Are Nature still, but Nature methodiz'd.
> (*Essay on Criticism*, lines 88–9)

The rules, then, are practical experience reduced to an orderly system.

In the neoclassical conception, the rules constitute the basis of "art." This term had a somewhat narrower meaning in earlier centuries than it has in ours. Art consisted of a series of skills or techniques that could be taught; an artist was a person who had mastered those techniques. This concept was at the heart of the ancient quarrel about whether a poet was born or made. Everyone agreed that genius was necessary for poetic greatness, but was genius enough, or did it have to be guided by art? The ancient Augustans were poets of refined technique, and this required something more than untutored genius. Horace's advice was clear: study the Greeks night and day (*Ars poetica* 268–9). Art without genius was sterile, but genius without art was crude. The rules – art in a codified form – were necessary if a work was to appeal to a sophisticated taste.

Art, though, was not an end in itself. The greatest poets recognized its purpose and its limits. When a poet found himself too confined by traditional practices, he was free to reject them. And if his new attempt pleased men of taste, he had added to the stock of useful artistic knowledge. In Alexander Pope's phrase, a daring poet might "snatch a grace beyond the reach of art" (*Essay on Criticism* 155). Indeed, the most percep- tive critics were aware that there was often something mysterious or ineffable in the way a literary work affected its audience. Bouhours perhaps captured this quality best in his idea of the *je ne sais quoi*, the inexpressible "I know not what" of a fine piece of writing. And Boileau, with his translation of Longinus' treatise *On the Sublime* (1674), introduced the age to a new and powerful concept. For Boileau, as for Longinus, the "sublime" was achieved through rhetorical techniques and thus was clearly linked to the tradition of "art"; but its effect was the crucial element. The sublime was something extraordinary or marvelous in a work, something that lifts, ravishes, transports the reader. And this, like the *je ne sais quoi*, could not really be taught. Such ideas opened up the true space for genius in the neoclassical scheme. Racine sums up the contemporary attitude: "La principale régle est de plaire et de toucher. Toutes les autres ne sont faites que pour parvenir à cette premiere" (the primary rule is to please and to touch; all the others were made to attain this end; quoted in Yarrow 1967: 203).

   In the end, though, one cannot help but sense that these writers were suspicious of the imagination. The respect for the rules and the deference to the Horatian idea of careful craftsmanship were reinforced at every turn during this time by the tendency towards rationalism. Most writers of the day agreed that the poet's most important faculty was not his imagination but his judgment. This was the element of restraint, the faculty that pruned away all excesses and produced a finished work of art. The term "judgment" is sufficiently general to allow a variety of elements in its com- position, including the even-less-concrete notion of "taste," but underlying it is always at least a hint of reason. It was, after all, the century of Descartes, and reason had become for many the only means of access to the truth, and for some, even to beauty. For thinkers like these, the creative mind was not opposed to the rational but supported by it.

   Judgment was the faculty that governed the next basic element of neoclassical aesthetics: propriety, or decorum, in French *la bienséance*. Although the concept can be found in Aristotle, it has a strong Horatian provenance. Indeed, the first 50 lines of the *Ars poetica* offer a primer on the topic: the elements of a work must fit together, the author must know what to include now and what to defer until later, and so forth. But during the seventeenth century the idea was exalted to the highest level of importance. René Rapin called decorum the essential principle of literary creation, claiming that without it all the other rules were false (Bray 1927: 215). The term implied a vague but universal principle of fitness. Propriety had a social character as well. Not only must the work be skillfully assembled, it must also be fit for its intended audience. It is not enough, for instance, for a satirist to imitate the tone or manner of Juvenal; he must also fashion a poem suitable for his audience – in this case an aristocratic readership, at least nominally Christian, with a distaste for blatant vulgarity. The principle of decorum would here overrule the utility of imitation. Juvenal's nymphomaniacs and homosexual prostitutes were suitable sub- jects for those who could read Latin, but they were not fit to be mentioned in French or English.

Finally, the concept of social decorum was closely allied to the demand for an art of moral instruction. Horace tells us that every poet wishes either to be of use to his readers (*aut prodesse*) or to delight them (*aut delectare*), but the writer wins every vote who mixes the useful with the sweet (*Ars poetica* 333, 343). Horace is far from dogmatic here; the delightful and the useful each has its own audience. But the French critics who formulated the modern theory generally agreed that instruction was necessary; after all, the poet lived in society and had an obligation to it (Bray 1927: 63–84). And to a devout Christian like Samuel Johnson, merely to delight was an unacceptable goal if that delight might encourage sin. In his "Preface to Shakespeare" Johnson sums up the modern rethinking of Horace: "The end of writing is to instruct; the end of poetry is to instruct by pleasing" (1958: 7:67).

These principles provided the general context within which poets and critics thought about literary matters. Roman authors were held in particularly high regard, and their works provided the most important models for imitation. In both France and England, the discursive genres came to dominate. Satire, with its direct link to the Roman tradition, became very popular among contemporary poets, but other discursive forms flourished as well, including poetic essays and epistles. In addition, each nation developed a suitably "refined" verse form appropriate to such topics. French poets, adhering to the rules set down by Malherbe, made the "Alexandrine" couplet an elegant vehicle for discursive verse, while Edmund Waller and Sir John Denham, two poets of the mid-seventeenth century whose verse was praised by contemporaries for its smoothness and musicality, brought in the vogue of the English "heroic" couplet. These verse forms would dominate poetry for the next century.

3   Imitation and Satire

The modern poet who set the pattern for several generations of French and English satirists was Boileau. Horace and Juvenal were his models, and he used them with great ingenuity. The poems themselves are best called "imitations": Boileau would take an idea or situation from Roman satire and develop it in terms of his own contemporary world. For instance, his first and sixth satires (1666) derive directly from Juvenal's Third Satire. In Boileau's first, a disgusted poet explains why he is leaving Paris, and in his sixth Boileau describes a day's adventures in the city – the noise, the mud, the crowds, the danger. Many of the elements are familiar from Juvenal, and some passages are direct translations. But Boileau has made the material his own, adjusting Juvenal's moral complaints to fit his own time and adding rich (often comic) detail to his picture of contemporary Paris. He has also created a new satiric voice, blending the urbanity of Horace with the direct social criticism of Juvenal. And in his most imaginative poems he totally transforms his source. In the wonderfully ironic argument of Satire IX (1668), Boileau accuses his *esprit* (wit) of getting him into trouble. In his wit's reply we hear Horace's own justifications of satire; but Boileau has added a new charm to the familiar material. Finally, Boileau's imitations went beyond satire; in his epistles (1670–98), which praise moderation and encourage the search for self-knowledge, an attentive reader will often hear Horace speaking French.

Boileau's most skillful disciple in this art was Alexander Pope, whose *Imitations of Horace* (1733–8) offer a brilliant reimagining of Horatian material. Pope chose four satires and five epistles that he rendered into elegant English couplets. In each case he follows Horace's text – in fact, he had the Latin printed on the pages facing his version – and yet everything is made new. The setting of the poems is modern England, the cast of characters contemporary society. Like Boileau he had created his own persona, an urbane English gentleman-poet. Horace's reflections are filtered through this new sensibility, his criticisms turned with epigrammatic wit. As a result, everything at the same time is and is not Horace. When Pope's satire turns political, as in the "Epilogue to the Satires," the tone sometimes seems more reminiscent of Juvenal than of Horace, but this is not surprising. Like Boileau, Pope creates his own voice, and he can laugh, rail, or sneer at the world depending on the world's folly or vice.

Samuel Johnson's imitations of Juvenal's Third and Tenth Satires also deserve notice. Johnson's *London* (1738) captures some of Juvenal's contempt for the corrupt metropolis, but Johnson's true genius was for moral reflection rather than biting satire, and it was in Juvenal's Tenth Satire that he found matter proper for his own temperament. *The Vanity of Human Wishes* (1749) is a deep and powerful reworking of Juvenal's reflections on human folly. Johnson maintains the basic structure of Juvenal's poem, with its many examples of misguided desires, but he asserts his own control over the poem's tone. Gone are the sneering and disgust; in their place are sober reflection and an underlying note of sadness. Johnson does not explicitly bring Christianity into the poem, but his religious faith inflects his handling of the material at many points, especially the conclusion, where he follows closely Juvenal's Stoic prayer for resignation, yet accommodates it thoroughly to Christian beliefs.

4   Epic and Mock-Epic

It is one of the curiosities of literary history that in an age that fostered imitation and in which Homer and Vergil were revered as the greatest of poets, epic languished. (Those who recall that *Paradise Lost* first appeared in 1667 may find this claim puzzling, but this is in itself a problem of literary periodization. As his choice of blank verse makes clear, Milton was working in the Renaissance tradition rather than in the "modern" neoclassical style. He stands completely outside the intellectual milieu under consideration in this essay.) And yet, if neither Dryden nor Pope wrote his own epic, both paid homage to the greatest of the genres through translation, Dryden in his *Aeneid*, Pope in his *Iliad*. To the neoclassical poet, though, translation posed a problem: how was the author to capture not just the sense, but the genius of the original? Prose would never do, for that would sacrifice every trace of the poem's artistry. To render verse into prose was to falsify the very nature of the original. And so in his version of the *Aeneid*, Dryden sifted Vergil's meaning through centuries of commentary, then adopted the diction of English epic gleaned from (among others) Spenser and Milton, and deployed that language in the "heroic" couplet, with all the rhetorical flourishes typical of that style. In doing so Dryden distorted the precise character of Vergil's style, but his *Aeneid* remains a great English poem.

In his translation of the *Iliad*, Pope followed Dryden's practice, turning Homer into a poet of "Augustan" elegance. Perhaps no other poem ever pointed out so clearly the tensions inherent in poetic translation: Samuel Johnson, responding to the sustained brilliance of the verse, called it a "poetical wonder, ... a performance which no age or nation can pretend to equal" (*Lives of the English Poets* 3.236), while the great classicist Richard Bentley supposedly remarked, "It is a pretty poem, Mr. Pope, but you must not call it Homer" (*Lives* 3.213). Both were to a large extent correct.

But if it was not an age of epic, it was an age of parody, and the mock-epic thrived. In *Le Lutrin* (The lectern, 1674) Boileau ridiculed a dispute that arose between two church dignitaries after the treasurer of Sainte-Chapelle placed a *lutrin* in front of the choir, hiding the choirmaster from public view. Boileau retells the petty yet acrimonious dispute that followed in the heightened diction and tone of epic. The poem's first lines give a sense of the style:

> Je chante les combats, et ce prelat terrible,
> Qui par ses longs travaux, et sa force invincible,
> Dans une illustre église exerçant son grand coeur,
> Fit placer à la fin un lutrin dans le choeur.

> Arms and the priest I sing, whose martial soul
> No toil could terrify, no fear control;
> Active it urged his outward man to dare
> The num'rous hazards of a pious war:
> Nor did th' immortal prelate's labors cease,
> Till victory had crowned 'em with success;
> Till his gay eyes sparkling with fluid fire,
> Beheld the desk reflourish in the choir.
> (*Boileau's Lutrin*, trans. J. Ozell, 1708)

Boileau employs much of the machinery of epic as well: the goddess Discord provokes the dispute; the hero consults Chicane, the Sibyl of the law courts; and the rivals battle in a library. The work teems with parodic echoes of Vergil and Homer, all of which contribute to its humor.

In England the mock-heroic flourished. John Dryden's *Mac Flecknoe* (1682), Samuel Garth's *The Dispensary* (1699), and Alexander Pope's *The Dunciad* (1728; 1743) all use the language of heroic verse to ridicule the actions of recognizable contemporaries. Perhaps the greatest of all the mock-heroic poems, though, is Pope's *The Rape of the Lock* (1714). As with *Le Lutrin*, the story arose from a real incident, a young nobleman's clipping a lock of hair from the head of a young lady. The poem is remarkable for its elegance and its subtlety as Pope's retelling of the incident mingles ironic humor with serious reflections on the relations between the sexes. At least a portion of the poem's genius lies in its echoes of ancient epic, which often appear in startlingly new contexts and invite the reader to muse on their transformation.

5   The Ode

In 1656 Abraham Cowley published his *Pindarique Odes*, a collection of 15 poems
emulating Pindar's grand manner. It was a bold experiment. No less an authority than
Horace had warned poets of the sad fate of anyone who attempted to rival Pindar
(*Odes* 4.2). For Cowley, though, the style was an end in itself. Its long digressions,
bold figures, and irregular meters were thought to mimic poetic fury. The new
Pindaric ode was the artificial expression of overpowering feeling.

   The ode was easily reconciled to neoclassical theory. No one could deny that strong
passions were natural, so there must be a poetically appropriate articulation of such
feelings. And Pindar himself sanctioned the attempt. As a result, most of the important poets of the day tried their hand at the ode's irregular measures and heightened
tone. Dryden was undoubtedly the most successful. He tended to reserve the genre
for special occasions calling for strong emotions, like the death of the young painter
and poet Anne Killigrew. The ode also became the conventional form for writing
about music, which, according to Renaissance theory, had an almost irresistible power
to sway the passions. Two of Dryden's finest odes, *A Song for St. Cecilia's Day* (1687)
and *Alexander's Feast* (1697), are in this subgenre and were in fact written for musical
accompaniment.

   To modern readers, though, the Pindarics of the age seem stiff and artificial. Their
diction is often conventional rather than immediate, and even the emotion generally
seems contrived. Indeed, they were so out of keeping with the genius of the day that
they betray less spontaneity and passion – the presumed justification for their form –
than a satire by Boileau or an epistle by Pope.

6   The Drama and Its Criticism

The area in which neoclassical theory sparked the most controversy was undoubtedly
the drama, particularly tragedy. Aristotle himself had discussed tragedy at length in
the *Poetics*, and Renaissance critics, first bowing to his authority, then seeking to
rationalize his precepts, developed his remarks into a series of rules. Most notorious
of these were the three "unities" – those of action, time, and place (Bray 1927: 240–
88). The sixteenth-century Italian critic Castelvetro, adding a psychological justification for several of Aristotle's principles, argued that the spectator judges the truth of a
drama by its fidelity to his own experience of time and place. Hence not only must a
play's action be unified, but the stage can represent only one place, and the action
itself should approximate the amount of time spent in the theater (Bray 1927: 256).
The unities thus enforced the illusion of reality.

   But the unities were not the only rules derived from ancient theories. French critics
of the seventeenth century, for example, argued that each character should be restricted
to its "type," a concept traceable to both Aristotle and Horace. Different times of life
and different social positions, they noted, all have their typical qualities: a youth differs
from an old man in his habits and desires, a farmer differs from a merchant, and so on.

Under the theory of types, each character takes on added significance, for he exemplifies his age and status. The play, then, does not merely depict the encounters of individuals but the interaction of broad social forces. The characters are not particular people but representative, even universal, figures (Bray 1927: 221–2).

The primary effect of the dramatic rules was to put pressure, both artistic and social, on the playwright. The rules themselves encouraged a form of artistic purity – a play should have a simple, clear plot with representative characters. For Racine the rules appear to have been a spur to his genius, for they allowed him to explore directly and intensely the passions of his characters. Since the rules were generally known, though, a writer who neglected them risked being attacked by critics who knew no other basis for judging plays. Nevertheless, no author appears to have abided by them in all cases; the demands of plot and character often overcame the imperatives of theory. English playwrights like Dryden tended to take a middle ground: they did not adhere to the unities with any rigor, but they sought to prune extravagances and to tighten structure. The best contemporary discussion of these matters is undoubtedly Dryden's *Essay of Dramatic Poesy* (1668), a dialogue in which four speakers debate the merits of ancient and contemporary drama, with a full consideration of the value of the rules.

Of all the critical controversies brought on by the application of neoclassical rules, the most important is the dispute over Shakespeare's plays. If Shakespeare knew of Castelvetro and his theory of the "unities," he paid no heed to them. It is not unusual in his plays for years to pass between scenes or for the action to shift from one nation to another, and his characters often violate the expectations set by their social roles. To many critics of the late seventeenth century, such looseness signaled a lack of "art." Thomas Rymer, one of the most influential critics of the age, denied Shakespeare's plays any merit (see especially his contemptuous analysis of *Othello* in *A Short View of Tragedy*, 1693). Indeed, Shakespeare's artlessness was so widely accepted that many of his plays were rewritten by contemporary playwrights, and these "improved" versions held the stage, to the exclusion of Shakespeare's actual texts, throughout the eighteenth century.

But Shakespeare still had his partisans, and it was the last of the major neoclassical critics, Samuel Johnson, who vindicated Shakespeare's position as the greatest English dramatist. In his "Preface to Shakespeare," Johnson returns to the most basic of Aristotelian principles, that art is an imitation of nature: "Shakespeare," he tells us, "is above all writers, at least above all modern writers, the poet of nature; the poet that holds up to his readers a faithful mirrour of manners and of life" (1958– : 7:62). If Shakespeare violates the rules, he does so triumphantly; he dismisses the intermediaries of "art" and goes directly to nature. Some critics had complained that Shakespeare's characters were not proper "types," that his kings did not always act like kings and that a Roman senator was portrayed as a buffoon. To these Johnson replies:

Shakespeare always makes nature predominate over accident.... His story requires Romans or kings, but he thinks only on men. He knew that Rome, like every other city, had men of all dispositions; and wanting a buffoon, he went into the senate-house for that which the senate-house would certainly have afforded him. (1958– : 7:65–6)

As for the unities, Johnson dismisses them by attacking Castelvetro's premise and appealing to common sense. The audience is not disturbed or confused if a play breaks the illusion of reality: "The truth is, that the spectators are always in their senses, and know, from the first act to the last, that the stage is only a stage, and that the players are only players" (1958– : 7:77). And so ended the tyranny of literary theories over the practice of irregular dramatists.

7   The Politics of Augustanism

The emperor Augustus had always been a controversial figure. Vergil and Horace had honored him for bringing the civil wars to an end, even if it was at the cost of Roman liberty. Tacitus had depicted him as a ruthless politician who had removed all his enemies through war or proscription and then ruled the state as a tyrant. Poets like Juvenal and Martial, distressed at the lack of literary patronage during their own age, looked back to the reign of Augustus as a time when men of wit and taste both governed Rome and supported writers of genius. Augustus, then, could be either enlightened monarch or pitiless tyrant, depending on the use a poet or historian wished to make of him.

In seventeenth-century France, the court of Augustus was to be emulated. Indeed, the comparison of modern France with Augustan Rome had patriotic implications: Louis XIV was now the incomparable monarch, a modern rival to Augustus. In England, though, the political situation was more complicated, and Augustus served several different political purposes. For some Oliver Cromwell was a modern Augustus who had destroyed the state and set himself up as tyrant. Conversely, in *Astraea Redux* (Justice restored, 1660), a poem celebrating the Restoration of Charles II, Dryden could proclaim the advent of a new Augustan age that promised to rejuvenate English "arms and arts" (line 322). In the end Dryden and his contemporaries would be disappointed by Charles's rule, but the myth of the Augustan court, with its men of taste dispensing enlightened patronage to writers of genius, remained an ideal for literary men, one that poets of all political parties could exploit. The writer in search of patronage, for example, could employ the Augustan myth in his approach to those in power and, if disappointed, bewail the times in which no Maecenas was to be found.

During the 1730s, with George II on the throne, Alexander Pope made imaginative use of the idea of the Augustan age in his satiric imitation of Horace's epistle to Augustus (*Epistles* 2.1). Pope was one of the literary men who opposed the policies of the king and his chief minister, Sir Robert Walpole. English freedom, these authors argued, was being undermined by a corrupt administration, and true merit went unrecognized at court. In this heated political context, Pope addressed the king (who had been christened George Augustus) as Horace had addressed the emperor, praising him for his victories, his reformation of the nation's morals, and his support of the arts – none of which, as far as Pope was concerned, could be said truly of King George. Pope's poem, though, is neither a naive evocation of the Augustan myth, nor a simple attack on the monarch he despised. It is a serious engagement with Horace's thoughts on the place of poetry in the modern world. It remains a political poem, but its deepest concerns are social; and the figure at the center is neither George nor Augustus, but Horace.

8 Ancients versus Moderns

As the seventeenth century progressed, it became clear to many educated members of French and British society that they were living through a period of great intellectual vitality. Descartes had created a new philosophy of reason premised on the rejection of all authority, including ancient philosophy; and with the development of such tools as the telescope and the microscope, knowledge of the natural world was expanding rapidly. The modern world was also in possession of entirely new technologies, from advances in shipbuilding and navigation to gunpowder and the printing press. French elites began the century hoping to emulate the splendor and sophistication of the Augustan court; by its close many felt that they had surpassed it. In 1687 Charles Perrault made the case for the superiority of the modern world in his poem *Le Siècle de Louis le Grand* (The age of Louis XIV). Perrault, though, was not content simply to press the claim for the achievements of modern art and science; he also denigrated the classical past. By the refined standards of modern taste, he says, Homer's work is crude. In addition, Plato is boring and Aristotle's physics is all wrong. Although the poem pleased many of his contemporaries, it offended Boileau, Racine, and La Fontaine, for whom the ancients remained an incomparable source of wisdom and beauty. For the next 13 years Boileau and Perrault kept up a running skirmish in verse and prose, sometimes defending their preferred authors, sometimes insulting their opponent's taste, in what has come to be called the *querelle des Anciens et des Modernes,* the quarrel between the Ancients and the Moderns.

Similar sentiments had been growing in England, where enthusiasm for Baconian "natural philosophy" had given birth to the Royal Society in 1660. Three years after the *querelle* began in France, Sir William Temple offered a new defense of the ancients in his *Essay upon the Ancient and Modern Learning* (1690). Temple, a former ambassador and one of the most respected men in England, had a gentleman's knowledge of the classics; that is, he read the Roman writers for pleasure and moral instruction. He was skeptical by temperament and so did not believe that the new science was likely to improve the world in any significant way. The *Essay* betrayed many of the deficiencies of his learning, and it soon gave rise to a scholarly critique, William Wotton's *Reflections upon Ancient and Modern Learning* (1694). A new quarrel was about to commence and new contenders about to engage, for Wotton's friend and supporter was the irascible scholar Richard Bentley, and Temple's secretary an unknown young man named Jonathan Swift.

In his *Essay* Temple had stated that the oldest writing was often the best, offering the *Epistles* of Phalaris as a notable example. Bentley read such things with contempt, and when a second edition of Wotton's *Reflections* appeared in 1697, it was accompanied by "A Dissertation upon the Epistles of Phalaris," a scholarly demolition job of unmatchable learning. The *Epistles*, Bentley instructs us, were neither the work of the ancient tyrant Phalaris nor among the oldest Greek writings; they were trite and artificial, a rhetorical exercise by a Sophist of much later date. By now, though, the public had become interested in the quarrel, and the public had no means of evaluating Bentley's scholarship. What they saw was a "pedant" (Bentley) impugning the taste of a gentleman (Temple); what was this but a breach of social decorum? This particular perception was reinforced a hundredfold when, after Temple's death, Swift entered the fray with two great satires, *A Tale of a Tub* and *The Battle of the Books* (1704), where modern learning is presented as pedantry, small-mindedness, and solipsism verging on madness. The ancients, it appeared, had triumphed.

The quarrels between the ancients and the moderns, in both France and England, embodied social and cultural tensions that are not always apparent. In both nations they pit the modern world – optimistic, scientific, progressive – against a world of traditional ideas and values. For Boileau the ancients offered crucial insights into art and life; to denigrate their achievements was to put at risk the recent strides in modern culture. Swift, like Temple before him, was deeply skeptical about progress: was the new learning, whether the scientific advances of the Royal Society or Bentley's emendations of some classical text, likely to make men better? To men like these the ancients offered something else – education for character, and knowledge as a means to moral insight. Nevertheless, the scientific revolution would continue, and Bentley's scholarship would be vindicated. In the end the game would go to the moderns.

9   The Reaction against Neoclassicism

During the early decades of the eighteenth century, some English writers became discontented with the reigning literary fashion. They chafed under the formal constraints of the closed couplet and found the ends of Augustan verse – refined style and sophisticated wit – unsatisfying. For some, like James Thomson in his poem *The Seasons* (1730), blank verse offered liberation. Blank verse also had a classical pedigree: it had been associated with the Latin hexameter since Surrey first translated portions of the *Aeneid* into unrhymed pentameters, and Milton had reaffirmed that linkage in his choice of blank verse for *Paradise Lost*. Thomson's matter, though, was new as well: his poem celebrates man's interaction with the natural world and marks a new stage in the poetic description of nature. And yet here, too, an alert reader finds frequent reminiscences of Vergil and Ovid throughout. Few poets of this age, even when turning to new materials, would wish to separate themselves completely from the classical past.

At the same time, a new classical influence was beginning to make itself felt: a heightened interest in Greek literature. Although Boileau, Dryden, and Pope all knew at least some Greek, their taste had been formed by reading the Roman poets. But Greek instruction had improved, and now a handful of writers had come to prefer Homer and the Greek tragedians to Vergil and Horace. For this new generation the Greeks seemed to offer a simplicity, nobility, and emotional honesty not found in the polished artificiality of Augustan verse.

This enthusiasm is perhaps most obvious in the odes of William Collins and Thomas Gray, where the ability of Greek poets to move the passions becomes a frequent theme. But the shift in taste had its greatest impact on criticism, especially on the new aesthetics developing in Germany. It was Johann Winckelmann who taught modern Europe to see idealized beauty and artistic perfection in Greek statuary; and his assertion that the characteristic greatness of Greek art lay in its "noble simplicity and quiet grandeur" posited a new basis for aesthetic judgment and a new standard of taste (1987: 33).

Winckelmann's remarks in the *Reflections* on the statue of Laocoön provided a starting point for G. E. Lessing as he probed the differences between poetry and the visual arts. Lessing declared that painting and sculpture are spatial arts, poetry a temporal art. The true poet, then, will represent action and eschew description, a lesson he draws not only from reason but from Homer (*Laokoon* 1766: ch. 16). It is of particular significance that Lessing turned to Homer to demonstrate his thesis. Throughout the neoclassical age, Homer was honored as the father of poetry, but the *Aeneid* was considered a finer (at least a more polished) poem than either the *Iliad* or the *Odyssey.* Homer, it was agreed, abounded in genius, but he lacked "art." In explaining what true poetry *should* be, Lessing cited passage after passage from the *Iliad.* He had returned Homer to the center of artistic achievement.

10   Neoclassicism and Enlightenment

The eighteenth century was the age of Enlightenment, a period that we associate with social criticism, anticlericalism, and scientific discovery; and the classics often appear to have no place in this culture of reason and progress. But as Peter Gay has demonstrated, virtually all of the important Enlightenment figures were deeply immersed in classical learning. These men were of course virulent and aggressive "moderns," but in case after case we find that their rejection of contemporary prejudices or their contempt for Christianity had been nourished by their readings in the ancient moralists and philosophers. Voltaire, for instance, said that he took his article on "Superstition" for the *Dictionnaire philosophique* (Philosophical dictionary) from Cicero, Seneca, and Plutarch; and David Hume declared that he preferred the catalogue of virtues in Cicero's *De officiis* (On duties) to that in *The Whole Duty of Man* (Gay 1966: 1:51, 66). Indeed, Cicero alone, through his dialogues examining the various ancient philosophical systems, provided justifications for the modern versions of skepticism, Stoicism, or epicureanism espoused by so many of the *philosophes.*

Few books on the Enlightenment, though, even mention neoclassicism, and an unsuspecting reader might conclude that literature and the arts did not exist during the Age of Reason. It is true that in England during the seventeenth century a suspicion of figurative language gave rise to a plainer prose style, with some effect on poetry as well, and that a number of French thinkers of the eighteenth century were directly hostile to verse because it interfered with simple, clear expression (Niklaus 1970: 58), but the educated classes of both nations continued to read poetry and to attend the theater despite the disapproval of their more austere contemporaries.

During the first half of the eighteenth century, neoclassicism actually constituted the basic aesthetic theory of the Enlightenment. We have already seen the general tendency towards rationalism that underlay so many neoclassical judgments, and in such works as Alexander Pope's *Essay on Man* we recognize the inherent compatibility between Enlightenment ethics and neoclassical aesthetics. But here, too, as in so many aspects of the Enlightenment, Voltaire offers the most instructive example. Our modern image of Voltaire – the author of *Candide*, the enemy of established religion, the sage of Ferney – misses almost completely the way he was perceived by his contemporaries. To his age he was France's greatest living poet and dramatist, the master of the alexandrine couplet, which he wrote by the thousands, not only for his epic poem *La Henriade*, but for his tragedies as well. It was in fact through his tragedies that he preached his message of freedom and toleration most directly to his contemporaries, and it was his success as a poet that earned a readership for his philosophical prose. Throughout his long life he remained committed to neoclassical principles in art, whether in his remarks on poetry or his general adherence to the dramatic unities. In the works of Voltaire Enlightenment and neoclassicism merge.

But neoclassicism and Enlightenment influenced one another in more subtle ways as well. In England, for instance, the concept of "polite letters" – that is, a literature of formal polish aimed at a sophisticated audience – had always been associated with an idea of social progress. A truly refined literature, many believed, could improve the manners, the morals, and the intelligence of its readers. In his *Spectator* essays (1711–14) Joseph Addison, perhaps the finest practitioner of "polite letters" in his day, made no secret of his purpose:

> It was said of Socrates that he brought philosophy down from heaven, to inhabit among men; and I shall be ambitious to have it said of me that I have brought philosophy out of closets and libraries, schools and colleges, to dwell in clubs and assemblies, at tea-tables and in coffee-houses. (*Spectator* 10)

Addison is hardly to be ranked among the *philosophes*, but this was an educational project worthy of the Enlightenment.

Nevertheless, as the eighteenth century progressed, the neoclassical style began to seem antiquated and the rules of art in conflict with the Enlightenment spirit of freedom. In addition, the rise of "sensibility" introduced a new emphasis on feelings that came into conflict with the primacy of reason. These powerful trends would lead inexorably to Romanticism. And finally, Rousseau's *Discours sur les sciences et les arts* (Discourse on the arts and sciences, 1750), with its argument that modern civilization corrupted rather than ennobled human nature, attacked the very premises of neoclassicism. As a literary movement neoclassicism had stressed artistic refinement and respect for tradition; its dominant principle was propriety. It made no secret of its elitist presuppositions; its aim was not just to entertain but to civilize its audiences. But to Rousseau, social polish and artistic decorum were mere screens for dissolute morals and a corrupt taste. Neoclassicism was part of the problem he sought to remedy. It is perhaps a fitting irony that Rousseau's *Discourse* is shot through with illustrations from the classical world; the angle of vision, though, has been changed.

Sparta is there preferred to Athens. Rousseau's heroes are Socrates, praised not for his philosophy but for his "ignorance," and Cato the Elder, who opposed the introduction of Greek refinement into Rome. And so it was that with an appeal to the classics, neoclassicism was brought down.

FURTHER READING

The indispensable work for understanding the historical development of neoclassical theory is Bray (1927). For the particular way these ideas developed in England, see Johnson (1967). For many years the period of English literature from 1660 to 1798 was called the "Augustan Age." That terminology came under attack towards the end of the last century. Some background on the dispute as well as a defense of the term "Augustan" can be found in Kaminski (1996). Readers in need of a general introduction to French literature will find clear, readable surveys of the important authors and literary trends in Yarrow (1967) and Niklaus (1970). David Hopkins has provided an excellent, brief survey of classical translation and imitation during this period in Womersley (2000). Stack (1985) provides a detailed analysis of Pope's imitations of Horace. Two important works (often in disagreement) survey the reputation of Augustus Caesar and his place in the political debates of the eighteenth century: Weinbrot (1978) and Erskine-Hill (1983). The disputes between the Ancients and the Moderns receive thorough coverage in Levine (1991). And finally, for a wide-ranging discussion of Enlightenment thought, including the influence of ancient philosophers, see Gay (1966).

CHAPTER SIX

Romanticism

Bruce Graver

1 Introduction

In the 1940s, when Gilbert Highet wrote his account of the classical tradition in the Romantic era, he avoided the word "Romantic." For Highet, the late eighteenth and early nineteenth century in Europe "was a time of revolt, and it would be better called the Revolutionary than the Romantic era" (Highet 1949: 356). Political rebels invoked classical history to justify their principles of government; writers, insofar as they showed classical influences, did so in unorthodox ways, or deliberately championed Greek culture as a way of rebelling against the prevailing emphasis on Rome and the Latin classics. Throughout, Highet resisted yoking the terms "Romantic" and "classical," as if to do so would be an act of violence on both words. Highet's study appeared in the same year as Rene Wellek's seminal essay "The Concept of Romanticism in Literary History," a work that restored the word "Romantic" to scholarly respectability. In his essay Wellek articulated a "system of norms" (Wellek 1963: 129) that characterized Romantic literature, and that can be located in the literary works of Europeans and Americans writing in the late eighteenth and early nineteenth centuries. These norms are "imagination for the view of poetry, nature for the view of the world, and symbol and myth for poetic style" (161) and show an enormous debt, not just to German literature, but to Wellek's understanding of German Idealist philosophy, a very different basis for understanding Romanticism than the political upheavals that inform Highet's "Time of Revolution." Yet Wellek, like Highet, had a difficult time using the words "Romantic" and "classical" in the same breath. Schiller's "Die Götter Griechenland," for instance, is not really classical, but "a typical romantic dream." Herder is "an extremely irrationalistic pre-romanticist," in spite of his role in championing historical criticism of the Homeric poems. And Goethe, who "for a time expounded a classical creed" and "wrote some works ... [with a] classical spirit," nonetheless wrote his best works, such as *Faust*, *Werther*, and *Wilhelm Meister*, when his view of nature, imagination, and poetic style were indistinguishable from Schelling's, and hence Romantic (162).

Wellek's concept of Romanticism has given shape and direction to Romantic scholarship since the 1950s. Since his essay appeared, studies of Romantic writers have focused on the interaction of the creative imagination with nature, on nature itself, on Romantic myth and myth-making, and on Romantic concepts of the imagination. Few of these studies have looked to the ways in which Romanticism engaged itself with the classical tradition, in more than nominal ways. Even in the 1980s, when it became fashionable to write of Romanticism and history again, and the French Revolution became the great backdrop against which all Romantic writing was to be seen, the resulting criticism was too often ignorant of classical models, classical methods of education, and contemporary developments in classical scholarship. The result is an extraordinary gap in Romantic scholarship, which only a handful of studies have attempted to fill. Yet to be educated in the Romantic age meant to be learned in the classical languages: students began to study Latin by the age of eight and moved on to elementary Greek by their teens, and university education across Europe concentrated primarily on the study of classical authors. What is more, during this period classical scholarship itself was undergoing immense change: new historical methods of literary criticism reshaped the ways in which ancient texts were read; there was a revival of Greek studies at European universities, which led to the pan-European phenomenon of Romantic Hellenism; archaeological discoveries, especially at the recently-excavated sites of Pompeii and Herculaneum, altered long-held preconceptions about the cultural achievements of ancient societies; and the removal from the Parthenon of the so-called "Elgin Marbles" inspired a passionate debate about the nature of ancient art that challenged neoclassical ideals. All this informed the works of Romantic writers, whether it is Goethe writing his *Roman Elegies*, Madame de Staël describing Pompeii and Herculaneum in *Corinne*, or Keats viewing the Parthenon Marbles. Indeed, one could argue that what we have called "Romanticism" is a kind of classicism, reinterpreted through the magnifying lens of empirical research.

In this chapter I will look at two subjects widely regarded as central to Romanticism: literary primitivism and emotion. The rise of historical criticism in the eighteenth century, which resulted primarily from developments in classical, especially Homeric, scholarship, made possible the interest in primitive epic and folksong that is characteristic of Romantic poetry. Romantic ideas of emotion developed from the renewed interest in classical, especially Stoic, emotion theory. I make no pretense here of giving a comprehensive overview of Romantic debts to the classical tradition. But by exploring the classical origins of both of these Romantic concerns, I hope to demonstrate that Romanticism and classicism are not the antithetical terms we have come to consider them to be.

2   Homeric Criticism and Romantic Primitivism

The reevaluation of Homer and the Homeric poems, which culminated in F. A. Wolf's *Prolegomena to Homer* in 1795, was arguably the most important scholarly development of the eighteenth century. Eighteenth-century Homeric scholars were primarily responsible for introducing historical criticism to the study of secular literature, and, by so doing, ended the dominance of French neo-Aristotelian formalism. By the century's end, Homer himself had even disappeared: the Homeric epics, scholars argued, were not created by a single blind bard, but instead were collections of set-pieces, composed orally by many different writers and preserved centuries after their composition by editors who were responsible for transcribing and arranging the epics in a readable, coherent form. Besides reshaping the contemporary understanding of the Homeric epics, this line of criticism had profound cultural effects. Antiquarians throughout Europe began to investigate and preserve the last remnants of the oral poetry of their own countries, in hope of discovering epics equal to Homer's. As a result of their efforts, thousands of works that survived only in rare manuscripts or in oral tradition were published for the first time, including the poems of Ossian, the first scholarly collections of medieval ballads, and medieval epics and romances, such as *The Poem of the Cid*. Critics such as Herder argued that these newly discovered works should serve as models for contemporary writers, and, almost immediately, serious young poets began experimenting with ballads, romances, and folksongs as their preferred genres. Their aim was to recover the immediacy and power of primitive verse; by so doing, they permanently transformed the character of European literature.

We can trace this transformation by considering the arguments of three Homeric scholars: Thomas Blackwell, Robert Wood, and F. A. Wolf. In *An Enquiry into the Life and Writings of Homer* (1735), Blackwell called Homer a "stroling indigent Bard," his translation of the Greek *aoidos*, a word used in the Homeric poems to describe "a Set of Men, who distinguished themselves by Harmony and Verse. The wonderful Tales which they told, and the Melody with which they accompanied them, made the Delight of these simple Ages . . ." (Blackwell 1735: 104). These bards traveled throughout Greece, from household to household and from city to city, singing or chanting their poems to the accompaniment of the lyre, as a form of after-dinner entertainment. Thus they were able to observe a wide variety of places and scenes, as well as customs and manners, all of which they would reproduce in their poems. What distinguished Homer from the others, thought Blackwell, was his skill in reproducing what he had seen: he "took his plain natural images from Life" (34). That he performed his poems in public was also important: he was compelled to use "a simple, intelligible Stile," so as to communicate with his audience effectively, and at the same time would employ "the boldest Metaphors and glowing Figures," to capture and hold their attention (116–17). In fact, Blackwell came very close to articulating an oral theory of composition: the Homeric poems, he wrote,

> were made to be recited, or sung to a Company; and not read in private, or perused in a Book, which few were then capable of doing. . . . His Stile . . . cannot be understood in any other Light; nor can the Strain and Manner of his work be felt and relished unless we put ourselves in the place of his Audience, and imagine it coming from the Mouth of a Rhapsodist. (Blackwell 1735: 118)

To understand the Homeric poems, then, we must investigate both the historical circumstances that his poems represent and the customs of the society in which they were produced. This is the core of the argument of Blackwell's *Enquiry*. With it, this obscure Scottish scholar, the future Principal of Marischal College, Aberdeen, over-turned two centuries of literary formalism.

Some 30 years after the publication of *An Enquiry into ... Homer*, Robert Wood refined and extended Blackwell's argument in his *Essay on the Original Genius and Writings of Homer* (1775). No professional scholar, Wood was an educated amateur traveling throughout the Eastern Mediterranean on diplomatic missions who spent his spare time checking out the actual geography of the Homeric poems, measuring the distance of sea voyages, and drawing the first modern topographical survey and map of the plain of Troy. Like Blackwell, Wood historicized the Homeric epics:

> Homer's great merit seems to be that of having transmitted to us a faithful transcript, or (what is, perhaps, more useful) a correct abstract of human nature, impartially exhibited under the circumstances, which belonged to his period of society, as far as his experience and observation went. (Wood 1775: xiii)

To understand this "transcript," we must understand "his period of society," and from his poems attempt to judge the extent of "his experience and observation." In this respect, Wood followed Blackwell very closely. But, in his chapter entitled "Homer's Language and Learning," he struck out in a new direction. Assuming that Homer was an *aoidos*, Wood argued, first, that if writing was known in Homeric Greece, it was pictographical, not alphabetical, and thus unsuited for lengthy compositions like an epic poem. He then maintains that Homer himself was probably illiterate and must have composed his poems orally. We owe their survival not to their author but to the memory of Ionian rhapsodes, who preserved the poems for centuries as scattered fragments, something like ballads. After the invention of alphabetical writing, an effort was made to collect and assemble these fragments, probably late in the sixth century BC, and only at that time did the poems take something like their current form. What we call the "Homeric" poems, then, may owe as much to the efforts of later editors as to the "original genius" of a bard named Homer (Wood 1775: 248–78).

Having shown that Homer composed his poems orally, Wood considered "whether [the poet] might not derive some advantages from this illiterate state of things" (Wood 1775: 279). He then developed a primitivist argument that focuses on Homer's style:

> When the sense was catched from the sound, and not deliberately collected from paper, simplicity and clearness were more necessary. Involved periods and an embarrassed style were not introduced, till writing became more an art, and labour supplied the place of genius. (Wood 1775: 281)

For Wood, Homer's is "the language of Nature," a language which

> still retains its powers in the province of Poetry, where the most finished efforts of artificial language are but cold and languid circumlocution, compared with that passion-ate expression of Nature, which incapable of misrepresentation, appeals directly to our feelings, and finds the shortest way to the heart.... It was therefore an advantage to the

Father of Poetry, that he lived before the language of Compact and Art had so much prevailed over that of Nature and Truth.... Thus the simplicity, without meanness or indelicacy, of the Poet's language rises out of the state of his manners. (Wood 1775: 283–4)

There are a number of things to note here: first, his assertion that writing tends to corrupt language, inducing poets to depart from simple clarity and indulge in "cold and languid circumlocution"; second, his articulation of an expressivist poetics, closely allied to his primitivism, which M. H. Abrams considers to be one of the central features of the Romantic enterprise (Abrams 1953: 80–1); and third, his insistence on Homer's indebtedness to "the state of his manners" for his poetic achievement. As Wood stated near the end of his *Essay,* "It has been the great object of this Essay to carry the Reader to the Poet's Age, and Country," to read Homer historically and investigate his culture anthropologically (Wood 1775: 300). Expressivism and historicism are thus inextricably bound together.

Wood's *Essay* was published in 1769, in a private edition of about a half dozen copies, and its author died shortly afterwards. Luckily, one of these copies was sent to Johann Michaelis at the University of Göttingen. Michaelis, the greatest living biblical scholar, recognized the significance of Wood's arguments and asked his son to prepare a German translation of the *Essay,* to rescue it from obscurity. The translation was published in 1773, to great acclaim. C. G. Heyne and the young Goethe reviewed it enthusiastically. Herder put its arguments about the power of primitive poetry at the heart of his famous essays on Ossian (Foerster 1947: 96–112). At Göttingen itself, Heyne introduced a generation of students to Wood's arguments, and in the late 1770s, one of them, F. A. Wolf, began to seek concrete scholarly evidence to prove the "many shrewd and fine observations" of the English amateur (Wolf 1985: 71). Wolf first formulated his "unorthodox thoughts on Homer" in an essay presented to Heyne in 1779 (Wolf 1985: 232). But it was Villoison's publication of Homeric scholia (1788) that finally gave Wolf the evidence he was lacking and led him to write what has been called the greatest philological work of the eighteenth century, his *Prolegomena to Homer* (1795). In that work, as Anthony Grafton has noted, Wolf wrote the first "history of the Homeric text" (Wolf 1985: 7–15): he showed how the practices of rhapsodes and scholiasts would have affected our received texts of the Homeric poems, he outlined the difficulties inherent in purifying the poems of their many accretions, and he concluded that, very probably, "the very songs from which the *Iliad* and *Odyssey* were assembled do not all have one common author" (Wolf 1985: 70). After Wolf's *Prolegomena,* our idea of Homer could never be the same.

The historical criticism of the Homeric poems made possible a broad critical reexamination of the European poetic tradition. If the *Iliad* and *Odyssey* had been produced by a preliterate oral culture, then there might be similar cultural monuments preserved in obscure manuscript collections or still alive in oral traditions in remote parts of Europe. In Scotland, James Macpherson, who studied at Marischal College while Blackwell was its Principal, collected fragments of ancient Gaelic poetry, knit them together into two epic poems (*Fingal* and *Temora,* published in 1762 and 1764), and ascribed them to a legendary Gaelic bard named Ossian. For the next century, Ossian became a household name across the European continent. Thomas Percy, skeptical of Macpherson's procedures, compiled manuscripts of older English and Scottish poems, most of them ballads. These were, he argued, composed by ancient British minstrels, itinerant bards who performed their works at the households of noble patrons during the later Middle Ages. He published his three-volume collection *Reliques of Ancient English Poetry* in 1765, introduced with lengthy scholarly dissertations and supplemented with a full critical apparatus. Percy's *Reliques* were read and admired widely, both in Great Britain and on the continent (Groom 1999: 61–105). They were translated into German by Herder, for whom "Ossian," "Homer," and "minstrel" became almost interchangeable terms. They were imitated by a generation of young German poets, among them Goethe and Bürger, whose imitations of folk ballads achieved extraordinary popularity. In the 1790s many of these modern German imitations of ancient English ballads were translated back into English and published in prominent literary journals. Walter Scott, later the editor of an important ballad collection of his own (*Minstrelsy of the Scottish Border*), first made his literary reputation as a translator of German ballads. And in 1798, spurred in part by their reading of German literature, two young Englishmen decided to publish their own collection of ballads, *Lyrical Ballads and Other Poems*, one of the foundational works of British Romanticism (Graver 2005: 39–41).

In *The Hidden Wordsworth*, Kenneth Johnston raises once again an old scholarly question: "Why the *Lyrical Ballads*?" "Wordsworth," Johnston notes,

> had, as of March 1798, written only one and a half ballads in his entire life.... His interest for several years had not been in short poems at all, let alone ballads. He was determined to write long poems, narrative poems in blank verse ... taking his inspiration not from the ballad revivals of Bishop Percy ... but from the epic examples of Milton and Spenser. (Johnston 1998: 568–9)

Much the same may be said of Coleridge: he had written sonnets, odes, effusions, philosophical or meditative blank verse, and verse drama, but very little in the way of ballads before "The Rime of the Ancient Mariner." Johnston here assumes a sharp generic division between the ballad and the epic: the former is a product of folk culture and a low poetic kind; the latter is both highly sophisticated and fiercely literate, the most ambitious of poetic genres. But in light of eighteenth century Homeric scholarship, Johnston's generic division does not seem as sharp as he implies. By 1798, scholars across Europe had come to consider the *Iliad* and *Odyssey* not as sophisticated literary epics but as repositories of traditional material, composed orally by an anonymous bard or bards, preserved in the memories of rhapsodes, and assembled at a much later date by scholarly editors. The closest English equivalent to Homeric epic is not *Paradise Lost*, but a late medieval ballad like "Chevy Chase." It follows, then, that to write a collection of ballads (and to publish them anonymously) is to approximate the writing of epic, albeit epic of a very different kind from those conceived of by Milton, Spenser, or Vergil. In this light, the experiments of the *Lyrical Ballads* take on a new appearance. It has often been said that Wordsworth, in his "Preface to *Lyrical Ballads*" and especially in his 1802 "Appendix on Poetic Diction," articulates a primitivist view of poetic style. It is less often noted that when he refers to "the earliest Poets of all nations" (Wordsworth 1992: 761–2), he includes Homer in the mix and thus allies his poetical experiments with the earliest literary art of ancient Greece.

In many of the *Lyrical Ballads*, Wordsworth and Coleridge explore the relationship of preliterate folk culture to the modern world of literacy and published books. Maureen McLane argues that the *Lyrical Ballads* mark "the emergence of a new literary orality.... [The poems] offer a way to rethink the relation of orality to literacy and specifically the relation of the oral to the literate within literature" (McLane 2001: 425–8). Coleridge's "Rime of the Ancient Marinere" is a good case in point. His mariner is an illiterate itinerant, invested, like a Celtic bard, with preternatural powers. The wedding guest is a representative of the noble class that would employ itinerant minstrels, and the narrator of the poem is intended to be a minstrel of a somewhat later period who presents the telling of the tale in dramatic form. We owe the preservation of the ballad to an editor of an even later date, who is the fictive author of the introductory "Argument" and the notorious marginal gloss that Coleridge first published in 1817. The whole poem thus seems a complex scholarly hoax on the antiquarian fascination with the minstrelsy and preliterate folk culture. Wordsworth, too, explores over and over again the relationship between the oral traditions of folk culture and the literate poet who turns these traditions into published verse. In "The Brothers," for instance, the parish priest of Ennerdale is a repository of oral history, which the narrator of the poem has taken upon himself to preserve. In "Michael," Wordsworth uses Miltonic blank verse to relate a plain tale about a remarkable Grasmere shepherd. This tale is also a product of oral tradition: he was told it "while I was yet a Boy, / Careless of books," and he retells it in this highly literate form specifically for "youthful Poets, who among these Hills / Will be my second Self when I am gone" ("Michael," lines 27–8, 38–9, in Wordsworth 1992: 253). Oral culture is translated to literary form for the sake of writers of literature, and they in turn will inherit Wordsworth's role as a preserver of oral tradition. But of all the *Lyrical Ballads*, "Hart-leap Well" problematizes the relationship of oral and literate culture most fully: not only does it dramatize the relationship of the modern poet to oral tradition, but it raises questions about the contemporary concepts of minstrelsy and primitive poetry, derived from Blackwell, Percy, and others.

"Hart-leap Well" is divided into two nearly equal parts. Part 1 recounts in heroic terms a tale of a medieval stag hunt, beginning abruptly, *in medias res*, with the leader of the hunt, "Sir Walter," calling for his third horse of the day.

> The Knight had ridden down from Wensley moor
> With the slow motion of a summer's cloud;
> He turn'd aside towards a Vassal's door,
> And, "Bring another Horse!" he cried aloud.
>   ("Hart-Leap Well," lines 1–4, in Wordsworth 1992: 133–9)

Mounted on a new "Courser," Sir Walter "like a falcon flies," to pursue a "poor Hart" (lines 9, 11, 29), leaving the rest of his party far behind. Just before expiring, the hart leaps "Nine roods" in three bounds, to die beside the spring that gives the poem its name, and in honor of "the gallant brute," Sir Walter has a basin constructed around the spring, erects three stone pillars to mark the hart's leaps, and orders a "Pleasure-house" to be built, for summertime merrymaking (lines 50, 65, 57). Here, he vows,

> I will come hither with my paramour;
> And with the dancers, and the minstrel's song,
> We will make merry in that pleasant bower.
>
> Till the foundations of the mountains fail
> My mansion with its arbour shall endure.
> (lines 70–4)

Thus ends the story of Sir Walter and the hart. But not the poem. In the last stanza of Part 1, the narrator makes a promise to "add another tale" in "a second rhyme" (lines 95–6). And in that "second rhyme," Part 2 of the poem, he proceeds very differently. First of all, it takes place, not in the past, but in contemporary England, and depicts the chance encounter, at the site of the original hunt, between the narrator of the poem and a Yorkshire shepherd. The shepherd retells the tale of the hart's death, and both he and the poet moralize about it from a modern perspective. For the shepherd, "the spot is cursed" (line 126), made forever barren because of Sir Walter's brutality. For the poet-narrator, Sir Walter has violated the "sympathy divine" of "Nature" (lines 163–4), and the bleakness of the landscape is not so much a curse as a sign of what happens when we disrupt the balance of natural environments. Yet "Nature," he continues, "once more / Shall here put on her beauty and her bloom," once the "monuments" Sir Walter erected have decayed (lines 171–2, 176). He concludes with a moral:

> One lesson, Shepherd, let us two divide,
> Taught both by what she shows, and what conceals,
> Never to blend our pleasure or our pride
> With sorrow of the meanest thing that feels.
> (lines 177–80)

In other words, if we don't hunt down harts (or, for that matter, albatrosses), don't build pleasure houses (or pleasure-domes) to celebrate our power, and don't enclose springs that naturally irrigate meadows, the world may be a better place.

But this moral is rather beside Wordsworth's point, a point that, like Coleridge's in the "Rime," has much more to do with the debates about minstrelsy and cultural primitivism than with animal rights or ecology. In "Hart-Leap Well" Wordsworth juxtaposes competing versions of the minstrel, Percy's ancient minstrel and Wordsworth's modern one, and does so to explore the relation of each to oral tradition. Part 1 of the poem is a modern imitation of Percy's *Reliques*, and its placement in *Lyrical Ballads* ("Hart-Leap Well" is the opening poem of vol. 2 of the collection) as well as its subject matter are meant to recall "Chevy Chase," the first poem in Percy's collection. Until the final stanza of Part 1, Wordsworth's narrator seems an impersonation of Percy's ancient minstrel, celebrating the deeds of a noble patron from the patron's point of view, with a tale that the patron himself must have been the source for. We can even imagine this part of the ballad being sung as a kind of after-dinner entertainment in the ancestral seat of Sir Walter and his descendants, or perhaps in the very pleasure-house he built to commemorate the hunt. Part 2 of the poem, however, retells the story from the perspective of an illiterate rustic, who sees things, not like Sir Walter, but through the eyes of the "unhappy hart." For the shepherd, the hunt was just another sign of how the ruling class exercises arbitrary power, exploiting wildlife, the land, and, by implication, those who work the land, in pursuit of idle and destructive pleasures. Wordsworth's narrator is literally a "stroling indigent bard," a modern incarnation of Blackwell's Homer en route between Richmond and Askrigg, who records both versions of a local legend: the shepherd's version, given in the shepherd's own voice, and Sir Walter's version, which he recreates from what the shepherd told him. This is creative editing indeed! And it is also partisan editing. The poet concludes the poem by taking the shepherd's side, effectively undercutting the ruling-class point of view expressed in Part 1 of the poem. By undercutting it, Wordsworth rejects Percy's model of the minstrel.

But what, then, are we left with? What kind of minstrel, if minstrel he is, does Wordsworth represent himself as being? Surely not one who sings of "low and rustic life" to "low and rustic" people ("Preface" to *Lyrical Ballads*, in Wordsworth 1992: 743) – people who never had the five shillings for the 1798 *Lyrical Ballads*, let along the higher price for the two-volume editions of 1800, 1802, and 1805. Rather, I suggest that Wordsworth is attempting to recover a more genuinely Blackwellian concept of the poet – an itinerant, to be sure, but one without any particular ties to a noble household, one who, like Blackwell's Homer, "is a keen observer of his world," taking his "plain, natural images from life" as he sees it, not as it is seen by those who read his books – a poet, that is, of the sort who might write to the leader of the Whigs, Charles James Fox, and enjoin him with a straight face to read his poems and learn of the "domestic affections" of rural laborers, so that even the powerful can come to recognize "that men who do not wear fine cloaths can feel deeply" (quoted in Wordsworth 1992: 401).

3   The Stoicism of Romantic Emotion

Romantic writers, we have often been told, stressed the intrinsic value of emotive experience and the passions at the expense of logic and reason. What is less often stated, however, is the extent to which the Romantic discussions of the passions, and Romantic works that explore the power of the emotions, depend upon classical, especially Stoic, discourse about emotion. Sometimes this dependence is direct, as in Wordsworth's "Ode to Duty," with its epigraph from Seneca (Wordsworth 1983: 407). Sometimes it is indirect, as in Joanna Baillie's *Series of Plays in which it is attempted to delineate the Stronger Passions of the Mind*, which reflect the neo-Stoic theories of emotion expressed in the treatises of Adam Smith and other late eight-eenth-century Scottish moral philosophers. Even when, as in Madame de Staël's *Corinne*, an attempt is made to rethink the nature of emotion, it is, for the most part, the Stoic view that is being criticized and reshaped. And rightly so. Not only did the Stoics give the most thorough analysis of the emotions of all the ancient writers, but Stoic writings were among the first philosophical treatises that educated Euro-peans of the eighteenth century would encounter, either in translation or in the original classical languages. Romantic theories of emotion begin with the Stoics, and thus are fundamentally, and paradoxically, classical.

Two familiar passages from one of the greatest Romantic lyrics, Wordsworth's "Tintern Abbey," illustrate this paradox very well. Both passages focus on the emotion of joy, and relate it to a perception of the nature of things. The first ends the second verse paragraph: "While with an eye made quiet by the power / Of harmony, and the deep power of joy, / We see into the life of things" (lines 48–50 in Wordsworth 1992: 116–20). The second passage comes some 40 lines later in the poem: "And I have felt / A presence that disturbs me with the joy / Of elevated thoughts; a sense sublime / Of something far more deeply interfused ..." (lines 94–7). In the first passage, Wordsworth asserts that joy, working in concert with harmony, has the power to quiet the organs of perception, producing a "serene and blessed mood" (line 42) that enables deeper, more comprehensive cognition. In the second passage, something rather different is described. Joy is part of an emotive response to the sublime; it disturbs, rather than calms or quiets; it is specifically evoked by the "elevated thoughts" the sublime sense or presence generates. This joy is also cognitive, but here cognition is a product of distress or disturbance rather than contemplative serenity, and it is right to question whether a perception produced by disturbance has the same validity as one that is the product of harmonious calm. Yet most readers of the poem would agree that the perception, in both cases, is the same: "the life of things," "a motion and a spirit that ... rolls through all things" (lines 50, 101, 103). Can Wordsworth have it both ways?

We can begin to understand what Wordsworth is doing here by examining the various discourses about emotion that were available to him. Burke's *Philosophical Enquiry into the Origin of our Ideas of the Sublime and Beautiful* obviously is impor-tant, but just as important – indeed, I will argue far more important – is classical Stoic analysis of emotional experience, presented in the works of Cicero and Seneca that were familiar to him from early youth. The Stoic writers provide a systematic account of emotional experience that can serve as a model for understanding how Wordsworth treats particular emotions, whether fear, as in *Peter Bell*, grief, as in "The Ruined Cottage," or maternal love, as in "The Mad Mother." It is especially important that we give joy this kind of analysis: it and grief are at the emotional centers of most of his poems. Joy surprises, quiets, and disturbs in Wordsworth's poetry; it also makes possible the years that bring the philosophic mind. But what, precisely, *is* joy, according to Wordsworth, and how do we understand and judge its effects?

We can begin to find answers to these questions by looking at the third and fourth books of Cicero's *Tusculan Disputations*, where the Stoic view of the emotions is given its fullest expression. According to the Stoics, emotions are the result of judgments or beliefs. Thus emotions are cognitive, in that they invariably have ideational content. If, for instance, someone we love dies, we feel grief because we believe that death itself is an evil and that this death has harmed us in some way; if someone threatens us with death, we feel fear if we believe death is evil and if we believe them likely to carry out the threat. The problem with emotion, from the Stoic point of view, is that these judgments are usually made too hastily or are based on false premises, and the resulting emotions are irrational. In order to avoid irrational behavior, the Stoic attempts to discipline affective response so that judgments are based on right reason rather than irrational impulses of the mind (Graver in Cicero 2002: xix–xxiii). In the case of grief, the belief that death is an evil must be addressed, and in the *Tusculans*, which were written largely as therapy for Cicero's own incapacitating grief for his daughter Tullia, Cicero offers a number of methods for correcting false beliefs, including logical argumentation, rhetorical persuasion, and various meditational techniques (Graver in Cicero 2002: xiii–xv). The professed aim is to eradicate emotions, or failing that, to blunt their force. Only by so doing can human beings hope to live well.

The chief method of discipline, and perhaps the most important part of Cicero's discussion, is his classification of the various emotions, which constitutes a major part of *Tusculans* 4. By understanding the nature of individual emotions and their relationship to each other, Cicero believes we can better learn to control our responses to potentially emotive events. Following Zeno, he defines emotion as a "movement of the mind contrary to nature," or "a too-vigorous impulse." These impulses arise from beliefs about what is good and evil: "Those arising from goods are desire and gladness, gladness being directed at present goods and desire at future goods; while those arising from evils are fear and distress, fear being directed at future evils and distress at present ones" (Cicero 2002: 43). Emotions arising from perceived goods elevate or elate the mind; those arising from perceived evils lower or contract it. Into these four categories – desire, gladness, fear, and distress – all the common emotions can be classified. Thus pity is "distress over the misery of another who is suffering unjustly," anger is "desire to punish a person who is thought to have harmed one unjustly," and vainglory is "pleasure which exults and makes a display of arrogance" (Cicero 2002: 45–6). But whatever the emotion, Stoics believe it to signal a "loss of control, which is a rebellion in the mind as a whole against right reason." Emotions are "reason's enemy, ... throwing [the mind] into disturbance and riot" (Cicero 2002: 46–7). Therefore, they must be eradicated.

But where does joy fit into this schema, and what does that tell us about "Tintern Abbey"? For Cicero in the *Tusculan Disputations*, joy is not an emotion at all and is contrasted with its emotional equivalent, *effrenata laetitia* (unbridled gladness). "There are two ways we may be moved as by the presence of something good," he writes:

> When the mind is moved quietly and consistently, in accordance with reason, this is termed "joy"; but when it pours forth with a hollow sort of uplift, that is called "wild or excessive gladness," which they define as an "unreasoning elevation of mind." (Cicero 2002: 44)

Joy (*gaudium*) in such a case is, by definition, rational; it is an affect of a motion of the mind that accords with reason, and hence with nature. Cicero uses the Stoic term *boulesis* (volition) to describe this kind of mental action (Cicero 2002: 44); Greek Stoics more regularly used the term *eupatheia* (good emotion, proper feeling) to describe it (Graver in Cicero 2002: 136). Eupathic joy is an affective response to right moral decisions or accurate perceptions of the nature of things, and it contrasts with unbridled gladness (*effrenata laetitia*), which is the reaction of the immature or foolish to perceived pleasure. Even when this gladness is directed at genuine goods, it is dangerous, because it throws the mind into a state of uncontrolled elation or elevation. Seneca expands on this idea in the *Moral Epistles*. "Believe me, true joy is a serious matter," he counsels Lucilius.

> Do you think that it is with a relaxed and cheerful countenance that one despises death, opens his home to poverty, reins in pleasure, and rehearses the endurance of pain? One who is pondering such things is experiencing a great joy, but hardly a soft or seductive one. This is the joy I want you to possess: you will never run out of it, once you learn where it is to be found.... Cast aside those things that glitter on the outside, those things that are promised you by another or from another, and trample them underfoot. Look to your real good, and rejoice in what is yours. What is it that is yours? Yourself; the best part of you. (Seneca, *Moral Epistles* 23.4–6, in Graver forthcoming: ch. 2)

The truly wise person, the Stoic sage, is in a constant state of joy. But few would lay claim to this degree of wisdom. As Seneca elsewhere admits of himself, most people are in the process of seeking wisdom, a process of constant self-discipline and self-discovery. That is why so much Stoic writing takes the form of therapeutic counseling: those somewhat further on the path toward wisdom take it upon themselves to serve as guides to others, partly to help and partly as a means of sharpening their own powers of self-control.

In "Tintern Abbey," Wordsworth preserves the Stoic distinction between emotion and eupathic affect. This is first evident when he compares his past and present responses to nature. The joy of the "serene and blessed mood" corresponds almost exactly to the quiet, consistent movement of the mind "in accordance with reason," characteristic of Stoic wisdom. To "see into the life of things" is to experience, if only for a few moments, Stoic *eupatheia*. On the other hand, the passionate response to nature of his youth, with its "glad animal movements," "aching joys," and "dizzy raptures" (lines 75, 85–6), is *effrenata laetitia*, gladness wild and unbridled, like the roe to which Wordsworth compares himself. What is more, his emotive responses seem self-contradictory and confused. Desire for what he loves seems more like flight "from something that he dreads" (line 72); the "sounding cataract" haunts "like a passion" (lines 77–8); joys are "aching," bringing pain as well as pleasure, and a far cry from the kind of joy Seneca and Cicero described. We can measure Wordsworth's psychic growth by comparing these passages with the meditative calm of the opening verse paragraph, where not even the apples "disturb" "the wild green landscape" (lines 12–15). The frantic physical exertions of the past have given way to repose and an eye that moves from a fixed point steadily, and perceptively, through the natural world. Similarly, the distinction between emotion and *eupatheia* is evident in Wordsworth's "exhortations" (line 147) to his sister that close the poem. Here William plays Seneca to Dorothy's Lucilius, looking forward to the time when her "wild ecstasies" will mature into a "sober pleasure" (lines 139–40). This will happen, he believes, when her "mind has become a mansion for all lovely forms," her "memory a dwelling-place for all sweet sounds and harmonies" (lines 140–3), counseling her both to discipline her emotive responses and to discover, like Lucilius, that which is truly good, that best part of herself. And her maturation will strengthen his own: nothing, he asserts, "shall ... disturb our chearful faith that all which we behold is full of blessings," and nature will lead them "from joy to joy" (lines 133–5, 126). As a result of experiences such as this, and the bonds they form between human beings, both William and Dorothy can look forward to a future in which their perceptions, and their affective responses, are more in accord with nature than they are on July 13, 1798, the fictive date of the poem.

Thus far, Wordsworth follows the Stoic discourse on emotion very closely, openly invoking both its ideas and its characteristic vocabulary. But, as I noted above, the way Wordsworth experiences joy in the present is problematic, at least from a Stoic point of view, and here we can begin to see some of the ways in which he is modifying and departing from the Stoic model. "And I have felt a presence," he writes, "that disturbs me with the joy of elevated thoughts, a sense sublime of something far more deeply interfused...." Joy, at least the eupathic joy of the Stoics, does not disturb: it results from a quiet, consistent movement of the mind, in accordance with reason. When Wordsworth presents joy as a disturbance, he admits that his usual state of mind is unsettled, and when he specifies joy as an affective response to the sublime, he indicates what the source of his instability might be: Edmund Burke. For Burke, the normative response to the sublime is fear and distress; in Burkean terms, Wordsworth's joy is abnormal. But in Stoic terms, to respond to natural phenomena with fear or distress is an irrational impulse: the joy Wordsworth feels is the response of the wise, but it comes in fits and starts that disrupt his otherwise flawed perceptions. That is, Wordsworth is suggesting that his usual experience of joy is far short of ideal Stoic *eupatheia*: it interrupts and disturbs typical emotive responses, with some of the same force as emotions themselves. Even the eupathic joy of his "serene and blessed mood" is not wholly a Stoic consistency, in that it occurs only in moments of particularly intense meditation, when the body is "laid asleep" (line 46). And afterwards Wordsworth's faith in those moments of joy is not unwavering: he is concerned that it may be "a vain belief" (line 51). Wordsworth needs a way to guarantee the validity of the eupathic joy he believes himself to have felt, so that he can look forward to sustaining it, somehow, in the future.

His solution marks his most radical departure from Stoic thought. For Wordsworth refuses to reject emotional experience. Rather, the more powerfully emotional an experience has been, the deeper an impression it makes on the memory, and the deeper the impression, the more opportunity one will have to return, in thought, to the memory itself and understand its genuine significance. Using this Lockean model of memory and mind, Wordsworth develops a meditative technique for disciplining emotional experience that turns on its head an ancient meditative technique for relieving mental pain: the pre-rehearsal of future ills. Following the Cyrenaics, Cicero recommends the pre-rehearsal of future ills (*praemeditatio futurorum malorum*) as a means of strengthening ourselves against extreme mental pain. To avoid extreme grief, for instance, we should spend time regularly imaging the death of our children, or parents, or a spouse, or friends, and rehearse how we should respond (Cicero 2002: 24–8). Pre-rehearsal works very well for those facing torture, or attempting to overcome a phobia, such as fear of airplane flight. But to spend one's time meditating on the possible death of loved ones seemed, even to Cicero, a bit morbid. Wordsworth may have pre-rehearsal in mind when he suggests to Dorothy that "neither evil tongues, / Rash judgments, nor the sneers of selfish men" shall "disturb our chearful faith" (lines 129–30, 134–5). But rather than pre-rehearse sneers, or imagine the possibility that the two of them may, someday, be separated, Wordsworth charges her to remember "That on the banks of this delightful stream, / We stood together" (lines 151–2). That is, we can sustain ourselves best against mental pain by concentrating our thoughts on past moments of emotional intensity, deriving from them "life and food / For future years" (lines 65–6). In "Tintern Abbey" it is a past moment of intense pleasure; we know from *The Prelude* that moments of intense pain can be just as valuable. For Wordsworth, there can be no *eupatheia* without intense emotions, which imprint themselves so deeply in the memory that he can, again and again, return to them and "drink, / As at a fountain" (*Prelude* 1805, 11.383–4, in Wordsworth 1979: 436).

I would like to close by turning to another familiar passage, so familiar that we have probably stopped thinking about it, where Wordsworth also invokes the Stoic distinction between emotion and *eupatheia*:

> I have said that Poetry is the spontaneous overflow of powerful feelings: it takes its origin from emotion recollected in tranquillity; the emotion is contemplated till by a species of reaction the tranquillity gradually disappears, and an emotion, similar to that which was before the subject of contemplation, is gradually produced, and does itself actually exist in the mind. ("Preface" to *Lyrical Ballads*, in Wordsworth 1992: 756)

In light of Stoic emotion theory, this passage takes on a new significance, and it is a significance we need to explore, if we are to understand the aesthetics, and the moral psychology, of Romantic emotion.

FURTHER READING

Good introductions to the classical tradition in romanticism may be found in Webb (1993) and Graver (2005), with information on the classical scholarship of the period available in Brink (1985). Highet (1949) and Wellek (1963) offer an introduction to the perceived conceptual tension between "romantic" and "classical"; Abrams

(1953) also remains useful. On Homer and oral poetry, see Blackwell (1735), Wood (1775), and Wolf (1985), accompanied by the modern discussions in Foerster (1947), Groom (1999), McLane (2000), and Trumpener (1997). On Stoicism and the emotions, see Cicero (2002) and Graver (forthcoming). Wordsworth deserves special attention in the context of this essay: see Wordsworth (1979, 1983, 1989, 1992, 1998), with the critical commentary of Johnston (1998) and Clancey (1999).

CHAPTER SEVEN

Victorian

Norman Vance

The long classical tradition, from Homer to Byzantium, fascinated the Victorians in its own terms. It was contemplated, and studied with a new rigor, in an increasingly international context that involved European hopes and fears in the aftermath of the French Revolution, German (and sometimes American) philological, textual and historical scholarship, French neoclassical taste and its various transformations, and the archaeological discoveries of many nations.

Less rigorously, selective and often ahistorical and idealized readings of the matter of ancient Greece and Rome also continued to provide modern writers and artists, liberal humanists, statesmen, and a rapidly expanding reading public with literary models, matter for dreams and fantasies, versions of civility and successful living, and metaphors and allusions to describe and reflect on contemporary life and thought. Alfred Tennyson, Poet Laureate since 1850, wrote poems on Homeric themes and was deeply influenced by the language and themes of Latin poetry, particularly Vergil, Horace, Catullus, and Lucretius (Markley 2004). Matthew Arnold's narrative poem *Sohrab and Rustum* (1853) embodied his perception of the grandeur and rapidity of Homer, which he discussed at length in *On Translating Homer* (1861). The painter J. M. W. Turner and others presented classical ruins and Roman history in terms of the romantic sublime, while Sir Lawrence Alma-Tadema devised visually opulent ways of imagining and depicting the cultural and domestic life of classical times (Liversidge and Edwards 1996: 38–53; Becker 1996). William Gladstone, four times Prime Minister, quoted Vergil in the House of Commons and published substantial studies on Homer in the intervals of public life (Bebbington 2004). Parallels and differences between the empires of Rome and Great Britain were debated at length in the later years of Victoria, controversially proclaimed Empress of India in 1876.

But earlier postclassical appropriations and transformations of classical material, constituting an already rich and complex tradition, contributed significantly to Victorian classicism. Tennyson's poem ''Ulysses'' drew on Dante's Ulysses as well as Homer's Odysseus. The classically trained sculptor, designer, and illustrator John

Flaxman (1755–1826) had prepared designs illustrating the *Iliad* and the *Odyssey* in the 1790s. This mode of visualizing Homer was still current when, in his novel *Far from the Madding Crowd* (1874), Thomas Hardy alluded to Flaxman's group of the suitors of Penelope in the *Odyssey*. John Henry Newman's long essay on Cicero in the first volume of his *Historical Sketches* (1872), originally an encyclopedia article published in 1824, drew extensively on Conyers Middleton's much-reprinted *History of the Life of M. Tullius Cicero* (1741, new edn. 1837). The tendency of Matthew Arnold and other Victorians to belittle Vergil by comparison with Homer can be traced back to the taste of the late eighteenth century and romanticism, which privileged original genius. Victorian versions of the Romano-British hero Caractacus derived from several centuries of British theatrical tradition as well as from classical sources. The discovery of everyday Roman life preserved forever in the buried ruins of Pompeii led to Bulwer Lytton's novel *The Last Days of Pompeii* (1834) and later dramatic and operatic treatments of the same theme (Mayer 1994: 19–20; Vance 1997: 278–9), and to Edward Poynter's heroic painting of a Pompeian sentinel, *Faithful unto Death* (1865), but this was an eighteenth-century discovery, dating from 1748.

1   Scholarship

So what is distinctively Victorian about Victorian classicism? What made it different? In the first instance, it was often more scholarly. In Oxford and Cambridge and the great public schools, the dominance of the classical curriculum was increasingly challenged, particularly from the 1860s, but it was not finally dethroned by science and modern studies until the end of the century: it was indeed strengthened by more systematic teaching and examining, a steady retreat from the older gentlemanly emphasis on Latin and Greek verse composition to allow time for more extended classical reading, and a new research-driven professionalism influenced by rigorous German scholarship (Stray 1998: 117–40). The study of early Roman history, hampered by the semilegendary nature of the Roman sources, was revitalized by the sometimes-speculative or intuitive work of the scholar and diplomat B. G. Niebuhr in his *Römische Geschichte* (Roman history, 1811–12, rev. edn. 1827–32), translated by Connop Thirlwall, J. C. Hare, and William Smith (1828–42) and used extensively by Thomas Arnold in his *History of Rome* (1838–43). Theodor Mommsen's extensive researches on imperial Roman history, particularly his monumental *Römische Geschichte* (1854–6), were taken seriously in Britain, although his unstinted praise for Julius Caesar encouraged some unsympathetic English readers to misread and dismiss him as a Prussian militarist reconstructing Caesar as an immoral Bismarckian hero. Text-editing, involving the collection and patiently systematic comparison of ancient manuscripts to reconstruct the best possible text, had been brought to a fine art that was almost a science, mainly by German scholars such as Karl Lachmann of Berlin, and in Britain this was reflected in substantial editions with full commentary such as H. A. J. Munro's *Lucretius* (1864), based in part on Lachmann's work, and John Conington's *Virgil* (1858). The Danish scholar and sometime Minister of

Education Johan Nicolai Madvig had published extensively on the syntax of both Latin and Greek, and this work was adapted and made available to English classrooms by the indefatigable textbook compiler Thomas Kerchever Arnold. The German philologist Wilhelm Freund's pioneering Latin dictionary on historical principles (Leipzig, 1834–5) was edited and translated by the American scholar Ethan A. Andrews in 1850 and then in 1879 substantially revised and expanded into a durable standard work, published by Oxford University Press, by Andrews' compatriots Charlton T. Lewis and Charles Short. Franz Passow of Breslau, who in 1807 had been appointed to a professorship of Greek literature at the Weimar Gymnasium by Goethe himself, had produced a major Greek dictionary in 1819–24, building on the work of his Breslau colleague J. G. Schneider, and this was used as the basis for the monumental *Greek–English Lexicon* compiled by the Oxford classicists Henry Liddell and Robert Scott (1843; 8th edn. 1897).

Yet words on the page were only one of the clues to classical civilization. New archaeological discoveries in Italy, Greece, and the Middle East and increased awareness of the evidence for and the importance of ritual, religion, visual culture, and social life in the ancient world greatly enlarged the scope of classical studies: from about the time Victoria came to the throne in 1837, the new German *Altertumswissenschaft*, or multidisciplinary science of antiquity, began to influence British classical studies. W. A. Becker, Professor of Classical Archaeology at Leipzig from 1842, had assembled materials for both Roman and Greek social history in his two extraordinary, encyclopedic volumes, cast in the form of fiction, *Gallus, or Roman Scenes of the Time of Augustus* (1838; English trans. 1844) and *Charicles, or Illustrations of the Private Life of the Greeks* (1840; English trans. 1845). Both must be among the most heavily footnoted "novels" ever published, although they ran through many editions and supplied many more readable novelists and historians with invaluable background material.

But Victorian classicism was never just a matter of rigorous scholarship and the accumulation of detailed information. The ultimately ahistorical liberal humanism that it supported among teachers and educational thinkers such as Matthew Arnold was indeed sometimes unhappy with academic developments and the increasing archaeological evidence of what Homeric society might actually have been like (Turner 1981: 180–3). Among the general public a distinctive and vivid, if unscholarly, sense of connection with the world of Greece and Rome, particularly Rome, was stimulated by contemporary developments, notably steam engines, religion, popular publishing and the politics of class, nation, and empire.

2   Steam Engines

Britain's steam-powered industrial revolution led not just to material riches but also to an enhanced sense of civic and indeed national pride that found visible expression in dignified Victorian public buildings. While various styles were adopted, some architects and some city fathers continued to favor classical designs because they recalled the achievements of the Greek city-states and the majesty of imperial Rome. Cuthbert

Brodrick's design for Leeds Town Hall (1858) featured classical columns of the local stone, millstone grit. The enormous commercial success of early-Victorian Liverpool was reflected in the building of St. George's Hall (1842–54), acclaimed as one of the finest neoclassical buildings in Europe. H. L. Elmes's design for the main hall was self-consciously modeled on the *tepidarium* (tepid bathing-room) of the Baths of Caracalla in Rome. There were other classical buildings in the city. A painting by the Liverpool artist Samuel Austin depicting Vergil's Aeneas being received at the court of Dido, Queen of Carthage actually depicts many of these buildings, as if to suggest that the trade passing through the modern port of Liverpool invited comparison with that of ancient Carthage, Rome's great rival (Vance 1997: 74).

Steam power also improved communications. Steamships and railroads increased opportunities for travel not only to Rome, Pompeii, and Athens but also to classical sites closer to home, such as Hadrian's Wall or the Roman antiquities of Bath or Colchester. Before, and even, for a time, after, the famous Greek travels of Lord Byron and his protagonist Childe Harold, Greece had been more of a dream than an actual place, almost out of reach of northern Europe, tempting some so-called travel writers to stay at home and recycle the work of their predecessors rather than furnish fresh material from firsthand observation (Constantine 1989).

The Grand Tour of the eighteenth century which had allowed young aristocrats to see the grandeur that was Rome at first hand had been prohibitively expensive, a leisurely, once-in-a-lifetime experience for the privileged few. But the coming of the railroads and passenger steamers gradually made the journey to Italy quicker and cheaper, something that could be contemplated by middle-class novelists such as Charles Dickens or George Eliot as well as by wealthy noblemen. Karl Baedeker's compact and indispensable handbook *Central Italy and Rome*, available to English travelers from 1861, responded to and stimulated a new classical tourism, economically providing the expert advice on art and antiquities that might once have been supplied by a special guide or an accompanying tutor. Baedeker's *Greece* came later, in 1889.

The pioneer travel agent Thomas Cook conducted tours to Italy from 1863, after the completion of the rail-link between northern Italy and Rome, and the journey became even shorter with the opening of the Mont Cenis railroad tunnel through the Alps in 1871. It was now much easier for classicists to pursue their researches on the ground or in the Vatican library: the British Archaeological Society of Rome was established in 1865, and French, American, and British Schools in Rome followed in 1873, 1894, and 1901. The British School in Athens was opened in 1886.

Roman antiquities within Britain had begun to attract more visitors during the Napoleonic Wars, when continental travel was difficult even for the wealthy. The growth of the railroad network soon after encouraged this new interest by making it easier to visit the widely scattered sites and local museums testifying to Roman occupation. Traces of the Roman presence in Dorchester, which contributes to the sombre backdrop of Hardy's novel *The Mayor of Casterbridge* (1886), are still on display in the Dorset County Museum. Some of the artifacts were unearthed during the building of Hardy's new house in Dorchester in 1884. The massive excavations entailed by Victorian railroad construction as well as by road-making and building programmes constantly brought to light additional evidence of Roman settlement.

The scholarly London pharmacist Charles Roach-Smith took to haunting building sites, prepared to make an offer for almost anything Roman that the spade might turn up. His extensive collection of Roman artifacts, now in the British Museum, provided the basis for his book *Illustrations of Roman London* (1859).

In 1832, in rapidly expanding industrial Manchester, remains of the old Roman fort of Mancenion were accidentally uncovered at the foot of the new Altrincham railroad viaduct and carefully protected by Lord Francis Egerton. The dramatic juxtaposition of bustling modernity and Roman remains stimulated the popular imagination and helped to encourage a sense of connection: it became apparent that, like the British of modern times, the Romans in Britain had been great civil engineers and improvers, building connecting roads if not railroads throughout the country, attaining new standards of personal comfort with running water, elaborate public baths, and underfloor heating, and developing a well-attested material culture.

3   Religion

Archaeological evidence of Roman religious practice in Britain had also survived. A chapel of Mithras, for example, had been found in 1852 at Housesteads (Borcovicus) on Hadrian's Wall. The Romans in Britain were not usually Christian, and Christianity spread among the Greek-speaking people of the Mediterranean long after the classical period usually studied at school and university. Despite other points of contact, this tended to mark the classical world as distinctly "other" in a self-consciously religious age, increasingly defensive about its faith in the face of new scientific and historical challenges to it. But the challenges of scientific modernity, often aggressively presented as a war on outmoded superstition, could be paralleled in antiquity. The poet Lucretius, dismissed as a "filthy dog" by John Calvin but admired for his scientific materialism and his impatience with the old gods by Karl Marx, could be enlisted among the moderns. Tennyson's ingeniously allusive poem "Lucretius" (1868) reinstates a tradition of hostility stemming from Jerome and early Christianity by representing the great rationalist as dying a madman's death (Vance 1997: 83–111).

For orthodox Victorians a sense of difference from Roman religion – or the lack of it – could be used as a mode of cultural and moral self-congratulation. For all their military and political achievements, the Romans who colonized Britain had not seen the light of the gospel and had depended on and upheld the institution of slavery, which had (since 1834) been abolished throughout the British empire after a religiously inspired crusade against slavery. The moral severity associated with early Rome and exemplary figures such as Horatius or Virginia, celebrated in Lord Macaulay's *Lays of Ancient Rome* (1842), had its uses in the Victorian schoolroom. But archaeological discoveries of luridly decorated Samian ware or Pompeian wall paintings suggested that by the time of the Empire Roman morality, particularly sexual morality, knew little of the decency and restraint Christianity encouraged. It was recognized by prudent and prudish schoolteachers that some Latin texts such as the erotic poems of Catullus or the probably satirical *Satyricon* of Petronius needed to be approached with considerable caution. W. E. H. Lecky, the austere Victorian historian of European morals, was disgusted by the *Satyricon* and observed that even at its best, during the Roman Republic, the Roman religion, unlike Christianity, was never an "independent source of moral enthusiasm." Under the Empire amoral luxury "rose to excesses which the wildest Oriental orgies have never surpassed" (Lecky 1897: 1:215n, 168–9).

For this and other reasons, it could be argued, the eventual decline and fall of Rome and of Greco-Roman civilization was inevitable and well deserved. The visionary radical William Blake, unimpressed by classical religion, morality, and mythology, hostile to the tradition of Roman imperial tyranny and its imitations in later kingdoms and empires, had complained that "The Greek & Roman Classics is the Antichrist" (Blake 1967: 825). But for Victorian rebels such as the poet Algernon Swinburne, that was part of the attraction. His poem "Hymn to Proserpine," nostalgic for the harsh but colorful paganism of the classical world before Christianity became the official religion of the Roman Empire, regretted the gray, conventionally Christian modern world that had taken its place. Thomas Hardy's self-taught hero Jude, in the novel *Jude the Obscure* (1895), comes to experience an impossible tension between the classical and the Christian components of British higher education. Swinburnian paganism and the tragic vision imparted by his classical studies ran counter to the official pieties and the Christian hope espoused by the Church of England. In moments of despair bleak snippets of Greek tragedy came to his lips rather than the consolation of the Scriptures.

Less abrasively, in *Culture and Anarchy* (1869), Matthew Arnold had tried to find a route round and beyond what he saw as "Hebraism," the narrowness and moral censoriousness of much of Victorian religion, by balancing it with an idealized and simplified "Hellenism." This was a harmonious and rational wisdom for life developed from J. J. Winckelmann's notions of the serenities of Greek art and a selective reading of Homer, Sophocles, and the Stoic philosopher Epictetus that could be presented as prior to and independent of the later development of Christianity. Richard Jebb (1841–1905), Professor of Greek at Cambridge, the great Victorian editor of Sophocles, felt that there need be no real antagonism between the more liberal versions of Christianity and Arnoldian Hellenism (Turner 1981: 33). But Jebb, great-nephew of an Irish bishop, was in some ways old-fashioned. Such antagonisms were ceasing to matter very much. The sometimes-awkward cohabitation of classicism and Christianity in schools and colleges was now less of a problem because Oxford and Cambridge were becoming more secular places. Jebb's Cambridge colleague A. W. Verrall (1851–1912), Fellow of Trinity College, was one of the new breed of nonclerical dons. His interests, unconfined by religious orthodoxy, included the work of the Society for Psychical Research, of which his wife was an active member. An authority on Euripidean tragedy, he controversially but influentially developed a view of Euripides as rationalist skeptic that resonated with late-Victorian agnosticism.

Verrall's Euripides was attractive without being too disconcerting. It was different in Germany. Friedrich Nietzsche's *Birth of Tragedy* (1872), dissatisfied with the classicism of Winckelmann, was much more radical and much less comfortable reading, proposing the origins of tragedy in a synthesis of the rational or Apollonian and darkly irrational or Dionysiac energies. But post-Christian Hellenism in Victorian

Britain was largely unaffected. It developed into an influential agnostic aestheticism in the work of Walter Pater, in the essays eventually collected as *Plato and Platonism* (1893) and *Greek Studies* (1895) and in his earlier book *The Renaissance* (1873), which included a substantial essay on Winckelmann. A controversial "Conclusion," tactfully omitted in the second edition, quoted Heraclitus on the perpetual flux of things and outlined a philosophy of heightened aesthetic consciousness as the supreme good in a world deprived of the certainties of Christianity and the hope of resurrection. In his only novel, *Marius the Epicurean* (1885), subtitled *His Sensations and Ideas*, Pater follows his hero through a range of sensations and systems of belief in the Rome of Marcus Aurelius and leaves him, uncommitted and dying, on the threshold of Christianity, which can be seen as possibly just another set of sensations and beliefs. Perhaps the Greek or Greco-Roman world could provide an alternative, even an antidote, to Victorian orthodoxies in religion and morality. Like Pater's work, Goldsworthy Lowes Dickinson's *The Greek View of Life* (1896) and John Addington Symonds's *Studies of the Greek Poets* (1877–9) and *A Problem in Greek Ethics* (1883), a pioneering discussion of homosexuality, were in a sense agnostic explorations, extended essays in non-Christian or post-Christian ethics and aesthetics. In his early poetry and in his life, Oscar Wilde presented himself as part of the same tradition. He had studied the classics in Dublin and Oxford and traveled in Greece with his mentor, the legendary Irish classicist J. P. Mahaffy: his eloquent if ultimately unavailing courtroom defense of male love as an ennobling mode of personal identity rather than a crime invoked Plato and the Greeks as well as Michelangelo and Shakespeare (Dowling 1994: 1–3).

If Plato could shake hands with Shakespeare, then perhaps Greek life and thought were not, after all, completely alien from (formally) Christian Britain. Connop Thirlwall, the Cambridge ancient historian and religious liberal who became Bishop of St. David's, was disposed to take a fairly tolerant view of Greek religion in his *History of Greece* (1835–44). It all began as nature-worship, which sometimes involved debased conceptions of divine nature, but he felt there was some evidence of reverence for a superior being and a growing sense of divine unity that could sometimes at least indirectly encourage moral behavior (Thirlwall 1845: 217–22).

Swinburne's mentor and friend Benjamin Jowett, Oxford Professor of Greek and later Master of Balliol, had worked on the Greek texts of Plato and of St. Paul and developed a liberal, idealist, theological outlook accommodating cultural change that owed much to them both. The synthesis was, however, vulnerable and unstable: Jowett's contribution to the controversial *Essays and Reviews* (1860), "On the Interpretation of Scripture," was widely attacked by more conservative churchmen.

Mr. Gladstone's quite extensive Homeric researches, starting with his three-volume *Studies in Homer* (1858), criticized at the time but still of interest to modern scholars, represented a development of his deep-seated religious convictions. The Old Testament testified to God's presence in the life of ancient Israel, but Homer's account of ancient Greece in the heroic age, the earliest surviving narratives of civilized society, could be read as evidence of a parallel if partial revelation to the Greeks. Such a reading required Homer to be substantially true, a single author rather than an ahistorical composite of multiple layers of tradition as Lachmann and others had suggested, as accurate on matters of fact and as generally reliable as the Bible was expected to be by literal-minded precritical readers. Gladstone's version of Homer and Homeric geography led him in the 1870s into uncritical opportunist endorsement and appropriation of Heinrich Schliemann's reckless archaeological claims after investigating allegedly Homeric sites. But it is now accepted that even if Schliemann and Gladstone got it quite badly wrong in detail, there are probably traces of an actual rather than a purely fictional history and geography behind the Homeric poems.

It was easier and less contentious to apply Roman materials to Christian purposes. There were parallels to Victorian missionary activity in Africa and India in the spread of Christianity throughout the Roman Empire. The gospel account of the crucifixion by the Roman authorities in Palestine, St. Paul's missionary journeys and detention in Rome, and the subsequent persecutions of Christians by the Roman emperors Nero and Diocletian dramatically brought the matter of Rome and the matter of Christianity together. Could ancient Britain be linked with this early Christian Roman world? Paul had Christian friends in high places, "saints in Caesar's household" (Philippians 4:22), and one of them might have been Pomponia Graecina, wife of Aulus Plautius, who had conquered Britain in the time of the emperor Claudius. Perhaps Pomponia persuaded Paul to visit Britain? There was also a tradition, uncomplicated by hard evidence, that Joseph of Arimathea, a disciple of Jesus, eventually settled at Glastonbury. Seductive but unscholarly speculation and legend linking early Christianity with Roman Britain, invoked by Anglican apologists such as Bishop Stillingfleet in *Origines Britannicae* (1685), could be revived in historical fiction if not in serious critical history. Claudia and Pudens, mentioned in the New Testament as friends of St. Paul, might – or might not – have been the same as the British Claudia and Pudens mentioned in the poetry of Martial. F. W. Farrar, Dean of Canterbury and a serious biblical scholar, decided they were not, except for the purposes of his novel *Darkness and Dawn; or, Scenes in the Days of Nero* (1891).

There was evidence that Caractacus, leader of British resistance to the Roman occupation, had been carried off as a prisoner to Rome, and that provided a model for fictions such as G. J. Whyte-Melville's *Gladiators* (1863) and G. A. Henty's *Beric the Briton* (1893), which linked proto-British heroism with the majesty of imperial Rome. Religiously inflected Roman melodramas of courage and martyrdom were established in British popular culture well before the American Lew Wallace's novel *Ben-Hur; or, The Days of the Messiah* (1880) and the films based on it. Shakespeare's frequently revived Roman plays *Julius Caesar* and *Coriolanus* provided a kind of model that could easily be Christianized. Bulwer Lytton's *Last Days of Pompeii*, which helped to set the fashion for nineteenth-century novels of Roman life, had included a little liberal Christianity in the last of its five books, corresponding to the five acts of a Shakespearean drama, when Glaucus and his wife Ione become Christians. Knowledge of the later Roman Empire derived from a classical education could be usefully combined with more specifically religious concerns by popular novelists with axes to grind. Charles Kingsley's *Hypatia* (1853), an anti-Catholic novel criticizing fifth-century Alexandrian monks, was answered by the now-Roman Catholic John Henry Newman's early-Christian conversion-novel *Callista: A Tale of the Third Century* (1855). The recently investigated catacombs beneath the city of Rome and the saints and martyrs of the early fourth century, the time of the persecutions of Diocletian, were brought together in fictional form in Cardinal Wiseman's novel *Fabiola* (1855). In an early example of what Hollywood was to call "novelization," Wilson Barrett rewrote his Christians-and-lions martyr-play *The Sign of the Cross* as a novel in 1897, the same year that Wiseman's *Fabiola* was dramatized as *From Cross to Crown*. Edwin Long's popular painting *Diana or Christ?* (1889) shows a Christian maiden at the edge of a Roman arena, obviously about to choose Christ and encounter martyrdom.

4 Publishing

Long's painting was widely familiar because it was not only exhibited at the Royal Academy but was subsequently engraved and published by Thomas Agnew (Mayer 1994: 3). A century earlier the views of Roman ruins of Piranesi or Pannini had been expensively engraved and bound in elegant folio volumes intended for gentlemen's libraries, but the processes were now cheaper and more reliable, so classical-subject paintings and the visual evidences of Greek and Roman antiquity could be conveyed to a much wider audience. With the development of line-illustrations and photographic reproductions, instead of expensive plates that had to be separately inserted into printed texts, and with improvements in printing and binding processes, the matter of Greece and Rome could reach people more vividly and more inexpensively than ever before. From the 1880s the slim blue volumes of Macmillan's Elementary Classics series, intended for schools, were illustrated with maps and drawings and photographs of busts, mosaics, or Greek vases.

Without pictures, classical books could be even cheaper. Hardy's self-taught Jude, like the young Hardy himself, had suffered from a lack of affordable and user-friendly classical texts. The Teubner series published in Leipzig from 1828 provided reliable texts, but these had only textual notes, in Latin. A. J. Valpy's reissue (1819–30) of the seventeenth-century French Delphin Classics editions was better than nothing, but not much. But all that was about to change. The growth of public examinations as a rite of passage not merely to and from universities but also to professional employment brought with it a demand for inexpensive examination texts. Cambridge University Press's Pitt Press series, inaugurated in 1875, was designed for students taking the Cambridge local examinations. It provided up-to-date, annotated editions of "set books," including English, French, and German as well as classical texts.

Other publishers were quick to exploit this market. Rivingtons' *Catena Classicorum* series began in 1867. Elementary or abbreviated versions of substantial classical histories and editions became common. Sir Charles Oman's *History of Greece* (1890) was followed by an *Elementary History of Greece* (1899), both published by Rivingtons. A. W. Verrall's edition of the *Medea* of Euripides (1881) was followed by his friend M. A. Bayfield's school edition (1892), both published by Macmillan.

But Macmillan's Elementary Classics were not for everyone. The Prefaces are usually impersonal or couched in ungendered language, but when the word "beginner" is used, the beginner is usually assumed to be a boy, particularly when the text is Greek. Latin had always been more widely taught than Greek and it was often a matriculation requirement for university when Greek was not. George Eliot had taught herself Greek and brooded on the fate of Antigone in *Middlemarch* with some knowledge of Sophocles' play, and Elizabeth Barrett Browning had read Homer in the original, but they were exceptional.

Demands for a national education system led to an Education Act in 1870, but secondary education that could include some Latin and even Greek continued to be the preserve of the middle and upper classes. Elementary education for those under 13, which was all that was available to a majority of the population, boys as well as girls, included neither Latin nor Greek, apart perhaps from a few etymologies of English words. Most readers, especially women readers, encountered the classics, if at all, only through translation. H. G. Bohn's Classical Library, published between 1848 and 1913, eventually ran to 116 volumes of translations, anticipating later popular series such as Everyman's Library, founded in 1906, which included classical authors in translation.

Both the Bohn and Everyman volumes often reprinted earlier translations, such as Thomas Moore and Leigh Hunt's versions of Catullus, John Mason Good's Lucretius (1805), and Shelley's version of Plato's *Ion*, so that readers were given some sense not just of the texts themselves but of a tradition of interest in them. That sense of a classical tradition was both witnessed and heightened by William Blackwood's popular series Ancient Classics for English Readers (1870–1932), which provided elementary introductions to classical authors with translated passages and paraphrase or summary of classical texts. Contributors included the novelist Anthony Trollope (on Julius Caesar) as well as professional scholars. There was some overlap with Macmillan's series of Literature Primers, issued from 1875, which included some classical volumes. Richard Jebb contributed *Greek Literature* (1877), and Mr. Gladstone himself supplied *Homer* (1878).

5   Politics

Gladstone's classical scholarship, like Trollope's, led to some carping from more learned if less readable professional scholars in an increasingly professional age. But his understanding of the ancient world was informed by and in turn illuminated his knowledge of contemporary politics. The inviolable rights of a Roman citizen under the empire were invoked during the Don Pacifico debate in 1850 in the House of Commons, when it was suggested that the (technically) British citizen Don Pacifico should enjoy similar protection from imperial Britain. But Mr. Gladstone knew too much about ancient as well as modern empires to be entirely happy with the parallel, suggesting that lofty notions of citizenship on the Roman model entailed potential injustice to others.

As Gladstone acknowledged, however one interpreted them, many of the key terms in the political vocabulary of the nineteenth century derived from the classics.

"Empire" (*imperium*), "liberty," and "republic" came from the Latin. "Politics" itself, originally the affairs of the *polis* or city-state, came from the Greek, as did "oligarchy," "tyranny," "aristocracy," and "democracy." "Aristocrat" and "democrat," first noted in English about 1790, came not directly from the Greek but from the French, and popular views of aristocrats, democrats, and democracy continued to be influenced by attitudes towards the French Revolution of 1789. Whatever one might think of democrats, the Greeks had also given English the word "demagogue," with more or less worrying examples to go with it.

The political battles of the nineteenth century were easily projected onto ancient history. The still-visible ruins of imperial Rome and of other ancient empires could be read as evidence of catastrophe, but they assured European revolutionaries that even the greatest tyrannies would come to an end. Rome had not always represented tyranny. Republican Rome, represented as a repository of political virtue and ideal liberty in the nostalgic rhetoric of Tacitus, was the supreme imaginative resource of revolutionary France. Roman heroes, such as the Gracchi, who had championed the people against the patricians, became honorary Jacobins. But counterrevolutionary writers such as Edmund Burke and, later, Thomas Carlyle became adept at giving an ironic twist to Roman analogies. Carlyle's *The French Revolution* (1837) is a kind of prose epic that alludes to Vergil's *Aeneid*, the great Roman epic of nation-building, but only to suggest that the revolutionary project of building an anti-aristocratic nation might be not so much epic as tragic farce.

Hostility to revolutionary politics on the French model colored English political thinking, and perceptions of Roman history, for much of Victoria's reign. Thomas Arnold of Rugby, an authority on both Greek and Roman history, liberal rather than radical in politics and with a headmaster's attitude towards insubordination, allegedly summed up his attitude towards the popular political disturbances of his own day by commending the Roman practice of flogging the rank and file and flinging the ringleaders from the Tarpeian Rock. Rick-burning and civil unrest associated with demands for parliamentary reform in the 1820s and early 1830s had prompted classically educated parliamentarians to brood darkly on the Roman experience of revolutionary conspiracy such as that of Catiline or of actual or threatened civil war. Debates on the Corn Laws promoted reflection on the disastrous (though rather different) Roman Corn Laws that the Gracchi had tried to reform. Spartacus, the Thracian gladiator who led an almost-successful slave revolt in Rome, became a popular figure in radical circles. Chartist agitation for further parliamentary reform in the 1840s stimulated interest in earlier heroes of the people, and the Chartist Ernest Jones included Spartacus in his extended discussion of "The Gladiators of Rome," published in 1852 (Vance 1997: 46).

The main events of Greek history and the different forms of political organization in different Greek city-states were also read in the light of postrevolutionary Europe. Connop Thirlwall complained, unavailingly, about the modern writers who used Greek history to talk about "questions of modern politics, which never arose in the Greek republics" (Thirlwall 1845: 464). Defeating tyrants such as Napoleon was all very well, but what exactly was a tyrant? For the Greek historian William Mitford, as for the Greeks themselves, a tyrant was not necessarily either evil or oppressive but simply a citizen who had by whatever means acquired the power of sovereignty over other citizens, a power that could be used for good or ill. Democracy on the Athenian model had had rather mixed success, Mitford felt, and was not necessarily a good thing, as it could take the form of corrupt populism, unbalancing the constitution. But political liberals, and campaigners for parliamentary reform and more representative government in Britain, preferred a different reading of Greek history. Macaulay reviewed Mitford, unfairly, with political as much as scholarly hostility. George Grote, a more liberal historian of Greece, writing in the 1840s and 1850s, spoke for the philosophical radicals of his generation and his vision of British constitutional politics when he suggested that the troubles of Athens derived not from too much democracy but from too little (Turner 1981: 192–207; 213–22).

By the 1870s political concerns had shifted from parliamentary reform to imperial debate. France had already shown how ancient and modern empires could interact. Charles-Augustin Saint-Beuve, appointed to the Collège de France by the emperor Napoleon III, lectured in 1855 on Vergil, the poet of Roman imperialism sponsored by the emperor Augustus, though anti-imperial sentiment caused the lectures to be discontinued. It is tempting to assume that enthusiasm for empire in late-Victorian and Edwardian Britain was universal and uncontroversial and that Roman analogies were explored only to ensure the better running of the British empire. There is some evidence that seems to support this view, such as Lord Cromer's lectures to the Classical Association on *Ancient and Modern Imperialism* (1909) and Sir Charles Lucas's *Greater Rome and Greater Britain* (1912). But the analogies, sometimes difficult or troubling, highlighting problems of rights and of overextension, could serve to articulate misgivings about the idea of empire. Vergil's *Aeneid*, anticipating a time when Rome would rule the known world, might sustain dreams of empire, but it also dramatized the pain and the human costs of empire-building. The Victorian historian E. A. Freeman, committed to the essential continuity of ancient and modern European history, insisted that "The true glory of the Latin tongue is to have become the eternal speech of law and dominion" (Freeman 1872: 39), but Freeman himself was uneasy about the imperial Roman model of "dominion," an English version of the Latin *imperium*, not to mention the *imperator* or emperor who might wield such power. J. M. Robertson summed up a tradition of radical dissatisfaction with the legacy of empire on the Roman model when he insisted that "The imperial people was *ipso facto* a community diseased ... with the *imperator* comes in due time the decadence of empire, the humiliation and paralysis of the spirit that had aspired to humiliate its kind" (Robertson 1899: 155, 157).

The most effective critique of empire was possibly the refusal of politics and the retreat into the alternative empire of art represented by the late-nineteenth-century cult of "decadence." Both France and England had had experience of modern imperialism, but particularly after the collapse of the French Second Empire in 1870, French and English writers looked increasingly to the art rather than the politics of Greco-Roman civilization. Particularly in the theatre, French taste had stayed close to the classics until challenged by Victor Hugo and the romantics. Critics such as Desiré Nisard, hostile to the new French romanticism, praised the Roman poets who flourished when Rome was at its best and condemned their "decadent" successors, with the implication that France, like Rome, could not be depended on to maintain standards of taste (Nisard 1834).

It was often suggested or implied that the sometimes-spectacular dissipations and the long, slow, political and moral decline (or *décadence*) of imperial Rome and its outposts in the great cities of Alexandria and Byzantium, not really helped by torpid, institutionalized Christianity, fostered different and inferior kinds of writing, brittle, self-consciously literary, artificial, with strange forms and a vocabulary that was more exotic and colorful, or for the purists more polluted, than the lexicon of Cicero. In fact, dissipated conduct could be found even in the early days of the Empire, and moral decline, political decline, and literary decline did not collude as neatly as the myth-makers might have wished.

Even so, poets and writers seeking to shock or challenge the values of their own age evinced a perverse fascination with the decadent culture of a dying Empire. Leconte de Lisle had celebrated the Alexandrian philosopher Hypatia, not as an historical figure so much as an emblem of the beleaguered beauty and truth to be embraced by the artist at all costs (Dzielska 1995). In his poem "Langueur" (1883) Paul Verlaine identified himself with the Empire at the end of the decadence. The surviving minutiae of classical art had perhaps more enduring value than the political legacy of imperial Rome. J. K. Huysman's impossibly decadent fictional hero Des Esseintes had the same taste for overelaborate late-Roman poetry as Verlaine and Mallarmé. The Irish writers George Moore and Oscar Wilde, strategically French rather than English in their tastes, made the shocking new aesthetic of "l'art pour l'art" available to English audiences in *Portrait of a Young Man* (1889) and *The Picture of Dorian Gray* (1891).

In a sense the Victorian chapter in the history of the classical tradition drew to an end with "Ars Victrix," Austin Dobson's neat translation of Théophile Gautier:

> All passes. Art alone
> Enduring stays to us.
> The Bust outlasts the throne;
> The Coin, Tiberius.
> (Dobson 1902: 205)

FURTHER READING

The Latin and Greek branches of the classical tradition in the Victorian period have often been separately treated in general accounts: for the former see Vance (1997) and the wide-ranging essays in Edwards (1999); for the latter see Jenkyns (1980), particularly strong on literary and artistic themes, and Turner (1981), which pays more attention to historiography and political thought. Both Roman and Greek influences on ideas of decadence are considered in Potolsky et al. (2004). Stray (1998) provides a wide-angled overview and a detailed account of the institutional contexts of classical teaching, Sandys (1908) includes a survey of European classical scholarship in the period, and Lloyd-Jones (1982) contains essays on individual classical scholars. There is some material of Victorian interest in Haynes (2003), which explores the influence on later writing of Latin and Greek vocabulary, syntax, and metrics. The classical dimension of the Victorian visual tradition is reviewed in Wood (1983) and Liversidge and Edwards (1996; generously illustrated) and in studies of individual artists such as Alma-Tadema (Becker et al. 1996) and Leighton (Ormond 1975). Kestner (1989) offers controversial and sometimes eccentric readings of particular images. Issues of gender and sexuality, considered by Kestner, are pursued by Prins (1999b) and Dowling (1994). Negotiations of classical materials by individual authors, discussed in older general accounts such as Bush (1937) and Highet (1949), occasionally the subject of monographs such as Delaura (1969), Wheeler (1979), and Markley (2004), are often most easily approached through good annotated editions such as Kenneth Allott's edition of Arnold (1965, 1979), Christopher Ricks's edition of Tennyson (1969, 1986), Kenneth Haynes's edition of Swinburne's *Poems and Ballads & Atalanta in Calydon* (Penguin, 2000), and the World's Classics paperback editions of Victorian novelists such as Thomas Hardy and George Eliot.

CHAPTER EIGHT

Modernism

Kenneth Haynes

1 Introduction

One major current of European and North American modernism was a new attention to archaic, preclassical, and primitive aspects of classical antiquity.[1] As a visual
icon, the archaic *kouros* was to the first half of the twentieth century what the
Laocoön group was to the late Renaissance and Baroque or the Elgin marbles to
the Romantic period. This orientation toward an ever-more-remote antiquity – from
Hellenistic sculpture to the marbles of classical Athens to preclassical Greek figures –
parallels a broad feature of the classical tradition in western Europe since the
Renaissance, where in successive periods the dominant focus of attention moved
from the Rome of seventeenth-century classicism to the Athens of nineteenth-
century Hellenism to the preclassical Greece of the modernists.

The archaic art and literature exploited by modernists encompassed much more
than the Mediterranean world. Primitive art of all sorts, stimulated especially by
African and Pacific works but also by pre-Columbian figures, Paleolithic cave painting, and folk art, was a major influence on painters and sculptors for the 30 years or so
from Picasso (with *Les Demoiselles d'Avignon*, 1907) to the artists of *Die Brücke* to
surrealists and others (on modernist primitivism, see in general Rubin 1984; Barkan
and Bush 1995; Cardinal 1996; Flam 2003). This wide influence contrasts with
previous, more isolated instances of primitivism, such as Gauguin's. Often it is not
possible to distinguish Mediterranean sources from other primitive influences. Bran-
cusi, for example, turned equally to Cycladic art, Romanian folk culture, and African
or African-influenced work. In this mingling of primitive sources the differences
among particular primitive societies were usually ignored, and a similar aesthetic
(and sometimes mythology or spirituality) was found in or imposed on very diverse
groups; the basis for such similarity was most often no more than an opposition
to certain features of the modern age. This, too, has a precedent in earlier periods of
the classical reception. Romantic Hellenism, for example, merged with Romantic

medievalism, although they had no more in common than their distance from the Augustan classicism of the eighteenth century. In both cases, the scholarly corrections that ensued to place works in fuller historical and anthropological contexts were themselves dependent and consequent on the initial enthusiasm and attention.

If the primitivist current within modernism was not limited to Greek and Roman works, neither was the classical tradition within modernism limited to the archaic. Poetry ranging from Ezra Pound's "Homage to Sextus Propertius" (1919) and Constantine Cavafy's poems of Alexandria, and prose such as Hermann Broch's *Death of Virgil* (1945) and Marguerite Yourcenar's *Memoirs of Hadrian* (1951), are obvious reminders that modernist writers could be inspired by any period of classical antiquity.

Such inspiration was partly a matter of the particular affinities of a writer, but the national context was also involved. What the ancient classical world meant in the early twentieth century in countries like Great Britain and Germany, with their strong nineteenth-century traditions of Hellenic enthusiasms and education, differed from what it meant in the more Latin-based culture of Italy and France, and it had yet another range of meanings for Orthodox countries like Greece and Russia.

Finally, a number of modernists had little interest in the classical world, and some were actively hostile to it; the futurists, for example, vehemently espoused the modern experience of speed and technology over the deadening weight of tradition.

This chapter will be organized by period of the classical world: the archaic first and at greatest length, followed by classical and postclassical Greek, and then by classical and postclassical Latin. Most of the examples discussed will be written works, and the discussion will involve both literary history and literary criticism. Foreign titles will usually be given in English, and references to secondary literature will mostly be restricted to works in English.

2 The Archaic

In what ways does the modernist discovery of the archaic differ from previous episodes of primitivism, influential since at least the eighteenth century (Boas 1973) and a major component of Romanticism?

First, sensational archaeological discoveries from the 1870s on transformed the contemporary understanding of antiquity. Heinrich Schliemann believed that he discovered the Homeric city of Troy in his excavations in 1871–3, and despite some scholarly skepticism a wide public enthusiastically greeted his discoveries, as they did later in the decade when he published his findings at Mycenae. In the 1880s British and German archaeologists began to investigate the Cycladic civilization more thoroughly than ever before (for an overview, see Etienne and Etienne 1992; on the archaeology of the Cycladic civilization specifically, see Doumas 1991). Lastly, toward the end of the nineteenth century and for the first quarter of the twentieth, Arthur Evans excavated at Knossos in Crete the remains of what he called the "Minoan" civilization. Previously, it was easy to believe that Greek art began with the Parthenon; now the art of three more ancient civilizations had been added to it. In addition, the status of Homer and Greek legendary stories was fundamentally altered, as a concrete historical dimension was restored to what had been mere myth (Graver, in this volume).

Second, in the last quarter of the nineteenth century the interpretation of primitive religion became a central preoccupation of anthropological theorists (J. G. Frazer, J. E. Harrison, W. R. Smith, E. B. Tylor) in contrast to the more political and sociological concerns just after mid-century (Bachofen, Maine, Morgan). This shift in emphasis (Kuper 1988) brought attention to the various and controversial phenomena of animism, fetishism, ritual, sacrifice, and totemism. Anthropological attempts to synthesize this material prepared the way for the uses of mythology in major American and British modernists – Eliot, Joyce, Lawrence, Pound, and Yeats (Feder 1971; Manganaro 1994). Of all such attempts, *The Golden Bough* by J. G. Frazer had perhaps the greatest literary impact (discussed at length by Vickery 1973). The study, published in two volumes in 1890 and reaching 12 volumes by 1915, sought to identify a central pattern of ritual not only in classical antiquity but in mythology everywhere: the dying and resurrecting sacred king who embodies the spirit of vegetation. The work was unsettling not only for treating classical and primitive myths on equal footing but also for its implicit connection of Christianity and myth. Because of the work of Frazer and others, mythology seemed to have universal application.

Frazer held a fellowship at Cambridge, and partly due to his example a group of classicists later known as the "Cambridge Ritualists" introduced the anthropological study of religion into classical scholarship (Ackermann 1991; Calder 1991; and for a bibliography, Arlen 1990); the career of Jane Harrison, in particular, has been closely studied (Peacock 1988; Beard 2000; Robinson 2002). They were influential not only in insisting on the religious and ritualistic aspects of Greek culture but also, along with Nietzsche and to some degree Pater, in drawing attention to the darker, unenlightened, and chthonic phenomena of classical antiquity.

In German-speaking countries, a similar combination of classics and anthropology in the nineteenth century would come to influence modernist writers. In particular, the work of J. J. Bachofen, who began his career as a professor of Roman law but gained fame for his speculations in the 1860s about an original matriarchal society and about the Orphic mysteries, was much read in the 1920s and 1930s, influencing not only writers such as Hauptmann, Hofmannsthal, Mann, Rilke, and others but also the political debates of the time and even the development of psychoanalytic theory (Davies 2005; Gossman 2000: 111–200; and Ryan 1999: 167).

Third, some of the most influential thinkers of the modern period – Freud, Marx, and Nietzsche – had a familiarity with classical antiquity that left a fundamental imprint on their analyses of the conditions of modern life (on Freud and antiquity, see Armstrong 2005; Barker 1996; and Gamwell and Wells 1989; on Marx and antiquity, see the bibliography by McCarthy 1999). Nietzsche is the most obvious case, since he began his career as one of the most promising classical scholars of his day, later abandoning the profession of classics to assume the mantle of the prophet of modernity. In his first book, *The Birth of Tragedy* (1872), he wrote, "And now the mythless man stands eternally hungry, surrounded by all past ages, and digs and grubs for roots, even if he has to dig for them among the remotest antiquities" (§23, trans. Walter Kaufmann). In the last third of the book he celebrates the rebirth of German myth in Wagner, but already by the time of his next work, the aphoristic *Human, All-too-Human* (1878), he changes tack and instead of attempting to recuperate myth, embraces the possibilities opened up by the end of myth. His attitude would change again in subsequent works. Still, however it is interpreted, the exhaustion of myth as a condition of modern life is a constant theme in Nietzsche's writings, one that anticipates and exposes the modernist self-entanglement with the archaic.

The imaginative forms of social solidarity that were evident in archaic societies provided a ground against which to diagnose the pathologies of modern life and to understand the radical pressures exerted on the social structures of the day by industrialization, positivism, Darwin, and the erosion of traditional belief. Even without classical training, other thinkers, notably French sociologists such as Durkheim, Lévy-Bruhl, and Mauss, had a wide influence on writers who were attempting to come to grips with the strained relations of past and present. The sense of strain became a sense of crisis with the world wars and the economic disruptions of world depression, and the relation of modern culture to its past became a question of great urgency. Under these conditions, T. S. Eliot, in his essay "Tradition and the Individual Talent" (1919), gave a new emphasis to the word "tradition," one in keeping with his own sense of the necessity of cultural and ritual survivals in modern life (in *The Waste Land* he is as skeptical as he is desirous of those survivals). Ezra Pound, although he did not have Eliot's sense of tradition, shared his urgency about the past, attempting to reclaim what he saw as the essential texts and jettisoning others. The modernist attitude towards classics, generally speaking, was one of urgency, of rescue rather than reappraisal.

The most sustained literary engagement with the archaic may be Pound's *Cantos*, a long work begun around 1915 and abandoned in the 1960s. It opens with a version of the "Nekuia," Book 11 of the *Odyssey*, in which Odysseus visits Hades. Pound believed that it represented the oldest stratum of the poem, and, in common with the anthropological turn of some of the classical scholarship of his day, he emphasized the ritualist and mythic dimension of the descent to the underworld (Pound 1971: 274; relevant passages by Jane Harrison are quoted in Bush 1976: 126–8). Yet Pound does not translate from Greek; instead, he uses Andreas Divus' Latin translation of 1538. Moreover, he includes some archaic English words: "fosse" for ditch; "dreory," a coinage meant to restore the etymological sense of "dreary" (dripping with blood); "bever" for drink; "pitkin", a coinage based on an obsolete diminutive, and others. The archaic vocabulary here is deployed only intermittently; he avoids the monotony of the more consistently archaizing diction of Morris, Rossetti, or Doughty, for example, reserving it for special effects. (Later, in the *Pisan Cantos* and the *Confucian Odes*, Pound shows himself the twentieth-century master of archaic diction.) The rhythm of the translation is largely blank-verse, but some lines are deliberately modeled on the rhythm of *The Seafarer*, with alliterative words in stressed positions. Canto I is meant to be triply archaic: the most ancient part of an ancient poem is translated from a Latin version of the Renaissance (which also served as the basis for Chapman's Homer) into an English that recalls Anglo-Saxon.

The outward-directed artists and men of action whom Pound celebrates (Odysseus, Sigismundo Malatesta, Mussolini, and many others) constitute only part of his study. Pound seeks to identify primeval experiences that recur in history, to read history as myth. The descent into the world of the dead is necessary for rebirth and renewal, a return to the roots that sustain life. The experiences of ritual and initiation are represented on several occasions, in Cantos XVII and XLVII, as well as in the *Pisan Cantos*. Over the course of the latter, the sacred marriage of Demeter and Zeus celebrated at Eleusis is recreated elliptically,[2] initially in fragments, with a more sustained affirmation toward the end of the sequence.

The *Cantos* grapples with what Pound believes to be the religious underpinning of civilization, where by "civilization" is meant the life, the political, economic, religious, and artistic life, in the great cities at or just before their prime. Canto I ends with fragments from the Homeric hymns to Aphrodite, in Latin and English; its reference to "Aphrodite, Cypri monumenta sortita est" becomes clear only later, when the vision is more fully articulated in the *Pisan Cantos* ("the hidden city moves upward" in Canto LXXXIII, and a series of puns in Canto LXXXII culminates with "let the herbs rise in April abundant"; see Carne-Ross 1985: 37–8). Pound is equally concerned to denounce the enemies of this organic vision; the denunciations take powerful poetic form in the "usura" Cantos (XLV and LI) but elsewhere are no more than anti-Semitic ravings against Jewish financiers.

The relation of the *Odyssey* to Joyce's *Ulysses* (1922) is more controversial than in the case of Pound's *Cantos*. On a few occasions Joyce supplied a schema of the work (one of these was published in Stuart Gilbert's *James Joyce's Ulysses*, 1930), in which each episode is given a title that recalls an episode from Homer. The Nekuia, for example, corresponds to chapter 6 of *Ulysses*, called "Hades" in the schema, in which Leopold Bloom attends the funeral for Paddy Dingham. Bloom's thoughts wander: "The Botanic Gardens are just over there. It's the blood sinking in the earth gives new life. Same idea those jews they said killed the christian boy" (Joyce 1986: 6.771; cf. 8.729). Ronald Bush, in a discussion of Pound's Canto I, contrasts Pound's technique with Joyce's, noting that Joyce employs the Flaubertian technique of description mainly to represent how "the experience of death and renewal feels *today* for *un homme moyen sensual*" (Bush 1976: 130–1) – in sharp contrast to Pound's attempt at a direct evocation of archaic ritual.

However, to describe in more general terms the relation between Homer and Joyce is difficult. Not only do the different chapters have greatly varying relationships to Homer and to myth, but critics are divided about how to interpret them. In answer to the question about which books on the Ulysses theme were studied by Joyce, his brother Stanislaus answered, "Virgil, Ovid, Dante, Shakespeare, Racine, Fénelon, Tennyson, Phillips, d'Annunzio, and Hauptmann, as well as Samuel Butler's *The Authoress of the Odyssey* and Bérard *Les Phéniciens et l'Odyssée*, and the translations by Butler and Cowper" (Stanford 1964: 276n6).[3] The translations are significant in that Joyce, for all his enthusiasm for Greek, did not read or pretend to read the language. Hugh Kenner emphasized in two respects the impact of Butler's Homer on Joyce. First, Butler was "the first creative mind – Joyce's was the second – to take the archaeologist's Homer seriously" (Kenner 1969: 293). The archaeological context was one in which the concrete and everyday details of ordinary life were restored to prominence in a poem that most Victorians had treated as sublimely removed from the quotidian. Second, Butler's translation into plain prose had the "texture of a naturalistic novel, the same texture a reader of Joyce encounters" (Kenner 1969: 296). The influence of Bérard's study on Joyce was fully explored by Michael Seidel (1976). The Homeric names of the episodes of *Ulysses* are the same as the chapters in Bérard's study, and the geography that he offered for Odysseus is carefully translated into the geography of Dublin. Moreover, he emphasizes a Phoenician, that is, Semitic, background to Odysseus' wanderings, and so Joyce had an "archaeological" precedent for casting the Jew Bloom in the role of a modern Odysseus.

The links between *Ulysses* and the *Odyssey* are multifarious, cunningly made, and endlessly elaborated. But how should they be understood? In an essay of 1923, Eliot made a case for myth, arguing that Joyce's continuous parallel between contemporaneity and antiquity is "a way of controlling, of ordering, of giving a shape and a significance to the immense panorama of futility and anarchy which is contemporary history" (Eliot 1975: 177). Yet it remains an open question what kind of order, if any, is yielded by the intricate systemization. Other readings emphasize the parodic elements of the novel: the middling perceptions of Bloom, the inflated "epic" language of chapter 12, the Homeric framework itself as pseudoclassical in the way favored by the Irish Literary Revival (argued by Platt 1998: 98–127), and most centrally the illusions and self-deceptions of Stephen Dedalus. It may be that the novel offers neither myth nor a parody of myth, neither order nor a parody of order, but unsettles the difference between them. For Guy Davenport, Joyce's labyrinthine symbolism is "a mimesis of symbolism: a dramatic perception, ultimately tragic, that man's ideas, his art, his noblest configurations of sense, are no more than symbols. They are forgeries of meaning" (Davenport 1987: 60).

Homer was a major presence among the Greek modernists, for whom he was both an import of Western European Hellenism and a domestic legacy available, in however questionable a degree, in the Greek language, landscape, and folk experience. Nikos Kazantzakis's *Odyssey* (1938) is in open competition with Homer, iconoclastically pitting "demoticism at its lexical extreme" (Ricks 1989: 3) against Homer's poetic language and canceling the stable appeal of Ithaca by inventing a series of amoral wanderings after Odysseus' return home. The title of George Seferis's *Mythistorema* (1935) has its ordinary meaning, "novel," but also insists on "myth-history"; in Seferis generally, recent Greek history, in both its ordinary and tragic dimensions, coexists with a mythology from the ancient world. In *Mythistorema*, the connections to the *Odyssey* are looser than in Joyce's *Ulysses* but perhaps more intense: David Ricks has called the rewriting of the Nekuia in the final poem of the sequence, so that it affirms the poet's vocation as agent between the living and the dead, "perhaps Seferis' most distinctive contribution to European poetry" (Ricks 1989: 137; see also Beaton 1991: 108–9). Angelos Sikelianos was most concerned with the mythological and cosmological implications of Homer's world, as in poems like "Homer," "Achelous," and "Secret Iliad," but more generally with a poetic recreation of ancient myth in which the poet acts as a kind of priest.

Rainer Maria Rilke's fascination with the archaic included texts like *Gilgamesh* and the Egyptian *Book of the Dead* as well as the Greek *kouros*,[4] which he celebrated in the sonnet "Archaic Torso of Apollo" (1908). A fifth-century funeral relief that he saw in the Museo Nazionale in Naples in 1904 inspired his poem "Orpheus. Eurydice. Hermes" of the same year; it is also recalled at the end of the second *Duino Elegy* (1912). The figure of Orpheus fascinated Rilke. He was attracted to Bachofen's account of Orphism, and after his trip to Egypt he became interested in the similarities of Orphic mysteries with ancient Egyptian death cults. Such an attempt at comparative mythology was a common exercise of the time, and he read widely in it (Ryan 1999: 176–7), attempting his own synthesis of myth in the tenth *Duino Elegy* and many of the *Sonnets to Orpheus* (1922). Symbolists at the end of the nineteenth century often invoked Orpheus as the figure for the poet, and his mythology was further developed in the first half of the twentieth century by a large number of writers, artists, and musicians: Apollinaire, Benn, Cocteau, Dufy, Klee, Redon, Stravinsky, Tsvetayeva, and many others (Strauss 1971; Segal 1989: 155–98; and Brunel 1999).

The archaic becomes important at this time in another respect: the fragmentary writings of the pre-Socratic philosophers are evaluated anew, above all in the philosophy of Martin Heidegger after the publication of *Being and Time* (1927). From the 1930s onward, Heidegger abandons his previous attempt to give an a priori account of how Being becomes intelligible within human experience and instead seeks to give a history of Being. This history consists of distinct epochs that constitute a series of "falls," marked by increasing *Seinsvergessenheit* (the forgetting of Being) that culminates in the nihilism of modernity. One critical event was the translation of Greek philosophical terms into Latin ones. In *Introduction to Metaphysics* (given as a lecture course in 1935 and first published in 1953), Heidegger writes that all the translations of Greek philosophical language into Latin destroyed "the authentic philosophical naming force of the Greek": this translation was "the first stage in the isolation and alienation of the originary essence of Greek philosophy," which would become definitive for the Middle Ages and modern philosophy (Heidegger 2000: 14). In other writings, such as "Plato's Doctrine of Truth," given as class lectures in 1931–2 and published about a decade later, Heidegger emphasizes the philosophy of Plato – notably the allegory of the cave – as the decisive rupture that would impoverish philosophy by reducing truth to no more than the agreement of language with reality.[5]

Wherever the fall is identified, for Heidegger the history of Being has its numinous origin in pre-Socratic Greece. Critical for Heidegger was the Greek word *alētheia*, which he understood, through a debated etymology, as "unconcealment" or "disclosure" (on the history of Heidegger's understanding of truth in this sense, see Young 2002: 5–6). The usual translation of the word as "truth," understood as the agreement or correspondence of propositions to facts, is inadequate since it depends on the existence of things in the first place, and facts about them, and propositions that refer to them. Truth understood as correspondence depends on there already being present a world, a disclosed horizon; it is, therefore, derivative of a more primordial truth. This more primordial truth was experienced above all in pre-Socratic Greece, uniquely open to the self-presencing of Being, in contrast to the subsequent reduction of Being to ontology, to objects reliably present (Young 1997: 112). Heidegger repeatedly turns to the fragments of pre-Socratic philosophers, in lectures, in his *Introduction to Metaphysics*, and in essays on Anaximander, Heraclitus, and Parmenides (collected and translated into English in Heidegger 1984; for Anaximander, see also Heidegger 2002: 242–81).

3   Classical and Postclassical Greek

The long involvement of American and European dramatists with Greek tragedy throughout the first half of the twentieth century yielded many plays. The emphases varied, from myth to psychology to politics, as did their dramaturgy and dramatic language, but the plays on Greek themes by Anouilh, Cocteau, Eliot, Giraudoux, Hauptmann, Hofmannsthal, Jeffers, and O'Neill have had at best only a mixed reception. In conjunction with other arts, especially music, a few of these responses to Greek tragedy have been more enduring.

At the beginning of the twentieth century, Hofmannsthal abandoned the lyrics and short verse plays that had made his reputation; in his short essay "Letter of Lord Chandos" (1902), the fictional author expresses a radical skepticism about the possibilities of language in order to explain his decision to cease his literary activity. Shortly afterwards, he began to write plays on classical themes (*Electra*, 1904; *Oedipus and the Sphinx*, 1906; and *King Oedipus*, 1907) in which myth, ritual, and gesture were to create a new language. *Electra*, the first and most famous of these, announced on its title page that it was "freely after Sophocles." Hofmannsthal turned Sophocles' play into a study of psychological extremity. The transformation was motivated by the example of Wilde's *Salome*, a drama of decadent sexuality that Hofmannsthal saw in 1903; by reading Freud and Breuer on hysteria in women; and by a study of Rohde's *Psyche* (1898), a work in which the Furies were interpreted psychologically as an extreme manifestation of a diseased mind (Goldhill 2002: 151). However, fame is attached not to the play but to the revised form it took when Strauss adopted it for his opera. The libretto is about two-thirds the length of the original, Strauss having made cuts to streamline the play and to simplify the psychologies explored by Hofmannsthal (Gilliam 1991: 36). The music with its contrasting moods (four confrontations with Electra constitute the largest part of the opera), expressive dissonance, thematic unity, and extensive network of motifs realizes Hofmannsthal's ambitions more fully than his own words alone (Gilliam 1991: 1–17 and 67–106; Murray 1992). Even more drastically, 40 years later, the staging and language of Gerhart Hauptmann's *Atreides Tetralogy*, his rewriting of the *Oresteia* in the context of the last years of Hitler's Germany, were not equal to his dramatic ambitions, although the darkly fatalistic atmosphere of the tetralogy has been admired (Maurer 1982: 123–30).

French rewritings of Greek tragedy were often concerned with politics. In Giraudoux's *Electra* (1937), Aegisthus is not only the accomplice to the murder of Agamemnon, but also a successful ruler who has brought prosperity to his city. He embodies and explicitly defends the political expediency against which Electra's revenge seems pointlessly destructive. The same conflict is heightened in Anouilh's *Antigone* (1944), where Antigone's defiance of Creon may be no more than an absurd rebellion against bourgeois values. *Antigone* is probably the best of the plays on mythological themes he wrote at this time (including *Eurydice*, 1941; *Orestes*, 1945; and *Medea*, 1946): its "stagecraft" and "argumentative cunning ... far exceed what is a fundamentally tawdry, reductive treatment of the Antigone theme" (Steiner 1984: 193). Besides his rewriting of the story of Oedipus in *The Infernal Machine* (1934), Cocteau produced a colloquial French version of *Antigone* in 1922, with incidental music by Honegger and scenery designed by Picasso. A few years later he wrote the French text that was translated into Latin (by Jean Daniélou) to serve as the libretto for Stravinsky's "opera-oratorio" *Oedipus Rex* (1927–8). The Latin feels at once stately ("Divum Jocastae caput mortuum!", Head of Jocasta, divine, dead) and liturgical, and the opera, designed to have a static and "neoclassical" monumentality, nonetheless recreates the movement of Oedipus' fate, musically translated into the progress from "florid melisma into stony syllabic simplicity" (Taruskin 1992: 577; see also Walsh 1993).

Gide (*Oedipus*, 1931) and Sartre (*The Flies*, 1943) also based plays on ancient Greek tragedy, as did D'Annunzio (*The Dead City*, 1898). T. S. Eliot took the plots of *The Family Reunion* (1939) and *The Cocktail Party* (1949) from Aeschylus' *Eumenides* and Euripides' *Alcestis*, respectively, and rewrote them in the language of the contemporary drama of social manners. Eugene O'Neill's trilogy *Mourning Becomes Electra* (1931) transplants the *Oresteia* to a New England setting immediately after the Civil War. Robinson Jeffers adapted and imitated a number of Greek tragedies. The list of such adaptations in the first half of the twentieth century is long and dispiriting.

The Hellenism of Osip Mandelstam, in contrast, is one of the great achievements of modernist literature. Though he was not as erudite in classical philology as the Symbolist poets Innokenty Annensky (who translated Euripides), Vyacheslav Ivanov (translator of Sappho and Aeschylus), or Valery Bryusov, he absorbed and in some cases "corrected" (Mandelstam 1979: 477) their influence to become the greater poet. As a student at the Faculty of History and Philology at the University of St. Petersburg, he loved Greek in a personal, passionate, and idiosyncratic way (see the memoir by his Greek tutor quoted in Brown 1973: 47). His Hellenism is likewise personal. He contrasts Hellenization with an "inner" or "domestic" Hellenism:

> an earthenware pot, oven tongs, a milk jug, kitchen utensils, dishes; it is anything which surrounds the body. Hellenism is the warmth of the hearth experienced as something sacred ... the transformation of impersonal objects into domestic utensils, and the humanizing and the warming of the surrounding world with the most delicate teleological warmth. (Mandelstam 1979: 127–8)

This amalgam of "loftiness and distance with the familiar homeliness" (Brown 1973: 255) is not contrasted with Rome or Christianity but encompasses them within his commitment to the Mediterranean world and European high culture; it exists in an intimate relation to the "Judaic chaos" (Mandelstam 1986: 83–8) that drives him to embrace it.

Stone (1913), Mandelstam's first book of verse, includes several poems on classical themes; two poems (Nos. 62 and 78) invoke Homer in a mood of languid, golden slowness. *Tristia* (1922) is more haunted by death. The figure of Persephone appears throughout the book, knit to the darkened fate of St. Petersburg and of the living, fleshly word after the Revolution. In this book and in his subsequent poetry, classical references are deployed indirectly and suggestively, with complex effect (Bryusov even complained about the inaccuracies of the mythology; see Brown 1973: 266). The title poem "Tristia" invokes Ovid,[6] other ancient writers, and Pushkin in its study of leavetaking. Although lament and nostalgia are dominant moods in the book, they are counterpointed by moments of quiet contentment and of the joyful recognition of one's condition in time that is made possible by high literacy. *Poems* (1928) collects the previous books and adds a few new poems, including the great anguished ode "The Horseshoe Finder," which Mandelstam offers as the defeated end of the tradition of the ode inaugurated by Pindar (on this theme, see Cavanaugh 1995: 163–8). In the final poems of the *Voronezh Notebooks*, references to the classical Mediterranean world are placed under the extreme pressure of Stalin's terror; Rome is depicted in a sinister light.

Constantine Cavafy wrote a few early poems on Homeric themes, avoided almost totally the Greece of the fifth century, and set the majority of his classically inspired poems in the Hellenistic empire or later. Marguerite Yourcenar, who translated a selection of his poetry into French prose, divided the latter into cycles:

> the *Ptolemys-Seleucids* cycle, which we might also call the *Fall of the Hellenistic Mon-archies-Triumph of Rome*, the largest, since it includes at least two dozen poems and the ones most charged with pathos and irony; the four *études de moeurs* in the *Hellenized Jews* cycle; seven poems in the fine Alexandrian *Caesar-Caesarion-Antony* cycle; ten poems in the *Sophists-Poets-Ancient Universities* cycle, which constitutes the equivalent of Cavafy's *ars poetica*; two poems on Nero ...; some twenty poems in the *Pagan-Christians* cycle ...; two poems about Apollonius of Tyana; seven poems on, or rather against, Julian the Apostate; seven in the *Orthodoxy-Byzantine Chronicles* cycle. (Yourcenar 1985: 166–7)

Classical Greek poetry plays only a small part in his own verse; he draws on the lesser-known Greek prose writers and evidently on works like E. R. Bevan's *House of Seleucus* (1902; see Yourcenar 1985: 163) in creating his new myth of Alexandria. This city – historical, erotic, mythical – and the dispersed and disempowered inhabitants of its empire yield the characters and events over which his skeptical intelligence ranges with oblique ironies and sympathies (see further Keeley 1976).

Because of "Sailing to Byzantium" (1928) and "Byzantium" (1933), Yeats is the modernist most closely associated with Byzantium. In the nineteenth century, something like a "Byzantine revival" had occurred in the wake of the Gothic revival, with a particular appeal to the international Arts and Crafts movement (see Bullen 2003). Yeats read W. G. Holmes's *The Age of Justinian and Theodora* (1905) and a few other works on the topic (Gordon 1962: 81–9), but the symbol he made of Byzantium depends largely on the nineteenth century's aesthetic and organic view of the city. In *A Vision* (1925), he wrote that perhaps in early Byzantium alone "religious, aesthetic and practical life were one." He was conscious of historical parallels and connections between Ireland and Byzantium and perhaps saw Ireland's break from England as an echo of Byzantium's break from Rome (Foster 2003: 326).

Modernist poets did not translate extensively from Greek. Yeats adapted Jebb's translation of *Oedipus Rex* in 1912, and two decades later, after consulting "half a dozen translations," he produced a version for the Abbey in December 1926; he continued to revise, closely studying Paul Masqueray's French translation, and in 1928 he published *Sophocles' King Oedipus* (Clark and McGuire 1989: 3–40). In his *Collected Plays* of 1934 he added Sophocles' *Oedipus at Colonus*. He included a chorus from *Oedipus at Colonus* in *The Tower* (1928), and one "From the *Antigone*" in *The Winding Stair and Other Poems* (1933). Other translators include not only Annensky and Ivanov but also H. D., whose imagistic translations include choruses from Euripides' *Iphigenia at Aulis* in 1916 and from *Hippolytus* in 1919 (she translated Euripides' *Ion* in 1937), and Salvatore Quasimodo, who translated a selection of ancient Greek lyric in 1940 and subsequently turned to Homer and the tragedians (he also translated Latin verse).

4   Classical and Postclassical Latin

In 1917 Wilfred Owen denounced the "old Lie: Dulce et decorum est / Pro patria mori" (a sweet and seemly thing it is, to die for one's country, Horace *Odes* 3.2.13); the slaughter of a generation of the educated class in the trenches during the Great War cast into radical doubt the value of the classical literature that had served as the basis for their education. Pound found within Latin literature itself a means to attack the bloated poetic and political inheritance of his age (on Pound's involvement with the poetry of classical Rome during World War I, see Davidson 1995; on Pound and Vergil, see Davie 1986). The goal of his *Homage to Sextus Propertius* was to present "certain emotions as vital to me in 1917, faced with the infinite and ineffable imbecility of the British Empire, as they were to Propertius some centuries earlier, when faced with the infinite and ineffable imbecility of the Roman Empire" (Pound 1971: 231). The analogy between the British and Roman Empires – and between what Pound understood as Propertius' relation to Horace and Vergil on the one hand and the modernist relation to the English poetic tradition on the other – provided the ground for rethinking and relaunching the literary mode of imitation. The poem consists of translations, adaptations, and mistranslations of passages from Propertius' later elegies, designed in various ways to create an atmosphere of life confined within a deathly stasis (the deliberate "howlers," for example, mock the deadening pedantry of scholars). The *Homage* traces the dramatic situation of a Propertius who struggles to find words for life and love at a time when the available language comprises the deceptions of public life, the clichés and self-deceptions of romantic attachment, and a discredited poetic tradition (Sullivan 1964; Bush 1983).

After World War I and with the rise of fascism, Vergil began to be read in a new and more darkly political way (Ziolkowski 1993). From 1936 to 1945, a period that saw his detention in Nazi custody as well as his emigration to the United States, Hermann Broch worked on *The Death of Virgil*, a long prose fiction recreating the last 18 hours of Vergil's life. Broch had only rudimentary Latin, and before this project he had shown little interest in Vergil or Rome. The initial impetus for the book came from reading Theodor Haecker's *Virgil, Father of the West* (1931), a study that drew parallels between Vergil's age and contemporary Europe and, continuing a tradition of reading Vergil as an *anima naturaliter Christiana* (a spirit Christian by nature), emphasized the presence of love in his works (Haecker's work also had a significant influence on T. S. Eliot; see Reeves 1989: 96–116). With further details from Donatus' life of Vergil, which a friend translated for him, Broch examines Vergil's intention to destroy the *Aeneid*. Art is autonomous, and no duty can be imposed on it (Broch 1983: 334); therefore, the artist's devotion to his art necessarily withdraws him from the domains of politics and even from "the round of human action and the human need for help" (Broch 1983: 225). As history changes, this withdrawal may cease to be justified. In the third section of the book, Augustus and Vergil argue, with increasing anger, about Vergil's intended sacrifice. Vergil at last relents, and although this is not explained, it is clear "by renouncing his wish, he is able to commit an act of human love, thus anticipating in his own way the kingdom of love and spirit which is to come" (Ziolkowski 1993: 205).

From 1938 to 1944, Miklós Radnóti wrote eight eclogues[7] that are commonly considered one of the great achievements of modern Hungarian poetry. The initial impetus for these was a commission to translate Vergil's *Eclogue* 9 in 1938. He was attracted not only to the Vergilian themes of dispossession, exile, and the poet's task, but also to formal aspects of classicism, such as writing in hexameters (all but two of his eclogues are written in dactylic hexameter). The formal and thematic concerns form a unity. In the seventh eclogue, written during his imprisonment in a labor camp in Yugoslavia, he asks:

> – O home, O can it still be?
> With the bombing? And *is* it as then when they marched us away?
> And shall those who moan on my left and my right return?
> Say, is there a country where someone still knows the hexameter?
> (Ozsváth 2000: 205)

The hexameter is a synecdoche for civilized life, which was ended by the labor camps and continued to exist only in memory and in the formal, metrical commitment to Vergil and to the Hungarian hexameter tradition (George 1986: 433). The eighth eclogue, written a few months before his murder in a forced march, combines the classical and the biblical pastoral modes, and fury sustains both the prophet Nahum and the poet who bears witness to the torched cites of Europe (Géfin 1999; Adams 1965).

The modernist reception of Ovid was broad but often indirect, inseparable from the encounter with myth (for a survey see Ziolkowski 2005); from this perspective a critic may have been justified in claiming Ovid as a "chief ancestor of literary modernism"

(Tomlinson 2003: 101). For Pound, Ovid's *Metamorphoses* was "a sacred book; one of the cornerstones of his creating imagination" (Davidson 1995: 116; see also Feder 1985). Eliot's *Waste Land* responds as much to Ovid as to Vergil (see Medcalf 1988; Reeves 1989: 28–58; Martindale 1995–6; Tomlinson 2003: 121–41). Picasso's illustrations of the *Metamorphoses* were an unusually close response to the text. In a short period, he produced 30 etchings to a selection of myths made by Albert Skira. For Picasso, the linear style of the illustrations was a means to unite modern and ancient styles. He admired ancient art, especially fifth-century vase painting, and as he believed that line drawing alone was intrinsically abstract, it was also modern (Cowling 2002: 543). He made full use of the nonrepresentational "overlappings, foreshortenings, and other uncertainties" (Florman 2000: 34) of the illustrations.

Other Latin writers had a narrower impact, significant in more isolated cases, as with Seneca and T. S. Eliot, or with Petronius and F. Scott Fitzgerald (*The Great Gatsby*, 1925) or Cocteau (*The School of Widows*, 1936). One of the fullest engagements with imperial Rome was Marguerite Yourcenar's *Memoirs of Hadrian* (1951), an historical novel she began in 1924, abandoned, and took up again in 1948, in a period of relative optimism, after war had ended and the United Nations was founded. The novel is written in the form of a monologue and a political testament, in which Hadrian is depicted as a wise sensualist and citizen whose flexibility, openmindedness toward other cultures, and large scope of thoughtful action ensured a limited peace until drawn into war in Palestine (see Yourcenar 1980: 113–29).

Yourcenar was unusual in the degree to which she was immersed in classics and classical languages. The lack of direct access to classics was more common, and it sometimes – as with the exemplary instances of Broch, Joyce, and Mandelstam – seems to have acted as a positive incitement to engage classical texts in new ways.

FURTHER READING

Every important modernist figure has been the subject of more criticism and scholarship than can be surveyed. Of the thousands of scholarly and critical works on James Joyce, for example, there are hundreds devoted to various aspects of his relation to classics. Yet for all this volume, no reasonably comprehensive survey of the classical tradition and modernism has been attempted, and the broad shape and scope of the modernists' engagement with the classics remain unknown. An additional stumbling-block is that in many cases we lack the fundamental scholarship necessary for critical inquiry, including, for example, scholarly editions of most of the major works of Eliot and Pound, or the publication of many of their letters. Most often the useful secondary literature has examined more focused subjects. In two studies, Ziolkowski investigates modernists in their relation to Vergil (1993) and Ovid (2005), both in detail and with a wide perspective. In an earlier generation, critics investigated the reception of individual classical themes or figures and usually covered the modern period, at least to some degree (see for example Stanford 1964 on Ulysses, or Strauss 1971 on Orpheus).

NOTES

1 Of the competing accounts of modernism, a narrow definition of the term might limit it largely to works of 1910–40; a more expansive definition might place its origin in France in the last third of the nineteenth century, or in Britain or Germany of the 1890s. This chapter has adopted the chronological limits of the first half of the twentieth century as its working basis.

2 With details from Frazer, as noted by Carne-Ross 1979: 209–10.

3 Stephen Phillips published his verse drama *Ulysses* in 1902; D'Annunzio's long poem *Maia* (1903), a chronicle of his journey to Greece, imagines contemporary encounters with ancient characters, including Ulysses.

4 It is not known for certain which *kouros* served as Rilke's model, although several possibilities have been discussed.

5 The deficiencies of Heidegger's account as an historically plausible interpretation of Plato are discussed in Friedländer 1958: 221–9.

6 Ovid was a "lifelong favorite of Mandelstam's who may have felt that his fate in Soviet Russia was that of Ovid in exile" (Terras 1966: 259); see also Ziolkowski 2005: 67–73.

7 It is not known for certain which of his poems corresponds to the sixth eclogue.

PART II

Places

CHAPTER NINE

Africa

William J. Dominik

1 Introduction

The classical tradition in sub-Saharan Africa (hereafter "Africa") is immense and longstanding. The role and extent of the classical heritage in African literature, law, and architecture can be traced throughout the subcontinent. There are dozens of dramas, collections of poetry, individual poems, prose works, and titles of works that reveal classical influences. On a general level this heritage among African writers is most evident in the use of classical themes, subjects, allusions, figures, names, words, and expressions, including those written in Latin and Greek, and even meters. The influence of classical literature and mythology upon modern African literature is most evident in African dramaturgy. A large number of writers in modern Africa make use of classical elements in their poems and prose works. Latin literature was written as early as the sixteenth century by African scholars who translated classical literature and composed poetry and prose works on contemporary topics. Other areas in which the classical heritage is evident on the subcontinent are law and architecture. The African intellectual environment has been pervaded by the debate concerning the extent of the role of black Africa in the development of the Greek and Egyptian civilizations.

2 Drama

The influence of classical literature and mythology in the development of African drama is evident mainly among numerous west and South African playwrights, whose identities range across the ethnic and racial spectra and include white, black, Afrikaaner, Yoruban, Ijaw, Ghanaian, Congan, and Cameroonian. Greek drama and mythological sources have been used in modern African drama for means quite different from the causes of imperialism and colonialism that they have sometimes served in the literature, art, and music of nineteenth- and twentieth-century Europe. Some African dramas derived from classical sources, almost all of which are tragedies, explore political issues relevant to colonial and postcolonial society, while others touch upon issues pertinent to tribal Africa and feature religious and folk rituals. These plays are written in languages such as English, Afrikaans, French, Zulu, Xhosa, seSotho, Yoruban, and Tamil and explore all types of relationships between various characters who emerge as complex and fragmented figures. They are hybrid dramas that reflect not only their postcolonial and classical origins but also the split identities of their authors.

2.1   Political drama

The second half of the twentieth century gave rise to the birth and development of political drama as a genre on the African subcontinent. Greek and Roman literature and mythological sources are used in modern African drama for the expression of a range of political viewpoints. These dramatists adapt the storylines, themes, motifs, and characters of classical literature and history in order to deal with political issues involving power, freedom, and justice and to expose their opposites of powerlessness, oppression, and injustice. Many African dramas derived from classical sources constitute both an explicit challenge to established political authority and a form of political protest and resistance in societies whose writers have composed their works in a climate of political oppression and injustice. Some of these plays also serve as a type of political and social protest against colonialism and neocolonialism, while others promote political ideologies and nationalist causes. While some of the dramas discussed below preserve the broad outlines of particular Greek plays, others incorporate classical motifs and elements without reproducing the narrative details of a particular classical drama or myth. An example of the latter is the Congan Sylvain Bemba's *L'enfer, c'est Orféo* (Hell, it's Orpheus, 1970), which evokes the tale of Orpheus in its title, main character (Orféo), and quest motif to deal with the period of Portuguese decolonization in Guinea Bissau.

2.1.1   Antigone.   The themes of Sophocles' *Antigone* resonate broadly in several modern African dramas featuring themes of political oppression and resistance, racial and cultural prejudice, social and economic injustice, and the triumph of the human spirit in the face of overwhelming odds. The most well known of the African dramas derived from Sophocles' *Antigone* is *The Island* (1973), by the South Africans Athol Fugard, John Kani, and Winston Ntshona. *The Island* incorporates the *Antigone* mainly in the performance of a short and radically adapted version of the original. In *The Island* Creon, played by Kani, embodies the oppressive power of apartheid, while Antigone, played by Ntshona, represents individual freedom and human rights. Fugard, Kani, and Ntshona also weave into the fabric of *The Island* themes drawn from or coincidental with Sophocles' *Antigone* – the theme of conflict between the state and the individual, for instance, and the distinction between human law and divine justice. But *The Island* is primarily a political drama that has appropriated and adapted a classical form to explore the human costs of a particular form of political power. The evil of the political power exercised is in the form of apartheid and embodied literally in the cruelty of the prison guard Hodoshe, who victimizes the innocent prisoners. The fate of Winston, who is serving a life sentence for burning his passbook, mobilizes the feelings of the reader against the system of apartheid, which dehumanizes and attempts to suck the life force out of its victims. The performance of *The Island* constituted a political act because the regime recognized that it was not merely a damning portrayal of apartheid but also a call for resistance and action against it.

The main theme of *Odale's Choice* (1967), by Kamau Brathwaite, a Caribbean dramatist who lived in Ghana for many years, is the defiance of tyranny, symbolized by the figure of Creon, whose name provocatively remains European although he is an African; the names of the other characters adapted from the *Antigone* are Africanized. Odale must choose whether or not to challenge Creon's tyranny and to bury her brother Tawia (Polynices), who has been captured in battle, slain by Creon, and denied burial. Odale refuses to accept Creon's oppression and, as Antigone does, gives her brother a rough burial in accordance with African and Greek customs. Creon decides to banish rather than execute Odale; she rejects Creon's pardon, however, until Tawia can be buried, whereupon Creon sentences her to death and orders her body to be laid next to her brother's corpse. Odale's choice is to die in the process of resisting tyranny rather than to submit to it by accepting Creon's pardon without the burial of her brother. Because of its lack of application to a specific country or culture, its message of resistance in the face of political oppression is applicable to any number of African countries.

The Nigerian Femi Òsòfisan's *Tegonni: An African Antigone* (1999b) is set in northern Yorubaland at the end of the nineteenth century, a period of British colonialism. The main theme involves the confrontation between oppressive tyranny and racism, represented by Lieutenant General Carter-Ross, the British colonial governor of Nigeria, and the oppressed who courageously defy tyranny, represented by Tegonni, a Yoruban princess. As in Sophocles' original, two brothers warred over who was to succeed their father and died. Oyekunle, the rightful heir, has died along with his brother Adeloro, who was backed by the British in his attempt to usurp the throne and is granted a burial with honors. Carter-Ross has ordered Oyekunle's body to be displayed in the market square as a warning to all those would defy the British, but Tegonni manages to give Oyekunle a minimal burial. The governor decides to pardon her if she apologizes for her action, but when Tegonni refuses to conform, he orders that she be sold into slavery; in the resulting melee Tegonni is shot. Òsòfisan not only uses *Tegonni* to explore issues of colonialism, imperialism, racism, slavery, and capitalism, but also connects these issues to modern Africa, especially Nigeria, where military oppression and a lack of political freedom continued long after the departure of the colonial powers. The related issues of political oppression and economic exploitation, therefore, are not simply or even ultimately attributable to race: even indigenous Africans cooperated with the Europeans against their own people because of the political and economic benefits. Ultimately the choice of whether to resist tyranny, as Antigone does, or submit to it is an individual choice.

Silvain Bemba's *Black Wedding Candles for Blessed Antigone* (1990), the fourth African drama based on Sophocles' *Antigone*, is a translation of Bemba's 1988 play entitled *Noces posthumes de Santigone* (Posthumous weddings of Santigone; 1995). Melissa Yadé, the fiancée of President Titus Saint Just Bund of Amandla, a fictitious African country, is a black student at a university in Birmingham, England. During the course of her dramatic performances, Melissa does not merely play Antigone in Sophocles' *Antigone* but gradually merges her identity with Antigone, which prefigures her role as an agent of justice later in Bemba's play. Meanwhile back in Amandla, Titus is killed in a military coup. Melissa returns to Amandla and is treated as her husband's widow. Transformed completely into Antigone by this stage, Melissa denounces the oppressive regime that has replaced the government of her husband and declares her intention to have a public funeral for him. She is led away and boards a plane out of her country, which plunges into the sea, killing her along with the other passengers.

2.1.2 Orestes.   A few South African anti-apartheid productions are based upon the story of Orestes. In *Orestes* (1978) Fugard conflates the situation of Orestes to the predicament of John Harris, a white South African who as a form of political protest against apartheid in 1964 left a suitcase filled with dynamite near a bench marked "For Whites Only" in the Johannesburg Railway Station; it exploded, killing a little girl and burning an elderly woman. Harris's deed raises the questions of the extent to which violence is justified by an honorable cause and whether Orestes' killing of Clytemnestra falls into the same category. While Orestes at least had recourse to a homicide court on the Areopagus that ended his family's blood vendetta, there seemed to be no politically effective way for Harris to express his anger at the injustice of apartheid; nor in such a system did he have the chance, as Orestes did, of absolution, and he was subsequently executed.

The story of Orestes and its application to apartheid South Africa are further explored in *The Song of Jacob Zulu* (1993) by Tug Yourgrau, a white South African-born playwright raised in the US. Yourgrau was impressed by the similarity in circumstances between Orestes and Andrew Zondo, on whom his main character Jacob Zulu is based. Andrew Zondo, the black teenage son of a Zulu Christian minister, became an ANC guerrilla and planted a mine in a garbage can that caused the deaths of 5 men and injured over 50 others shortly before Christmas, 1985. In developing the story of Zondo's trial and execution for the stage, Yourgrau (1993: viii, x) was particularly inspired by Aeschylus' *Oresteia* and Sophocles' Oedipus cycle. *The Song of Jacob Zulu* rejoices over the end of apartheid and expresses hope for a system of true justice in a similar vein to the *Oresteia*. As in Aeschylus' trilogy, the trial of a young man becomes the backdrop against which a humane legal system can emerge from a destructive cycle of blood violence and vengeance.

Mark Fleishman and Jennie Reznek's ironically entitled *In the City of Paradise* (1998a, 1998b) examines the problem of how to stop the cyclical pattern of violence and revenge in the postapartheid era. Fleishman and Reznek's production is based mainly upon the story of Orestes and Electra in Aeschylus' *Oresteia*, Sophocles' *Electra*, and Euripides' *Orestes* and *Electra*. After Orestes and Electra avenge Clytemnestra's murder of their father, Agamemnon, by killing Clytemnestra and Aegisthus, they are put on trial for matricide and convicted. As the chorus begins to attack Orestes and Electra, the herald announces that the judges have decided to grant amnesty to them and all others who give a truthful account of their deeds so that the cycle of violence and vengeance is broken. Tyndareus and his wife Leda refuse to accept the decision, however, which casts a shadow over the proceedings and suggests that national reconciliation will remain an elusive goal until South Africans are ready to forgive the perpetrators of violence and abusers of human rights under apartheid.

2.1.3 Medea. The South Africans Guy Butler, Mark Fleishman, and Jennie Reznek detect an allegory of their country's political situation in the story of Medea. Butler's *Demea* (1990) transposes the main characters, setting, and time of Euripides' *Medea* to the Eastern Cape of the late 1820s, prior to the time of the so-called "Great Trek." At the time of *Demea*'s conception in the late 1950s, it seemed to Butler that the English speakers in South Africa, represented by the figure of Jonas (an anagram of Jason) Barker, were voting for the racist Afrikaner nationalist party, symbolized by Johannes Kroon (an adaptation of Creon), at the expense of the colored and black population, represented by Demea (an anagram of Medea). Jonas, a trader and former British officer, intends to lead a party of racially mixed trekkers north, but instead decides to join a group of white trekkers led by Kroon, who is an advocate of racial separatism, and to marry his daughter. Butler portrays Jonas's abandonment of his wife Demea, a Tembu princess, and their two sons as a betrayal of the black and colored community by Anglophone South Africans. In a scene reminiscent of the end of the *Medea*, Demea arranges for her sons to be in Kroon's laager of the trek party, which she knows will be attacked by African warriors and lead to their deaths. Demea's motivation is based not only on her desire for revenge against her desertion by Jonas but also purportedly to save her children from racial abuse.

Fleishman and Reznek's *Medea* (1994a, 1994b) is based mainly upon the *Medea* of Euripides, and to a lesser extent also upon Seneca's *Medea*, Apollonius' *Argonautica*, and Valerius Flaccus. The postapartheid production draws parallels between Jason, driven by his ambition to become king, and those who abused their power under the aegis of apartheid, and between Medea, the exploited barbarian, and the marginalized nonwhite races. After Medea joins Jason, she attempts to integrate herself into the Greek social order for his benefit but is pushed aside by a society that has never really embraced her. Sacrificed by an ambitious Jason and banished by Creon, she seeks revenge against her oppressors by staging the murder of their sons. Medea's act is given the motivation of saving her sons from the abuse and humiliation she has suffered. The human cost of Jason's single-minded pursuit of power is given graphic illustration through the deaths of the sons that Medea has borne him, a loss that applies within the context of the modern production to the circumstances of both the oppressor and the marginalized under the apartheid system.

2.1.4 Dionysus/Bacchus. Two African dramatists use the figure of Dionysus to comment on the abuse of power and political freedom. The Nigerian Wole Soyinka has adapted in spirit and in its treatment of Dionysus the *Bacchae* of Euripides in his

The Bacchae of Euripides: A Communion Rite (1973). While the main episodes of the Greek original are retained in broad outline, the chorus is Africanized, as in other African dramas inspired by Greek tragedy, in this case with slaves whose leader, Soyinka recommends, should be wholly negroid (Soyinka 1973: xiii). Soyinka makes Euripides' treatment of oppression and religious conflict relevant to the African context by transferring his setting toward the end of the Peloponnesian War to the postcolonial period. Pentheus is likened to an African military dictator through his position as general and oppression of his people; the Greeks are linked by the slave chorus to their masters in the form of colonial oppressors; and Dionysus is identified with the political power of the marginalized, who are embodied in the chorus of slaves. Soyinka transculturates the Greek tale of Pentheus and Dionysus into a story of a confrontation between an African tyrant and a revolutionary who strives to free his people from the yoke of political and religious oppression.

In *Bacchus in die Boland* (1954) the Afrikaans playwright Bartho Smit uses Bacchus to satirize the complex political circumstances of South Africa. There are clear allusions to the subject of Euripides' *Bacchae*, although most characters in the drama have names of South African historical figures. Bacchus comes to Boland to confront Willem Adriaanse, a Boland wine farmer who maltreats his works and neighbors. Willem challenges Bacchus to a wine-drinking contest and passes out from drinking too much wine. In Saturnalian fashion Bacchus rehabilitates Willem by compelling him to hand over his farm to his servants and to play the role of a colored worker. Eventually Bacchus restores the old social order, whereupon Willem resolves altruistically to divide up his land with his subordinates, whom he has come to view as his fellow men. But his servants reply that it is against the law and that they would rather work for their pay. In exasperation over the failure of Bacchus, Willem Adriaanse, who has to deal with an even more difficult situation than before, chases Bacchus off his farm. The political reality of South Africa in *Bacchus in die Boland* is manifest: the victims of apartheid must be ready to embrace transformation as much as its perpetrators. It is not merely the oppressor who must change, but the entire lawbound community, which is not yet ready for the sort of solution attempted by Willem Adriaanse. Until the mindset of the victims of apartheid changes, the old order will remain in power, just as it does at the end of the drama. At the end of the play Willem tells Bacchus that he will have to come back later and try again, words that would eventually prove prophetic when, 20 years after the publication of *Bacchus in die Boland*, South Africa finally took the first step toward fulfilling Bacchus' vision of an equal society when it elected its first government aspiring to the principles of democracy and nonracialism.

2.1.5 Oedipus and the Trojan women. African playwrights use the stories of Oedipus and the Trojan women to draw attention to the ruinous consequences of political and military conflict. The Nigerian Ola Rotimi transfers a Greek model of tragedy and the Oedipus myth to a Yoruban setting in *The Gods Are Not to Blame* (1971). The play, whose plot structure roughly follows that of Sophocles' *Oedipus*

Rex, features Odewale (Oedipus), king of Kutuje (Thebes); Ojuola (Jocasta), queen of Kutuje; Aderopo (Creon), son of Adetusa (Laius) and Ojuola; and Baba Fakunle (Teiresias). Odewale is made king for arriving in Kutuje and freeing the people from the Ikolu tribe. Adetusa's bodyguard reports that Adetusa was slain by robbers at the crossroads between Ede and Oshogbo, but a flashback reveals that Odewale killed Adetusa when the latter tried to take over his land and insulted his ethnicity. The duel between Odewale and Adetusa not only exemplifies the intertribal tension and ethnic prejudice of Africa but also serves as a dramatic parable for the internecine conflicts in various regions of the subcontinent, including the Nigerian civil war, during which Rotimi's play was composed. The title of the drama and the final scene suggest that it is the African rulers and people, not foreign powers, who must assume responsibility for their problems. The Cameroonian Jacqueline Leloup also adapts the myth of Oedipus to an African context in *Gueido* (1986). This play commences with the birth of a long-awaited son (Guéidô) to a chief. A soothsayer discovers by interpreting a sign on the wrist of a child that he is afflicted by a curse and will kill his father and commit incest with his sister; subsequently the village exiles Guéidô along with his mother. Eventually Guéidô confronts and supplants the chief, then marries his daughter. After Guéidô discovers that he has fulfilled the curse, he drinks some poison and dies.

Femi Òsòfisan's *The Women of Owu*, first performed in 2004, is an adaptation of Euripides' *The Trojan Women*. Set in southwest Nigeria in 1821, the play starts the morning after the fall of Owu, a city that had been besieged for seven years by Ife and Ijebu forces in alliance with Oyo mercenaries. Although the pretext for the war was to free the economically prosperous market of Apomu from the control of Owu, a strong personal motivation is apparent. Iyunlowe, wife of Okunade, had been abducted by an Owu prince. *The Women of Owu* highlights the senseless nature of war and its destructive effects, especially upon innocent women and children. Nor are the conquerors to be spared, since Orisaye, a Cassandra-like figure, prophesies that they will wander from one battle to another before dying, a prediction that recalls the wanderings of Odysseus on his return journey to Ithaca.

2.1.6 Tyrants and generals. A few Afrikaans dramas derived from the classical world dealing with political issues feature important historical figures who were tyrants or generals. These plays end with disastrous consequences not only for their protagonists, who are unable to rise above the challenges presented by their political dilemmas, but also for their numerous victims, who are defenseless against the misuse or nonuse of power. D. J. Opperman uses the figure of Periander, a tyrant of Corinth in the early sixth century BC, in his verse tragedy *Periandros van Korinthe* (1960, first published 1954) to examine the relationship between poetry and power. The subject recalls the role of poetry in Greek society explored in Plato's *Apology* (22a–b), *Ion* (530a–542b), and *The Republic* (376e–403c, 595a–608b). The combination of political and artistic power is shown to be particularly dangerous, since Periander as a poet explores the limits of human wickedness and as king has the power to put his designs into action. This idea is reminiscent of Plato's idea in the *Republic* that poetry is positively harmful to morality and is capable of transmitting evil (376e–403c *passim*). As an exploration of a political theme, *Periandros van Korinthe* upholds the cause and principles of democracy, but an intertextual reading of the play with Opperman's *Vergelegen* (Hinterland, 1956), which defends segregation and Afrikaner nationalism over integration and civil rights, suggests that Opperman is advocating a form of democracy with participation limited in scope, the type of government that existed in South Africa under apartheid.

N. P. van Wyk Louw's *Germanicus* (1956) is based upon figures prominent in Tiberian *Annals* 1–3, such as Germanicus, his wife Agrippina, Livia, Piso, and his wife Plancina. Set early in the reign of Tiberius in the second decade of the first century AD, the play examines the consequences of political passivity and inaction. The various characters of the play, especially Piso and Tiberius, attempt to involve Germanicus in the pursuit and maintenance of power – for themselves and for Rome. While the inaction of Germanicus is attributable to his belief that the goal of ruling justly does not justify the violent means required to gain power, the basis of his passive acquiescence in his own demise, which is contrived by Livia, Tiberius' mother, is the Stoic belief that one gains the ultimate freedom through death. The despairing portrait of power in the *Germanicus* seems to preclude the possibility of achieving a just and political order free of corruption without resorting to inhumane means to achieve it. On the surface a reader could be tempted to apply this to the situation of indigenous blacks under apartheid, where the perpetration of violence formed an important part of the struggle for freedom and justice. During the 1980s, the South African authorities had an increasingly difficult time in containing an upsurge in political violence across the country. Tiberius reminds Germanicus of the difficulty of maintaining power in the face of hydra-headed resistance (Scene 6, pp. 71–2). The circumstances of the Roman empire under Tiberius and Germanicus, who after quelling one rebellion in the empire must immediately turn to suppressing another, resemble the situation under apartheid. Tiberius' grim conclusion about stumbling further into the filth until they sink and the waters wash over them resonates with relevance for South Africa.

Caesar: 'n Drama (1961) by André Brink is a reenactment of the conspiracy and assassination of Caesar on the Ides of March, 44 BC. The drama deals with the issue of whether the use of violence is justified as a means of preventing tyranny and the loss of freedom. Numerous historical characters such as Caesar, Calpurnia, Cleopatra, Antony, Cicero, Brutus, and Cassius are present throughout the play. Obstinacy and pride, along with an excessive desire for power, lead to Caesar's downfall. The conspirators, who associate the Republic with the concept of freedom, fear that absolute power will enslave Rome to the will of Caesar and result in the loss of political freedom. On the Ides of March the conspirators stab Caesar as he enters the senate house, whereupon he falls and dies ironically at the statue of Pompey, the figure of republican liberty that he had defeated at Pharsalus. The publication of *Caesar: 'n Drama* coincided with South Africa's declaring itself a republic. Since there are several passages in which characters speak about the freedom of the republic and democracy, the play seems to constitute a criticism of the South African regime. Cicero declaims to Caesar on the people's love of freedom, sentiments that could be applied to the situation of politically aware black Africans under apartheid. The subsequent murder of Caesar is portrayed as a blow struck for freedom and democracy, but to Caesar the perceived advantages of democracy – the freedom to speak, worship, and vote as one pleases – are deceptive. There is also a description of the loss of political direction, the anarchy and political vengeance that can result when "freedom" is finally gained. While Caesar exposes the trappings of democracy as illusory, his murder suggests that violence may be necessary to bring about political change. There is a potential application of the words and action of this play to apartheid South Africa, where many whites viewed democracy with suspicion and some black activists considered violence a transformative tool.

2.2 *Nonpolitical drama*

Some African dramas adapted or inspired by plots and characters of Greek drama are concerned with religious and other nonpolitical subjects. The Ijaw Nigerian J. P. Clark recalls the ritualistic origins of Greek drama in *The Song of a Goat* (1964), a play about sterility and fertility. *The Song of a Goat* forms the first part of a trilogy of plays that features the working out of a family curse, a Nigerian version of the Sophoclean *Oresteia*. Zifa, a fisherman and part-time ship's pilot, has become impotent after the birth of his first son. His wife, Ebiere, upon the advice of the crippled village Masseur, who serves as the local oracle, encourages Tonye, his younger brother, to take over Zifa's matrimonial functions. Orukorere, a Cassandra-like figure, prophesies disaster but is disregarded as a raving woman. Ebiere and Tonye engage in intercourse not only without the approval of Zifa but also without the sacrifices necessary to make it acceptable in the eyes of the gods and ancestors. During the sacrifice of a goat Zifa discovers his misfortune. As a result Tonye hangs himself, Ebiere miscarries, and Zifa drowns himself, an event that takes place off-stage in the customary Greek manner.

The plot of Ghanaian Efua Sutherland's *Edufa* (1967) is reminiscent of Euripides' *Alcestis* and includes the standard chorus of Greek drama. Sutherland provides a detailed account of the circumstances in which Ampona becomes a victim of the calculating materialism of her husband Edufa. After Ampona is tricked under false circumstances into declaring her love for Edufa, thereby unwittingly ensuring her own death through the charm her husband is wearing, she takes vengeance by giving him beads that will deprive him of his fertility. Notwithstanding the ambiguous portrayal of Ampona, Sutherland draws particular attention to the contrast between Edufa's façade as an emancipated, civilized man who rejects traditional culture in the form of sacrifices and omens but yet consults diviners when approaching death fills him with fear. *Edufa* ultimately seems to argue for a sensible balance between and application of modern and traditional beliefs.

Although South African playwrights have been mainly concerned with political matters in their dramas, some deal with religious and other issues. The *Demetrios* (1943) of the Afrikaans writer D. F. Malherbe is based upon Acts 19:23–8, which tells the story of the silversmith Demetrios. The play, which is set in Ephesus, features the exploitation of people's religious beliefs for financial gain by Demetrios and other silversmiths, who sell small silver temple shrines of Roman Diana. The struggle for religious power sets the worship of Diana and the wisdom of the Greek philosophers against the new Christian gospel as proclaimed by Paul, which is rapidly gaining ascendancy in the hearts and minds of people throughout Asia Minor. Athol Fugard's *Dimetos* (1977) has its ultimate origin in a work of Phylarchus, a third-century BC Greek historian, although Fugard's version is derived from the myth of Dimoetes in the *Narrationum amatoriarum libellus* (Little book of love stories) of the first-century BC poet Parthenius. Fugard's drama highlights forbidden love and the latent human passions of its characters. Dimetos has a secret love for his niece Lydia, a Phaedra-like figure. Danilo, in Dionysian fashion, suddenly appears on the scene. He attempts to seduce Lydia, who then hangs herself. Later a corpse washes upon the rocks, which as it decays almost causes Dimetos to have a mental breakdown. Even African dramas that are not heavily classical sometimes contain many such elements, an example being Douglas Livingstone's radio play *The Sea My Winding Sheet* (1978), which contains a large range of Greek gods and heroes.

3   Poetry and Prose

Some scholars of African literature consider the epic *Os Lusíadas* (The Lusiads, 1572) of Luís Vaz de Camões to be one of the first African poems, although it is written in Portuguese. *Os Lusíadas*, which Camões claims was modeled on Vergil's *Aeneid*, features the giant Adamastor, who combines aspects of Polyphemus and Prometheus. This classically based epic has served as the inspiration for several South African poets, including Roy Campbell in his poem "Rounding the Cape," which was published in *Adamastor* (1930). Campbell's reworking of the epic *Os Lusíadas* contains a large number of classical deities, as do other adaptations of this epic. In Campbell's poem, Adamastor, who desires Thetis, Peleus' wife, is cast in the role of the black "other" who suffers at the hands of a white populace ignorant of the atrocities it has perpetrated. This slippage in the characterization of Adamastor by Campbell parallels the practice of African dramatists who politicize their dramas by refiguring classical myth.

Numerous other writers in Africa reveal classicist leanings through their use of Greek and Roman references. Some of the poems by the Senegalese statesman Léopold Senghor in his anthologies, including *Chants d'ombre* (Songs of shadow) (1945) and *Elégies majeures* (Major elegies, 1979), are pervaded by Greco-Latin poetry and Greek philosophical thought. The Zimbabwean poet Musaemura Bonas Zimunya makes use of classical allusions in *Thought Tracks* (1982a), *Kingfisher, Jikinya and Other Poems* (1982b), and *Country Dawns and City Lights* (1985); in the first and third collections, his use of certain phrases and a variety of meters resembles the Latin poets, particularly Catullus (Maritz 1996). Other poets have adapted the heroes, themes, and subjects of classical authors. Wole Soyinka uses the archetype of Ulysses in an eponymous poem in *A Shuttle in the Crypt* (1972), while in "Idanre," published in *Idanre and Other Poems* (1967), the god Ogun embarks on an archetypal journal into the abyss reminiscent of a descent into Hades. In South Africa, many writers have written works based upon classical sources, including Etienne Leroux, who in *Hilaria* (1959) uses a mythological parallel of Cybele and Attis' revival and the Eleusinian Mysteries; Karel Schoeman, for whom Vergil's *Aeneid* serves as a guide for the chief character Versluis in *'n Ander land* (Another land, 1984); and N. P. van Wyk Louw, whose operatic libretto *Asterion* (1957) contains elements from Greek tragedy and myth.

Modern African novelists sometimes use characters and episodes from Greek mythology and literature. This is not all that surprising, since in the first part of the twentieth century there was no tradition of novel writing on the subcontinent. This is the case with the Nigerian novelist Daniel Olorunfemi Fagunwa. In Fagunwa's *Ogboju Ode Ninu Igbo Irunmale* (The forest of a thousand daemons: a hunter's saga, 1938), the hunter Akara-Ogun is an Odysseus figure, while in *Ireke-onibudo: Pelu Opolopo Alayeo* (The sugarcane of the guardian, 1949), characters such as Oluigbo, Ireke, and Itanforiti are modeled respectively upon Polyphemus, Jason, and Chiron. The novelist Ibrahim Issa of Niger in his *Grandes eaux noires* (Big dark waters, 1959) draws upon Homeric images to explore the historical possibility that Roman soldiers destroyed the kingdom of a local ruler along the Niger River after the Second Punic War in 182 BC. Ayi Kwei Armah, a Ghanaian novelist, incorporates echoes of Juvenalian satire and Platonic morality, including the allegory of the cave, in his work entitled *The Beautyful Ones Are Not yet Born* (1968). In the novel *Le dernier des Cargonautes* (The last of the Cargonauts, 1984), Sylvain Bemba uses the tale of the Argonauts as the basis of his account of the life of Emmanuel Mung'Undu, who is modeled upon the figure of Jason. In this work Mung'Undu endures a life of exile and adventure through the deeds of his despotic father, an African Pelias, before finally dying through the agency of a Medea-like woman.

The classical tradition among modern writers in Africa is also evident on a superficial level in the titles of their works. Numerous poets in Cape Verdes and on the mainland use titles for their collections of poetry and individual poems based upon classical elements. The title of an anthology such as *Jardim das Hespérides* (Garden of the Hesperides, 1928) by the Cape Verdean poet José Lopes, who also wrote poems in Latin, bears witness to this influence. So does van Wyk Louw's *Tristia* (1962), named after Ovid's work, which contains poems with Latin titles such as "Ars Poetica," entitled in imitation of Horace's poem of the same name. Titles of individual poems that show this influence include "Creation of Caryatid" by Wole Soyinka (1967) and "Daphne en Apollo" and "Echo en Narcissus" by the South African D. J. Opperman (1945). Many other collections of poetry, individual poems, prose works, and the titles of these works contain classical allusions, names, and words and phrases in Latin and Greek.

4   Literature in Latin

The earliest and probably the best-known African poet who wrote in Latin was Juan Latino, who was born in west Africa and came to Spain in about 1530. Latino wrote mostly panegyrics containing mythological allusions and phrases from classical poetry. His major work, *Austrias* (1573), written in hexameters, commences with an invocation to Apollo, narrates the victory of Don Juan of Austria at the Battle of Lepanto, shows him addressing his troops in the supposed words of Julius Caesar (*alea iacta est*, the die is cast), and compares the battle between the Turkish and Spanish fleets to a battle between the Greeks and Trojans. Miguel de Cervantes, a contemporary of Latino, paid the *Austrias* homage in *Don Quixote* (ch. 6) for the qualities of its verse. In *Epigrammatum liber* (Book of epigrams, 1573), written almost entirely in elegiac couplets based upon an Ovidian pattern, Latino celebrates the birth of Prince Ferdinand in 1571 and the victory of Don Juan over the Turkish forces.

Other well-known African writers who wrote in Latin include Anton Wilhelm Amo and Jacobus Eliza Johannes Capitein, who were educated in Holland. Amo wrote works on legal and philosophical subjects entitled *De jure Maurorum in Europa* (On the rights of the Moors in Europe, 1729), *De humane mentis Ἀπάθεια* (On the impassiveness of the human mind, 1734), and *Tractatus de arte sobrie et accurate philosophandi* (A treatise on the art of philosophizing soundly and truthfully, 1738). Capitein published some of his sermons and an oration entitled *Dissertatio politico-theologica de servitute libertati Christianae non contraria* (1742), which argues on theological grounds somewhat curiously, given that he was formerly a slave, that Christian freedom is compatible with slavery.

In South Africa, Latin was used in numerous historical and legal documents of the sixteenth and seventeenth centuries – namely, in accounts of the early Cape Hotten-tots and in South African law. South-African born Gysbert Hemmy, for instance, delivered a Latin oration entitled *De Promontorio Bonae Spei* (On the Cape of Good Hope, 1767) at the Hamburg Academy. He also composed *De testimoniis Aethiopum, Chinensium aliorumque paganorum in India Orientali* (1770) as his doctoral thesis, which discusses the ability of non-Europeans to testify in legal proceedings.

5   Law

The influence of Roman law upon Roman-Dutch law in South Africa is one of the most significant cultural influences upon African society. The common law of South Africa is based on Justinian law as received in Europe from the time of the glossators in the twelfth and thirteenth centuries and interpreted by the Roman-Dutch jurists of the seventeenth and eighteenth centuries. South African judges have applied certain aspects of Roman law, which were rearticulated in the Roman-Dutch sources brought to South Africa after 1652, in a wide range of legal situations. Roman law passages have sometimes been argued in court, and judges have sometimes referred to the *Corpus iuris civilis* (The body of civil law), the comprehensive code of Roman law compiled under Justinian, in making their judgments. In a case heard in the Cape of Good Hope in 1860, for instance, the judge based his verdict regarding interest payments upon Justinian's code ([1860] 3 *Searle* 365).

The Roman influence upon South African law is apparent especially in the areas of Roman legal concepts and institutions, which have been entrenched in South African law after being preserved in Roman-Dutch law; legal thoughts and distinctions, which have been used to inform and elucidate South African legal issues; and Roman principles and actions, which have been retained in South African law. While judges have sometimes opted to use the Roman law in instances where it has undergone a change in Roman-Dutch law, they have occasionally upheld the key principles of Roman laws and applied them to circumstances that had no legal precedent in the Roman world. This application and extension of Roman legal principles to a variety of situations in South Africa reflects the enduring influence and relevance of Roman law on the subcontinent.

6 Architecture

The most visible influence of classical antiquity upon Africa is in the field of architecture. Classical architecture, with its qualities of monumentality and historicism emblematic of European colonial power and tradition, has influenced the design of numerous public buildings in South Africa. Hundreds of public buildings have been modeled upon various features of Greek and Roman architecture. From about 1780 a revival of classicism can be detected in South African architecture and included not just the exterior of a building but also its interior design and furnishings. Greek columns with their three orders became very common in public and private buildings, as did other Greek features such as porticos and pediments; Roman architectural features, particularly the arch, apse, and dome, were also used. A trend in architecture in the period of Greek revivalism between 1820 and 1837 was an emphasis upon the portico with its classical colonnades. Examples of buildings with this emphasis include the Royal Observatory (1827), St. Andrew's Presbyterian Church (1827), and St. George's Cathedral (1834), all in Cape Town, and the Anglican church (1828) in Simonstown.

A particularly vigorous phase of classical revivalism followed in the years following 1837, as exemplified in the Commercial Exchange (1840) in Port Elizabeth, with two pedimented corner pavilions flanking a Doric portico in the centre, and the Trinity Presbyterian Church (1842) in Grahamstown, with its Doric portico and columns and bare pediment. From about the middle of the eighteenth century classical revivalism made no pronounced distinction between Greek and Roman features, although some buildings were clearly designed after a Roman model: the Dutch Reformed Church in Craddock (1864), for example, was built with the broad, heavy proportions of a Roman temple.

The neoclassical movement continued in different phases through the next one hundred years. Two impressive examples of classical revivalism from the second half of the nineteenth century are the Public Library (1860) in the Gardens of Cape Town and the Town Hall (1884), now the General Post Office, in Durban. Classical revivalism persisted in the twentieth century until after World War II. Some of the numerous examples include the Rhodes Building (1902) in Cape Town, based on a plan of a Roman palazzo; the City Hall (1914) in Johannesburg, with its Ionic columns and half-domed entrance; and the Central Block (1933) of the University of the Witwatersrand in Johannesburg, with its Corinthian portico the focal point of an axially planned campus in the Roman manner. The axial design of this campus mirrors the layout of many South African towns founded in the nineteenth century that follow the rigid grid pattern of Roman town planning. The Voortrekker Monument (1949) in Pretoria, dedicated to Afrikaaner nationalism and culture, has a marble frieze consisting of 27 bas-relief panels that bring to mind the ideological program of the Altar of Augustan Peace and the battle and migratory scenes on the Columns of Trajan and Marcus Aurelius; in addition, the form, function, and structure of the interior cupola of the Monument are reminiscent of the Pantheon, with its method of natural lighting by means of the central *oculus*.

7   The Politicization of the Classical Tradition

Classicists generally like to defend their discipline as a cornerstone of western civilization, but in Africa some scholars have viewed the classical tradition as imperialist and racist. The postmodern questioning of the self-definition and transmission of the classical tradition has resulted in a fierce debate over the origins of western civilization. In the western academic mainstream and popular culture, the views of Martin Bernal (1987, 1991), who openly challenges the European model based upon the Greek origins of western civilization, have received wide publicity. Long before Bernal arrived on the scene, however, African scholars had been challenging the positivistic, self-legitimating claims of the European model. According to these scholars, the nonwestern cultures of Africa, mainly Egypt, are the source of the scientific rationalism of the ancient Greeks in various fields such as astronomy, medicine, science, and mathematics; furthermore, Egypt was either a black African civilization or influenced heavily by black Ethiopian culture. The Senegalese scholar Cheikh Anta Diop (1955, 1967, 1981), for example, claims that ancient Egypt is black in origin and that the Greek civilization is primarily based upon it. At the United Nations Educational, Scientific and Cultural Organization colloquium on "The Peopling of Ancient Egypt and the Decipherment of Meroitic Writing" held in Cairo, Egypt in 1974, Diop and the Congan Théophile Obenga, who represented sub-Saharan Africa, maintained that the people, culture, and especially language of ancient Egypt were derived from black Africa (cf. Mokhtar 1980: 795–823). The Ethiopian-born Yosef ben-Jochannan (1970, 1988) argues not only that Africa is the source of Judaism, Christianity, and Islam but also of western civilization. Both ben-Jochannan (1988: 375–452) and Obenga (1995) make a case specifically for the African origins of Greek philosophy.

Various figures in the black African consciousness movement have used some of these arguments not only to promote the idea of an African renaissance but also to push their political and ideological agendas. Just one example of this was a seminar held in Durban, South Africa in 1997 by Pritzi Dullay entitled "Vulamehlo: Open Your Eyes. An Essential Seminar." The seminar set out the arguments of various Afrocentric scholars on the subcontinent and elsewhere that Africa, not Europe in general or Greece in particular, was the cradle of civilization and home to humanity's greatest achievements. The proclaimed objectives were to show that whites had stolen the black African legacy and that it was now time to reclaim this legacy for the black African race. This workshop exemplifies the extent of the politicization of the classical tradition in contemporary Africa.

8 Afterword

This chapter has examined the influence of the classical world upon African culture in several areas. The politicization of the classical tradition reflects the postmodern tendency to decenter the cultural works and ideas of Greece and Rome from their western orientation and to destabilize them in terms of their position of cultural dominance. At the same time the globalization of the classical tradition reflects the expansion of the concept of the classical tradition to geographical areas such as Africa and to modern critical disciplines such as postcolonial studies. The classical tradition is a complex, sometimes fragmented, web of interconnected works, images, and ideas, which naturally has contributed to its becoming an area of cultural contestation. Consistent with broader cultural shifts occurring elsewhere in the world, cultural politics in Africa has resulted not only in a lessening of the Eurocentric focus on the study of the classical tradition but also the treatment of the modern work as equal to the original classical work. In the African context the concept of the classical tradition is open to challenge on the basis that it is neither entirely classical nor a cohesive tradition, but rather a fragmented form of cultural hybridity in which classical and postcolonial elements from different cultures – not just African and European – converge and diverge. Cultural developments in Africa have shown that classical texts, images, and ideas continue to provide the basis for much reflection on the subcontinent and to serve as a stimulus for political and social transformation. This cultural phenomenon will continue to ensure that there are rich opportunities for scholars interested in the role of the classical tradition in Africa not only in examining the extent to which Africans adapt classical works, images, and ideas but also on the problem of western aesthetic responses to Africanized literary and dramatic forms.

FURTHER READING

The bibliography for the classical tradition in Africa is extensive. Dominik (1999, 2003) provides brief overviews (in German, with bibliography) of the reception of the classical tradition in Africa. Wetmore (2002) and Budelmann (2004) discuss adaptations of Greek drama by postcolonial playwrights, while Mezzabotta (2000) and Dominik (2006) specifically treat South African postapartheid and Afrikaans drama, respectively. Beinart (1952) neatly summarizes the role of Roman law in the practice of South African law. On the influence of classical architecture upon modern South African architecture, see Lewcock (1963), Greig (1971), and Fransen (1987).

CHAPTER TEN

Central-Eastern Europe

Jerzy Axer with the assistance of Katarzyna Tomaszuk

1   Introductory Remarks

Traditional syntheses of the history of European culture have used the concept of the classical tradition conceived as "ancient heritage" to justify an identity founded on the belief that there existed a cultural canon and that passing it on ensured the proper upbringing of future generations. The idea of heritage harmonized with the "grand narrative" of European history and led to a negative judgment regarding any noncanonic reaction to the western European model of discovering antiquity – to the Italian model during the Renaissance, the French model during the Enlightenment, and the German model of *Altertumswissenschaft* (classical scholarship) in the nineteenth century.

In the humanities today, the growing interest in reception is opening up new possibilities for understanding the cultural tradition of regions, nations, and states. The canon is becoming a nonoperational concept and is unattractive to the contemporary consumer of culture; resistance, transformation, and noncanonical consumption are now perceived in a positive light. This creates a new opportunity to write the cultural history of regions like central-eastern Europe. In central-eastern Europe the lasting character of the classical tradition can be traced to its position at the margins of Europe and to the late development of nation-states. Instead of being seen as peripheral to the reception of antiquity, this area now occupies the space of cultural borderlands through encounters, exchanges, and free choices.

Central-eastern Europe is a fuzzy, ideologically marked concept. I shall use this name to denote the part of Europe that joined western Christianity in the tenth century, extending its reach east of the borders of the revived Roman empire. From then on, a systemic acculturation of the Mediterranean tradition began. The region comprised, from the beginning, three monarchies: the Czech monarchy of the Premyslids (in the western Christian community from the first half of the tenth century), the Polish monarchy of the Piasts (baptism 966), and the Hungarian monarchy of the Arpads (baptism 997). The Hungarian Kingdom's expansion gradually took over the area of today's Slovakia, and in the early twelfth century a personal union between ruling families led to the incorporation of Croatia. In the late Middle Ages, Lithuania federated with Poland and together with dominions in Ruthenia (today's Belarus and Ukraine) became part of this region. Such a delineation of borders means that the sphere of influence of the eastern empire – Byzantium and the Orthodox church – is excluded from this study, except for cultural forms created at the meeting point of the two churches (in Transylvania and Ruthenia). This geography continues to make sense in reference to subsequent centuries, because the Latin world separated itself from Turkish Islam with equal decisiveness and, in parts, on the same border that had divided it earlier from Byzantium. Meanwhile on the east, Kievan Rus was destroyed by the Mongolian invasions, and another eastern Europe was born and started gaining importance: Muscovy, whose ambition was to replace Byzantium in its imperial role and build its identity in opposition to the Latin west.

The approach proposed here differs significantly from the tradition of writing about the reception of ancient culture where "reception" is seen as identical with "heritage." I also question the practice of describing the classical tradition in the individual nation-states in reference to their present borders. During the periods most important for the reception of the classical tradition, the map of this part of Europe was completely different (see maps 10.1–10.4). In the time of Renaissance

Figure 10.1 Central-Eastern Europe ca. 1000

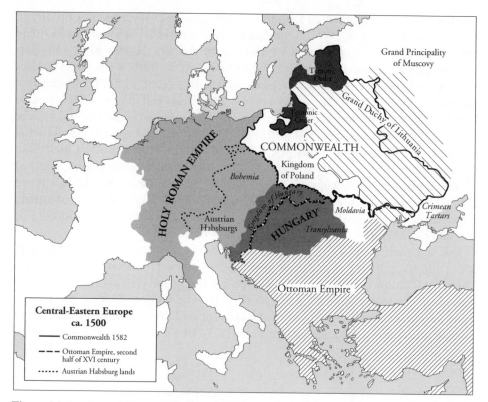

Figure 10.2   Central-Eastern Europe ca. 1500

humanism, the territorial reach of the countries today called Poland, Hungary, and Lithuania was much bigger, while other countries (Belarus, Ukraine, Slovakia) did not exist as states at all. In the other period that is important for our inquiry – the nineteenth century, a time of scientific reflection on antiquity and the formation of modern nations – none of the countries in the region enjoyed sovereignty or had a national educational system. Thus western European learning, pro-state on principle, was imposed on peoples nurturing a constant hope of overthrowing the state in which they were living and of mythologizing their own past so as to raise new generations in loyalty toward the nation they identified with, not the contemporary state.

The systems of culture that developed in central-eastern Europe were dominated by gentry whose role as the sole representatives of society before the monarchy created a base for the cultivation of freedom that sought antecedence in Roman *libertas* (freedom), but made the cultures in question difficult to adapt to the conditions and structures of a modern, ethnic nation-state.

A region demarcated in this way lies "between" east and west, at any time and within every understanding of these concepts. This situation created a paradox: in this region of Europe enslavement was common, but so was the opportunity to choose and select – a typical borderland experience.

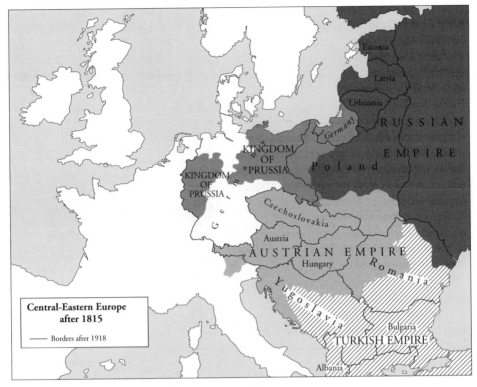

Figure 10.3 Central-Eastern Europe after 1815

2   Cyrillic-Methodian Tradition (Eighth to Tenth Centuries)

This issue is especially valuable for studies on the reception of the classical tradition in central-eastern Europe; the growth and decline from the ninth through the twelfth centuries can be interpreted in connection with the attempts to develop a Slavic paradigm for adapting ancient Christianity that would be independent of Byzantium and Rome, the universalizing cultures. The Thessaloniki Saints' mission to the Khazars and Moravia, and their disciples' activity in Bohemia and Slovakia, and especially in Croatia and Bulgaria (Clement of Ohrid's school, ninth to tenth centuries), resulted in the Greek alphabet being adapted to the Slavic languages and in the development of a Slavic liturgy different from both Greek and Roman rites. Regardless of the Saints' intentions and the political plans of Constantinople and Rome, this mission resulted in the emergence of a "third way" between the two universal empires.

On the territory of the former Great Moravian State, there remained a lasting tendency to seek a Slavic identity that was subsequently invoked for various political

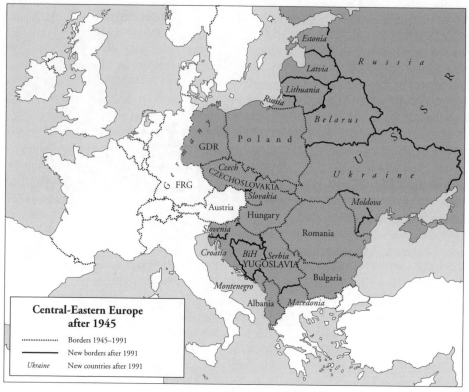

Figure 10.4   Central-Eastern Europe after 1945

aims. Also worth a special mention is Kievan Rus, whose Christianity invoked its own ancient genealogy, separate from Byzantium, while also aspiring to represent all Slavs. *Nestor's Chronicle* (twelfth century) says that Paul the apostle taught the Slavs directly and that St. Sophia's Church in Kiev, not in Constantinople, is the equivalent of the Jerusalem Temple. Moreover, the *Chronicle* polemicized Byzantine historiography by telling the story of humankind in general and not of the empire (Avenarius 2000).

Thus in central-eastern Europe, interpreting the Cyrillic-Methodian mission as having served to build the autonomy of the region reveals a continuity whereby domestication and resistance contribute to the acculturation of the classical tradition in the region. The competition between the western and eastern churches, and Russia's assumption of the role of Byzantium's heir, influenced the anachronistic ideologization of Cyril and Methodius' mission and its consequences. Scholars in the nineteenth and twentieth centuries invoked it to justify both Russian expansion and Catholic proselytizing. Individual nations (particularly Romania) also used the mission to emphasize their own unique place between east and west, or to demonstrate hostility toward the "other side," depending on the governing ideologies, be they nationalist, Nazi, or communist.

3 Middle Ages (Tenth to Fifteenth Centuries)

Except for the southern part of the Hungarian kingdom, all of central-eastern Europe in the late Middle Ages was outside the *limes Romanus* (the Roman border). There was no ancient heritage in material form here, only imports and acculturation processes.

The first wave of the western Latin tradition came with baptism, which depended on the decisions and choices of local rulers. Bohemia's bond with the west was already seen as a foregone conclusion when Otto III's idea of a universal empire emerged. The opportunity to join this empire was extended to the Polish Piasts and Hungarian Arpads as well as to the Polabian Slavs. The Poles and Hungarians accepted, but without also accepting a feudal allegiance to the empire. Two kingdoms were thus formed, the Polish and the Hungarian, and two archbishoprics, in Esztergom and Gniezno, marked the eastern boundary of Latin Europe for centuries.

Kievan Rus treated the Byzantine model with equal freedom, accepting baptism (988/9) and thus opening itself up to the ancient heritage. If the existence of this state had not been interrupted by the Mongol invasions, it might have ended up with an interesting Latin-Greek subculture (Szücs 1985). Such a tradition was in fact later revived in the Ukraine.

Becoming part of the Roman church, these three new Christian kingdoms effected radical changes in social structure, turning to political and organizational forms developed by the first generation (fifth to eighth centuries) of peoples in post-Roman western Europe and, in the case of Poland and Hungary, selecting some elements from the proposed model and rejecting others. This way of taking advantage of the ancient heritage, which was received here exclusively as a part of medieval Christian culture, was implemented within three increasingly far-reaching waves of occidentalization.

The first, from the tenth to the eleventh centuries, was limited to the kings and powerful lords as well as their courts. They adopted western organizational models for public life, traveled abroad, and organized the import of manuscripts and art works. One needs to appreciate the importance of the decision of the Poles and Hungarians to offer their states to the *patrimonium* (patrimony) of St. Peter while bypassing the empire, which underlined the distinctiveness of their own political communities from the *populus Romanus* (Roman people) of the empire.

The second wave, in the twelfth century, brought major royal and aristocratic foundations, the expansion of churches and convents, and the birth of local literature and historiography. Romanesque art reached the Vistula River via Hungary, and the activity of the Cistercians and Norbertines developed the sense of belonging to European prehumanism.

The third wave of occidentalization involved fourteenth-century humanism. The gateway for the most intensive penetration was Hungary under the Anjous, but Charles IV also elevated Prague to the status of a leading European metropolis.

From the thirteenth century, the transfer of western culture, including its reception of antiquity, was greatly facilitated by German-language immigration into Transylvania,

Poland (starting from Silesia), Bohemia, western Pomerania, and Prussia. The German civil law of urban communities thus linked the whole region to the west.

From the thirteenth century, Poles, Hungarians, and Czechs studied at Italian (chiefly Bologna and Padua), German, and French universities. Universities were established in Prague in 1348, then in Kraków (1364, reestablished in 1400), and then in the Hungarian kingdom, in Pécs (1367) and Presburg (*Academia Istropolitana*, 1467).

4   The Renaissance and Humanism (Fifteenth to Seventeenth Centuries)

4.1   The history and geographical reach of neo-Latin Literature

From Dante and Petrarch to our times, neo-Latin literature is among the most important indicators of the reception of the classical tradition in its national and regional diversity. Interdisciplinary studies on this huge store of prose and poetry are only just beginning (IJsewijn 1990; IJsewijn and Sacré 1997; Ludwig 1997; Ludwig 2004–5). Neo-Latin literature emerged on the foundation of the ideas and linguistic principles of the Italian humanists, as an expression of the will to return to ancient Rome's moral magnitude and to a revival of ancient standards in Latin style. Expanding geographically and developing over time (within the *Respublica Litteraria* [Republic of letters]), it addressed a much broader audience and created a dialogue between the language communities of its authors and the educated public all over Europe.

This literature functioned on several levels. Writing poems and telling the histories of their states and nations in Latin according to western models, the Polish, Hungarian, Czech, and Lithuanian elites declared themselves to be part of Europe, translating their cultural experience into the universal code of ancient signs. This resulted in the rapid spread of all the literary genres developed by humanism according to ancient models, and also the ability to imitate the poetic works not only of Ovid and Vergil, but also Horace, and in prose, not only of Cicero and Livy, but also Tacitus. The use of neo-Latin literature as a tool for expressing one's cultural identity in international dialogue gradually moved eastwards, also enabling the communities that wanted to emphasize their autonomy from the dominant cultures in the central-eastern European region to make similar declarations. This is best seen in the example of the Ruthenians in the Polish Commonwealth and Croats in the Hungarian kingdom (with the Croatian relationship to the Mediterranean and Slavic traditions, however, going beyond the geographical range of our study). Meanwhile, along the border between Catholicism and the Orthodox religion, and between Christianity and Islam, neo-Latin literature acted as a particularly useful medium for formulating ideas of *antemurale Christianitatis* ("bulwark of Christendom") as well as expressing one's stand in the dispute between *Slavia Latina* (Latin Slavdom) and *Slavia Graeca* (Greek Slavdom). These changes involved a search for identity in the language of humanism.

4.2   Ethnogenetic myths

The problem of identifying what separated the "younger Europe" (to use Kłoczowski's conception) both from the west and from the east, and what linked the "younger Europe" both to the west and to the east, revealed itself fully between the Middle Ages and humanism. For the people of this time the point was to define one's place in world history and to translate this awareness into Renaissance anthropological language, which used signs of the classical tradition. That is, the goal was to include local states and peoples on the map of ancient Mediterranean space-time as a way of consolidating their internal integration and international position in fifteenth- and sixteenth-century Europe.

In the nineteenth and twentieth centuries, the earlier search for the place of the peoples of this region in Europe's cultural and political reality was interpreted within the framework of the idea of nation-states. The national-socialist ideology, then the communist system, transformed into various forms of national communism, drew from various myths of origin to carry out "ethnic purges" in the historical memory. A more fruitful interpretive approach takes into account the multitude of communication communities functioning here in the late Middle Ages and early Renaissance, and the fact that many people belonged to several of them simultaneously. From this perspective, the strongest information carriers are language, symbols, and semiotics of behavior. This approach increases the importance of Latin texts and signs referring to the classical tradition. Naming the border between central-eastern Europe and the Germanic Holy Roman empire and making the border between Latin and Byzantine Slavs less impermeable were fundamental problems for translating one's identity into the new language.

The Polish, Hungarian, and Lithuanian declarations were the clearest. In the Polish republic, the Sarmatian origins of Poland and the name of Sarmatia for the state became popular from the late sixteenth century, a reference to fourteenth-century genealogical constructions legitimizing the restored Polish kingdom (1320) by introducing themes of military victories over the ancient rulers, Julius Caesar, and Alexander the Great. Presenting the emerging concept of the Polish Commonwealth, Kraków humanists translated the Ptolemic formula differentiating between European and Asian Sarmatia into contemporary political geography, identifying Poland, Ruthenia, Lithuania, and Moscow right up to the Don as *Sarmatia Europaea*. Beyond that was *Sarmatia Asiatica vel Scithia*. In the west, the treatise of Miechowita and the map of Wapowski popularized this image of central-eastern Europe's place in Mediterranean civilization. Soon Muscovy was moved to *Scithia*, and together with the Tartars formed the hostile border of the Polish-Lithuanian community of Jagiellonian states.

The Hungarians chose a genealogical identification with the Huns. Attila, vanquisher of the ancient west, became a precursor of the Hungarians' acculturation in this world. At Matthias Corvinus' court, the Italian humanist Antonio Bonfini wrote the history of the kingdom, linking ancient Hun genealogy with the Huns' subsequent kinship with the Slavs and turning the monarch into the creator of a Mediterranean-central-eastern European power, distinct from Germanic and Romanic models. This claim was strengthened by the use of Latin by the community of noblemen as the language of the emerging nation that united the three peoples it contained (*unio trium nationum*, 1438).

After their late baptism, the Lithuanians hastily worked on their particular myth of origin. Their non-Slavic language was a major factor. At the court of the Polish and Lithuanian branch of the Jagiellons, an idea began to form, with some Italian inspiration, that Lithuania was created by emigrants led by the Roman commander Palemon, who reached the Baltic coast by escaping from Nero's persecution (or from Sulla's, or from Caesar's civil wars). By the end of the sixteenth century the myth was firmly in place, and in popular awareness it built a continuous genealogy of the Lithuanian nobles and rulers stretching back to antiquity. Lithuania thus became the Third Rome – an excellent argument in the rivalry with Moscow and an important asset in competing with the Polish nobility within the Commonwealth.

Much less clear are the Czechs' myths of origin, probably because their state was bound to the empire from the twelfth century (chronicles of the time place the Czechs in ancient Germany; they also tried to trace their origin to Celtic Bohemia). In terms of the reception of ancient culture, the main point was that the Czech identity was linked to a certain anti-antiquity – a folk, local, and Slavic identity serving as an alternative to the Latin (meaning the imperial and German) one.

Today's Ukraine was in a special situation. On the one hand, the Polish concept of two Sarmatias recognized the Ukrainians as *Roxolani*, one of the peoples forming the Sarmatian confederation in late antiquity. On the other, it was felt that they belonged to the tradition of another community, one that also had an ancient genealogy: the Byzantine church and the mythical Tsargorod. Ruthenian elites opposed Polonization by bonding with Kievan Rus, an older heir to Byzantium than Moscow.

In their dialogue with western intellectuals, the Polish elites unhesitatingly recognized the Hussite and Protestant Czechs (together with Orthodox Moscow) as alien, despite their Slavic origins. The decisive consideration was loyalty to the Holy See, as the only depository of ancient Roman tradition, to which Poland acceded – this was always emphasized – not from weakness but as a sovereign partner. In 1467 Jan Ostroróg presented the pope with proof: Julius Caesar had been crushed three times on the Polish plains.

The Hungarians in the fifteenth century saw Moldova as ancient Moesia. As for the Romanians in Wallachia, the Italians suggested the usefulness of their identifying themselves as Romans by origin, descendants of the conquerors of Dacia from Trajan's time. This viewpoint was convenient for Corvinus (a ruler of Wallachian origin, who could thus consider himself a Roman aristocrat by direct descent) and for the idea of including the Wallachians, and the Romanians from Transylvania, in the Latin community. Circles linked to the Wallachian hospodars' court, on the other hand, were inclined to seek autonomy in the anti-Latin Orthodox-Slavic-Byzantine tradition.

An analysis of the results of translating the sense of national identity into the language of new Renaissance humanism, the language of ancient tradition, seems to confirm the distinctness of the region enclosed between the borders of the west, identified with *Imperium Romanum*, of the east, with its mission of restoring Byzantium, and of the Turkish empire's militant Islam. The task itself stemmed from preparations for a direct meeting with a west beyond Germany, with states and nations whose ethnogenetic myths enjoyed a Vergilian patronage (France, England) or a Vergilian-Dantean one (Italy). In this territory, the space-time of Troy and the legendary beginnings of Rome were superimposed on the tradition of barbarian kings and kingdoms that had directly adopted the heritage of the Roman empire. Central-eastern Europe had to take up the dialogue in the same language.

4.3 Humanism

At the Hungarian-Croatian court, Latin-language humanism flourished thanks to its ties to Italy, which were strengthened in the fourteenth century during the d'Anjou dynasty's rule, and then under Sigismund of Luxembourg. There were many eminent Italians in Croatia (e.g., Vergerio, Giustiniani, and Feliciano).

A magnificent development of humanist culture in the second half of the fifteenth century took place during Matthias Corvinus' reign. This was the time of the archbishop of Esztergom and the royal chancellor Vitéz, who established the *Academia Istropolitana* in Presburg as well as a printing house in Buda, and his nephew Pannonius, a translator from Greek into Latin and an excellent poet. The ideal of the orator-poet that developed at the royal court in Hungary led to the conjunction of poetry and epistolography, characteristic for early humanism; this was considered the tool of diplomacy.

Hungarians working with Italians largely bypassed the stage of imitating Italian artists and intensively absorbed the works of Roman as well as Greek authors directly. The Bibliotheca Corviniana was founded (1485), and historiography developed to consolidate the Hungarian identity by presenting King Matthias as the synthesis of Roman, Greek, and Hun traditions (Bonfini). Florentine Neoplatonism flourished through the influence of Ficino in Buda. The greatness of Italian-Hungarian humanism waned after the brief reign of the Jagiellon dynasty, when it seemed as if all of central-eastern Europe would unite under one dynasty capable of rivaling the Habsburgs. The Turkish victory at Mohacs (1526) resulted in the disintegration of the kingdom into three parts (1541): the west and north came under Habsburg rule, Transylvania became an independent duchy ruled by Hungarian noble families, and the rest was occupied by Turkey. Humanist culture survived at the court of the Transylvanian dukes.

In sixteenth-century Hungary, Italian influences were replaced by German, and Neoplatonism by Erasmianism and the Reformation. Latin-language historiography and epic poetry became the dominant literary forms, both closely linked to the country's dramatic history: Schesaeus' *Ruinae Pannoniae* (Decline of Pannonia), Istvánffy's *Historiarum de rebus Hungaricis libri* (Books on the history of Hungary), and Olahus' *Athila* and *Hungaria* (Bene 2006; Conley forthcoming).

Bohemia went a different way. Its situation was more similar to France's than to that of neighboring countries, with poetry and prose in the national language, both religious and lay, emerging as early as the fourteenth century (Goleniščev-Kutuzov).

Bohemian humanism was always closely connected to that of Germany and Hungary. The same universities (Prague, Vienna, Wittenberg, and Kraków) and the same courts (Prague, Vienna, and Kraków) influenced all three. The strong ties linking the Czechs to European humanism were created as early as the fifteenth century, with Hassensteinius as the leading figure; philologists of high quality, like Pisecký and his pupil Gelenius, appeared. Olomouc became an excellent humanist center. Right up to the early seventeenth century, thousands of people in Bohemia created works in Latin. Czechs, Moravians, and Germans (e.g., Bruschius, Cropacius, and Bartholdus) wrote an impressive amount of lyrical, religious, and historical poetry of a very high standard, at home and abroad, and around 1600 Prague was still one of the greatest cultural centers in Europe. Latin-language theater flourished, and outstanding academic treatises were written (e.g., the Jesuit Balbinus wrote a defense of the Czech language). Czechs participated intensively in the *Respublica Litteraria Europaea*, and Comenius, a philosopher and educational theorist active mainly as an émigré (in Poland, Sweden, Hungary, and the Netherlands), gained fame.

The Hussite wars in the fifteenth century ended the effort to build an "open society" in Bohemia. The defeat of the Czech Protestants at White Mountain (1620) meant that the attempt to give the Czech state a sovereign form of the nobleman-nation's republic failed. From that time up to the national revival (early nineteenth century), the Czech reception of antiquity in terms of academic thought and higher culture can be viewed as a reflection of the changes occurring in the German-speaking part of the Austrian empire.

Things were different in the Jagiellons' "core" countries, in Lithuania and Poland. From the mid-fourteenth century, the Polish kingdom included Ruthenian lands in the southeast. At the end of the century, it was united with the Grand Duchy of Lithuania through a personal union (with the Jagiellons accepting baptism from the west and assuming the Kraków throne). This union was transformed in 1569 into a federation, with the commonwealth encompassing the Lithuanian-Ruthenian lands right up to Kiev and the Black Sea. It adopted the name *Respublica*, and in its "Golden Age" (sixteenth and early seventeenth centuries) was an example of a tolerant, open, multiethnic, and multidenominational culture (Axer and Kieniewicz 1999). The coexistence of Catholic and Protestant cultures was guaranteed by the Warsaw Confederation (1573). With regard to the Orthodox culture, various forms of osmosis took place: Gothic art shifted the border of western Europe to the line connecting Vilnius and Lviv, while Byzantine painting traveled westward to the churches of Lublin, Sandomierz, and Kraków. Generally, though, the Commonwealth kept moving the borders of Latinity eastward.

The beginnings of humanism in Poland may be seen as derivative. The visit of Sigismund I, when he was heir to the throne, to his brother Ludwik's court in Buda led to the conversion of Wawel castle into a Renaissance residence designed by Italian architects, a process in which the king's wife Bona Sforza also played an important role. At that time the Polish Renaissance involved copying Italian artists, not imitating ancient models directly, not only in architecture, sculpture, and painting, but initially also in Latin-language literature, which imitated the prose and poetry of Italian neo-Latinists, then only through them the works of ancient authors. Such were the beginnings of Latin oratory, which subsequently became a Polish specialty on a European scale.

The "golden age" in Polish culture did not start until the late fifteenth century. Earlier Długosz had offered his independent interpretation of the country's history (*Annales seu Cronicae incliti Regni Poloniae* [Annals or chronicles of the celebrated Kingdom of Poland]). The arrival at the Kraków court (via Buda) of Buonaccorsi and Conrad Celtis brought first-rate models. In the sixteenth century the university and court in Kraków brought in great humanists (Cox, Roisius) and hundreds of students from Germany, Bohemia, Hungary, and Italy.

Neo-Latin poetry (Hussovianus, Dantiscus, Cricius, and Janicius) dominated until the 1540s. After that, bilingual writers began appearing. The greatest of these, Jan Kochanowski, experimented with transferring ancient forms and genres into the national language, competing with the latest experiments of Italian poets and philologists (e.g., his *Threnodies, Aratea, Trifles*). Szymonowic was another excellent poet in both languages. In the next century the Jesuit Sarbiewski, "Horatius Sarmaticus," gained European fame; Lubomirski, a poet, prose writer, and playwright, wrote in the spirit of Lipsius' neo-Stoicism. In some fields Polish neo-Latinists were ahead of Europe: as Kochanowski had written the complete Latin version of Cicero's *Aratea* before Grotius, so Fredro published his collection of Latin aphorisms in Gdańsk (1664) before La Rochefoucauld. Western Europe learned about eastern Europe from the historical works of Kromer, Miechowita, and Pastorius. Coialovicius' Latin translation of Stryjkowski's *Chronicle* was particularly important for Lithuanian identity. Major political treatises were written by Modrevius, Orechovius, and Zamoyski, and oratory and epistolography developed vigorously. Scientific literature was less prolific, but it did include Copernicus' *De revolutionibus orbium caelestium* (On the revolutions of the heavenly spheres).

Until the end of the eighteenth century, Latin was the only language enabling a broader European audience to access Polish culture and literature.

4.4 *The region's place within* Respublica Litteraria Europaea

The community of scholars and artists that functioned from the time of Erasmus for almost three hundred years reached the eastern part of the continent, encompassing the Czech and Hungarian kingdoms and Poland-Lithuania early on, in the first quarter of the sixteenth century. The ideal of a "republic of letters" was implemented by means of intensive contacts among its citizens. "Networking" took place primarily through the exchange of letters, the main language being Latin, with the auxiliary languages (Italian, German, Spanish, and French) depending on the region. This correspondence was conducted largely over and above ethnic and religious divisions, and without political control. Outstanding humanists being visited by followers and enthusiasts; preparing examples of the *Album amicorum* (book of friends), showing the range and intensity of contacts within the Republic; including testimonials from friends in the introductions to books; inviting famous scholars to academic centers; opening libraries and book collections for foreigners; establishing academic societies involving foreigners (from Celtis's *Sodalitas Litteraria Vistulana* [Vistula Society of Letters] to the academies of London, Paris, Berlin, and St. Petersburg) – all these practices manifested the existence of *Respublica Litteraria*. To this one may add a system of awards, competitions, and scholarships. Scientific periodicals and a new literary form, the review, emerged in the seventeenth century (Burke 1999).

Representatives of the central-eastern European region formed a not-very-numerous group in the Republic, but were perceived by the community as an important and attractive circle. If we look at the "networking" by letter within this community, we can see that the intensive participation of Hungarians, Poles, Lithuanians, Croatians, Ruthenians, Czechs, Germans from Prussia and Transylvania, Slovaks, and so on proves not only the existence of outstanding individuals capable of holding dialogue on equal terms with the Italians, French, Dutch, Germans, Spanish, and English, but also shows the strategy of the leading personalities and the strongest national communities in *Respublica Litteraria Europaea*, who documented their authority and success by identifying the greatest possible number of partners in regions they considered exotic.

The extraordinary popularity of Ioannes Dantiscus (1485–1548), whose volume of correspondence (around 6,300 letters) is more than two times that of Erasmus and one and half times that of Lipsius (including his unpublished letters), is explained not only by the broad range of his roles in life, but also by the readiness of princes and kings, poets and philologists, merchants and conquistadors, to maintain an epistolary conversation with a man thanks to whom the *Respublica Litteraria Europaea* itself stretched to the eastern and northern frontiers of Christian Europe (Skolimowska 2004). Up to the mid-seventeenth century the *Respublica* did not include the Scandinavian peninsula, nor up to the first half of the eighteenth century, Russia, nor up to the end of the eighteenth century, the Balkans (except for the multinational elite of the seventeenth-century Osman court). Thus the region of central-eastern Europe was valuable for its experiences and contacts with those cultures, from both political and academic viewpoints. The great kindness with which humanists from central-eastern Europe were treated by their western partners, as well as the opinions voiced in the letters of their correspondents, which local scholars often treat as proof of the exceptional quality of humanism in these various areas, have to be viewed from this perspective as well.

For the reception of classical culture in central-eastern Europe, the participation of citizens of the countries of this region in the *Respublica Litteraria Europaea* had a dual importance: it consolidated the sense of belonging to the west and facilitated contacts with the highest-quality academic and artistic use of classical cultures, as applied in the leading centers of humanism. At the same time, it awakened an interest in the eastern fringes of Latin culture among European elites. The Latin language facilitated such interaction, as Latin was the language of the Hungarian and the Polish political nations. From the mid-sixteenth century onward, this gave representatives of the region a certain asset in their contacts with the west, where Latin was being withdrawn from public life. The replacement of Latin by French and the institutionalization of the activity of the *République des Lettres* (Republic of letters) coincided with the final partition of the region.

5   Subcultures of the Reception of the Ancient Tradition in the Region (Sixteenth to Eighteenth Centuries)

5.1   Slavia Romana *versus* Slavia Byzantina

Disputes over what to call the parts of this region from the perspective of the reception of the ancient tradition reveal problems with the definition: the result is always an asymmetrical arrangement. *Slavia Romana* stresses ties to Rome (ancient and Christian) and requires two corresponding concepts: *Slavia Byzantina* (political) and *Slavia Orthodoxa* (religious). *Slavia Latina* would correspond to *Slavia Graeca*. This pair neutralizes the political and religious differences. Greek, however, did not play the same role in spreading the classical tradition among eastern Slavs as Latin did among the western Slavs.

The borderline between the two Slavic areas depends on the criterion applied. The line is easiest to draw in reference to Catholicism and Latin as the language of culture and education. It will run differently when drawn according to architectural orders or the influence of Roman law. It is most interesting – and most difficult – to draw it according to the declarations of identity revealed in the sources (Axer 1994a). This movable border cuts across the Commonwealth. Along it, hybrid subcultures developed, adapting both systems for the reception of ancient culture.

Early testimony to this phenomenon in Belarus (then the Grand Duchy of Lithuania) is provided by Nicolas Hussovianus' *Carmen de bisonte* (1523), which he offered to the pope. The author declared that the bison he described was not a bison according to the western model (as described by Caesar and Pliny), because his background as a writer included Greco-Ruthenian books and local hunting experiences. Hussovianus agreed to an extension of the Latin world on the condition that the local heritage be respected, for he believed it enriched Europe. Strikingly, there is no sense of betraying the Ruthenian-Byzantine world, but rather of faith in the possibility of drawing from both traditions and hope for their synthesis (Schama 1995; Axer 2004c).

This trend can be followed in the territory of today's Ukraine, where a Latinized community of Ukrainian clergy (its influence stretching to Moscow in the seventeenth century), a separate Greek-Catholic Church (founded in 1596), and a Ukrainian lay, Latinized gentry developed in the sixteenth and seventeenth centuries (Ševčenko 1996; Yakovenko 1995). Under these conditions, a Latin Ukraine subculture was able to develop, combining the concept of *Roxolania* with the Kievan tradition open toward Moldova and Constantinople and seeking independence within its own Orthodox education system, adapting Jesuit educational techniques to its own needs (e.g., Petro Mohyla's Kiev Academy) (Ševčenko 1984).

The situation changed in the middle of the seventeenth century, when civil wars (Khmelnitsky's uprising) led to the Ukraine's being divided between Russia and Poland. The isolation of the Latinized Ukrainian elites, with their kinship to the Polish environment of freedom and their deep communion with Ruthenian historical memory and the Orthodox faith, was revealed. Symbolic here is the fate of the Kievan governor Adam Kysil, who testified to his double identity in Latin but ultimately became the embodiment of betrayal for both sides (Sysyn 1986). Along the Baltic, from the Bay of Gdańsk to Lake Ladoga, local cultures overrun and reorganized by German conquerors (the Teutonic Order) in the late Middle Ages, and adopting Lutheranism as the dominant religion during the Renaissance, developed an interesting subculture of German Protestant humanism superimposed on the local culture. In Ducal Prussia, a university was established in Königsberg; in the area where Polish, Swedish, and Russian influences crossed (today's Latvia and Estonia) the Jesuit colleges were created (i.a. in Dorpat, Dyneburg, Riga). This area would become a bridge between Germany and Russia, important for the reception of the classical tradition in the Russian empire during the eighteenth and nineteenth centuries.

In German-speaking Royal Prussia, which belonged to Poland, an active center of Catholic reform existed in Ermland (Dantiscus, Hosius, Cromerus, Treterus), where the reception of Christian antiquity remained in constant dialogue and dispute with the Protestant communities of Gdańsk and Toruń. Silesian humanism should be recognized as a separate subculture.

Transylvania developed its own neo-Latin subculture, continuing until the end of the nineteenth century. Apart from the Hungarians, this involved the Saxons, who maintained regular contacts with Germany and Italy. Local historians from the period became part of the new Latin Wallachian (Romanian) identity in the nineteenth century.

5.2   *Latin and the noble-nations*

The "nobleman-nations" of central-eastern Europe are a particularly important phenomenon in the history of Hungary and the Polish Commonwealth: in the sixteenth and seventeenth centuries, Poland assimilated Lithuanian, Ruthenian, Prussian, and Livonian nobles; in Hungary after the Battle of Mohacs, there was a strengthening of the sense that the sole carrier of Hungarian identity in the divided country was the Hungarian gentry (*una eademque nobilitas Hungarica* [one and only Hungarian gentry]).

Studies on the reception of the ancient tradition have failed to appreciate the fact that the nobility used Latin to its advantage and turned it into their own supra-ethnic language of the political nation, treating it as a characteristic of their own civic and collective identity. In Hungary, Latin was the official language until 1844. In this case, not changing to Hungarian as the national language could be seen not as cultural backwardness, but as a dramatic effort to hang onto a language that would be comprehensible to Europe.

In Croatia this identification served to declare unity with the Magyars under the Josephine rule (1790), and after 1847, when Hungarian policy threatened to Magyarize the language and culture, to defend Croatian identity (Rapacka 2004).

In the Commonwealth, Latin became a component of political language through a different mechanism. Used in public life much longer than in western Europe, it also entered into a special relationship with the vernacular languages of this multinational state, particularly with the language of the dominant Polish people. This bilingualism effectively delimited the state's political uniqueness, serving its purpose well in epistolography and oratory, whose role went far beyond the usual western European practice (Axer 1998).

In the nineteenth century *Latinitas* (Latinity) became a component of the mythologized national identity of the Poles, Hungarians, and Croats, as did the liberties and privileges of the nobles.

5.3 *The Roman republic as a model*

The history of republican forms in Europe, with the Roman Republic as the initial model and the French republic as its modern culmination, also includes the twelfth- and thirteenth-century waves of medieval republicanism. The republicanism of noble-nations in sixteenth- and seventeenth-century central-eastern Europe should be considered along the same lines (Szücs 1985).

The Polish nobility went the farthest in building a republican model. The Hungarian nobility entered into a compromise, adopting the nonancient concept of "the kingdom's mystical body." With time, the Prussian nobility abandoned republican liberties for a western-type model of the state. The Lithuanian nobility decided to join the Polish model, as did the Ukrainian elite (regardless of whether this was a process of voluntary confederation or the Poles' internal colonization of eastern Europe). In the Polish republic, a set of concepts from republican Rome (mainly from Cicero) helped in the self-interpretation of the concepts of *respublica* (republic), *civis* (citizen), and *libertas* (freedom), along with the whole system of values declared by the nation-state.

This domestication of the traditions of the Roman Republic became especially important in the final period of the Polish republic, its partition by Russia, Prussia, and Austria. The "republican camp," seeing salvation in restoring the old political forms and at the same time seeking aid from France, used the same political language to describe the utopian model of the past as the precursors of the French Revolution (Rousseau, Mably) had used to describe the utopia of the future. The republicanism of the noble-nation losing its sovereignty also harmonized with the language of the Founding Fathers in the US (Walicki 1989; Axer 1994b).

The diverse noble cultures of central-eastern Europe form interesting subcultures of the reception of ancient models of freedom and the republican language of public debate, and can be superimposed on the previously mentioned hybrid forms of reception resulting from ethnic and religious diversity.

5.4 **Societas Jesu** *versus civic education*

The Jesuit Order, brought to central-eastern Europe in the sixteenth century (to Bohemia in 1555, to Hungary in 1561, and to the Polish Commonwealth in 1564), had a huge impact both on spreading the supranational, post-Trent version of the reception of antiquity and on its domestication in this region. A fundamental role was played by the Jesuits, who assumed a major (Hungary) or decisive (Polish Republic) role in organizing general education, based on a curriculum binding for all colleges in Europe

(*Ratio atque institutio studiorum Societatis Iesu* [Method and system of the studies of the Society of Jesus], 1599). The college network covered the whole region, reaching eastwards as far as Smolensk. Catholics and Protestants, as well as Orthodox and Uniates in the late Renaissance, found a good general, modern education at these schools.

The Jesuit college unified the models and signs of culture, invoking the classical tradition that had become a component of the noble-nations' identity. The Jesuits also turned to the burgher, and even peasant, communities. Hence a common language of signs developed, with a still-under-appreciated influence on the mentality of local and regional communities that extends up to the present. The Jesuits' teaching of classical languages (particularly Latin), along with Greek and Roman history, created a new language of communication in political life that led to a redefining of the limits of *Latinitas* as the community of the Catholic religion and a unified version of the ancient tradition. Only German neohumanism in the nineteenth century constituted a similar attempt at reshaping the teaching of the classical tradition on a European scale. However, whereas neohumanism laid the foundations for educating the *cives rei publicae* (citizens of the republic), Jesuit schools provided civic education to citizens of the states as they were then: citizens of the noble-nation republic in the Common-wealth, but loyal subjects of the Habsburg monarchy in Protestant Bohemia.

College curricula were adapted to the needs of the region: following the model constructed in the west and using western innovations in terms of teaching and communication strategies (especially in preaching and theater), the Jesuits were sensitive to local conditions and capable of modifying their strategy. Their educational programs referred not only to the larger regional identity but also to the identities of individual national and ethnic subcultures. To meet these goals, they would deviate from the general *Ratio studiorum* and, in addition to Latin, use national languages: Polish, German, even Latvian.

An unusually clear picture of these efforts emerges from studies of the scripts and programs of theaters affiliated with the colleges. Within the Commonwealth, the most thoroughly studied in this respect, there were 56 colleges in the seventeenth century that staged approximately four thousand performances. Jesuit theater par-ticipated not only in religious polemics but also in strictly political public debates and in shaping the collective memory. Due to the "Jesuit dark legend," however, the impact the Jesuits' activity had on building a sense of community, civic attitudes, and local patriotism is often underestimated.

The process of domestication of the ancient tradition, so effectively assisted by the Jesuit Order, changed its character as the academic quality and intellectual ambitions of the college faculties weakened. From the mid-seventeenth century, Jesuit colleges began displaying growing conformism, moving toward accepting cliental obligations and expanding their success within existing systems.

The Order's dissolution (1773) was a smaller blow to the educational system of this region than it was in western Europe. Particularly in the Commonwealth, the landing was a soft one. The Jesuits had tried to modernize the educational canon from the 1740s, and outstanding individuals (Bohomolec, Naruszewicz), who played an important role in the Enlightenment reform of the cultural paradigm, had appeared among them. The Commission for National Education took over the Order's libraries and adapted their curricula, maintaining the link between the Latin language, literature and Roman history, and literature in the national languages. Some Jesuit colleges (e.g., in Vilnius, Lviv, Olomouc, Wrocław, and Zagreb) were also transformed into universities in different periods.

5.5 Auctores – *regional readings*

The reading of the Latin classics in central-eastern Europe is poorly researched. Western studies on Ciceronianism, Vergilianism, Horatianism, and Ovidianism touch this region only incidentally. Local scholars, anxious to confirm their own traditions as "being European," focus on proving that western European models of the reception of *auctores* found worthy followers in their respective cultures.

It is therefore worth noting the development of a special "regional" way of reading the major Latin authors, along with the lack of this sort of originality in reading the Greeks, at least in the Catholic territories. This confirms the domestication of ancient culture in its Latin variation and its strong ties to the noble-nation's ideology. One can also see the unifying role of Jesuit education in creating models of reception and a shared resource of reading matter and quotations.

The reception of Cicero is the best studied. The rhythm of reception was different in the Commonwealth than in the west. Already in the Renaissance, the orations were the main object of study, as practical instructions that facilitated functioning in public life and the parliamentary system. This approach did not appear in the west until the French Revolution.

The texts of Cicero, Tacitus, and Livy mainly concern the Republic in crisis and reminiscences about the Republic, so references to this tradition were invoked by the nobility, particularly during political crises. These references survived the downfall of the state, becoming part of the national myth, and were subsequently used as well by artists and scholars working to regain independence.

In the Renaissance and Baroque culture of the Commonwealth, the choice of works from the Vergilian corpus is almost as striking. A lack of interest in the *Aeneid* (imperial ideas drew no response) was accompanied by wide reading of the *Bucolics* and especially the *Georgics*, because the Polish nobleman was primarily a farmer.

Ovid, too, was read in a unique way in this region, as the only Roman poet who – because he had been exiled "to Scythia" – could become the forefather of local poetry.

6 Multiple Antiquities, Multiple Modernities (Eighteenth through Twentieth Centuries)

6.1 *The Enlightenment*

The final wave of fascination with Greco-Roman antiquity (in the French version) brought a new trend in art and architecture to this region beyond the boundaries of the Roman empire: the intentional seeking of direct contact with the material heritage of antiquity. The region came within the influence of the collections of antiquities in Vienna, Berlin, and St. Petersburg. In Poland, King Stanisław August (1764–95) encouraged the remodeling of original historic buildings (the Royal Castle and the Łazienki Palace in Warsaw).

In the Commonwealth, Enlightenment ideas and literature accompanied attempts to reform the noble-state and reshape historical memory, with the help of signs from the ancient tradition, in a process whereby references to the republic were replaced with references to the principate. The partitioning of the Commonwealth by Russia, Prussia, and Austria was the culmination of the process, ongoing since the seventeenth century, of dividing central-eastern Europe among the eastern and western powers. Consequently, in this region the nineteenth-century building of new national identities differed from western Europe's: for the nations without states, reinterpretation and mythologization of the past (invented tradition) would replace other integrating factors.

6.2   *Romanticism, neohumanism, and philhellenism*

In the early nineteenth century, German neohumanism began to dominate the region's reflections on antiquity. Its characteristic philhellenism harmonized with Romanticism. Hybrid forms of the reception of antiquity emerged, stemming from new stimuli merging with domesticated Latin culture, which reached deep into social structures, and with French elite culture. One interesting example is the multiethnic community of the Philomat and Philaret Society (Poles, Ukrainians, Lithuanians, and Belarusians), founded at Vilnius University (1817–25) around a philhellenic seminar transplanted there from Göttingen. Disbanded by the Russian police (the university was soon closed), it left a lasting trace as an attempt to build a "civic society" with ancient legitimization.

One Philomat, the Polish Romantic "bard" Mickiewicz, lecturing at the Collège de France in Paris (1842–6), presented the idea of the rebirth of Europe through rejection of both the classicist French version of Latin tradition and the Byzantine tyranny of the Russian empire. Mickiewicz saw the heritage of the Commonwealth, and more broadly Slavic central-eastern Europe (for political reasons he counted Hungarians and Lithuanians among Slavs), as a chance, first, for a new evangelization of Europe, in the spirit of freedom and fraternity of a classless society seeking a model in ancient Roman Christianity, and second, for spreading the idea of freedom, which would allow the parliamentary system to be replaced by the consensus on which the republicanism of the nobles had theoretically been based (Axer 2005).

Philhellenism also functioned in Russian political thought and imperial propaganda. As Tsar Alexander's foreign minister (1803–5), the Polish Prince Czartoryski linked the idea of resurrecting Greece with the concept of uniting central-eastern Europe as an autonomous part of the empire, seeing this as a chance for the rebirth of the Commonwealth. Later, philhellenism served as a foundation for revolutionary slogans and the community of peoples deprived of their own state (e.g., Czartoryski's émigré activity in Paris after 1830) (Axer forthcoming).

6.3 *Imperial education versus home education*

Education offered a paradox important for the reception of ancient culture in the region. While academic reflection on Greco-Roman antiquity was part of civic education in the west, in this region foreign schools were there to teach loyalty toward foreign empires. In opposition to this system, home education mythologized the local cultural tradition (e.g., neo-Sarmatism in Poland).

In western European literature, art, and journalism, the classical tradition consolidated the positive attitude of the citizens toward their state and strengthened its position in disputes with other powers (e.g., "Latin" France vs. "Hellenic" Germany). In central-eastern Europe, antiquity served to express attitudes of indifference or hostility toward foreign authority (e.g., in Sienkiewicz's *Quo Vadis*, 1896, which presented Russia as Nero's Rome, with the fate of the Poles associated with the fate of the first martyrs). It would seem that the relationship between teaching the classics and the process by which the elite accumulated power and created control mechanisms, a relationship characteristic of western Europe, does not really work in central-eastern Europe. The modernization that new nations of central-eastern Europe achieved was based on a construction of the past meant to legitimize the present. In this region, "multiple antiquities meant multiple modernities" (Klaniczay and Werner 2005).

7 Modern Times (Twentieth and Twenty-First Centuries)

7.1 *After the Treaty of Versailles (1919–39)*

From the viewpoint of the reception of the classical tradition, the region where independent states emerged – Poland, Lithuania, Latvia, Estonia, Czechoslovakia, Yugoslavia and a pared-down Hungary – became similar to western Europe during this time. National universities developed courses of study focused on antiquity and vigorously educated their own faculty. In the part of Ukraine and Belarus remaining within the Soviet Union, meanwhile, many academic circles were shut down in the 1930s, and part of the faculty were physically eliminated (Isayevych 2002).

At this time, references to antiquity were marginal in the definitions of their own identity constructed by nations in this region. A proposal that was ahead of its time for the concept of a battle of civilizations (similar in its intentions to the later ideas of Toynbee and Huntington) was developed in Poland (Koneczny 1962). It declared the primacy of the value of Latin civilization and its radical opposition to "Byzantine" civilization (understood as any system in which authorities have the advantage over individuals). The continuation of the Polish academic "cult" of Cicero (Morawski 1911) was characteristic, referring implicitly to Old Polish republican traditions and maintaining its validity for subsequent generations (Kumaniecki 1957).

The death of Zieliński (1856–1944), the greatest Polish classicist, was the symbolic end of the epoch. Dreaming of a scientific synthesis of antiquity and Christianity that reconciled German *Altertumswissenschaft* with Slavic messianism, raised in Russia, educated in Germany, a professor in St. Petersburg and from 1920 in Warsaw, *civis totius mundi* (citizen of the entire world), Zieliński died in Hitler's Bavaria writing his *Journal* in Polish.

One can recognize another subculture of the reception of the classical tradition emerging during the Austro-Hungarian monarchy: that of the submissive nations in opposition to the dominating ones. This type of reception then developed in the countries that later emerged there, in the *Latinitas* linked to Catholicism and pan-Slavism (Slovakia) or messianism and nationalism. Later this subculture also invoked Italian or German Fascist thought (Hungary, Romania), which in turn was related to anti-Bolshevik and anti-Semitic slogans. After World War II, this *Latinitas* served the communist regimes as an excuse to oppose the classical tradition, forcing many intellectuals to emigrate (Eliade, Cioran, and Kerényi).

7.2   Post-Yalta order (1945–89)

The division of Europe decreed after World War II meant that antiwestern ideology encompassed the whole region and "real socialism" reigned, while the classical tradition as a component of (elite) western culture was opposed and eliminated from education. The restrictions varied, though. In territories incorporated into the Soviet Union (Lithuania, Latvia, Estonia, western Ukraine and western Belarus, and Moldova), purges and physical elimination of the elites also involved circles teaching and studying ancient cultures, and artists drawing from these sources. Teaching of the classics at universities was practically eradicated in Vilnius, Lviv, Tartu, and Riga; archaeology was meant mainly to supply proof of autochthonic Slavism in the largest possible part of this area. The political pressure was almost as great in Czechoslovakia, increasing further after 1968. In Hungary it was the other way around: after 1956, classical studies developed gradually. In Poland, while the number of students was reduced, the faculty potential was not touched. After 1957 classical studies regained quite substantial contacts with the international community, since support for Mediterranean archaeology and classics was supposed to contribute to the communist government's reputation in the west. The regime in Poland viewed the ancient tradition as relatively neutral compared to the Sarmatian or Romantic traditions.

The entire region was subject to ideological indoctrination and political control. There was, however, no serious plan for imposing any cultural unity. Against the ancient tradition, state ideology used the nineteenth-century polemics of activists demanding Slavic rebirth, especially among the Czechs. In Hungary and Poland, the cultural traditions of the noble-nations were opposed with particular intensity. On the other hand, there were some attempts to incorporate ancient themes into the new ideology. Slave uprisings were invoked as a kind of anticipation of proletarian revolutionary movements. The Renaissance, presented as lay, materialist, and antichurch, also gained an important place in education at the cost of the Middle Ages and Baroque era, accompanied by appropriate reinterpretation of the ancient tradition in that era. Communist authorities tried to build a new version of the reception of antiquity in art, especially in architecture. This was "socialist classicism," drawing from the classicism of Mussolini, Hitler, and Stalin. In Poland, due to the "golden age" tradition, this style was combined with local Renaissance elements. Attempts were also made to reorganize urban spaces in order to transform the chronotopos, the space and times aspects that were important to the identity of the residents (e.g., Warsaw was rebuilt from wartime destruction). Since the regime was antireligious and antichurch, there was no extensive return to what had been so important in Russia's nineteenth-century policy – namely, replacing the Latin tradition with the Byzantine tradition. Latin was opposed, however, as the language of the Catholic Church.

Resistance to these practices, especially in Poland and Hungary, often assumed forms similar to the nineteenth-century use of the classical tradition to fight against the educational system and censorship of the partitioning powers. In Soviet-bloc societies, Greco-Roman antiquity served the purpose of more or less open dissociation from communism. People emphasized the European nature of their national traditions, and allusive literary texts and theater performances were created. The ancient tradition was also a part of the "Aesopian speech" in literature (e.g., Herbert, Parnicki, and Bocheński in Poland) and in drama and theater (e.g., 21 stagings of *Antigone* in Czechoslovakia). There are perceptible similarities here to the reception of antiquity in apartheid South Africa (Hardwick 2003a).

Antiquity served as a refuge for outstanding prose writers and poets who did not seek confrontation with the authorities, but wanted to avoid serving them. These issues require further study, but there seems to have been a clear subculture of the reception of the ancient tradition in the countries of this region in 1948–89.

7.3   *After the disintegration of the Soviet Union (after 1990)*

When the post-Yalta order collapsed, the classical tradition and the entire cultural heritage became the subject of thorough revaluation. The short time that has elapsed since then allows for only an outline of trends that seem characteristic of the region. In Lithuania and Croatia, less so in Ukraine, in a unique way in Belarus, despite the peasant roots and traditions of nineteenth- and twentieth-century independence movements in these countries, Latin texts – chronicles, poems, and plays – were seen to contain that layer of national tradition and historical memory that invaders (Russians, Poles, Serbs, etc.) had not managed to destroy in the past. This "nationalization" of the classical tradition occurring after the "autumn of the peoples" in newly formed states constitutes a kind of "catching-up" with nineteenth-century nationalism, an interesting sociopolitical move.

Meanwhile, in the countries that retained their statehood during Soviet domination (especially Poland and Hungary), antiquity in the new political situation stopped serving as a tool for playing games with censorship or as an arcadia providing refuge from reality, and Latinity stopped being identified with Europeanism. Opening up to the west caused an immediate triumph of mass culture and a rapid modification of educational programs according to Old Europe's standards, assigning a marginal place to the classical tradition and languages. This process could be called a "catching-up" with the 1968 Paris revolt.

Whether central-eastern Europe will invoke its own reception of the ancient tradition in mass culture, or will only use the alphabet provided by global culture (especially American cinema) for its references to antiquity, is hard to determine today.

8 Conclusions

In central-eastern Europe, in the space between east and west, in the periods when the nations of this region enjoyed freedom of choice, the reception of ancient culture did not lead to the development of a canon that would limit the freedom of individuals or communities in a degree comparable with the restrictions imposed by other factors. At the same time, the system of values linked to this tradition was often a declaration of identity for individuals and communities, and a sign of nonconformity. Consequently, the role of the Latin language and the broader Latin culture in this region of Europe is different from the role described by Waquet (2001), which is based on western European (mostly French) experience. In this region, Latin was a sometimes a tool of oppression, but at least as often it was a weapon in the hands of those fighting for survival, the excluded, those demanding a right to develop their own forms of community life and to preserve their own identity (Axer 2004c).

The situation in Russia can be viewed as a certain antithesis of this kind of freedom, which does not mean not appreciating the greatness of Russian culture and the originality of how the ancient heritage was reshaped within it. I share the view (Okenfuss 1995) that even the last European wave of Latinization (the Enlightenment) was never accepted there, and that pagan Latin writers were included in Russian culture only in the nineteenth century, as school reading under the strictly controlled educational reform of Nicholas I. The tragedy of the Decembrists – Latin republicans ("Slavophiles Westernizers") – is symbolic (Lotman 1984). Anyone preparing a study of the classical tradition in Russian will find that this attitude to humanism provides one explanation for the unique fate of the Russian intelligentsia, which served the state but simultaneously was alienated from it.

Perhaps the recent trend to reorient classical studies toward studies on reception will encourage in central-eastern Europe an interest in the continuity of the region's own tradition. Such an approach enhances the value of the cultural space once called "the peripheries" and makes hybrid forms of culture in the "borderlands" particularly interesting.

FURTHER READING

Little attention has been paid in the west to the classical tradition in central-eastern Europe (there is, for example, nothing in the syntheses of Highet 1949 or Bolgar 1973). There are many studies in the languages of the region on the classical heritage in literature and the visual arts that present a national approach. For studies according to the contemporary political division of the region, see the articles in Cancik, Schneider, and Landfester (1996–2003), vols. 13–15: Belarus (Schevtschenko); Czech (Martínková, Svatoš, Stehlíková, Vidmanová); Estonia (Lill, Nagel); Hungary (Borzsák, Ritoók); Latvia (Cīrule, Feldhūns); Lithuania (Ulčinaitė, Zabulis); Moldova (Gussejnov); Poland (Axer, Brzozowski, Domański, Kalinowski, Kiss, Kolendo,

Mikocki, Myśliwiec, Sarnowska, Stabryła, Wołodkiewicz); Romania (Barnea, Bulgăr, Petecel, Piatkowski); Slovakia (Škoviera); and Ukraine (Gussejnov).

My proposal for understanding the classical tradition in the region derives from a new "research questionnaire." Abandoning the previously dominant philological perspective and the criterion of faithfulness to this model, I have decided on a historicocultural approach, focusing on processes of reception and change. Therefore, the literature listed below mainly concerns the cultural identity of the region and its history. For general accounts: Kłoczowski (2004); Mączak, Samsonowicz, Burke (1985); Wandycz (2001); Banac and Sysyn (1986); Adamska and Moster (2004). On the limits, divisions, and definitions of the region: Halecki (1950); Picchio (1984); Szücs (1985); Graciotti (1998). On the Renaissance and humanism: Burke (1988); Fiszman (1988); Goleniščev-Kutuzov (1989); Porter and Teich (1994); Rabil (1988). And finally, on Latinity in the region: Axer (2004c); Birnbaum (1986); Kieniewicz (2001); Merisalo and Sarasti-Wilenius (1994); Merisalo and Sarasti-Wilenius (2003); Waquet (2001).

CHAPTER ELEVEN

France

Philip Ford

1 Introduction

Throughout the centuries, the classical tradition has played an important role in the intellectual and cultural history of France. Until relatively recently, its place in the educational system has been of central importance, and this has resulted in a significant presence of Greek and Roman sources in French writing and art. Yet, at the same time, not all periods have reacted in the same way to the Greco-Roman past, and many of the more interesting moments of literary history have taken place against the backdrop of tensions arising from a reassessment of the nation's debt to the ancient world. At various periods, individual authors have been more or less popular. In the following pages, we shall explore in particular some of these moments of tension in order to suggest the impact of the classical tradition in French literature.

Before doing so, however, it will be necessary to identify what in particular constitutes the classical tradition in this context. In the first place, it goes without saying that a knowledge of the two central languages of classical antiquity will be an obvious touchstone for the degree to which classical culture permeates any given society, and if Latin was a more or less permanent presence over the centuries, Greek, in line with its position in other European countries, enjoyed a more variable fortune, and its relative prominence at any point is an excellent indication of the general health of the classical tradition. Secondly, and clearly linked with the language question, the popularity of individual classical authors will be an indication of the kind of classical tradition that readers and writers favor at particular periods, with some authors going in and out of fashion, while others maintain a more permanent presence. Finally, there is the whole question of attitudes toward the classical past: the degree to which antiquity is seen as a model to be imitated or an outmoded and stifling albatross, to be abandoned at the earliest opportunity.

2 The Middle Ages

The gradual decline of classical culture in late antiquity resulted in a period of literary stagnation from the end of the sixth century until the reign of Charlemagne (768–814). The reforms of the Frankish Church that Charlemagne instituted involved the recruitment of scholars from Italy, Spain, and the British Isles, including Alcuin (ca. 735–804), who helped to systematize the teaching of the central pillar of medieval education, the trivium (grammar, rhetoric, and dialectic). He and other scholars were rewarded with lucrative Church livings in exchange for which they did much to raise the educational and religious standards of the kingdom. Convinced that the only way to achieve the ecclesiastical reform that he desired was through education, Charlemagne was largely responsible for encouraging amongst his subjects the first touchstone of the classical tradition, a firm knowledge of the Latin language. To this end, he required in the *Admonitio generalis* (General exhortation) of 789 that priests should educate all boys in their parish in a reading knowledge of Latin. Charlemagne was also responsible for a massive increase in book production: more than 7,000 Latin manuscripts survive from the ninth century, compared with only 1,800 for the entire period before this (Barbero 2004: 234). Although many of these texts were religious in nature, classical Roman prose-writers, including Cicero, Livy, and Sallust, as well as poets such as Lucan, Horace, Martial, Tibullus, and Juvenal, were in circulation. Moreover, as Alessandro Barbero writes, "Literature from late antiquity was read with pleasure, and moreover the court poets could be considered direct followers of that tradition, which was perceived as still alive and not merely a matter of imitation" (Barbero 2004: 236).

After the death of Charlemagne, literary writing declined, although the monastic and cathedral schools continued to maintain the status of classical literature. It is not until the twelfth century that we see the next crucial moment in French intellectual history, with Paris becoming the educational capital of Europe (Benson 1984: 113–72). However, as was the case with the Carolingian reforms, the main impetus for progress was not a love or admiration of the classical past for its own sake, but rather a desire to use the Latin language, as well as classical authors, in order to reinforce the hold of Christianity. The Latin Aristotle, in many cases translated from Arabic texts, provided the foundations for Scholasticism, a system that, thanks to the Church, even managed to outlive the Renaissance (Marenbon 1987: 50–7).

This period also witnesses the beginnings of a vernacular literature in France, and if Latin writing was largely devoted to religious topics (twelfth-century lyric verse by the Goliardic poets being a notable exception; cf. Raby 1957: 2:322–41), French writers did turn more to classical themes for inspiration, particularly in the area of epic poetry: the *Roman de Thèbes* (Story of Thebes, ca. 1150), inspired by Statius' *Thebais*; the *Roman d'Eneas* (Story of Aeneas, ca. 1160), which draws on Vergil and Ovid; and Benoît de Sainte-Maure's *Roman de Troie* (Story of Troy, ca. 1165) (Cormier 1973; Benson 1984: 593–612). Chrétien de Troyes (flourished 1160–85) began his poetic career with imitations of Ovid, including the poem *Philomela*, which he drew from book 6 of the *Metamorphoses* (Frappier 1982: 49–50). Ovid also played a significant part in the thirteenth-century bestseller *Le Roman de la rose* (The romance of the rose), and as a source of classical mythology as well as ideas on love, he became in more general terms a leading figure in medieval literary circles. Nevertheless, the treatment that he received in the fourteenth-century *Ovide moralisé* (Ovid moralized) is emblematic of the way in which the Middle Ages accommodated classical writing: the frequently shocking stories concerning the interaction between the divine and the human realms are reduced to banal Christian allegorizations (Moss 1982: 23–7). This general tendency to defuse classical writing by denying its alterity, to interpret it with methods derived from biblical exegesis, characterizes much of this period, and it is only with the arrival of a more rigorous philological approach to the classics developed in fourteenth- and fifteenth-century Italy that classical literature began to enjoy a more authentic revival in France.

3   The Renaissance

The French Middle Ages had been largely Greekless, an indication of the limits within which the classical tradition had been confined. The closing years of the fifteenth century, however, saw the beginnings of a movement that would transform French literature, culture, and thought through the introduction of a language and literature that were less intimately bound up with the Catholic Church than had been the case with Latin. Yet, paradoxically, a desire to return to the original languages of the Bible was one of the motives for this interest in Greek, and French evangelism is closely tied up with the development of humanism.

The lead of Italy was crucial in the spread of Hellenism in France. Not only did the first printed editions of Greek writers emanate from Italy (first in Florence and subsequently in Venice, with the Aldine press proving to be particularly productive), but it was Italy that supplied many of the scholars who helped with the dissemination of the Greek language. These included exiles from Constantinople after its fall to the Turks in 1453. At the same time, French scholars began to develop an interest in classical antiquity, both Greek and Roman, for its own sake, and the printing press provided the necessary technology to enable a limited democratization of learning. According to the words that Rabelais attributes to Gargantua in the early 1530s, "The whole world is full of learned people, highly educated teachers, well-stocked libraries, so that I believe that neither in the time of Plato or Cicero or Papinian was there such an opportunity for study as we see nowadays" (Rabelais 1994: 244, my trans.).

Of the various scholars in this early period, it is Guillaume Budé (1468–1540) who had the most significant impact. Largely self-taught in Greek, he made the most of the resources at hand, both human and literary, in order to extend his knowledge of the classical tradition. Benefiting from brief periods of intense study with the eminent Greek scholar Janus Lascaris (1445–1534; Grafton 1997: 135–83), Budé developed a profound knowledge of the Greek language and culture that permeates all his writings. As well as contributing to the teaching of Greek through his *Commentarii linguae Graecae* (Commentaries on the Greek language) of 1529, he also reflected at a more profound level on the balance between classical culture and Christianity, in particular in the *De transitu Hellenismi ad Christianismum* (On the transition from Hellenism to Christianity) of 1535. It was also thanks to his lobbying of the king, François Ier, that the Collège des lecteurs royaux was established in 1530, with the express purpose of teaching the three ancient languages, Latin, Greek, and Hebrew (Fumaroli 1998). In sharp contrast to the religious authorities and the University of Paris, which were highly suspicious of the new learning (in 1523, the Sorbonne tried to suppress the spread of Greek, and Rabelais's Franciscan superiors confiscated his Greek books; Rabelais 1994: LXIV), the Collège royal provided public lectures aimed at students of all levels of knowledge and ability. With royal support, interest in classical culture flourished, and the newly refurbished palace of Fontainebleau was beginning to be filled with frescoes celebrating the ruling dynasty in the guise of Greco-Roman gods and heroes.

At the same time, humanist colleges were educating an emerging urban middle class for whom language skills were a central requirement. If dialectic had been the most highly prized element in the medieval trivium, the requirements of a more meritocratic society in the sixteenth century led to a greater emphasis on the communication skills offered by rhetoric. Following Erasmus' recommendations in the *De copia* (On abundant variety), there was an expectation that, to achieve rhetorical expertise, students would read and assimilate the whole corpus of classical literature, and this soon had an impact on writing of all kinds, both in the vernacular and in neo-Latin (Cave 1979: 3–77; Moss 1996). Indeed, it is the early neo-Latin poets – Jean Salmon Macrin, Nicolas Bourbon, Étienne Dolet, and many others – who prepared the ground for the introduction of classical topoi, genres, and styles into French poetry. The Collège de Guyenne in Bordeaux, where Montaigne studied in the 1540s, also helped introduce the classical theater to France, with the Scottish poet and humanist George Buchanan (1506–82) both translating Euripides and composing original biblical tragedies (*Jephthes* and *Baptistes*) for performance by the students (Ford 2001: 58–60).

By the 1540s, the stage was set for a massive advance in the presence of the classical tradition in all aspects of French culture. Thanks to the work of early Hellenists such as Budé, Jacques Toussain (ca. 1498–1547), and Pierre Danès (1497–1557), knowledge of Greek was spreading, with Parisian printers such as Robert Estienne (1503–59) providing reliable editions of Greek authors, encouraged by royal favor (Girot 2002: 7–30). Marsilio Ficino's editions and commentaries of Plato were also having an impact thanks to the interest of humanists such as the Lyon polymath Symphorien Champier (1471–1537/9) and Jacques Lefèvre d'Étaples (died 1536), whose Platonizing evangelism had a strong impact on the king's sister, Marguerite de Navarre (Walker 1972: 63–131). Scholasticism was seen by the new brand of thinkers as standing in the way of both educational and religious progress.

But it is the Limoges-born humanist and poet Jean Dorat (1508–88) who had the most profound effect on the direction that French writing followed in the middle years of the century. Tutor to Ronsard, Du Bellay, and Jean-Antoine de Baïf, he was instrumental in forming the poetic values of the Pléiade, whose aesthetic ideals were based on raising the status of French poetry through the imitation of classical, and principally Greek, sources. Convinced that ancient poets such as Homer, Hesiod, and

Orpheus had acted as intermediaries between the divine and the human worlds (like the biblical David), Dorat saw the role of the poet in society as that of presenting divine truth in allegorical form. Under his influence, the Pléiade set about the composition of highly allusive, at times obscure, poetry that aimed to rival the works of Italian authors such as Petrarch, Ariosto, and Tasso. Dorat, who took up the post of professor of Greek at the Collège royal in 1556, was also responsible for introducing his pupils to a form of syncretism that tended to emphasize the similarities between classical pagan thought and Christianity: Homer was aware, thanks to the sibylline prophecies, of the coming of the Messiah, and Plato's ideas were in perfect harmony with those of the Scriptures (Demerson 1983).

It was Du Bellay, in the *Deffense et illustration de la langue françoyse* (Defence and illustration of the French language) of 1549, who expounded many of these ideas in their most memorable form. For him and his colleagues, the assimilation of classical writers was a *sine qua non* of poetic composition, and like the Romans with the Greeks it was necessary for modern authors to

> transform themselves into them, devour them, and after properly digesting them, turning them into blood and sustenance, to choose, each one according to his own genius and the subject he wanted to tackle, the best model, whose rarest and most exquisite qualities he would carefully observe (Du Bellay 1904: 99, my trans.)

This thoroughly classicizing form of imitation would mark the poetry of virtually the entire century, and was extended to other genres such as drama, notably in the tragedies of Étienne Jodelle, Jean de La Taille, and Robert Garnier (Jondorf 1990: 9–28), where classical themes often mirrored the dire situation France faced during the Wars of Religion (1562–98).

As well as Dorat, other French humanists such as Henri Estienne, Denis Lambin, and Adrien Turnèbe were working to disseminate classical literature through their teaching and publications, and there can be no doubt that the sixteenth century witnessed at all levels of society the results of this educational and cultural ethos. Classical mythology was used to celebrate the Valois dynasty in the visual arts, court entertainments, public occasions such as royal entries and marriages, and literature, so that it became commonplace to depict the members of the French court as Greco-Roman gods and heroes, as in the *Tour de la Ligue* (Tower of the League) in the château de Tanlay (Yates 1977: 121–48). At its height, this enthusiasm for the classical world is characterized by an unrestrained exuberance which first finds its expression in the works of Rabelais, but which was not without its critics. In particular, the Catholic Church, after the Council of Trent, became increasingly hostile toward the syncretism espoused by Dorat and his followers, while a new canon of classicism was being elaborated by J. C. Scaliger, which would prepare the way for seventeenth-century neoclassicism.

Scaliger's *Poetices libri septem* (Seven books on poetics) was published posthumously in 1561, and its impact in Renaissance France was gradual. Taking his inspiration from Aristotle's *Poetics*, the Italian-born humanist explores all areas of poetry and drama, but one of his main concerns is to demonstrate the superiority of Latin literature over

Greek. For him, elegance, sophistication, and verisimilitude are more important literary qualities than the raw energy of earlier writers, with the result that Vergil is held up as the supreme model of poetry over Homer and his Greek followers (Michel 1986: 63–73). This aesthetic approach would be readily taken on by the Jesuit colleges, which in the second half of the sixteenth century began to offer serious rivalry to the humanist colleges in France and which, in line with the post-Tridentine reforms, revived a form of scholasticism in their teaching and exercised considerable caution in the choice of classical texts included in the curriculum (Farrell 1938). The seeds of a far narrower view of the classical tradition were being sown, and their effect would not be limited to the popularity of individual Greek and Latin authors, but would determine the way in which sixteenth-century vernacular authors were viewed in the closing years of the century, in particular leading to a sudden and dramatic decline in the popularity of the Pléiade (Faisant 1998).

Yet one of the greatest authors and thinkers of the latter part of the century would escape these trends. Montaigne's enthusiasm for the classical past was wholehearted and down to earth. His favorite ancient writers, for the most part historians and poets, come over in his *Essais* (Essays) as privileged interlocutors, with whom he engages in a dialogue shared with his readers. It is precisely the self-revelation of the ancients that he prizes and exploits in order to reveal something of his own nature. They provide him with consolation after the loss of his closest friend, Étienne de La Boétie, and, in his numerous citations and adaptations of their works, they often reveal more about the author than he is prepared to state explicitly. Intertextuality becomes in the hands of Montaigne a means of encouraging the complicity of the reader (Coleman 1979: 108–79).

The sixteenth century is thus the period at which the classical tradition reaches its peak. For the first time, there is a widespread knowledge amongst the educated classes of the two languages of classical civilization, and a thorough knowledge of Greek and Roman literature for its own sake, and not simply as an adjunct to Christianity. For nationalistic reasons, Greek is prized more than Latin, partly because Latin is closely associated with the rival Italian culture, partly because scholars such as Henri Estienne claimed that French was derived from Greek (Estienne 1565). All the main forms of writing – poetry, theater, and prose – are thoroughly imbued with classical notions, owing in part to the central role of the commonplace book, and the various literary genres take classical texts as their models. The ideas and ideals of the classical world – Platonism, skepticism, Stoicism, Epicureanism – all make an appearance in Renaissance thought and help shape attitudes to the often-turbulent events of the times. Above all, there is an attempt, whether by scholars such as Budé and Dorat or the general reader such as Montaigne, to understand ancient authors in their own right, to engage with them as individuals, and to consider what they had to say to be every bit as valuable as the works of Christian writers.

4 Neoclassicism

The gradual progress made by Jesuit colleges in educating French youth in the sixteenth century accelerated in the following century, no doubt aided by their principle of offering free education to nonboarding pupils. In some respects, they continued many of the traditions of the humanist colleges that they were supplanting, including the composition and staging of annual plays in Latin, but in other respects the return to scholasticism and the restrictions on authors included in the curriculum led to a narrowing of what constituted the classical canon (Snyders 1964: 74–83). Didactic poetry was particularly prized, leading to a burgeoning of the genre both amongst the Jesuits themselves and more generally (Haskell 2003: 1–69). The Jesuits did not, however, have a monopoly on education, and from 1637 the rival Jansenist movement provided one of the best classical educations available in France at their *petites écoles*, set up in various locations by lay members of the order. Unlike the Jesuits, they paid considerable attention to Greek as well as Latin, providing a more rounded knowledge of the classics, while their austere view of religion had a surprisingly profound effect on the intellectual elite of seventeenth-century France.

If poetry was the greatest beneficiary of the classical tradition in Renaissance France, there can be no doubt that it was the theater that benefited most in the seventeenth century. Although the tradition of humanist drama was prolonged until the 1630s by the prolific playwright Alexandre Hardy (ca. 1572–1632), who is credited with some six hundred plays, two main influences helped shape the direction that tragedy in particular would take in the course of the century. On the one hand, Jesuit drama would espouse a Senecan approach to the genre, with Martin Antonio Delrio's *Syntagma tragoediae Latinae* (Essay on Latin tragedy) of 1593–4 offering a commentary on the plays of Seneca that was inspired by Aristotle's *Poetics*, but seen through Jesuit eyes. Certain Stoic notions are privileged: the inevitability of Providence, the importance of reason in the control of the emotions, and the role of the *sententia* or gnomic expression as a means of moral education. The other powerful influence in the early decades of the century was Cardinal Richelieu, who quickly grasped the propaganda potential of drama as a means of changing society. He commissioned the abbé d'Aubignac to produce a summary of the classical theory of tragedy, and although *La Pratique du théâtre* (Theatrical method) did not appear until 1657, the debate that Richelieu provoked was instrumental in the formation of the neoclassical theater (Phillips 1980).

The effects of both these influences may be seen in the theater of Corneille (1606–84), who was educated at the Jesuit college in Rouen between 1615 and 1622 before training as a lawyer. His greatest tragedies show his characters grappling with fate, but their reliance on reason rather than the emotions frequently allows them to overcome what may appear to be impossible odds, nowhere more notably than in *Cinna*, where the Stoic Auguste triumphs over his feelings of vengeance and wins around the other characters (Maurens 1966). Although Corneille was criticized for the happy endings of many of his tragedies in apparent defiance of Aristotle, d'Aubignac justifies such dénouements by appealing to the actual practice of the Athenian theater and by defining tragedy in terms of the nobility of its characters rather than the downfall of the tragic hero. However people viewed these issues, there is no doubt that the debate was governed by classical notions of the theater, whether it be Aristotle's enormously influential description of tragedy in the *Poetics*, or the plays of the Greek and Roman tragedians themselves. Verisimilitude, as defined by Aristotle, emerged as one of the central issues in what developed into the *querelle du théâtre* (quarrel over the theater): in an increasingly austere religious climate, only plays that carried a convincing moral message were defendable, and to be convincing a play had to avoid anything that might weaken the suspension of disbelief (Phillips 1980: 18–22). The three unities of time, place, and action, decorum in the presentation of the characters, as well as the plots themselves, were all governed by this central consideration.

Moral improvement presented more of a challenge for comedy, where the traditions of the Roman stage, often mediated by Italian *commedia erudita* (learned comedy) and the *commedia dell'arte*, were adapted to suit modern tastes. Writers such as Pierre Larivey (ca. 1540–1612) and Jean Rotrou (1609–50), who frequently drew on Plautus and Terence as well as Italian dramatists, helped prepare the way for the genius of Molière (1622–73), whose often-controversial plays got him into trouble with the authorities on more than one occasion. Although the basic plots of his plays are typical of the Roman theater – one or more young men are in love with apparently unsuitable young women, but aided by servants to win over their disapproving fathers – Molière's originality lies in his use of contemporary stereotypes: the *précieuse*, the religious hypocrite, the doctor, the social climber, the *femme savante* (bluestocking). Nevertheless, many of his plays such as *Amphithryon*, *L'Avare* (The miser), and *Les Fourberies de Scapin* (The trickeries of Scapin) owe much to the Roman tradition (Howarth 1982: 106–24).

The author who comes closest in spirit to the ancient stage is the Jansenist-educated Jean Racine (1639–99). His mastery of Greek as well as Latin allowed him to develop a far greater feeling for the Greek theater, and in particular Euripides (Phillippo 2003), than many of his contemporaries, while his assimilation of Aristotle's *Poetics* leads to some of the most moving works to be produced in the seventeenth century. In many ways, the Jansenist concept of predestination fitted in perfectly with the Greek notion of fate, and it is this heroic struggle with the inevitable that Racine presents in his tragedies, whether they be inspired by classical mythology and history, or the Bible. As in the Greek theater, there is a sense in many of his protagonists (Polynice and Etéocle in *La Thébaïde*, Oreste in *Andromaque*, Néron in *Britannicus*, Phèdre, and Athalie) of an inherited pollution (Dodds 1951: 35–7), which they can do little or nothing to control. Though aware of their corrupt nature (another Jansenist theme), their lucidity in no way allows them to counter their emotions, in contrast to Corneille's more Stoical heroes. Racine exploits to the full all of Aristotle's precepts in the *Poetics* in a form of tragedy that emphasizes at the same time the wretchedness and the nobility of unredeemed Man.

The form of classicism that ultimately triumphed in seventeenth-century France can be seen to have its roots in the aesthetic judgments of Scaliger, with verisimilitude, reason, and elegance being its prime qualities. Yet there were other aspects of the classical past that appealed to early seventeenth-century writers, and amongst these it is important to recognize the influence of Lucretius and Epicureanism in the development of libertinism in France. Developing from the skepticism of the late Renaissance, this movement embraced many of the new scientific ideas of men such as Galileo in seeking a rational explanation for natural phenomena. Pierre Gassendi (1592–1655) was the principal exponent of these ideas in France, and we see his influence in the works of writers such as Cyrano de Bergerac (1619–55), notably in his fictional works *Les Etats et empires de la lune* (The states and empires of the moon) and *Les Etats et empires du soleil* (The states and empires of the sun), as well as in Molière's *Dom Juan*.

In the realm of poetry, it is the more didactic genres, such as the fable (La Fontaine, 1621–95) and satire (Boileau, 1636–1711), that have their clearest roots in the classical past. Boileau was also responsible for writing what may be considered as the ultimate summary of French classicism in the four-book didactic poem *L'Art poétique* (The art of poetry) of 1674. For generations of French schoolchildren, this work has embodied in a readily memorizable form the aesthetic judgments of the period. Alongside Boileau's translation of pseudo-Longinus' *Treatise on the Sublime*, it also embodied the classicizing tradition in the so-called *Querelle des Anciens et des Modernes* (quarrel of the Ancients and the Moderns), which rumbled on from the mid-1660s until the early years of the following century (Adam 1974: 158–64). It was at its height between 1687 and 1700 when the two sides formed rival factions, the *Modernes* led by Charles Perrault and Fontenelle, the *Anciens* under Boileau, supported by the likes of Racine, La Fontaine, and La Bruyère. At stake was nothing less than the role of Greek and Roman literature as literary sources, with the *Modernes* supporting a notion of cultural progress that saw no place for the intellectual claims of the past.

The seventeenth century, then, is a period of retrenchment for the classics in France. The expectation that an educated reader would have read all of classical literature no longer holds, and the classical canon came to favor Latin over Greek texts, didactic and moral works over the more exuberant kind. There are exceptions: the *libertins* (free-thinking) poets and writers, and even La Fontaine; but the form of classicism that ultimately emerges is sober and rational, Aristotelian rather than Platonic. If the Renaissance had attempted to integrate the thinking of the Greco-Roman world into the Christian world view, the seventeenth century largely turned its back on syncretism, so that even the mention of the pagan gods in Christian contexts was gradually eradicated. In language terms, French made inroads into the use of Latin as a literary language outside of Jesuit circles. All this led in turn to a rejection of the literary heritage of the French Renaissance, summed up in Boileau's view of Ronsard, criticized for "speaking Greek and Latin in his French poetry" (*Art poétique* 1.126).

5   The Enlightenment

If the main thrust of eighteenth-century ideas would ultimately be favorable to the *Modernes*, this did not mean that the literary ideals of classicism disappeared overnight. The classical tradition continued in epic poetry (including Voltaire's *Henriade* of 1723–8), didactic poetry, and the ode; tragedy (in particular Crébillon [1674–1762] and Voltaire again), and even comedy (Lesage). But the dynamic force of writers such as Racine, who knew how to exploit and bend the rules of classicism to emotional and aesthetic ends, was largely missing, and writing classical literature became more a question of applying a formula. The Romantic authors of the late eighteenth and early nineteenth centuries would reject the classical norms in favor of a freer form of writing.

The eighteenth century was a period of upheaval in the realm of education. Until they were closed down in 1762, Jesuit colleges continued to provide many pupils with a sound classical education, but the universities went through a relatively stagnant period, acting largely as a conservative force, as they had done in the sixteenth century. Nevertheless, there was interest in classical literature both within the universities and outside, as is demonstrated by the *Querelle d'Homère* (Quarrel over Homer), which lasted from 1711 to 1717. A continuation of the *Querelle des Anciens et des Modernes*, this new controversy centered on Anne Dacier's translations of the *Iliad* (1711) and the *Odyssey* (1716), and the reactions to them of the *Modernes*, such as Houdar de La Motte and abbé Jean Terrasson. At stake was not only the status of Homer as a model of epic poetry, but also the question of how best to translate the Homeric epics into French (Létoublon and Volpilhac-Auger 1999: 89–103). The eighteenth century also witnessed the most significant event in Homeric publication since Henri Estienne's 1566 edition of the Greek epic poets. Jean-Baptiste Gaspard d'Ansse de Villoisin's edition of the Venetus A manuscript of the *Iliad* (1788), with its 532 pages of previously unpublished scholia, revolutionized the way in which Homer would be read and interpreted in future years, even calling into question the identity of "Homer" as a single poet (Létoublon and Volpilhac-Auger 1999: 41–61).

This academic interest in the classics was also mirrored in the ideas that helped nurture the French Revolution, looking back as it did to the democratic values of the Roman Republic or Athenian democracy as an alternative to the monarchical systems that had dominated since ancient times. Education was seen as central to the new Republic, and in 1793 wide-sweeping reforms resulted in all 24 French universities being abolished and the innovative *écoles centrales* (central schools) being established in 1795. These latter were replaced in 1802 under Napoleon by the *lycées* (high schools), and a new, strictly secular university system was set up in 1808. The introduction of the *baccalauréat* (baccalaureate) saw a return to humanist values, with a renewed emphasis on Greek as well as Latin literature. These new republican values are clearly seen in the art of the period, with painters such as David (1748–1825) drawing on classical themes to celebrate the new political regime. The effects of these reforms may be seen in the new generation of writers that grew up in the nineteenth century.

6   The Nineteenth Century

Although nineteenth-century Romanticism might be seen as the antithesis of the classical tradition, it is seventeenth-century neoclassicism that Victor Hugo and his followers were rejecting rather than the Greco-Roman tradition as such. Freed from the interference of the Church, state education permitted a wider range of classical texts to be studied in the schools, and a sense of the excitement and, in many cases, the transgressive nature of the ancient world was felt by a new generation of school-boys (girls' *lycées* only being established in 1880). Sainte-Beuve (1804–69), a defender of Romanticism, helped reestablish the reputation of the Pléiade and their aesthetic values in the *Tableau historique et critique de la poésie française et du théâtre français au XVIe siècle* (Historical and critical description of French poetry and theater in the sixteenth century), published in 1828 (Faisant 1998: 535–70). As a result, the field of poetry in particular witnesses a burgeoning of classical influences in this period, alongside a revival of pagan values.

The nineteenth century also sees a shift in the balance between Greek and Latin sources. If the seventeenth and eighteenth centuries had largely favored Roman authors, the nineteenth century opts for the Greeks, for their originality and grandeur. As Hugo states in the *Préface de Cromwell* (1827):

> All ancient tragedians repackage Homer. Same stories, same dénouements, same heroes. All of them draw on the Homeric stream. It is always the *Iliad* and the *Odyssey*. Like Achilles dragging Hector, Greek tragedy circles around Troy. However, the epic age is reaching its end. Like the society it represents, this poetry is being worn out by revolving on itself. Rome copies Greece, Vergil imitates Homer. (Hugo 1968: 65, my trans.)

For Hugo, then, Homer is a poetic giant that later authors could not emulate.

Often, it is the more mystical aspects of classical culture that appeal to Romantic and post-Romantic writers. Gérard de Nerval (1808–55), for example, an admirer of Ronsard, is strongly influenced by Neoplatonism and a syncretist view of religion, to which he gives expression in his essay *Isis*, and his best-known work, *Les Chimères* (The chimeras), is imbued with a mixture of classical and biblical imagery. His friend Théophile Gautier (1811–72) also draws on classical imagery in a natural and unself-conscious way in his *Émaux et camées* (Enamels and cameos), while Baudelaire's *Les Fleurs du mal* (The flowers of evil), first published in 1857 and dedicated to Gautier, demonstrates a considerable debt to the classics. His parodic poem "Franciscae meae laudes" (Praise of my Frances) demonstrates a certain facility with Latin, which he would have gained from his education at the Lycée Louis-le-Grand in Paris, but, more crucially, his entire concept of the status of poetry and the poet appears to be marked by Platonic notions that would not have been out of place amongst the Pléiade. Beauty is an absolute ideal that the poet seeks, but that can be reached only by some form of inspiration allowing the release of the soul from the body: the poet's soul or mind is often represented as a bird soaring above the mundane world, as in "Élévation," where it moves "above the lakes, above the valleys, the mountains, the woods, the clouds, the seas, beyond the sun, beyond the ether, beyond the confines of the starry spheres" ("Spleen et idéal" 3).

In general terms, then, the nineteenth century saw the revival of interest in classical literature revitalizing poetry and restoring it to the status it had enjoyed during the Renaissance. Intertextuality was central to this endeavor, and, thanks to the renewed place of the classics in the educational system, the reading public was able to appreciate the highly allusive poetry being produced. Classical influences were not altogether absent from the novel, although concerns with social issues tended to privilege more contemporary themes. Flaubert's *Salammbô* (1862), set in the Carthage of Hamilcar, is an exception to this general rule. The musical world was also involved: in 1858 Berlioz completed his opera *Les Troyens* (The Trojans), based on his childhood reading of Books 2 and 4 of Vergil's *Aeneid* (Létoublon and Volpilhac-Auger 1999: 439–53).

Thus the nineteenth century reestablishes to a considerable degree the prestige of the classical tradition in French literary circles. The new spirit of *laïcité* (secularism), which started at the time of the Revolution but which survived the vicissitudes of political life throughout the period, freed Latin from the control of the Church and allowed a renewed interest in human and humanist values. Much of twentieth-century education was a continuation of these ideals, and the institutions put in place by Napoleon, such as a centralized educational system, the regional *académies* (school districts), and the *grandes écoles* (prestigious higher education institutions where admission is determined by national entrance examinations), have survived to this day.

7   The Twentieth Century

So it is that the generation of authors who were writing before and immediately after World War II was thoroughly steeped in the classical tradition. At the same time, a renewed interest in Greek mythology brought the classical tradition to a wider audience. The excavations of Troy and Mycenae by Heinrich Schliemann in the late nineteenth century had awakened people to the possible historical links between Homer's epics and Greek history, while in a very different field, Freud had suggested the power of myth in his analysis of sexuality. Scholars such as Jean Seznec, working in the Warburg tradition, provided scholarly studies of the history of mythography (Seznec 1953).

It is in the world of the theater, however, that the classical tradition made its clearest mark in twentieth-century literature, not least because of the allegorical potential of Greek myth. Jean Cocteau's *La Machine infernale* (The infernal machine) of 1934 takes on the story of Oedipus, emphasizing the inescapable nature of the tragic plot, but playing with modern, anachronistic allusions. Jean Giraudoux stages a debate on the merits of war and peace in the ironically named *The Trojan War Will Not Take Place* of 1935, while both Sartre and Anouilh take mythical plots for their wartime plays, in particular *The Flies* (1943, Sartre's treatment of the story of Orestes) and *Antigone* (1942, Anouilh's rewriting of Sophocles). The device of choosing a classical setting and retelling an ancient story allows the authors to deal with themes that, in Nazi-occupied France, might not otherwise have got past the censors. Though both writers are concerned with conveying their theories of existentialism, they also comment on the question of totalitarianism and individual freedom in a moving and convincing manner.

In other genres, classical sources continue to inspire poets; for example, Apollinaire's *Le Bestiaire, ou cortège d'Orphée* (The bestiary, or the parade of Orpheus) of 1911, and his *Calligrammes* of 1918, modeled on the *Technopaegnia* of the Greek Anthology (poems formed to represent an object such as Pan pipes or an axe). Other writers such as André Gide use discreet allusions to classical literature in order to approach the question of homosexuality in their writing (for example in *L'Immoraliste* of 1902), a device followed more explicitly in Christiane Rochefort's *Printemps au parking* (Spring in the car park, 1969) with its allusions to Socrates and

Phaedrus. There is thus a sense in which classical intertextuality can act rather as it had done in Montaigne, to alert the careful reader to underlying themes.

With the postwar changes that education has undergone in France, the increasing prestige of science and mathematics, and the recent threats to the teaching of Greek and Latin in French *lycées* (where their position is now quite precarious), the educated general reader, whom writers in the first half of the twentieth century could rely on, is becoming a threatened species. Nevertheless, the classical past continues to exercise its charm, not least in the highly successful comic book figures of Asterix and Obelix, created by René Goscinny and Albert Uderzo.

8   Conclusion

The history of the classical tradition in France has thus been a checkered one. While proficiency in Greek has varied considerably over the centuries, Latin, either with or without the support of the Church, has been a more constant factor. The classical past has represented many different things to French writers and artists: individuality, exuberance, primitivism on the one hand, sobriety, reason, balance on the other. Each epoch has tended to select those elements that it finds most congenial and to form them into its own image of the classical past, a process that will no doubt continue in the future.

FURTHER READING

France (1995) is a good starting point for a general view of the classical tradition in France (see in particular the articles on "Classical influences," "Education," and "Latinity"). Le Goff (1988) provides an excellent overview of the medieval period, while Benson and Constable (1984) contains useful chapters on education (pp. 113–72) and literature (pp. 593–612). For the sixteenth century, Sandy (2002) offers detailed studies on many aspects of the role of classical culture and a full bibliography, while Norton (1999) contains some useful chapters relating to France. Fumaroli (2002) provides an exhaustive study of the impact of classical rhetoric on early modern French writers. Bray (1966) and Adam (1996) still provide an excellent introduction to the seventeenth century, including many aspects of the classical tradition, while, despite its apparently narrow title, there is a great deal of general interest in Létoublon and Volpilhac-Auger (1999). For the modern period, educational trends can be followed in Prost (1986).

CHAPTER TWELVE

Germany and German-Speaking Europe

Volker Riedel

1   The Middle Ages

Classical, predominantly Roman, culture had continued to influence most Germanic
tribes, especially the Ostrogoths but also the Franks under Merovingian rule, following
the late classical and early medieval Christianization of Europe. However the first
major reorientation of the Roman Catholic Middle Ages to its classical inheritance
took place later, from the second half of the eighth to the beginning of the tenth
century, under the Carolingians. Charlemagne (768–814, crowned emperor 800)
initiated this cultural renewal, the so-called "Carolingian Renaissance." Reaching
back to late antiquity in particular, it led to a synthesis of Germanic traditions, classical
culture, and Christianity. Charlemagne undertook a far-reaching reform of the educational system, as part of his attempt to emulate the former Roman emperors and to gain
preeminence for the Frankish state in western Europe, as a counterweight to the
Byzantine empire in the east. He attracted scholars from across Europe to his court,
including the Anglo-Saxon Alcuin (ca. 730–804), the Lombard Paul the Deacon
(ca. 720 – ca. 799), and the Visigoth Theodulf (ca. 760–821). Alcuin, the most
significant scholar of his age, wrote theological treatises and textbooks on grammar,
rhetoric, and dialectic as well as on lyric verse and fables. Yet his main legacy lies in
advancing education by rediscovering classical achievements (especially the concept of
the *septem artes liberales* [seven liberal arts] as constituting the basic curriculum), which
exerted a lasting influence throughout the Middle Ages. Monasteries and cathedral
schools played an important role, in particular the Benedictine abbey of Fulda and its
abbot, the first Germanic theologian and polyhistorian Hrabanus Maurus (ca. 776/
84–856, abbot 822–42), the most influential scholar of the late Carolingian era.

   Collections of glosses and interlinear versions had already been created around 760,
but under Charlemagne and his successors numerous works of Roman literature were

copied. A new script that followed Roman models – the Caroline minuscule – was invented, and Vergil and the Roman historians served as models for poetic and historical writings. Einhard (ca. 770–840), a Frankish scholar, followed Vitruvius in his concern for architectural construction and Suetonius in his *Vita Caroli Magni* (Life of Charlemagne). Biblical poetry such as the Old Saxon *Heliand* (ca. 830) and the Old High German *Book of the Gospels*, which Otfrid von Weißenburg completed around 865, was influenced by Fulda, and thus by late classical traditions. Notker I of St. Gall (Notker Balbulus, ca. 840–912), who composed the *Gesta Karoli* (Deeds of Charles) and the *Vita Sancti Galli* (Life of St. Gall), was the major lyric poet of the early Middle Ages who invented the genre of Latin sequences. Early Romanesque architecture, such as the palace chapel in Aachen and the monastery of Lorsch, followed late classical and early Christian models, as did the visual arts of illuminations, frescoes, small-scale sculpture, jewelry-making, coins, and gems.

   Subsequently the Frankish lands were divided, the German empire was established, and the Saxon house of the Ottonians came to power (first quarter of the tenth to the first quarter of the eleventh century). A renewed, more pronounced orientation toward classical antiquity began under Otto I (936–73, crowned emperor 962) and his successors, which extended into the first years of the reign of the Salian Henry II (1039–56, crowned emperor 1046). The expression *renovatio imperii Romanorum* (renewal of the Roman empire) was used, but Greco-Byzantine influences were also acknowledged. This so-called "Ottonian Renaissance" did, however, retain a greater independence from antiquity than that of the Carolingians. In northern Germany, the chapterhouse of Magdeburg and the monastery at Corvey on the Weser River were centers of spirituality, as were the monasteries of St. Gall and Reichenau on Lake Constance in the South. Literature was composed mostly in Latin. In Saxony, Hrotsvitha von Gandersheim (ca. 935 – ca. 975) modeled her six plays in rhythmic prose on Terence, although she approached his work from a Christian perspective. Widukind von Corvey (died 1004), who wrote the chronicle *Res gestae Saxonicae* (Saxon deeds), was another important Saxon author. Key figures in St. Gall were Ekkehard I (after 900–73), Notker III (Notker Labeo or Notker Teutonicus, ca. 950–1022), and Ekkehard IV (ca. 980–1060). Ekkehard I was possibly the author of the *Waltharius*, a poem, written in Latin hexameters and revised by Ekkehard IV, that often echoes Vergil. The polyhistorian Notker III was the only poet of his generation to translate into German, composing, for instance, a treatise on music in the tradition of Boethius, as well as writing in Latin. Ekkehard IV distinguished himself as a linguist, lyric poet, and chronicler of the monastery of St. Gall. On the island of Reichenau, Hermann von Reichenau (1007–54) wrote among other works a history of the world (*Chronica*) from the birth of Christ up to his own time. The *Ecbasis cuiusdam captivi* (The escape of a certain prisoner) (ca. 936), the oldest animal epic in German literature, uses motifs from Aesop's fables and the *Physiologus* and regularly quotes Vergil, Horace, Ovid, and other Roman writers. In all likelihood it was the work of a monk from Toul in Lothringia. Traditions stemming from late antiquity were continued in architecture in, for example, the cathedral and imperial palace of Magdeburg and in Bamberg Cathedral, but also in illumination (which was now flourishing on the Reichenau) and in jewelry-making.

Under the Frankish dynasty of the Salians from the second quarter of the eleventh to the first quarter of the twelfth century, the power of the monarchy was strengthened. Subsequently, the emperor, the German nobles, and the papacy started to vie for supremacy in the empire during the investiture struggle. These disputes between church and state were conducted in part utilizing Roman rhetoric and dialectic. Most literary production was of a spiritual nature, as part of the movement toward religious renewal and monastic reform. Echoes of classical poetry can be found in the Latin verse epic *Ruodlieb* (mid-eleventh century), composed in leonine (rhyming) hexameters, and in the Latin-German *Hohelied* (High song) poetry and exegesis of Williram von Ebersberg (1048–85). The Romanesque architecture and plastic arts of the eleventh and twelfth centuries employed Roman models and techniques: the cathedrals of Speyer, Worms, and Mainz are based on the Roman basilica and use round arches, columns, pillars, barrel vaults, cupolas, and portals. In sculpture, simple imitation, such as crafting reliefs, was widespread, while metalwork most closely followed antique models.

Medieval culture reached its zenith between the mid-twelfth and the mid-thirteenth centuries during a period of change and innovation in Europe, the "twelfth century (or Hohenstaufen, after the ruling family) renaissance." This Swabian dynasty saw the empire as extending across Germany, Italy, and Burgundy, and as independent of the papacy, in accordance with a theory developed since the late tenth century and systematized from the end of the eleventh century. Partly based on Jerome and Orosius, four empires were seen to follow one after the other: the Babylonian, that of the Medes and Persians, the Greek, and the Roman. The theory then states that the rule of the Roman Empire – the final one before the world comes to an end – had been passed on by the Romans to the Franks and then on to the Germans, through the *translatio imperii* (passing on of the empire). Roman law was researched extensively, increasingly so in the late medieval and early modern period, and its influence is still palpable today. In 1157 during the reign of Frederick I (Barbarossa, 1152–90, crowned emperor 1155), the empire was first called *Sacrum imperium*, as well as simply *imperium* or *imperium Romanum*; later *Sacrum imperium Romanum* (Holy Roman empire) was commonly used. Frederick II (1212–50, crowned emperor 1220) even replicated elements of the emperor cults of late antiquity and introduced religious overtones to his rule.

As a consequence of the Crusades, medieval culture at its high point became better acquainted with Byzantine and Arabic, and through them Greek, culture. Following Augustine and Boethius, the theology and philosophy of the early Middle Ages had been characterized more by Neoplatonic, and less by Aristotelian, influences. But Aristotle's works, which had been translated from Greek into Arabic, were now again made more widely accessible by translating the Arabic itself into Latin. Albertus Magnus (ca. 1193–1280), the most significant German scholar of this period, wrote theological and scientific treatises. Through them and his pupil Thomas Aquinas, he ensured that a Christianized Aristotelian approach provided the foundation for the flourishing of Scholasticism. Supported by the knights, the literature of the Hohenstaufen period turned to worldly, and in particular courtly, concerns, with its most important works composed in German. Epic verse was the dominant genre, beginning with the *Alexanderlied* (Song of Alexander), written around 1130/50 by Lamprecht, a priest from Trier, after a French model. The *Eneit* of Heinrich von Veldeke (between 1140 and 1150 – before 1210) followed the French *Roman d'Énéas* as well as using Vergil's own *Aeneid*, showing the way for the courtly and artful epic of the high Middle Ages. The poem presents exemplary knightly behavior, fulfilling the requirements of courtly ceremony, itself founded on the *hohe Minne* (courtly love): in a departure from Vergil, increased attention is paid to Aeneas' love for Lavinia, which is juxtaposed to the hero's passionate relationship with Dido. This epic was completed around 1200 at the court of the Count of Thuringia, a center for the reception of classical literature. From Thuringia, we also have the *Trojaroman* (Story of Troy) of Herbort von Fritzlar (after 1190) after Benoît de Sainte-Maures' *Roman de Troie*, and the rendition of Ovid's *Metamorphoses* in German rhyming couplets by Albrecht von Halberstadt (ca. 1210/17). Ovidian influences are also at work in goliardic verse (Archipoeta [born ca. 1130/40]), in the *Carmina Burana* (mid-thirteenth century), in the works of *Minnesänger* (minnesingers), and in the Latin animal epic *Ysengrimus* (Wolf), a satire on courtly and monastic lives (1146–8). Otto von Freising's (ca. 1114–58) universal history *Chronica sive Historia de duabus civitatibus* (Chronicle or history of two states), modeled on Augustine, marks the high point of medieval historiography. Classical influences were less visible in architecture and sculpture, although stones from antique buildings were increasingly reused. However, a bronze head of Frederick I, the Head of Cappenberg, cast soon after 1155, portrays him wearing the fillet and laurel crown of a Roman emperor, and under Frederick II larger-scale sculpture developed at a greater pace.

The Gothic style, which was predominant in Europe from the thirteenth to the fifteenth century, was less closely connected to antiquity. Although architects retained the basic shape of the basilica of the early Christian Roman church, classical decorative architectural elements and imagery were only employed in a limited way. A clear indication is the shift from the round to the pointed arch. Sculpture, drawing, and painting only occasionally looked back to antiquity, and even then in only rudimentary fashion. There were, however, many illustrations to classical texts, as demanded by their subject matter, and antique models for sepulchral sculpture and epitaphs gained in importance. Latin itself continued to play a crucial role during the late Middle Ages. With the rise of the urban centers and their citizens, it now came to be taught more in the Latin schools of the towns than in the monastic and cathedral schools.

2   The Renaissance

The court of Charles IV (1346–78, crowned emperor 1355) of the house of Luxembourg in Prague was the first to show signs of the Renaissance, even if only briefly and limited to this area of the empire. The Italian humanists Francesco Petrarca and Cola di Rienzo both resided there temporarily. The humanism of the Renaissance actually began to take hold in Germany from the middle of the fifteenth century. The invention of letterpress printing contributed to this, as did the humanists' dominance in Italy and their contacts with German scholars, and the passing of the title of emperor from the Luxembourg to the Habsburg dynasty (1438). The fall of Constantinople to the Turks (1453) and the subsequent expulsion of Greek scholars brought a deeper understanding of Greek to western Europe, which up to then had been influenced mostly by Latin. The Renaissance was marked by a number of important changes: from a culture of courts and knights to that of an urban citizenry, from the emperor's and pope's claims to universal rule to the emergence of the nation state, of geographically based rule, and of different confessions. During the Middle Ages the classical inheritance provided the basis for culture, insofar as it could be reconciled with Christianity. The "rebirth" of antiquity, however, brought a very different, new approach, as illustrated by the increasingly secular nature of people's lives, the exploration of the globe and of humanity, and the regard for the individual, nature, and the nation. A new, historical perspective on antiquity also emerged, as did the emulation of classical Latin, the development of anticlerical tendencies, and the emergence of modern national literatures in their different vernaculars.

Even though the claim to resurrect the Roman Empire had failed with the disintegration of the rule of the Hohenstaufen, it was renewed by the Habsburg emperor Charles V (1519–56, crowned emperor 1530). Only thereafter did the term *imperium Romanum* lose its claim to universality and come to designate one empire among many, in which sense it continued to be used as a formal title until 1806.

Philosophy and natural sciences, legal and state theory, the arts and especially literature, concomitant with philology and pedagogy, all now reached back to classical thought. Philosophers left behind the now-mechanistic Aristotelian approach of scholasticism and gave increasing importance to Plato and Neoplatonism.

Even before the main period of German humanism, Nikolaus von Kues (Nicolaus Cusanus, 1401–64) spent many years in Italy where he discovered, among other manuscripts, 12 comedies by Plautus. He strove for a synthesis of scholasticism, mysticism, antiquity, and modern natural sciences. The crucial mediator, however, between Italian and German humanism was Enea Silvio Piccolomini (1458–64, Pope Pius II), who lived in Germany for 21 years altogether, including 10 in Vienna, which became a cultural center under Frederick III (1440–93, crowned emperor 1452). These towns and universities in southern and western Germany were also centers of humanism: Basle, Strasbourg, Schlettstadt, Heidelberg, Tübingen, Augsburg, Ingolstadt, and Cologne; in the sixteenth century they were joined by Erfurt, Wittenberg, and Leipzig in central Germany.

While early German humanism (up to around 1485) owed much to Italian influence, it soon developed its own national confidence as well. It focused mostly on absorbing what was already available, through collections of models and translations, but began to innovate in lyric poetry, historiography, and rhetoric. Its most significant literary contributors were Albrecht von Eyb (1420–75), Peter Luder (ca. 1410 – after 1474), Heinrich Steinhöwel (1412–82), and Rudolf Agricola (1444–85). Albrecht von Eyb composed a number of writings about the city of Bamberg, edited the anthology *Margarita poetica* (a rhetorical textbook and compendium of classical and humanist quotations and maxims), and translated two of Plautus' comedies. Peter Luder, the first representative of German humanism at a university, was famous for his 1456 inaugural lecture at Heidelberg and for his *Elegia Petri Luderi poetae clarissimi ad Panphilam amicam suam singularem* (Elegy of the most famous poet Peter Luder to his most particular [girl-]friend Panphila), which contains many reminiscences of Vergil and other Roman authors. In it Luder shows a considerable poetic self-confidence, introducing the elegiac genre and meter to Germany. The main work of Heinrich Steinhöwel is the *Esopus*, an edition, translation, and commentary of a range of classical, medieval, and humanist fables and stories, which is marked by a distinctly secular perspective. Rudolf Agricola was the first German humanist to win international acclaim with his voluminous and wide-ranging works. His speech in praise of philosophy and the other sciences given at the inception of the academic year at the University of Ferrara in 1476 stands out, displaying an optimistic view of life.

   The time between 1485 and 1520 can be described as the high point of humanism in Germany. In addition to the editing and translating of texts, new works were increasingly being created, from plays, a number of lyrical genres, letters, and treatises to a range of satirical and humorous writings. The first significant German poet composing in Latin and the greatest lyrical talent of German humanism was Conrad Celtis (1459–1508). From 1497 he was active in Vienna, which continued to be a cultural center under Maximilian I (1493–1519, crowned emperor 1508). His programmatic ode *Ad Apollinem* (To Apollo) proclaims the Muses to be at home in Germany forthwith, while his inaugural lecture of 1492 at Ingolstadt asks his audience to strive for fame, virtue, and true immortality following the examples of classical philosophers, poets, and orators. Celtis wrote plays (such as *Ludus Dianae* [Play of Diana]), elegies (the *Quattuor libri amorum secundum quattuor latera Germaniae* [Four books of loves according to the four sides of Germany], his greatest work), odes, and epigrams. Sebastian Brant (1457–1521) employed in his *Narrenschiff* (Ship of fools) countless classical examples; particularly impressive are Odysseus and Heracles. Jacob Locher (1471–1528) translated this work into Latin and wrote poems, speeches, and plays (such as the *Iudicium Paridis de pomo aureo*, or Paris awarding the golden apple). The motif of a contest (judgment of Paris and Heracles at the crossroads) was one of the most popular in the literature and paintings of the sixteenth and seventeenth centuries. The first German rendition of Vergil's *Aeneid* by Thomas Murner (1475–1537) was a significant achievement. Desiderius Erasmus of Rotterdam (1466–1536) received recognition as the undisputed leader of German humanism; the most important among his many and varied writings are the *Adagia* (a collection of Latin sayings, maxims, parables, examples, and metaphors with a commentary and index), the witty *Morias encomion seu laus stultitiae* (Praise of folly), and his critical edition of the New Testament.

   During the height of humanism, German sculpture, design, and painting developed with particular confidence, taking classical subjects and forms as their guideline and focusing on the secular world. The newly discovered physical nature and beauty of the human form stood at the center of German Renaissance art. Albrecht Dürer (1471–1528) was the artist whose theory and practice were most strongly influenced by antiquity. The Isenheimer Altar by Mathis Gothart-Nithart (Grünewald, ca. 1460–1528) also deserves to be mentioned.

The polemical and anticlerical phase of German humanism began around 1510. It culminated in the Hebrew controversy between Johannes Reuchlin (1455–1522) and the converted Jew Johannes Pfefferkorn of Cologne (1469–1521), who called for all Jewish writings to be burned. All major German humanists supported Reuchlin. The satire *Epistolae obscurorum virorum* (Letters of obscure men), published in 1515 and 1517, attacked scholasticism and its nonclassical Latin as well as the feigned spirituality of the clergy. The main author of the second part of the "Dark Men's Letters" was Ulrich von Hutten (1488–1523), who shortly afterwards started to write in German instead of Latin. His letter of October 25, 1518, to the Nuremberg patrician Willibald Pirckheimer (1470–1530), one of the most brilliant figures of the humanism of the Renaissance in Germany, includes these words: *O saeculum! O litterae! Iuvat vivere* (O times! O literature! It is pleasant to be alive). The circle of humanists in Erfurt around Konrad Mutianus Rufus (1471–1526) also gained recognition; it included Crotus Rubeanus (1480–1539), another author of the "Dark Men's Letters," Helius Eobanus Hessus (1488–1540), who was noted for his eclogues, heroides, and elegies, and the epigrammatist Euricius Cordus (1486–1535).

From about 1520 German humanism was more or less marked by the Reformation and mirrored the changes and differentiated developments that accompanied it. Even though the Reformation had been prepared for, to an extent, by humanism, and even though Martin Luther (1483–1546) as well as Huldrych Zwingli (1484–1531) and Johann Calvin (1509–64) had been influenced by it, the *studia humanitatis* (liberal arts) became the medium and foundation that led to the *studia sacrarum litterarum* (religious studies). Luther showed concern for ensuring that the Greek and Latin languages, and comedy after the model of Terence, were taught, as well as famously translating the Bible into German. He himself translated 13 of Aesop's fables in such a way as to emphasize their moral, didactic nature, in contrast to Steinhöwel. His friend and fellow reformer Philipp Melanchthon (1497–1560) wrote textbooks on rhetoric, grammar, and dialectics, as well as publishing editions, commentaries, and his own poetry. As *praeceptor Germaniae* (Germany's teacher), he founded the new, Protestant range of schools and universities. This period saw the creation of a literature of debate and controversy, often satirical, employing classical elements (e.g., from Aristophanes, Lucian, and the rhetorical tradition). Latin, then German, educational drama developed, as did numerous lyrical writings, now taking the form in particular of learned poetry by scholars and priests, which significantly limited the scope of subject matter covered by humanist poetry. Philology continued to flourish, and a number of translations were published, foremost among them being the rendition of the *Odyssey* by Simon Schaidenreisser (ca. 1500–72). Animal fables and epic were especially valued. Even passion plays and the songs of *Meistersänger* (master-singers) featured classical motifs (Hans Sachs [1494–1576]).

Biblical, classical, and civic-urban elements combined in the visual arts (Lucas Cranach the Elder [1472–1553], Hans Holbein the Younger [1497/8–1543]). Classical elements were used as features in secular buildings such as town halls (e.g., Görlitz) and palaces (Dresden, Heidelberg), and in Saxony the first Protestant palace chapels were designed (Torgau, Augustusburg).

The humanism of the post-Reformation in particular witnessed major scientific and technological achievements. Georgius Agricola (1491–1555), a geologist and mineralogist, founded the modern science of coal and iron mining utilizing the works of Hippocrates, Aristotle, Theophrastus, Pliny the Elder, and other classical authors. Influenced by the scientific approach of Hippocrates and Galen, the doctor, chemist, and philosopher Paracelsus (1493–1541) breathed new life into medicine. The mathematician and astronomer Nicolaus Copernicus (1473–1543) took inspiration from the Pythagoreans, Plato, Aristarchus of Samos, and Proclus, and developed his heliocentric view of the universe as a continuation of and improvement on Ptolemy and in critical dialogue with Aristotle's physics. Even the cosmology of Johannes Kepler (1571–1630) was still rooted in Renaissance Platonism and in its classical sources, which influenced both the mathematical understanding of the universe and the concept of a universal harmony.

3   The Baroque

Antiquity played a less significant role in Germany during absolutism and the Baroque period (seventeenth and first half of the eighteenth century) than it had done in the Renaissance. Latin gradually gave way in some areas to a modern German literary idiom, and classical authorities were valued less as the natural sciences increasingly relied on experimentation and individual observation. Received paradigms paled in view of the upheavals of that period ("Aber wenn der Tod uns trifft, / Was hilft da Homerus' Schrift?", or "But when Death reaches us, / What use is Homer's verse?" [Paul Gerhardt; cf. Riedel 2000: 83]). However, the engagement with antiquity remained notable in politics, philosophy, literature, music, visual arts, and architecture. This engagement served to develop, and partly already to question, a courtly-aristocratic culture in particular in the decades following the Thirty Years' War (1618–48).

Philosophy and political theory, as well as literary works on historical topics, were dominated by a (neo-)Stoicism influenced heavily by Seneca and first expounded in the treatise *De constantia* (On constancy) by the Dutch philosopher Justus Lipsius (1547–1606). This (neo-)Stoicism was closely linked to a Tacitean way of thinking. It had its origins in the crisis of the European monarchies during the religious and civil wars of the sixteenth and seventeenth centuries and consciously borrowed from authors of the Principate.

Martin Opitz (1597–1639) held the greatest significance for Baroque literature. His speech *Aristarchus sive de contemptu linguae Teutonicae* (Aristarchus or on the neglect of the German language) called for German to be used, and his *Buch von der Deutschen Poeterey* (Book on German poetry), partly based on Aristotle, Horace, and Quintilian as well as the poetics and poetry of the Renaissance, laid the intellectual foundation for later writers. He led the way for lyric and the novel (including pastoral poetry), and his translations of Seneca's *Troades* and Sophocles' *Antigone* became models for later tragedy. Lyric poetry mostly followed Horace (Paul Fleming [1609–40], Jacob Balde [1604–68]). The best-known playwright of the time was Andreas Gryphius (1616–64), who wrote four original tragedies on historical-political subject matter, among them *Papinian*, which was set in the late Principate and reflected the contrast between legal ideals and practice under absolutism and the uneasy situation of a bourgeois hero serving at court.

The history of the early Baroque period was marked by the Thirty Years' War, while its outlook on the world was shaped by the predominance of the *vanitas* concept, and its aesthetics by a classicism following the influence of the poets of the Renaissance. The high Baroque of the second half of the seventeenth century reflected the postwar period and an increasingly feudal society. The language employed was elegant, sometimes bombastic, and motifs relating to the enjoyment of life and love replaced those of death and the grave, changing from *docere* (teaching) to *delectare* (giving pleasure) and from Horace to Ovid. Christian Hofmann von Hofmannswaldau (1617–79) modeled his poetry on Ovid in particular; Daniel Casper von Lohenstein (1635–83) wrote four tragedies on Roman subjects (*Cleopatra*, *Agrippina*, *Epicharis*, and *Sophonisbe*), which thematized conflicts between reason and passion and exemplified the ambiguity of political action while praising exemplary conduct. His novel *Großmütiger Feldherr Arminius* (Magnanimous General Arminius), marked by heroism and gallantry, sets Germans against Romans. Other novels (such as the *Römische Octavia* [Roman Octavia] by Herzog Anton Ulrich von Braunschweig [1633–1714]) and epics likewise bear witness to a courtly approach to Roman history. In contrast, the most important work in prose of this time, *Der Abentheurliche Simplicissimus Teutsch* (The adventurous greatest German simpleton) by Hans Jacob Christoffel von Grimmelshausen (1621/2–76), is rooted in the traditions of popular poetry, although even this novel contains numerous traces of classical writings, especially the *Odyssey.* The last of the well-known Baroque poets, Johann Christian Günther (1695–1723), preferred those of Ovid's poems that deal with more serious subject matters.

In music and musical theater, opera, which had first been developed around 1600 in Italy, claimed to revive Greek drama. Opitz had already introduced this genre to Germany with his libretto of 1627 for the opera *Dafne*, composed by Heinrich Schütz (1585–1672). Classical myth and history continued to supply the subject matter for most operas and also influenced oratorios and cantatas: Georg Philipp Telemann (1681–1767) wrote the operas *Orpheus und Eurydike*, *Der geduldige Sokrates* (Patient Socrates), and *Omphale* as well as the cantata *Ino*. The works of Georg Friedrich Händel (1685–1759) include the operas *Giulio Cesare*, *Xerxes*, and *Deidamia* along with the pastorals *Apollo e Dafne* and *Acis e Galatea*, as well as the oratorios *Semele* and *Hercules*. Some of the cantatas of Johann Sebastian Bach (1685–1750) also feature antique myths (*Der zufriedengestellte Äolus* [The satisfied Aeolus], *Streit zwischen Phöbus und Pan* [Contest between Phoebus and Pan], and *Wahl des Herkules* [Hercules' choice]).

Greek myth and Roman history offered the most popular motifs for painters and sculptors, and again Ovid's *Metamorphoses* was a particular favorite. A number of aristocratic courts started archaeological excavations and collections, and such collections of antiques became a usual feature of a ruler's displays at his court. Pediments, columns, and friezes were retained, and architects followed the prescriptions of Vitruvius, although they did move further away from classical models in other respects. Garden design and architecture was informed by classical myth, particularly when the subject matter suited the cult of the ruler (Hercules), and important Baroque gardens were created in Vienna, Dresden, Kassel, and Stuttgart.

Brandenburg/Prussia had an especially strong relationship to classical antiquity. Friedrich Wilhelm (the "Great Elector," 1640–88) was influenced by (neo-)Stoic thought and had already given Roman culture a key role at his court. Statues imitating antique sculpture and pseudoclassical paintings adorned the palace at Berlin, and classically inspired figures were set in the "Lustgarten" (Pleasure garden). Friedrich III (1688–1713, as Friedrich I King in Prussia from 1701) continued this policy with increased vigor. Among the sculptures commissioned by him, the most noteworthy is a statue of himself wearing the dress of a Roman emperor with reminiscences of portrayals of Apollo and Alexander, together with an equestrian sculpture of his father based on that of Marcus Aurelius. He renovated and extended the palace in Berlin, added to the collection of antiques, encouraged the creation of the *Thesaurus Brandenburgicus*, the greatest catalogue of antiquities of its time, and founded the academies of the arts and sciences.

4   From Classicism to Romanticism

Classical antiquity was most influential during the Age of Reason, the "Weimarer Klassik" (Weimar classicism) and the romantic period (from the mid-eighteenth to the early nineteenth centuries). This period was characterized by the gradual development of a bourgeois society, by the growing perception of the *Querelle des anciens et des modernes* (quarrel of ancients and moderns), and by the resulting tensions between accepting the classical heritage as normative on the one hand and as historical on the other. Traditional rules were discarded while the source material received renewed attention, and classical life – rather than art – was seen as exemplary. This entailed looking less toward classical Rome and more toward Greece, thus emphasizing issues relating to the human condition in general rather than political concerns.

During this period, the reception of antiquity in Germany was closely linked to the rise of classical studies and to the development of a neohumanist notion of education and educational reform. Following the great achievements of Renaissance humanism, at the beginning of the eighteenth century classical philology had focused mostly on compilations, polyhistory, and collections of trifles. However, the increasingly philological and historical approach to antiquity prompted first a reform of how the classics were taught at school and university by philologists such as Johann Matthias Gesner (1691–1761) and Johann August Ernesti (1707–81). Christian Gottlob Heyne (1729–1812) and Friedrich August Wolf (1759–1824) then became the founders of an approach that looked for an encompassing exploration of antiquity that meant to form both the mind and taste. This so-called neohumanism called for a return to the classical sources of European literature, as had the humanism of the Renaissance. It, too, centered on the notion of humanizing society through education and mastery of the languages, but in contrast to earlier humanism, it looked back primarily to Greek, not Roman, art, literature, philosophy, and ways of thinking. One of the most important neohumanists was Wilhelm von Humboldt (1767–1835), a linguist, art historian, educator, and liberal politician whose reform of humanist secondary education and founding of the University of Berlin left their mark on the German systems of secondary and higher education. Friedrich Immanuel Niethammer (1766–1848) and Friedrich Thiersch (1784–1860) helped realize the same ideas in Bavaria. During the 1820s the influence of neohumanism saw large sections of German society sympathize with the Greek struggle for independence from the Turks (philhellenism).

Until the middle of the eighteenth century the interests of the courts still held sway over people's thought and actions, which were guided by the key principles of French classicism and clearly belonged to the Rococo period. The architect Georg Wenzeslaus von Knobelsdorff (1699–1753) knew how to combine elegance and austerity, Rococo and classicism in his buildings such as the Berlin opera, the city palace of Potsdam, and the palace of Sanssouci during the reign of Friedrich II (1740–86). Antiquity was ever present in the gardens of Sanssouci, serving to heighten the perceived status of the monarch's rule. Johann Christoph Gottsched (1700–66) attempted to reform German literature, especially drama, with his *Versuch einer critischen Dichtkunst* (Attempt at a critical art of poetry) and his *Deutsche Schaubühne* (German stage), guided by the rules and models of the "ancients." Lyricists like Friedrich von Hagedorn (1708–54) and Johann Wilhelm Ludwig Gleim (1719–1803) followed the examples of Anacreon and Horace.

A new start can be clearly discerned from the mid-eighteenth century onwards. In literature there are the three great writers of the high Age of Reason: Friedrich Gottlieb Klopstock (1724–1803), Gotthold Ephraim Lessing (1729–81), and Christoph Martin Wieland (1733–1813), as well as the thinker Johann Joachim Winckelmann (1717–68). Klopstock's epic *Der Messias* (The Messiah) introduced the hexameter and Greek mode of expression to German literature, and his odes did the same for other classical meters. Although he increasingly came to prefer Germanic to classical mythology, he remained an admirer of the "ancients" throughout his life. In his works on literary theory (the best known of which are *Laocoon* and *Hamburgische Dramaturgie* [Hamburg art of theater]), Lessing took his lead primarily from classical poets and Aristotle's *Poetics*, thereby clearly shifting the emphasis from Roman to Greek antiquity, without, however, rejecting the Romans in principle. His poetry repeatedly treated subjects from Greek and Roman history (*Philotas, Emilia Galotti*) or followed classical models (as in his fables and epigrams). Finally, Wieland allowed himself to be heavily influenced by antiquity in his considerable literary oeuvre: in his novels *Die Geschichte des Agathon* (The story of Agathon), *Die Geschichte der Abderiten* (The story of the Abderites), *Peregrinus Proteus, Agathodämon,* and *Aristipp und einige seiner Zeitgenossen* (Aristipp and some of his contemporaries); in verse epics such as *Musarion*; in Singspielen (small-scale, often comic operas) like *Alceste* and *Die Wahl des Herkules* (The choice of Hercules); in translations (Cicero, Horace, Lucian); and in essays. Unlike many of his contemporaries he avoided any overbearing enthusiasm, any value judgment between Greece and Rome, and any one-sided preference for classical Athens.

Winckelmann clearly provided the main inspiration for the "classical" German view of antiquity (including its illusionist tendencies). The founder of classical archaeology and of art history was the first to set the monuments of classical art in an historical context; he described the essence of this art (in contrast to the Baroque) as "eine edle

Einfalt und eine stille Größe" (a noble simplicity and a solemn magnificence); he took his lead primarily from Greek art and saw political freedom as lying at the root of its beauty. Certain more normative views, which are evident in his early treatise *Gedanken über die Nachahmung der griechischen Werke in der Malerei und Bildhauerkunst* (Thoughts on the imitation of Greek works in painting and sculpture), gave way to a historical perspective in his main work *Geschichte der Kunst des Altertums* (History of classical art).

Johann Gottfried Herder (1744–1803) helped define the reception of antiquity during the Storm and Stress period and Weimar classicism, building on and grappling with Winckelmann and Lessing. His view of antiquity was characterized by a tension between admiring it and viewing it from a historical perspective, by the greater attention he paid to classical life than art, by an emphasis on the differences between Greece and Rome, and by his interest in Greek myth as well as the toning down and humanization of classical paradigms. The most important figure in German literature around 1800 in general, as well as for its relations to antiquity, was Johann Wolfgang

Figure 12.1 Johann Joachim Winckelmann monument in Stendal. Photo: The Winckelmann Museum, Stendal

Goethe (1749–1832). Already as a young poet in the first half of the 1770s, he felt a strong connection to the Greeks, whom he saw as exemplary for a natural way of life, for a forceful voicing of one's own claim to live, and for an attitude of rebellion (*Prometheus, Die Leiden des jungen Werthers* [The sorrows of young Werther]). During his first decade in Weimar he proclaimed a harmonic and humane view of the Greeks (*Iphigenie auf Tauris* [Iphigenia in Tauris]). The "rebirth" he experienced in Italy (1786–8) was primarily a "rebirth" under the overwhelming influence of antiquity, which he felt in its landscape and artifacts. The years between his return from Italy and 1805 saw his most intense engagement with antiquity. He was receptive to love elegy, the art of the epigram, and the didactic poetry of the Romans, but his predominant interest was in the Greeks (epic poetry, lyric, drama). His book *Winckelmann und sein Jahrhundert* (Winckelmann and his century) marked the culmination and conclusion of Goethe's theoretical efforts (which did not always avoid a normative classicism). The final quarter century of his life shows a continuing appreciation of the "ancients" as well as an extension of his interests and thinking beyond antiquity, as shown, for example, in *Faust II*.

The friends of the young Goethe during the Storm and Stress period (Jakob Michael Reinhold Lenz [1751–92], Friedrich Maximilian Klinger [1752–1831], Friedrich Müller [1749–1825]) were familiar with antiquity, as were Johann Jakob Wilhelm Heinse (1746–1803), the poets of the Hainbund of Göttingen (among whom Johann Heinrich Voß [1751–1826] stands out for his translation of Homer), and Friedrich Schiller (1759–1805). Roman political motifs predominate in Schiller's early work; in later works, such as the poems *Die Götter Griechenlandes* (The gods of Greece), *Das Ideal und das Leben* (The ideal and life), or *Das Glück* (Fortune) and theoretical writings like *Über Anmut und Würde* (On grace and dignity) and *Über die ästhetische Erziehung des Menschen in einer Reihe von Briefen* (On the aesthetic education of man in a series of letters), it is especially Greece that for him embodies a world of harmony, beauty, and unity of opposites. He was, however, well aware of the differences between ancient and modern times and of the fact that Greek art is unique and not to be repeated (*Über naive und sentimentalische Dichtung* [On naive and sentimental poetry]), and his late poems often exhibit elegiac traits.

Winckelmann also showed the way for the development of visual art and architecture toward harmony and symmetry, clear organization, and delimitation. Among his friends were the painter Anton Raphael Mengs (1728–79) and the architect Friedrich Wilhelm Freiherr von Erdmannsdorff (1736–1800), who created the first purely classicist building in Germany in the palace of Wörlitz near Dessau. Other important exponents of classicism, which remained the dominant style in sculpture and architecture until the middle of the nineteenth century, were the painter and etcher Johann Heinrich Wilhelm Tischbein (1751–1829), and the sculptors Johann Heinrich von Dannecker (1758–1841), Gottfried Schadow (1764–1850), and Christian Daniel Rauch (1777–1857). Significant architects were Carl Gotthard Langhans (1732–1808), who designed the Brandenburg Gate in Berlin under inspiration from the Propylaea of the Acropolis; Karl Friedrich Schinkel (1781–1841), who left his mark on the townscape of Berlin and Potsdam (Schauspielhaus, Altes Museum, Alte Wache and Nikolaikirche) by using classical elements freely and creatively; and Leo von Klenze

(1784–1864), whose buildings define the city of Munich by echoing the architecture of Greek temples. The gardens of Wörlitz and Weimar were shaped largely by references to antiquity, and universities first began to collect casts of ancient sculptures.

Enthusiasm for antiquity, mythical subject matters, and classicist inclinations likewise were the hallmarks of the operas of Christoph Willibald Gluck (1714–87). They were meant to match Greek tragedy in their truth, simplicity, and greatness, and their protagonists were characterized by humanity and dignity (*Orfeo ed Euridice, Alceste, Paride ed Elena, Iphigénie en Aulide, Iphigénie en Tauride, Écho et Narcisse*). Other composers like Joseph Haydn (1732–1809) with his opera *L'Anima del Filosofo (Orfeo ed Euridice)*, Wolfgang Amadeus Mozart (1756–91) with *Idomeneo* and *La Clemenza di Tito*, Ludwig van Beethoven with the ballet *Gli uomini di Prometheus* (The men of Prometheus), and Franz Schubert (1797–1828) with his song *Lied des Orpheus, als er in die Hölle ging* (Song of Orpheus as he descended to hell) took their plots from classical mythology and history.

During the eighteenth century, classical thinking and schools lost their fundamental importance to philosophy, while it remained characteristic to refer back especially to Plato but also to Heraclitus, the Neoplatonists, and classical natural law. This is true of Immanuel Kant (1724–1804), Johann Gottlieb Fichte (1762–1814), Friedrich Schleiermacher (1768–1834), Friedrich Wilhelm Schelling (1775–1854), Georg Wilhelm Friedrich Hegel (1770–1831), and Arthur Schopenhauer (1788–1860).

In contrast to the writers of Weimar classicism, those of the next generation (Friedrich Hölderlin [1770–1843] and the young Friedrich Schlegel [1772–1829]) often felt an even stronger and more impassioned affinity to Greece, under the influence of the French Revolution and its consequences. They did, however, also introduce some more or less obvious changes. While Hölderlin did not yet question the exemplary nature of Greek art or life in any way, his view of antiquity is determined less by "Apollonian" harmony than "Dionysian" dynamism. In his novel *Hyperion* and in many of his poems, he reflects the fall of the ancient world in his tragic-elegiac attitude. Classical antiquity was also part of the past for Jean Paul (Johann Paul Friedrich Richter, 1763–1825) and for August Wilhelm Schlegel (1767–1845), in the novel *Titan* and the elegy *Rome*, respectively. Heinrich von Kleist's (1777–1811) *Amphitryon* introduces tragic conflict into a subject matter traditionally employed for comedies, and shows a world characterized by deceit, confused emotions, and loss of identity. In his *Penthesilea* he focused for the first time on the "dark side" of an archaic-barbaric antiquity and explicitly freed himself from a "classical" view of the Greeks. Friedrich Schlegel was the leading theorist of the early Romantics. He developed from a critic to a defender of modernism and called for the creation of a "new mythology." The philosopher Schelling and the classicist Georg Friedrich Creuzer (1771–1858) also contributed greatly to this novel renaissance of myth. In general, romantic writers, especially after 1800, turned away from using classical themes to Christian, medieval, oriental, and modern (national) subject matters. We can even see classical antiquity become less valued in favor of Christianity (for instance in the novella *Das Marmorbild* [The marble image] by Joseph Freiherr von Eichendorff [1788–1857]). As heir of the "Kunstperiode," the Austrian writer Franz Grillparzer (1791–1872) was the only one to attempt to portray common human experiences through classical materials (*Sappho,*

Das goldene Vließ [The golden fleece], *Des Meeres und der Liebe Wellen* [The ocean's and love's waves]). Romantic painting likewise did not view the art of the "ancients" as providing guiding rules and principles, least of all aesthetic norms.

5 The Nineteenth Century

The nineteenth century (including the first decades of the twentieth century) represents the "great time" of German classical studies, which had been developed on strict historical foundations with meticulous research into philological, historical, and archaeological details since August Boeckh (1785–1867). Well-known scholars of this time included the ancient historian Theodor Mommsen (1817–1903), the philologists Friedrich Ritschl (1806–76), Friedrich Leo (1851–1914), and Ulrich von Wilamowitz-Moellendorff (1848–1931), the historians of philosophy Eduard Zeller (1814–96) and Hermann Diels (1848–1922), and the archaeologists Ernst Curtius (1814–96), Heinrich Schliemann (1822–90), Wilhelm Dörpfeld (1853–1940), and Adolf Furtwängler (1853–1907). It was during this period that academic projects on a grand scale, such as the "Bibliotheca Teubneriana" series of classical texts, the compendia *Realencyclopädie der classischen Altertumswissenschaft* (Factual encyclopedia of the study of classical antiquity) and *Handbuch der classischen Altertumswissenschaft* (Manual of the study of classical antiquity), the dictionary *Thesaurus linguae Latinae* (Treasure of the Latin language), and the collections of inscriptions *Inscriptiones Graecae* (Greek inscriptions) and *Corpus inscriptionum Latinarum* (Collection of Latin inscriptions), were initiated. Excavations commenced in Troy, Olympia, Aegina, and Pergamon. Scientific academies, universities with their departments of classical studies, museums (especially in Berlin and Munich), and collections of antiquities and casts became important centers of academic life.

In contrast to fundamental research with a positivistic bend, the Swiss scholars Johann Jacob Bachofen (1815–87) and Jacob Burckhardt (1818–97) aimed at a new appreciation of classical culture as a whole, which included turning away from an idealizing view of the Greeks. New theoretical approaches were also developed in philosophy: in the sociocritical reading of antiquity by Karl Marx (1818–83) and Friedrich Engels (1820–95) as well as in Friedrich Nietzsche's (1844–1900) ecstatic "Dionysian" view of antiquity, which was markedly different from the harmonic "Apollonian" understanding of the classical period.

These scholars threw light on the "dark side" of antiquity. The detailed research in the field of classical studies also mostly avoided the preceding period's tendency to emphasize the heroic. Yet traditional views still prevailed in popular writings and in the educational system, which mostly continued Humboldt's approach, though with somewhat less breadth. Although the position of the "Humaniora" remained secure, changes in literature that had been developing since 1800 gained currency, and a "realistic" rendering of a bourgeois environment became dominant. The reception of classical antiquity lost much of its importance during the course of the nineteenth century – not so much quantitatively as in its perceived role as offering a dominant worldview and/or as in its artistic standards. On the one hand, we see a flattening, trivialization, and derivative imitation of the classics – Gustav Schwab (1792–1850), for instance, explicitly recounted the "*schönsten* Sagen des klassischen Altertums" ("*most beautiful* myths of classical antiquity"); on the other, the tendency to use antiquity for nationalistic purposes grew steadily (clearly from 1866, the year of Prussia's victory over Austria), as in the novel *Ein Kampf um Rom* (A battle for Rome) by Felix Dahn (1834–1912).

Significant works with classical motifs were, however, still being produced. Heinrich Heine (1797–1856) definitely recognized antiquity as part of the past and often satirized it, but he also saw it, in the end, as the goal of his elegiac longing. Christian Dietrich Grabbe (1801–36) portrayed historical processes in a number of plays on Roman subject matters without any illusions. Democratic convictions and a sharp anticlerical stance were met by a strong inclination toward the formal and classical in August Graf von Platen-Hallermünde (1796–1835). Because he felt that his inner nature resonated in sympathy with that of Anacreon, Theocritus, Catullus, Horace, and Tibullus, Eduard Mörike (1804–75) liked to render personal subjects in quasi-classical tones. Friedrich Hebbel (1813–63) wrote *Gyges und sein Ring* (Gyges and his ring), using Herodotus and Plato, a tragedy exploring issues of power, tradition, and achievement. In his *Ring des Nibelungen*, Richard Wagner (1813–83) consciously combined a story from Germanic myth with the world of the gods of the *Iliad* and the structure of Aeschylus' Prometheus plays.

The work of Wagner is significant for the history of literature, as well as of music and of the theater. While German music of the mid-nineteenth century for the most part was not concerned with antiquity, the first production of an original classical play (in translation) took place in 1841 with Sophocles' *Antigone*, directed in Potsdam by Ludwig Tieck (1773–1853). This new trend toward a classical revival in the theater was continued by other productions directed by Tieck in Potsdam as well as by performances in Munich, Meiningen, and Vienna.

Classical subject matters also played a role in painting without being dominant. Anselm Feuerbach (1829–80) strove to renew Greek beauty by means of a grand style and decorative composition (*Medea, Amazonenschlacht* [Battle of the Amazons], *Iphigenie, Gastmahl des Platon* [Plato's feast]). The Swiss painter Arnold Böcklin (1827–1901) tried to revive fundamental moods and concepts of antiquity (*Triton und Nereide, Im Spiel der Wellen* [In the play of the waves]). The genre of historical painting was cultivated by Karl Theodor von Piloty (1826–86) (*Die Ermordung Cäsars* [Caesar's murder], *Tod Alexander des Großen* [Death of Alexander the Great]). Hans Makart (1840–84) created a *Triumph der Ariadne* (Triumph of Ariadne) and a *Tod der Kleopatra* (Death of Cleopatra). Max Klingner (1857–1920) employed classical ideas and forms in a unique, creative manner (*Amor und Psyche, Urteil des Paris* [Paris' judgment], *Kassandra*).

6   The Twentieth Century

During the twentieth century, classical studies and education were characterized by a marked decline in the teaching of the ancient languages, in particular Greek, and by the conservative stance of many practitioners, which led to close relations to those in power, both under the rule of the Kaiser and under the National Socialists. As a consequence, those secondary schools that taught classics were often criticized for being remote from the real world and for having a submissive attitude. This attitude is also evident in the last attempt so far to derive guiding principles for society from antiquity: the "Third Humanism" founded by Werner Jaeger (1888–1961). Mainly a reaction to Germany's defeat in World War I, to the November Revolution and democracy, it bore quasi-religious traits and was directed – in contrast to neohumanism – toward the state, not the individual.

The ideology of National Socialism represented a low point despite the fact that overall it saw itself less indebted to antiquity than did Italian fascism. Nevertheless its leading exponents – foremost among them Hitler himself – appealed to Sparta and Rome, interpreted classical history according to their theory of race, and aimed for heroic-monumental state architecture. After 1945 classical traditions were seen in close relationship to Christianity ("Abendlandideologie" [Ideology of the occident]) as part of how West Germany understood itself politically, while they did not assume any direct ideological role in the German Democratic Republic.

Still Greek and Roman times remained important in the twentieth century. Significant research continued to take place in philology, archaeology, and ancient history. Numerous translations and editions of texts prove that antiquity remained of interest to many readers. Philosophers of many different schools (from Edmund Husserl [1859–1938] and Martin Heidegger [1889–1976] to Ernst Bloch [1885–1977], Max Horckheimer [1895–1973], and Theodor W. Adorno [1903–69]) engaged with questions raised by Greek philosophy, mythology, and literature. When founding psychoanalysis, Sigmund Freud (1856–1939) reached back to the ancient myths ("Oedipus complex"), and the arts, first and foremost, were characterized much more by classical motifs than in the nineteenth century. The dominant mode was a critical and questioning approach to the models, following Marx, Nietzsche, and Freud: influenced by their own experiences of extreme crises, many writers, painters, sculptors, and composers viewed antiquity as a time of incredible social and political tensions. They stressed the *harshness* of ancient myths, questioned conflicts from a psychological perspective, and understood antiquity less in an "Apollonian" than in a "Dionysian" fashion. It was no longer a single author, work, genre, or period that was crucial for the reception of antiquity, but the received subject matters were seen as a freely available reservoir of motifs, a trend that had begun since the Romantic period. Linked to the general tendency for art to become more political, Rome again assumed a larger role despite the primacy of Greece.

The newly awakened interest in antiquity started with the postnaturalistic literature of the turn of the century. In drama Gerhart Hauptmann (1862–1946), Frank Wedekind (1864–1918), and Hugo von Hofmannsthal (1874–1929) played a part; in lyric, besides Hofmannsthal, Stefan George (1868–1933) and Rainer Maria Rilke (1875–1926); and in prose writing, Heinrich and Thomas Mann (1871–1950 and 1875–1955, respectively). In his travelog *Griechischer Frühling* (Greek spring) and his drama *Der Bogen des Odysseus* (The bow of Odysseus), Hauptmann turned his attention toward the darker aspects of antiquity. His late Atrides tetralogy still reflected, in its ever-present engagement with Aeschylus, Sophocles, Euripides, and Goethe, the experiences of World War II. Wedekind portrayed human sexuality as an elemental force destroying societal norms in *Erdgeist* (Earth spirit) and *Die Büchse der Pandora* (Pandora's box); in *Heracles* he showed a suffering and disappointed hero. Hofmannsthal's *Electra* virtually offers an exemplary psychological interpretation of myth reaching back to, and turning away from, Sophocles, Goethe, and Shakespeare. With *Ödipus und die Sphinx* (Oedipus and the Sphinx), *Ariadne auf Naxos* (Ariadne on Naxos), and *Die ägyptische Helena* (The Egyptian Helena), he likewise turned toward a subtle and sensitive exploration of the dark recesses and undercurrents of the soul. While George employed a fair amount of pathos and force in his attempts to see classical norms valued, Rilke reenacted human liminal experiences in a very moving way in poems such as *Alcestis* or *Orpheus. Eurydice. Hermes.* He also sought to suspend the tragic nature of life, love, and art in the "Raum der Rühmung" (Room of glorifying) in the *Sonetten an Orpheus* (Sonnets to Orpheus). In his novel *Die Göttinnen* (The goddesses), Heinrich Mann celebrated "die große heidnische Sinnlichkeit" (the great pagan sensuality) by means of the mythological roles of Diana, Minerva, and Venus. His novella *Die Rückkehr vom Hades* (The return from Hades) reflected the precarious relationship of the artist and his public. Thomas Mann's novella *Der Tod in Venedig* (Death in Venice) narrates a modern journey to Hades. In it, hints of Plato's thoughts on love and beauty move from an atmosphere of a classicism echoing antiquity to Dionysian intoxication, ending in chaos and barbarism. Reminiscences of antiquity also pervade his novels *Der Zauberberg* (The magic mountain), *Joseph und seine Brüder* (Joseph and his brothers), and *Doktor Faustus.*

Expressionism referred back to antiquity more strongly than some theoretical pronouncements would lead one to expect: thus in the poems of Georg Heym (1887–1912) and Ywan Goll (1891–1950), in the antimilitaristic plays *Die Troerinnen* (The Trojan women) by Franz Werfel (1890–1945) and *Antigone* by Walter Hasenclever (1890–1940), in Hans Henny Jahnn's (1894–1959) *Medea,* which combined both antiracism and social criticism with basic instincts and archaic behaviors, and in a number of pieces by Georg Kaiser (1878–1945). References to antiquity pervade the prose writings of Franz Kafka (1883–1924), partly under the surface, such as the labyrinth- and Oedipus-motifs, partly in new deconstructive interpretations that alter and remove the heroic (in *Das Schweigen der Sirenen* [The silence of the sirens], *Prometheus, Poseidon*). This is also true in the works of Albert Ehrenstein (1886–1950) and Gottfried Benn (1886–1956). Benn began as a "dionysischer Rauschkünstler" (Dionysian intoxication-artist) under the influence of Nietzsche, but later identified himself more with the artist Orpheus, advocated an Apollonian-intellectualizing view of antiquity, and emphasized the tragic content of the ancient myths. Immediately following the establishment of the Nazi dictatorship, he proclaimed his allegiance to a total state founded on violence, terror, and leadership in his essay *Dorische Welt* (The Doric world), using Sparta as an example.

Antifascist authors who were active primarily during the Weimar Republic and the years of exile became radicalized in their social and political pronouncements, focusing particularly on Roman antiquity – for instance in Ödön von Horvárth's (1901–38) comedy *Pompeji*, in Lion Feuchtwanger's (1884–1957) novels *Der jüdische Krieg* (The Jewish war) and *Der falsche Nero* (The false Nero), or in Hermann Broch's (1886–1951) novel *Der Tod des Vergil* (The death of Virgil). Broch used the figure of the Roman poet and his relations with Augustus to deal with issues such as the meaning and value of art and its relationship to politics, from the experiences of fascism and exile. He debated fundamental questions concerning the antagonism of truth and beauty or of glory and insignificance, and he reflected on the responsibility of the creative individual who can be both revered as a bringer of salvation and manipulated by power.

Among the "left"-leaning writers of the first half of the twentieth century, Bertolt Brecht (1898–1956) was the one who showed the most engagement with classical motifs. He reinterpreted traditional history and mythology in a distancing and non-heroic manner (*Berichtigungen alter Mythen* [Corrections of old myths], *Die Geschäfte des Herrn Julius Cäsar* [The affairs of Mr. Julius Caesar], *Das Verhör des Lukullus* [The trial of Lucullus]). Yet he also showed the exemplary nature of classical events for social behavior today (*Die Horatier und die Kuriatier* [The Horatii and the Curiatii], *Briefe über Gelesenes* [Letters on what has been read], *Coriolanus* [after Shakespeare]), and proved his sympathy for personalities of the ancient world in a simple and unaffected way (*Der Schuh des Empedokles* [The shoe of Empedocles], *Der verwundete Sokrates* [The wounded Socrates]). With *Die Antigone des Sophokles. Nach der Hölderlinschen Übersetzung* (The Antigone of Sophocles. After the Translation by Hölderlin), Brecht

Figure 12.2 Bertolt Brecht at the dress rehearsal of his play *The Antigone of Sophocles* in Chur (Switzerland, February 15, 1948), with Helene Weigel as Antigone and Hans Gaugler as Creon. Photo by Ruth Berlau, reproduced with permission of Hilda Hoffman. Bertolt-Brecht-Archiv, Berlin

gave the impetus for the reception of antiquity in the following decades in a number of ways: in the visible role of the dramatic, in the close affinity to the genre of adaptations, in the sociocritical emphasis, the politicization, and "Durchrationalisierung" (thorough rationalization) of the material, in the nuanced relationship between continuation and contrast, and not least also in the appreciation of Hölderlin.

The reception of classical motifs in the literature of the late forties and early fifties is marked for the most part by the historical experiences of the war and postwar period: by terror and death, exile and return, conformity and opposition, a fresh start and disillusionment. At first elements of identification and affirmation predominate, as an echo of traditional "humanist" attitudes as well as an attempt to "appropriate" the classical "inheritance" for socialist purposes. Later, however, the critical-questioning approach clearly prevails. The increased literary interest in classical subject matters in general, and the critical interpretation of the traditional myths in particular, owe much to the reception of antiquity in French theater since the end of the twenties (André Gide, Jean Giraudoux, Jean Cocteau, Jean Anouilh, Jean-Paul Sartre, Albert Camus) and in the works of the American dramatist Eugene O'Neill and the writers of lyric and essays, the Englishman T. S. Eliot and the American Ezra Pound.

The work of the Swiss authors Max Frisch (1911–91) and Friedrich Dürrenmatt (1921–90) is rooted in the postwar period. They employed the Odysseus- and Oedipus-motifs in the novels *Stiller* and *Homo faber* (Man the maker) and expressed a non-heroic view of history in the plays *Romulus der Große* (Romulus the great) and *Der Stall des Augias* (The stable of Augias). Heinrich Böll (1917–85) calls the militaristic interpretation of antiquity in German schools to account in his story *Wanderer, kommst du nach Spa …* (Wanderer, when you come to Spa …); Arno Schmidt (1914–79) has taken a critical attitude to classical myths and events, and transformed them into travesty, in a range of stories in the volumes *Leviathan oder Die beste der Welten* (Leviathan or the best of worlds) and *Kühe in Halbtrauer* (Cows in half mourning). While the reception of antiquity was generally in decline in West German literature after the fifties, it remained a constant presence in the work of the classical philologist Walter Jens (born 1923) from Tübingen. In the literature of the German Democratic Republic, classical influences became evident, first in the fifties, especially in lyric poetry. The use of traditional motifs in a positive, affirmative manner, which Johannes R. Becher (1891–1958) had been developing since the thirties and which he now continued in a fairly linear fashion, proved in the end to be less effective. In contrast, the early poems of Stephan Hermlin (1915–97) have elegiac and questioning traits, and the late lyrics and essays by Erich Arendt (1903–84) show a characteristic development from positive identification to distancing, a distancing that applies both to the classical heroes and to the socialist present (*Odysseus' Heimkehr* [Odysseus' return]) and other poems from the cycle *Ägäis* [Aegean]). The rejection of history goes hand in hand with an endorsement of nature and art (*Gesang der sieben Inseln* [Song of the seven islands], *Stunde Homer* [Hour Homer]). Pensive reflections are also characteristic of Georg Maurer's (1907–71) and Johannes Bobrowski's (1917–65) lyric poetry, and Peter Huchel's (1903–81) poems are characterized particularly by elegiac moments of resignation (*Polybius, Der Garten des Theophrast* [The garden of Theophrastus], *Das Grab des Odysseus* [The grave of Odysseus]).

It is notable that engagement with antiquity during the second half of the twentieth century became a key characteristic of writers in the German Democratic Republic. It allowed them to create a poetry addressing fundamental concerns, to escape a narrow definition of realism, and to debate the issues of their own time without prejudice. Since about 1960 this literature has been influenced not only by fascism and war but also by the circumstances of the postwar period. Drama was the dominant genre at the beginning of this phase: the production of Peter Hacks's (1928–2003) reworking of Aristophanes' *Frieden* (Peace) in 1962 in Berlin was one of the most successful plays in German-speaking countries after 1945. With plays such as *Amphitryon, Omphale*, and *Numa* or later with the *Die Vögel* (Birds) (after Aristophanes), *Senecas Tod* (Death of Seneca), and *Pandora* (after Goethe), Hacks explored the tensions in the relationship between utopia and reality with the help of classical subject matters. For the most part he adopted a positive stance toward both literary tradition and socialist society. The works of Heiner Müller (1929–95), on the other hand, offer an example of a more critical approach to traditional subjects. In plays like *Philoktet, Heracles 5, Ödipus Tyrann* (Oedipus tyrant) (after Sophocles), *Der Horatier* (The Horatian), and *Zement* (Cement) (after a novel by Fjodor Gladkow), Müller employed the ancient myths to portray the problems of the (mostly socialist) present – especially the conflicting interests of individuals and of society – in sharp focus. In lyric poetry, a differentiated engagement with traditional subject matters continued with authors such as Günter Kunert (born 1929), Karl Mickel (1935–2000), Heinz Czechowski (born 1935), and Volker Braun (born 1939) (who were also active in other genres). Over the last decades, these authors have been joined by Durs Grünbein (born 1962), whose interest lies mainly in Roman history, with his historical-philosophical perspective and sobering diction. Among writers of prose narrative, Franz Fühmann (1922–84) and Christa Wolf (born 1929) should be mentioned. Fühmann echoed the guilt and delusion of German soldiers in World War II in his story *König Ödipus* (King Oedipus) and created an intelligent adaptation of Homeric epic (*Das Hölzerne Pferd* [The wooden horse]). In his "mythological novel" *Prometheus*, and in a number of stories, he questioned the conflict between "Geist und Macht" (spirit/mind/intellect and power). In *Kassandra*, Christa Wolf challenged war and the politics of power, violence, and ideological manipulation – a challenge that means grappling with a patriarchal world and with the dangers of a one-sided rationalism, and that does not flinch in questioning the price to be paid for the progress of society and technology, and that repudiates all "heroism." However, human interactions and the use of political power are discussed in even more fundamental and subtle ways in *Medea. Stimmen* (Medea. Voices). This work also reflects experiences since the collapse of the "socialist camp" in Europe and its return to the "Western World," and enacts a radical turn away from the Euripidean version of Medea as child-murderer.

Since the seventies interest in classical subjects has also been renewed in the German literature of the Federal Republic of Germany, Austria, and Switzerland and in countries inhabited by German exiles. This work similarly tends to take a critical approach, as do Peter Weiss (1916–82) and Botho Strauß (born 1944) as well as the Austrian writers Christoph Ransmayr (born 1954) and Michael Köhlmeier (born 1949). Weiss's novel

Die Ästhetik des Widerstands (The aesthetic of resistance) sets the antifascist resistance in the context of a process of two thousand years of social conflict. It poses the question of a radical "appropriation" of the artistic "inheritance" in order to resolve one's own existential questions – the great frieze of the Pergamon altar and the interpretation of Heracles with all his duality play a significant role in this. Strauß lets the mythological appear among the everyday in a number of his pieces and offers an emphatically conservative reading of Homer in *Ithaca*. In Ransmayr's novel *Die letzte Welt* (The last world), Ovid's *Metamorphoses* virtually piece themselves together out of the life of the poet, who, victimized by a tyrant, has been exiled to Tomi, and out of the investigations of the narrator. Köhlmeier mixes divine and human action from stories related to the Homeric epics with a modern ambience in his Odysseus novels *Telemach* and *Kalypso* and leaves much room for irony and persiflage.

The reception of antiquity in other forms of art is more or less closely related to literature. In theater, there were the epoch-making productions of the *Oresteia* by Max Reinhardt (1873–1945) and of *Oidipus* by Leopold Jessner (1878–1945) during the Weimar Republic. In the eighties, Peter Stein's (born 1937) staging of the *Oresteia* at the Berlin Schaubühne, the Schwerin project "Entdeckungen 'Antike' " (Discoveries "antiquity") by Christoph Schroth (born 1937), and the five Theater Festivals of Stendal stand out. The rendition of authentic classical plays (in translation), the staging of adaptations, and the production of modern plays on classical topics regularly form part of the play-lists and sometimes are in fact linked with each other.

Classical (mostly mythical) subjects have become increasingly popular again in music, especially musical theater. Richard Strauss (1864–1948) is among the first. His operas *Elektra*, *Ariadne auf Naxos* (Ariadne on Naxos), and *Die ägyptische Helena* (The Egyptian Helena) were created to the libretti of Hugo von Hofmannsthal. Later Walter Braunfels (1882–1954) composed *Die Vögel* (The birds, after Aristophanes), Egon Wellesz (1885–1974) *Alkestis* and *Bacchantinnen* (Bacchantes) (after Euripides), Ernst Křenek (1900–91) *Orpheus und Eurydike*, *Das Leben des Orest* (The life of Orestes), and *Pallas Athene weint* (Pallas Athena cries), and Rudolf Wagner-Régeny (1903–69) *Prometheus*. Heinz Röttger (1909–77) and Aribert Reimann (born 1936) adapted in *Die Frauen von Troja* (The women of Troy) and *Troades* works by Euripides and Franz Werfel, respectively. Paul Dessau (1894–1984) created the opera *Das Verhör des Lukullus* (The trial of Lucullus) after Brecht. Carl Orff (1895–1982) often set original Greek and Latin texts to music (like the *Prometheus* of Aeschylus, Sophocles' *Oedipus*, the *Catulli Carmina*, or the medieval *Carmina Burana*); he chose Hölderlin's translation for his *Antigone*, after Sophocles. Rolf Liebermann (1910–99) wrote the operas *Penelope* and *Freispruch für Medea* (Acquittal of Medea), Hans Werner Henze (born 1926) the ballet *Orpheus*. From the last decades we have the opera *Ödipus* (after Sophocles and Heiner Müller), the cello concerto *Styx und Lethe* (Styx and Lethe) by Wolfgang Rihm (born 1952), and *Kassandra. Starrend von Zeit und Helle* (Cassandra. Rigid with time and brightness) and a *Musiktheater in sechs Gedichten von Erich Arendt* (Musical theater in six poems by Erich Arendt) by Peter Michael Hamel (born 1947). Then there are the operas *Die Heimkehr des Odysseus* (The return of Odysseus) and *Omphale* (after Hacks), a dramatic score to the Oedipus-tragedies of Sophocles, and musical renditions of Catullus by Siegfried Matthus (born 1934), as well as the operas *Gastmahl oder Über die Liebe* (Banquet or on love) and *Antigone oder Die Stadt* (Antigone or the city) by Georg Katzer (born 1935).

The fine arts also utilized classical subjects. From the first half of the twentieth century the sculptor Gerhard Marcks (1889–1981) and the painter Max Beckmann (1884–1950) ought to be mentioned. Marcks engaged with classical myths during his whole life (*Orpheus-Mappe* [Orpheus-portfolio], *Ödipus und Antigone, Gefesselter Prometheus* [Prometheus bound]); Beckmann preferred to work on mythical subject matters during his exile in the 1940s (*Mars und Venus, Perseus, Prometheus, Odysseus und Kalypso*). Gustav Seitz (1906–66), Hans Arp (1888–1966), and Bernhard Heiliger (1915–99), among others, engaged with classical motifs on occasion during the second half of the century. The reception of classical antiquity flourished in the arts of the German Democratic Republic, as it did in its literature. It provides nothing less than the foundation for the work of the sculptor Wieland Förster (born 1930), who reflects painful experiences of the individual and society through the motif of the labyrinth and through figures like Daphne, Nike, and Marsyas, and for the painter Wolfgang Mattheuer (1927–2004), who repeatedly turned to the myths of Sisyphus and Icarus. Bernhard Heisig (born 1925), who also paid special attention to the figure of Icarus, and Werner Tübke (1929–2004) created further works illustrating this trend. Besides Icarus, Prometheus, the judgment of Paris, and Cassandra are favorite themes (on whose reception through the ages there have already been a number of exhibitions).

During the very times of crisis, of historical change and seeming distance from antiquity, subjects from the Greek and Roman past can serve as the focal point for topical debates by stimulating a turning away from conventional interpretations and an emphasis on ruptures and discontinuities. This is proof that the heritage of antiquity retains a life and influence beyond all monumentality and classicality.

FURTHER READING

On Goethe and the Greeks, see Trevelyan (1941); from the eighteenth to the twentieth centuries, see Butler (1935); on the classical tradition in twentieth-century Germany, see Ziolkowski (1993). Much good material remains accessible only in German: see especially the collections edited by Baumbach (2000), Faber and Kytzler (1992), and Seidensticker and Vöhler (2001), along with the books by Cancik (1998) and Riedel (1996, 2000, 2002). Much useful information is available in Cancik, Schneider, and Landfester (1996–2003), *Der neue Pauly: Enzyklopädie der Antike*, whose last five volumes are devoted to the classical tradition, with a pronounced German slant. These volumes are being translated into English and published by E. J. Brill, with the first volume having been published in 2006.

This chapter has been translated by Kathrin Lüddecke.

CHAPTER THIRTEEN

Iberian Peninsula

Luisa López Grigera

1 Introduction

Primitive inhabitants of the Iberian peninsula – Iberians and Tartesians – possessed alphabets; and Phoenicians, Greeks, and Carthaginians established a commercial base there. The Romans, after conquering the peninsula at the end of the third century BC, converted it into a province – Hispania – in which two emperors were born, as well as various writers: Quintilian, Martial, the two Senecas (father and son), and the elder Seneca's nephew Lucan. In the period of Christian antiquity in Spain, there was Prudentius. The last great figure, in Visigothic times, was Saint Isidore of Seville. When the Roman empire fell, the classics took refuge in the monasteries, but in Hispania that world was destroyed in 711 by the Muslim invasion, which isolated the Peninsula from the rest of Europe. In small enclaves of the north (Asturias and Navarre), Christian groups began to organize the "Reconquest" of the "bull's skin," as Strabo called the peninsula with its peculiar shape. But in those dark centuries the Muslim world maintained contact with the classical tradition by way of translations of Greek and Oriental works into Arabic.

At the beginning of the thirteenth century Spain encompassed the Christian kingdoms of Castilla-León, Aragon, Navarre, Portugal, and the Muslim Al Andalus, which at that time had fragmented into small kingdoms, easily conquered by the Christians in the middle of that century. One Moorish kingdom survived until 1492: Granada. The marriage of the Catholic monarchs Isabel of Castille and Ferdinand of Aragon consolidated the union of those two kingdoms, to which was annexed Navarre, while the kingdom of Portugal remained independent, although from 1580 to 1640, due to a lack of direct heirs, Philip II, King of Spain and the son of a Portuguese princess, united it to the crown of Spain.

2   The Classical Tradition in Spain

2.1   *General studies*

It is only fitting to consider the classical tradition in the vernacular languages, whose presence is detected from the start of the twelfth century. Even scholars of the eighteenth century recognized that presence and esteemed it as being of great significance. But ever since the emergence of post-Kantian ideas about the work of art as an "original expression of personal experience," the presence of the classics in Spain has been underappreciated. Even neo-Latin texts were evaluated pejoratively. Only a few critics from the beginning of the twentieth century dared to speak about "literary sources." Even still, Marcelino Menéndez Pelayo (1856–1912) recopied hundreds of pages grouped together in *Biblioteca hispano-latina clásica* (Classical Spanish-Latin library [1950–3]) and *Biblioteca de traductores españoles* (Library of Spanish translators [1952–3]), fundamental works for the study of the classical tradition in Spain. Literary movements such as modernism and creationism returned to recreate the classics at the beginning of the twentieth century. And scholars such as María Rosa Lida de Malkiel studied this tradition in Hispanic literatures. Several of her studies are gathered together in *La tradición clásica en España* (The classical tradition in Spain, 1975), which includes a review (339–97) of G. Highet's *The Classical Tradition* (1949), which she chastises for its exclusive interest in things Greek and Roman and for what she calls the author's "ignorance of things Spanish" (368). An unjustifiable ignorance: although the classical tradition in Spain might be "less important than in Italy or England," since "in the Golden Age (the sixteenth and seventeenth centuries), Spanish dominated Europe, it is impossible to ignore it without falsifying the literary histories of the countries which it influenced" (368). She also points out errors, such as attributing to the poet Juan de Mena (1411–56) a translation of the *Iliad* of Homer, when what he really translated was a post-Homeric version, "the Latin *Ilias*" (369). Her entire book remains fundamental for work in this area.

2.2   *Studies of individual authors*

In imitation of the Italians, the Spaniards (according to Juan Gil) "forged at the end of the fifteenth century the idea of a mythical extension of the Iberian Peninsula across the centuries, forming a direct bridge between the Spain of their time and the Roman Hispania" (2004: 234). They inherited the direct tradition of the Greek and Latin classics, although in the Middle Ages the first of these arrived by way of Arabic translations. Even in the fifteenth century, which was a first Renaissance, arising soon after the Italian one (Nader 1979; Di Camillo 1989), the Greek tradition was known – with some exceptions – through Latin and Italian translations. Already in the sixteenth century the Greeks were edited and translated into Spanish directly.

Despite the poor Latin of Christian Hispania, there have been attempts (Menéndez Pelayo in his *Bibliografía hispano-latina clásica* (*BHLC*) (1950–3) to detect even there the presence of the classics, in manuscripts, editions, commentaries, translations, and imitations of almost all the Greek and Latin authors. For some of them there are more recent studies, such as those published in the *Enciclopedia virgiliana* (della Corte 1988), which contains three entries about Spain and one about Portugal. Juan Gil studies the Vergilian tradition *ab ovo* (1988: 953b), that is to say, the early reception, revealed in inscriptions of the Roman era and also of the Visigothic period, during which "the fame of the poet continues living, but as a classic more venerated than read" (953b). The manuscripts preserved in Spain in the High Middle Ages and the translations and adaptations done later in Castille reveal, according to Gil, a continuity of interest. Margherita Morreale studies the presence of Vergil in all periods and aspects: manuscripts, translations, and imitations. From the seventh and ninth centuries she registers a reference to a manuscript of the *Aeneid* carried by Saint Eulogius from a monastery in Pamplona to Córdoba, the capital of the Muslim kingdom. From later centuries she recalls the presence of Vergil's works in the Monastery of Ripoll, along with an ancient codex registered in the Cathedral of Salamanca in the thirteenth century, and others of the *Bucolics* and the *Georgics* loaned to King Alfonso the Wise in 1270 by the monastery of Albelda (957a). But she warns that the Wise King's version of the story of Dido and Aeneas proceeds more from other texts than from Vergil's. In medieval literature she finds Vergil the astrologer, the enamored poet, and Dante's guide through hell. "The imitations and translations [of Vergil]," says Morreale, "begin in Spain with the Vergilian *Églogas* of Juan del Encina (1468–1529)" (958a–b). And they continue by way of pastoral poetry such as that of Garcilaso de la Vega. Nevertheless she considers that "the most constant literary genre, and the one most universally linked to Vergil, is that of erudite epic poetry, which for the years 1550–1700, with numerous titles (close to 180), represents what was for the upper classes the equivalent of the *comedia* for the commoners" (965b). She notes that in the eighteenth century there arose an indirect imitation of the *Georgics* in *The Seasons*, by James Thomson (1726–30), which produced secondary imitations in Spain, where the *Georgics* had not exerted much influence during the Golden Age (966a–b). But the translators' interest, she says, "was concentrated on the work most consonant with Enlightenment and Neoclassicism, the *Aeneid*" (966b). There is a third study for Catalonia, where Vergil makes an entrance by way of the presence in Naples of the Aragonese King Alfonso the Magnanimous in 1443. The king who fomented humanism in his Neapolitan court also guided the arrival of this movement in his Hispanic lands.

On Seneca in Spain, the book *Séneca en España* by Karl Blüher covers a good part, although first-hand information is scarce. Seneca was very influential during the first, fifteenth-century Renaissance. In the library of Pope Pedro de Luna there were 38 manuscripts of Seneca and 20 of Cicero. Before Luna, the papal library had 11 codices of Seneca and 5 of Cicero. Blüher, however, also ignores the influence of Seneca on Góngora. Some critics had considered the influence of Lucan upon Góngora, since he, too, was from Córdoba, but they neglected what was known by his contemporaries: that in the style initiated by the *Polifemo* (Polyphemus) and the *Soledades* (Solitudes) there is a notable influence of the Latin authors of the Silver Age (López Grigera 2005).

Vives Coll, in his *Luciano de Samosata en España (1500–1700)* (Lucian of Samosata in Spain, 1959) offers data that could be complemented and reinterpreted, but that still form a base for the study of an author who influenced the Peninsula so greatly. The Latin translations and imitations done in Italy in the fifteenth century were diffused rapidly in Spain, where there were no direct translations, apparently, until the sixteenth century. Lucian's influence begins, according to Vives Coll, with Juan Luis Vives (1492–1549), Alfonso de Valdés (died 1532), Pero Mexía (1496?–1552?), and Cristóbal de Villalón, among others in the sixteenth century, and continues in the seventeenth with Cervantes, Quevedo, Diego de Saavedra Fajardo (1584–1648), and Gracián. But we should also mention, for the sixteenth century, Antonio de Guevara (died 1545?) with his *Marco Aurelio* (1528), which should be situated in the tradition of Rabelais, and also Francesillo de Zúñiga. Another important omission is Lope de Vega with his *Gatomachia* (Battle of the cats), one of his great poetic works; still another we should not forget is the drama of the Portuguese Gil Vicente.

Juan Gil has studied Martial in Spain (2004). Martial was a poet who produced scarcely an echo in the Middle Ages and who, in the Renaissance, because he had been born in Spain, suffered strong politically based rejection in Europe. In his own country, Martial received a very diverse reception. In Salamanca the existence of manuscripts is known in the medieval period; and Hernando Columbus, the younger son of the "discoverer" of America, read and studied Martial carefully "when he was still very young" (250). On the various Latin imitations, which Gil studies carefully and with great erudition, we shall not detain ourselves here, since the Castilian ones are many and important. The revalorization of Martial appears concurrently with that of Latin Silver Age poetry in the last third of the sixteenth century. The Jesuits prepared expurgated editions for students' use, as the composition of epigrammatical poetry was one of their pedagogical objectives. Garcilaso, Cetina, and Herrera imitated him. In the seventeenth century Quevedo, Góngora, and Argensola did the same with more dedication. And Baltasar Gracián (1601–58) proposes him as a model in his *Agudeza y arte de ingenio* (Wit and the art of ingenuity). Gil studies the edition of Martial done by Lorenzo Ramírez de Prado (1583–1658), without moral expurgations but with harsh reflections upon earlier, expurgated editions. Gil closes his essay by remembering how Martial provided material for the false chronicles of the Toledan Jesuit Jerónimo Román de la Higuera (1538–1611), who "canonized" as Christian saints a number of characters mentioned by Martial.

3 Periods

3.1 The Middle Ages

In spite of the apparent precariousness of Peninsular humanism, the classical tradition began with King Alfonso X (1221–84), who, according to Francisco Márquez Villanueva, compiled such a strong "summary of Latin materials" that it is "from that moment fundamental and impressive" (2004: 67). The father of Castilian prose, he directed the translation and compilation of works on science and history. Among those whose classical sources are better known are the *General estoria* (General history) and the *Estoria de España* (History of Spain). The first of these, which begins with the creation of the world, contains biblical translations of the Old Testament and its commentators and glossators; but although its foundations are sacred, says Charles Fraker, "*General Estoria* is a secular history ... happenings in the narrative are moved along not by the hand of Providence but by natural means" (1996: 4). It includes an almost complete translation of Lucan's *Pharsalia* and a large number of passages from Ovid, especially the *Heroides* and the *Metamorphoses* (Brancaforte 1990). In the *Estoria de España* there are also various materials from antiquity.

> But King Alfonso was no protohumanist. Without doubt, he possessed an alert literary sensibility – always capable of surprising us – but it would be unjust to expect of him any archaeological sense of the Greco-Roman past. As a product of his times, he lacked eyes and ears for the classical tradition, which his vast project used only on an auxiliary plane and not as an objective or goal of the culture which he desired for his kingdoms. (Villanueva 2004: 66)

Dido, the Carthaginian queen who appears in several works of Roman literature, plays an important role in the reception of the classical tradition in medieval Spain. Lida de Malkiel notes that

> Chapters 57 to 60 of the *Crónica general* (General chronicle) are nothing but a narration of the Virgilian episode, plus a prolix version of Ovid's letter. It is worth noting ... that the account is not taken directly from the *Aeneid*, but instead through Ovid and the *Historia Romanorum* (History of the Romans), Chapter II from Archbishop Rodrigo of Toledo. (1975: 5–6)

On studying the "chaste Dido," without Vergilian roots, she affirms that

> with characteristic medieval eclecticism [...], Alfonso the Wise, after paraphrasing in Chapters 51 to 56 of the *Crónica general* the story of Dido according to Justinian, notes: "But others tell how this queen Dido killed herself, to the great sorrow of Aeneas, her husband, because he abandoned her, as you will hear later." (1975: 61)

To the so-called "mester de clerecía" the classical tradition arrives by way of great French poems: the *Libro de Alexandre* (Book of Alexander), as Ian Michael has demonstrated (1970), with other sources stemming from the *Res gestae Alexandri Macedonis* (Deeds of Alexander the Great) and a Latin translation of Pseudo-Calisthenes, with elements of the *Alexandreis* of Walter of Châtillon and of the *Ilias latina* (Latin *Iliad*). According to Marden (1976), one of the best specialists, the novel *Libro de Apolonio* (Book of Apollinius), a thirteenth-century translation of the Latin version *Historia Apollonii regis Tyri* (History of Apollonius of Tyre), proceeds from the Latin text directly and not by way of French translations. In the same versificatory structure, monorhythmic tetrastrophic alexandrines, we find (a century later) the *Libro de buen amor* (Book of good love), which is a curious miscellany of multiple sources, as many eastern as western:

it is perhaps the work in which there converge all, or almost all, of the medieval literary traditions; or if you will, it is the work created by the school system of the Middle Ages, just as the *Guzmán de Alfarache* (Guzman of Alfarache) [a Counter-Reformation picaresque tale] is the product of the Renaissance [pedagogical] method; [...] both proceeded from the common root of rhetoric and from its accompanying concept of the ultimate end of all literary work. (Arcipreste de Hita 1983: xx–xxi)

Its classical sources, although indirect, are studied by Lecoy, who notes that the Aesopic fables, possibly by Phaedrus, reach Juan Ruiz through "Walter l'Anglais" (1938: 117). This work also contains classical ideas, some of them from Ovid, on the art of love.

3.2 *The fifteenth century*

Although the high Renaissance is the era of the Catholic Monarchs (1476–1516), according to current researchers, in the fifteenth century a kind of early Renaissance arises in different areas of Spain: Batllori recalls that

the master of Rhodes, Juan Fernández de Heredia (ca. 1313–95), surrounds himself, in the East and in Avignon, with wise Greeks; he orders for the first time the translation of Thucydides and Plutarch into a Romance language of Hispanic origin – Castilian or his Aragonese dialect – and imitates the ancient Hellenic historians in his historical works in the vernacular. (1987: 4)

That is to say that the conquests of Aragon in the Byzantine East "explain why Catalan-Aragonese humanism has been more Hellenist than Latinist" (1987: 4). Around this time Pero López de Ayala (1332?–1407) "was writing history of a Renaissance form and substance in 1395" (according to Nader 1979: 13), and the key to explaining this is his education in the papal court at Avignon, during the same years of Petrarch's residence there. Furthermore, during an ambassadorial mission to said court in 1394–5, he met with Juan Fernández de Heredia (ca. 1480–1549), who in "Avignon, maintained a team of scholars in his household to edit, transcribe, and translate his collection of Greek, Latin, and vernacular histories" (Nader 1979: 82–3). His collection of Greek and Latin manuscripts, together with the aforementioned rich collection of classical codices of Pope Pedro de Luna, had already passed in the fifteenth century to the libraries of the Kingdom of Aragon.

According to Di Camillo, Renaissance humanism arose in Spain not much later than in Italy, with many points of contact but with one great difference: the Spaniards, interested in the classical imitation of the Spanish language, instead of writing in Latin, tried to Latinize their Spanish in terms of vocabulary and syntax. This decision, however, had a serious consequence: "The preferred use of vernacular over Latin has often provided grounds for certain historians and literary critics to deny, without further inquiry, the presence of any serious humanistic activity in fifteenth-century Spain" (1988: 66).

The most representative figure of this period is Alonso de Cartagena (1385?–1456), educated in Salamanca, who distinguished himself in the Council of

Basel. He translated Cicero, among others. For Di Camillo (1988) the Renaissance of the fifteenth century stems from the *letrados,* the social class of highly placed administrative functionaries at the royal court, coming out of the universities, while for Nader (1979) the Mendoza family, of high nobility, was the point of entry for this movement, beginning with Pero López de Ayala (1332–1407). That family produced great figures in the fifteenth and sixteenth centuries: Iñigo López de Mendoza, the Marqués de Santillana (1398–1458), the most illustrious figure of Castilian letters of the fifteenth century, and his descendants (one of his great-grandsons, Don Antonio de Mendoza, first viceroy of Mexico, brought the printing press to America and stimulated the creation of its universities in 1551). Santillana, politician and poet, surrounded himself with manuscripts and erudite translators who translated both classical authors and the latest vernacular creations from Italy.

Slightly earlier was his mentor, the noble Don Enrique de Villena (1384–1434), translator of Cicero and Vergil. In addition to the *Traducción y glosas de la Eneida* (Translation and glosses of the *Aeneid*), he composed the treatise *Los doce trabajos de Hercules,* first in Catalan and then in Castilian. Juan de Mena (1411–56), whom Lida de Malkiel calls the "poet of the Spanish pre-Renaissance," wrote in a highly Latinate Spanish, both in terms of vocabulary and in terms of syntax, as may be noted in his most important work, *Laberinto de fortuna* (Labyrinth of fortune), composed of three hundred stanzas of *arte mayor.* His sources are Latin poems written in France, in addition to Vergil, Ovid, and Lucan.

The *Celestina,* a masterpiece of world literature composed at the end of the fifteenth century and translated into almost all the western languages in the sixteenth, is strongly rooted in the classics, as is demonstrated by a recent edition of *La Celestina comentada* (Annotated Celestina), the work of a lawyer who was a contemporary of Rojas. Lida de Malkiel points out not only its thematic sources but also its structural ones. One finds the influence of Aristotle and Petrarch in Act I; but according to Peter Russell, "more important is the influence of medieval Senecanism [. . .] which was quite different from classical Senecanism" (Rojas 1991:106). Undeniable, too, is the influence of the theater of Plautus and Terence, especially by way of the commentaries of Donatus.

The period of the Catholic Monarchs (1476–1516) saw a series of humanists educated in Italy: Alonso de Palencia (1423–92), Antonio de Nebrija (1442?–1522), and Hernán Núñez Pinciano (1475?–1553). The poet Juan del Encina (1468–1529), traditionally and erroneously seen as a popular poet, infuses his *Églogas* with a strong presence of the Latin classics.

3.3   Golden Age

The period stretching from the arrival of Charles V in Spain until the death of Calderón de la Barca in 1682 has been called the "Golden Age." (This label suggests a period of decline from that year until the Enlightenment of around 1726; but recent studies find around 1680 an interesting pre-Enlightenment.) During the Golden Age, the height of Spanish culture, the presence of the Greek and Latin classics was fundamental. As George Kennedy has emphasized, "The recovery of classical texts, including a knowledge of Greek, by the great humanist scholars of the Renaissance is surely the most important event in the history of the classical tradition" (1994: 11).

3.3.1 Ciceronianisms and anti-Ciceronianisms Menéndez Pelayo studied Ciceronianism in the first quarter of the sixteenth century in "Apuntes sobre el ciceronianismo en España y sobre la influencia de Cicerón en la prosa latina de los humanistas españoles" (1950–3: 3:177–271). Eugenio Asensio (2005a: 1) completed the history of the movement until the middle of the sixteenth century; he recalls its beginnings in the early 1500s, under the leadership of Bembo, with an early presence in the University of Salamanca, where the Belgian Longolius was living during those years and proselytizing for a pure Ciceronianism. That relative triumph vanished, in large part, with the appearance in 1528 of the *Ciceronianus* of Erasmus (a work that was reprinted in the University of Alcalá in 1529). From that point on, the only true Ciceronians, in my opinion, were Garcilaso de la Vega and his friend Boscán (López Grigera 1983: 4–9). The second historical moment that Asensio studies is the middle of the sixteenth century, which felt the influence of Vives' disciple, Honorato Juan, who contributed to the defense of Ciceronianism and to aiding the decline of Erasmianism around 1560, especially in the University of Valencia (2005a: 244).

Around 1568, upon the emergence of an "Attic" style, there appear to have been echoes of a nascent neo-Stoicism. The stylistic theories of Lipsius would thus find fertile ground. But I believe (López Grigera 2003) that the change of style was not due only to the imitation of Seneca propagated by the Belgian, but also to the influence of the Greek rhetoricians Demetrius and Hermogenes, who allow a grave style that uses the short phrase in place of the circular periodic sentence (128–30). Another imitation tied to that of Seneca was that of Tacitus, which had great relevance in Spain. The presence of Malvezzi in the court of Philip IV and the translation of his works into Spanish, in addition to the aphoristic writers, such as Antonio Pérez (died 1611), and the application of his techniques and style to historiography, deserve special mention. An earlier Tacitean historian was another great-grandson of the Marqués de Santillana, Don Diego Hurtado de Mendoza (1503–75), in his *Historia de la guerra de Granada* (History of the war of Granada). Other Taciteans included Francisco de Quevedo (1580–1645) and his friend, the Portuguese Manoel de Mello (1608–66).

3.3.2 Rhetoric and poetics The introduction to the history of rhetoric by Menéndez Pelayo (1962) is the most complete one, although it was written at the end of the nineteenth century. Of the later ones, of varying quality, the one by Karl Kohut (1973) is excellent. Also useful are those by Rico Verdú (1973) and García Berrio (1980). In 1983 I traced an outline for the sixteenth century, and Elena Artaza did another for the first half of the seventeenth (Artaza 2000). Artaza is fundamental for understanding the *Ars narrandi* (Art of narrating) in the Spain of the sixteenth century.

3.3.3 Translations To the study by Menéndez Pelayo, the *Biblioteca de traductores españoles* (1952–3), has been added the *Hispano-Classical Translations Printed between 1482 and 1699* of Theodore Beardsley (1970), with reference only to the printed translations; it would have been better to include those preserved in manuscripts prior to the eighteenth century.

3.3.4 Poetry The great Spanish humanist Francisco Sánchez de las Brozas (1523–1601), in his critical edition of the poetry of Garcilaso de la Vega, laments the misinterpretation of source studies:

> To say that with these annotations there is made more affront to the poet than honor, because by them are discovered and made manifest the thefts, which were before hidden, is an opinion certainly not worthy of a response, if we spoke with the very wise. But to satisfy those who are not so [wise], *I say and affirm, that I do not take for a good poet one who does not imitate the excellent ancients.* And if they ask me why, among so many thousands of poets, as our Spain has, so few can count themselves worthy of this name, I say, that there is no other reason, than that because they lack knowledge, languages, and doctrine to know how to imitate. (Cited in Gallego Morell 1972: 23)

Garcilaso de la Vega (1500?–1536), whose short poetic oeuvre reveals laborious polishing, is the great classic of peninsular lyric poetry. Together with Juan Boscán (1490?–1542), he fostered the imitation of Pietro Bembo's neo-Petrarchan school, to whom they were introduced by Andrea Navagero. Garcilaso and Boscán were also friends of Baldassare Castiglione, whose *Il cortigiano* (The courtier) Boscán translated into a model of Castilian prose. The poetry of both friends, published in 1543, not only exerted enormous influence on the Spanish poetry of subsequent centuries, but also had repercussions throughout Europe: Abraham Fraunce, in his *The Arcadian Rhetoric*, illustrates the tropes and figures with examples from Homer, Vergil, Sydney, Torquato Tasso, Boscán, and Garcilaso. The edition of 1570, done by El Brocense (Sánchez de las Brozas), carries annotations of "rhetoricia," that is to say, of erudite sources, while the Sevillian poet Fernando de Herrera (1534?–1597) can be considered a "grammarian." The classical sources of Garcilaso – who read and wrote Latin, although we do not know whether he also knew Greek – are Ovid, Horace, Vergil, Martial, Tibullus, and Theocritus (either directly, or by way of Petrarca, Poliziano, Bembo, and other Italians such as Bernardo Tasso and Sannazaro). The British Library preserves the letter by Bembo, congratulating him in 1535 for his Latin poetry (López Grigera 1988).

Fray Luis de León (1527–82), poet and prose stylist, was a professor of Hebrew in Salamanca. His philosophical poetry, almost all of it written in an Inquisitorial jail (an ordeal from which he was freed after having been completely absolved), was edited by another great poet, Francisco de Quevedo. It was divided into three books: Book 1, original poetry; Book 2, "Translations and Imitations" of Vergil's *Eclogues* and first *Georgic*, Horace's *Odes*, Pindar, Tibullus, Petrarch, and Bembo; and Book 3, translations and imitations of the Psalms and Proverbs.

Of the studies of the classical sources of his poetry, the edition and study by Juan Francisco Alcina (de León 1986) is especially interesting. About the "Horatianism" of Fray Luis, in his translations of odes and epodes, there is no doubt; but he is Horatian also through imitation, as much in his Latin poetry as in his Spanish verse. His is an imitation not of themes but of "Horatian procedures [that] give color to all his poetry" (39); "of Horatian origin [is] the taste for apparent lack of unity and the intertwining of themes" (39) and the "taste for the symbology of nature" (40). This is an art of intricate structures, apparently simple: it is a composed imitation. It almost lacks metaphors. Alcina is right to say that Fray Luis does "more than create; what he does is re-write" (41). And, as Rafael Lapesa has demonstrated (1980: 114), his use of "semantic cultisms" makes comprehension difficult because it gives traditional Castilian words the meaning they used to have in some of the Latin classics, thus giving (at times) a double meaning to the words.

Under the influence of Fray Luis de León, San Juan de la Cruz (1542–91), one of Spain's great lyric poets, basically imitates the *Song of Songs*, but also Garcilaso and – according to Thompson (1985: 111) – Theocritus, by way of Garcilaso.

Lope de Vega (1562–1635), a great dramatist and one of the best poets of his time, counts among his greatest poems two with classical themes: in the first canto of *La Filomena* (1621), he develops the history of Tereus and Philomela, and in *La Circe* (1624), written in octava rima, he imitates part of the *Odyssey*. His burlesque poem *La gatomachia* (1634) is one of his masterpieces. As was frequent in those centuries, his directly imitative works were predominantly inspired by Italians, especially Torquato Tasso.

Luis de Góngora (1561–1627), one of the greatest Spanish lyricists, in his post-1613 work initiates a style to which Lope refers with the burlesque term *culterano*, but he also undoubtedly imitates the classics, as much the Latins as the Greeks. In his greatest poems, *Polifemo* and the *Soledades*, he imitated Seneca and the Silver Age authors. Eunice Jones has demonstrated the strong influence of Claudian upon this great Cordoban poet. His contemporaries had already recognized the influence of the Greek lyricists as well as poets of the Latin Silver Age (López Grigera 2005).

Francisco de Quevedo (1580–1645), educated by the Jesuits to be able to imitate the classics, continued along these same lines. His translations appear to obey the advice of Cicero and Quintilian to translate in order to enrich one's own language. He imitated Pindar, Statius, Martial, Juvenal, and Persius. Some books from his personal collection have been discovered with marginalia that show his interest in imitation: for example, his copies of Pindar, Lycophron, Florus, and Aristophanes have all come to light. In Santander there is an exemplar of Aristotle's *Rhetoric* that belonged to him, with interesting annotations and references to his own poetry (López Grigera 1998). His copy of Statius' *Sylvae* is also preserved and has been studied by Craig and Hilaire Kallendorf (2000). Their study is of great interest because Quevedo imitated Statius, especially in his "Silvas," the study of which was begun by Eugenio Asensio (2005b: 2). In his translation of the *Anacrontea*, Quevedo reveals a philological preoccupation with the Greek text. His amorous sonnets, in turn, are considered among the best in Spanish poetry.

3.3.5 Prose fiction   In the sixteenth century the modern novel is born: in Spain there emerges, in the middle of the century, the "picaresque" genre and – simultaneously – the pastoral. The short novel of the Italian type flourished at the beginning of the seventeenth century: its most important authors are Miguel de Cervantes, Lope de Vega, and María de Zayas (1590–1650). Juan de Zabaleta (1600?–1677?) ended up burying the genre of Spanish narrative fiction with his portraits of manners in which the verbal forms of the "narrated world" disappear, replaced by the current ones of the "world, commented upon." The masterworks of the Spanish novel are *La vida de Lazarillo de Tormes y de sus fortunas y adversidades* (The life of Lazarillo de Tormes and his fortunes and adversities), published in 1554, and the *Quijote*, published in two parts, in 1605 and 1615. The *Lazarillo*, apparently the autobiography of a *pícaro*, or a socially marginalized rogue, boasts of its classical erudition, citing Cicero and Pliny directly in the prologue and also making reference to Ovid. The anonymous novel's narrative technique proceeds from Aristotle and Hermogenes (Artaza 1988), and Marasso (1947) also believes that "the end of the *Lazarillo* parodies the end of the *Georgics*" (212). The *Guzmán de Alfarache* (1599 and 1604) achieved unprecedented success that lasted over a century. The pastoral, from 1560 to 1630, imitated in prose the classical bucolics, combined with more or less Neoplatonic theories of love, as seen in the works of Pietro Bembo, León Hebreo, and Flaminio Nobili. The oldest pastoral novel of this period, *La Diana*, was written in Spanish by the Portuguese Jorge de Montemayor. On a parallel track, and with equal success, there developed a tradition of the Greek novel. Great writers such as Lope de Vega and Cervantes composed pastoral and Greek novels. The rise of a middle-class reading public, especially women, fomented the proliferation of novels containing amorous adventures.

Miguel de Cervantes (1547–1616) deserves special mention. He once lamented that it was "I who in vain toil and keep vigil, / in order to appear that I have as a poet / the glory which heaven did not choose to give me" (*Viaje del Parnaso* [Journey to Parnassus] vv. 25–7). Ironically, he is now considered to be the greatest prose writer of the Spanish language. His novels, which he wrote relatively late in life, are the pastoral *La Galatea* (1585), *El Quijote* (1605 and 1615), the *Novelas ejemplares* (Exemplary novels, 1612), and the *Persiles* (1616). Within the *Novelas ejemplares* there are three, "Rinconete y Cortadillo," "El Licenciado Vidriera" (The glass licentiate), and the "Coloquio de los perros" (Colloquy of the dogs), which fall within the genre of Menippean satire, especially the last two of these. The *Quijote* also contains much that could be considered Menippean. Its reception was special: the first part, which appeared in early 1605, met with great success, as much in Spain as in America, where some complete editions were carried over to the "New" World. But the book's first readers saw it as full of jokes to make them laugh; soon after it was published, Don Quixote and Sancho became characters in public festivals. Nevertheless, its success was inferior to that of *Guzmán de Alfarache*, which even until the eighteenth century was considered superior to the *Quijote*. In the nineteenth century, the *Quijote* was elevated by the German Romantics, who saw it as an incarnation of the best artistic ideals, and it was transformed, in popular opinion, into a sublime work, admired as the fruit of a "lay genius" who improvised ingeniously without any classical influence (all pure originality). But ever since Américo Castro published his *El pensamiento de Cervantes* (The thought of Cervantes, 1925), things have changed radically. Now it is accepted that Cervantes received a humanistic education, and his classical sources have been studied. (Already in the eighteenth century and at the beginning of the nineteenth, annotators had noted these sources.) In the twentieth century, Arturo Marasso has fearlessly revalorized that classical tradition; the first thing he notes is Cervantes' relationship to Vergil:

> Spain had entered into its plenitude with the glory of a Platonic spirituality – Horatian, Vergilian, Latin. If Cervantes had not been imbued, since he was a child, with this spirit, he would not have attained universality or become what he is, in the wise play of his ironic and captivating intelligence. The Vergil of Cervantes is many times a Vergil intentionally deformed, but not for this reason is the great poet's stimulus any less. (1947: 15–16)

He believes that the influence of Vergil is stronger in the *Quijote* of 1615 than in that of 1605, upon which the "sphere of the chivalric romance" exerts greater influence:

> The Vergilian cycle can group itself predominantly thus in this work: the windmills, an allusion to the Cyclops (*Quijote* VIII, *Aeneid* III); Crisóstomo, the episode of Dido transferred from classical tragedy (*Quijote* XI–XIV, *Aeneid* IV); the epic catalogue (*Quijote* XVIII, *Aeneid* VII); the adventure of the dead body (*Quijote* XIX, *Aeneid* XI); the fulling mills (*Quijote* XX, *Aeneid* III, VI); and the helmet of Mambrino (*Quijote* XXI, *Aeneid* VIII).

Meanwhile, in the second part, "the knight-errant Don Quixote is transformed almost completely into the heroic Don Quixote" (18). Marasso demonstrates with precision that Cervantes parodies the Spanish translations of Diego López and Hernández de Velasco more than the Latin text, and recalls that Vicente de los Ríos, in his *Análisis del Quijote* of 1780, affirmed that "the stay of Don Quijote in the house of the Duke and Duchess corresponds perfectly to the detention of Aeneas in Carthage" (148).

3.3.6 Menippean satire In 1528, there appeared a work titled *Libro aureo de Marco Aurelio* (The golden book of Marcus Aurelius), by Antonio de Guevara (1480?–1545). Humanist Europe, anxious to discover the works of the philosophical Roman emperor, read avidly this fiction that a Franciscan friar, adapted to courtly life since a child, wrote (apparently as a mirror for princes). It is a work laden with invented erudition. It probably had at least two types of reception: the common reader (like today) would devour these fictional stories, but the erudite one would laugh out loud at the fraud. It was thus that this work, according to Casaubon, was the most-read book in Europe, second only to the Bible, and was translated into almost every language. This work should be situated in the Menippean genre, like that of his contemporary and near companion of religion, François Rabelais.

From the sixteenth century onward, there are various Lucianesque dialogues, some published later; but only in the seventeenth century do the great works of this genre arise: three *Novelas ejemplares* by Cervantes, and the *Sueños* (Visions) and *La hora de todos* (The hour of all, or the last reckoning) by Quevedo. The *Coloquio de los perros* of Cervantes is a masterpiece: a man convalescing from syphilis relates – although he doubts whether he dreamed it or heard it – a dialogue between two dogs in the hospital of Valladolid. One of them, on narrating his life, passes through all the social classes of Sevillian life. In the *Sueños* of Quevedo – the *Sueño del juicio final* (Vision of the last judgment), the *Sueño del alguacil endemoniado* (Vision of the demoniac constable), the *Sueño del infierno* (Vision of hell), the *Sueño del mundo por de dentro* (Vision of the world from inside), and the *Sueño de la muerte* (Vision of death) – the classical tradition is more evident, although in some of them, biblical sources are predominant. But apart from the fact that the genre is clearly Lucianesque, the narrator himself comments at times upon his debt to various classical authors, from Cicero to Claudian.

3.3.7   Prose, non-fiction   Although the principal sources of ascetic and mystical prose are biblical and patristic, nonetheless it is worth noting the presence of classical authors: in Book 1 of his *Introducción al símbolo de la fe* (Introduction to the symbol of faith), Fray Luis de Granada (1504–88), to prove rationally the existence of God, uses two Latin authors: Cicero and Seneca. Saint Augustine and Saint Jerome are also important sources in these works. But Francisco de Quevedo, who had recently taken minor orders, is neo-Stoic in his early ascetic treatises: his *Doctrina moral* (Moral doctrine) was strongly influenced by Seneca and Epictetus (Rothe 1965). Two decades later, we find less neo-Stoicism in his writing and more patristics (Ettinghausen 1972).

The historiography of the Renaissance and the Baroque reached its height upon having to recount the extraordinary deeds of the "discovery" and conquest of America. The classical tradition in historiography may be noted already at the middle of the fifteenth century in Alfonso de Palencia (1423–92), educated in Italy, a disciple of George Trebizond. From the last third of the sixteenth century we have the *Historia de la guerra de Granada* (History of the war of Granada) by Diego Hurtado de Mendoza, with the strong influence not just of Tacitus, but also of Thucydides. At the end of the seventeenth century we see a figure of great interest, a poet, dramatist, and historian who may be situated within the group of so-called pre-Enlightenment innovators: Antonio de Solís (1610–86), who wrote the *Historia de la conquista de México* (History of the conquest of Mexico). The Carmelite Jerónimo de San José (1587–1654) also published in 1651 his treatise on historiography, *Genio de la historia* (Genius of history).

3.3.8   Drama   Edward Wilson attributes to Juan del Encina the creation of a theater "on a neo-Aristotelian model half a century before the *Poetics* became widely known in Europe" (Moir & Wilson: 4), but we must remember that in 1498 Giorgio Valla had published his translation of the *Poetics* of Aristotle and that, as Patricia Garrido Camacho (1999) has shown, all the writers of the end of the fifteenth century and beginning of the sixteenth had made use of the *Rhetorica ad*

Herennium (Cicero 1981) and the rhetorical works of Cicero, which contained certain classical dramatic principles (27–9). Juan de Encina also could have gleaned some of these ideas from the commentaries of Donatus on the comedies of Terence (46–7). Garrido recalls that these theories are gathered into "the two great vocabularies, el *Papias vocabulista* (Papias the lexicographer) and the *Universal vocabulario* (Universal word-list) of Alfonso de Palencia" (47). For her, "the influence of the *Poetics* of Aristotle on the first half of the sixteenth century, in terms of the treatment of anagnorisis, appears unquestionable." In effect, there is an early presence of "recognitions" such as those prescribed by Aristotle in some works of the Portuguese Gil Vicente and Bartolomé de Torres Naharro (flourished 1517). And we do not need to interpret them as the influence of Italian theater.

In the second half of the sixteenth century the influence of theories and models from classical theater is undeniable. Tragedy is where it is noted most, according to Wilson: "it was not till the 1570s that a school of deliberately classicising Spanish tragedians grew up." But "when this school did appear, its main stylistic source was not Greek tragedy but Seneca, the great model of all the Renaissance and seventeenth-century European schools of tragedy" (Moir & Wilson 1971: 29). Lupercio Leonardo de Argensola (1559–1613?), Andrés Rey de Artieda (1549–1613), Cervantes, and others followed it.

With Lope de Vega (1562–1635) the Spanish theater experienced a great change, which has been erroneously interpreted according to Romantic principles as an expression of that which is genuinely Spanish, "national and popular"; this is something that should be reconsidered, because the classical influence on his work is clear, although Lope's dominant themes are in fact national and local. Nonetheless, as criticism has insisted, his dramas are more of action than of characters – and this is precisely what Aristotle recommends in his *Poetics*.

4   Spanish and Portuguese Literature of the Eighteenth and Nineteenth Centuries

On the influence of the classical tradition in the eighteenth century there can be no doubt. Leandro Fernández de Moratín (1760–1828) was able to compose dramatic works following the supposedly Aristotelian "three unities," but literary history, the fruit of post-Kantian Romanticism, underestimated this century precisely for its lack of originality. Still, at the end of the nineteenth century, the children of the Romantics returned their gaze to classical antiquity. And the so-called "generation of '98" was firmly grounded in the classics. Men such as Miguel de Unamuno (1864–1936) and Antonio Machado (1875–1939) found their roots in the thought, artistic theories, and styles of antiquity. Vergil returned to Catalan letters with the Renaixença, the movement in defense of the Catalan language, at the beginning of the second third of the nineteenth century, according to José Luis Vidal (1988: 973–5). Marcelino Menéndez Pelayo (1856–1912) published important studies of the classical tradition in Spain and America. And one cannot escape mentioning a novelist like Juan Valera (1824–1905), who recognized the value of Rubén Darío and his classical roots, since he himself had just finished a Spanish translation of Longus' *Daphnis and Chloë*.

The classical tradition in Portugal begins in the Renaissance. Medieval Portuguese literature such as the *Cantigas de amor* (Songs of love) and the *Cantigas de amigo* (Songs of lovers), written in Portuguese and Galician, do not appear to bear the influence of classical tradition. Furthermore, in the Renaissance, the majority of Portuguese writers wrote in Spanish: a good part of the theater of Gil Vicente (1470?–1536), almost all the work of the poet Sá de Miranda (1481?–1558), the work of Jorge de Montemayor (1520?–1561), and a good part of the works of even Luis de Camoëns (1524?–1580) were written in Spanish. From the seventeenth century the great prose writer Francisco Manuel de Melo (1608–66) also wrote in Spanish.

I trace the bare outlines of what has been studied for this material, which is not much, since Romantic literary criticism has predominated, exalting original nation-alistic Portuguese works more than the classical tradition. But I should pause over the great epic poet Luis de Camões. A recent study by José V. de Pina Martins, "El humanismo en la obra de Camões," considers that this humanism "would have to be defined by what the poet owes to his masters, Homer and Vergil" (1982: 14). With irrefutable authority, he affirms that the reading of the poet "was immense in the area of Greco-Roman literature," although he recognizes that Camões was "a reader of anthologies, since any cultured man of the sixteenth century, travelling as he did, could not take along an entire library" (14–15). Concerning his Platonism, Pina Martins recalls that

> in the monologue of the main character of one of his works, the *Auto llamado Filodemo* (Auto called Philodemus), he speaks of Plato, of Bembo, Garcilaso, Laura and the sonnets of Petrarch. This offshoot, which denounces the existence of anti-Platonic and anti-Petrarchan cultural currents, implicitly proves that the poet was very sensible to the impact and the work of Platonism and Petrarchism. (19)

However, Pina Martins warns that even more than a manifestation of Petrarchism, Camões' style is a *stilnovismo* movement, which becomes fashionable in Italy starting in 1527 (22). On the other hand, he notes that in the lyric poetry there may be detected the strong presence of Ovid (29). In his *Estudios portugueses* (Portuguese studies, 1974), Eugenio Asensio notes multiple classical sources for Portuguese authors of the Renaissance and Baroque.

FURTHER READING

Unfortunately, very little on the classical tradition in Spain has been published in English. Di Camillo (1988) offers a useful overview of Spanish humanism and its roots in the classics, while Beardsley (1970) surveys Spanish translations of Greek and

Latin authors published in the sixteenth and seventeenth centuries. Ettinghausen (1972) and Kallendorf and Kallendorf (2000) trace the classical roots of Francisco de Quevedo, who can serve as a representative of Golden Age culture. For those who can read Spanish, the works of Menéndez Pelayo (1950–3, 1952–3, 1962) and Lida de Malkiel (1975) remain fundamental. Several studies trace the influence of particular classical authors in Spain: Seneca (Blüher 1983), Martial (Gil 2004), Terence (Gil 1984), Lucian (Vives Coll 1959), and Vergil (Gil 1988, Morreale 1988, and Vidal 1988). Finally, two excellent works on the classical roots of the key writers of Spain and Portugal, Marasso (1947) on Cervantes and de Pina Martins and Asensio (1982) on Camões, deserve mention.

This chapter has been translated by Hilaire Kallendorf.

CHAPTER FOURTEEN

Italy

David Marsh

1   The Late Middle Ages

By the year 1200 a patchwork of distinctively Italian societies was emerging that shared the traditions of Roman law and the faith of the Roman church, and which soon found a *koinē* or common language in Tuscan Italian. In a land so markedly shaped by Roman institutions and Greco-Roman civilization, the classical tradition had deep roots to which cultural movements would constantly return for nourishment and support.

As in the rest of western Europe, the classical inheritance in medieval Italy was preserved largely through ecclesiastical institutions such as monasteries and cathedral schools, whose collections and curricula were notably enhanced by the so-called "Carolingian renaissance" of the ninth century. Typically, classical works were read in the selections excerpted in encyclopedias and anthologies, or in the corpus of texts recognized as school "authors." With the rise of universities in the later twelfth century, Italy was in the vanguard with two schools noted for a specialized curriculum: Salerno for medicine, and Bologna for law. The teachers in such institutions were markedly international, as foreign faculty competed for the most prestigious positions (Scaglione 1990).

The language of instruction and the professions remained Latin, and the slow emergence of vernacular literature in medieval Italy reflects the persistence of Latin as the vehicle of diplomatic, legal, and religious expression. It is only after 1200 – by which time a varied literature already existed in French, Provençal, and Spanish – that a distinctly Italian language developed, based on the language of Florence. The ascendance of Tuscan Italian owed its success in part to the ease with which it could assimilate Latinate vocabulary and syntax, which is brilliantly demonstrated in the prose and poetry of Dante Alighieri (1265–1321).

A generation earlier, Dante's teacher Brunetto Latini (ca. 1220–94) had employed French prose in writing his philosophical compilation *Li livre dou tresor* (The book of the treasure), a work that reflects the Gallic enthusiasm for encyclopedic compilations (Picone 1994). But shortly after 1300 Dante showed in his prose *Convivio* (The banquet) that serious philosophical questions could be discussed in the Tuscan dialect. (By so doing, he emulated the achievement of his admired Cicero, who had rendered Latin a suitable vehicle for Greek philosophy.) In this work, Dante describes how he had attended "the schools of the religious and the disputations of the philosophers." Naturally, Dante's philosophical authorities include a number of Aristotelian and Scholastic thinkers such as Averroes, Albertus Magnus, and Bonaventure, but his writings also indicate a familiarity with the Roman poets Vergil, Statius, and Ovid, as well as the philosophical works of Cicero, Seneca, and Aristotle (which he read in Latin).

Dante's greatest achievement was his *Comedy*, an epic allegory couched in a poetic language capable of describing vividly both the horrors of hell and the raptures of heaven. Whereas Dante's philosophical prose followed the model of Cicero, the inspiration for this epic allegory derived from Vergil's *Aeneid*, and in particular from allegorized interpretations of Aeneas' descent into the underworld. For more than half the poem, Dante is guided by Vergil, who is hailed as the poet's "teacher and author"; and in Limbo Vergil introduces Dante to Homer, Horace, Ovid, and Lucan – thus making him an heir of the classical tradition. In point of fact, Dante knew Homer only indirectly and makes little use of Horace. But in *Inferno* 25, when describing grotesque metamorphoses, he boasts that his work challenges Ovid and Lucan. His "medieval" masterpiece explicitly rivals the poets of classical antiquity.

2 Humanism: The Early Renaissance

Beginning in the late thirteenth century, the movement that came to be called humanism – the study of classical history and literature as the basis for new cultural ideals – arose in the literary and intellectual circles of northern Italy (Rabil 1988; Witt 2000). Initially fostered by jurist-poets such as the Paduans Lovato dei Lovati (1241–1309) and Albertino Mussato (1261–1329), the enthusiasm for Latin history and poetry inspired Francesco Petrarca (Petrarch) (1304–74) to invent a career as a cosmopolitan man of letters and self-styled "moral philosopher" that set a pattern for generations to come. Although it was his Italian poetry that would change the course of European lyric, Petrarch was symbolically crowned as poet laureate in 1341 for undertaking a Latin epic that sought to rival Vergil's *Aeneid*. And in classical studies, his exemplarity as humanist scholar was established by his discoveries of neglected manuscripts and by the philological acumen he demonstrated in emending the text of the Roman historian Livy.

The search for classical texts that lay neglected in monastery libraries had in fact begun with the Paduan poets. By visiting Pomposa and other northern Italian monasteries, Lovati brought to light the tragedies of Seneca (soon to be imitated by his pupil Mussato) as well as poems by Lucretius, Statius, Catullus, Tibullus, and Propertius. In 1333, Petrarch found a copy of Cicero's oration *Pro Archia* (In defense of Archias), a text much valued for its defense of poetry and poets. In his enthusiasm for ancient history – evident in his Latin epic about Scipio – Petrarch devoted himself to writing biographies of Roman heroes and to assembling all the extant corpus of Livy. In the next century, Poggio Bracciolini (1380–1459) continued the search. While attending the Council of Constance (1414–18), he made several notable discoveries: Valerius Flaccus' *Argonautica*, Silius Italicus' *Punica*, and a complete text of Quintilian's *Institutio oratoria* (Institutes of the orator) (Sandys 1921). Poggio used such new-found sources in composing his series of neo-Ciceronian dialogues on moral topics (Marsh 1980). He also learned enough Greek, despite a busy diplomatic career in the papal Curia, to make rather free translations of works by Lucian, Diodorus Siculus, and Xenophon.

The study of ancient Greek had begun abortively with Petrarch, who owned a codex of Homer but was unable to find a suitable teacher. By contrast, Petrarch's friend and admirer Giovanni Boccaccio (1313–75) brought the Calabrian scholar Leonzio Pilato to Florence in 1360, where in the next two years he produced Latin prose versions of Homer's *Iliad* and *Odyssey* accompanied by textual notes. Despite some disparaging remarks about him in Petrarch's letters, Pilato, who had spent some years in Crete, offered a valuable collation of Homeric texts and scholia, from which Boccaccio gleaned matter for his *Genealogia deorum gentilium* (Genealogy of the pagan gods).

This residence of a Hellenist in Florence set an example for the next generation. In 1396, the chancellor of the Florentine Republic, Coluccio Salutati (1331–1406), summoned the Byzantine scholar Manuel Chrysoloras (ca. 1349–1415) to offer public lessons in Florence. Finding no textbooks in Italy, Chrysoloras composed a brief outline of Greek grammar in the form of a catechism appropriately titled *Erotemata* (Questions). His most illustrious pupil was Leonardo Bruni (1370–1444), who, like Salutati, eventually became the chancellor of Florence. As a "civic humanist," Bruni wrote a Latin history of Florence that reveals a debt to Roman historians and provides a new beginning for Renaissance historiography. Even more influential were his many Latin translations from the Greek. Beginning with St. Basil's *Discourse to Young Men* (1400), a Christian apology for pagan literature, Bruni in the next 30 years translated Xenophon's *Hieron* and *Apology*, three of Demosthenes' orations, seven of Plutarch's *Lives*, five of Plato's dialogues, and Aristotle's *Economics*, *Ethics*, and *Politics*. When his translations of Aristotle drew fire from Schoolmen accustomed to medieval versions, Bruni replied in 1428 with a Latin treatise *De recta interpretatione* (On correct translation).

In 1400, Chrysoloras left Florence, but his contribution to Italian humanism did not end with his departure. Guarino Guarini of Verona (1374–1460) traveled to Constantinople and lived in the house of Chrysoloras from 1403–8 before returning to Italy, where he taught Greek, first in Venice and Verona, then finally in Ferrara, in the service of the Este rulers (1430–60). Guarino translated several works of Isocrates and Lucian, 15 of Plutarch's *Lives*, and all of Strabo's *Geography*. Two decades later, another Italian, Francesco Filelfo (1398–1481), likewise spent five years in Constantinople in the house of Chrysoloras' nephew, whose daughter he married. On his return to Italy, he taught in Florence and Milan; among his many translations are Latin versions of Aristotle's *Rhetoric*, four of Plutarch's *Lives*, and Xenophon's *Agesilaus*, *Spartan Constitution*, and *Education of Cyrus*.

Such intellectual commerce between Italy and Constantinople eventually guaranteed the survival of Greek scholars and manuscripts. In 1423, the Sicilian Giovanni Aurispa (1376–1459) brought to Italy 238 Byzantine codices, including the tenth-century codex (now Laurentianus 32.9) that remains an essential witness for Aeschylus, Sophocles, and Apollonius of Rhodes. Most of this commerce took place by way of Venice, whose empire in the eastern Mediterranean was to contribute Italian elements to modern Greek; and with the advent of printing it was Venice that naturally became the capital of Greek imprints. Aldo Manuzio (1449–1515), who was renowned for his elegant pocket-sized editions of Latin and Italian classics, also published some 27 first editions of Greek classics, many of them edited by the Cretan Marcus Musurus (ca. 1470–1517) and his colleagues.

As early as Leonzio Pilato, the teaching of Greek had entailed the paraphrasing of texts in Latin, and Italian humanists undertook numerous translations to make ancient works accessible to a wider readership. In this field, they were encouraged by the example of Cicero, whose dialogues had purveyed the tenets of Greek philosophical schools to an educated Roman elite. More important, the demands of accurate translation provoked lively discussions not only about the relations between style and meaning, but also about the historical development of languages as well. The foundations of modern philology were laid when the language of texts as canonical as Aristotle and the New Testament Vulgate was analyzed by Lorenzo Valla (1405–57), who later translated the Greek historians Herodotus and Thucydides for Pope Nicholas V. Giannozzo Manetti (1396–1459) was a wealthy Florentine – today we would call him "an independent scholar" – who, like Valla, enjoyed the patronage of both Alphonse of Aragon and Pope Nicholas V. Besides applying his knowledge of Greek to Aristotelian and biblical texts, he also studied Hebrew and translated the Psalter – a controversial enterprise that he defended in his treatise *Apologeticus* of 1454.

The humanists' engagement with classical texts proved beneficial to vernacular literature as well. By the 1430s, Leon Battista Alberti (1404–74) could assert that Latin and Italian possessed equal dignity as vehicles of literature and philosophy, since each language was the normative means of communication in its day; and he sought to demonstrate the fact in neo-Ciceronian dialogues written in Italian, such as his four books *Della famiglia* (On the family). This reassessment of the medieval view of Latin as an unchanging and eternal language inaugurates the Renaissance cultivation of vernacular languages, which were subsequently enriched by infusions of classical ideas and vocabulary.

The humanist movement also effected a shift in educational practice, which occurred largely outside the established institutions of the universities. To the university disciplines of medicine, law, and theology, Petrarch had preferred the classical *studia humanitatis*, which concentrated on grammar, rhetoric, history, moral philosophy, and poetry. In the 1430s, Guarini in Ferrara and Vittorino da Feltre in Mantua established schools that adopted this curriculum. Eventually, what is now known as an undergraduate "liberal arts" education developed from such schools, while universities continued to offer advanced (today's "graduate") professional training (Grafton and Jardine 1986). Contributors to the humanist program included scholars like Pier

Paolo Vergerio and Leonardo Bruni, who wrote treatises on the subject but never taught in classrooms (Kallendorf 2002). In the Quattrocento (fifteenth century), humanist educators taught Latin and Greek as the classical foundation of the educated individual. But even vernacular education perforce included a large "classical" component, since the works of Italian poets from Dante to Ariosto were imbued with allusions to the culture of antiquity (Grendler 1989; Black 2001).

Even before the advent of printing, many humanists published dialogues and epistles, genres in which learning and discussion are presented in the social context of the author's friends and correspondents. (The principal Roman model for both was, of course, Cicero, whose letters and philosophical dialogues were widely imitated during the Renaissance.) The same process of relativization evolved in the humanists' reflections on history. In the vanguard was Leonardo Bruni, whose Latin *Historia populi Florentini* (History of the Florentine people) advances historiography from medieval chronicle and exemplary anecdote to an analysis of political institutions and motivations. At mid-century, Bruni was succeeded both as chancellor and historian of Florence by Poggio Bracciolini, whose political acumen and historical vocation were certainly less inspired. In the vernacular, the engagement with Livy's Roman history, which had begun with Petrarch, was carried forward by Niccolò Machiavelli (1469–1527), who also followed in the footsteps of Bruni and Poggio Bracciolini as both chancellor and historian of Florence.

The rediscovery of ancient Greek texts in Quattrocento Florence naturally stimulated the study of philosophy. Here, too, Bruni was in the vanguard. By 1415, he had translated seven of Plato's dialogues, and in the next 20 years he was to translate Aristotle's *Nicomachean Ethics*, *Economics*, and *Politics*. In 1433, Ambrogio Traversari (1386–1439) completed his Latin version of Diogenes Laertius' *Lives of the Philosophers*, a text that offered new insights into Greek schools of thought (Grafton 1988; Schmitt 1988). In the next generation, Marsilio Ficino (1433–99) published a complete translation of Plato's works in 1484, and numerous works by Plotinus and other Neoplatonists between 1492 and 1497. In addition to paraphrases and commentaries on various texts, he also composed an elaborate "Platonic theology" that attempts to reconcile ancient philosophy with Christian belief (Ficino 2001–6).

The impact of classical texts during the Quattrocento was facilitated by two new cultural mechanisms. First, libraries guaranteed the consolidation of humanist acquisitions, as manuscripts that had lain unknown in monasteries were transferred to, or copied for, private collections that soon passed into public libraries. In Florence, the book collector Niccolò Niccoli (1363–1437) bequeathed some 800 codices to the library of the Dominican convent of San Marco; and the collection of the Medici family eventually passed into the Biblioteca Medicea-Laurenziana, now housed in a building designed by Michelangelo. In Rome, the Vatican Library – officially, the Biblioteca Apostolica Vaticana – was consolidated under Nicholas V (1447–55) and officially institutionalized by Sixtus IV (1471–84). In the course of time, it would acquire the libraries of prelates, princes, and potentates, and amass one of the most important collections of classical manuscripts and printed books in the world (Grafton 1993). In Venice, the exceptional library of the Greek cardinal Bessarion (1403–72) formed the basis of the city's Biblioteca Marciana.

Second, the advent of printing accelerated the diffusion of humanist learning and promoted the emergence of classical philology as scholars collated and edited texts for publication. The new technology of movable type, invented by Gutenberg around 1450, arrived in Italy in 1465, and soon Italians were "classicizing" the new print culture. Based on the humanistic script devised by Quattrocento humanists like Poggio Bracciolini, typographers created a "Roman" font to replace the "Gothic" characters of German printers. And they eagerly sought to provide new and improved editions of classical texts. In the preface to his 1469 edition of Apuleius, the prolific editor Giovanni Andrea Bussi coined the term *media tempestas,* or "middle age," referring to the centuries that separated contemporary humanists from classical antiquity.

In the Renaissance, as later in the Risorgimento, the city of Rome was the symbolic center of Italy, historically and geographically, which came to dominate much of the entire peninsula. In 1309, the papacy moved to Avignon, and the failed attempt by Italian cardinals to restore it to Rome resulted in the Great Schism. In 1417, a Roman of the powerful Colonna family was elected as Pope Martin V, and by mid-century Pope Nicholas V began to reshape the physical and cultural landscape of the Eternal City. As Rome gradually emerged from the backwater of the fourteenth century into the *caput mundi* of the sixteenth century, it was transformed by men inspired by the classical past.

In the Middle Ages, Rome had been a natural destination for pilgrims and travelers, but medieval guidebooks like the *Mirabilia urbis Rome* (Wonders of the city of Rome) contained numerous inaccuracies about classical sites and institutions. With his fervid interest in Roman history, Petrarch was the first to study critically the ruins of Rome, which he described in his writings and put to literary use in his epic poem about Scipio Africanus. And he pointed the way toward modern numismatics by collecting Roman coins and adducing them as evidence for understanding ancient history. In the Quattrocento, the description of extant monuments was continued and elaborated by humanists like Poggio Bracciolini, whose dialogue *De varietate fortunae* (On the variability of fortune) contains a survey of ancient Rome, and Flavio Biondo (1392–1463), whose *Roma triumphans* (Rome triumphant), *Roma instaurata* (Rome restored), and *Italia illustrata* (Italy illustrated) offer detailed commentary on Roman monuments and institutions. Another member of the papal Curia, Leon Battista Alberti, surveyed Rome's most notable monuments from the Capitoline hill and charted them on a polar-coordinate map. Epigraphy, or the study of inscriptions, developed from the research of men like Biondo and his contemporary Ciriaco d'Ancona (1391–1452), who traveled to Greece and sketched details from ruins (Cyriac of Ancona 2003). In the sixteenth century, printing and the papacy joined forces to promote the antiquarian movement in the Eternal City (Stinger 1985; Weiss 1988; Jacks 1993).

At the same time, new Latin translations of Greek writers like Plutarch and Diodorus Siculus greatly expanded the humanists' repertory of historical data. In the field of architecture, Alberti based his Latin *De re aedificatoria* (On the art of building, 1452) on Vitruvius' *De architectura* as well as on his own analysis of ancient monuments. And the discovery in Rome of the Domus Aurea in the 1480s inspired artists like Pinturicchio and Raphael to devise the elaborate ornamental patterns called *grottesche* after the grottos in which they were found. If during the Renaissance, popes paid lip service to preserving ancient monuments, while in fact quarrying them for new projects, the papacy began to take an interest in the conservation of artworks. Pope Sixtus IV founded the Capitoline Museum, the first public collection in Europe (Ridley 1992).

3   The High Renaissance and Baroque Era

As in other fields, the Cinquecento (sixteenth century) witnessed the codification of a classical style in architecture and city planning. More than a century after Alberti, the most influential printed treatise was the 1570 *Four Books of Architecture* by Andrea Palladio (1508–80), who had already published surveys of Roman antiquities and churches in 1554. Both Palladio's work and the 1615 *Idea of Universal Architecture* by his pupil Vincenzo Scamozzi (1552–1616) were translated into French and English; and in England his original texts were studied by Inigo Jones (1573–1652), the first of the British neoclassical architects.

After the Council of Trent (1545–63), Italian missionaries were instrumental in disseminating Christian and classical ideals throughout the world. The Jesuit order excelled in "propagating" classical learning through the curriculum outlined in its *Ratio studiorum* (Plan of studies) and soon became an international brotherhood of scholars and missionaries. In 1634, the German Jesuit Athanasius Kircher (1601–80) settled in Rome, where he founded a museum of antiquities and published some 40 volumes that established him as a paragon of classical erudition. Yet over the course of time the Jesuit order had no lack of scholarly Italians, such as the historian Lodovico Antonio Muratori (1672–1750) and the philologist Angelo Mai (1782–1854), who continued the humanistic tradition of discovering unknown texts.

The diffusion of classical ideals was also promoted by the foundation of Italian academies – a name derived from Plato's school, adjacent to a grove dedicated to the hero Academus – in which learned men gathered to discuss literary or scientific questions. During the Quattrocento, the term "academy" often designated an informal group of scholars united by a common interest, such as the Platonic Academy of Florence led by Marsilio Ficino. In Naples, under Alphonse of Aragon (1442–58), an erudite circle formed around the humanist Antonio Beccadelli (1394–1471), called Panormita after his native city of Palermo ("Panormus" in Latin). After his death, the direction of the Accademia Antoniana was assumed by the humanist poet and diplomat Giovanni Pontano (1426–1503), who formalized the structure of the organization, which continues today as the Accademia Pontaniana.

In the sixteenth century, the formal institution of Italian academies multiplied and soon inspired the creation of analogous institutions in France and England. The seminal gatherings of the Quattrocento at first often lacked a formal name, membership lists, and rules of order. Early in the next century, the idea of an erudite *sodalitas* persisted and inspired Raphael's fresco *The School of Athens* (1509–11) in the Vatican. By 1540, academies were proliferating in Italy's urban centers, and by 1600 there were some 377 academies in Italy. By 1700, the number of Italian academies had grown to nearly 1250. Among the most prominent of these were the Roman Accademia dei Lincei (1603), which still meets and publishes today (website: www.lincei.it), and the Florentine Accademia della Crusca, whose 1612 *Vocabolario* (Dictionary) established it as the linguistic arbiter of the Tuscan language. In addition to its critical editions of Italian texts, the academy has since 1996 posted a website (www.accademiadellacrusca.it) that features a vast array of information about the Italian language.

Italian academies were soon imitated in other countries, and the city of Rome proved to be a powerful magnet for learned societies from various nations. Whereas academies in Italy were usually local civic organizations, their French and English imitators tended to be nationalized (Findlen 1999). In 1632, Cardinal Richelieu founded the French Academy, which affirmed the Aristotelian "unities" of time, space, and persons; and Pierre Corneille, inducted as a member, defended his 1636 tragedy *Le Cid* by citing the neo-Aristotelian rules endorsed by the Academy. By this time, the French artists Nicolas Poussin (1594–1665) and Claude Lorraine (1600–82), favored by Louis XIII, had settled in Rome; and in 1666 Louis XIV founded the French Academy in Rome that offered a "classical" experience to aspiring artists such as Jacques-Louis David (1748–1825) and Jean-Auguste-Dominique Ingres (1780–1867). (In 1803, Napoleon transferred the Academy to the Villa Medici, overlooking the Spanish Steps, and instituted the prestigious prize for musical composition that would be held by composers like Berlioz and Debussy.)

Academies and courts were essential in the development of "classical" theater and in that quintessentially Italian invention, the opera. During the Middle Ages, the ancient Roman comedies by Plautus and Terence were often read but seldom imitated. In the "heroic" age of manuscript discoveries during the early Quattrocento, Nicholas of Cusa discovered 12 unknown comedies by Plautus (1429) and Giovanni Aurispa found Donatus' commentary on Terence (1433). Such discoveries inspired Neo-Latin dramatists like Enea Silvio Piccolomini (1405–64), later Pope Pius II, whose *Chrysis* of 1444 is a cento (composite pastiche) of Plautus and Terence (Grund 2005). In the next century, Ludovico Ariosto (1474–1533) adapted these Roman models in five Italian comedies that exercised an influence far beyond the court of Ferrara. His comedy *Suppositi* (1509) was the model for the English *Supposes* (1582), written by George Gascoigne (ca. 1525–77), which in turn influenced Shakespeare's early comedies, *The Comedy of Errors* and *Taming of the Shrew* (ca. 1589–94). Gascoigne also translated Ludovico Dolce's *Giocasta*, an Italian tragedy based on Euripides' *Phoenissae*.

The Greek text of Aristotle's *Poetics*, which expounded the principles of classical drama, was first printed in the 1508 Aldine edition of *Rhetores Graeci* (Greek rhetoricians) ; but it was only 40 years later that Italian theorists turned their attention to ancient Greek tragedy, producing a vast series of treatises in Latin and Italian on poetics. After the appearance in 1548 of the *Explicationes* by Francesco Robortello (1516–67), the next decades saw the publication of Latin and Italian translations and commentaries on Aristotle's treatise by Bernardo Segni (1549), Bartolomeo Lombardi and Vincenzo Maggi (1550), Piero Vettori (1560), Lodovico Castelvetro (1570), Alessandro Piccolomini (1575), Antonio Riccoboni (1585), and

Lionardo Salviati (1586). Mediated by works like Julius Caesar Scaliger's Latin *Poetices libri septem* (Seven books on poetics) (1561) and Jean Vauquelin de La Fresnaye's versified *Art poétique* (1605), neo-Aristotelian standards shaped the French tragedies of Corneille and Racine (Weinberg 1961; Schmitt 1983).

From the outset, Italian opera not only sought to reinvent Greek musical drama, but was also a vehicle for the celebration of Greek mythology and ancient history. As the Greek name suggests, the notion of *melodrama* (in Italian *dramma per musica*) arose in a learned society – namely, the Florentine Camerata dei Bardi, whose members sought to discover the principles of the musical drama in antiquity. In the first generation of Italian opera, the three extant operas of Claudio Monteverdi (1567–1643) dramatize Greek myth (*Orfeo*), Roman history (*L'incoronazione di Poppea* [Coronation of Poppaea]), and episodes from Homer's *Odyssey* (*Il ritorno di Ulisse in patria* [Ulysses' return to his homeland]). A century later, the erudite librettist Apostolo Zeno (1668–1750) drew upon the classical historians Herodotus, Thucydides, Plutarch, and Livy for his opera libretti. His successor as Imperial Poet in Vienna was Pietro Metastasio (1698–1782), whose 27 libretti on classical themes shaped the course of *opera seria* (serious opera) in theaters from Vienna to London. His *Clemenza di Tito*, for example, was set by more than 50 composers, including Mozart (Smith 1970).

Like Italian artists, Italian opera composers were conspicuously itinerant; and the eighteenth century witnessed an unparalleled diffusion of Italy's musical culture. For example, the Venetian Baldassare Galuppi, who set several of Metastasio's works, spent 1738–43 in London, and 1765–70 in St. Petersburg, where he premiered his setting of Marco Coltellini's libretto *Ifigenia in Aulide* (Iphigenia in Aulis). Later in the century, Gluck effected his opera reforms in collaboration with the Tuscan poet Raineri de' Calzabigi (1714–95), who wrote mythological libretti for *Orfeo ed Euridice* (Orpheus and Eurydice), *Alceste* (Alcestis), and *Paride ed Elena* (Paris and Helen).

Throughout the Baroque, Italy likewise supplied Europe with classicizing standards in painting and architecture. In his pastel apotheoses of saints and Olympian gods, Giambattista Tiepolo (1696–1770) celebrated the iconic supremacy of the *ancien régime* (traditional monarchies) in palaces from Würzburg to Madrid. Meanwhile, Italian architects created the monuments of sovereign states from Madrid (the Royal Palace by Giovanni Battista Sacchetti, 1740) to St. Petersburg (the second Winter Palace by Domenico Tressini, 1716; and the General Staff Building and Winter Palace by Carlo di Giovanni Rossi, 1819).

4   The Enlightenment and Modern Era

Inevitably, the courtly and ecclesiastical ascendance of the classical heritage was challenged by new ideas. After 1700, the classical tradition found itself under attack from two camps in particular. The rationalists of the Enlightenment reacted against the identification of Greco-Roman culture with the values of Catholic education and monarchism. And the avatars of Romanticism stridently decried classical rules as stifling the vital inspiration of Nature.

All the same, it is a commonplace that Italy never experienced a reformation or revolution; and the cultural offshoots of the Enlightenment and Romanticism, rather than taking root, were merely grafted onto the more liberal branches of society. In this context, the *New Science* of Giambattista Vico (1668–1744) attempts to reconcile a devout affirmation of divine Providence with a recognition of the prerational impulses that inspired primitive poetry and civilization (Vico 2001).

Vico's insights into primitive myth stripped classical mythology of its ideological trappings and suggested instead that poetic narratives derived their power from a darker, more universal force in the human mind. Nevertheless, neoclassical taste and style in Italy – fostered by conservative political hegemonies – weathered the Napoleonic storm. Indeed, Napoleon's occupation of Rome, like that of Egypt, led to the development of systematic and state-run archaeology (Ridley 1992). The playwright Vittorio Alfieri (1749–1803) translated works by Aristophanes and Terence, and based many of his tragedies on Greek myth (*Agamemnon, Antigone, Merope, Orestes*) or on ancient history (*Brutus, Horatius, Philip, Regulus, Scaevola, Timoleon, Virginia*). The virtuoso sculptor Antonio Canova (1757–1822), today celebrated for his neoclassical monuments representing various popes and potentates in idealized form, lived in Rome from 1781, where he served as museum director, superintendent of antiquities, and president of the Accademia di San Luca, Italy's premier Academy of Fine Arts. Inspired by ancient works, Canova helped to shape the neoclassical movement in the arts; he was also granted the title of marquis for his role in restoring to Rome works such as the *Apollo Belvedere* (imitated in his own *Perseus*) and the *Laocoön Group*, which Napoleon had taken to Paris in 1799. And the fiery patriot Ugo Foscolo (1778–1827), born on the Greek island of Zakynthos, began his career in Venice with the tragedy *Thyestes* and ended it in London, translating parts of Homer and revising an unfinished *Hymn to the Graces*, which was inspired by Canova's sculptures. Complete translations of the Homeric epics were made by Foscolo's friends Vincenzo Monti (1754–1828; *Iliad*, 1811) and Ippolito Pindemonte (1743–1828; *Odyssey*, 1822), whose versions defined Greek epic for many generations of Italians.

In mid-century, a fortuitous discovery gave classical archaeology in Italy a major boost. Just four years after Vico's death, workmen digging near the Sarno canal southeast of Naples discovered bronzes and marbles from the ancient town of Pompeii, which had been buried by the eruption of Vesuvius in AD 79 and which now became a sort of outdoor laboratory of practical archaeology. In the latter half of the eighteenth century, the story of Pompeii's destruction, recounted by Pliny the Younger, exercised a great fascination over educated Europeans like Goethe, who visited the "mummified city" in March of 1787. In the same period, the keen German interest in Italian antiquities was incarnated in the figure of Johann Winckelmann (1717–68), whose writings inaugurated modern scholarship on classical art and led to his appointment by Pope Clement XIII in 1763 as Commissioner of Antiquities in Rome. Archaeology in the Kingdom of Naples was at first sporadic, but eventually Italian scholars began to conduct more systematic excavations. During a long and illustrious career, Rodolfo Lanciani (1847–1929) discovered many antiquities at Rome, Tivoli, and Ostia and published a topographical survey of classical, medieval, and modern Rome titled *Forma urbis Romae* (Plan of the city of Rome, 1893–1901). By the second half of the nineteenth century, the study of Italian antiquities was being vigorously promoted by German, French, and Italian scholars (Moatti 1993).

Like Petrarch, Giacomo Leopardi (1798–1837) contributed both to classical philology and to Italian lyric poetry, although he enjoyed none of the international celebrity of his humanist predecessor. During his lifetime he published critical observations on editions of the classics as well as a slim volume of lyric poems, or *Canti*, and a series of *Operette morali* (Little moral works) whose title intentionally echoes the canonic essays of Plutarch. In this collection, Leopardi often imitates Lucian by composing dialogues based on Greek mythology. Yet his sense of irony is more world-weary than cynical, and in the classical past he finds little of the sublime as celebrated by Vico. Leopardi also compiled a vast *Zibaldone di pensieri* (Miscellany of reflections), an intellectual diary of notes on his readings in classical and Italian literature, as a sort of reference work that he even provided with an index. This philosophical and philological miscellany reveals Leopardi in dialogue with German classical scholars like the historian Reinhold Niebuhr.

As a nationalist movement, the nineteenth-century Risorgimento had little use for the Hellenic enthusiasms of Foscolo or Byron. The poet Giosue Carducci (1835–1907), Italy's first professor of Italian literature (1860) and her first Nobel laureate in literature (1903), sought to revive "classical" metrics in his Italian *Odi barbare* (Barbaric odes) of 1877, several of which celebrate the glories of the Roman past. At the same time, classical education prepared men of letters like Giovanni Pascoli (1855–1912) and Pope Leo XIII (Vincenzo Gioacchino Pecci, 1810–1903, pontiff from 1878) to craft Latin odes worthy of the Horatian tradition. Even the "decadent" poet Gabriele D'Annunzio (1863–1938) composed a lyrical evocation of the Hellenic world in his *Maia* (1903), a poem of some 8,400 lines inspired by a trip to Greece in 1895. The first half of the work commemorates a tour of Patras and the Peloponnese; but the poet never mentions Athens, and the poem concludes with a celebration of Rome, the Sistine Chapel, and Carducci's patriotic odes on Italy's greatness!

5   The Twentieth Century and Beyond

Europe's faith in its classical tradition was irreparably damaged by the crisis of belief and culture caused by World War I. Yet in Italy, the social and financial unrest of the 1920s fueled the propagandistic exploitation of "Roman" ideals by Benito Mussolini and his Fascist party. During the 20-odd years of this regime, the *renovatio imperii* (renewal of the empire) inspired not only imperialistic ventures in Greece and Africa, but the renewal of Roman festivals, a "Roman" calendar dating from the advent of Fascism, and a style of public architecture intended to evoke a "masculine" revival of classical monumentality. Under the Duce, ancient Rome was glorified as an exemplar of heroic militarism, and the valor of its history was revived both in oversized statues and buildings and in the practice of the "Roman" salute. The complex of buildings on the outskirts of Rome known as EUR – the site of a world fair, or *Esposizione Universale di Roma*, planned for 1942 but canceled by the war – offers a notable instance of the Fascist reworking of classical architecture. Still, the Roman enthusiasms of the regime led to achievements more lasting than displays of patriotic propaganda. Mussolini clearly identified with Augustus as an autocratic ruler establishing Italian prosperity at home and power abroad; and in 1937, the bimillennium of the emperor's birth, Mussolini commissioned the restoration of the *Ara Pacis* (Altar of Peace), which depicts Augustan achievements. He also sponsored extensive excavations of classical monuments and famously surpassed the emperor Trajan by draining the Pontine Marshes, a malarial wetland that by 1940 hosted a series of "Roman colonies": Aprilia, Latina, Pomezia, Pontinia, and Sabaudia.

During the early twentieth century, the mythical Mediterranean persisted in Italian poetry, bridging the late Romantic effusions of Gabriele D'Annunzio (1863–1938) and the Hermetic seascapes of Eugenio Montale (1896–1981; Nobel prize 1975). Inevitably, the early Italian cinema exploited the Roman past, at first evoking its Romanticized depictions by Victorian and *fin-de-siècle* artists. The epic style of Mario Caserini's *The Last Days of Pompeii* (1913) and Giovanni Pastrone's *Cabiria* (1914) and *Maciste* (1915) influenced D. W. Griffith's epic *Intolerance* (1916). After World War I, the Italian movie industry declined, but in 1937 Mussolini founded Cinecittà (the Italian Hollywood, outside of Rome), whose productions were inaugurated by Carmine Gallone's *Scipione l'Africano* (Scipio Africanus), a Fascist-sponsored epic with a decidedly less republican vision of history than Petrarch's *Africa*!

After World War II, Italy regained its standing as a major film producer and profited from the renewed fascination of moviegoers with the classical world. During the 1950s and 1960s, Italy provided inexpensive scenery and extras for what were called "sandal and spear" epics, and Hollywood producers bankrolled such iconic successes as William Wyler's *Ben Hur* (1959) and Stanley Kubrick's *Spartacus* (1960), which were "shot on location," as it were. During the same years, Federico Fellini (1920–97) was portraying the Americanization of his adopted city in *La dolce vita* (The sweet life) (1959); but within a decade he, too, turned to the classical past as the inspiration of his poetic and dreamlike vision of the Roman past in *Satyricon* (1970) and *Roma* (1972).

Around 1960, the gifted poet Pier Paolo Pasolini (1922–75) undertook an Italian translation of Vergil's *Aeneid* that he soon abandoned, and a version of Sophocles' *Antigone* that was never published. But the classical tradition was also central to his intense and well-publicized involvement with the theater and motion pictures. In addition to his original dramas, Pasolini translated Aeschylus' *Oresteia* (1960) and rendered Plautus' *Miles gloriosus* in Roman dialect as *Il vantone* (The braggart, 1963). After his first black-and-white films, based on his own fiction about contemporary Rome, Pasolini took on larger projects in color including *Oedipus Rex* (1967) and *Medea* (1969) – adaptations of Greek tragedy that anticipated Fellini's more whimsical evocations of ancient Rome. But the ancient world was only one of various eras and cultures that inspired Pasolini, and his film career, cut short by his violent murder in 1975, ended with a so-called *Trilogy of Life* (1970–4) that drew on Boccaccio, Chaucer, and the *Arabian Nights*.

As if in reaction to the Romantic movement, Greek antiquity also exercised its fascination, albeit sporadically, over postwar Italian writers. The Lucianic tradition inspired the *Dialoghi con Leucò* (Dialogues with Leucothea) by Cesare Pavese (1908–50). Written between 1945 and 1947, this series of 27 brief dialogues – originally titled *Uomini e dèi* (Men and gods) – evokes the works of Lucian and of his imitator Leopardi. In poetic exchanges, pairs of figures like Oedipus and Tiresias or Circe and Leucothea examine the meaning of mythological events in a sort of lyrical existentialism that, while grounded in ancient myth, holds implications for the contemporary human condition. The presence of Hermes signals Pavese's own "hermetic" reworking of Greek mythology as a vessel for autobiographical symbolism, which is comparable to Dante's *Vita nuova* (New life) as a figural rereading of the poet's experience. Yet Dante's cosmological framework is here replaced by an archetypal mythology that derives from the historic vision of Vico, the anthropological symbolism of Sir James Frazer's *Golden Bough*, and the collective imagination of Carl Jung.

An even more impressive monument to Frazer, and to the poet and mythographer Robert Graves, is found in Roberto Calasso's *Nozze di Cadmo e Armonia* (Marriage of Cadmus and Harmony, 1988). This rhapsodic prose poem unites the threads of Greek mythology in a poetic prose-poem whose opening pages emblematically echo Vico's observations on Europa. Like Pasolini and Pavese, Calasso seems drawn to Greek antiquity because it is remoter than the Roman past and thus more susceptible to personal interpretation. At the same time, the twentieth-century *revitalization* of the classical tradition entails its *relativization*. Unlike the Roman heritage embraced by Italian thinkers from Petrarch to Pascoli, classical antiquity was now viewed as only one of many valid cultural paradigms. It is not surprising to find that Calasso's later novel, *Ka* (1996), deals with the origins of Buddhism.

During the postwar period, Italo Calvino (1923–85) achieved worldwide fame for his innovative narratives. Yet when he was invited to deliver the Norton lectures at Harvard University in 1985, he abandoned Borges and French deconstruction in favor of the classical tradition. Not surprisingly for a writer concerned with narrative invention and structure, Calvino turned to ancient Greek rhetoric. Interrupted by his sudden death, his *Six Memos for the Next Millennium* actually consists of five lectures on literary criteria – lightness, quickness, exactitude, visibility, and multiplicity – that reflect the rhetorical categories of the second-century orator Hermogenes (Kirby 2000). Significantly, the very first lecture, "Lightness," begins with a retelling of the myth of Perseus and Medusa, with quotations from Ovid and Montale.

6 Conclusion

The most striking feature of the classical tradition in Italy is its continuity. In part, this is fostered by the extensive survival of the physical record of Roman civilization, which has inspired countless poets, architects, and tourists. The persistence of Latin-based culture, ensconced in the rites and liturgy of the Roman church, and in traditional disciplines like law and medicine, exercised a conservative restraint on Italian culture. Upon this foundation, the new ideals of the Renaissance added further layers of classically inspired culture in the arts, letters, and education. By the sixteenth century, Italy's classicizing trends were setting the pace for much of Europe. With the Counter-Reformation, Rome again asserted a cultural hegemony that dominated those lands not lost to Protestantism, while the ecstatic creations of the Baroque could occasionally cross borders drawn by religion.

In the eighteenth century, the quest by Italians to understand the Roman world led to the rise of anthropology (the insights of Vico) and archaeology (the unearthing of Pompeii), but elsewhere in Europe the study of the ancient Greek world inspired a new vision of noble sublimity. The Romantic generation in Italy shared in this movement, in which a rarefied ideal of Hellenic antiquity was seldom clouded by an actual inspection of Greece's inscriptions and monuments, much less by a confrontation of its political plight. The Risorgimento gave renewed impetus to the Roman past, and by 1871 the new nation of Italy perforce made Rome its capital. Whereas the crisis of World War I undermined European faith in the classical tradition, in Italy it aided the rise of Mussolini's Fascist party, which soon played the trump card of the "Roman" destiny of the Italian people. Outside Italy, scholars who regarded the Fascist vision as tainted analyzed the great cost at which Augustus and the empire had triumphed. After World War II, Italian writers and filmmakers increasingly turned to Greek myth, perhaps in reaction against the "Roman" ideal. But soon the ancient monuments of the Italian peninsula and its capital proved powerful enough to fuel a postwar boom in tourism and cinema centered around the grandeur that was Rome. Bread and circuses, indeed.

CHAPTER FIFTEEN

Latin America

Andrew Laird

Times will come in later years when Ocean will loosen the chains of things and a huge mass of land will lie revealed, Tethys will uncover new worlds, and Thule will not be the furthest of lands.

Seneca, *Medea*

The Classical Tradition is a golden chain which enables us to "take our journey back", as Edwin Muir puts it. And at the end of all our journeying are those same everlasting Forms of Beauty that have always been there and always will be.

No one, of course, has ever believed this nonsense. There are much messier stories to tell of the "real" Classical Tradition, and classical studies as a discipline have always been much more "open," again in every sense ... one of the functions of the classical ideal has always been to enable rebellion from it, to function as a dreary father figure. . . .

Don Fowler, *Roman Constructions*

1   Tradition versus Innovation: Conflicting Classical Legacies

The premiere of the first opera specifically commissioned for performance in the Americas was held in Peru on October 19, 1701. Tomás de Torrejón y Velasco, the director of music in Lima Cathedral, composed *La púrpura de la rosa* (The blood of the rose) to honour the eighteenth birthday of Philip V of Spain and the first anniversary of his reign.[1] The libretto, already regarded as a literary masterpiece in its own right, had been written in 1659 by the great poet and dramatist of the Spanish Golden Age, Pedro Calderón de la Barca. Developing the story of Venus and Adonis from Ovid's *Metamorphoses* 10.503–739, Calderón had attributed the killing of Adonis by a wild boar to the machinations of the god Mars, who is jealous of Venus' love for the mortal youth. A purple rose grows from the blood of the fatally wounded Adonis, and at the end of the drama Venus and Adonis are reunited in heaven by the personified figure of Love (*Amor*).

Calderón's libretto, with its numerous choral passages, was evidently suited to Torrejón y Velasco: the proficiency of the Peruvian choristers who sang in Quechua, Latin, and Spanish had inspired other composers like Juan Pérez Bocanegra and Juan de Araujo to hybridize European music with Andean as well as African influences. In transmitting a Greco-Roman myth to its viceregal audience, *La púrpura de la rosa* thus involved not only Spain's best-known poet and Peru's leading composer, but very probably drew from the talents of indigenous singers and musicians as well. The production of this opera at the beginning of the eighteenth century may seem to provide impressive evidence of a classical tradition existing in at least one part of the vast area now known, however controversially, as "Latin America" (Pym 2000: 191; see also Bolaños and Verdesio 2002).

But is this evidence for a classical tradition in Peru so impressive? To what extent can Torrejón y Velasco's endeavor really be considered American? The opera represents the tidy transplantation of European courtly culture and political values to the quintessentially colonial setting of the palace of Don Melchor Portocarro Lazo de la Vega, the Viceroy of Peru who commissioned it. And it is also important to heed a more general point: the occasional artistic adaptation of a Greek or Roman story, whether mythical or historical, should not necessarily be taken to indicate the existence of a "classical tradition" in any strong or meaningful sense. *La púrpura de la rosa* is more properly an example of "classical *reception*" – and fairly indirect reception at that: it was the librettist Calderón de la Barca and certainly not Ovid who provided the impetus for Torrejón y Velasco's composition. Calderón's stature as a playwright in Spain and its dominions was roughly equivalent to that of Shakespeare in England, and we might compare popular responses to *Venus and Adonis*: for better or worse, that poem will always interest more people for being a text by Shakespeare than for the crucial influence of Ovid on its contents.

I have opened this discussion with the problematic example of *La púrpura de la rosa* because I suspect that its predominant constitution – of European myth, European poetry, and European music – exemplifies what many believe or imagine to be the character of the classical tradition in the Americas. It is assumed that Greco-Roman civilization is not an authentic element of Latin American culture, but a concern only for those artists or thinkers who hold some allegiance to the Old World or whose interests extend beyond the continent they inhabit.

What is more, much Latin American literature of the twentieth century would seem to support this incorrect assumption – or rather the cosmopolitan careers of the globetrotting authors themselves would seem to support it. For example, *Elogio de la madrastra* (Praise of the stepmother) by Mario Vargas Llosa, a Peruvian writer who has spent much of his life in France, specifically presents its erotic retelling of the Gyges story from Herodotus' *Histories* as an ekphrasis of a Flemish painting, *The Wife of Candaules, King of Lydia*, by Jacob Jordaens. And while Gabriel García Márquez in his 2002 memoir *Vivir para contarla* (Living to tell the tale) acknowledges Sophocles as one of the two greatest influences on his writing in Colombia during the 1950s, the second author he names is William Faulkner, whom he read along with Hemingway, Joyce, and Virginia Woolf. The modernist poetry, essays, and fictions of Jorge Luis Borges are well known for their elegant incorporation of ideas and curiosities from classical antiquity, but the writer's Argentine background probably had little to do with this aspect of his work: Borges attended the Collège Calvin in Geneva – where he added German, French, Latin, and Greek to his native Spanish and English – before moving to Italy and Spain in the 1920s. Again, the novelist Alejo Carpentier, who published widely on a number of Greek and Latin authors after his return to Cuba, had lived as an exile in Paris (Miranda Cancela 2003: 117–35). And Carlos Fuentes, who has incorporated Scipio's conflict with Hannibal in Numantia in his 1993 novel *El naranjo* (The orange tree), was educated in the United States and Switzerland and served as Mexican ambassador to France.

But there have been many other individuals from earlier centuries, if not less well traveled then less well known outside Latin America, whose ideas and achievements were influenced directly by the legacy of Greece and Rome, to the extent that classical antiquity came to have a very conspicuous place in the continent's history.

Two contrasting figures – both important protagonists in the political formation of their respective nations – merit specific discussion: the Byronic hero of Cuban independence, José Martí (1853–95), and the scholarly president of Colombia, Miguel Antonio Caro (1848–1909). José Martí began his prolific career as a poet and political essayist in the 1860s when he was still at school in Havana: his work for underground newspapers led to his exile to Spain at the age of only 17. Although he managed to return to Cuba on three occasions, Martí was compelled to spend most of his life abroad: he lived in Mexico and taught literature and philosophy at the University of Guatemala before eventually settling in New York, from which he campaigned relentlessly for his country's independence. He died in combat after leading a brigade of revolutionaries from the US to Cuba in 1895. Martí's legacy has been extraordinarily influential: one poem alone, *Guantanamera*, inspired the well-known popular song; his prose writing is much admired; his advocacy of a solidarity between the peoples of Hispanic America, the importance he attached to indigenous histories, and his opposition to racism and colonialism continue to inform progressive thinking (Martí 2002: 288–95). More recently, emphasis has also been laid on the importance of Hellenism or – to use the substantivized adjective Martí himself preferred, *lo griego* (the [idea of what is] Greek) – for his revolutionary vision (Miranda Cancela 2003: 8).

In the 73 volumes of his collected writings, there are more than a thousand references to the Greco-Roman world. José Martí had a profound admiration for Aeschylus, Aristophanes, Hesiod, and especially Homer; he publicized Heinrich Schliemann's excavations at Troy and Mycenae in the New York daily *La América*; and he made Spanish translations of some Anacreontic poems from the Greek Anthology. But, as the Cuban scholar Elina Miranda Cancela has also observed, it was neither scientific antiquarianism nor the Wildean aesthete's search for beauty in a romanticized past that enthused Martí, but the potential of Greek culture to enhance understanding of the present and to shape the future (Miranda Cancela 2003: 29–45). Though he was not oblivious of ancient imperialism, Martí saw a clear parallel between the Greek struggle for freedom in his own time and the predicament of colonial Cuba. José Martí's unselfconscious absorption of the classical tradition and his vision of its heroism are evident in a stanza from one of his best-known political poems, "Sueño con claustros de mármol":

> I dream of marble cloisters
> where in silence divine
> the heroes, on foot, repose;
> at night, by the soul's light,
> I speak to them: at night!
> They are in line, I pass
> between the lines: their hands
> of stone I kiss: there open
> eyes of stone: there move
> lips of stone: there shake
> beards of stone: they grasp
> the sword of stone: they weep:
> the sword vibrates in its case!
> Mute, I kiss them on the hand.
> (Martí 1891: poem 45, stanza 1, my trans.; see also Martí 2002: 282–5)

The circumstances, character, and aspirations of Miguel Antonio Caro could hardly be more different from those of Martí. Though Colombia continued to lack political stability, the country had secured independence from Spain in 1819, more than 20 years before Caro was born in Bogotá. Caro attended a Jesuit school and became proficient in Latin: while he never had any formal higher education, the early interest he developed in language, philology, and literature endured for the rest of his life. His first volume of poetry came out in 1866, and, at the age of 18, he published a Latin grammar in collaboration with Rufino José Cuervo: *Gramática de la lengua latina* (Bogotá, 1867). A treatise on the use of the participle followed in 1870.

Caro began his public career by founding a conservative periodical, *La tradicionalista*, to attack the ideas of the *radicales*, liberal thinkers in Colombia who opposed interventionist government and who advocated federal republicanism and a separation of Church and State, along with secular education. In Caro's view, their idealism was making the nation ungovernable: the federal system had devolved power to the dictatorial whims of autonomous territories, each of which had its own politics, exchequer, and army. Having sought an alliance with Rafael Nuñez, the leader of the moderate liberal wing, Caro had a major involvement in the constitutional assembly in 1886. As vice-president when Nuñez assumed the presidency of Colombia in 1892, Caro was able to become the architect of a series of centralizing reforms, known as the *Regeneración*, which restricted individual liberties and strengthened accord between the government and the Catholic Church. On Nuñez's withdrawal from public life in 1894, Caro himself became president until 1898.

While José Martí has a place in history for his political activities rather than his humanistic devotion to classical culture, the reverse might apply to Miguel Antonio Caro. Even in Colombia, Caro is at least as much remembered for what he contributed to his country's literary and pedagogical legacy as he is for his involvement in its political history. As well as holding two chairs in philosophy and founding a Catholic university in Bogotá, he was National Librarian and President of the *Academia Colombiana de la Lengua* (Colombian Academy of the Language, an institution modeled on the *Real Academia Española*, the Spanish royal academy). Caro's best known work is a Spanish verse translation of the complete works of Vergil, but he produced many other translations into Latin verse as well as Spanish, literary criticism, and poetry of his own (Rivas Sacconi 1993). It is tempting to imagine that the discipline of Latin verse composition and the codification of language and grammar held a special attraction for a man who sought to impose order on a society he considered to be tumbling into chaos. And Caro's particular devotion to the Augustan poet Vergil seems all too appropriate for an ideologue whose program of *Regeneración* has more than a glancing resemblance to the reformist legislation of the emperor Augustus himself.

Though Martí and Caro were contemporaries, it is not customary to compare them, because of the dissimilarity of their respective historical and political positions. The perspectives these two nineteenth-century Americans had on the Greco-Roman world, how they conceived of it and approached it, are correspondingly divergent: the adventurous radicalism of a Hellenist creatively driven by the grand vista of antiquity stands in virtual opposition to the conservativism of a philological Latinist with a Catholic education. That polarity may at first look as if it conforms to a frivolous opposition commonplace in classical studies today: between *Greek*, which is held to foster original thinkers who are concerned with bigger issues raised by the "predicament of culture," and *Latin*, which is stereotyped as appealing to those who confine themselves to the exacting but very methodical techniques of textual criticism and historical commentary.

In fact, Martí's and Caro's different attitudes to antiquity point to a more serious tension – between *innovation* and *tradition* – which underlies every narrative about the later legacies of Greece and Rome. That tension goes well beyond the problem of how to explicate ancient authors: it is between those who regard antiquity, Greek or Roman, as a springboard for the present, universalizing its texts and artifacts as material to *use* or think with, and those who instead seek – or affect – to *preserve* an idea of the ancient past, transmitting its contents (or even imposing them) on to the age in which they live, irrespective of the concerns and preoccupations their present age may have. That tension between innovation and tradition has perhaps manifested itself in Latin America more acutely than anywhere else, and it came to the surface very rapidly, as soon as classical learning took root in the early 1500s. And that tension in American interpretations of Greco-Roman culture came to have more consequence and significance than many Europeans could have envisaged.

2   Indigenous American and *Mestizo* Influences on the Classical Tradition

The impact of ancient Greece and Rome on the New World is usually considered in terms of a very wide range of discourses about the Americas from the European Renaissance. The celebrated "Controversy of the Indies," for instance, was a battle of books and speeches, conducted in Valladolid in Spain in 1550–1, in which the Spanish humanist Juan Ginés de Sepúlveda appealed to Aristotle's notion of the natural slave to argue that the "barbarian" Indians should be subjugated. Bartolomé de las Casas used his own knowledge of ancient philosophy to counter that all humans were rational: challenging the application of the term "barbarian" to the Indians, he insisted that war and slavery should not be imposed upon them. That debate did not just involve Aristotelian thought: the historical precedent set by the Roman empire also played a major part in the arguments of both sides (Lupher 2003).

Ethnographers like Peter Martyr (Eatough 1998, 1999a), Bernardino de Sahagún (León Portilla 2002; Mason 1994; Lupher 2003), and Gonzalo Fernández de Oviedo informed debates like this by applying classical paradigms to the cultures they described. Conversely, reports about the pagans in the newly conquered territories were occasionally used to shed light on pre-Christian Greece and Rome. The Spanish humanist Juan Luis de La Cerda, for example, applied knowledge gleaned from the New World in his magisterial Latin commentary on the complete works of Vergil (Laird 2002: 190–1). And in a Spanish translation of Vergil's *Georgics* (1596), the Galician Juan de Guzmán, supposedly resident in the New World, offered a *silva de varia lección* (a miscellany of variegated reading) of indigenous American words by way of comment on 48 of Vergil's verses (Morreale 2002). But far more frequently, it was "recognition" of aspects of the classical past in American phenomena and cultural practices that found expression in European literature and poetry. From the sixteenth to the eighteenth centuries, a number of neo-Latin epics recounting Columbus' feats in Vergilian style abounded in Italy and elsewhere: Fracastaro's *Syphilis* (1530) and Stella's *Columbeid* are the earliest and best known examples (Eatough 1984, 1999b; Hofmann 1994). Columbus' own son Ferdinand made a significant annotation to the lines of *Medea* – quoted in the first epigraph to this chapter – in his copy of Seneca: "this prophecy was fulfilled by my father ... the Admiral in 1492" (Elliott 1988:1; see also Rossi 1998). The extent to which the Renaissance preoccupation with antiquity determined the way in which the Americas were conceived and regarded has been subjected to a great deal of attention – and by very prominent figures such as Antony Grafton (Grafton, Shelford, and Siraisi 1992), Stephen Greenblatt (1991), and Tzvetan Todorov (1984).

The classical tradition is often regarded as a monument that can stand only awkwardly on American soil, simply because European imperialism and elitism first put it there. But Greek and Roman antiquity has perfused the culture and imagination of Latin America. Classical motifs and themes abound in visual art, architecture, literature, and all kinds of intellectual discourse. Well-known architectural examples include the colonial Catedral Metropolitana of Buenos Aires, the Palacio del Gobierno in Quito (remodelled with a neoclassical façade after Ecuador's independence in the 1830s), and the imposing mid-twentieth-century statue of "The Archeress of the North Star" in Mexico City, popularly known as *Diana la cazadora* (Diana the huntress). The American classical tradition, however, pertains not only to *criollos* (Spanish Americans in the ethnic sense) and the Portuguese colonial class in Brazil. The classical tradition is also an important part of the continent's rich *mestizo* (mixed race, multicultural) and indigenous heritage – and that aspect of it certainly merits much more emphasis and academic attention than it has so far received. But it is also important to remember that *criollos*, those people of Spanish origin born in the Americas, were not generally accorded the same status as Spaniards in Spain during the colonial period (roughly 1520–1800). The same situation did not obtain in Brazil, where there was no creolization of the colonial state, despite the emergence of a Brazilian as opposed to Portuguese identity from the early 1700s (Bethell 1987). Thus even an account confined to the role of the classical legacy in the *criollo* experience would constitute an account, however selective, of an American inheritance. As the present volume is the first-ever guide to the classical tradition in English to give any consideration at all to Latin America, the basic emphasis here on cultural productions *from* the countries in the region should need no justification.

At the same time, the confused political, ethnic, and cultural scenario that prevailed after the European incursions has meant that the definition of what – or who – is American can never be conceived too rigidly. Juan Correa (1646–1716), an important painter in colonial New Spain (Mexico) and one of the very few artists to treat classical themes, is a case in point. His mother's parents were *bozales*, or native Africans, and his father's parents, a Spaniard and a *mulata*, or possibly a *morena* (Moor), were both from Cádiz. Correa's paintings were celebrated for depicting individuals from Christian and pagan literature *de color quebrado* (in a burnt color) (Velásquez Guttiérez 1998: 9n1). An animated detail from his ambitious screen *The Four Elements and the Liberal Arts* presents the Daughters of the Sun – from Ovid's *Metamorphoses* 2.344–66, where they are turning into poplar trees – as *mulatas*, crowned with headdresses of shooting leaves.

A very different case is that of the poet Alonso de Ercilla y Zuñiga (1533–94), a patriotic Spaniard who dedicated his epic *La Araucana* to Philip II. Even though Ercilla was a conquistador in Peru, even though he returned to Spain and died there, and even though his epic poem recounts its author's own part in punitive expeditions to crush the rebellious Araucanian Indians of Chile, Ercilla is nonetheless staunchly regarded as the national poet of Chile, even as a virtual founding father of the nation: an "inventor and liberator," in the words of the deeply humanitarian Chilean communist Pablo Neruda (1971, quoted in Kallendorf 2003: 395). This apparently puzzling accolade is in no small part explained by the way in which classical literary models are used in *La Araucana* itself. Allusions to Roman poets and historians are frequently compounded in order to provide analogies that give an epic stature to the indigenous warriors, as in the following excerpt from a lengthy description of the Araucanian sacking of Concepción:

> Not with so much severity did the Greek people
> penetrate into the Trojan settlement
> scattering Phrygian blood and live fire,
> cutting it down to the utmost foundation,
> as in anger, vengefulness, and blind frenzy
> the barbarian people – not content with plunder
> makes ruin, destroys, lays waste
> and yet still cannot take fill of its malevolence.
>
> (Canto 7, octave 48, my trans.)

The grim tenor of the description and its hyperbolic, moralizing tone recall the style of the Roman poet Lucan, but the particular situation presented here evokes Aeneas' pathetic description of the fall of Troy in the second book of Vergil's *Aeneid*. Only a few lines later, Ercilla's *araucanos codiciosos* (avaricious enemies) are likened to columns of ants carrying their booty: this turns to different effect the simile Vergil had used to convey positively the industry of the ancient Tyrians as they built Carthage under Dido's leadership (*Aeneid* 4.402–7). Although the high esteem Alonso de Ercilla has for the Araucanians is made very clear in the opening stanzas of his poem and in his prose preface, different readings of the ways in which he transforms his literary sources – and indeed different readings of those sources themselves – have informed a range of opinions about the quality of the poet's sympathy for the indigenous Chileans (Quint 1993: 131–210; Kallendorf 2003).

Correa's paintings were relatively exceptional for giving *afromestizo,* or indigenous American likenesses, to figures from Scripture or classical literature. A kind of reverse of that process – in which indigenous American cultures, achievements, and individuals were represented in terms of paradigms and precedents from Greek and Roman civilization – was in fact nothing less than routine, from the mid-sixteenth century onwards. During the 1530s the philanthropic humanist Vasco de Quiroga, a devotee of Plato, Lucian, and Thomas More, sought to defend Indian autonomy by constructing "Utopian" communities in Mexico City and Michoacán (Zavala 1965). Indeed, from soon after the first conquests until well into the nineteenth century, there were those who sought actually to *equate* American populations with early Mediterranean peoples. In the 1550s Vinko Paletin, a Croatian Dominican, insisted that the Mayan inscriptions at Chichen Itza were in Punic and that the Carthaginians had once possessed the Indies – this was to show that the Roman Empire had proper title to these Punic territories, which, via the papacy, could pass to the Spaniards! (Lupher 2003: 167–86). Some comparable claims were made in the 1660s by another Dominican, Gregorio García, who argued that the natives of America were descended from the lost tribes of Israel and that the Carthaginians had constructed the Incan and Mayan monuments – García's more laudable aim here was to indicate that Spaniards and the native Americans had common ancestors (García 1980 [1607]; Brading 1991: 195–200, 382).

However, it was by no means only Europeans living in the Americas who perceived connections between indigenous American culture and European antiquity. Educated Indians and *mestizos* sought to ennoble, or simply to make sense of, their complex heritage in terms of classical models. This is evident in the famous writings of the Inca Garcilaso de la Vega (1539–1616). Garcilaso was the illegitimate son of the niece of the Inca Huaina Capac; his father was a prominent conquistador. A native speaker of Quechua, he had mastered Spanish and Latin in Cuzco before he traveled to Spain in 1560, never to return to Peru. Garcilaso's first publication in 1590 was a translation of a Neoplatonic work in Italian that also drew heavily from Jewish philosophy: *Dialoghi d'amore* (Dialogues of love) by Leone Ebreo.[2] This was followed by *La Florida del Inca* – an account of De Soto's expedition to the southeastern part of North America – in 1605, and the *Comentarios reales de los Incas* (The royal commentaries of the Incas) in two volumes: the first came out in 1609, the second, tactfully retitled *La historia general de Peru* (The general history of Peru), in 1617. Garcilaso was well aware of comparisons of the Incas to the Romans which had been made already by Spaniards, and he maintained that, for the purpose of writing Inca history, "all comparisons are odious" (Garcilaso de la Vega 1966: 1.1.xix.51, quoted and trans. in MacCormack 1998a: 11). Nonetheless, the idea of Rome, along with its history and its historians, from Livy to Isidore of Seville, pervades the *Comentarios reales*. After expressing his objection to the Spaniards' attempt to rename Cuzco "New Toledo," the Inca Garcilaso writes as follows:

> For Cuzco in relation to her empire was another Rome in relation to hers, and the one can thus be compared to the other, for they resembled each other in the most noble respects: first and foremost, in having been founded by their first kings; secondly, in the many diverse nations which they conquered and subjected to their empire; thirdly, in the large number of such good and truly excellent laws which they established for the government of their states; and fourthly, in producing so many and such excellent men and raising them with good civic and military teachings. (Garcilaso de la Vega 1966: 1.1)

And Sabine MacCormack has shown how the letter and spirit of Livy's Preface to his *Histories* was closely followed by Garcilaso, who sets out his own historical pro-gramme in almost exactly the same way:

> We will carefully recount the Inca's more historical doings, leaving aside many others as being irrelevant and prolix. And although some of what has been said, and of what will be said, may appear to be fabulous, I decided not to omit recording these matters, in order to avoid discounting the foundations on which the Indians build to explain the greatest and best achievements of their Empire. For it is on these fabulous beginnings that the grandeur that belongs to Spain was in effect founded. (Garcilaso de la Vega 1966: 1.1.xix.50–1, trans. in MacCormack 1998a: 18–19)

But as MacCormack also points out, such literary borrowing from ancient histo-rians should not be taken to imply that Garcilaso, who treated his Peruvian sources with considerable care, was producing a fictionalized or imaginary history of his people. His *methods* as well as his expression were informed by Polybius, Tacitus, Suetonius, Plutarch, and others, who regarded historical truth as bound up with the "moral dimension in human action and in historical processes" (MacCormack 1998a: 12).

An earlier Mexican *mestizo* writer, Diego Valadés, made an impressive attempt to use classical thought and learning to interpret indigenous traditions of knowledge. Yet in spite of the fact that his achievement was in many respects even more remark-able than that of Garcilaso de la Vega, Valadés is nowadays far less well known – perhaps because, unlike the Inca, he wrote his major work in Latin (Laird 2006b; Abbott 1996: 41–59). Diego Valadés, whose father was also a Spanish conquistador and whose mother was a member of the indigenous Tlaxcaltec nobility, was born in Tlaxcala between 1520 and 1533 and died in Italy, some time after 1582. He studied theology and philosophy in the Franciscan schools of Mexico City, and learnt the

Mexican languages of Nahuatl, Otomí, and Tarascan in order to work as a missionary. In 1571 he went to Spain and then to Paris before becoming Procurator General of the Franciscans in Rome. His *Rhetorica Christiana* (Art of Christian Rhetoric) was printed in Perugia in 1579. Consisting of nearly four hundred folio pages in Latin, illustrated by the author himself, this book is commonly deemed the first by an American writer to have been printed in Europe.[3] The title, which suggests an inventory of the requirements for successful preaching, had been imposed on Valadés by his superiors: the work is more of a doctrinal treatise that places special emphasis on the value of "artificial memory." Valadés had realized that indigenous Mexican calendars involved both natural memory and something akin to the mnemotechnic theories he found espoused in Cicero, Augustine, and other classical, patristic, and humanist authors. That led Valadés to construct an alphabet of words from Mesoamerican "hieroglyphs," which could be charged with new meanings. To make his case, he drew from a constellation of influences, ranging from the tenth-century Islamic philosopher Al-Farabi and the Aristotelian commentator Alexander of Aphrodisias to classical humanists of the Renaissance such as Petrarch and Politian. This striking fusion of humanist learning and an aboriginal Mexican heritage reflects Valadés' own transculturation: his origins as a Tlaxcaltec *mestizo* did nothing to diminish his standing as a scholar in Rome, able to correspond with Pope Gregory XIII – to whom he dedicated his *Rhetorica Christiana*.

The fact that Franciscan colleges had been set up in New Spain in order to teach Latin, rhetoric, philosophy, music, and theology to youths of the indigenous nobility in the early 1500s meant that there were a number of "Indians" who were conversant with the language. The students produced grammars, dictionaries, and sermons. They translated classical authors like Pseudo-Cato and Aesop as well as Christian texts into Nahuatl, the language of the Mexica or "Aztecs" (Osorio Romero 1990; Laird 2009: 182–196). Latin was, of course, a shibboleth of the Roman Catholic Church, and its dissemination by no means always entailed enthusiasm for the culture of pagan antiquity. Nonetheless, in the Spanish and Portuguese colonies of the sixteenth and seventeenth centuries, the Latin language continued to retain its association with ancient Rome and its function as a medium of secular humanism and literature, to a much greater degree than it ever would in North America. By the 1530s, the Indians studying at Santa Cruz de Tlatelolco in Mexico City had access to a wide range of pagan authors, including Cicero, Vergil, Seneca, Juvenal, Sallust, and Livy. One student, Pablo Nazareo, a prince from Xaltocan, translated the cycle of lessons for the church year from Latin into Nahuatl. In a Latin letter he wrote to Philip II of Spain in 1566, Nazareo quotes four verses from Ovid's *Ars amatoria* (Art of love) and shows his knowledge of their provenance by adding the words *ut ait Ovidius ille libro tercio de arte* (as Ovid says in the third book of the *Ars*) (Gruzinski 2002: 94; Osorio Romero 1990). The same letter compares the king to Phoebus Apollo. Even if one leaves aside speculation about how far the Indians integrated their knowledge of European paganism and ancient history into their own thinking, it is clear enough that classical culture – not just the Latin language – had pervaded Mexico surprisingly soon after the Spanish conquest.

3   The Emergence of a Hispano-Latin Literature in America

In periods of history during which the influence of Greek and Roman culture was potent or even overwhelming, there is often little or no contemporaneous conception of there being such a thing as a classical tradition – at least not in the way that it is conceived by those who now make it an object of study. One criterion for establishing the existence of a "classical tradition" (in the strong sense) for any given time is to consider how far Latin remained alive in speech and writing. Another criterion is to determine the extent to which aspects of Greco-Roman antiquity are spontaneously incorporated into the mainstream of cultural production. For the greater part of Latin America's modern history, both criteria are fully satisfied. First, the Latin language did not merely survive, but flourished long after the conquest until the end of the eighteenth century – and in some quarters even after that. An immense corpus of material in Latin is the key to a fuller historical understanding of the colonial period in Spanish America and Brazil. Numerous documents and early printed books remain to be catalogued, let alone read and interpreted: not just school texts, grammars, and theological tracts, but also epics, didactic poems, elegies, letters, dialogues, and treatises on subjects ranging from indigenous languages, ethnography, and natural history, to political philosophy and Platonism.

Secondly, the legacy of Greek and Roman civilization could hardly have been more conspicuous in vernacular poetry, theater, and other kinds of public performance. The two most prominent features of the cultural life of Latin America in the seventeenth and eighteenth centuries were the Baroque conventions of the *certamen poético* (poetic contest) (Leonard 1983: 130–44) and the *máscara*, a kind of carnival or masque to mark a special occasion (Leonard 1983: 117–29). The grand poetic tournament, involving both civic and ecclesiastical patronage, was a sumptuous event, and the idea of a highbrow talent show as a public pageant has obvious precedents in the cultural practices of Greece, Rome, and the Italian Renaissance. The *máscara* consisted of a parade of people – of all social classes and races – in costume, along with bands of musicians, cars, and floats. The actual theme of the *máscara* was nearly always classical: poems and orations were delivered, and visual artists were commissioned to represent appropriate Greco-Roman subjects and motifs. Leading savants and writers who organized such an occasion – be it a viceregal or episcopal reception, a funeral or a local feast day – would also commemorate it with a formal account: the *relación* (*relaçao* in Portuguese).

The first book to be printed in Brazil provided just such an account: Luiz Antonio Rosado de Cunha's *Relaçao de Entrada* (1747) recorded the entrance into Rio de Janeiro of Antonio do Desterro Malheroto, the new bishop of the city (Elliott 1988: 13). The text provides an account of the triumphal arches in Corinthian and Doric styles that were put up along the parade route. Each of the seven arches was devoted to a figure from classical myth: Juno, Iris, Venus, Neptune, Orpheus, Minerva, and Jupiter. In spite of the innocuous content of Rosado de Cunha's volume, it had been printed illegally: no presses were officially established in Brazil until 1808, owing to severe restrictions imposed by the Portuguese crown. In Spanish America, conditions had been rather different – a *relación* of the ceremonial entry of the new Spanish viceregal couple into Mexico City in 1680 was printed in that very year. Two of the greatest figures in Mexican intellectual history produced poems to mark this particular event: Carlos de Sigüenza y Góngora (1645–1700), the scientist and antiquarian who was Professor of Mathematics at the University of Mexico, and Sor Juana Inés de la Cruz (1648–95), a Jeronymite nun-poetess, now an icon of Spanish colonial literature and feminist *avant la lettre* (Juana Inés de la Cruz 1997: xi–lxiii; Paz 1988). Both compositions – Sigüenza's *Theatro de vertudes políticas* (Theater of political virtues) and Sor Juana's *Neptuno alegórico* (Neptune allegorized) – are panegyrical, describing two temporary triumphal arches that had been specially erected for the festivities. The inspiration for the *Neptuno alegórico*, in which Sor Juana's best Latin verses are embedded, was the depiction on one of the arches of Neptune and his consort Amphitrite (Andrews and Coroleu 2007: 23–44).

The year 1680 in Mexico also saw the publication of a volume entitled the *Centonicum Virgilianum monimentum* (Vergilian centonic monument) by Bernardo de Riofrío: this collage of 365 hexameters from Vergil related the famous story of the Virgin of Guadalupe, who reputedly appeared to an Indian named Juan Diego at Tepeyac, near Mexico City, in 1531. Riofrío's cento was prefaced by an original poetic narrative in Latin by Bartolomé Rosales, in which the shade of Vergil himself appears and announces that he has been reborn in the New World (Laird 2007: 216–217). All these works illustrate the interplay between Latin and Spanish in the literature of seventeenth-century America: writing in Spanish was conspicuously Latinate in expression, whilst poetry and prose in Latin reflected the Baroque styles of vernacular writing.

From the middle of the following century the Jesuit Colleges of New Spain fostered a neoclassical movement. The reputation of this period as a "Golden Age" of Latin literature rests on some outstanding scholars and poets like Abad, Alegre, and Landívar who remain little known in the English-speaking world. Although their literary works (mostly begun in Mexico but published in Italy after the 1767 expulsion of the Jesuits from the Spanish territories) cover a wide range of themes and subjects, they all have two major characteristics in common: the absorption of Enlightenment thinking – on science, aesthetics, and even political theory – and a pronounced emphasis on their authors' Mexican or American cultural identity. Diego José Abad (1727–80) wrote a magnificent Latin didactic epic in 43 books entitled *De Deo, Deoque Homine carmina heroica* (Heroic verses on God, and on God as Man), which drew from his expertise in philosophy and science as well as in classical literature and theology (Kerson 1988). Numerous references in the poem to "Mexico" – *not* "New Spain" – indicate Abad's attachment to his American birthplace. That is underlined by the pseudonym under which the 1773 and 1775 editions of the *De Deo* were published: *Selenopolitanus* (Citizen of the moon) is a Hellenization of *Metzli* (City of the moon), the Nahuatl word for Mexico (Kerson 1991; Laird 2004). Abad used the same *nom de plume* when he published an elegant but forceful tract – in Latin – as a response to the prejudice he encountered in Europe that "only Italians could write Latin properly" (Kerson 1991). Francisco Xavier Alegre (1728–88), a native of Veracruz, is considered Mexico's greatest Hellenist: he translated the entire *Iliad* and the Homeric *Batrachomyomachia* into Latin hexameters. As well as many volumes of prose, Alegre wrote original poetry in Latin: the *Alexandriada*, an epic on the capture of Tyre by Alexander the Great that ends with an encomium of Mexico (Laird 2003), and his lost *Lyrics and Georgics in Praise of Blessed Mary of Guadalupe*; he also translated Boileau's well-known neoclassical treatise *L'art poétique* (The art of poetry) into Spanish (Deck 1976; see also Kaimowitz 1990).

Rafael Landívar (1731–93) was born in Guatemala when it was still annexed to New Spain. He is now regarded as the nation's greatest poet: the success of his *Rusticatio Mexicana* (Life in the Mexican countryside) in various Spanish translations has meant that many are unaware that this compelling panorama of natural wonders and country life in the American isthmus was actually composed in Latin. Landívar drew from classical and Renaissance authors who specifically addressed rustic themes (e.g., Hesiod, Vergil, Varro, Columella, Politian, and Jacques Vanière, French author of the highly influential *Praedium rusticum*, or Country estate) as well as writers as diverse as Lucretius, Horace, Ovid, and Thomas More (Laird 2006a). Landívar's work is further distinguished by its accommodation of the sublime (Higgins 2000). However Landívar's emphasis on the value of indigenous knowledge, customs, and tradition, and the fact that America itself is his central theme, best account for the continuing popularity of his didactic poem. Its fusion of indigenous folklore with European literary convention make the *Rusticatio Mexicana* an important but hitherto unrecognized precursor of "magical realism" in modern Latin American literature. The work may have been conceived in part as a response to influential European naturalists of the time like Cornelius de Pauw and George-Louis Leclerc Buffon, who regarded the Americas and all of their inhabitants as inferior to Europe and Europeans (Cañizares-Esguerra 2001).

In this respect the *Rusticatio Mexicana* has something in common with the lengthy *Ancient History of Mexico*, originally published in Italian in 1780 by Francisco Xavier Clavigero (1731–87), another of Landívar's Jesuit comrades in exile. Clavigero began his work with a positive account of Mexico's natural history, before going on to commend the pre-Columbian civilizations of the Americas and the intellectual capabilities of the Indians. He observed – as Cicero did for Latin – that even if Nahuatl had no equivalents for some Greek philosophical categories, the language could accommodate the meaning of the Bible and advanced mathematical calculations: Clavigero himself produced a grammar of the Nahuatl language. The Jesuit historian compared the indigenous Mexicans to the Greeks of his day, who could not be like those who "lived in the times of Plato and Pericles" (Clavigero 2003: 65). Greece was then under the rule of the Ottoman Turks: in making this comparison, Clavigero was aligning the imperialist Spaniards with the dreaded Turks. That remark was probably enough to prevent his history from being published in Spanish, until Mexico secured independence from Spain in 1821 (Brading 1991: 454).

4   Conclusions

The history of the classical tradition in Latin America cannot be isolated from political history any more than in other parts of the world. Even after Spain and Portugal had yielded control of their vast dominions, the legacy of European antiquity continued to play a significant ideological and cultural role in the emergence of many new American nations: painting and sculpture that idealized indigenous subjects in specifically Hellenistic or Roman styles abounded in the mid-nineteenth century (Barajas Durán 2002).

There is no doubt that views of the Greco-Roman world had severely limited the conceptual horizons of the first missionaries and ethnographers who tried to make sense of the "New World," affording them crude, if not utterly useless, frameworks and taxonomies for interpreting the alien cultures they encountered. But very rapidly, and for a much longer period of time, classical learning provided a means by which not only *criollos*, but also indigenous Americans, *mestizos*, and other groups have been able to articulate and celebrate their distinctive identities.

It has been argued that multiculturalism really began in the wake of the conquests of the Americas. Whether or not that was so, a cultural transition – from a stagnant Baroque version of the Renaissance to a kind of postmodernity – has certainly accompanied the Latin American nations' political independence from Spain and Portugal (Lange-Churión and Mendieta 2001). That relatively rapid transition ensured that the continent's dialogue with Greece and Rome remained essentially different from the classical legacy that had begun in Europe so much earlier, and had reached the United States so much later. As well as providing a new terrain for interdisciplinary enquiry, the cornucopia of classical traditions in the Hispanic or Latin American heritage could secure an important role for Greco-Roman studies in today's academic curricula, which are naturally bound to reflect the cultural diversity of society at large (George 1998). And this cornucopia offers a powerful moral and methodological challenge to those European and North American scholars who still believe that there is only *one* classical tradition, and that it belongs to the Old World alone.

FURTHER READING

Although European perceptions of the Americas in relation to classical antiquity are often discussed (e.g., Grafton, Shelford, and Siraisi [1992]; and Haase and Reinhold [1993]), only one overview of the classical traditions to have emerged *within* Latin America has been produced to date: Elliott [1988], an exhibition catalogue for the John Carter Brown Library.

However, treatments of mainstream Latin American culture and history indicate the centrality of the Greek and Roman legacy: e.g., Brading (1991); Cañizares-Esguerra (2001); Henríquez Ureña (1945); Leonard (1992); Paz (1988); and Gruzinski (2002: 91–106). Some more specifically relevant studies of nations, individuals, and topics include Lupher (2003), Anadón (1998, with an essay on pp. 8–31 by S. MacCormack, "The Incas and Rome"), and Abbott (1996, which has a chapter on Diego Valadés, pp. 41–59). My own discussions in Haskell and Ruys (2009), and in Andrews and Coroleu (2007), will address various classical influences in New Spain.

The first chapter of Laird (2006a: 9–30) relates the development of classical human-ism in Mexico from the Spanish conquest until the end of the colonial period.

For traditions of classical culture and education in nations that could not be treated fully, or even mentioned, in this chapter, see Castillo Didier (2003) on Chile, Eichmann Oehrli (2003) on Charcas-Bolivia, Herrera Zapién (2000) on Mexico, Miranda Cancela (2003) on Cuba, Nuñez (2003) on Brazil, and Rivas Sacconi (1993) on Colombia. Sparisci Lovicelli (2003) is a short study of rhetoric in nine-teenth-century Costa Rica.

NOTES

1   There is a score for Torrejón's opera in the Bodleian Library in Oxford (Ms. Add. A.143, folios 170–93) in addition to the one in the Biblioteca Nacional in Lima (Ms. C 1469): for further background see Lohmann Villena (1945). René Clemencic had to rewrite some missing instrumental parts for the first world recording of the work, which was made by the Ensemble Vocal La Cappella and the Orchestre Baroque du Clemencic Consort in Italy in 1990 (Nuova Era 6936). A second recording by Andrew Lawrence-King's Harp Consort was produced in 1997 (Deutsche Harmonia Mundi 05472 77355 2).

2   Leone Ebreo (Leon the Hebrew) was in fact a pseudonym adopted by the Portu-guese Jewish humanist Judah Abarbanal; Garcilaso correspondingly drew attention to his own distinctive ethnic status on the title page of his translation of Abarbanal's work by naming himself *Inga* (Inca).

3   The first book to be published by an American in Europe was reputedly the *Arte de la lingua latina* (Art of the Latin language, Barcelona 1568) by Pedro Juan Antonio, an indigenous Mexican who had gone to Spain in 1562 to study law at Salamanca.

CHAPTER SIXTEEN

Low Countries

Gilbert Tournoy

1 From Antiquity through the Middle Ages

Vergil and his Roman fellow citizens knew where the Morini, one of the tribes inhabiting part of the territory of the Low Countries, were to be found: they were a people at the extreme end of the Empire or even the world (*Aeneid* 8.727: *extremique hominum Morini*). This region hardly ever formed a political unity, only a geographical and cultural one. It is situated along the Channel and the North Sea from Boulogne to Emden in the north, the southern border following an imaginary line from Boulogne to Trier, the eastern one from Trier to Emden. It covers the modern kingdoms of Belgium and the Netherlands, the Grand Duchy of Luxembourg, and a major part of northern France, including cities such as Arras (Atrecht), Boulogne, Cambrai (Kamerijk), Cassel, Douai (Dowaai), Lille, St. Omer (St. Omaars), Thérouanne, and Valenciennes. It was forged into a political unity by the Burgundian duke Philip the Good (died 1467), with the exception of the prince-bishopric of Liège, which remained independent until the French Revolution.

Latin culture was introduced into the region by the invading and occupying Roman legions. For several centuries Latin was the only official language for administration, but there is no evidence that there was ever any literary output by a local author in antiquity, except for a few inscriptions and wooden tablets written by soldiers belonging to the *cohors Batavorum* (the cohort of the Batavians) or the *cohors Tungrorum* (the cohort of the Tungri) originating from this region. Whatever may have blossomed was completely eradicated, as was observed by the fifth-century author Sidonius Apollinaris in his letter to Arbogast, the governor of Trier: *Quocirca sermonis pompa Romani, si qua adhuc uspiam est, Belgicis olim sive Rhenanis abolita terris, in te resedit* (The splendor of the Roman language, if anywhere it still in some fashion survives, rests with you, for it has long since been effaced from Belgic and Rhenish lands; letter 4.17.2).

This letter was all too flattering: it took several centuries before the Latin language and culture could make a vigorous comeback, during the Carolingian era. Not unlike in the rest of Europe, monasteries and cathedral schools were to become the main centers of intellectual life. Beyond a single important center in the northern part of the Netherlands (Utrecht), a host of abbeys and priories were founded in the south from the early eighth century onwards: Arras, Aulne, Cambrai, Douai, Echternach, Ghent, Lobbes, Marchiennes, Saint-Amand-les-Eaux, Saint-Omer, Stavelot, Sint-Truiden, and so on.

It was thanks to the activity of the scriptoria of these monasteries that classical authors were transmitted to posterity. It is obvious, however, that they chiefly took an interest in copying and studying manuscripts with a religious or devotional content. Even before Alcuin of York composed at Tours (ca. 800) his Life of Willibrord (the English missionary who became the apostle to the Frisians), an early copy (now at Stuttgart, Württembergische Landesbibliothek, codex HB XIV.1) of which was transcribed at Echternach during the ninth century, the St. Truiden abbey had already generated two similar hagiographical works: the biographies of Eucherius and of the abbey's founder, Trudo, this last one by Trudo's fellow-countryman Donatus Hasbaniensis.

In that early period a somewhat higher cultural level was reached in the western part of the Low Countries, where Hucbald of St. Amand (ca. 840–930) bequeathed to his abbey a conspicuous number of books, among them Vergil, Seneca, Priscian, and also the Latin translation of Plato's *Timaeus* by Chalcidius. He moreover brought off an amazing *tour de force*, treating in verse a theme that had been introduced by Synesius of Cyrene (ca. 370–413). His *Ecloga de laudibus calvitii* (Eclogue on the praise of baldness) is a philosophical eulogy of baldness, in which every single word starts with the letter "c." Several centuries later it inspired the Dutch poet Janus Dousa, about 1577, to undertake a creative imitation in a caustic satire against a Franciscan friar. This *Sacri calvitii encomium* (Eulogy of the sacred baldness), however, he never completed.

At about the same time as Hucbald composed his *Ecloga*, bishop Radbod from Utrecht (died 917) produced a charming nature-poem on the swallow, *De hirundine*, which witnesses to his rhetorical schooling. Furthermore, an enhancement of the relatively limited knowledge of classical antiquity and the poor quality of local instruction was provided by Celtic scholarship. Towards the middle of the ninth century there arrived at Liège the learned Irish teacher Sedulius Scottus. He even had a fair knowledge of Greek, although the *Proverbia Grecorum* (Greek proverbs) in his *Collectanea* (Collected works) most probably stem from an Irish source. He was the very first author to write a "mirror for princes" (*De rectoribus Christianis*, Concerning Christian rulers), in verse, and his fame as a poet earned him the title of *Maro Leodii* (the Vergil of Liège).

The tradition of sound instruction continued at Liège. Trying to teach Latin to his pupils at the Cathedral School of Liège in an attractive way at the turn of the tenth century, Egbert of Liège wrote for them a manual in verse, the *Fecunda ratis* (Fertile ship), divided in two parts, the *Prora* (Prow) and the *Puppis* (Stern). It presents a strange mixture of proverbial, satirical, and other pieces, derived from biblical and classical sources (especially the Roman satirists) as well as from vernacular ones, amongst them the presumed ancestor of Little Red Riding Hood – *De puella a lupellis servata* (Concerning the girl preserved from the wolves). It was in that scholarly environment that manuscripts of classical authors were studied and copied, as is proved, for instance, by the extensive twelfth-century list of a Liège school library or by the surviving manuscript books and catalogs containing mainly classical texts originating from monasteries such as Lobbes, Gembloux, or St. Amand.

Classical authors who were almost completely unknown during the Middle Ages in the rest of Europe were read and imitated in the Low Countries. A prominent scholar in this respect was Ratherius of Verona, born in the Liège area and educated at Lobbes (ca. 890–974), three times bishop of Verona, but also bishop of Liège and abbot of Lobbes and Aulne. He not only had some knowledge of Greek, but was one of the very few people of the Middle Ages who read Plautus and Catullus. Similarly, the versatile writer Sigebert (ca. 1028–1112), a teacher in the neighboring school of the abbey of Gembloux, was one of the very few in the entire period from the ninth until the fifteenth century to have seen and used Lucretius' *De rerum natura* (On the nature of things). One who was extremely well versed in classical Latin literature was Nivardus of Ghent, the enigmatic author of the *Ysengrimus*. This satirical work, which proved to be of central importance for the development of medieval beast-literature, was composed ca. 1148/9 in sophisticated elegiacs, showing a great familiarity in the first place with Ovid, but also with Vergil, Horace, Juvenal, Lucan, Statius, and others.

More than classical authors, however, it was writers of Late Antiquity who were most eagerly read in the twelfth century. The foundation for the prosimetric *De planctu naturae* (On the lamentation of nature) of the *doctor universalis* (universally learned) Alan of Lille (ca. 1120–1203) was supplied by the *Timaeus* of Plato, read in the Latin translation of Chalcidius, while the literary model was provided by Boethius' *De consolatione philosophiae* (On the consolation of philosophy). A blend of literature and philosophy is equally present in Alain's long allegorical poem *Anticlaudianus* (Against Claudian), which according to the prose prologue can be read on three levels: as a simple adventure, as a tale with a moral message, or in an allegorical way. It provides a reply to the *In Rufinum* (Against Rufinus, in which the hellish Furies conspired against *Iustitia*, justice), composed by Claudius Claudianus, the last great poet of classical antiquity, who was very influential not only in the Middle Ages and the Renaissance but even down to the twentieth century: he occupies a place of honor in the historical novel by Hella S. Haasse (born 1918), *Een nieuwer testament* (A newer testament, 1966).

Vernacular literature, Dutch and French, has been influenced by the classics almost from the beginning. In the second half of the twelfth century, Hendrik van Veldeke composed his *Eneide*, a free adaptation of the French *Roman d'Eneas* (Romance of Aeneas), based on Vergil and Ovid. A century later the Flemish poet Jacob van Maerlant (ca. 1225 – ca. 1300) imitated Walter of Châtillon's *Alexandreis* in his *Alexanders yeesten* (Deeds of Alexander), whilst his *Historie van Troyen* (ca. 1264) goes back to Benoît de Sainte-Maure's poem *Roman de Troie* (Romance of Troy), and his *Wrake van Jerusalem* (Revenge of Jerusalem) to Flavius Josephus' *Bellum Judaicum* (Jewish war). The theme of the *Les neuf preux* (the "nine worthies"), which from around 1300 rapidly spread in literature and art not only in the

Low Countries but all over Europe, appeared for the first time in his rather short poem *Van neghen de besten* (Concerning the nine worthies),

One of the sources for the principal poem of the famous court poet Dirc Potter (ca. 1370–1428), *Der minnen loep* (The course of love, 1411), a kind of introduction to love in four books, was Ovid's oeuvre, especially the *Heroides* and *Metamorphoses*. A hundred years later Cornelis van Ghistele (1510–73) not only translated the comedies of Terence (1555), the *Aeneid* (1556), and Sophocles' *Antigone*, but also composed a tragedy, *Van Eneas en Dido* (Of Aeneas and Dido, 1551). Dirk Volckertz Coornhert (1522–90) was interested especially in ethical texts: he translated Cicero's *De officiis* (On duties, 1561), Seneca's *De beneficiis* (On kind deeds, 1562), and Boethius' *De consolatione philosophiae* (On the consolation by philosophy, 1585). With his *De dolinghe van Ulysse* (The wandering of Ulysses), a translation of the first 12 books of Homer's *Odyssey* published in 1561, he opens the long series of Dutch translators of Homer.

Vernacular literature in French found a friendly home at the Burgundian Court, where classical antiquity became a constant source of inspiration for ducal aspirations, for decorations on tapestries, and for festivities. When Philip the Good founded his Order of the Golden Fleece in 1430, unlike most other founders of similar orders, he turned to classical mythology for his symbols, continuing in this way the interest of his grandfather Philip the Bold (1342–1404), who already in 1393 had bought two tapestries representing the story of Jason. At the request of Philip the Good, his chaplain Raoul Lefèvre composed an *Histoire de Jason* (ca. 1460), in which the hero, Jason, displays all the qualities of a noble knight and at the end marries Medea. It was also for Philip that Lefèvre compiled a *Recueil des histoires de Troie* (Anthology of the accounts of Troy, 1464), intended to replace the *Historia destructionis Troiae* (History of the destruction of Troy) by Guido delle Colonne (ca. 1287), the condensed Latin prose version of Benoît de Sainte-Maure's *Roman de Troie* (Romance of Troy). Almost immediately, William Caxton, staying at that time at Bruges, started an English translation, which he completed at the request of Philip's spouse, Margaret of York. He had it printed – the first book ever printed in English – most probably at Bruges, at the end of 1473 or the beginning of 1474. Back in England he also published an English version of the *Histoire de Jason* around 1477, while a Dutch translation appeared at Haarlem in 1485.

Still at the Burgundian court, Jean Miélot undertook the translation into French of Cicero's famous letter to his brother Quintus concerning the duties of a governor, at the request of Philip the Good, who intended it for his son Charles. In 1462 Miélot also translated in 1462 the *Romuleon* of Benvenuto da Imola, a fourteenth-century Latin compilation of Roman history based on Livy, Sallust, Suetonius, Vergil, Valerius Maximus, and so on, an undertaking repeated more skilfully in 1466 by Sébastien Mamerot. Charles the Bold outdid his father in the liveliness of his interest in historical works recording the deeds of the great heroes of antiquity, and he enjoyed passing his leisure time listening to them being recited. He even had a medal struck by Giovanni Filangieri di Candida, representing himself as an ancient Roman. To him Charles Soillot dedicated his translation of Xenophon's *Hieron* in 1467 in order to illustrate the dangers of tyranny. In 1468 Vasco de Lucena made a French version of

Quintus Curtius's *Historia Alexandri* (History of Alexander), introducing some chapters taken over from the Latin version of Plutarch's *Life of Alexander* translated by Guarino Veronese. Two years later he translated Xenophon's *Cyropaedia* (The education of Cyrus), following the Latin version by Poggio Bracciolini (1470). Jean Du Quesne translated for Charles the *Commentarii* (Commentaries) of Julius Caesar.

2   The New Learning

No less important than the Burgundian Court were the newly founded University of Louvain (1425) and the steadily growing contacts with Italy at ecclesiastical, economic, diplomatic, and scholarly levels. Merchants, clerics, diplomats, and wandering scholars set out from Italy or returned from there full of enthusiasm for the new learning. Petrarch was the most celebrated, but not the first, Italian to make known the treasures of the ecclesiastical institutions at Liège where, during his travels of 1333, he discovered in addition to the spurious *Ad equites Romanos* (To the Roman knights), Cicero's important authentic oration *Pro Archia* (In defense of Archias), that glorification of poetry that he put to use in his own *Collatio laureationis*, the speech he gave when he was crowned poet laureate. He was preceded by his friend Matteo Longhi, archdeacon of Liège, who in 1325 had brought to Avignon a rare copy of Statius' *Achilleis* (now Antwerp, Museum Plantin-Moretus, M 85).

Whilst, in Italy, Petrarch gave the decisive impetus for the return to classical antiquity, in the Low Countries Geert Groote essentially focused on a return to the sources of the Christian life. His followers, the Brethren of the Common Life, aimed at a better understanding of the Bible and of Christian authors in the first place, which could hardly be achieved without a sound knowledge and appreciation of the classics. It was in their schools that the young Erasmus first caught the *odor melioris doctrinae* (scent of better learning). But before Erasmus was born, the dean of the Cathedral at Utrecht, Willem van Heze, heard that a colleague of his, Jacob of Borselen, was planning to set out for Italy. Van Heze gave Jacob two book-lists, one with the orations of Cicero, which were already in his possession, the other with the works of Cicero and of other authors that van Heze wished to acquire. When Poggio Bracciolini was presented with these lists and noticed in the first one a title he did not recognize, a fifth Catilinarian by Cicero, he was greatly interested, although he immediately suspected, and rightly so, that it could be a hitherto unknown oration by Cicero or an oration composed by someone else. Still, in his letter of December 31, 1451, he praised Willem as a man of great erudition and dedication to humanistic studies, and promised to procure for him whatever texts he wanted, hoping to wheedle out of him a copy of the unknown oration.

In spite of his obvious inclination toward the classics, Willem van Heze does not seem to have had much impact on his cultural circle. Much more important in that respect was the role of Rudolph Agricola, from Baflo near Groningen (1444–85). Back in his homeland after a 10-year stay in Italy, first at the University of Pavia, then at the Court of Duke Ercole d'Este in Ferrara, he felt at a loss and extremely unhappy. Every day, so he wrote in a letter of September 20, 1480, to his friend Alexander

Hegius, his practice, and hence his love, of studying was diminishing. From the moment he left Italy, his knowledge of ancient authors started to slip from him and his ability to express himself elegantly was fading away. But perhaps he was suffering at that time from a kind of postpartum depression after having finished the three books of his *magnum opus*, the *De inventione dialectica* (On dialectical invention, first published in Louvain in 1515), one of the first responses to scholastic logic and the generally recognized starting point of the history of philosophy in the Low Countries. Agricola also left more than 50 elegant letters and some exegetical notes and valuable conjectures on some of the Latin authors he cherished (Pliny the Younger's *Letters*, Pliny the Elder's *Natural History*, Seneca, Tacitus). No less important was his enthusiasm for Greek literature, which earned him the title of founder of Greek studies in the Low Countries. Agricola may have started the study of Greek at Pavia, but it was at Ferrara that he really plunged into it, playing the organ at the Court in order to finance the purchase of Greek books, and even refusing the call from the University of Louvain to occupy the newly established chair of poetics. By doing so he became the first northern European to have acquired such a sound knowledge of Greek that he was able to translate a number of literary texts by Lucian, pseudo-Plato, Isocrates, and Aphthonius into Latin.

Agricola transmitted his enthusiasm to Alexander Hegius and even to the young Erasmus, who caught a glimpse of the famous Frisian at Deventer and testified that *Rodolphus Agricola primus omnium quandam aurulam melioris literaturae nobis invexit ex Italia* (Agricola was the first to bring a breath of better literature from Italy; Allen vol. 1, p. 2). Erasmus continued in the same line as his predecessor but did not go to Italy for his studies. He was also more than 30 when he learnt more than the foundations of Greek, stating that "Latin scholarship, however elaborate, is maimed and reduced by half without Greek. For whereas we Latins have but a few small streams, a few muddy pools, the Greeks possess the purest of springs and rivers running with gold" (Allen, letter 149). This late start did not prevent him from making available to the world an impressive number of Greek authors, editing or translating Aristotle, Euripides, Isocrates, Libanius, Lucian, Plutarch, and Xenophon.

In the field of Latin literature he did the same for Cicero, Quintus Curtius, Livy, Plautus, Pliny, Seneca, Suetonius, and Terence, not to mention the Fathers of the Church, such as Ambrose, Augustine, Basil, Chrysostom, Cyprian, and Hilary. In this way Erasmus made a massive contribution to the work of making Greek and Latin literature available to the general public. This contribution continued with his impressive collection of *Adagia* (Proverbs), and in his original works, such as the *Colloquia* (Colloquies), the *De recta Latini Graecique pronuntiatione* (On the correct pronunciation of Latin and Greek), or the *Ciceronianus*, where he came down heavily against what he saw as narrow linguistic purism obsessively focused on the usage of Cicero. But restoring classical antiquity was not his main goal. Although from childhood he was swept "by some mysterious force of nature into liberal studies" (Allen, vol. 1, p. 2), he considered the study of classical literature not as an end in itself, but as a means to be placed at the service of Christianity. Erasmus' longstanding admiration for Lorenzo Valla and the discovery in 1504 of Valla's *Adnotationes in Novum Testamentum* (Annotations to the New Testament) at the Premonstratensian abbey of Park (Louvain) convinced him that it was by no means impossible, but even advantageous to apply the philological method to the study of the Bible. His ultimate goal was to contribute to the advancement of Christianity through the presentation of the gospel in a purer and more elegant wording. So he embarked upon a risky undertaking: a new Latin translation of the New Testament, which he published in 1516. Remarkably enough it was the accompanying new Greek edition, rather hastily put together on the basis of a few manuscripts now generally regarded as of inferior quality, that was to remain the *textus receptus* (received text) for the next three centuries.

It was also thanks to the continuing efforts of Erasmus (and the financing by Jerome Busleyden) that the study of the so-called three sacred languages – Greek, Hebrew, and Latin – officially began in 1517, when the *Collegium Trilingue* (trilingual college) obtained a firm footing at the University of Louvain. But even before this date, thanks mainly to the foundation of the chair of poetics and the series of Italian scholars who occupied it until 1500, the new learning was introduced into the University of Louvain and became firmly rooted there. At the beginning of the sixteenth century, Martin Dorp (1485–1525), who called himself a fellow-countryman of Erasmus, studied and taught at the Lily, the most humanistic of the four colleges in the faculty of arts. On September 3, 1508, he staged Plautus' *Aulularia*, adding the missing fifth act, and in 1509 the *Miles gloriosus* (Boastful soldier). He also wrote a few didactic dialogues, among them one dealing with the popular theme of Hercules at the crossroads. Dorp was taught Latin by Johannes Despauterius (ca. 1480–1520), the author of a Latin grammar which for centuries was to be used throughout western Europe. Even more successful were the manuals of Greek grammar composed by Nicolaus Clenardus (1495–1542), which in less than two hundred years went through more than five hundred editions.

The most important event of that period, however, was the foundation of the *Collegium Trilingue*, on which other similar institutions throughout Europe, such as the Collège de France, were modeled. It could boast of a series of excellent professors who acquitted themselves honorably in Latin and Greek scholarship. Hadrianus Barlandus (1486–1538) was the first professor of Latin at the *Trilingue*. He had already proved himself to be an excellent teacher, not only by staging plays by classical authors like Plautus and Terence, the *Hecuba* of Euripides (in the Latin version by Erasmus), and *Dido* in a dramatic setting, but also by providing his pupils with Erasmus' Latin version of several dialogues by Lucian or a collection of Aesopic fables. His successor, Cornelius Goclenius (died 1539), also distinguished himself pedagogically. He translated a dialogue by Lucian (1522) and published a new edition of Lucan's *Bellum civile* (Civil war, 1531). Goclenius was succeeded by Petrus Nannius, who not only left a 10-book *Miscellanea* (Miscellany) commenting upon a host of Latin authors (Cicero, Horace, Livy, Terence, and Vergil), but also the first edition of the Latin version of Athenagoras, as well as the partial or complete translation of several other Greek authors (Aeschines, Apollonius of Tyana, Athanasius, Chrysostom, Demosthenes, Plutarch, Synesius of Cyrene). Nannius' successor was Cornelius Valerius (1512–78), who commented upon Cicero and Lucretius, but above all passed on his encyclopedic knowledge to the next generation, among them the Hellenists Guilielmus Canter (1542–75) and Andreas Schottus (1552–1629), and the most prominent of all, Justus Lipsius (1547–1606).

In the field of philology Lipsius' most outstanding achievement was his edition of Tacitus, which remains down to the present day a cornerstone for Tacitean scholarship, even if Lipsius relied more on his own intuition than on the painstaking work of collating manuscripts, an approach considered inadequate by modern standards. Another philological masterpiece was the edition of Seneca's *Opera omnia* (Complete works) in 1605. But philology was not his ultimate goal: in a letter to Woverius, Lipsius proudly boasted, *ego e Philologia Philosophiam feci* (I made Philosophy out of Philology; *Centuria quarta miscellanea*, letter 84, quoted in Tournoy 1998), paraphrasing the famous letter in which Seneca criticizes those scholars for whom scholarship is an end in itself (*Epistulae morales ad Lucilium*, letter 108.23–38). Already as a young scholar Lipsius had started to study the philosophical works of Seneca, who was to become the principal source of the ethical system he later developed. In his *De constantia* (On constancy, 1583/4), he attempted to combine Stoicism and Christianity. Twenty years later, in 1604, he crowned his philosophical program with the publication of his *Manuductio ad Stoicam philosophiam* (Handbook of Stoic philosophy) and his *Physiologia Stoicorum* (Natural science of the Stoics). In these two manuals, dealing with Stoic moral philosophy and with Stoic physics, respectively, Lipsius tried to reconcile secular ethics and Christian faith, thus laying the foundations for the rapidly growing success of neo-Stoicism throughout Europe. Lipsius mainly confined himself to Latin, considering Greek *decorum magis quam necessarium* (not so much a necessity as an adornment; Tournoy 1998). But on the other hand, serious scholarship without Greek was not an option for him. So in 1595 he published his *De militia Romana* (On Roman warfare), a commentary in five books on the sixth book of Polybius, and intended to be used as a practical manual for modern warfare. In fact most of his publications aimed at making antiquity relevant to his own society, exactly as his teaching aimed at using classical authors to prepare young people for the roles they would play in society. Even art had for him a merely pedagogical function, as shown by the letter in which he urged Otto van Veen (Vaenius) to paint the death of Arria (*Centuria tertia ad Belgas*, letter 82). In it he meticulously described the composition according to the details mentioned in Pliny the Younger (*Epistulae*, book 3, letter 16) and even suggested that the epigram by Martial (1.13), in which the heroine's death is glorified, should be added.

Lipsius' influence is also evident in the engravings cut by Cornelis Galle after the drawings Peter Paul Rubens designed for the second edition of Seneca by Lipsius, and in the title-page of the 1637 edition of Lipsius' *Opera omnia* (Collected works), again by Rubens. It was mainly in Italy that the great Antwerp artist became acquainted with classical monuments and sculptures. In Mantua he had painted a huge painting, the *Council of the Gods*, in which an accumulation of antique sculptures studied and copied by Rubens can be detected. After his return from Italy in 1608, Rubens's interest in antiquity turned into a cornerstone of his art. With his oeuvre the representation of classical mythology reached its most exuberant expression. Rubens in fact produced a wealth of paintings and cartoons for tapestries with mythological and historical subjects, such as the cycle of paintings retelling the history of the Roman consul P. Decius Mus (after Livy 8.6–11), or the paintings of *Prometheus Bound*, *The Death of Adonis*, *The Judgment of Paris*, *Venus Frigida*, *Juno and Argus*, *Jupiter and Callisto*, *The Three Graces*, and so on. The influence of the classics on Rubens can still be admired today in the house he bought in 1610, in the courtyard and the garden, decorated with paintings and busts of mythological and classical figures.

With the closing of the era of Lipsius, an end had come to the glory days of the *Collegium Trilingue* and to the highest levels of scholarship at Louvain University. For a century the *Collegium Trilingue* had proved to be a breeding-ground for a considerable number of scholars in all fields of scholarship, such as the lexicographer Kilianus (1528/9–1607); the lawyers Gabriel Mudaeus (1500–60), Viglius van Aytta (1507–77), Josse Damhoudere (1507–81), and Franciscus Balduinus (1500–73); the orientalist Andreas Masius (1514–73); the founder of Latin epigraphy, Martinus Smetius; the anatomist Andreas Vesalius (1514–64); the diplomat and discoverer of the *Monumentum Ancyranum* (the text on the wall of the temple of Augustus at Ankara that celebrates the emperor's achievements), Augerius Busbequius (1522–91); the cartographers Gerard Mercator (1512–94) and Gemma Phrisius (1508–55); and the botanists Carolus Clusius (1526–1609) and Rembert Dodonaeus (1517–85).

3   The Seventeenth Century

Political circumstances and bitter religious controversies forced the southern Netherlands to remain under Spanish control, while the northern part acquired its freedom. This caused the two parts to diverge more and more from one another during the centuries to come. While the south would decline, economically as well as culturally, for centuries, the north experienced its Golden Age, which approximately spanned the seventeenth century. To start with, a new university was established in 1575 at Leiden to counter the influence of Catholic Louvain. One of the founding members, the poet and humanist Janus Dousa (1545–1604), was even able to convince his friend Justus Lipsius to accept a chair there, which greatly contributed to the fame of the young university. So did his successor Joseph Scaliger (1540–1609), with his innovative research in the field of chronology and his new edition of Manilius. From the southern Netherlands came a host of talented teachers, often prompted by religious reasons. The first professor of Greek was Bonaventura Vulcanius from Bruges (1538–1614), who devoted himself to Hellenistic and Byzantine authors (Callimachus, Moschus, Bion, Agathias, Theophylactus). Another Greek scholar was his fellow-countryman Franciscus Nansius (1525–95), who applied himself to Nonnus' hexameter version of St. John's Gospel and taught in Leiden and Dordrecht. Daniel Heinsius (1580–1655), born in Ghent, was most influential in the field of literary theory, thanks to his *De tragoediae constitutione* (On the structure of tragedy), which appeared as an appendix to his Latin translation of Aristotle's *De poetica* (On poetry, 1611). In collaboration with Hugo Grotius he contributed to the rise of Senecan tragedy (*Auriacus, sive libertas saucia* [Auriacus, or liberty afflicted] 1602, treating of the death of William of Orange; and *Herodes infanticida* [Herod the baby-slayer] 1642). At the Synod of Dordrecht (1618–19), where the controversy introduced by Arminianism into the Dutch Reformed Church was discussed, Heinsius was appointed to watch over the quality of the Latin used. Heinsius also edited several Greek authors, providing them with an excellent Latin translation, but his edition of Ovid has proved to be of especially lasting value. He was, moreover, a poet himself, in Latin, Greek, and also in Dutch (*Nederduytsche poemata*, Dutch poems), thus considerably stimulating the development and renewal of vernacular poetry.

Born of Antwerp parents, Joost van den Vondel (1587–1679) was the most prominent poet and playwright in Dutch literature. In his most popular play, *Gysbreght van Aemstel* (1637), which was produced more than a hundred times during his lifetime, Vondel borrowed several features from the second book of the *Aeneid*. The translation of Vergil's entire oeuvre, first in prose (1646), later in verse (1660), was a high point of his literary career, but he also translated Horace and Ovid's *Heroides* and *Metamorphoses* in his *Heldinnebrieven* (1642) and *Herscheppinghe* (1671). His biblical epic *Johannes de Boetgezant. Begrepen in zes boeken* (John the preacher of penitence. Contained in six books, 1662) was intended to compete with the first part of Vergil's *Aeneid*, and even to surpass it by Christianizing it. Biblical drama was, however, his main and most important commitment. After a tragicomic play, treating of the exodus of Israel from Egypt (*Het Pascha*, 1612), he turned to Flavius Josephus for the subject of *Hierusalem verwoest* (Jerusalem destroyed, 1620). These were followed by many others. The most exalted of these and the most original in conception is *Lucifer*, being entirely set in heaven, from which Milton may have drawn inspiration. He reworked a classical theme for only three of his dramas: *Palamedes oft Vermoorde onnooselheyd* (Palamedes or murdered innocence, 1625), *Salmoneus* (1657), and *Faëton of Reuckeloze stoutheit* (Phaethon or reckless rashness, 1663). He produced, however, many translations of classical tragedies in the 1620s and 1630s: the *Amsteldamsche Hecuba* and *Hippolytus*, renderings of Seneca's *Troades* and *Phaedra*; *Elektra* and *Herkules in Trachin*, vernacular versions of Sophocles; and *Ifigenie in Tauren* (Iphigenia in Taurus) and *Feniciaensche* (the Phoenissae), renderings of Euripides. For the Greek plays he depended heavily upon Latin versions, as, for example, the *Phoenissae* by Hugo Grotius.

Pieter Corneliszoon Hooft (1581–1647), born at Amsterdam, made a journey through Italy in 1600, during which he addressed to the Chamber of Rhetoric a metrical letter called *In Liefd' Bloeyende* (In love flowering), in which he expressed his admiration for the achievements of Latin and Italian literature. Perhaps already before that date he produced the first classical tragedy in Dutch, *Achilles ende Polyxena* (Achilles and Polyxena), based essentially on Dictys Cretensis and Dares Phrygius, and stylistically indebted to Seneca. It was followed by several other plays of classical inspiration, such as *Theseus ende Ariadne* (Theseus and Ariadne, 1602 or 1603), *Paris oordeel* (The judgment of Paris), and *De gewonde Venus* (The wounded Venus, 1607). Again in Senecan style, he dramatized the origin of the Batavi (who lived between the Rhine and the Meuse) in his *Baeto*, and in the same year 1617 he also adapted Plautus' *Aulularia* in his *Warenar*. In 1628 Hooft started his masterpiece, his

Neederlandsche Histoorien (History of the Netherlands), voicing personal judgments on persons and their actions and pointing out lessons to be drawn from history. In the first 20 books, published in 1642, he dealt with the period from the abdication of Charles V in 1555 to the death of William of Orange in 1584. The last seven books (21–7) were published posthumously. The deliberate imitation of classical historians, especially Tacitus, as well as the solemnity of its manner made it into a model of Dutch prose style.

The last of the Amsterdam triad that should be mentioned is Gerbrand Adriaensz Bredero (1585–1618), who was probably the least influenced by the classics. His comedy *Moortje* ("Blackie," 1615), however, goes back to Terence's *Eunuchus*, or rather to a French version of it.

Hugo Grotius (1583–1645) has already been cited for the metrical version of Euripides' *Phoenissae* that he produced in 1630. He started his literary and political activities, however, much earlier. At the age of 15, he graduated in law from the University of Orléans; in that same year he ventured to comment upon the contemporary political situation with his *Scutum auriacum* (Shield of orange) and *Pontifex Romanus* (Roman priest). In 1598, he published an edition with a commentary of Martianus Capella's handbook of the seven liberal arts, as well as the *Phaenomena* of Aratus of Soli, for which he could make use of the manuscript holdings of the rich Leiden library. He produced a Latin translation of Theocritus in collaboration with Daniel Heinsius, and in 1614 edited Lucan. As early as 1601 he was appointed by the States of Holland as their Latin historiographer. During that same period he also worked on a comparison between the Athenian, the Roman, and the Batavian societies, producing in reality a eulogy of the Dutch nation (*Parallelon rerumpublicarum*, a parallel among republics). In this work his clear preference for the style and method of Tacitus is evident, as it also was in his *De antiquitate reipublicae Batavae* (On the antiquity of the republic of the Batavi, 1610) and, especially, in his *Annales et historiae de rebus Belgicis* (Annals and histories of 'Belgian' affairs), a description of the Dutch Revolt from 1559 until the Twelve Years' Truce (1609–21). In his main works, *De iure praedae* (Commentary on the law of prize and booty, 1604/5) and the expanded version *De iure belli et pacis* (On the law of war and peace, 1625) he laid the foundations of modern international law.

Another child prodigy was Constantijn Huygens (1596–1687), who wrote Latin poetry at the age of 11 and French poetry from 16 onwards. In 1625 he published a witty collection of Latin, French, Italian, and Dutch poems (*Otiorum libri sex*, Products of leisure, in six books). As a real "universal man," he designed his own residence at The Hague, his own country house (Hofwijck), and the decoration for the "Oranjezaal" in the Ten Bosch residence at The Hague, representing the *stadholder* Frederik Hendrik in the company of the Muses and the gods of Olympus. In 1647 he published 39 of his own musical compositions (*Pathodia sacra et profana*, Songs of passion, sacred and profane); he also wrote thousands of epigrams in Latin and Dutch, as well as a Latin panegyric of Oxford and a Latin autobiography (*De vita propria sermonum inter liberos libri duo*, Two books of conversations concerning my own life among my children). He gave his son Christiaan Huygens (1629–95) a many-sided education, enabling him to grow into one of the most famous mathematicians and physicists of his time. Christiaan unraveled (part of) the many secrets surrounding the planet Saturn (*Systema Saturnium*, Saturnian system, 1659), published the first book on probability theory (1657), and constructed the first pendulum clock in 1656, discussing the theory of the pendulum motion in his *Horologium oscillatorium* (1673). While in previous generations Latin had been predominant in the field of literary as well as scholarly and scientific output, C. Huygens's oeuvre, written partly in Latin and partly in the vernacular – as was the case for Descartes or Newton – is typical of the period in which European culture was moving more and more towards the vernacular and increasingly freeing itself from the long predominance of classical antiquity. Still, it can be pointed out that the Treaty of Münster (1648), which ended the Eighty Years' War and officially secured independence from Spain for the northern Netherlands, was drafted in Latin.

At a scholarly level the flowering of the Dutch Golden Age also involved the establishment of many new institutions of higher learning. Not so in the south, where the only newly established university, that of Douai (1559), was lost to the French in 1667, together with the rest of southern Flanders. Only a few colleges of monastic orders, especially the Augustinians and the Jesuits, grew into strongholds of the Counter-Reformation. Nevertheless, West Flanders produced a trio of gifted poets, Sidronius Hosschius (1596–1653), Jacobus Wallius (1599–1690), and Guilielmus Becanus (1608–83), who could even, in the opinion of some, compete with Ovid or Vergil. In the north, however, high schools and universities appeared in almost every province: a university at Franeker (1585), Groningen (1614), and Utrecht (1636); at Harderwijk (1648), Deventer (1630), and Amsterdam (1632), a *Gymnasium* or *Athenaeum Illustre*, all these becoming thriving centers of classical learning and literature.

4   Eighteenth Century to the Present

Nevertheless, the eighteenth and part of the nineteenth century marked a period of scholarly and cultural decline, not only in the south but even in the north. The Austrian and Napoleonic Wars, the short-lived reunification of the Netherlands in 1815, and their separation again in 1830 took a heavy toll. Under Napoleon some universities, such as those of Louvain (1797), Franeker (1811), and Harderwijk (1811), were closed.

Still, on the whole, Greek authors continued to be relatively well studied, edited, and equipped with learned commentaries, especially in the north. The Hellenist Carel Gabriel Cobet (1813–89), professor of Greek at the University of Leiden (1848–83), dominated classical scholarship for almost half a century. Through his many pupils he had an enormous influence until far into the twentieth century, but his hypercritical approach in the matter of textual transmission and his outspoken predilection for the pure Attic language led him to propose massive and faulty interventions in works of authors from other regions and periods.

But much more than the scholarship of that time in the field of Greek and Latin classics, which all in all was no more than average in quality, it is vernacular literature that deserves closer attention. Carel Vosmaer (1826–88) was one of the few Dutch authors who was deeply influenced by the classics. His archaeological novel *Amazone* (1880) has its setting in Rome and Naples; his romantic idyll *Nanno* is modeled on Greek verse. He translated the *Iliad* and the *Odyssey* into Dutch hexameters. As an editor of the leading journal *De Nederlandsche Spectator*, he played an important part in the revival of Dutch literature and set a trend for the next generation, known as the "Tachtigers" (The Movement of Eighty). This was an innovative and influential group of writers belonging to the same social circle at Amsterdam who aspired to extreme individualism and aestheticism. Several members had a classical training or were even active in the field of classical studies. Willem Kloos (1859–1938), for example, started as a student of classics, focusing mainly on the Greek poets. His earliest poetical works (*Rhodopis*, 1880; *Ganymedes op aarde*, Ganymede on earth, 1885; *Sappho*, 1893) were pervaded with the Greek conception of life. Later on he also treated Greek authors such as Callimachus and Pindar, and translated some Greek tragedies (Sophocles' *Antigone* and Euripides' *Alcestis*). Herman Gorter (1864–1927) even obtained his doctoral degree with a dissertation entitled *De interpretatione Aeschyli metaphorarum* (On the interpretation of Aeschylus' metaphors, 1889). His epic poem *Pan* (1912) and his study on *De groote dichters* (The great poets) reveal his lasting love for the classics. Jan Hendrik Leopold (1865–1925) was not only a poet of the utmost sensitivity and harmony but was also active as a philologist, publishing on Herodotus, Marcus Aurelius, and the Latinity of Spinoza. That most refined poet Pieter Cornelis Boutens (1870–1943) translated Plato's *Symposium* at the age of 18, and his own oeuvre remained permeated with Platonic ideas in matters of love and eroticism. He also translated the *Odyssey* and part of the *Iliad*, along with some Greek tragedians and Sappho.

To the same generation belonged Louis Couperus (1863–1923), who was above all a wonderful narrator. Time and again he goes back to classical antiquity for his tales and novels (*Dionyzos*, 1904; *De berg van licht*, The mountain of light, 1905/6, a historical novel narrating the life of the emperor Heliogabalus; *Herakles*, 1913; *De verliefde ezel*, The amorous ass, 1918, a retelling of Apuleius; *Izkander. De roman van Alexander den Groote*, Izkander, the novel of Alexander the Great, 1920). He also translated Plautus' *Menaechmi* and two *Idylls* of Theocritus.

During the twentieth century several more classical scholars developed into fine poets whose work was entirely imbued with classical echoes and motifs: Ida Gerhardt (1905–97), Anton van Wilderode (the pseudonym of Cyriel Coupé, 1918–98), and Jos de Haes (1920–74). For her doctoral dissertation Gerhardt translated two books of Lucretius, and later on also some Greek epigrams and Vergil's *Georgics*. In the entire oeuvre of Jos de Haes there is an intense yearning for purity, mixed with constant feelings of guilt and incapacity. He left a collection *Reisbrieven uit Griekenland* (Travel letters from Greece, 1957), together with translations of Pindar, *Pythische oden* (Pythian odes, 1945) and of Sophocles, *Philoktetes* (1959). Anton van Wilderode often suggested an imaginary ideal world in his poems, playing with classical figures and themes (*Najaar in Hellas*, Autumn in Greece, 1947; *De overoever*, The opposite shore, 1981; *Een tent van tamarinde*, A tent of tamarind, 1984). He also translated several of Horace's poems and Vergil's entire oeuvre.

The two most prolific writers of the modern period were Simon Vestdijk (1898–1971) and Hugo Claus (born 1929). Many of Vestdijk's poems have a mythological background: in some novels, such as *Else Böhler, Duitsch dienstmeisje* (Else Böhler, German house maid), which revived the Perseus and Andromeda story, he treated mythological themes, and three of his novels are even set in ancient Greece. In 1981 Paul Claes (born 1943) investigated the traces of classical influence in Claus's oeuvre in his doctoral dissertation, entitled *De mot zit in de mythe: antieke inter-textualiteit in het werk van Hugo Claus* (The moth is in the myth: ancient intertext-uality in the work of Hugo Claus). He also developed into a gifted author himself and a translator of classical authors such as Sappho and Catullus. He even tried his hand at a Latin translation of Claus's poetry.

Thus Latin and Greek language, values, and models did not entirely disappear from the Low Countries. It cannot be denied, however, that not only in the Low Countries, but all over Europe, a general classical decline can easily be detected. The main cause for this decline is that, from the beginning of the nineteenth century, if not earlier, the ideal of an education based on humanistic principles gradually crumbled away. At the universities in Belgium and the Netherlands, Latin as a teaching language was replaced by the vernacular, French in Belgium, Dutch in the Netherlands. Still, dissertations were presented in Latin until the beginning of the twentieth century, and in some minor institutions, such as Roman Catholic seminaries or faculties of theology, the teaching of Latin persisted until after World War II. In the secondary schools, teachers complained that their pupils had to study not only several vernacular languages but also mathematics and sciences, so that their study program was overloaded and their knowledge of Latin and especially of Greek rapidly declined. A vivid illustration is to be found in the letter sent by Domien Cracco (1790–1860) to the bishop of Bruges in 1842 (*Epistola de ratione docendi in gymnasiis*, Letter on the course of study in secondary schools). This situation deteriorated over the years in the nineteenth and twentieth centuries, and continues nowadays more rapidly than ever. The amount of time reserved for the teaching and study of Latin, and especially of Greek, has been reduced to an unworkably low level or has even been dropped altogether. Other decisive elements have been the process of democratization in the field of higher education and new – but not better – pedagogical insights, which have led to the opening of universities in the 1960s even to those who had not studied Latin and Greek at their secondary school. Even worse: due to the predominant impact of mathematics and the physical and social sciences, the study of Latin and Greek has become an almost unsur-mountable disadvantage for anyone wishing to go on to academic studies in fields other than the humanities. The Catholic Church also played some role. The second Vatican Council, by allowing the use of the vernacular for the liturgy instead of Latin, contributed in that way to the elimination of Latin from everyday affairs and its confinement to an even more remote corner of life. In this way Latin today has evolved into a curiosity, surfacing only at a few traditional events, such as diplomas bestowed *honoris causa* (honorary degrees) and congratulatory letters exchanged between universities, heraldic devices for newly appointed noblemen, and medals or inscriptions at the foot of a statue.

More than four hundred years ago, on July 2, 1602, Justus Lipsius wrote to Isaac Casaubon that scholarship, especially in Greek, was declining rapidly, so that "they were just holding on to vanishing Latin literature. So what hope could there be for Greek?" (Tournoy 1998). And three years later, on September 21, 1605, he wrote to his Bruges friend Janus Lernutius that they were heading for the last frontier of illiteracy. It is to be feared that after four centuries, his prophetic vision is about to come true.

FURTHER READING

For the Middle Ages, see Manitius (1911–31), Brunhölzl (1975–92), Raby (1957), Mann (1987); and Ziolkowski (1993) on the Latin tradition; Dolbeau (1979), Derolez et al. (1966–2001), Alessio, Billanovich, and de Angelis (1985), and Fiesoli (2004) on manuscripts and their readers; on Greek, Berschin (1980). On the coming of humanism to the Low Countries, the works of IJsewijn (1975, 1988, 1990, 1993) remain fundamental. Akkerman and Vanderjagt (1988) provide an up-to-date look at Agricola, with an edition of his letters available in Agricola (2002). The *Collected Works of Erasmus* (1974–) is ongoing, with many of the most important works already having appeared; Allen (1906–58) remains the standard edition (in Latin) of the letters, and Mann Phillips (1970) is useful on Erasmus and the classics. De Vocht (1951–5) describes the rise of the *Collegium Trilingue*. On Lipsius, see Tournoy (1998), Mouchel (1996), and Oestreich and Mout (1989). The connections between Rubens and the classical tradition are traced in Stechow (1968) and Morford (1991), with Rowland (1963) and the exhibition catalogue *Hollands classicisme in de zeventiende-eeuwse schilderkunst* (Dutch classicism in seventeenth-century painting) carrying forward the analysis of the relationship between classical scholarship and art. Nellen (1985) has written authoritatively on Grotius. On the classical tradition in modern, and more specifically in Dutch, literature, see Bogaerts (1969), Claes (1984, 2000), Van der Paardt (1982, 1991), De Rynck and Welkenhuysen (1997), and the series of bibliographical notes on Dutch translations of Greek and Latin authors in the journal *Hermeneus* from 1974 onwards.

CHAPTER SEVENTEEN

Scandinavia

Minna Skafte Jensen

1 Introduction

"Scandinavia" is here understood as the area covered by the modern states of Iceland, Norway, Sweden, Finland, and Denmark. In historical times, the majority of the people have spoken a group of closely related Germanic languages, while the northern- and easternmost parts are peopled by Finno-Ugrian-speaking Sames and Finns. During the ninth century Norwegian Vikings settled in the Faroe Islands and Iceland, and around 985 arrived in Greenland, already populated by Inuit peoples. A small Norwegian colony survived there until around 1500.

Thus the Scandinavian peoples are related by both language and history, but they nevertheless have distinct national identities. Over the centuries the Scandinavian states have engaged in continuous rivalry, often in open war. After some centuries of independence Iceland and Greenland accepted Norwegian sovereignty in 1262. The Swedes gradually conquered the Finns. A general Scandinavian union was established in 1397, formally among equal states, but to all practical purposes under Danish sway. Sweden withdrew in 1523. In 1658 Denmark permanently lost some of her richest areas to Sweden. Norway stayed under Danish rule until 1814, only to be annexed by Sweden, which on the other hand had lost Finland to Russia in 1809. Norway finally gained independence in 1905, Finland in 1917, and Iceland in 1944. The Faroe Islands and Greenland are still parts of the Danish state.

2 Middle Ages

There are scattered mentions of Scandinavian matters in ancient sources, notably the elder Pliny, Tacitus, and Ptolemy.

The runic alphabet (*futhark*), known from around AD 200 on, must be derived from the Greco-Roman letters and thus represents a very early ancient influence.

Many local finds of Roman workmanship testify to lively trade relations between Rome and Scandinavia during the first centuries AD. In particular, two beautiful cups decorated with scenes from the Trojan cycle were found in Hoby, Denmark. The Swedes maintained a travel route via Novgorod to Byzantium. The magnificent ships from around 850 found in Oseberg, Norway, testify to Byzantine influence on local woodcarving (Shetelig 1949: 104–5, 123). Vikings met with Roman-inspired communities during their raids to the British isles and Normandy. But coherent ancient influence only came with the Christian missionaries during the ninth and tenth centuries. By around 1100 Scandinavia had accepted the new religion.

During the Middle Ages the ancient culture that was transmitted by means of the church and its schools was almost exclusively Roman. A selection of Roman authors – mainly Terence, Cicero, and Vergil – was taught in schools, and Latin was a living, spoken idiom among the educated classes. Students traveled to seats of learning abroad in order to qualify for posts in the government and church at home, and Scandinavia had its role to play in the international Christian organizations. Also in the field of law, Scandinavia was part of a common European trend. Already in 1164 a Norwegian synod assembly produced canons influenced by *Decretum Gratiani* (Gratian's decree; i.e., canon law), and this influence continues in the many provincial laws issued in Norway, Denmark, and Sweden during the following two centuries (Landau 2005).

It is impossible to say how widespread runic writing became, since in most cases only texts on stone have been preserved. But in Bergen, Norway, rich finds of inscriptions on wood from the late Middle Ages include many private, informal messages and suggest that vernacular runic literacy was considerable even among the common people. Some Latin phrases (e.g., a quote from Vergil) occur (Liestøl & Johnsen 1980–90: 11–13). Thus runes and Latin letters coexisted for centuries. In general, however, the picture we meet in the manuscript tradition is that of a culture in which the spoken language is vernacular, the written one Latin. Iceland is the great exception to this rule. Here the Roman alphabet was used right from its introduction for writing in both Latin and Icelandic, and a rich literature of sagas as well as Eddic and Scaldic poetry has survived, testifying to a lively interaction between oral narrative traditions and Latin literature. There is even a saga of the Trojan War, based on the tradition of Dares and Dictys.

As elsewhere in Europe, Latin evolved away from its classical form under influence from the vernaculars. Most written literature was composed in this idiom. However, around 1200 two ambitious representatives of "the Renaissance of the twelfth century," both Danish, returned to classical models. Anders Sunesen composed a paraphrase of the beginning of *Genesis*, *Hexaëmeron* (A poem of the six days), in 8,040 hexameters, and Saxo Grammaticus in his huge national history modeled his prose on authors such as Valerius Maximus and Martianus Capella, while the interspersed poems move in classical meters (Friis-Jensen 1987). His overall purpose was to demonstrate that the Danish kingdom had a glorious past, well able to compete with Rome. Significantly, the Icelander Snorri Sturluson (ca. 1178–1241) chose the vernacular for his history of the Norwegian kings.

In Sweden, St. Birgitta (ca. 1303–73) established her own monastic order, which gradually spread to other countries and even to Rome. Her revelations were translated from her original Swedish into Latin by her confessors.

The church as an institution represented an unbroken link to Roman culture, and so did its buildings. Churches and monasteries, first in Romanesque and then in Gothic style, were erected all over Denmark and Sweden, with the most lively building activity concentrated in the twelfth and thirteenth centuries. Christian art, too, was international and in the final analysis inspired from ancient Rome. Churches were decorated with lively paintings, brilliantly colored; normally these are anonymous, but in the Stockholm area the signature of Albertus Pictor is well known. In Norway, too, monumental churches were constructed, most notably the cathedral of St. Olav in Nidaros (later Trondheim). But there smaller, local churches were most often wooden buildings in a style of their own. About 1290 a small cathedral in stone was even begun in Kirkjubøur in the Faroes, but never finished; its ruins are still to be seen.

Universities were opened in Uppsala in 1477 and Copenhagen in 1479.

3   Renaissance

With the Renaissance a new dialogue with the ancient tradition began. The movement reached Scandinavia early in the sixteenth century, but was soon overtaken by the Lutheran Reformation, itself a child of the Renaissance with its return to the original Bible. It remained typical of Renaissance influence in Scandinavia that the Reformation was transmitted via Wittenberg.

The Reformation was first embraced by Sweden, where King Gustav Vasa broke the ties to the pope in 1527. In Denmark the movement began in the church, and during the 1520s and 1530s a lively and sometimes violent dispute developed, almost entirely in the vernacular. Finally in 1536 King Christian III established Protestantism in all his lands. In Norway the change met little reaction, but the Icelanders were by no means ready to leave the Catholic Church, and the opposition was silenced only when bishop Jón Arason was beheaded in 1550.

The main reformers, Olaus Petri (1493–1552) in Sweden, Hans Tausen (1494–1561) in Denmark, and Michael Agricola (1509–57) in Finland, all studied in Wittenberg, and so did their successors. There they were taught by Luther's colleague and friend Melanchthon, mentioned again and again in Scandinavian literature of the period. One of Europe's most competent Hellenists, he was intent on establishing a workable synthesis of Christian and pagan culture. In the efforts to have the Bible translated into the vernaculars, the scholars, of course, followed Luther's German translation, but also the Hebrew and Greek originals. The Bible appeared in Swedish in 1541, Finnish (only the New Testament) in 1548, Danish in 1550, and Icelandic in 1584, whereas the populations of Norway and the Faroe Islands were supposed to read the Danish Bible, a fact that for centuries hindered the development of their respective vernaculars as written languages. The universities had not functioned during the upheavals, but when they were reopened they included chairs of Hebrew and Greek.

Lutheran reformers insisted on service being read in the vernaculars. Nevertheless, the second half of the sixteenth century brought a tremendous revival of classical Latin. In poetry all the classical genres – epic and elegy, didactic poetry, pastoral, satire, iambics, and lyrics – were used, as well as typical neo-Latin forms such as *propemptica* (valedictory poems), *hodoeporica* (poems describing a journey), panegyrics, and praises of cities. Paraphrasing the Bible, an activity well-established in medieval times, achieved new importance, with the psalms in particular being recomposed again and again. It was somehow disquieting that God seemed to have given to pagan authors a finer sense of stylistics than was to be found in the Bible; at the same time, to unite biblical content with classical form was at the heart of Melanchthonian ideology.

A recurrent motif was that of inviting the muses. Already in antiquity these goddesses had moved from Greece to Rome, and while Italians still considered them at home in their country, poets north of the Alps had been inviting them northwards from around 1500. Now young Scandinavians offered them a refuge from war-ridden Central Europe, and their arrival symbolized poetry in classical meters. Among the first were the Danes Johannes Georgius Sadolinus (1528–1600) and Johannes Franciscus (1532–84) as well as the Swede Laurentius Petri Gothus (1529–79). Sadolinus (1552), Franciscus (1554), and Gothus (1561) all issued collections of elegies, with Ovid's letters from his exile as the great model. Gothus also composed an historical poem over an incident in Herodotus, *Strategema Gothici exercitus* (A stratagem of the Gothic army, 1559) with allusions to the poet's own times: the Scythians are identified with the Swedes and the tyrant Darius with the Danish King Christian II (Aili 1995: 137).

In the following decades conditions for poetry were more favorable in Denmark, where King Frederik II supported art and literature, than under the more turbulent years of Gustav Vasa's reign in Sweden. Especially Sadolinus developed into an interesting poet who composed on many different topics and in a variety of meters, inspired also by poets who were not yet much read in Scandinavia, such as Catullus and Martial (Jensen 2004: 153–7). In Norway, a small group of scholar-poets established a humanist milieu around the Latin school in Oslo (Ekrem 1995: 70–3).

In some cases poets identified closely with classical models. This is especially evident in the case of Erasmus Laetus (1526–82) and the astronomer Tycho Brahe (1546–1601). Laetus became the Danish Vergil by composing bucolics, a didactic poem on shipping, and two national epics, as well as quite a few other poems, most of them in hexameters. Tycho Brahe, on the other hand, chose Ovidian forms. Already in his first publication, *De nova stella* (On the new star, 1573), he included an elegy in which he relates how he met the muse Urania, who entrusted him with the mission of elevating the study of astronomy to the level it had had in antiquity. Later in life he composed other elegant imitations of Ovid, for example a heroid (letter from an abandoned heroine) composed in the name of his sister Sophie. And when toward the end of his life he lost royal support and left Denmark in search of new patrons, he expressed his frustration in an elegiac letter addressed to the personified Dania, taking on the role of the exiled Roman poet (Zeeberg 1994).

One of the common features underlying this exuberant outpouring of Latin poetry was the wish to demonstrate that Scandinavians were as fully civilized as any people in

Europe. This same impulse lay behind the monumental descriptions of the Scandinavian peoples by the Swedish brothers Magnus, who had emigrated to Italy to
escape Protestant persecution. Johannes Magnus (1488–1544) composed *Historia
de omnibus Gothorum Sueonumque regibus* (A History of all the Gothic and Swedish
kings, printed 1554), and Olaus Magnus (1490–1557) wrote *Historia de gentibus
septentrionalibus* (A history of the Nordic peoples, 1555), an ethnographic description of Scandinavian culture. Polemic against erroneous ideas about his nation
dominated the works of Arngrímur Jónsson (1568–1648), *Brevis commentarius de
Islandia* (A brief note on Iceland, 1593) and *Crymogaea sive res Islandicae* (Crymogaea; i.e., Iceland, 1609), describing Icelandic conditions and history in elegant
modern form (Benediktsson 1991; Pétursson 1995: 104–6).

   The nationalist drive took a special turn in the competition over history that
developed between Sweden and Denmark. Already in 1434 when the Swedish bishop
Nicolaus Ragvaldi had represented the Scandinavian union at the international
church assembly in Basel, he had demanded special honors with a reference to
Jordanes' *Getica* (AD 551). Here the island of Scandza is described as the home of
the Getic/Gothic people. The island was identified with the Danish province of
Scania, and the fact that the component "Goth-" exists in the names of various
Swedish landscapes pointed in the same direction. Now Johannes Magnus used the
same argumentation to stress the venerable old age of the Swedish nation. According
to him, Noah/Janus had lived in Scythia. He divided the world between his sons, of
whom Japhet/Atlas received Europe. His son Magog had three sons: Suenno,
ancestor of the Swedes, Gothar, progenitor of the Goths, and Ubbo, founder of
Uppsala. The Danes were also Goths, but descendants of Swedish criminals who over
the years had been sent southwards in exile. Magnus' work provoked an official
Danish answer, *Refutatio calumniarum cuiusdam Ioannis Magni* (Refutation of a
certain Johannes Magnus' slanders, 1561), composed by Johannes Svaning, and two
years later an anonymous Swedish reply, *De iniusto bello a Danorum rege contra Suecos
gesto* (About the unjust war of the Danish king against the Swedes). A decade later
both of Erasmus Lætus' two epics propagated the Danish views, and in 1612 the
Swedish historian Johannes Messenius (1579–1636) published a new answer, *Retor-
sio imposturarum* (Rejection of the deceits) (Borst 1957–63: 1100–1; Skovgaard-
Petersen 1991, 1993; Hillebrecht 1997; Skovgaard-Petersen 2002: 91–124). A
similar conflict was fought over the history of the runes.

   All power and prestige were concentrated in Latin literature. But an interest began
in recording the vernacular ballad tradition common to Norway, Sweden, Denmark,
and the Faroes. These poems are mostly concerned with Nordic themes, but the story
of Paris and Helen also occurs. In 1591 the Danish Anders Sørensen Vedel published
the world's first printed ballad collection. In Finland a collection of pious Latin songs,
Piae cantiones, was published by Theodoricus Petri in 1582. In spite of its title, the
collection also contains a great many secular songs and is related to medieval students'
poetry as known in other parts of Europe. It may be considered another recording of
an oral tradition.

   While the handling of ancient traditions in literature extended rather broadly
through the various social classes, their place in art and architecture was mostly

restricted to monarchs and nobility. As a result of the Reformation, decorations left the church walls, but princes and noblemen invited foreign artists, and elegant castles were constructed and decorated, often with themes from ancient myth or history. Medieval castles in Bergen and Oslo were modernized in Renaissance style. When Oslo was destroyed by fire in 1624, King Christian IV had the city moved and rebuilt, modestly changing its name to Christiania, a name it retained until 1925. Among the many splendid works of art commissioned by him are some painted ceilings (by Gerrit Honthorst) in his Elsinore palace, Kronborg, showing scenes from Heliodorus' *Aethiopica* (1635). Court culture excelled in ancient motifs with regular use of classical figures such as personified virtues, when, for instance, processions were organized through the streets to celebrate birthdays, coronations, or funerals.

4 Baroque

Toward the end of the sixteenth century, almost all the surviving ancient authors had been introduced in Scandinavia, and poets mastered the classical forms. A certain mannerism made itself felt with a growing interest in various kinds of formal games, such as *chronosticha*, *acrosticha*, and *telesticha*. For example, with great virtuosity the Norwegian Halvardus Gunarius (ca. 1550–1608) celebrated the crowning of the Danish King Christian IV in Oslo with a hexameter poem in which every single word begins with a "C" (printed in the collection *Akrostichis*, 1606). The Latin *parodia*, a form combining extremely close imitation with new content, appeared in such works as the parodies of Horace's *Odes* (1615) by the Danish Bertil Knudsen Aquilonius (1588–1650). Epigrams, preferably of the type that contains a pointed ending, became trendy, and anagrams, mostly built on personal names, flourished. An especially happy one was that of the Swedish king "GVSTAVVS" to "AVGVSTVS," an expression of the widespread appeal of *translatio imperii* (power transfer): the power of imperial Rome had gradually been transferred toward the north and was now finding its natural home in Stockholm (Tengström 1973: 55).

Both Denmark and Sweden involved themselves in the Thirty Years' War – with catastrophic results for Denmark, while it inaugurated Sweden's ascent as a great power. Foreign poets composed huge epics to celebrate King Gustav II Adolph's military prowess (Helander 2003). Under this king and his daughter Christina, with the nobleman Axel Oxenstierna as their chancellor, the Stockholm court became a magnet for artists and other intellectuals from all over Europe: Johann Comenius, Isaac Vossius, René Descartes, Nicolaus Heinsius, and Hugo Grotius all had close contact with the Swedish court, and in 1667 Samuel von Pufendorf was appointed professor at the new university of Lund. There he composed his main work, *De iure naturae et gentium* (On the laws of nature and the peoples, 1672). Christina was praised by local and foreign poets as the quintessence of both learning and the more usual female virtues, and identified with Minerva and Diana (Kajanto 1993).

Sweden also had a great many native authors in this period. Johannes Messenius (1579–1636) composed a description of the five oldest towns of the nation, *Sveopentaprotopolis* (1611), and also transmitted his learning to a broader public in a series of vernacular dramas on the nation's history (1611–14). Because of Catholic sympathies he spent his last 20 years in prison, but nevertheless succeeded in writing a huge description of Sweden, *Scondia illustrata*, published in 1705. The adventurous Lars Wivallius (1605–69) is generally acclaimed as the first Swedish lyricist, and his Latin poetry is of the same high standard. Olof Verelius (1618–82) left a manuscript containing Sweden's first novel (closely following a Spanish-French model), *Peregri-natio cosmopolitana* (A journey to the city of the world, published 1730). The first pages, in which the first-person narrator tells of the gentle education he received as a child, has been seen as an influence from Comenius. The protagonist visits a symbolic city in which hypocrisy reigns supreme and also has the choice between the steep path of virtue and the broad road of vices. He soon ends in hell, but manages to escape (Bergh and von Platen 1994). The most famous Swedish implementation of the theme of the crossroads, however, is the great didactic poem *Hercules* by Georg Stiernhielm (1598–1672), in Swedish hexameters.

Whereas in the Danish empire there was still only one university, that of Copen-hagen, the Swedes opened universities in the areas under their power, such as in Åbo/Turku, Finland, in 1640, and in Lund, in the recently conquered Scania, in 1668.

In Iceland the vernacular still coexisted with Latin in a specially balanced way. Most popular were the vernacular narrative poems *rímur*, of which more than a thousand survive in written form. The bishop Brynjólfur Sveinsson (1605–75), although Lu-theran, composed a Latin hymn in various meters to the virgin Mary (Pétursson 1995: 117), while Hallgrímur Pétursson (1614–74) composed his *Fifty Passion Hymns* in Icelandic (Magnússon 1989). The learned Thorsteinn Björnsson (1612–75) worked to copy all sources for Icelandic history in a single collection, and when as an old man he lost his eyesight, he composed Latin poetry (Springborg 1991).

In the rest of Scandinavia the vernaculars only now began to establish themselves as a serious written medium. Experiments were made with composing Latin literary forms, such as panegyrics, satires, didactic poetry, or biblical paraphrases, in the vernaculars. Claus Christoffersen Lyschander (1558–1623), Anders Arrebo (1587–1637), and Thomas Kingo (1634–1703) in Denmark, Petter Dass (1647–1707) in Norway, and Georg Stiernhielm in Sweden composed their most important works in their own languages but retained the ancient frames of reference dominated by Roman mythology. For instance, Arrebo's main work is a *Hexaëmeron* (A poem of the six days), and when Kingo started out composing love-lyrics in pastoral form praising the charming Chrysillis, he followed a well-known ancient pattern established by Vergil and imitated by innumerable others; Kingo, however, did it in Danish. Dass, in contrast, distanced himself more from ancient models. He composed a vernacular praise poem, *The Trumpet of Nordland*, but used the form to celebrate not a city, but everyday life in the countryside. The title of Stiernhielm's collected poems, *Musae Suethizantes* (1668), is significant, not least its Swedish subtitle: "That is, the goddesses of song now at last learning how to sing and play in Swedish."

The question of metrics became important. Classical Latin poetry is based on syllabic quantities, while the rhythm in Nordic verse depends on stress. Aquilonius argued that composers should follow the quantitative system even when they com-posed in Danish, but his opponents won the day, and both in Sweden and Denmark poets worked to establish rules for a vernacular poetics, able to compete with the classics. Peder Jensen Roskilde (1571–1641) wrote a *Prosodia Danicæ linguæ* (Prosody of the Danish language, 1629) and published a translation of Vergil's *Bucolica* in Danish meters in 1639. Andreas Arvidi (ca. 1620–73) published his *Manuductio ad poesin Suecanam* (A guide to Swedish poetry, 1651).

The controversy over origins developed into a question of languages. Throughout the Middle Ages Latin had undisputedly been the sacred language, but when it was gradually realized that the Bible had originally been composed in Hebrew and Greek, Latin lost some of its authority, and which language was the original one gradually became an important question. This international discussion had its special Scandinavian variants. In *De Danicae linguae cum Graeca mistione* (About the fusion of the Danish language with the Greek, 1641) Aquilonius argued that Greek was derived from Danish, referring to the fact that in Homer the Greeks are called *Danaoi*; besides, the Greek language is full of Danish words, of which he listed a multitude of examples. Georg Stiernhielm argued that the European languages, including Greek, Latin, Armenian, and Persian, all go back to Japhet's language, Scythian, which is the same as Gothic or Swedish. Stiernhielm also provided an edition of Wulfila's Bible, the only important witness to the true Gothic language, which had been brought to Uppsala as booty from Prague. Another Swede, Andreas Kempe (1622–89), advanced an especially charming version: in Paradise, God spoke Swedish to Adam and Adam answered in Danish, but the serpent spoke French to Eve! Gothicism reached its peak with Olof Rudbeck (1630–1702), who in his *Atlantica* (1675) maintained that Sweden is not only the home of Japhet's/Atlas' descendants, but also the place that Plato called Atlantis. Petrus Bång introduced the Finns into the genealogies, suggesting that they might be descendants of Japhet's oldest son Gomer (1675), whereas Daniel Juslenius in his history of Åbo/Turku (1700) argued that this town had been founded by Magog in person, and that the Finnish language went right back to the tower of Babel (Borst 1957–63: 1335–40; Kajanto 1995: 181–3).

Much energy was invested in historiography. The monarchs engaged historians to write their national histories, and in Denmark the final result was two monumental Latin descriptions, both inspired by Tacitus: Isaac Pontanus' knotty production, full of quotations and discussions of sources (1631), and Johannes Meursius' eloquent work (1630–8) (Skovgaard-Petersen 2002). The Icelander Thormod Torfaeus (1636–1719), who lived most of his life in Bergen, composed a huge *Historia rerum Norvegicarum* (History of Norway, 1711). It was gradually realized that Icelandic manuscripts were a treasure trove of information about early Nordic history and myth, and again there was a competition between Sweden and Denmark to get hold of the valuable books and of Icelanders able to read them. In Denmark Thomas Bartholin (1659–90) and Arni Magnusson (1663–1730) cooperated over *Antiquitates Danicae* (Danish antiquity, 1689), which all over Europe became the standard handbook of Nordic mythology.

In architecture noblemen and monarchs excelled in having fabulous castles built, decorated by the best painters and sculptors of northern Europe. In Sweden the architects Nicodemus Tessin, father and son (1615–81 and 1654–1728), were preeminent. Both contributed to the royal palace Drottningholm, just outside

Stockholm (1662 onward), inspired by classical monuments and decorated with symbolic figures from antiquity. Their style still dominates the center of Stockholm, where they erected several important buildings.

5 Enlightenment and Neoclassicism

In the early eighteenth century, one figure towers over everybody else in Scandinavia: the Norwegian Ludvig Holberg (1684–1754). He was a prolific writer in both poetry and prose, composing scholarly works as well as fiction. Inspired by Samuel Pufendorf, he wrote in Danish *Natural and Popular Law* (1712–14). His mock-epic about the shipwrecked merchant *Peder Paars* (1719–20) could not have existed without the *Aeneid*, but the epics of his close contemporaries were probably his main target. From 1722 onward he composed a long series of Danish comedies, inspired by Molière and, at a slightly greater distance, by Plautus and Terence. His satirical epigrams in Latin are in the tradition of John Owen and Martial, and his *Moral Epistles* were inspired by Seneca and the younger Pliny. His utopian Latin novel about *Nicolaus Klimius* (1741) has, again, both modern and ancient models, notably Jonathan Swift and Lucian.

In Sweden the most remarkable personalities, Emanuel Swedenborg (1688–1772), Carl von Linné (1707–78), and Olof von Dalin (1708–63), were very different in kind. Swedenborg, who by education was a scientist, developed into a religious mystic. Linné established a classification of the world's flora, which is still the basis for modern botany. His *Systema naturae* (1735) uses a binary nomenclature directly inherited from Aristotle. Dalin, however, worked for the education of his fellow countrymen, among other things publishing a national history in Swedish (1747–62).

The enlightenment implied a critical attitude toward classical models in literature and scholarship, and brought an end to the more irrational phenomena. But the mere fact that almost all professional discussions were composed in Latin meant that ancient categories still kept a firm hold on the minds of educated people, and, in the long run, what happened was less a movement away from antiquity than a change in the way antiquity was perceived. Other authors were selected or other aspects studied, and especially, a new interest in Greek rather than Latin appeared. Greek had been well known ever since the Renaissance, but it never achieved a status equal to that of Latin. Greek authors had been studied mainly in Latin translations. Many attempts had been made to master ancient Greek as a spoken and written language, and some individuals had become proficient at expressing themselves in Greek. For instance, the Finnish Johann Paulinus Lillienstedt (1655–1732) composed a Greek poem in 379 hexameters, praising the wonders of his nation, *Magnus principatus Finlandia* (The Grand Duchy of Finland, 1678). But Latin was still the language chosen by default for science, scholarship, and prestigious literature. Now, on the contrary, an enthusiasm for everything Greek arose. Greek ideas of democracy and political liberty, including freedom of speech, were taken as the great inspiration for social progress in modern societies, and the originality of Greek literature was celebrated in contrast to the imitative quality of Latin works. Vergil lost ground to Homer.

German "new humanism" became very influential in Scandinavia and led both to an intensified study of ancient Greek and to a professionalizing of classical studies in general. While antiquity gradually lost influence as an immediate model, there was a growing interest in historical and philological research on ancient themes, and in the universities the chairs of Greek and Latin grew independent of theology. The Norwegian Georg Sverdrup (1770–1850) was a professor of Greek in this modern sense at the University of Copenhagen before he proceeded to Oslo, where he was one of the founders of the new university in 1813. He was also a member of the commission that prepared the constitution of Norway after it became independent.

In another field the new admiration for originality had a tremendous impact: in the growing interest in the literature of the noneducated, the socially or geographically marginalized. At the university of Turku, Henrik Gabriel Porthan (1739–1804) was professor of eloquence, and in a series of dissertations on Finnish poetry (1766–78, well before Herder's *Popular Voices in Song*, 1807) he argued that the tradition of stories and poems existing among illiterate Finns was of great artistic value. In his works on rhetoric he taught pastors how to preach in Finnish, and his voluminous notes to the *Chronicle of the Medieval Bishops of Finland* (1784–1800) were the first serious study of Finnish history. He put an end to speculations about the biblical pedigree of the Finnish people by demonstrating that they had immigrated from Russia, and in 1801 he even sketched a study of Finnish dialects. This whole achievement was performed in Latin (Kajanto 1984). However, Rasmus Rask (1787–1832), the first modern linguist in Scandinavia, published his study of the history of old Norse (1818) in Danish. During this same period, the learned Faroese J. C. Svabo (1746–1824) worked on a dictionary of the Faroese language with translations into Danish and Latin, and was the first to collect ballads in the Faroe Islands.

A revolt against classically inspired rationalism took place in some of the lyrical poetry of the day, for instance with the Danish Johannes Ewald (1743–81). But poems such as *The Beatitudes of Rungsted* (1772) and *To the Soul, an Ode* (1780) are formally inspired by Pindar and Horace, and *Philetus, a Narration* (1770) is modeled on Vergil's first eclogue in its celebration of contemporary agricultural reforms (Friis-Jensen, unpublished).

In the meantime ancient tradition had become dominant in art and architecture. In Sweden the neoclassical sculptor Johan Tobias Sergel (1740–1814) won international fame with his representations of classical themes, but his masterpiece is a colossal statue of the Swedish King Gustav III in central Stockholm. His friend, the Danish painter Nicolai Abildgaard (1743–1809), also preferred ancient subjects for his pictures. His painting *The Wounded Philoctetes* (1774–75) is a remarkable interpretation of the Sophoclean figure with its concentrated expression of wild desperation. Abildgaard worked regularly for the absolute monarch, but it has recently been argued that in his own choice of motifs he revealed his sympathies for the French revolution (Kragelund 1999). No Scandinavian artist has, however, been more internationally respected than Bertel Thorvaldsen (1770–1844). Among his best known works are *Jason with the Golden Fleece*, *Venus*, and *The Three Graces*. He spent four decades in Rome, where he became a central figure among local and foreign artists, and still today his works decorate many European cities. In Munich he was entrusted to restore the sculptures from the temple of Aphaia in Aigina. When in 1838 he returned to Denmark, he was welcomed as a hero and given his own museum.

Neoclassical art was often commissioned by well-to-do bourgeois patrons. Houses, furniture, and indoor decoration took on classical garb. Great creative architects, such as the Danes C. F. Harsdorff (1735–99), C. F. Hansen (1756–1845), and Gottlieb Bindesbøll (1800–56), worked during this period. In Copenhagen most of the center was rebuilt after catastrophic fires in 1794–5, and this was when the city center achieved the dominant neoclassical character it still retains. Harsdorff and Hansen were also called in to remodel the center of Christiania, together with the Norwegian H. D. F. von Linstow (1787–1851). Another type of neoclassicism came to dominate the center of Helsinki. To celebrate Finland's new status as an autonomous duchy within the Russian empire, Czar Alexander I sent his German architect Carl Ludvig Engel (1778–1840) to plan a suitable center for the new capital, and the result was truly monumental, dominated by the great church of St. Nicholas.

6   From Romanticism to the Twentieth Century

When during the first decades of the nineteenth century, Romanticism came to dominance, it meant a total reversal of values. The respect for originality led to an admiration for whatever was first and oldest, but paradoxically it also gave priority to everything new. The Danish philosopher Søren Kierkegaard (1813–55) was part of this movement, although he remained deeply affected by his classical learning. In his novel *Either–Or* (1843), the dialogue between aesthetics and ethics is at the same time between pagan and Christian ideas.

In everyday practice Latin and the grand constructions it had been connected with were gradually rejected. This involved a criticism of ancient mythology and an attempt at introducing Nordic mythologies instead. Nationalism was nothing new, but it changed form and spread to broader sections of the populations. The leading personalities were poets, the Danish Adam Oehlenschläger (1779–1850) and N. F. S. Grundtvig (1783–1872) as well as the Swedish Esaias Tegnér (1782–1846) and P. D. A. Atterbom (1790–1855). (Tegnér was also a professor of Greek at the University of Lund.) They shared an enthusiasm for everything Nordic and for the common people – although the latter were felt to need suitable education. Grundtvig invested great energy in establishing a new kind of people's high schools, primarily meant for youngsters from the countryside.

For the artists a new goal arose: to give visual form to the mythic figures. Whereas ancient mythology had consisted of both stories and images and there was a firm tradition of how Jupiter, Minerva, and Diana looked, artists now had to determine how to represent Odin and Väinämöinen – no mean job. That they did so in naturalistic ways was ironically a survival of ancient tradition. This was also the case in Greenland when the Danish governor Hinrich Rink (1819–93) met Aron, an Inuit from Kangeq (1822–69). The Inuit had no traditions for drawing or painting, but Aron was quick to learn the various techniques, and the brilliant series of illustrations he produced, both for old stories and for the everyday life of his own times, had as their model the naturalistic way of painting that via the Renaissance goes right back to antiquity (Thisted 1999, 2001).

An unusual ancient influence was that of Homeric scholarship on the composition of the Finnish national epic. Elias Lönnrot (1802–84), who collected oral traditional songs among the poorest inhabitants of Karelia in eastern Finland, was well informed about German criticism, and F. A. Wolf's ideas about how the *Iliad* and the *Odyssey* had been built on the basis of the performances of illiterate rhapsodes were productive in his own creative work. As another Homer, he arranged the songs he had recorded so as to form one long, continuous narrative, changing as little as possible in the process. In 1835 he published the *Kalevala*.

With the Napoleonic Wars the conflict between Sweden and Denmark had lost importance. Compared with the threat from great powers such as Russia, Britain, and Germany, internal Scandinavian disagreement paled into insignificance, and a wave of pan-Scandinavian feelings supplanted old rivalries.

In the universities, the emancipation of classical scholarship developed further. This was the period of the great Johan Nicolai Madvig (1804–86), professor at Copenhagen University for half a century and for long periods its rector, also serving as Minister of Culture in an especially critical period. He embraced all aspects of encyclopedic philology, and especially in the fields of language studies and textual criticism broke new ground.

The story of the classical tradition during the nineteenth and twentieth centuries is one of gradual retreat. The central debate concerned the place of Latin in the schools, and it is still going on. Traumatic descriptions of the Latin school abound in autobiographies, and bitter criticism was launched especially by the Norwegian Alexander Kielland in his novel *Poison* (1883) and the Dane Hans Scherfig in *The Neglected Spring* (1940). In the nineteenth century professional classicists such as Madvig were among those who were the most critical of undue idealization of ancient culture and had purely rational reasons for wanting to keep Latin in the educational system. In more recent times, classicists have mostly argued for retaining the last remnants of this tradition in the school curriculum. The older universities still have chairs of Greek and Latin, and classical scholars have become energetic participants in interdisciplinary projects. In his studies of Latin syntax, the Swedish Einar Löfstedt (1880–1955) was inspired by general linguistics. In Iceland, Jakob Benediktsson (1907–99), with his encyclopedic knowledge and precise classical scholarhip, was a central figure in the humanist landscape.

Characters from ancient mythology or history have now and then been called upon in contemporary conflicts, such as in the Norwegian Henrik Ibsen's drama *Catilina* (1850) and in the Swedish Viktor Rydberg's novel *The Last Athenian* (1859). The historical novel has had interesting representatives in Scandinavia: the Danish Nis Petersen's *The Street of the Sandalmakers* (1931), the Finnish Mika Waltari's *Sinuhe the Egyptian* (1945), and T. Vaaskivi's *The Autocrat* (1942) as well as the Swedish Eyvind Johnson's *The Clouds over Metapontion* (1957).

Exactly when the ancient tradition disappeared as an undisputed common frame of reference cannot be determined. But its afterlife has been more and more dependent on translations, and especially Greek authors are richly represented in the Scandinavian languages. In Denmark Christian Wilster's translations of Homer (1836–7) have become national classics in their own right, often alluded to in later literature. He chose hexameters and modeled his language on Oehlenschläger's, but showed great creative energy in his coining of new words to represent the characteristic Homeric epithets. Twenty years later Sveinbjørn Egilsson chose an Old Icelandic meter, *fornyrðislag*, for his translations. There is still a market for new translations, and Attic dramas are often played in modern staging.

In art and architecture ancient themes are mainly allusive or indirect. Now and then mythological motifs turn up, sometimes to add an extra layer of meaning to a picture, as when the Norwegian Edvard Munch called a painting of a naked couple *Amor and Psyche* (1907), in other cases ironically, as in *The Judgment of Paris*, a picture by the Danish Harald Giersing showing the painter with three models (1909). The Scandinavian "villa," normally a modest house meant for a single family, has little in common with its Roman model. A special variation, though, the "atrium-house," is actually modeled on the typical Roman house, closed to the outside but opening into a central courtyard.

7 Epilogue

Perhaps the most important aspect of the classical tradition in Scandinavia, as elsewhere, was the way in which Greek and Roman culture over the centuries influenced languages and mentalities. The Latin language, the most important medium for this influence, underwent important shifts from its place as the normal idiom for written and special parts of oral communication in the Middle Ages, through the conscious and very energetic revision of its use with a return to classical standards in the sixteenth century, followed by a long period in which this revised form of Latin became again the normal idiom for most prestigious communication, and a transitional period in which Latin literature worked as a matrix for experiments in the vernaculars, until its gradual decline during the nineteenth and twentieth centuries. As in other marginal areas, the classical tradition in Scandinavia was characterized by a constant competition with classical Rome and its more central modern representatives. Special to Scandinavia, however, are traits such as the runic writing system, the Lutheran reform, the competition between Sweden and Denmark, the "Gothic theory," and the old Norse and Finnish mythologies.

CHAPTER EIGHTEEN

United Kingdom

Richard Jenkyns

1   Remoteness and Aspiration

When an Englishman turns to Latin poetry, he finds that his land is obscure, remote, and exotic. Catullus extravagantly tells his friends that they are willing to follow him to the ends of the earth, to where the eastern waves beat upon the Indian shore and to the "shaggy and most distant Britons" (Poem 11). Horace flatters his master by predicting the conquest of the farthest and most improbable peoples: Augustus will be held to be a god upon earth when he has added the Persians and the Britons to his empire (*Odes* 3.5.1–4). And one of Vergil's herdsmen, in an excess of despair, declares that exile will take him to Scythia or the Sahara or to "the Britons separated from the entire world" (*Eclogue* 1.66). Nineteen hundred years on, when Tennyson wrote his homage *To Virgil*, he echoed these lines, but with a significant adjustment:

> I, from out the Northern Island,
> sunder'd once from all the human race,
> I salute thee, Mantovano . . .
> (lines 35–7)

In the little adverb "once," much of the history of the British engagement with classical antiquity is encapsulated – the awareness that the British had been peripheral to the classical story, to which they might add the hope that they might be able to latch on to the central tradition of European culture, or the confidence that they had indeed done so. In Tennyson's time the British might claim that far from being sundered from all the human race, they were at the head of it; even so, his "Mantovano," "man of Mantua," recalls that Vergil is not only what T. S. Eliot was to call him, the classic of all Europe, but also an Italian, a foreigner. At the same time, Tennyson remembers that Dante had addressed Vergil with the selfsame word, and thus he engages also with the Vergilian tradition that has been carried down into the literature of the west.

Throughout its history, Britain's outlook upon classical antiquity has been affected by its distinctive relationship to the Mediterranean world. Contrasts of climate, history, and culture differentiate the south of Europe from the north, and the massive barrier of the Alps has kept the British symbolically and practically separate. In addition, they have always been inevitably conscious that they live in an island, part of Europe but not part of the continent; and after the Reformation they were divorced confessionally from the Catholic south. All these things contributed to an idea of the classical world that often combined admiration with a sense of otherness.

However remote Britain may have seemed to Catullus, Vergil, and Horace, a hundred years later the Romans conquered the southern half of the island. But though this part of Britain was to remain under Roman control for some three and a half centuries, it was always at the edge of empire, and after the Romans left, the dissevering from Mediterranean civilization was almost complete. In some parts of Europe the transition from antiquity to what we call the Middle Ages can seem to be an almost continuous process. The languages of Italy, Spain, Provence, and even northern France evolved from Latin. In the Romanesque architecture of France and southern Europe we can often detect a modification of the Corinthian order in the capitals and sometimes in the bases of the columns. Even in Germany we may catch the distant resonances of Roman grandeur: Charlemagne based his imperial chapel at Aachen on one of the masterpieces of late antiquity, the church of San Vitale in Ravenna; and another building of the same period, at Lorsch, plainly derives its organization from the Roman triumphal arch. But in Anglo-Saxon and Anglo-Norman architecture, Romanesque though it may be, even the faintest echo of antiquity is seldom to be found. Any classical element in the visual culture of England would henceforth have to be a matter of recovery, not continuity.

The case of Westminster Abbey, Henry III's showpiece church, may illustrate England's relationship at once to modern Europe and to the classical tradition. One of Henry's aims was to emulate Louis IX of France, and the Abbey is famously the most French in style of all English medieval churches. But it also looked to Rome – and that meant both the Church and the ancient past. Richard Ware, Abbot of Westminster, traveled to Rome to receive his commission from the pope, and came back with "marbles of Thasos" and porphyry, stripped from the ruins of classical buildings. He also brought with him Italian craftsmen, who used the porphyry in making King Henry's tomb. On the side of this tomb is what is unmistakably a miniature classical portico, with pediment and pilasters, seeming to anticipate the arrival of the Renaissance in England by more than two hundred years. By its uniqueness, this extraordinary work may suggest the remoteness of medieval England from classical antiquity; but by its presence it also suggests an aspiration.

That aspiration is exemplified in another way by the inscription, in bronze letters, that surrounded the pavement before the high altar, made by the imported Italian artists from the stones that Abbot Ware had acquired. The content of this inscription is a weird and more or less incomprehensible allegory; but it is written in verse, and in classical Latin meter. Or rather it is written in a mixture of Latin meters, mingling hexameters with elegiac couplets. That is something that any classical Roman would have considered bizarre. So in these words, too, we find a great distance from ancient Rome combined with an aspiration toward it. It is like observing the centripetal tendency in a planet at the outermost edge of the solar system.

Architecture is the master art of the Middle Ages, and Gothic is its master style. The earliest Gothic, as it appears in northern France in the middle of the twelfth century, may still be felt to have something "classical" about its aesthetic – in balance, proportion, and even in some of its forms. And the same may be said of the twelfth-century Gothic of the choir of Canterbury Cathedral. The cylindrical columns around the apse and their superbly carved capitals, whose concave profile and crisply executed leaf forms are in a line of descent from the Corinthian order, might be said to continue the classical tradition by other means. But the first architect of Gothic Canterbury was William of Sens, a Frenchman, and the craftsmen who carved the capitals may have been imported from France also. As soon as the first indigenous Gothic style appears in England, the story is different. The stiff-leaf capitals and clustered columns of Wells Cathedral are wholly new and original. Twice more English Gothic would create something radically new – first in the early fourteenth century, with the Decorated style, which would be taken up on the Continent and developed into the Flamboyant style, and then in the middle of the century with the Perpendicular style, which would remain wholly English and endure for the best part of two hundred years.

The consequence of this for the British relationship to the classical tradition was to be profound. The idea was planted that Gothic was the natural – almost it might seem the native – style for England. This was an argument that Pugin, the most passionate champion of the Gothic Revival, was to use in the nineteenth century. Gothic, he said, was Christian architecture; despite this, the classical style might be just about acceptable in southern Europe, but in the north it was not only pagan but alien. Back in the sixteenth century, the long and noble history of English Gothic meant that when the Italian Renaissance began to impinge on the English consciousness, it came as something wholly external. It also came out of a brilliant new culture. Engagement with the Renaissance would be at once an engagement with modern Italy and with the classical past.

In the case of literary culture, the story is somewhat different. There is a sense in which England was part of the Latinate culture that was the common possession of all western Christendom. John of Salisbury, Roger Bacon, and William Occam wrote in Latin just as Aquinas did, and as Bede or even St. Patrick had, many centuries before. As for the vernacular, there never was an English without vocabulary of Latin origin. Even before they crossed the Channel, the peoples who were to become the Anglo-Saxons had derived many words from Latin; among them are such plain, everyday nouns as "mat," "belt," "pipe," "sack," "sock," "candle," "pan," "butter," "kitchen," "pin," "plant," "pit," "beer." More words entered Old English from Latin before the Norman Conquest: for example, "cat," "chest," "anchor," "pear," "fan," "spend," "cook." After the Conquest English acquired many words from French, which had itself derived them from late spoken Latin. Other words came into English from written Latin, either directly or via France. Hence the phenomenon of the etymological doublet: two English words deriving from the same Latin source. Some of these doublets are merely curious (and sometimes surprising): "treason" and "tradition," "forge" and "fabric," "spice" and "species." Others have affected the texture and flavor of the language. Take the pairs "frail" and "fragile," "poor" and "pauper," "abridge" and "abbreviate." In each case the second word looks and feels Latinate, while the first does not.

Such doublets have enriched the word store of English and increased its expressive range. This phenomenon apart, the history of England formed a language of distinctive character: the base is Germanic, but the bulk of the abstract vocabulary derives from Latin or Greek. Yet there remain plenty of abstracts that descend from the Anglo-Saxons. When Tyndale translated St. Paul, he wrote, "Now abideth faith, hope, and love, even these three: but the chief of these is love" (1 Corinthians 13:13). When the revisers who produced the King James Bible came to this verse they changed "love" to "charity." St. Paul's word is *agapē*, which he uses to denote Christian love, as distinct from *erōs*, physical desire, and *philia*, a general word for all kinds of personal affection. The Vulgate renders *agapē* by "caritas," the word that gives us "charity." Tyndale chooses the plain, straight word; the revisers choose a word directed to St. Paul's particular nuance; the mixed origin of the English language gives them the choice.

The development of English as a literary language was bound in the long term to lead to a decline in the writing of Latin; but as long as Latin was learnt, people had a direct access to the literature of ancient Rome. Just before the end of his *Troilus and Criseyde* Chaucer writes,

> But litel book, no makyng thow n'envie,
> But subgit be to alle poesye;
> And kis the steppes, where as thow seest pace
> Virgile, Ovide, Omer, Lucan, and Stace.
>
> (V.1789–92)

This expresses a sense of subordination, and perhaps also of isolation and remoteness: all these poets are very distant in time, and distant in place as well. And yet Chaucer is echoing Statius, a poet more highly regarded in the Middle Ages than he was to be later. As he concludes his epic *Thebaid*, Statius admonishes his poem not to seek to rival the divine *Aeneid*, but to follow at a distance and to worship its footsteps. And so in the very act of marking his separation from the great names of classical antiquity, Chaucer is inserting himself into the stream of a classical tradition.

The Latin heritage was a common possession of western Christendom as a whole: Chaucer can use Statius as readily as Dante can. The same was not true of visual culture: paintings, statues, and buildings do not travel as easily as words. The effect of the Italian Renaissance, or at least of its visual elements, was to provincialize northern Europe as a whole. When François I of France brought Primaticcio to Fontainebleau and Leonardo to the Loire valley, he acknowledged an inferiority. Even in the seventeenth century the churches of Paris follow, a little staidly, the models of Baroque Rome. England was further from Italy, but even here we find royal patronage importing the new style, and reaching, through that newness, toward the recovery of antiquity. Italians carve the choir stalls at King's College Cambridge; the Italian Torrigiani makes the tombs in Henry VII's Chapel at Westminster. Henry VII's

Figure 18.1 The Tower of the Five Orders. © Brian Harding / Eye Ubiquitous / CORBIS

Chapel is indeed spectacularly international: Flemings to carve the stone figures, a German for the metalwork, Englishmen for the architecture, and an Italian for the royal monuments themselves. Here Gothic and Renaissance collide, combine, and curiously harmonize. The architecture, wholly English and wholly Gothic, was equal to anything in contemporary Europe; nonetheless, for whatever reason, it marked the end of a story. The future, even in England, would lie with classical forms.

A visitor entering Henry VII's Chapel when it was new might well have supposed that England was on the brink of developing a brilliantly cosmopolitan visual culture. He would have been wrong: in the event the Reformation and its consequences cut England off from the Continental mainstream, and the movement of English art toward classicism was to be slow and fitful, and as a result to be marked by a sense of deference toward classical antiquity and its supposed rebirth in modern Italy. The Tower of the Five Orders, part of the Bodleian Library in Oxford, built in the early years of the seventeenth century, illustrates the English condition. This spectacular frontispiece has a different classical order on each of its five storeys, a display of learning suitable for a university library; but the orders are inaccurate in detail, and the columns are added as purely surface decoration to a tower that is unmistakably still Gothic in its construction. This is the classical language of architecture spoken in a quaint and half-barbarous accent.

2   Britain and Rome

As it happened, English literature was in a fairly undistinguished state for much of the sixteenth century; but for whatever reason, it burst into brilliant flower in the later part of Elizabeth I's reign. The Elizabethans' literature makes ample use of classical motifs and allusions; like their visual art, it aspires toward the classical, but in this case combines that aspiration with a robust and native self-confidence. Spenser's national epic, *The Faery Queen*, may serve to illustrate the point. It is in part a medievalizing work; as Ben Jonson noted with disapproval, his language affected the ancients – that is, English poets of the Middle Ages (*Timber: or Discoveries*). But at the same time it looks to modern Italy: Spenser's ambition was to write in English a grand epic romance comparable to those that Tasso and Ariosto had written in Italian. And it is also in a classical tradition: the poem begins:

> Lo I, the man whose muse whilom did mask,
> As time her taught, in lowly shepherd's weeds,
> Am now enforced a far unfitter task:
> For trumpets stern to change mine oaten reeds ...
> (*i*.1–4)

This echoes four lines with which, according to fourth-century commentators, Vergil had intended to begin his *Aeneid*. These lines are certainly spurious, but in the Renaissance they were commonly believed to be authentic. In them the poet declares that whereas he had previously written of country matters – that is, in the *Eclogues* and *Georgics* – he is now turning to epic. This fitted the idea (also derived from late antiquity) that Vergil had followed the perfect pattern of a poet's career, beginning with pastoral, the lowliest genre, moving to the middle style in the *Georgics*, and finally ascending to epic grandeur. With this pattern in mind, Spenser had written a pastoral sequence of poems, *The Shepherd's Calendar*, at the start of his career. In *The Faery Queen* he turns London into Troynovaunt, "New Troy," with a fanciful derivation implied from the Trinovantes, an ancient British tribe. Similarly, the name of the warrior maiden Britomart is borrowed from a Greek nymph, Britomartis, with another imaginative etymology suggesting British martial prowess. To a later and purer classicism such things would seem quaint and archaic, but in Spenser's synthesis the medievalizing and classicizing tendencies are not easily pulled apart.

The Elizabethans' access to the classical world was overwhelmingly through Latin; Greek was a comparatively uncommon accomplishment, and a wide range of Greek reading rarer still. C. S. Lewis's *bon mot*, that no sixteenth-century Englishman would have got a classical scholarship to a nineteenth-century university, may be an exaggeration, but it is not far from the truth. Sir Philip Sidney was noted for his knowledge of Greek: it was a part of the dazzling many-sidedness of this "renaissance man." But Sidney had been in Paris and conversed with the scholar Stephanus; his ancient Greek was part of his European modernity and exceptionally cosmopolitan quality. Ben Jonson was also unusual in the strength of his classical attainments; he had studied under William Camden, presumably at Westminster School.

It was Jonson who famously declared in the preface to the First Folio that Shakespeare had "small Latin and less Greek," and Milton was to evoke in *L'Allegro* the pleasure of hearing "sweetest Shakespeare, fancy's child, / Warble his native woodnotes wild" (133–4). (Milton, one might note in passing, was a formidable scholar, not only acquainted with Hebrew but the first person to correct a particular corruption in the text of Euripides' *Bacchae*.) Such judgments have sometimes encouraged the belief that Shakespeare did not have much of a classical education – perhaps not much of an education at all. This is mistaken: the years of Latin drill at Stratford Grammar School would have given him a thorough knowledge of the language. Parts of the curriculum, however, might seem strange to the modern student. Quite often the first Latin text to be read was the *Eclogues* of Mantuan, pastiches of Virgil's pastoral poems by a fifteenth-century Italian Carmelite; their pure Latinity and improving sentiments both commended them for school use. Holofernes, the comic schoolmaster in *Love's Labour's Lost*, burbles praise of Mantuan, quoting his very first line (4.2.95–6); this may indicate that Shakespeare, too, began his Latin reading here.

Shakespeare's access to Plutarch, the source for most of his Roman plays, was indirect: he read him in Sir Thomas North's English translation, which was itself made not from the original but from Amyot's French version. An English translation of a French translation of a Greek historian writing about Rome – the case of Shakespeare's Plutarch may seem to illustrate, once more, how far England was from the classical fountainhead. Yet this is only a half-truth: even in translation, and especially with prose authors, the reality came through pretty well. Shakespeare shows a sensitivity to the diversity within Plutarch's lives: his life of Julius Caesar is strongly political, whereas his life of Antony turns into a romantic tragedy and reserves its last chapters not for its notional subject but for Cleopatra. Accordingly, Shakespeare makes his *Julius Caesar* a study in the manipulation of power; and he makes Antony and Cleopatra the joint protagonists in a story of *égoisme à deux*.

Shakespeare also understands how to balance the Latin and Anglo-Saxon registers of the language. Planning the murder of Desdemona, Othello uses plain, short words until he comes to her skin, whiter than snow "And smooth as monumental alabaster" (5.2.5). All the Moor's feelings of love and admiration for Venetian beauty and civility are expressed in the momentary inflow of those classical polysyllables, before he returns to the simplest terms again: "Put out the light, and then put out the light" (5.2.6). Hamlet's dying speech is likewise very plain, except for the lovely, fluid Latinity of "Absent thee from felicity a while" (5.2.358). There speaks a prince; and in his next words, "And in this harsh world draw thy breath in pain, To tell my story," there speaks everyman (5.2.359–60).

The orders of classical architecture seemed to impose strict rules; but with classical literature it was otherwise: here was a storehouse of diverse treasures. The case of satire illustrates how classical sources provided not one pattern or ideal on which the modern writer should model his own work, but a range of possibilities. Verse satire, Quintilian had observed, was entirely Roman (*Institutiones oratoriae* 10.1.93); and with Lucilius surviving only in fragments, there were in effect only three authors that the English satirist could take for an example, Horace, Persius, and Juvenal. Donne's satires may strike us as awkward and angular, but they are made so deliberately, for in the poet's mind is the knotty, difficult verse of Persius. When the scholar Isaac Casaubon, a Huguenot refugee who was to become a canon of the Church of England, published his edition of Persius in 1605, the vogue for this poet was further increased. But the grand declamatory manner of Juvenal was another model; and Samuel Johnson's *London* and *The Vanity of Human Wishes* were to be avowedly "imitations" of Juvenal's third and tenth satires. Yet another model was the urbane and conversational manner first evolved by Horace in his satires (which he himself called *Sermones*, Conversations), and further developed by him in his *Epistles*. Here lay the inspiration for Pope's *Epistles*. So even within a genre as tightly defined as the verse satire, antiquity provided not so much a prescription as a range of possibilities.

The same may be said of pastoral. Here the dominant though not quite the only model was Vergil's *Eclogues*, but this single work generated a variety of response. The rough, clodhopping character of Spenser's *Shepherd's Calendar* is likely to strike the modern reader as unclassical, but Spenser himself would not have thought so. One school of thought, based upon the authority of the ancient commentator Servius, saw Vergil's *Eclogues* as allegorizing, moralistic, and affecting a rusticity of manner. Another school saw Vergil as the originator of pastoral in the form of arcadian idyll. Mantuan's *Eclogues*, smoothly Vergilian in language but coarser and sterner in content, could seem to belong to either school. Milton's *Lycidas* can be seen as a compendium of different versions of pastoral, compressed into the limits of a single poem.

Milton's prose and verse also exemplify the elaborated, almost Baroque classicism that was one strand in the English literature of the seventeenth century. In *Paradise Lost* he not only used a richly Latinate vocabulary but imitated some forms of Latin syntax too. Samuel Johnson disliked this, writing in his *Lives of the Poets*, "Of him, at last may be said what Jonson said of Spenser, that *he wrote no language*." That remark forms an ironic comment upon the development of classical taste. For the earlier Jonson, "affecting the ancients" referred to Spenser's medievalisms – to the respects in which he was unclassical; but Milton "wrote no language" through too great an imitation of classical Latin style.

In fact, Milton knew in his own fashion, as Shakespeare had known, the use of different registers of language. In a famous simile he declares that the paradise of Eden excelled in beauty even the fair field of Enna,

> ... where Proserpin gathering flowers
> Herself a fairer flower by gloomy Dis
> Was gathered, which cost Ceres all that pain
> To seek her through the world ...
> (*Paradise Lost* IV.269–72)

Inside the classical myth is enfolded the simplicity of "all that pain," so that we appreciate at once the fruits of a rich culture and the bare grief of a mother for her child. On occasion, Milton may perhaps even look with irony upon his own Latinisms. When Eve takes the apple, his account is extremely plain: "She plucked, she ate . . . all was lost" (9.781, 784). But once fallen, and "heightened as with Wine" (9.793), her diction becomes floridly classical:

> O sovran, virtuous, precious of all trees
> In Paradise, of operation blest
> To sapience, hitherto obscured, infamed . . .
> (9.795–7)

Milton includes in *Paradise Regained* an eloquent panegyric to the beauty and wisdom of ancient Athens; but it is put into the mouth of the Devil. Thus he dramatizes the double nature of the classical storehouse, at once a necessary source of enlightenment and a pagan or worldly temptation.

The late-seventeenth and eighteenth centuries can be seen, from one point of view, as the high-water mark of classicism in England. Classical taste was now purified, scholarly, and informed. This was by some called England's Augustan age even at the time, a label that indicates both an aspiration and an achievement. Yet from another point of view the classical past was beginning to lose a part of its significance. For centuries ancient texts had been essential to many areas of intellectual and even practical life, providing guidance on such varied matters as medicine, jurisprudence, philosophy, mathematics, and agriculture. England was at the forefront of the scientific revolution, which was rendering many of the old authorities obsolete: Harvey could tell you about the circulation of the blood, and Galen could not. In "Some Thoughts Concerning Education" John Locke argued that it was a waste of time and money to teach Latin to boys who would go into trade; on the other hand, "Latin I look upon as absolutely necessary to a gentleman." Classical knowledge was now becoming an accomplishment, not a necessity – except for social purposes. Augustanism itself implied a certain detachment; it is an attitude adopted, an aesthetic choice self-consciously made. Pope called his *Epistles* "Imitations of Horace," and Johnson imitated Juvenal; they put on classical costume, which, they suggest, they may put off once the performance is complete.

The changing character of the classical tradition in Britain in the eighteenth century is best understood in relation to a larger scene. Across Europe, the eighteenth century sees, sometimes slowly, sometimes abruptly, a shift in style, attitude, and belief. This change finds political expression in the French Revolution, social expression in the ideal of the noble savage and the natural man, visual expression in a revolt against the Baroque and a cultivation of austere simplicity. It also affected the way in which classical antiquity was regarded. There was a tendency now to see Roman art and life as pompously grandiose and elaborate, while Roman literature was considered too imitative of Greek models. Homer – now seen as grand, primitive, and natural – began his ascent toward his apotheosis in the Romantic age.

The Baroque manner itself depended on the classical tradition in that it exploited and indeed required the classical vocabulary of architecture; but it twisted, teased, and distorted classical forms. Originating in Italy, it spread across most of Europe, and even England had its Baroque period. Wren incorporated Italian influences into his personal style. Vanbrugh's highly idiosyncratic Baroque included towers and picturesque sky-lines that seemed to evoke the Elizabethan prodigy house or even the Middle Ages; as often in English history, an engagement with the classical tradition was an engagement with another time or place as well. But much earlier than the Continent, England turned away from the Baroque to a style that they called Palladian, harking back to Andrea Palladio and the Cinquecento, and through him to ancient Rome. Palladianism was not, of course, a reproduction of antiquity, but its practitioners saw themselves as the ancient world's true heirs. "The Italians can now no more relish the Antique simplicity," wrote Colen Campbell in 1715 in his *Vitruvius Britannicus.* Ironically, the British could now instruct the Romans, on this view, in the true Roman taste.

Accordingly, the shift toward neoclassicism, when it came later in the century, was a gentler and more pragmatic matter than on much of the Continent. But there was another reason why the British movement toward neoclassicism was more empirical than in other countries, and this is that it was, almost literally, an archaeological process. As British power and wealth grew, and as the Ottoman empire opened up a little to the west, British travelers began to explore classical sites and to publish their findings. In splendid folio volumes Robert Wood published the ruins of Palmyra in 1753 and Baalbek in 1757, and these editions inspired Robert Adam to publish in 1764 the late Roman remains of Diocletian's palace at Spalatro (now Split). He had indeed gone to Spalatro with the purpose of advancing his career as an architect, and the Adam style was to be a personal synthesis of forms and motifs found in these late-antique remains. Other recent discoveries were laid under contribution, too: the finds at Pompeii and Herculaneum, and the Greek vases found in Italy, which were at that time believed to be Etruscan. The houses built by Adam and his followers often have a Pompeian or an Etruscan room.

When Adam enlarged Kedleston Hall in Derbyshire, the centerpiece of his south front was based upon the forms of the Roman triumphal arch. The central hall is an adaptation of the Roman atrium. Yet one cannot quite call Adam a revivalist. It is partly that his sources were so eclectic, found in different lands and in periods separated by as much as 700 years, partly that Adam formed what he took into an original synthesis. The Adam style could be imitated by other architects, most brilliantly by James Wyatt. By a pleasing irony, when Catherine the Great imported the Scottish architect Charles Cameron to bring Adam's Roman style to Russia, where he made additions to the Summer Palace and built the imperial villa at Pavlovsk, her choice was an expression of Anglophilia. The Adam synthesis, devel-oped out of classical sources, had become distinctively British.

3   Britain and Greece

Among British travelers to the eastern Mediterranean, James Stuart and Nicholas Revett had an especial importance. They were the first to make entirely accurate measured drawings of the principal classical remains in Athens, and when the second

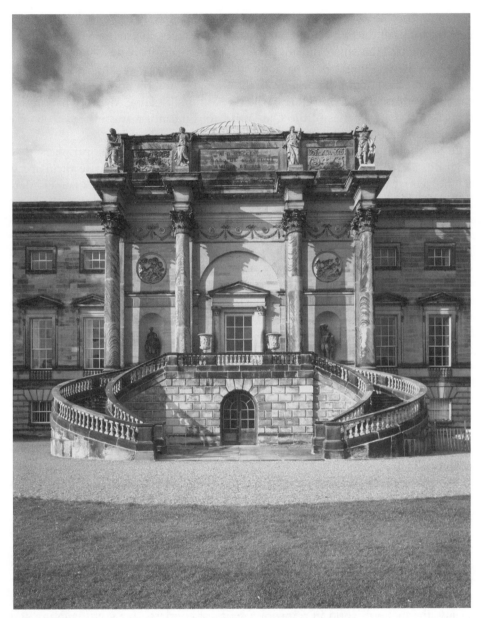

Figure 18.2 Kedleston Hall. Photo: © NTPL / Matthew Antrobus

and most important volume of their *Antiquities of Athens* was published in 1787, they made the Greek Revival possible. As an architect, Stuart's own use of his discoveries was eclectic: an Ionic order added to what was otherwise a Palladian façade; one garden building modeled on an Athenian building of the fifth century BC, another on an Athenian monument dating from several centuries later. But as the passion for Greece grew hotter in the early years of the nineteenth century and as

revivalism became an ideal, a purist architecture came into being, aimed at reproducing the forms of the fifth century BC as closely as was possible in modern conditions.
In England itself this vogue did not last long. In Germany there was some feeling that
the Greek Revival might be a patriotic style, the Germans and the ancient Greeks
having some kind of spiritual affinity. In the United States, the argument was put that
the austere, masculine architecture of the Greeks fitted a young, vigorous nation that
had cast off the fripperies of the Old World. In England, it was instead to be the
Gothic Revivalists who played the patriotic card.

In Scotland the story was somewhat different. Even more at the periphery than
England, the Scots had long prized the classical attainments that gave them access
to the central tradition of European culture. Indeed, the Christian names Alexander and Hector acquired a distinctly Scottish flavor; at one time even the name
Aeneas enjoyed some favor, inspired by a spurious etymology linking it to Angus.
Another element of Scottish classicism came about half by accident. In the seventeenth century the notion that whereas the Ionian Greeks were sophisticates and
city-makers, the Dorians were simple mountain folk led to the half-jocular application of the adjective "Doric" to rustic speech, and then to Scottish dialect. The
notion of the Dorians as rude highlanders helped this idiom to take root. And as
the Athens of the North, the Edinburgh of the Enlightenment staked a claim to be
not only "Doric" but Ionian too. The Greek style thus came to seem fitted to the
Scottish character, and it lasted longer north of the border. To some observers, the
Grecian buildings of Edinburgh only served to show how unsuited the classical
vocabulary of architecture was to the north. "The very climate," wrote Hippolyte
Taine, "seems to revolt against shapes proper to a dry, hot country; and the needs,
tastes and ways of northern men are even more hostile to them" (Taine 1957: 286).
Others have felt that Edinburgh's Greek buildings blend well with the plain
Georgian style of the older New Town to form one of the masterpieces of European
urbanism.

The adoration of ancient Greece that began in the eighteenth century, reached its
zenith in the Romantic age, and endured through the nineteenth century was a
phenomenon that affected all Europe, but in Britain it had some local characteristics.
The early champions of Hellenism were Germans – Winckelmann, Lessing, Goethe
among them – and to some extent this made the British engagement with Hellenism
also an engagement with modern German thought. A. W. von Schlegel's lectures on
the drama, first translated into English in 1815, were especially influential in popularizing German ideas. From here came the conception that Greece could be set
against the modern world in terms of a series of contrasts: between sculpture and
music as master arts of the epoch, between classic and romantic, south and north,
pagan and Christian. To these contrasts Britain, as the first industrialized nation,
added one more: between the grime, smoke, and materialism of the present age and
the pure, radiant light of Hellas. Another local variant of Hellenism came about
more accidentally: the arrival of the *Elgin Marbles* in London disturbed old preconceptions. Winckelmann had declared the nature of Greek sculpture (and indeed
literature) to be "a noble simplicity and a calm greatness" (Winckelmann 1987: 33);
but the pedimental figures from the Parthenon seemed thrillingly emotive. Hazlitt

rhapsodized over their passionate fluidity, and Keats wrote a sonnet declaring that they made him swoon, dizzying him with their grandeur. The *Marbles* made classicism romantic.

These ideas, and above all the sense that ancient Greece stood in contrast to the modern world, came to infuse much of Victorian literature and thought: it is recurrent, for example, in Ruskin and Pater, in Matthew Arnold and Swinburne, and in the novels of George Eliot. Greece became a yardstick against which contemporary life was measured and, more often than not, found wanting. Nowhere perhaps in Britain could one find the idea, sometimes found in Germany, that ancient Greece and the modern nation were spiritually kin. With Rome the case was different, for Britain was also distinguished from other nations by its empire, and the parallel between the *Pax Britannica* (British peace) and the *Pax Romana* (Roman peace) was inescapable. In fact, political comparison between Rome and England was not new, and can be traced back to the seventeenth century, though at first the resemblance was found in the Roman Republic rather than the Roman Empire. In an age of absolute monarchies, the parliamentary constitution of England, with a monarch sharing power with representatives of an aristocracy and gentry in part elected by a form of public suffrage, could seem to be a modern instance of the "mixed constitution" on which the Romans had prided themselves. Besides, in an age when education was dominated by the Latin and Greek classics, it was natural for a statesman's cast of mind to take on a Roman color. "*Otium cum dignitate* is my object," wrote Lord Chesterfield in a letter of February 9, 1748, upon resigning political office, referring to Cicero's gentlemanly ideal of freedom of action combined with public esteem. Lord Holland ventured to suppose that the principles of a liberal Spaniard could be likened to "those of Cicero and Mr Fox" (Mitchell 1980: 226); and in the middle of the nineteenth century the economist Nassau Senior was told by an Italian acquaintance that Cicero's letters were akin to the correspondence of a British statesman: "All the thoughts, all the feeling, almost all the expressions, are English."

A later and fictional Italian observer of the English scene is Henry James's Prince Amerigo, described in the first sentence of *The Golden Bowl* (1904) as "one of the modern Romans who find by the Thames a more convincing image of the truth of the ancient state than any they have left by the Tiber." In France, similarly, François Guizot, historian and statesman, spoke of the Romans and the British as the only two governing nations of the world. Palmerston traded on the comparison in a famous speech on the Don Pacifico affair, quoting the words *Civis Romanus sum* (I am a Roman citizen) from Cicero's denunciation of the corrupt provincial governor Verres. And Disraeli coined the phrase *Imperium et Libertas* (Empire and liberty), which enjoyed currency for a while. But the analogy between Rome and Britain was equivocal. Some readers remembered that Vergil – who could now be seen, in Lord Bryce's words, as "the national poet of the Empire, in whom imperial patriotism found its highest expression" (Bryce 1901: 1:72) – had set the Roman supremacy in conquest and government against the Greeks' superiority in such arts as sculpture, oratory, and astronomy. It was easy to feel that Britain was now in Rome's position, better than the countries of the Continent at winning and ruling an empire, but inferior to one or the other of them in artistic or intellectual power.

Most of Britain's public architecture was in the broad classical tradition for most of the Victorian age, Italianate in its middle years, turning to a revival of Wren's style later; once again, an engagement with the classical tradition was at the same time an engagement with another story. Through their echoes of Wren, the buildings of late Victorian and Edwardian Whitehall, for example, use the classical vocabulary to express a native patriotism. It is hard at any time to spot allusion to ancient Rome in such public monuments. It was partly, perhaps, that Roman imagery would have looked too Napoleonic. But it may also have been that the comparison with Rome was not altogether comfortable. Enemies of imperialism claimed that empire had led to economic parasitism and moral enfeeblement in ancient Rome, and was now doing the same in Britain; the apologists for empire tended to dwell as much upon the differences as the similarities.

The classical tradition was to be revitalized in the twentieth century above all through the influence of Nietzsche and Freud, so that once more the British response to the classical was also a response to the thought of the German-speaking world. This is a rich story, but it belongs in another place (see ch. 8, "Modernism"), as it is hard to see that the British now differed much in their response from other peoples. To be sure, one can think of occasions when writers have given their responses to classical literature a regional or national slant; the two most conspicuous examples, perhaps, are works by authors who, although born British subjects, may be thought to be British only in an extended sense: James Joyce's *Ulysses* and Derek Walcott's *Omeros*. But these are particular and personal experiments. For the most part, in the twentieth century the British engagement with the classical tradition was representative of the west as a whole rather than being tinged with local color, and that is hardly surprising. For the Britons were no longer sundered from the whole world; indeed, the language of this once remote island had become the medium by which nation spoke to nation, inheriting the role that Latin had enjoyed for so long.

FURTHER READING

The classical tradition in Britain preponderates in most of the essays in Jenkyns (1992). The books of Thomson (1948, 1951, 1956) are slight but can be useful as jumping-off points. Martindale (1988) and Martindale and Hopkins (1993) deal in the first case largely, and in the second case entirely, with the influence of the poet in question on English literature. Two other useful books are Bush (1932) and Ogilvie (1964). For the eighteenth century see Erskine-Hill (1983) and Weinbrot (1978). On aspects of Romantic Hellenism: Spencer (1954) and St. Clair (1967). Crook (1972) surveys Greek revival architecture and is amply illustrated. For the Victorian age as a whole, see Jenkyns (1980); Turner (1981) focuses on the intellectual legacy, principally examining historiography and philosophy; Jenkyns (1991) considers the legacy in terms of the visual arts; and Vance (1997) mostly addresses literary culture.

CHAPTER NINETEEN

United States

Ward Briggs

For at least the first three hundred years of America's history, the presence of the classical tradition in the realms of politics, literature, architecture, the decorative arts, and particularly the educational system depended in an almost Oedipal fashion on the degree to which Americans desired to emulate or reject the cultural presence of the classical tradition in Mother Britain. In the nearly continuous debate on the utility of classical study not only for the individual but for society as a whole, Americans nevertheless seized upon relics from the classical world – the structure of its governments, the sculpture of its heroes, the design of its buildings, and the performance of its tragedies – as symbols of their connection to states of largely imaginary freedom and virtue. Though the literature, art, and architecture of classical antiquity provided models of excellence and beauty for Europe and America, the centrality of the classics in the school curriculum has been continually challenged by those who denied its practical utility, first in an agrarian, then in a mercantile society. Nevertheless, since classics remained stubbornly at the core of the standard school and college curriculum (or was at least a common element in it) until the middle of the twentieth century, American writers, artists, and architects have had from their childhoods a cultural climate that provided stores of resources from the classical world that they have mined from the European discovery of the continent through the present day.

1 The Classics in Early American Education

The desire to see the new political experiment in democracy as a heritage from the ancient world is evident in the first history of the nation, Captain John Smith's *The Proceedings of the English Colonie in Virginia* (1612), which adopted a 12-book structure from Vergil's *Aeneid*, which "Aeneas-Smith" brought west to found a new land under divine guidance (Jones 1968: 25–6). Similarly Cotton Mather began the General Introduction to *Magnalia Christi Americana* (1702) with a direct imitation of the beginning of the *Aeneid*: "I write the *Wonders* of the Christian religion, flying from the Depravations of *Europe*, to the *American Strand*" (Mather, Introduction, 1-2, p. 89).

The classical tradition appears in the names of the earliest colonies like "Virginia," "Carolina," and "Pennsylvania," while the revolutionary fervor of the 1780s both there and in France resulted in any number of towns, north and south, being named after Athens, Troy, Rome, or Sparta (Highet 1949: 399–400). But the cultural and political differences between the regions are reflected in their use of the classical tradition.

The pioneers settling the North were essentially trying to escape the repressive and authoritarian structures and philosophy of England in order to found new and perfect communities along idealistic lines. Those who settled the South were largely trying to recreate the manorial system with themselves at the top of the ladder, which would have been impossible in England. The idealism of the North is reflected in its admiration of Plato from Mather through Emerson; in the South the practical Aristotle was the favorite natural and moral philosopher. Aristotle's authority had been weakened somewhat by the Renaissance and the Reformation, but he was still freighted with enough Catholic and medieval associations to make him suspect to Puritans. Of course, the Aristotle that many knew had been filtered through Cicero, the Stoics, Milton, Locke, Coke, and the British Whigs (Pocock 1975). Aristotle's notion of the "natural slave," though not a classification based on race, was familiar in both the North and South and would come into sharp focus in the years running up to the Civil War. The Massachusetts Congregationalist clergyman John Wise is typical of those who in 1717 opposed Aristotle's view of natural inequality, citing the *Politics* in paraphrase ("Nothing is more suitable to Nature, than that those who excel in understanding and prudence should rule and control those who are less happy in those advantages") (Wise 1956: 129). Southerners, on the other hand, further embraced Aristotle's views on the classification of governments, the value of an antimajoritarian mixed government, and the rejection of the notion of a social contract and natural rights in favor of the organic state. Aristotle thought that nothing enters the mind except via the senses, while Platonic ideals, which Jefferson called a "mysticism incomprehensible to the modern mind," were as unpalatable to Southerners as the independent Puritan "conscience," the "inner light" of Quakers, the fiery mysticism of Jonathan Edwards, and the transcendental idealism of Emerson.

Though the early settlers were themselves uniquely well educated (between 1630 and 1690 the colonies of the northeast could boast as many university graduates as all of England), classics in the schools was a point of early contention. The largely self-educated Puritans were initially skeptical of the value of classics as a university tradition too closely tied to the British establishment, while the Quaker educators of the Atlantic region thought classics was impractical. The religious revival known as the Great Awakening of 1740 developed strong anti-intellectualism, but in the middle of the eighteenth century, theologians relinquished the fight against classics to the utilitarians (Quakers began teaching the classics in the 1750s) and to those who sought a distinctly practical and American education, free from the excessive weight given Latin to the exclusion of other useful subjects. The low quality of instruction and the narrow expertise of the teachers (usually recent graduates awaiting their MA degrees and ordination) were always a counterargument to champions of the classics. Joseph Cogswell in 1819 bewailed the pitiful standard of teaching and preparation of the teachers: America has not "yet sent forth a single first rate scholar" (Cogswell 1819: 547). Defenders responded with efforts to reform the teaching profession, but noted the intrinsic value of learning the ancient languages for oratory, since the study of Greek and Latin produces examples illustrative of human conduct, mental discipline, logical thought, a trained memory, moral maxims, and argumentative structure. Moreover, ancient history itself had utilitarian value in that it taught the merits of republicanism, the need for civic virtue, the nobility of heroes, and the course of liberty, on the understanding that human nature is essentially uniform and that people behave similarly in similar circumstances, no matter the era.

Without regard to the arguments pro or con, most colleges followed the model of the earliest ones, Harvard (1636), William and Mary (1693), and Yale (1718), requiring matriculates to demonstrate a knowledge of Greek and Latin. In consequence, American grammar schools from the seventeenth through the later nineteenth centuries adopted a British curriculum whose appeal was not even countered by the unpleasantness of 1812. The wealthy continued to send their sons to Britain (Oxford or Edinburgh) for their university work, especially in the Anglophile South, where men like Charles Cotesworth Pinckney of Charleston (Westminster, Oxford) felt that a northern education was something to be feared.

Americans of the colonial and federal periods continued to encourage the study of the classics to acquire civic virtue of the kind lacking in the decadent monarchies of Europe, along with a concomitant hatred of tyranny. John Adams wrote his son John Quincy, "You will ever remember that the End of study is to make you a good Man and a useful Citizen" (Butterfield 1963–75: 4:117). Despite such formidable opponents of classical learning as Benjamin Franklin and Benjamin Rush, classics remained in the curriculum even after 1797, when the American Philosophical Society offered an award for the best proposal for reforming American education.

In America, as in Britain, whatever status a university education afforded was obtained by the study of the classics. For those of the middle class, like John Adams, George Whythe, or John Rutledge, facility in reading Cicero and Vergil, speaking and writing Latin prose, composing Latin verse, construing ordinary Greek as in the New Testament and Isocrates, and conjugating paradigms of Greek verbs was of necessity self-acquired. When John Adams despaired of learning Latin for his own advancement, his father offered him an alternative: Adams dug a ditch on his family's property for two days before he decided that he preferred Latin. He then dug instead into the standard texts of the time, James Otis's prosody and Ezekiel Cheever's grammar, and was admitted to Harvard. "If I have gained any distinction," he said later in life, "it has been owing to the two days' labor in that abominable ditch" (Chinard 1933: 11). The future senator Charles Sumner taught himself enough Latin to recognize a quotation in a speech by Daniel Webster and repeat it to his father. His father, impressed, then agreed to send him to Harvard. "I felt I too belonged to the brotherhood of scholars," wrote Sumner (Taylor 2001: 28). Acceptance into the gentlemanly brotherhood was the reward for being driven through Cicero, Vergil, Homer, Xenophon, Isocrates, and the Greek New Testament, with tedious drills and often brutal corporal punishment by usually incompetent teachers. That the wisdom and beauty of the ancient authors stayed with many of the boys so powerfully and for so long is testimony that the inherent value of the works was not lost even on children.

No small element in preserving the classical tradition in colleges was the debating society. Combining the best and worst of fraternities with the competitive spirit of intramural athletics before either existed, the Whig and Cliosophic societies at Princeton, the Linonian Society and the Brothers in Unity at Yale, and other such groups directed into the debate arena the students' drives both to bond and to compete. Their libraries were usually larger and more accessible than their colleges', and contained many classical authors in translation, from whom the debaters learned the appropriate structure of a good rhetorical argument, the use of examples from ancient history and literature, and the principles of proof, all with an eye to success on the great day of the school year, the grand spring debates, the equivalent of today's homecoming.

2   The Classics in American Political Discourse, from Washington to Lincoln

When John Adams enlisted Aristotle, Cicero, and Polybius in his fight against the Stamp Act of 1765, and when John Dickinson rallied farmers two years later against the Townshend Acts with quotations of Sallust, there began the great period of the use of classical models in political discourse that would conclude with Lincoln's Gettysburg Address in 1863.

Though Adams in 1811 claimed that the classical revival in nineteenth-century Europe was caused not by Napoleon but by the American Revolution ("That great event turned the thoughts and studies of men of learning to the ancient Greeks, their language, their antiquities, their forms of government" [Adair and Schutz 1966: 177]), and though one can trust Howard Mumford Jones's statement that both sides in the Revolution quoted the classics, one must not overstate the role of classical authors in the creation of the Constitution. The "classick pages" provided sources of propaganda, historical precedents, the theory and practice of a republic, and ancient heroes for the emulation of Roman virtue (Jones 1952: 227–72), even if Enlightenment philosophers selected the portions or interpretations of the ancients that supported their own theories. Thus the Founders' views of the mixed governments of Sparta and the Roman Republic contained an Enlightenment skepticism toward government, notions of separation of powers (as opposed to classes), and representative democracy, concepts unknown to the ancients. Indeed, though the personal library whose classical texts comprised more than 5 per cent of the total was rare in Colonial times, the Fathers were so steeped in classical lore that, in H. S. Commager's words, "it would have required explanation had the generation of the

Founding Fathers turned their attention elsewhere" (Commager 1975: 130). Gordon Wood's assertion that "Such classicism was not merely a scholarly ornament of educated Americans; it helped to shape their values and their ideals of behavior" (Wood 1969: 49) does not vitiate Bernard Bailyn's view that the real engine of the revolution was the European Enlightenment, English common law, and the writings of radical Whigs (Bailyn 1967: 23–6).

Citation of classical thought or example was so de rigueur for any public perform-ance or publication that the commonplace books of Madison, Hamilton, Adams, and many others show classical quotations aplenty. By far the most popular author was Plutarch, the favorites of his lives being Phocion, Timoleon, Cicero, Demosthenes, and especially Cato. After Plutarch, the favored reading was Polybius, Cicero, and the great historians. To read of the sacrifice and noble ideals in these works (Patrick Henry's "Lamp of Experience") gave the Founders a sense of common purpose with the ancients in the struggle for human freedom that was cut off at Philippi. The ancient authors gave their American readers the intellectual tools to think about government and a sense of the historical inevitability of their political experiment (Wood 1969: 8). Said John Adams, "When I read them I seem to be only reading the History of my own Times and my own Life" (Cappon 1959: 295).

The Founders, attempting to throw off a monarch's yoke, did not need the ancients to tell them about the evils of tyranny, yet John Adams thought a careful reading of the classics would instill such hatred of tyrants and immunity to mob rule that stability would be assured. Lacing the *Federalist Papers* with classical quotations and signing their contributions with classical pseudonyms, they understood, as Adams and Jefferson said later, that America was in a unique position to understand and enact these theories because it was the only nation since Greece and Rome that was untouched by feudalism. Commager noted the paradox of lawgivers who "were busy changing everything," scrutinizing ancient political theory for models of citizen participation and institutional stability, order, and reason (Commager 1975: 136).

Plato, in *Laws* and *Politicus*, noted that the three simple types of government inevitably degenerate – monarchy (rule by the one) into tyranny, aristocracy (rule by the few) into oligarchy, and democracy (rule by all) into ochlocracy (mob rule) – so he recommends a mixture of the three (*Laws*, 756e–757a, 832c; *Politicus*, 291d–e, 303c). Aristotle put mixed government at the core of his *Politics* (3.7), and Polybius (*Histories* 6.5–18) recommended giving equal amounts of power to each branch of government. The ideal of mixed government was endorsed by the Aristotelian Aquinas, John Calvin, Florentines like Macchiavelli and Guicciardini, who preferred the Spartan system to Athenian mobocracy, and Montesquieu. The American patriots focused on historical accounts of the democratic movement in Athens of the fifth and fourth centuries and the Roman Republic of the sixth through the first centuries BC. The admired Greek figures were Solon, Themistocles, Xenophon, and Demosthenes, as portrayed in Plutarch or Charles Rollin's *Ancient History* (1729). Admirable Romans were Cato the Younger, Brutus, Cassius, and Cicero, but most of all Cincinnatus, the embodiment of public service and civic virtue. The figures the Fathers disliked were Roman emperors and Greek tyrants like Alexander, Cleon, Catiline, Sulla, and Marc Antony, but most of all Julius Caesar (the Founders feared standing armies in part because Julius Caesar had used them to destroy the Roman Republic). Though the mixed constitution of the Spartan Lycurgus offered a model of longevity, harmony, and justice, Jefferson considered the Spartans "military monks" (Jefferson 1907: 15:482) and Adams despised their sharing of property. Athenian democracy may have produced a Pericles, but it also gave forth the demagogue Cleon (according to Thucydides, who was exiled by him) and it condemned Socrates, the mentor of Plato and Xenophon. The foremost proponent of mixed government was John Adams, who, drawing heavily on Cicero, *Republic* 2.23–30 in his "Thoughts on Government," described the process of trial and error that was Rome's ascent over time from a degenerate monarchy to a stable republic that was the model of mixed government. Constitutionalists in general agreed, preferring Rome's rule of the one (consuls), the few (senate), and the many (tribunate). Moreover, the pure virtue and frugality of the Roman agrarian life (Adam Smith supported the maintenance of the rural economy to keep the citizenry virtuous against mere mercantilism) prepared them for greatness.

In considering federalism, the Fathers looked to ancient Amphictyonic Leagues (associations of neighboring states pledged to the maintenance of a particular local temple), but even here there were differing views. Of the Delian Amphictyonic League, for instance, Hamilton and Madison (*Federalist* 6 and 18) thought it ruined by decentralization, while Monroe faulted its overly ambitious members. Hamilton thought the Achaean League insufficiently centralized, while Adams and Dickinson thought it subverted by outside (Roman) power and Madison thought it doomed by decentralization.

Throughout this period, the greatest champion of classical literature was Thomas Jefferson. As a boy he had studied 15 hours a day and carried his Greek grammar with him everywhere. As an old man he found that "the classick pages fill up the vacuum of *ennui*" (Jefferson 1907: 15:209). Homer was his ideal:

> When young any composition pleases which unites a little sense, some imagination, and some rhythm, in doses however small. But as we advance in life these things fall off one by one, and I suspect we are left at last with only Homer and Virgil, perhaps with Homer alone. (Jefferson 1907: 18:448)

Jefferson admired Demosthenes' *Phillipics* for their passion against tyranny, and he hated the Asiatic elaboration of Cicero, preferring the simplicity of the speeches that Sallust and Livy put in the mouths of Scipio Africanus, Cato, and Caesar. He championed Aristotle to Adams, but his Declaration of Independence favors natural rights and the social compact against Aristotle's organic theory of the state's origin. Jefferson also loved Tacitus' criticism of the Roman emperors. When he founded his university at Charlottesville, he put into practice his view that classics was the basis of all learning: regardless of his field of study, no student could be admitted to his Palladian precincts without Greek and Latin.

Of all the figures in American history, the most classicized is George Washington. As Cato called Cicero the father of his country, so Washington to this day is known as the father of his. Hamilton called him the American Fabius, Fisher Ames called him

Epaminondas, and his biographer Parson Weems compared him to Numa, Aristides, Epictetus, Regulus, Severus, Scipio, Fabius, Marcellus, Hannibal, Cincinnatus, Cato, and Socrates. Horatio Greenough portrayed him partially nude in Roman garb (too little garb for official taste, as it happened) as Phidian Zeus set in the Capitol (1847), shocking the chairman of the committee that commissioned it. Canova portrayed Washington as a Roman soldier (1818), and Ceracchi gave him a Roman hairstyle (ca. 1786). Washington, like Cincinnatus, was a gentleman farmer who enjoyed not only the work but also the reflection-inducing tranquility of the rural life. Nevertheless both men answered their country's call, and when given absolute control of the armies, won great victories and then showed the magnitude of their characters by giving up their total power. Washington had barely given up control of the Continental Armies when he was called back from the farm to preside over the Constitutional Convention and then to become the first president of the United States. The association was enduring: Byron called him "the Cincinnatus of the West" ("Ode to Napoleon Buonaparte" 1814: 168), and he was depicted as Cincinnatus by Charles Wilson Peale (1776) and John Trumbull (1780). John J. Barralet painted him surrendering power to Columbia, with Cincinnatus' ox and a plow in the background (1799; Wills 1984).

3 The Silver Age of American Classical Studies

The extraordinary fervor for classical learning and classical models of government was practically conterminous with the Revolution: Jefferson and Adams had found classical learning to be "indispensable" for the man who wishes to be a truly educated and useful citizen, but by 1789 Benjamin Franklin, not a college graduate himself and one of the most steadfast opponents of learning Latin and Greek, said that "learning the ancient [languages] for the purpose of acquiring Knowledge is become absolutely unnecessary" (Franklin 1907: 10:30).

Thus after 1790 began the period called by Meyer Reinhold (1984) the Silver Age of classical studies in America. Young America, with its own government, history (however brief), and independence, sought to be independent of the predominantly British and old-fashioned dependence on the classics, asking whether such studies could be truly "American." Now the calls for a national literature (the Connecticut Wit Joel Barlow rejected emulating Homer for his failed epic, the *Columbiad*), a national educational system (Benjamin Rush proposed a national college system), and ultimately a distinctly national brand of scholarship (by Emerson in "American Scholar," 1837), all required a step away from the studies that now seemed elitist, irrelevant, and useless. Some felt patriotic eschewing the classics; others simply reacted against its importance to the earlier generation. However useful classics had been in guiding the Founding Fathers, its purpose had been served; managing the new country required different models.

The changes were first felt in schools, where decades of incompetent or indifferent teaching had long made classics an easy target. By 1760, the rigorous British-style grammar school curriculum was gone, but the lack of American textbooks remained a problem. The various editions of Caleb Alexander's *A New Introduction to the Latin Language* (1795) from publishers like William Poyntell of Philadelphia and Wells and Lilley of Boston were so grotesquely disfigured by misprints as to be unusable. The debate also went on at the collegiate level, with little effect until students at Yale attempted to remove knowledge of Greek and Latin as formal entrance requirements. In writing the *Yale Report* of 1828, the classicist James L. Kingsley and Yale's president, Jeremiah Day, considered the traditional arguments of utility and Anglocentrism against those who asserted that at the root of their own language, literature, and culture lay the masterpieces of Greek and Roman literature and philosophy. The report asserted not only the core importance of classics for western thought but also the Revolution's belief that

> The models of ancient literature, which are put into the hands of the young student, can hardly fail to imbue his mind with the principles of liberty; to inspire the liveliest patriotism, and to excite to noble and generous action, and are therefore peculiarly adapted to the American youth. (Yale Report 1829: 345)

Thus the place of classics at the center of the collegiate curriculum remained settled until the end of the century.

In 1815, well before the *Yale Report*, four recent graduates of Harvard, George Bancroft, George Ticknor, Joseph Green Cogswell, and the newly appointed (and first) Eliot Professor of Greek, Edward Everett, recognized that America had no classical scholars. In 1816, Ticknor wrote, "We do not yet know what a Greek scholar is; we do not even know the process by which a man is to be made one" (Ticknor 1876: 1:53). The four friends went to Germany in pursuit of PhDs and an introduction to the German science of philology. Upon their return, Cogswell took the lead in trying to transplant the German system of seminars, original research, and publication, but the teaching corps of America was unprofessionalized in a land where "scholarship" had the English connotation of reading for one's own edification rather than for publication of some new and true fact. Everett, who had not only heard the great German philologists but had touched Greek marble in 1820, returned to Cambridge to present lectures to both academic and nonacademic audiences that were so beautifully expressed and full of the new matter from Germany that his student Ralph Waldo Emerson called them "a new morning" in America. But the experiment was short-lived, for the German system could not be transplanted this early and the American system remained for a half-century basically what it had been, the province of amateurs.

Almost contemporaneous with Ticknor and Everett's experiment and the assault on the predominance of Latin in the schools came an interest in Greek, a language that John Adams had been advised was "a meer curiosity" (Adams 1962: 1:55). Always marginalized and taught in schools only to the level of college admission, in other select quarters Greek was touted as the salvation of American education, propelled in part by the accounts and pictures brought back from Greece by Nicholas Biddle of Philadelphia in 1806, even though Rome remained a popular Grand Tour stopover (Vance 1989).

American Greek textbooks, grammars, and dictionaries (often derived from German models) began to appear along with Latin textbooks after the Revolution. The publication of an accurate fourth edition of Dalzel's *Collectanea Graeca majora* (1824) under the supervision of Harvard classicists in 1824 gave at last an accurate and usable (if boring) text that would be used in schools for the next half-century. In New England, the *North American Review* asserted the primacy of Greek, while in South Carolina, the diplomat and editor Hugh Swinton Legaré, a friend of Ticknor and a lover of Greek liberality who distrusted Greek politics, wrote of the appropriate model for the young nation much as the *Yale Report* had, "Much better to imitate the old and elegant humanity of Greece, than the barbaric pride of a Norwegian or Hunnish stateliness; and...despise that slavish and nauseating subserviency with which all European literature is steeped through and through" (Legaré 1828: 8). In the nineteenth century, in America as in Europe, the benefits of a classical education were slowly being extended to women. Through Colonial times, in America as in Europe, it was feared that teaching girls Latin would later distract them from their household duties. Boys needed classical languages for their professions; girls did not. Sarah Bradford complained in 1810 to Mary Moody Emerson, "I am sometimes almost tempted to wish I knew nothing about Latin...I am as careful to conceal my books and as much afraid of being detected with them as if I were committing some great crime" (Kerber 1997: 246–7). The notion that women were not up to learning ancient languages and certainly of practicing philology survived through the nineteenth century. But one day in 1878 a young woman named Abby Leach strode confidently into the office of Harvard's Eliot Professor of Greek, William Watson Goodwin, begging for the best classical education the country had to offer. Confident that as a woman she could not translate Greek, Goodwin offered her a page of Xenophon to translate at sight and she rendered it so flawlessly that Goodwin engaged a number of his colleagues to teach Leach and a group of other women at what was called The Annex, which later developed into Radcliffe College. The daughter of a wealthy Baltimore Quaker, Martha Carey Thomas was so determined to be the first woman to receive an American doctorate that she enrolled in one of B. L. Gildersleeve's first classes at the new Johns Hopkins University, but she was soon so overwhelmed by the workload and the restrictions put upon her as a woman (she was not allowed to attend the seminars, since she would be a distraction) that she fled to Europe, where she took a degree from Zurich in 1882. She became the pioneering second president of Bryn Mawr College. The honor of being the first woman to receive an American doctorate fell to Helen Magill, who received her PhD from Boston University in 1877 (she went on to pass the Cambridge Tripos with honors in 1881), but at age 37 she married Andrew D. White, former president of Cornell, and her professional life was over.

It was likewise thought that African-Americans, whose enslavement had been so assiduously argued from Aristotle, were incapable of learning Greek and Latin. John C. Calhoun said that if he "could find a Negro who knew the Greek syntax," he "would then believe the Negro was a human being and should be treated as such" (Crummell 1992: 292). Walter Hines Page, a former student in Gildersleeve's seminary and future editor of the *Atlantic*, visited a black secondary school in Virginia after the Civil War to hear the students reciting and translating Greek. Back in Richmond, no one believed that he had actually heard this. With the rise of an educated black middle class after Reconstruction and the establishment of predominantly black colleges and universities, there emerged a small but significant group of black classicists led by William Sanders Scarborough, who seemed as well connected with the black intelligentsia as his counterpart Gildersleeve was with the white Establishment (Ronnick 2004). Black writers from Phillis Wheatley to Derek Wolcott and Toni Morrison have embraced the classical past in their work.

4   The Bronze Age of American Classical Studies

Reinhold's "Silver Age" ends in 1830 as the self-made men of the frontier led by Andrew Jackson came to Washington. The democratic movement accomplished its goals without any appeal to classical models and never imagined enfranchising women or blacks. George Kennedy has deemed the period from 1828 (the year of the *Yale Report*) to the end of the Civil War as the Bronze Age of American classics (Reinhold 1984: 325). Some northern men trained in the classics went on to public service: Everett became a senator from Massachusetts, George Bancroft became a minister to Great Britain, Prussia, and the German Empire, and even a former professor of classics at Western Reserve Eclectic Institute (now Hiram College), James A. Garfield, became President of the United States. However, many of the prominent voices in the South, Henry Clay, Jackson, Calhoun, Sam Houston and Jefferson Davis on the political side, and William Gilmore Simms, Henry Timrod, and Edgar Allan Poe on the literary side, came from the middle class, and most did not enjoy classical educations (though Calhoun and Houston had fine appreciations of authors they read in translation). Americans who condemned European decadence joined religious evangelicals in shuddering at the admiration of paganism and the misadaptation of Greek style to American values embodied in the monumental statue of Washington that Horatio Greenough made for the Capitol.

   No deep classical education is required to enjoy the predominant classical presence in American cultural life, that of Classic Revival architecture. British interest in Roman architecture had been stimulated by the rediscovery of Pompeii (1748) and Herculaneum (1750–1) and by the publication of *Antiquities of Athens* (1751) by James Stuart and Nicholas Revett. Though the first classical revival structure was Stuart's Doric garden temple in Hagley, England (1758), a taste for Roman architecture predominated in the last half of the eighteenth century both in Europe and America. Thus Jefferson's Virginia State Capitol (1785) in Richmond imitated the Roman temple at Nîmes, and both Monticello and the Colonnade at the University of Virginia were based on Roman designs. As the century turned, Benjamin Latrobe's Bank of Pennsylvania (1799), modeled on an Ionic temple, began the interest in Greek architecture. Latrobe, like Jefferson, believed that architecture should make a political statement, and they both proclaimed the continuity of democratic traditions in their public buildings. The Greek style is also notably represented in the Second Bank of the United States in Philadelphia (1824) by William Strickland, while the Roman element persisted in Jefferson's University and T. U. Walter's Capitol dome in Washington.

Though some private buildings in the North presented façades with columns, pediments, and clapboard exteriors, the true models of private Classic Revival were the great plantation homes of the South ("Southern Colonial" style), encouraged by the illustrations in *Grecian Remains in Italy* (1812), by John Izard Middleton of South Carolina.

As the debate on the slavery question heated up in the 1840s, southerners found that the Abolitionists (led by clerics) had coopted the Bible as an authority on the sanctity and equality of the individual, black and white. Beginning with Professor Thomas Dew of William and Mary and followed by intellectuals like James D. B. De Bow, George Frederick Holmes, and George Fitzhugh, Greek views of a natural hierarchy of humanity were called into play. Herodotus was summoned by both sides on the matter of Negro inferiority (Wiesen 1980), but the most repeated source was Aristotle's *Politics* and his clearest proponent was a former Vice President of the United States.

John C. Calhoun of South Carolina had so despised the "Tariff of Abominations" passed in 1828 that he resigned as Vice President to return to the Senate and fight for the rights of his state. In the decade before his death in 1850, he composed two tracts on government, both of which drew heavily from Aristotle, who "took a place in his trinity of the Constitution, the Bible, and Aristotle" (Eaton 1964a: 144). The key passage begins, "Nature has clearly designed some men for freedom and others for slavery; – and with respect to the latter, slavery is both just and beneficial" (*Politics* 1.5). Most Greeks denied rights to those they felt were inferior (women, foreigners), and Aristotle's view that slaves should be barbarians justified for some the enslavement of Africans. Upon reading Calhoun, George Fitzhugh of Virginia, author of *Sociology for the South or, The Failure of Free Society* (1854) and *Cannibals All! or Slaves Without Masters* (1857), said, "All these things I thought original in me, I find in Aristotle" (Wish 1948: 263). Other Aristotelians included two men at the University of Virginia, the English and history professor Holmes and Albert Bledsoe, a pro-slavery mathematician.

The most notable use of classical models in the Civil War, and the last time such models were employed in a major political event, occurred at the dedication of the Gettysburg cemetery. Edward Everett, PhD in classics from Göttingen, former US Senator, and President of Harvard, chose to become a modern-day Pericles to deliver the definitive historical account and analysis of the battle (as Pericles did in Thucydides' history). He followed the classical model for two hours. Abraham Lincoln spoke for less than two minutes, but as Garry Wills (1984) has shown, his far more effective address far more efficiently followed the rhetoric of the Greek Revival and the *epainesis/parainesis* (thanks to and counsel of the dead) model set by ancient rhetoricians, though whether Lincoln had ever heard of such as Gorgias cannot be determined.

5   The Classics in Late Nineteenth- and Twentieth-Century American Education

In the two decades following the start of the Civil War, two signal events bolstered the classical tradition in America.

In July of 1862, the US Congress (without any southern states voting) passed the Morrill Act as an expression of the general and scientific press's growing displeasure with the classics-based curriculum of the elite institutions and as a means of sponsoring agricultural and technical instruction. The Act provided for the founding on Federal land of state colleges devoted to teaching "agriculture and the mechanic arts ... without excluding other scientific and classical studies." Classical study was thus ensured at the more than 70 land-grant institutions established by the Morrill Act in states north (MIT), south (Auburn), east (Cornell), and west (Wisconsin, California).

The second signal event for classics was the establishment in 1876 of the Johns Hopkins University, the first true American university on the German model. The first appointment to the faculty was Basil Lanneau Gildersleeve, the nation's greatest classics scholar. He began the professionalization of undergraduate teaching and encouraged the development of doctoral programs in classics by establishing the first graduate seminary, directing some 65 dissertations, creating the nation's first quarterly classics journal, and setting a level of instruction and scholarship matched by that of his eloquence in defense of classical studies and his native South.

As the investigation and interpretation of the classical world became more and more the province of specialized scientists like Gildersleeve, no one of whom could comprehend all the new knowledge of antiquity brought to light by highly trained archaeologists and philologists, amateurs and those without the advantage of a university education sought in the popular aspects of the classical world an expression of private cultivation and public cultural identity that would equal the popular classicism of imperial Europe.

The identification of classical study with a higher culture in the popular mind was manifest in the development of great private collections of antiquities, the endowment of museums and university archaeological digs, and the establishment of American schools in Athens and Rome (Winterer 2002). The chief manifestation of this trend was a production of Sophocles' *Oedipus Tyrannus* at Harvard in 1881. The play followed the model of the successful production of Aeschylus' *Agamemnon* the year before at Balliol College, Oxford. The American production was performed for over a week to over six thousand people (who were given English translations), including Longfellow, Emerson, Henry James, and Henry Adams, who thought his Harvard classical education was incomplete except for "two or three Greek plays" (Adams 1999: 55). The performance of ancient plays in the original took place not only at Harvard (where the tradition was continued notably in 1906, 1933, 1939, and 1956), but in numerous schools, especially Randolph-Macon Woman's College, where Professor Mabel Whiteside oversaw most of the 41 productions performed from 1909 to 1954. Greek drama was a continuing if not seminal influence on American drama as early as William Vaughn Moody, *The Fire Bringer* (Prometheus, 1904), culminating in Eugene O'Neill's "Desire Under the Elms" (Hippolytus myth, 1924) and "Mourning Becomes Electra" (1931), along with notable translations like Witter Bynner's *Iphigenia in Tauris* (1922), Robinson Jeffers' *Medea* (1946), and Robert Lowell's "Oresteia of Aeschylus" (1978). Broadway musicals from Rodgers and Hart's "The Boys from Syracuse" (1938) to Gelbart–Shevelove–Sondheim's "A Funny

Thing Happened on the Way to the Forum" (1962) continued the lighter side of ancient theater. American filmmakers have created versions of these shows, but in general films have tended to view the Romans merely as anti-Christians and the Greeks hardly at all (Solomon 2001).

Only two years after the Harvard *Oedipus*, Charles Francis Adams Jr. gave an important Phi Beta Kappa lecture entitled "A College Fetich," in which he held that Greek produced too little in the way of good effects for the amount of effort it took to learn and that modern students could easily find more rewarding courses of study. Five years after the *Oedipus*, in 1886, Harvard, following a trend begun by lesser institutions, abolished the Greek requirement for admission; Yale soon did the same, abolishing Latin as well in 1933.

At the dawn of the twentieth century at least half of all high-school students took Latin, but in 1916 Abraham Flexner proposed eliminating Greek and Latin because their only excuse for being in the curriculum was that they had always been there. Flexner's challenge was met by Andrew Fleming West, president of Cornell, who enlisted ex-presidents, industry titans, and intellectual heavyweights to render their opinions in a volume called *Value of the Classics* (1917). In 1924 a study by the American Classical League called *The Classical Investigation* encouraged students to study Latin not simply to learn grammar, but also to sip the delights of Latin literature. Through World War II, while the American university remained the privilege of the elite, classical studies remained a prominent fixture; it was only after the war that the opening of universities to greater numbers of students from across the social spectrum allowed the wishes of Franklin and Rush to come to fruition.

6   The Classics in American Culture

Outside the academy, the influence of antiquity was still to be seen. Architecture in the North had become increasingly the grand domed style of the Roman Empire. The beaux-arts buildings of the World's Columbian Exposition in Chicago (1893) began a trend in which government buildings were based on Roman imperial models, and Penn Station in New York (1910) mimicked the Baths of Caracalla. In the twentieth century, the International Style of Le Corbusier and Van Der Rohe used elements of classical simplicity and efficiency, while postmodern architecture in the 1970s simply chose decorative features (e.g., the Roman arch and Chippendale top of Philip Johnson's 1984 AT&T [now Sony] Building in New York). The arrival of Carl Jung in America in 1930 with his views on tribal myth and the artist as shaman transmitting great truths to the populace was crucial to the intellectual background of the Surrealists and Abstract Expressionists like Mark Rothko and Adolph Gottlieb (Oedipus as the blind seer), who would use classical myths to interpret the tragedy of World War II. Great classical nudes were the basis for Gaston Lachaise.

With classics at the heart of the curriculum, it is no surprise that its myths, history, and authors should be a feature of American literature. Just as the first work of Roman literature is a translation (Livius Andronicus' translation of the *Odyssey*), so the first work of American literature is a translation, George Sandys' (1578–1644) rendering of Ovid's *Metamorphoses* (1621–6). Sandys, called by Dryden "the best Versifier of the former age" (Dryden 1962b: 521), crossed the Atlantic in 1621 as an official with the Virginia Company; his translation was a source of mythological tales for Keats, among others. So pervasive were the classical models in the Colonial Period that not only did Captain John Smith and Cotton Mather employ reminiscences of the *Aeneid*, but even slaves like Phyllis Wheatley ("Maecenas") and Jupiter Ammon used classical elements in their poetry. By the end of the nineteenth century, many Americans were versed in the stories in Thomas Bulfinch's *Age of Fable* (1855), just as many in the twentieth century (notably Robert Kennedy) would be introduced to mythology by Edith Hamilton's *Mythology* (1942). Of all classical stories, that of Aeneas has held the longest sway (Shields 2001). Vergilian echoes continued from the introduction to Joel Barlow's *Columbiad* (1807) ("I sing the Mariner who first unfurl'd / An eastern banner o'er the western world") into the twentieth century: Willa Cather drew heavily on the *Georgics* in *My Antonia* (1918) (Ryder 1990), as Fitzgerald did for the ending of *The Great Gatsby* (1925). Vergil also structured Allen Tate's "Aeneas at New York" and "Aeneas at Washington" and Robert Lowell's "Falling Asleep Over the *Aeneid*." Just as Thoreau in the nineteenth century had felt a special attraction for the *Eclogues* and *Georgics*, so in the twentieth century Robert Frost left his failed Vermont farm to join the English Georgic poets; half a century later his poem for John Kennedy's inauguration, "The Gift Outright," echoes *Eclogue* 4. In the South the Agrarians (Tate, John Crowe Ransom, Donald Davidson, Robert Penn Warren, and others) called for a return to southern regionalism and an agricultural economy, much on the order of Vergil's poem.

It is impossible to do justice to all the American poets who have written on classical subjects. Thoreau recounted Whitman declaiming Homer from atop a Broadway bus, and Odysseus has inspired poetry by other Americans from Nathaniel Langdon Frothingham in 1859 through Madison Cawein to Maxwell Anderson, Joseph Auslander, John Peale Bishop, John Ciardi, Gregory Corso, Mark Van Doren, Horace Gregory, Robert Lowell, Archibald Macleish, Edgar Lee Masters, W. S. Merwin, Richard Wilbur, and, perhaps most brilliantly of all, Louise Glück in *Meadowlands* (1996). Helen of Troy has attracted poets as different as Stephen Vincent Benet, Bishop, Hart Crane, Edgar Fawcett, Anne Adams Fields, John Gould Fletcher, Masters, Edgar Allan Poe, Laura Riding, George Santayana, and Sara Teasdale. The loves of Sappho have appealed to poets beginning with Philip Freneau at the end of the eighteenth century ("The Monument of Phaon") and continuing in the next century with William Wetmore Story, Cale Young Rice, and William Alexander Percy. Sappho has also, of course, attracted female poets, beginning with Elizabeth Akers in the nineteenth century, followed by Zoe Akins, Teasdale, Edna St. Vincent Millay, and notably H. D., whose connection with Hellenism was especially deep and wide (Gregory). It is difficult to think of a nineteenth-century poet who did not tap a classical source, from Longfellow to James Russell Lowell to Bayard Taylor, in addition to hosts of now-forgotten poets of the same period whose subjects were almost exclusively classical (Boswell 1982).

In the twentieth century, virtually every major poet wrote on classical themes, including (in addition to those mentioned above) William Rose Benet, R. P. Blackmur,

Louise Bogan, Witter Bynner, James Dickey, Rolfe Humphries, William Meredith, Thomas Merton, Marianne Moore, Howard Nemerov, John Crowe Ransom, Kenneth Rexroth, Edward Arlington Robinson, Delmore Schwartz, and Karl Shapiro (Boswell).

T. S. Eliot, classically educated at Harvard, used Tiresias in *The Waste Land*, the *Alcestis* of Euripides was his model in *The Cocktail Party*, and he compared his Everyman Sweeney to Polyphemus. His influential address to the British Virgil Society, "What Is a Classic?" defined Aeneas at mid-century in conservative Christian terms. Ezra Pound "translated" Propertius and other classical authors. Conrad Aiken wrote "Medusa" and "Priapus and the Pool," among others. Robinson Jeffers' poem "Cawdor" draws on Euripides' *Hippolytus*, *The Tower beyond Tragedy* is a version of the *Oresteia*, and "Solstice" reworks the Jason-Medea myth.

Some romance novels looked to the ancient world. The most notable is Hawthorne's *Marble Faun* (1860), which involves American lovers in Rome and an Italian who resembles the faun of Praxiteles, embodies aspects of the Greek ideal, and is thrown to his death from the Tarpeian Rock. *Moby-Dick* has elements of the Europa, Arion, Damocles, and Prometheus myths.

The fine tradition of American historical novels set in antiquity began with Mordecai M. Noah's *The Grecian Captive* (1822) and John Howard Payne's *Oswaldi of Athens* (1831). The great exemplar is Union General Lew Wallace's *Ben-Hur: A Tale of the Christ* (1880). An Indianan, Wallace was skeptical of the wealthy new society of post–Civil War America. Packed with great period detail and setpieces like the chariot-race at Antioch and the naval battle that have made it a perennial Hollywood favorite, the novel depicts Rome as the new imperial America, in which the citizens retain many of the virtues of earlier generations amid the worship of power. The long line of American fiction based on the ancient world includes George Horton's *Like Another Helen* (1901), John Erskine's *The Private Life of Helen of Troy* (1925), Thornton Wilder's *The Woman of Andros* (1930), Howard Fast's *Spartacus* (1952), John Updike's *The Centaur* (1963), and Gore Vidal's *Julian* (1964).

FURTHER READING

The first study of American life to speak to the importance of the classical tradition is Samuel Miller's *A Brief Retrospect of the Eighteenth Century* (1803), but American intellectual history was not seriously studied until the 1920s. Meyer Reinhold notes that in 1925 Carl Becker asked "Will not someone write a book showing how the revolutionary state of mind of the eighteenth century was also nourished on an ideal conception of classical republicanism and Roman virtue?" (Reinhold 1984: 284). Seventy years later, Becker's wish was fully granted with the publication of Richard (1994), which is now the starting point for the study of classical influences on the Revolution. Richard encapsulates and supersedes much of Reinhold's *Classica Americana*, a collection of his seminal articles on the subject, but much of Reinhold's pathfinding work will always be of great value. Most surveys of the US classical tradition stop where Reinhold does, at the end of the "Silver Age" of the Classical Tradition, 1830, yet there is a rich vein still to be mined in the late nineteenth and early twentieth centuries. Howard Mumford Jones (1952, 1968, 1974) is the most frequent champion of the classical influence on American culture; Clement Eaton and Michael O'Brien (2004) have been particularly sensitive to classical influences in southern culture. Unfortunately Highet's magisterial *Classical Tradition* (1949) barely glances at American literature. For poets, individual studies like Gregory (1997) must be consulted. A full history of American classical scholarship is still a desideratum; in the meantime, see Calder (1994).

PART III

Contemporary Themes

CHAPTER TWENTY

Reception

Charles Martindale

Our literature is characterized by the pitiless divorce which the literary institution maintains between the producer of the text and its user, between its owner and its customer, between its author and its reader. This reader is thereby plunged into a kind of idleness – he is intransitive.

R. Barthes, *S/Z*: 4

What classics needs at the moment is more reflection on reading.

L. Edmunds, *Intertextuality and the Reading of Roman Poetry*: 166

1 Reception or Tradition?

In 1878 the painter James McNeill Whistler sued the art critic John Ruskin for libel. Ruskin had accused him of "Cockney impudence" for asking "two hundred guineas for flinging a pot of paint in the public's face." Among the issues at the trial were the degree of finish required in a painting and its status as representation. Of his *Nocturne in Blue and Silver* exhibited before the jury, Whistler averred, "It was not my intent simply to make a copy of Battersea Bridge.... As to what the picture represents, that depends upon who looks at it." Questioned by one of the defense counsels about the precise contents of the picture, Whistler replied with evident irony:

– Are those figures on the top of the bridge intended as people?
– They are just what you like.
– That is a barge beneath?
– Yes, I am very much flattered at your seeing that.

"My whole scheme," Whistler insisted, "was only to bring about a certain harmony of color" (Merrill 1992: 151). We have here what might be called a late nineteenth-century version of reception theory. The unconventional title of Whistler's picture can be seen as a provocation, encouraging the viewer to cooperate with the painter in performing, so to say, an interpretation of the work, one that "depends on who looks at it." Whistler was an avant-garde artist, but for centuries art theory had expected beholders to play an active role in responding to works of art. A concern with reception was not the invention of critical theorists in the 1960s. Indeed we might trace the modern phase to the "Copernican" shift advocated by the philosopher Immanuel Kant from the "thing-in-itself" to the thing as it appears to the minds and senses of human beings (which is, for Kant, all we can know).

The word "reception," however, in the specialized sense used within literary theory, is particularly associated with a group of German critics led by Hans Robert Jauss (died 1997) and Wolfgang Iser who worked together at the University of Constance from the 1960s; it often replaces terms like "tradition," "heritage," "influence," and so forth. Each of these keywords carries within it its own implied agenda and metaphorical entailments; each to some extent determines in advance its different "findings." The etymology of "tradition," for example, from the Latin *tradere* suggests a – usually benign – handing down of material from the past to the present. "Reception," by contrast, at least on the model of the Constance school, operates with a different temporality, involving the *active* participation of readers (including readers who are themselves creative artists) in a two-way process, backward as well as forward, in which the present and past are in dialogue with each other. When texts are reread in new situations, they have new meanings; we do not have to privilege the meanings that they had in their first, "original" contexts (even assuming these to be recoverable in principle). The distinction between the ancient world "in itself" and the way it has been received and understood in later centuries is thereby blurred, or even dissolved. But the boundary between "tradition" and "reception" is itself a shifting one, varying with the usage and practices of different writers. Many reception histories are highly positivistic in character (seeking to construct the-past-as-it-really-was-in-itself), while, half a century before Jauss first articulated his "aesthetics of reception" in his inaugural lecture at Constance in 1967, T. S. Eliot had argued, in the influential essay "Tradition and the Individual Talent," that "the past [is] altered by the present as much as the present is directed by the past" (Eliot 1920: 45), a cardinal principle for many versions of reception. Thus merely by putting a citation from Petronius as an epigraph to *The Waste Land*, Eliot changed the character of the *Satyricon*, rendering it modern again, indeed modernist (Kermode 2004: 77). My concern in this chapter is with the challenge reception theory in its classic form (whose roots can be traced back well beyond 1967) poses to what Jauss calls the "dogmatic historicism and positivism" (Segers 1979: 84) that still marks much of the scholarship describing the presence of antiquity in later centuries.

An example should make clearer some of the points at issue. Ben Jonson's "On My First Daughter" (22 in his *Epigrams* published in 1616) is an "imitation" (to use the term favored by the humanists) of an often-admired epigram by Martial (5.34) commemorating the dead slave girl Erotion:

Here lies, to each her parents' ruth,
Mary, the daughter of their youth;
Yet, all heaven's gift being heaven's due,
It makes the father less to rue.
At six months' end she parted hence
With safety of her innocence;
Whose soul Heaven's Queen (whose name she bears),
In comfort of her mother's tears,
Hath placed amongst her virgin train;
Where, while that severed doth remain,
This grave partakes the fleshly birth –
Which cover lightly, gentle earth.

Various elements (a father and a mother, mention of the age of the dead girl, her destiny in the afterlife, the concluding prayer to the earth) have been taken from Martial, while intractably Roman detail is omitted, including the picture of tiny Erotion, afraid, like many children, of the dark and recoiling from the huge dog Cerberus (a detail perhaps playful as well as sad, in view of the skepticism, at this date, about mythological accounts of the afterlife). Martial concludes with the traditional request that the earth should not lie heavy on the dead, a *topos* which has a special gracefulness in a poem about a child:

mollia non rigidus caespes tegat ossa nec illi,
  terra, gravis fueris: non fuit illa tibi.
(let not the hard clods cover her soft bones,
  and do not be heavy on her, earth – she was not so on you)
(9–10)

Jonson, reverting at the close to the small grave where his baby daughter is buried, gives this motif a Christian twist: Mary Jonson's soul is now in heaven, so only her tiny body is left under the earth. Out of Martial has come a fresh and English creation. A traditional account might say that Martial's poem (taken to have a fixed character which scholarship has determined) has influenced Jonson's (likewise so taken). But that is to make the hermeneutic process seem unduly straightforward, for both Jonson and us. We might rather say that Jonson, in writing his own poem, *was trying to find out* what sort of a poet Martial is, *constructing* him and his tone of voice, so to say. Writing of Jonson, Eliot observes that "to see him as a contemporary does not so much require the power of putting ourselves into seventeenth-century London as it requires the power of setting Jonson in our London: a more difficult triumph of divination" (Eliot 1920: 97). This is what Jonson, it may be claimed, did with Martial. The epigram could then be seen as providing a possible reading of Martial, one that we might accept or contest (some scholars question the seriousness of Martial's grief, citing in evidence another, rather more cynical epigram about Erotion, 5.37). The critic H. A. Mason, asking whether Martial is still in any sense a living classic, examines a variety of translations and imitations to see what kind of life might be found there (his conclusion is that Martial is alive in the work of Jonson and Cowley, but not in versions from the immediate postwar period). In particular he argues that "On My First Daughter," "as the best translation to date of the spirit of the epitaph on Erotion," brings us "nearer to the humanity of Martial" (Mason 1988: 309 – we should note, however, that this formulation reifies the "spirit" of the epigram). In other words, Mason uses Jonson and others as a way, indeed the best way, of exploring the character of Martial's poetry; we have then (Martindale reading) Mason reading Jonson reading Martial. Any imitation, as a sort of extended allusion, invites a reader to make another text part of her reading. Such intertextuality never merely resolves meaning; rather there is a dialectic of difference and similarity between the two texts, which is constantly reconfigured in new ways by new readers (Martindale 2000). When in my turn I read Jonson's epitaph, I become part of a three-way conversation between myself, Jonson, and Martial (with indeed numerous other more ghostly voices – past critics and readers including Mason, other intertexts – contributing to that conversation, many of them unrecognized by myself). And my account becomes a further link, however small, in what Jauss calls the "chain of receptions" (1982: 20). This chain is both enabling and constraining, as we make meanings intersubjectively, but not in circumstances of our own making (clearly there are readings that are unlikely, or impossible, within particular historical contexts). So, like the other ancient *auctores*, Martial (or should that be "Martial"?), as a man, as a body of texts, as an authority for different ways of living, has been diversely read in the West over the last two thousand years, by scholars, poets, and others, and our current images are shaped in response to that reception history.

Some complain that "reception" suggests a passive role for the reader (this may in part reflect the other associations of the word in English) and prefer "appropriation" (e.g., Hall 2004: 61). But we should remember that "reception" was adopted precisely to underline the dynamic and dialogic character of reading (indeed "appropriation," making one's own, downplays the possibility of dialogue, the capacity of the text to resist our attempts to master it, its capacity to modify our sensibility). "Tradition," by contrast, might imply that the process of transmission is comfortably uncontested. But readers can certainly be resistant, or antagonistic, or conflicted, as Tony Harrison's poem "Me Tarzan" reminds us:

> Outside the whistled gang-call, *Twelfth Street Rag*,
> then a Tarzan yodel for the kid who's bored,
> whose hand's on his liana ... no, back
> to Labienus and his flaming sword.
>
> *Off laikin' then t'fish 'oil* all the boys,
> *off tartin', off to t'flicks* but on, on, on,
> the foldaway card table, the green baize,
> *De Bello Gallico* and lexicon.
>
> It's only his jaw muscles that he's tensed
> into an enraged *shit* that he can't go;

down with polysyllables, he's against
all pale-face Caesars, *for* Geronimo.

He shoves the frosted attic skylight, shouts:

Ah bloody can't ah've gorra Latin prose.

His bodiless head that's poking out's
like patriarchal Cissy-bleeding-ro's.

Both the older Harrison (left-wing, anti-establishment) who writes the poem and his younger self depicted in it are divided in their response to the oppressive power of the classics (Rutter 1995: 127-8). The poem pits high culture (linked with Caesar and Cicero) against popular culture, and it works with three languages: Yorkshire dialect, Latin (associated with polysyllables like "patriarchal"), and standard English (in which most of the poem is written, and which, like the orthodox meter and rhyme-scheme, would seem to some quite as hegemonic as Latin). The clash of these languages generates various puns and plays. At one level "flaming" is a colloquialism, but it also suggests the sword of an epic hero (*fulmineus* is used in the *Aeneid* of Aeneas' sword), or the angelic sword that keeps Adam and Eve out of Paradise (and if the poem depicts a fall, is it a fortunate fall?). "Cissy-bleeding-ro" (bloody Cicero) is an unmanly pale-face in comparison with the "redskin" Geronimo (is education then gendered, and, if so, is this not incipient patriarchy in the boys?), but he is also the Roman statesman who bravely stuck his head out of the litter to receive his death blow. And, like his younger self, Harrison, despite his working class origins, in part resembles Cicero, a writer, set apart; and he is also by training a classicist, who has made a career by repeated turns to ancient literature – indeed this very poem is full of classical learning and allusions. But "Me Tarzan" reminds us that, even so, Harrison remains highly ambivalent about classical values (though ironically aspects of his "popular" culture will be almost unintelligible to many readers). Readers don't necessarily do what they are told, or respond as they are meant to.

Most versions of reception theory start from a proposition previously advanced within German hermeneutics, for example by Hans-Georg Gadamer in one of the last century's most profound philosophical explorations of the nature of literary under-standing, *Truth and Method*, published in 1960, and translated into English in 1975. This is the claim that interpretation always takes place *within history*, and is subject to the contingencies of its historical moment; there is no God's-eye position for the interpreter outside history. Indeed "history" itself cannot provide a stable ground for interpretation, since it is always differently understood, though history and theory can be used productively to interrogate each other. There is no permanently "cor-rect" reading of a text, but an ever-changing "fusion of horizons" (in Gadamer's somewhat awkward metaphor) between text and interpreter. There can be no final reading since that would imply that we have come to the end of history: "our knowledge of the past ... is limited by our knowledge (or ignorance) of the future" (Danto 1965: 18). Writing from the perspective of the early twenty-first century, Iser sees reception theory as a response to the conflict of interpretations, one that helps to "elucidate why and how the same literary text can mean different things to different people at different times" (Iser 2006: 68). He locates two main strands within that theory, both of which are needed for a fully developed account of reading and interpretation. The first is represented by his own work, which is concerned with reading as a *process* in relation to formal features of the text, including gaps in the text that a reader has to fill (his "implied reader" is thus a transcendental or virtual construct, not to be identified with any actual reader either now or in the past). Within this model "meaning is no longer an object to be defined, but is an effect to be experienced" (Iser 1980: 10). Iser's second strand derives from the work of his colleague Jauss, who sought a revival of literary history, and was concerned with documented historical readers and what they can tell us about the texts we read. Jauss's "aesthetics of reception" attempts to reconcile hermeneutics (the theory of interpretation) with poetics, historical with aesthetic criticism. In the notes to his translation of the *Iliad*, Alexander Pope observed that the commentators were "fonder of showing their learning in all kinds than their single understanding in poetry" (Shankman 1996: 46). But if the *Iliad* was produced in the past, it is valued (or not) in the present; an adequate account, if it is not to be of merely antiquarian interest, needs to attend to both aspects. Past works have the power to act in the present (any present of reading) in ways that could not have been foreseen at the time. Following Gadamer's dialectical approach, Jauss breaks down the barrier between the art object and the perceiving subject: the reader experiences "self-enjoyment in the enjoyment of something other." His version of reception thus "entails not only the introduction of the reader as a guide to value and interpretation, but implicitly a model for understanding encounters with the past in which we simultaneously form and are formed by artefacts" (Holub 1995: 344, 326). Hostile critics sometimes link reception with the consumerism characteristic of late capitalism. But reception does not claim that the customer is always right, just that she is always a party to the transaction. Validity remains an issue for reception scholars, as for other interpreters (indeed since criteria of validity are historically situated and always in dispute, they can themselves be seen as a crucial part of the processes of reception).

Why should we study previous readers? Jauss's metaphor of the "chain" reaching us from the work could suggest a way of doing reception history rather different from the norm, one that explores historical filiations without privileging original meaning. We could say that reception theory, while stressing the importance of history, also destabilizes or complicates it as a site of meaning. We usually get flat accounts in which each "age" encounters the past in isolation rather as though it were a *tabula rasa* (so the "Romantic" view of Vergil becomes quite other than the "Augustan" view). But much of the history of reading will be unknowable and subject to multiple contingencies; good accounts will acknowledge the difficulties and aporias and blind-spots of any such project, including the complex entanglements of history. It is no advance simply to substitute positivistic accounts of the text-in-itself by equally positivistic accounts of the historical-reading-of-the-text-in-itself; if the *Aeneid* has no single "originary" meaning, subsequent readings are equally subject to the slide in signification, in accordance *inter alia* with the particular needs and configurations of changing reading practices. To cope with this we might try to devise accounts that are not hierarchically arranged, but in which any text could speak to any other text on terms of equality (I shall shortly offer an extended illustration). Thus we might approach Vergil obliquely through Dante, say, or Homer through the Romantics, remembering that we too are involved in these *layerings* (we can call this "double-distancing"). The classicist and aesthetic critic Walter Pater (1839–94), another, perhaps unexpected, forerunner of reception theory, may best point the way to a revised practice (see Iser 1995; Martindale 2005; introduction to Martindale and Thomas 2006). Too often reception histories present us merely with quaint practices or the errors we have outgrown. The assumption is that such receptions tell us only about the receiving culture, little or nothing about the work received (though we tend to exclude our own receptions from these strictures, particularly if we are scholars). Rather than patronizing our predecessors, we might do better to put our minds into productive friction with other minds in our contemplation of past works. A reception history need not be part of a narrative of progress; *we* might be the learners.

2 Velázquez, Ovid, and the Contingencies of Reception

Most of my examples of receptions so far have been written texts (whether in the form of a piece of criticism or another work of art), but a reception could just as well be a painting, or a sculpture, or a piece of music, or a film. A reception involving two different media can help to clarify some of the theoretical issues at stake. Accordingly – and to show how I believe we might "do" reception – I have chosen as my final exhibit a painting by Velázquez, both because it can be interpreted as a profound and profoundly haunting reception of Ovid's *Metamorphoses*, and because the way it has been interpreted itself perfectly illustrates the contingencies of reception history. It is today usually known as *The Spinners* (Las hilanderas); what title Velázquez gave it, if any, is unknown (Fig. 20.1; see Harris 1982: 158–62; Barkan 1986: 1–18; Brown 1986: 252–3; Alpers 2005: 135–262). Titles, often nonauthorial in origin, can help to determine how texts are read, and thus constitute a significant, if often ignored, element in their reception. In the early eighteenth century, just before Velázquez' painting entered the Spanish royal collection, it was catalogued as "the women who were working in a tapestry workshop / on tapestries." Furthermore the work we see today is not the same as the one Velázquez originally painted, probably around 1657/ 8. This is not merely the result of changes in color relationships and in general condition that would affect any painting over time (in that sense with older paintings we are never looking at the "original"); in addition at some unknown date the painting was substantially enlarged at the top and sides. These enlargements (which include the oculus above the tapestry) have the effect of clarifying the spatial relationships between the background and the foreground, but also of diminishing the impact of the bright interior scene, which in the smaller version starts out more dramatically against the darker front. In that front, artfully disposed in varied postures, five women work at tasks preparatory to the making of a tapestry, including the carding and spinning of the

Figure 20.1   *The Spinners*, or *The Fable of Arachne*, 1657/8 (oil on canvas) by Diego
Rodríguez de Silva y Velázquez. Prado, Madrid, Spain. Photo: Bridgeman Art Library

wool. One of the two most prominent figures, an older woman with her head covered,
faces us as she spins; the other, younger, woman has her back to us and winds thread
into a ball. This is apparently a workshop where the craft activities necessary to produce
a work of art are performed. In the raised room at the back, approached by stairs,
perhaps an artistic atelier, a finished tapestry is displayed. There are five standing
figures, three elegantly dressed women seemingly in costume of Velázquez' day, who
are perhaps viewing the tapestry (though the right-hand figure looks out at us,
challenging us to respond, so to say), one of whom holds something which might be
a musical instrument (Stein 2002) but has also been identified as an implement for
winding completed yarn. There are also a helmeted figure raising her arm (in the
nineteenth century sometimes taken to be male) and a woman facing us with her arm
lowered. These last two figures have been seen as part of the tapestry, but a careful
inspection suggests that they too may stand in front of it. In 1940 they were identified,
by Enriqueta Harris, as Minerva, goddess of handicraft, and Arachne, the mortal
woman who challenged her to a contest in weaving and, though unbeaten in artistry,
was turned into a spider, a story superbly told by Ovid in *Metamorphoses* 6.5–145,
which illustrates both the envy the great artist can arouse and the danger of antagon-
izing a divinity. An inventory of 1664 of possessions of a Spanish courtier includes a

work by Velázquez listed as *The Fable of Arachne*, now thought to be our painting. Do we then have a genre or a mythological painting, or a combination of the two? (Such generic confusions notoriously characterize the poetry of Ovid as well.)

In the later nineteenth century the European popularity of Velázquez increased fairly dramatically, partly as a result of the interest of such artists as Manet and Whistler (previously the work of Murillo had been more widely esteemed, partly because most of Velázquez' major paintings were in Spain, but partly no doubt reflecting larger differences in taste). Yet, so far as we can tell, Velázquez' nineteenth-century admirers knew nothing of any connection between *The Spinners* and Ovid's Arachne (indeed Velázquez was regularly seen as an artist who rejected the classical tradition in favor of realist subjects). This did not stop the influential critic R. A. M. Stevenson (cousin of Robert Louis Stevenson), in what was only the second book on Velázquez in English, declaring it one of his very greatest paintings, the equal of the celebrated *Las meninas* (The ladies in waiting); indeed "more supple and insinuating in its grace of pattern, more enchanting and varied in its treatment of colour and detail" (Stevenson 1899: 59). Ignorance of the "true" subject of the painting (as modern scholarship construes the matter) did not prevent intense aesthetic pleasure or a fully successful reception at this date. The point is instructive and can be generalized. There are all sorts of allusions in ancient poetry we cannot recognize (because the works alluded to have been lost) and whose presence we do not even suspect: that does not diminish one iota the pleasure we now take, say, in Vergil (if new intertexts are found, they will be incorporated into subsequent readings, but for the moment they are not missed).

The Spinners is lucidly satisfying and self-sufficient, while at the same time deeply mysterious; that mysteriousness is more like the rapt mystery of a Vermeer than the bafflement of an allegory by Bellini or Botticelli or Bronzino (where the viewer has the sense that the picture could be decoded if only she had the correct key). Putting Ovid in play creates fresh opportunities for reflection and interpretation, but it does not resolve the ambiguities (indeed the ambiguous character of the image could itself be seen as part of its "Ovidian" character). Ovid has memorable lines on the elegant way Arachne prepares her wool, in which several of the activities shown by Velázquez are included (19–23). Perhaps, then, we can interpret the foreground scene as a depiction of the conflict, with the young woman with her back to us as Arachne and the old woman as the disguised Minerva (this would explain her oddly shapely and youthful bared lower leg) rather than a scene in a contemporary tapestry workshop (but then again the figures are not wearing historical costume). In the end we simply cannot be sure; we do not know whether we have here a history or a genre scene, or both. And the inset scene is also not without its puzzles. If it depicts the moment when Minerva confronts Arachne after the completion of their rival masterpieces, then who are the other three figures? If they are the original audience at the contest, why are they wearing seventeenth-century dress? Or perhaps they are rather modern visitors inspecting a recently made tapestry in an artist's atelier? And might Minerva and Arachne in that case be part of a dumb show, or theatrical performance of some kind? Once again Velázquez seems to confuse history and genre, producing an ambiguous image. As we have seen, the object carried by the woman on the left has been read as either a musical instrument (and as such a traditional antidote to spider-bite)

Figure 20.2 *Europa*, 1559–62 (oil on canvas) by Titian (Tiziano Vecellio) (ca. 1488–1576).
© Isabella Stewart Gardner Museum, Boston, Mass., USA. Photo: Bridgeman Art Library

or an implement used in the making of tapestries. Another painting by Velázquez
provides an analogy: *The Drinkers* in the Prado could be read as representing either
Bacchus and his crew in contemporary dress or, more simply, a group of low-life modern
drunkards. What we can say, in the case of *The Spinners*, is that invoking Ovid makes a
new kind of sense for the whole picture, providing possible links between foreground
and background (and so the women who worked on tapestries becomes the fable of
Arachne).

  The Spinners, in a witty touch worthy of Ovid himself, contains another Ovidian
painting hidden within it, apparently first noted in print by the artist Charles Ricketts in
1903. In Ovid the first scene Arachne depicts, with virtuoso realism, on her web is the
rape of Europa ("a real bull, real waves you would think them," 104), a story already
told by Ovid himself *in propria persona*, creating a characteristic moment of self-
reflexivity, a mise-en-abîme. In *The Spinners* the completed tapestry is largely concealed
by the figures in front of it, but enough is visible (two Cupids careering through the sky
on the left, a young woman with a pink drape cascading over her who rides on a white
bull with clearly visible eye on the right) to identify a reproduction of Titian's *Europa*
(finished by 1562), one of a series of Ovidian mythologies the Venetian master painted
for Philip II of Spain (Fig. 20.2; Barkan 1986: ch. 5; Llewellyn 1988; Goffen

1997: 267–73). It remained in the Spanish royal collection, and as such an object of Velázquez' curatorial responsibilities (as well as admiration), as was a copy of it by Rubens, whom Velázquez had met and whose work he esteemed. Rubens had painted a whole series of Ovidian works for the Torre de la Parada, a royal hunting lodge near Madrid, including a *Minerva and Arachne*, now lost and known only in an oil sketch, which shows the goddess assaulting her rival, with a tapestry on the left depicting Europa and the bull. Rubens also regularly produced designs for tapestries. So the tapestry in *The Spinners* could even be construed as a copy of a copy, and its presence certainly invites thoughts on copying, imitation, and creativity. Velázquez' brilliant technique owes something to Rubens, much to Titian and the Venetian school in respect of both brush-stroke and color. In a wide-ranging discussion Svetlana Alpers explores the presence in *The Spinners* of traces of a number of paintings by Titian, Rubens, and others. Velázquez may also be recreating a lost painting by an ancient artist, Antiphilus, depicting a group of spinners, which is mentioned in Pliny the Elder's *Natural History* 35.138 (Bedaux 1992). Such intertextuality is regularly seen as a hallmark of Ovidian poetry, and both painting and poem are indeed often read as meditations on art – there is a general link in Ovid and the Ovidian tradition between art and illusion and metamorphosis.

Titian's series of Ovidian mythologies ought to be as much an artistic reference point with educated persons as the plays of Shakespeare (that they are not is an index of how much Anglophone education still remains more literary than visual). They are similar in kind, though superior in execution and power, to such early modern mythological narratives after Ovid as Marlowe's *Hero and Leander* and Shakespeare's *Venus and Adonis*, and, like these, they display a fully revived paganism, a preoccupation with sex (on the borders of pornography?) in all its polymorphic perversity, freedom from obvious allegory, art for beauty's sake, and an emotional ambivalence. One aspect of Ovid's seriocomic masterpiece that has regularly worried his more straight-laced inter-preters is the uncertainty, or complexity, of tone. A single episode may be by turns ludicrous, pathetic, tragic, grotesque, gay, grave, and much else besides, or (discon-certingly) more than one of these at the same moment. Titian can be interpreted as providing a painterly equivalent for all this by combining, in a single image, qualities not often previously found together in painting. *Europa* is obviously erotic, as the woman's semi-naked body, splayed over the bull's back, is displayed to our voyeuristic gaze (her legs are parted in a way that draws that gaze towards her – concealed – genitals). It is also witty, with the ebullient flying Cupids overhead, the swirling red drape around Europa's head, and, above all, the bull's knowing eye-contact with us (like the drape a feature of the iconographic tradition that goes back to antiquity) – he knows that we know he is not really a bull; he knows too that the viewer, even if he or she affects disapproval, may well share his erotic interest in Europa. But the painting, a painting of rape (however happy the eventual outcome), has undercurrents too of menace and fear: Europa clinging for dear life to the bull's horn (her awkward posture perhaps alluding to the figure of Dirce in the once-famous ancient sculpture-group known as the *Farnese Bull* in Naples); the dangerous romantic landscape to the left, with the tiny figures of Europa's companions gesturing towards her; the dark clouds on the right, the darkening and tempestuous seas ahead into which the bull is heading, the sinister monstrous fish with prominent teeth in the waters below. The incorporation of these ambivalences into an image of swirling motion constitutes the full discovery of a baroque mode, prefigured by the leap of Bacchus in Titian's *Bacchus and Ariadne* in the National Gallery, London. In a *paragone* with poetry Titian shows the full range of his technique as a painter, the variety of brushstroke, from delicate and precise to loose and broad, the brilliantly contrasting colors (whites, blues, flesh-tints, the bold slash of deep pink), the virtuoso realism (the sunlight on the hair of the Cupid riding the dolphin, the dramatic foreshortening of the flying Cupids): "a real bull, real waves you would think them." Titian may have more that is interesting to tell us about the *Metamorphoses* than many of Ovid's academic critics (which is not to deny that some of that criticism also informs my reading of Titian).

Titian, we are told, read Ovid in the translation of his contemporary Lodovico Dolce, but he undoubtedly received advice as well from others more classically learned in conventional terms than himself. The art historian Rona Goffen argues that in depicting Europa, Titian was tacitly putting himself into the subject position of Ovid's Arachne (if, perhaps, without the presumption, at least in the full know-ledge of the envy, *invidia*, so often aroused by great art). What he offers us is "a tapestry woven in pigment applied with unprecedented freedom that recalls the artistic act of creation" (Goffen 1997: 272). Ovid's description of the skill of Minerva and Arachne as colorists would serve just as well for Titian, famous for *colore*:

> While they cheer the eye
> With glowing purple of the Tyrian dye,
> Or, justly intermixing shades with light,
> Their colourings insensibly unite.
> As when a shower transpierced with sunny rays
> Its mighty arch along the heaven displays,
> From whence a thousand different colours rise,
> Whose fine transition cheats the clearest eyes,
> So like the intermingled shading seems,
> And only differs in the last extremes.
> Then threads of gold both artfully dispose,
> And, as each part in just proportion rose,
> Some antique fable in their work disclose.
>   (61–9, trans. Samuel Croxall, from Samuel Garth's composite version of 1717)

Classical scholars likewise argue that Ovid links himself as an artist with Arachne. Not only does he use words throughout the episode that could be applied to poetry in general and to his own poetry in particular[1] (the link is made easier because poetry was regularly associated with spinning and weaving), but also he explicitly makes Arachne into an Ovidian metamorphic artist, whose work, lacking the classical formality of Minerva's, depicts the transformations of gods to seduce mortal women in riotous abundance, starting with Ovid's own Europa:

> There might you see the gods in sundry shapes
> Committing heady riots, incest, rapes.
>   (Marlowe, *Hero and Leander*, Sestiad 1, 143–4)

3   Conclusions

Reflecting on *The Spinners*, prompting as it does questions about the nature of perception and reality and about art and narrative, provides an excellent point of entry into Ovid's metamorphic world. Velázquez had more than one translation of Ovid in his personal library, but we do not know whether *The Spinners* involved a direct response to Ovid's text, or one largely or wholly mediated by the Ovidian tradition in the visual arts. Arachne after all was a well-known figure, and Velázquez could have found all he needed in works of art available in the royal collection. Claiming that the painting is an important reception of Ovid does not require us to resolve that issue. My point is rather that putting *The Spinners* and the *Metamorphoses* into conjunction with each other can produce, in the resulting pleasurable free-play of our mental faculties, what Kant, the philosopher of the aesthetic, calls "aesthetic ideas," ideas, that is, which do not involve immediate closure or strict determination. Poem and painting can then mutually illuminate each other, suggesting interpretive possibilities without closing discussion down. This process may suggest to us something about Ovid, or Velázquez, or Titian in Velázquez' reception of him, that we had not considered before. Titian's *Europa*, like most other paintings after Ovid, shows us how one Ovidian story could be interesting. *The Spinners*, with its lack of clear linear logic, gestures towards how Ovid's poem might be found exciting *as a whole*. It does this by finding an equivalent for Ovid's subordination of story to story by means of its unusual spatial representation, with the curious Chinese-box effect of receding images (on four planes) that are hard to make sense of. The painting also encourages us to explore the links between art, and the reception of art, and metamorphosis. One great change that *The Spinners* depicts (one that recalls Pythagoras' list of changes in the natural world in *Metamorphoses* 15) is the transformation of wool into a completed work of art; we see the beginning and end of that process (which requires a humble craft base as well as supreme artistry in execution), but there is no sign of loom or of anyone weaving the tapestry. The change is at once natural and miraculous, as extraordinary in its way as the change of caterpillar into butterfly, or ugly cygnet into swan. If we insist that the relationship of past and present can only be unidirectional, we shall miss much of the benefit that such "correspondences" (to use a word of the poet Charles Baudelaire) can bestow. But within a Jaussian framework of interpretation, *The Spinners* becomes not only the fable of Arachne, but also a fable about reception.

Reception theory provides a methodology for dealing with any body of material, from the past or present. But does reception have a special role to play within classics? I would argue that it does, for at least two reasons, the first pragmatic, the second a point of principle. The pragmatic consideration is that reception provides a way of compensating for the loss of so much of the archive. If we take the case of Sappho, only the tiniest fraction of her work survives, and that in fragmentary form. Yet the quality of some of those fragments is such that some have thought her one of the greatest poets of all time, including the poet Algernon Charles Swinburne (no mean judge, as someone who regularly corrected the mistakes of Benjamin Jowett,

Master of Balliol, as he translated Plato's Greek). Positivist attempts to give us "the real Sappho" in her original context founder, if there were no other reason, on the lack of reliable ancient *testimonia*; such attempts seem all too evidently fictions, fictions only lightly constrained by data, highly speculative in character, and with an unusually evident coloring of ideology. Much discussion centers round the issue of Sappho and sex; but that Sappho was a lesbian (or not) can be represented – precisely from a historicist perspective – as a modern invention, involving the assimilation of her sexuality (whatever that might have been) to current concerns, and one that is, in significant measure, the creation of Baudelaire and Swinburne. However, if we adopt a reception approach, a vein of great richness immediately opens up before us, with abundant material for us to work on and with. For much of antiquity one can write a reception history, or no history at all (so Prettejohn 2006 in connection with ancient art).

Even more important is the consideration of principle. Classics registers in its very title a claim that the products of antiquity are in some sense exemplary for Western culture; the word's first recorded use in something like its modern sense is in Aulus Gellius, where it denotes a first-class and tax-paying author (not a proletarian without property), an author who endures. Gadamer catches the paradoxical consequences of this:

> The classical preserves itself precisely *because* it is significant in itself and interprets itself; i.e., it speaks in such a way that it is not a statement about what is past – documentary evidence that still needs to be interpreted – rather, it says something to the present as if it were said specifically to it. What we call "classical" does not first require the overcoming of historical distance, for in its own constant mediation it overcomes this distance by itself. The classical, then, is certainly "timeless," but this timelessness is a mode of historical being. . . . But understanding it will always involve *more* than merely reconstructing the past "world" to which the work belongs. Our understanding will always retain the consciousness that we too belong to that world, and correlatively, that the work too belongs to our world. (Gadamer 1989: 289–90)

It is precisely in the writings of Dante, Milton, T. S. Eliot, and the rest that Vergil remains a classic; among the best reasons for reading Homer is that one of the most important narratives of the twentieth century is Joyce's *Ulysses*. Classicists who believe that their attention should be confined to antiquity ought in justice to rename themselves and their discipline. Gadamer's formulation suppresses the issue of agency, but the agents in the process he describes are of course readers, and more readers can always join in. Classics has often been condemned as elitist (and Aulus Gellius' "classic" obviously has class connotations), but, configured in this light as the constant (re)creation of readers, it can assert with pride its democratic credentials as well as its cultural value. In the words of the novelist Philip Pullman:

> When you're reading you are the equal partner in the making of meaning, we are in control of the speed process. . . . When we've finished reading, we bring away what we ourselves and the text have made together. If we don't contribute, if we don't take part, we get nothing. If we do, we get a world. That's what I mean by the democracy of the

text and it's why printing and publishing and libraries and literacy and booksellers and writers and books are more necessary than ever and why reading and democracy are not different things not even different aspects of something else; they are the very same thing. (quoted in Rebuck 2004: 35)[2]

FURTHER READING

The two best short introductions to reception theory are both by Holub (1984, 1995). Behind both Iser (1980) and Jauss (1982) lies Gadamer (1989, but first published in German in 1960). For reception theory and classics, see Martindale (1993) and Martindale and Thomas (2006); for the current constitution of the field, Beard and Henderson (1995) and Hardwick (2003a, with full bibliography). For the reception of Velázquez, see Stratton-Pruitt (2003).

NOTES

1 So e.g., *artis* (8); *studio* (12); *opus admirabile* (14); *decor* (18); *mollibat* (21); *levi teretem* (22); *gracili* (54); *docta* (60); *texitur ... tenues* (62); *deducitur* (69); *inscribit* (74); *elusam ... imagine* (103); *intertextos* (128); *livor* (129).
2 I would like to thank David Hopkins, Miriam Leonard, and Liz Prettejohn for help and advice.

CHAPTER TWENTY-ONE

Postcolonial Studies

Lorna Hardwick

A smell of dead limes quickens in the nose
The leprosy of empire....
Marble like Greece, like Faulkner's South in stone
Deciduous beauty prospered and is gone.

D. Walcott, "Ruins of a Great House"

1 Introduction

Postcolonial "classics" involves rereading and rewriting classical texts. Some of these rewritings are also great literature. Both senses of the word "classics" come together in the work of three recent Nobel prize winners, Seamus Heaney, Wole Soyinka, and Derek Walcott, all of whom have refigured Greek and Roman material in the contexts of their own classical traditions and in postcolonial contexts. They have used classical referents as a way of exploring their own cultural identities and those of their societies, as have other major figures such as Aimé Césaire, Tony Harrison, Michael Longley, Femi Òsòfisan, and Ola Rotimi.

The term "postcolonial" is used here to cover mental and cultural attitudes and practices rather than to describe the chronology of changes in political power and institutions. Writing, art, and thought can become "postcolonial" in advance of political independence. Equally, colonial attitudes can persist after notional independence (Ngugi 1986). This is true both of colonizing and colonized societies. Divisions between colonizers and colonized can also be fluid and include those who move between the two and those who occupy space between (Saïd 1988; Bhabha 1994).

Because of the association between classics and political and cultural elites (Stray 1998) and the appropriation of Greek and Roman culture by western colonizers, the processes of political and cultural struggle have been problematic for classical

Figure 21.1 *Oidipus*, performed in a disused quarry in Toowoomba, Queensland, Australia, 2000. The production was in the original Greek and used Greek theatrical conventions (chorus, masks). Courtesy Greg McCart. "Similarities between ancient Greek culture and contemporary Aboriginal culture in Australia, especially with respect to a religious affinity to the earth and to the immediate presence of gods or spirits, prompted the adoption of choral choreography grounded in Aboriginal dance and the use of Aboriginal music and dance in the production" (Greg McCart, <http://playingwithtragedy.usq.edu.au/content/index.php> as cited January 2006). To the left of Oidipus (not shown) is an aboriginal didgeridoo player. This part of the illustration has been deleted to comply with Australian legislation on the representation of Aboriginal people. We wish to acknowledge by means of this caption the musical contribution to the live performance.

learning, which has become in different contexts both an emblem of liberation and a symbol of imperialism and of neocolonialism.

Each postcolonial context is different, as are the histories of the transmission and use of particular works and the subjective experiences of the writers.

This web of theory and practice impacts on the central concerns of this chapter in four main ways: the language and idiom in which classical material is reworked; the role of classical referents in challenging and reshaping assumptions about genealogy, suffering, and victim status; the mapping of cultural exchange and the construction of identities; and the deappropriation of colonial classicizing and the reappropriation of texts and themes in the creation of new artistic forms and cultural narratives.

Inevitably, pressures of space restrict what can be discussed, so I have decided to concentrate on practice rather than theory, to focus on literature in Anglophone contexts, and to choose examples that allow discussion of the relationship between private and public voices. Further studies on art and architecture, on political philosophy, and on Francophone culture will be important in the future (and see already Davis 1997a).

Because this is a relatively new area of practice and research, narratives and analyses are still in the process of construction (Hardwick 2006a). I have therefore tried to include examples of the main approaches that will need to be brought together in a full study of the topic. The three main sections of the chapter each approach my subject from a different starting point and focus, respectively, on people, places, and paradigms. So the first part of the chapter examines through discussion of particular texts the relationship between an individual writer and the traditions of which he is a part, focusing, of course, on the classical. The second section offers an overview of the genesis of new classical traditions in African drama and their migration to the west. The third section brings together African, Caribbean, and European intersections between cultural memory, history, and the role of classical referents in the construction of postcolonial senses of identity. I suggest, tentatively, that practice is outrunning theory and that we are now experiencing the emergence of new traditions in the transmission and reception of the classics, in all senses of the word.

2   Postcolonial Classical Rewriting in Ireland: The Case of Seamus Heaney

In his poem "Bann Valley Eclogue" Seamus Heaney's invocation is "Help me to please my hedge-schoolmaster Virgil" (Heaney 2001: 11–12). Heaney is from a Catholic, nationalist, and rural background and the line encapsulates the relationship between the classical tradition in Irish cultural memory, the resistance of that tradition to colonial domination by the English, and Heaney's own use of classical texts as fields in which he can work through and revisit his cultural and political dilemmas.

   Classical texts and education were rooted in Ireland via early association with continental Europe and the coming of Christianity, in advance of the successive arrivals of colonizing Normans, Elizabethans, Cromwellians, and Williamites. It is this "indigenous" classical tradition that particularly distinguishes the anticolonial and postcolonial use of classical material in Ireland from that of other postcolonial situations, in which classical education and its associated traditions were something brought by colonizers, even if they were sometimes embraced with aspirational enthusiasm by the recipients.

   The hedge-schools to which Heaney refers were a dissenting response to the penal laws (ca. 1690–1795) imposed by the English in Ireland. These banned formal education for Catholic children. In defiance, informal schools were held in rural barns and sheds, and tradition had it that what was offered there included Greek and Latin literature. There is dispute about the historical facts surrounding the "hedge-schools," but they have a symbolic force in the cultural memory that is preserved in poems such as "A Poor Scholar of the Forties" by Padraig Colum (1881–1972) and "Lines in a Roman School book" by Desmond O'Grady (born 1935), which recalls times when poets

> . . . . kept alive
> the way of life that's ours by conversation –
> just as that other hedge school master talked
> in his muddled marketplace under the Attic sun and paid the price extorted.
>   (O'Grady, in Kinsella 1986)

The language of this extract shows the way in which Greco-Roman figures were appropriated for a rural anticolonialist tradition in which a combination of subversion and martyrdom lurked just beneath the surface. Anonymous epigrams translated from the Irish in the eighteenth century attest to the role of the hedge-schools as a vigorous link between indigenous culture and classical learning (Hardwick 2000a: ch. 5). The image of the fall of Troy was used as a touchstone for resistance to English domination of Ireland, with the Irish cast as Greeks.

The descendants of the Trojans, the Romans, were also regarded as agents through which the Irish might use classical culture to resist colonial domination. This tradition was drawn on by Brian Friel in his play "Translations" (Friel 1981). This was one of the first works created for the Field Day Theatre Company of Derry, which took "translation" both as its central focus and as an indicator of cultural and political change. Friel's play explored the impact on the rural Ireland of the 1830s of the Ordnance Survey that substituted English place names for Irish. It also explored the effects of the national schools that imposed English-medium education on all Irish children. The play highlighted the resistance of the hedge-school tradition and also illuminated the potential of Latin, and especially Vergil, as a cultural bridge between opposing groups who could not otherwise understand one another linguistically or culturally. Translation, literally and metaphorically, has been a crucial activity for Ireland, partly because Irish oral and written literatures developed in and through interaction between the Irish language and other European languages, including Latin, and partly because of the role of translations of various kinds in reliving and recreating symbolic stories and phases of history (Welch 1993; Cronin 1996). Retelling may point to cultural continuity and overlap; it may also highlight fracture and discontinuity (Deane 1991–2002: intro.).

Thus Seamus Heaney's classical work is situated in a classical tradition that is unique to Ireland, derived from and associated with an early interplay in Irish cultural history between the classical and the indigenous. This interplay constantly subverted any attempts by the English to use classical culture as a means of embedding Ascendancy domination. It meant that the Irish classical tradition could use Greek and Roman texts as allegories for political debate without fatal association with the colonizers. In 1840 the activist Thomas Davis conceded in his address to the Trinity College History Society in Dublin that even though knowledge of the ancient world should give way to that of the modern and there would not be time to learn the ancient languages, nevertheless translations of key texts offered moral and political insights of value to nationalists (Deane 1991–2002: 1271–2).

The late twentieth century was a crucial time in reassessing the situation of the north of Ireland, in which even after Irish independence in 1922 and the establishment of the Irish Republic in 1948, six counties still remained part of the United Kingdom (Britain and Northern Ireland). From the 1980s there was a plethora of translations and adaptations of Greek tragedy by Irish writers both north and south of the border. Some of these focused on the power struggles in the north between nationalists (mainly Catholics) and loyalists (mainly Protestants). Others focused on other aspects of social change such as gender roles (Dillon and Wilmer 2005; Hardwick 2000a: ch. 5; McDonald and Walton 2002). The vigorously political agenda of many of these modern rewritings led to heated debate about the aesthetic and cultural justification of creating close equivalences between the themes and situations of Greek drama and those of present politics. There was concern that apparently radical work might actually have the opposite effect if it transmitted a quasi-Aristotelian acceptance of the desirability of the cathartic effects of pity and fear on the spectators. It was suggested that this might actually undermine their sense of human responsibility for shaping a better future and might encourage acceptance of the inevitability of the cycle of revenge (Richards 1995: 191–200).

These issues also lead to a related question, that concerning the political and moral engagement of the writer and the power of drama and poetry to influence and to change. Seamus Heaney has visited and revisited these debates in both poetry and prose. He has recognized the power of the poetic imagination while being cautious about attributing to poetry a capacity to change the world. In "The Frontiers of Writing," he speaks of poetry as offering "a glimpsed alternative" (Heaney 1995: 186–203). He continues the discussion with the aspiration "To be at the same time a source of truth and at the same time a vehicle of harmony; this expresses what we would like poetry to be." The language resonates with his Christian Catholic background but is also related to the crisis of identity that he faced as a nationalist poet in the north of Ireland, especially in the violence of the Troubles during the last third of the twentieth century. In terms of identity he has asserted that "my passport is green" (Irish); yet he was criticized both for identifying too closely with republican nationalism and for not identifying closely enough with it. The conflict within Heaney was partly about political justifications for violence and partly about the tensions between the public and the private in poetry: "whatever the possibilities of achieving harmony at a political level, I wanted to affirm that within our individual selves we can reconcile two orders of knowledge, which we might call the practical and the poetic" (Heaney 1995: 203). Heaney's classical work is the crucial field for his exploration of the sometimes-conflicting pressures of the practical and the poetic at an individual level. This takes place through a process of visiting and revisiting Greek and Roman texts and forms, and in so doing he exemplifies as a postcolonial subject the process of engagement with past, present, and future.

In "Exposure," which is the closing sequence to "Singing School" in his collection *North* (Heaney 1975: 66–7), he describes his internal exile in County Wicklow in the Irish Republic. The Heaneys had moved from Derry (in the north) to Glanmore Cottage in Wicklow (in the Republic) in the wake of the Bloody Sunday atrocity (January 31, 1972) in which 14 civil rights protestors had been killed in Derry by British troops. In the poem Heaney expresses his agony of mind:

> As I sit weighing and weighing
> My responsible *tristia*
> ... I am neither internee nor informer
> An inner émigré, grown long-haired
> And thoughtful; a wood kerne
> ... Escaped from the massacre.
>   (Heaney 1975: 66–7)

The ambivalent invocation of Ovid's exile is combined with allusion to the disparaging reference in Edmund Spenser's *A View from the present state of Ireland* (1596) to the wood kerns, the starving soldiers of Cork, driven to the hills by the English army. The stress on weighing and balancing, of being neither of two extremes and yet as a consequence always in anxiety in the hope of reaching harmony, increases Heaney's need for further "classical ground" on which to work out his dilemmas. As he wrote in an early poem "Terminus":

> Two buckets were easier carried than one
> I grew up in between.
> ... Is it any wonder, when I thought
> I would have second thoughts.
> (Heaney 1998: 295–6, first published 1987)

Part of Heaney's dilemma is how to reconcile the violent traditions of both the agricultural and political aspects of the rural culture in which he grew up with his desire for harmony and reconciliation. In his poetry, memory of a rural childhood is never perfectly idyllic but is expressed with what has been called "an aggressive, even militaristic diction, emphasising at once the integrity of his culture and the violence that has become part of its daily ritual" (Burris 1990). In his classical work Heaney grapples with this tension in the wider sphere of cultural memory and politics. In the opening sequence to "Mycenae Lookout" (Heaney 1996), he exploits the image in the opening sequence of Aeschylus' *Agamemnon* (lines 36–9) of the ox on the Watchman's tongue. It is the ox on his tongue that prevents the Watchman from speaking out clearly about what he knows of the House of Atreus. The poem is one of the most violent of Heaney's creations. Its language straddles the worlds of Heaney the aspiring bringer of harmony and Heaney the radical pastoral poet who uses the language of violence and strife to convey the realities of the Irish rural tradition and of human history. This recreation of the ox on the tongue sees it as like "the dropped gangplank of a cattle truck / Trampled and rattled, running piss and muck." Despite the weight on his tongue, however, the Watchman is "still honour bound" to look beyond the limitations of his own existence, "beyond the city and the border." He is a repository of knowledge about the past of the house of Atreus and about its internal workings and the way in which they will lead to future disasters. Like the poet, he comments on, but does not intervene in, the action.

Heaney develops this relationship between classical allusion and open comment in his sequence of classically based poems "Sonnets from Hellas" in *Electric Light* (2001). "The Augean Stables" picks up the motif from the labors of Heracles and, in an elegiac sestet, associates the cleansing of the filth of the stables (resonant with the daily work in a farmyard) with the cleansing following a sectarian murder in Ireland, where they

> ... imagined
> Hose-water smashing hard back off the asphalt
> In the car-park where his athlete's blood ran cold.

The volume *Electric Light* is also remarkable for its specific engagement with Vergil. It includes variations on Eclogue 9 and a gently ironic reflection on the poet's internal exile in "Glanmore Eclogue." "Bann Valley Eclogue" specifically alludes to Vergil's "Fourth Eclogue" (Harrison 2007 forthcoming; Heaney 2003; Tweddie 2006). These poems have been said to exploit classical material in order for Heaney to leave behind his "roots" and to universalize. The implication is that by accepting his Latin education, Heaney "casts off provincialism" and becomes "magnificently authoritative" (Mackinnon 2001). Such judgments are misplaced. They miss the intertwining of the classical and the rural traditions in Heaney's work and how his "provincialism," that is, the way his poetic technique is rooted in the life-enhancing rural environment, is actually given greater authority in his dialogue with Vergil.

Heaney allied his rural ground with the Latin tradition of unidealized pastoral, a pastoral in which Vergil became the inspiration of what Richard Thomas has called "The Georgics of Resistance." Thomas contrasted those who, as in eighteenth-century English poetry, transformed Vergil through "an idealisation bred of comfort and tranquillity" with poets like Heaney who took from Vergil the combination of recognition of troubles, in which the agrarian and the political interacted, and a guarded optimism that better things might be possible (Thomas 2001b). In "Bann Valley Eclogue" Heaney uses Vergil's conversational question-and-answer technique to avert pessimism and personal and social disruption while still questioning complacency and nostalgia. "Bann Valley Eclogue" is not merely a cultural intertext, but also a linguistic one. Vergil's prompts are to explore the resonances of his own words in Heaney's contexts: "Here are my words you'll have to find a place for: / *Carmen, ordo, nascitur, saeculum, gens*. Their gist in your tongue and province should be clear: Even at this stage. Poetry, order, the times." The association of pollution, of blood guilt, with the reductive notion of earth is exposed: "Whatever stains you, you rubbed it into yourselves." Then the breaking of the waters in the forthcoming birth of a child will, like the overflowing of the waters of the Bann, wash the valley. In the closing lines of the poem, the poet returns to the images and associations of the rural Irish ground, but this is now enhanced and liberated through its encounter with the classical. Heaney's "classical ground" is the site for weighing and balancing, for redressing the sterility associated with nostalgia and for revitalizing the insights afforded by a pastoralism that is, like Vergil's, both powerful and dangerous. He excavates Irish identity and memory via the land, from the prehistoric bogs to the twenty-first century fields, interrogated by his "hedge-schoolmaster."

Heaney's process of engagement with classical texts and traditions, personal experience, and the Irish postcolonial context has been more problematic, however, in the more public area of drama. He has adapted two Greek tragedies, *The Cure at Troy: A Version* of *Sophocles' Philoctetes* (Heaney 1990), commissioned for touring by the Field Day Theatre Company, and *The Burial at Thebes: Sophocles' Antigone* (Heaney 2004), which was commissioned to mark the celebration in 2004 of the centenary of the Abbey Theatre in Dublin. Both of these Sophoclean texts are resonant for postcolonial situations (Hardwick 2006a and 2006b; Wilmer forthcoming).

Antigone was a key text in addressing the political situation in Ireland in the 1980s, notably in Tom Paulin's version *The Riot Act* (Paulin 1985). The play has also been adapted by the Barbadian writer Kamau Brathwaite (*Odale's Choice*, first performed 1962) and the Nigerian Femi Òsòfisan (*Tegonni: An African Antigone*, first performed 1994) as well as providing the central "play within a play" for the South African collaboration by Athol Fugard, John Kani, and Winston Ntshona, *The Island* (first performed 1973), which in its many revivals has become an icon of the struggle against apartheid. *Philoctetes* is particularly resonant for the Irish classical tradition because of the play's treatment of the key role of his bow in bringing about the fall of Troy, the city that early Irish poetry had identified with the power of the English.

In both his versions, Heaney followed quite closely the Sophoclean structure and the conventions of Greek drama. In *Cure* the vocabulary and speech rhythms of Heaney's Irish-English locate the play in the context of the Troubles in the North of Ireland.

The figure of Philoctetes was widely read as an image of sectarian intransigence, and the Choral Odes (written in verse but spoken, not sung) alluded to the sufferings of both communities. Heaney noted that he had used verse "in order to preserve something of the formal ritualistic quality of the Greek theatrical experience" but had also felt free to compose some new lines for the Chorus (Programme Notes 1991). The Chorus line "where hope and history rhyme" was taken up by politicians in the 1990s, culminating in press headlines at the time of the Good Friday Agreement (1998; Hardwick 2003a: ch. 6). Critics found the insertion into the Choral Odes of references to the bereaved from both communities ("the hunger-striker's father" and "the Policeman's widow") to be anachronistic, and Heaney later questioned their aesthetic value (Wilmer 1999).

Figure 21.2 *Cure at Troy* (Oxford Touring Company) was first directed by Helen Eastman at the Edinburgh Fringe Festival, 4–30 August, 1999, followed by performances at The Old Fire Station, Oxford, 4–23 October, 1999. Eastman later co-founded Floodtide Theatre Company with which she revised *Cure at Troy* (Battersea Arts Centre, 19–20 August, 2003 and on tour). This photograph is from the 2003 revival production at the Battersea Arts Centre. Director Helen Eastman. Photo: Floodtide Theatre Company, courtesy Helen Eastman. The lighting in the production – dark space with cast using torches and personal head lamps – was designed to bring out the allusions to light in the Sophocles and Heaney texts.

In *Burial* Heaney composed the Choral Odes without direct response to modern politics. Yet the richly textured language of the play alluded to various aspects of Irish colonial history and the stages of disengagement from colonialism. In discussing the background to the commissioning of the play and his composition of the work, Heaney has commented on two strands in Irish colonial and postcolonial history. The first is the oppression of Irish people by the English colonizers, expressed in an eighteenth-century poem in Irish, *Lament for Art O'Leary*, by Eibhlin Dubh Ni Chonaill. This poem is a widow's lament for her young husband, shot by the English and left to rot at the roadside, and calls for justice and revenge. Heaney took this as a paradigm for the situation in the *Antigone* in which Antigone demands proper burial for her brother. In interviews and program notes at the time of the production, Heaney also drew attention to a second "postcolonial" strand: the allusions to the 2003 invasion and the occupation of Iraq by a US-led coalition, in which the UK was also prominent. Heaney wove into Creon's speeches echoes of the words of United States President George W. Bush in a way that suggested correspondences between Creon's treatment of Polyneices and the "war against terror" ("whoever isn't for us / Is against us in this case"; Heaney 2004: 3).

Heaney also said that he was somewhat daunted by the precedent of W. B. Yeats's versions of Sophocles. *Oedipus Tyrannos* (1926) and *Oedipus at Colonus* (1927) were staged at the Abbey Theatre. Yeats was a cofounder of the Abbey and a moving force in Irish cultural nationalism (Saïd 1988b). His Oedipus plays represent another strand in the classical tradition in Ireland and, like Heaney but perhaps more loosely, Yeats had used the English translations of Richard Jebb (first published 1883–1900). Heaney described his version of the *Antigone* as a rewriting in his own English, and the text was widely praised as a brilliant poetic version. It ran into problems, however, when it was staged, directed by the Quebecoise Lorriane Pintal. The postcolonial aesthetics of Heaney's idiom and the braiding of his Irish-English lost impact because the mise-en-scène transplanted the Irish tradition of classical adaptation into another context, that of a Latin American dictator, in which the flamboyant costume of Creon and the brutalist set jarred with the words. This perhaps suggests the need for directors and writers to work more closely together. In terms of the subject of this discussion, the debacle reemphasizes the distinctiveness of the relationship between the Irish national memory and the Irish classical tradition and Heaney's development of both.

3   Texts and Counter-Texts: African Contexts

Heaney's Vergil was not only a Dante-esque guide to cultural memory, but also an interlocutor for the present and future. The use of classical texts as interrogators, explicit and implicit, rather than models is a characteristic of postcolonial classics. This suggestive questioning has been developed in late twentieth- and early twenty-first-century rewritings of Greek drama by African writers and directors. In South Africa the translation, performance, and adaptation of Greek drama, often in workshop contexts, was culturally and politically important in the resistance to apartheid. In the new South Africa, workshop theater has moved on from being an art form of protest and consciousness-raising and is reconstructing and revising cultural relation-ships. It has brought together different performance traditions and languages and built an intracultural theater, notably in the productions of Euripides' *Medea* (1994–6) and *In the City of Paradise* (1998, based on the Electra myth), directed by Mark Fleishman (Mezzabotta 2000; Steinmeyer forthcoming).

In West Africa, adaptations of Greek drama have also been important, but the context is different. Between 1960 and 2004 there were eight modern adaptations of Greek plays into English or French (Budelmann 2005). Most of these dated from the 1960s and early 1970s, and there was a preponderance of Nigerian writers using the English language. Classical education in schools and universities had given West Africa its own classical traditions, and unthinking mimicry of the imperial version of classical education

Figure 21.3 *Medea*, performed in three South African centers in the period 1994–6. Directed by Mark Fleishman and Jennie Reznek. Photo: Ruphin Coudyzer. Medea is played by Bo Petersen

and values was a source of satire (Gibbs forthcoming). The links between the University of Ibadan and the Universities of London and Leeds (which involved the West African writers Wole Soyinka and Christopher Okigbo and the British poet and dramatist Tony Harrison) fostered the exchange of ideas, cultural politics, and writing techniques, as did the French links of Femi Òsòfisan and the time spent in Boston by Ola Rotimi.

There are two important aspects in the "new traditions" developed by these writers. The first is the international movement of writers, directors, and productions, some of which were commissioned and first performed in Europe or the United States. Some aspects of this tendency are found in other areas of postcolonial culture, for example in the "diaspora" of Indian novelists to the west and the impact of British-born writers of Indian descent. The trajectory is in the direction of cosmo-politanism and hybridity between different cultural forms. The second important aspect of West African adaptations of Greek drama is that they involve a complex set of counter-discourses that not only, or even primarily, involve protest against former colonizers but allude critically to the sociopolitics of West Africa, both historically and in the more recent times after independence (Budelmann 2005). These critiques of postcolonial regimes in Africa have exposed dramatists such as Soyinka and Òsòfisan to accusations of cultural and political disloyalty.

The appropriation of Greek tragedy for African counter-discourse provides an important perspective on the dissociation of Greek tragedy from the literature of colonialism. Among the possible reasons suggested for this are some similarities between Greek and African (especially Yoruba) theater traditions, the importance of myth in Greek and African culture, the nature of the themes and debates in tragedy, and the difference between the Athenian *archē* (empire) and modern imperialism. A crucial point is that the Athenian dramatists were themselves refiguring and reinventing myth at a time of social and political change. To these one might add the desire of African dramatists to get African theater on the international stage and the European and North American interest in the exotic (a means both of assuaging postcolonial angst and of reappropriating Greek drama for metropolitan audiences).

A prime example of a play that relates to several of these contexts and offers several strands of meaning in different phases of its performance history is Ola Rotimi's *The Gods Are Not to Blame*, which takes Sophocles' *Oedipus Tyrannos* as its antetext. Rotimi, who died in 2000, believed in the importance of drama as an indigenous African artistic medium for expression and exploration (McDonald 2000: 95–108). He was educated in Nigeria and at the universities of Boston and Yale. He was twice a Fulbright Fellow and was for 20 years a university academic in Nigeria. *The Gods Are Not to Blame* was first performed by the Ori Olokun Acting Company in 1968 and published in 1971. It is set in a three-day period in Nigeria in the fifteenth century. Although it does not deal overtly with colonization or decolonization, it is concerned with the experiences of having land invaded and occupied and with intertribal conflict. Odewale/Oedipus says at the end:

> I do not blame the gods they knew my weakness: the weakness of a man easily moved to the defence of his tribe against others. I once slew a man on my farm in Ede. I could have spared him. But he spat on my tribe. He spat on the tribe I thought was my own tribe.... . I lost my reason.

This represents an implicit comment on, and slight shift from, the perspective in Sophocles, *Oedipus Tyrannos* 1329: "Apollo brought these sufferings upon me, but I myself accomplished them." Rotimi's play was sometimes interpreted as a metaphor for issues raised by the Nigerian Civil War of 1966, often called the Biafran Civil War (Macintosh 2001). It has also been read as using the Oedipus story as a metaphor for the impact of colonialism and of the psychology of its denial. The printed text of 1971 gives the Choruses in both the Yoruba and English languages, a practice further developed in the multilingual techniques in Femi Òsòfisan's *Women of Owu*, a rewriting of Euripides' *The Women of Troy* in an 1820s Nigerian setting that was premiered in Britain in 2004 (Budelmann forthcoming). Rotimi's play was revived in London in 2005 at the Arcola Theatre, a community theater in Hackney, by Tiata Fahodzi (Theater of the Emancipation). The director was Femi Elufowoju Jr., a British director of African descent who had already directed a highly regarded production of *Medea* in a West African setting with an all-black cast at the West Yorkshire Playhouse in Leeds in 2003. In preproduction interviews, Elufowoju spoke of the intense effect that Rotimi's play had had on him at his first theatrical experience in 1975, when as a boy of 11 he saw a revival performed in a reconstructed Greek amphitheater at a university campus in Ife, western Nigeria. He spoke of that production as "my baptism into African theatre tradition."

African theater tradition was the governing factor in Elufowoju's approach; indeed, in preparing the 2005 production, he revisited Nigeria to consult the original cast about crucial aspects of the play, such as the rhythms of the movements that go with the songs but are not in the text (Cripps 2005: 49). By 2005 the impact of the Biafran War was fading and audiences responded to the play more in terms of allusion to the role of African communities in facing contemporary problems, perhaps especially in the context of the "Make Poverty History" campaign that was high-profile at the time. The early scene in which Odewale advises the villagers on their responsibility for taking action to combat sickness among children drew an audible response from the multiracial audience (documented from the performance of June 11, 2005). Most important of all in this intersection of Greek, African, and British classical and theatrical traditions was the use of lament, especially as sung in Yoruba by the Antigone figure after the blinding of Oedipus. This marked a change in register in a way impossible in the emotionally and ritually constrained English language and tradition. The production as a whole is also significant as an indicator of the way in which the international migrations of ancient texts, modern writers, and theater performers, together with the cultural diversity of postcolonial audiences, create performances in which different strands of meaning are interwoven and activated according to the changing contexts within which they are received.

The postcolonial conversations in this play were, in this production, brought back to a site in the country that had imposed colonial regimes on Africa. Yet the production also demonstrated that Britain itself is now a postcolonial community, changing in terms of cultural identity and artistic diversity and collaborating in the invention of new classical traditions that engage with all these aspects. The lines of communication, however, are not merely two-directional. African/Atlantic/Caribbean intersections are never far from the core of developments in classical traditions.

Figure 21.4 *The Gods Are Not to Blame* by Ola Rotimi, Arcola Theatre, 06/05. Director: Femi Elufowoju, Jr. Mo Sesay, Golda John, Nick Oshikanlu. Photo: Marilyn Kingwill/ArenaPAL. Odewale/Oedipus (Mo Sesay) is on the left of the photograph

4   African/Atlantic/Caribbean Migrations

Cultural traffic across the Atlantic involves people, texts, arts works, and ideas. The relationship between classical traditions and this cultural process has been characterized in various ways. The term "The Black Atlantic" has been used to define a double consciousness in which people of African-Caribbean origin recognize different aspects of their identity, both as members of a diaspora, forcibly transported as slaves, and as members of culturally and politically proactive communities in the Caribbean, in America, and, through further migrations, elsewhere (including both Europe and Africa; Gilroy 1993). The resulting engagement with Greek and Roman material has attracted labels such as "Black Dionysus," used for African/American creative receptions of Greek drama (McDonald 2000; Wetmore 2003); "Black Athena," used to suggest that Greek material was already in some sense African in origin (Bernal 1987, challenged in Lefkowitz and Rogers 1996); and "Black Orpheus," a phrase used in various ways in scholarship and film to explore the relationship between emerging societies and their pasts (Wetmore 2003). All these labels draw not only on interactions between Greco-Roman and modern, but also on intersections between the histories and cultures of Africa, Europe, and America (north and south).

A central feature of this process is the contest between foundation myths and explanatory frameworks. Emily Greenwood has used the metaphor of the Atlantic triangle (more usually associated with economic history) to show how attempts to chart a unidirectional flow of "influences" are misleading. Although colonial education in the Caribbean embedded Greco-Roman culture in the "mythology of European superiority" (Greenwood 2004), classical material also provided counter-texts that were used not only to critique colonialism but also, especially from the last quarter of the twentieth-century, to react against the use of a counter-mythology of the African origins of Caribbean culture. Greenwood proposes a triangular model of cultural relationships that recognizes the multidirectional dynamics and tensions between Caribbean, African, and European transactions in the history of the region. The languages and idioms through which classical texts have been refigured recognize the paradox that the languages imposed by colonialism also become educational and literary forces and even languages of liberation.

In the Caribbean Anglophone context, Kamau Brathwaite sought to establish a "nation language" that would provide a fresh start from the conflicting pressures of multiple identities and the dislocation of both African and European antecedents (Brathwaite 1984). Derek Walcott adopted a different approach, juxtaposing the resources of the Anglophone poetic tradition in which he was educated with the Creole idiom, patois, and dialects of the St. Lucia in which he lived. Walcott referred to his ability to lead two lives – the interior life of poetry and the outward life of action and dialect – that could both be assimilated into his writing (Walcott 1998). This double consciousness and writerly capacity was developed through a series of poems, starting with his early poetic odyssey "Epitaph for the Young" (1949) and culminating in his long poem *Omeros* (1990), in which the hinterland to that double consciousness is explored with irony and with a ruthless assertion of cultural independence. The names used for the poor in the poem (Achille, Hector, Philoctete) are redolent of the practice of slave owners in naming slaves after classical heroes. Yet these figures take the foreground in the new epic. An exploitative tradition mutates into one of empowerment, with implications for both classical and modern. Walcott's "African Greeks" are emblems of his identification with the seafaring tradition of the ancient Mediterranean: "The Greeks were the niggers of the Mediterranean" (quoted in King 2000: 504). In *Omeros*, Philoctetes' wound is caused not by a snakebite but by a rusty anchor, the symbol of the fleets of slavery and empire (1.1). Yet Walcott refuses to confine his perspective to that of slavery and victim status. He uses classical tropes to challenge what he regards as the tyranny of obsession with the past (Williams 2001). The possibility of a return to African roots is explored and rejected through a variation on the classicising device of *katabasis* (descent to the underworld; *Omeros* 3.25–28; Hardwick 2002). The fisherman Achille makes a delirious return to his psychological underworld in Africa and finds that his name is forgotten; it is as though he never existed. In his dream he witnesses the African slave raiders colluding with the Europeans in abducting his ancestors.

Reappropriation of classical material, however, does present some problems for Walcott. In his *The Odyssey: A Stage Version* (performed 1992, published text 1993), he uses as narrator the blind blues singer Billy Blue, whose language braids together both Homeric and twentieth-century discourses. Yet when Odysseus finally returns home, ancient and modern prove to be irreconcilable. Penelope does not retreat to the upper room. She attacks Odysseus for turning the house into "an abattoir" and actually prevents the hanging of the maid, Melantho, played by a black actress. The scene reverses the cultural and aesthetic force of an Homeric and classical tradition of texts embedded in slavery (Homer *Odyssey* 22.457–72). For Walcott, it was as impossible to accept the primacy of this literary genealogy as it was for him to accept the primacy of African "roots." Thus his rewriting of classical material uses both classical literary devices to challenge the supremacy of African cultural foundation myths and Caribbean cultural forms to rewrite Homer and to challenge the aesthetic and moral force of classical traditions. Walcott brings together European, African, and Caribbean as strands in a new poetics, less concerned with the primacy of the genealogy of any one tradition than with creating a cultural identity that speaks in its own terms. A new classical tradition has been invented.

5   Conclusion

The transmission, interpretation, and cultural embedding of Greek and Roman material in outstanding works of literature and drama in postcolonial contexts has considerable implications for both. The emergence of literary figures who combine worldwide importance with deep local influence and whose work has been energized by engagement with classical material demonstrates that there is no single classical tradition, but rather a variety of migrations in which intersecting literary, dramatic, and cultural contexts sometimes clash and sometimes converge. Postcolonial contexts reveal both the appropriation of classical material by colonizers and its reappropriation to subvert, liberate, and create new work. The impact of classical traditions on the colonization and decolonization of the mind has been catalytic. The works created in the spaces where classical traditions and postcolonial perspectives can meet have added substance and examples to theoretical work in both fields. This is a relatively new strand in both artistic activity and research, but the evidence available to date suggests the need for approaches that not only use techniques of literary, performance, and contextual analysis but also develop lateral thinking and an appreciation of cross-genre exchange, the recognition of analogues, and collage, sometimes leading to the disruption of the conventionally recognized patterns of chronology and authority. Direct and extended engagement with classical texts and ideas in the original languages and contexts is no longer a core part of educational and cultural frameworks. The new and fluid traditions that have emerged in postcolonial contexts provide mediated representations of classical texts that will be significant in forming future perspectives on the ancient world as well as the modern one. Wilson Harris has commented in the forward to his odyssean novel *The Mask* of *the Beggar* that "European codes begin, it seems, to suffer a measure of transfiguration as they face faculties and creativities beyond their formal traditions" (Harris 2003: vii–viii). The creative intersections of the classical and the postcolonial are one aspect of this process.

FURTHER READING

The best follow-up to the discussion in this chapter is to read and/or view the classical rewritings by modern writers such as Seamus Heaney, Tony Harrison, Ted Hughes, Michael Longley, Femi Òsòfisan, Tom Paulin, Wole Soyinka, and Derek Walcott. For various approaches to contextualizing these rewritings, see McDonald (1992), McDonald and Walton (2002), and Hall, Macintosh, and Wrigley (2004). There is useful discussion of the analysis and critique of translations in France (2000), which has chapters on theory, historical development, and text types as well as language groups, ancient and modern. For specific focus on translations from classical languages, see Walton (forthcoming) and Hardwick (2000a). For discussion of translation in postcolonial situations, see Bassnet and Trivedi (1999). For an introduction to postcolonial theory, the best starting point is Azim (2001). For attempts to bring together classical receptions and traditions and postcolonial and other situations, see Wetmore (2002) and the chapters in Martindale and Thomas (2006) and Hardwick and Gillespie (forthcoming). For revision of the relationship between the concepts of classical tradition and reception, see Haubold (forthcoming), Haubold and Budelmann (forthcoming), and Martindale (chapter 20 in this volume).

CHAPTER TWENTY-TWO

Gender and Sexuality

Alastair J. L. Blanshard

1   Introduction

At the heart of the study of gender lies "social construction" – the idea that the capacities, expectations, and even the definitions of "men" and "women" are not derived from biology, but social practice. Given the foundational role of classical antiquity in formulating the distinctive "look and feel" of western European culture, it is understandable that the art, literature, and history of the Greco-Roman world was intimately involved in the articulation of normative definitions of masculinity and femininity.

The study of gender is political. It invites us to question the effects of social institutions. In this respect, it is far from clear that the classical tradition is something worth celebrating. Western culture has shown itself remarkably sympathetic to the misogyny of antiquity. The traditional privileging of male activity and its anxieties about female power in Greece and Rome have regularly found an audience who have been only too keen to hear and repeat its phallocentric maxims. Significantly, it is often difficult to separate out cause and symptom in these manifestations of classical patriarchal ideology. As a consequence, analysis of the relationship between gender and the classical tradition raises a number of questions about the value of the latter in western culture. Is such male chauvinism the inescapable product of the classical tradition – the bitter pill that needs to be swallowed when we drink from the fount of antiquity – or has the classical world just been excerpted and edited to validate contemporary prejudices? To put the question more directly, can we hold classical antiquity responsible for western antifemale attitudes? Are figures such as Aristotle the founders of the western philosophic tradition or female enslavement? Can we have one without the other? Such matters have divided feminist scholarship (Bar On 1994; Spelman 1983; Witt 1998), with some thinkers even arguing that such debates are themselves symptomatic of a patriarchal Aristotelian logic that fetishizes reason (Rooney 1994; Irigaray 1985, 1993). Whatever conclusions we reach on these questions, there should be some recognition that the story is never going to be a simple one of male oppressors and female victims. The images of masculinity promoted by the classical tradition are as limiting for men as they are for women. Moreover, alongside the repressive deployment of the classical past, there exist a number of moments where we see the tables turned and disempowered groups acting as agents in formulating their own counter-hegemonic classical tradition. It is a complicated field. The study of gender leads us inexorably to consider questions of power, resistance, sexuality, the body, and desire.

These issues cut across a number of disciplinary boundaries and categories. There is no single place where an unquestioned and definitive representation of either man or woman resides. The perception of either sex shifts, sometimes dramatically, sometimes subtly, as one moves from drama to painting to sculpture to poetry to prose. We should be wary of being too reductionist in our analysis. Each genre plays by its own rules. Comparing Rubens's erotic female nudes to the monstrous, splayed bodies found in drawings of gynecological autopsies should remind us just how fragile the notion of "flesh" is, let alone "woman." The nature of man and woman is the topic of a "cultural conversation" carried across time, place, and genre. Each part of the societal fabric has contributed to this discussion. Different moments brought different aspects into focus. Each contribution has often raised more problems than it solved. In what follows, I would like to outline some of the ways in which this conversation has been conducted as well as to focus on some of the important topics of debate.

2 Heroes and Monsters

The classical contribution to modern notions of gender comprises both the provision of influential theory and captivating examples. Classical texts have regularly been deployed to add authority to claims about appropriate gender roles. So, for example, the image of the *vir bonus* (good man) as sketched out by Cicero (especially in *De officiis*) exercised a decisive influence in the European humanist tradition (Narducci 2004; Monfasani 1992). It provided a paradigm for male behavior and established the practice of civic virtue as the most worthy male endeavor. Classical authors spoke to women as well. Richard Hyrde in his 1541 translation of Juan Luis Vives's *Instruction of a Christen Woman* describes domestic duties as "the womans party as Plato and Aristotle say full well." Xenophon's *Oeconomicus* was particularly influential in these matters (Hutson 1999). This text enjoyed widespread circulation in both Latin and vernacular translations and formed the basis of a number of textbooks on domestic duties. Xenophon's text begins as a dialogue between Kritoboulos and Socrates on the importance of household management. After both parties agree on the importance of such matters, Socrates relates what he has learnt from a young man called Isomakhos, who describes the paradigm of the well-run household. Indeed, Isomakhos and his partner come to embody the Renaissance ideal of husband and wife. The most significant passages for the study of gender roles concern Isomakhos' descriptions of the different duties of men and women and his claims that God made man suited to the outdoor life, travel, and the acquisition of goods through trade or labor. Women, in contrast, lack the necessary courage for such pursuits and are instead like queen bees – designed for the indoor life, the nursing of children, and the care of goods acquired by men (*Oeconomicus* 7.17–35). These sentiments found their way into a number of influential texts such as Heinrich Bullinger's *Der christliche Ehestand* (On the Christian marriage, 1540), and John Dod and Robert Cleaver's *A Godlie Forme of Householde Government* (1610; Hutson 1999: 82–4).

The use of such didactic texts was complemented by numerous role models and negative case studies. One of the earliest works of north Italian humanism is, for example, Giovanni Boccaccio's *De claris mulieribus* (On famous women, 1361–2), a collection of 106 biographies of famous women from antiquity (Kolsky 2003). This exemplary tradition has a number of strengths. These embodiments of vice and virtue provided a medium by which abstract claims and aesthetic notions could be realized and made substantial. They made convenient and attractive packages for conveying complex ideas. They relied on more than just classical prestige for their validity, however, for historical examples claimed to provide real precedents. Mythological figures could be said to embody poetic truths, reflect human nature, or, post-Jung, arise from the darkest recesses of human psychology. This means that classical ideas were remarkably virulent. When Xenophon falls out of fashion and classical texts are no longer above question, his ideas can easily be transmitted through another vehicle or pass under a different sign. Thus the relationship between Isomakhos and his wife that was celebrated in the Renaissance finds its corollary in the Victorian fascination with the Perseus and Andromeda myth. The image of the bound, naked woman waiting to be rescued by her lover from the ravages of a monster offered a potent blend of Romanticism and voyeurism. It promoted the notion of the passive, helpless woman and the active male hero. The monster, whose sexually predatory nature was barely repressed, warned of the dangers that lay outside the realm of comfortable domesticity. In image after image, we see Andromeda rescued just in time and returned to her proper place inside the home to assume the role of wife and mother (Munich 1989).

The tradition of turning to antiquity for specific historical role models can be traced at least as far back as the Carolingian period (Innes 1997). Greek and Roman myth as well as the works of Plutarch, Suetonius, and Livy meant that there was never any shortage of male role models. Every Homeric champion, mythic monster-slayer, victorious general, or skilled statesman has, at various times and places, managed to find adherents. One of the earliest manifestations of this practice can be seen in the list of "Nine Worthies." First devised in the fourteenth century, this list of champions was designed to embody the various aspects of chivalric virtue. The canonical list is attributed to Jean de Longuyon, who describes the "nine worthies" (*les neuf preux*) in his *Voeux du paon* (Vows of the peacock, ca. 1312). De Longuyon lists three pagan heroes worthy of emulation (Hector, Julius Caesar, and Alexander the Great) along with three figures from the Old Testament (Joshua, David, and Judas Maccabaeus) and three from Christian times (King Arthur, Charlemagne, and Godfrey of Bouillon). The "nine worthies" were a popular subject for masques, and the list could vary according to taste. For example, Shakespeare stages such a masque in the midst of *Love's Labour's Lost*, but includes four pagan heroes (Hector, Pompey the Great, Hercules, and Alexander the Great) in his lineup. Different ages have, of course, different preferences. Republican heroes such as Camillus and Coriolanus who enjoy such popularity in the Renaissance fade from popular consciousness in the nineteenth and twentieth centuries.

Two heroes have remained perennially popular in the male imagination: Alexander the Great and Hercules. Both establish martial prowess and love of adventure as the preeminent masculine virtues. Yet they were also more than just cyphers for "macho" values. Their respective traditions were so rich and varied that they could be deployed to address particular masculine concerns. Alexander's early death, his drinking, and his disillusionment on finding that there were "no more worlds to conquer" ensured that he could speak to men at their lowest ebb. The rise of the Romantic would be impossible without him (Spencer 1996). Hercules' humiliating servitude to Queen Omphale, in turn, struck a cord with the emasculated nobles of the French Regency. Forced to hang up their "clubs" in favor of the delights of the salon and its powerful mistresses, the French nobility turned to this incident to express the dangers of their predicament. During this period, we see an unprecedented explosion of images of Hercules and Omphale. Important canvases are produced by Francois Lemoyne (1724), Charles-Antoine Coypel (1731), and Francois Boucher (1734).

Although a corresponding list of nine female worthies (*les neuf preuses*), which included three virtuous pagan women (Lucretia, Veturia, the mother of Coriolanus, and Virginia) was constructed, the classical tradition has been less successful at providing virtuous paradigms for women. This is especially the case when compared with the contribution made by biblical models such as the cult of the Virgin Mary and female martyrs and saints. The one exception is, perhaps, Lucretia, whose suicide after being raped by Tarquin was a popular topic for art and drama. Shakespeare's *Rape of Lucrece* (1594) put the story into verse, and Thomas Heywood adapted it for the stage. Indeed, in his *Apology for Actors* (1612), Heywood praises the story for its beneficial effects on women ("women … that are chaste, are by us extolled and encouraged in their virtues, being instanced by Diana, Belphebe, Matilda, Lucrece").

It is in the production of negative exemplars that the classical world has provided more fertile ground. These classical women are abject: mixing revulsion and attraction, they encapsulate male fears. Anxiety about female power has been played out through images of Amazons and female monsters such as the harpies. At the beginning of the twentieth century, Electra inspired terror with her capacity for violence, rupturing comfortable notions about classicism in Strauss's operatic version of her story (1908; Goldhill 2002: 108–77; Scott 2005: 81–94). Freud, in the essays "The Medusa's Head" (1922; published 1940) and "The Infantile Genital Organization" (1923), turned Medusa into the poster-girl for the male fear of emasculation, the primeval *vagina dentata*. Women could bring down the greatest heroes. In the medieval period, Achilles was as much a victim of lust as wrath (King 1987: 171–218). Women such as Cleopatra have illicitly thrilled male audiences for centuries (Hughes-Hallett 1990). Attempts made by Dutch painters to domesticate and turn her into a housewife (Hamer 1993: 24–44) were short-lived and largely unsuccessful. She conforms too easily to popular notions about the east and female sexuality. The combination of sex, danger, orientalism, female despotism, and tragedy has made Cleopatra an irresistible subject for artists and cinematographers. She is the original *femme fatale*. In Pushkin's *Egyptian Nights* (1837), Cleopatra is a killer who demands a man's life as the price of a night's passion. It is a price all too many men are willing to pay. She is the specter who appears whenever men feel threatened by women. Her persona can be adapted to replicate every new threat. So, for example, in Theda Bara's cinematic portrayal (1917), she becomes the epitome of that terrifying arrival, the "new woman." Only modern consumerism seems to be able to tame her with her recent cinematic incarnations (1934, 1963), more designed to push product (cosmetics, fashion, jewellery) than politics (Wyke 2002: 244–78, 297–300).

3   Resistance and Dissidence

Classics has always provided a language by which contemporary women could explore their environment and reconcile themselves to their condition. It is a trend that we can see extending from colonial America (Gentilcore 1995) to women's historical fiction in the twentieth century (Hoberman 1997). Yet more than providing the courage to endure, the classical tradition has also been used by women to resist. The defiant Queen Christina (1626–89) appropriated the image of Alexander to signify her male soul within her female body (Biermann 2001; Kajanto 1993). From the very beginnings of feminism, the classical past was used to challenge and subvert attempts to regulate gender roles. Throughout the struggle for female emancipation, historical and mythical figures have been offered up to inspire activists, horrify them into action, or provide intellectual underpinnings to their philosophical endeavors. Indeed, the constant turn to antiquity is a recurring motif throughout successive waves of feminism.

One of the significant early struggles for female emancipation centered on the rights of nonaristocratic women to divorce their husbands and retain control of their property. In England and Wales this debate came to a head in the passing of the 1857 Divorce and Matrimonial Causes Act. Both sides of the debate were not averse to invoking classical material in support of their case (Hall 1999: 54–64). Prominent opponent William Gladstone, Member of Parliament and later Prime Minister, waxed nostalgically for the Homeric Age in which both divorce and prostitution were unknown – a position that he repeated a year later in his *Studies on Homer* (1858). Against such attempts to validate Victorian morality through recourse to Greek epic, we find the proponents of social change mobilizing their own classical allusions. Francis Talfourd, son of one of the radical MPs who supported increased rights for women, composed a burlesque entitled *Alcestis: The Original Strong-Minded Woman* (1850), in which the heroic Alcestis finds herself trapped in a disastrous marriage with a profligate Admetus. Other contemporary musical burlesques (e.g., Mark Lemon's *Medea; or, a Libel on the Lady of Colchis* and Robert Brough's *Medea; or, the Best of Mothers, with a Brute of a Husband*) deployed the figure of Medea to illustrate the situation of abandoned women spurned by their lovers and left desperate and destitute (Macintosh 2000).

Indeed, the figure of Medea and, in particular, her impassioned speech to the women of Corinth (Euripides *Medea* 215–66) became a favorite of the female suffrage movement. This speech had the status of an underground classic. It was largely omitted from performances of *Medea* until Augusta Webster (1837–94), poet and political activist, published her translation of the play in 1868 – just a year before her close associate John Stuart Mill published his famous treatise *The Subjection of Women*. Gilbert Murray famously described *Medea* to Sybil Thorndike as a play that "might have been written for the 'Woman Movement'" (Thorndike 1936: 74), and it was a popular item in the repertoire of the Actresses' Franchise League, whose members performed the "Women of Corinth" speech and the choral denunciation of the misogyny of myth (lines 410–30) at suffragette meetings (Hall and Macintosh 2005: 511–19).

Fueling this appropriation of classical imagery was the increased access women had to classical education. Traditionally classical learning represented a male preserve. Indeed its masculine exclusiveness was often attacked by female writers – George Eliot (1819–80) held it up to savage parody and Virginia Woolf (1882–1941) questioned whether these men could ever claim to really know Greek (Jenkyns 1980: 63–4; Fowler 1983). Although no period was ever without some women who knew Latin and Greek (the case of Thomas Ascham's tutelage of the future Queen Elizabeth I [1533–1603] in Greek, for example, while unusual was not unparalleled; see Grafton and Jardine 1986: 29–57), it was only with the mid-nineteenth-century reforms in women's education that we see a substantial increase in women's access to Greek and Latin texts (Hardwick 1997). It was a fruitful engagement. Classical myth, for example, had an important impact on the early American feminist Margaret Fuller (1810–50; Cleary 2000). The extraordinary thing about these early generations of female classical scholars is the willingness of a number of them to deploy classical culture to critique or subvert male repression.

During this period, a number of female authors and figures from antiquity were reclaimed. The figure of Sappho would prove inspirational (Prins 1999b). Numerous female students record how her lyrics seemed to speak directly to them. Even epic, traditionally conceived as the most masculine of genres, was not immune. In 1897, Samuel Butler published his infamous *The Authoress of the Odyssey*, in which he claimed that the author of the *Odyssey* was a women living in Sicily. His claims infuriated classical scholars, who ridiculed his conclusions. In making such a claim, however, Butler presents an eccentric reflection (or perhaps clever parody) of the concerns of his time.

Amongst those associated with the emancipation movement, there was a marked preference for strong, dramatic, dark women. The wild revels of the maenads exerted a powerful attraction on these free-spirited women (Prins 1999a), and scholars such as Jane Ellen Harrison (1850–1928) assisted in their fantasies with her exploration of the darker side of Greek ritual behavior. Medea was not the only villain to be reclaimed. Delphine de Girardin's *Cléopâtre* (1847) has Octavia bemoan the wife's lot and declare her envy of the liberated Cleopatra. The dancer and choreographer Martha Graham (1894–1991) chose Clytemnestra in order to dramatize "the private hell of a woman who has killed her love because her love killed her creative instinct – her child" (Freiert 1990). In one of her earliest works, the poet and novelist Amy Levy (1861–89) took the side of Xanthippe, the infamously shrewish wife of Socrates, and recast her as an early blue-stocking wronged by her husband, who cruelly derides her attempts to match him in philosophy (*Xanthippe and Other Verse*, 1881). In examining the fate of Xanthippe, whose soul "yearned for knowledge" but was left only "to bleed and quiver" by a husband who, "pregnant with noble theories and great thoughts, / deigned not to stoop to touch so light a thing / as the fine fabric of a women's brain" (lines 120–22), Levy found the perfect vehicle both to express the anguish of women's plight and indict the male chauvinism that caused it.

4   Perfect Forms and Unruly Bodies

Gender cannot escape the body. Biological differences between the sexes are all too quickly assimilated into differences of treatment and expectation. Through its domination of the twin spheres of aesthetics and medicine, the classical tradition has played an important role in determining the appearance, display, management, and pathologization of male and female bodies.

Classical art ensured that the body never left the gaze of western culture. The tradition of depicting stylized naked bodies to signify their heroic status is one of the most distinctive features of classical art (Bonfante 1989). Classical art served to legitimate such bodily display and permitted artists and viewers to use such displays as the focal point for their debates about masculinity and femininity. This can be seen most clearly in the genre of "history painting" as it developed from the mid-fifteenth century, and especially in its intensely neoclassical phase from 1760 onwards. The focus of these paintings was almost always a classical male nude in heroic pose who was offered to the viewer as a moral paradigm.

Nudes are almost always idealist. They depict us as we *should be* rather than as we are. As Quatremère de Quincy (1755–1844) famously remarked, "nudity should be regarded as a form of costume." Nudity contributes to the formation of gender categories by defining notions of beauty and encouraging imitation in its viewers. In its most extreme form women and men began to resemble classical statues (Dyer 1997). Although important since the Renaissance (Bober and Rubenstein 1986), this preeminence of classical statuary in western aesthetics was cemented in place by the influential critic and father of modern art history, Johann Joachim Winckelmann (1717–68; Potts 1994) and was facilitated by the large number of plaster casts that were dispersed in museums, art schools, and private collections throughout Europe and North America (Haskell and Penny 1981; Kurtz 2000). For women, white unblemished skin (in imitation of marble statuary) and the absence of body hair became essential components of female attractiveness. Similarly, the male body looked to the proportions and musculature of late classical and Hellenistic statuary for ideas of perfection.

For most of the history of the nude, it was the male form that attracted the most interest. Indeed, it was only in the nineteenth century that it ceded its place to the female nude as the primary object of artistic endeavor. The male form not only exemplified beauty; it also represented a series of ethical paradigms. Critical discussion of the male body constantly collocated it with notions of order, reason, proportion, structure, clarity, and luminosity. The male body became a text by which man's inherent worth could be read (Solomon-Godeau 1997: 177–224). Traditionally, two rival versions of the male nude have competed for attention. At one extreme, we find hypervirile, overmuscled forms that owe their origins to statues such as the *Farnese Hercules*. At the other, we find the smooth, slim-hipped, boyish physique that looks to figures such as the *Capitoline Faun* (Solomon-Godeau 1997: 22–4). We can see both types operational in the work of Jacques-Louis David. The figure of Leonidas who occupies center stage in David's *Leonidas at Thermopylae* (1814) exemplifies the "masculinized" male form. In Leonidas' broad chest, we can see allusions to the Beledevere torso. This headless fragment of antique sculpture was beloved by Michelangelo and Winckelmann, and its masculine pedigree was assured by its supposed origins in a statue of Hercules. Leonidas stands in contrast to figures such as the Paris found in David's *The Loves of Paris and Helen* (1788). Again the male nude form occupies a central position in the canvas. However, in this case, the male body is young, beautiful, and feminized. Both forms are equally idealized, and both find imitations in contemporary portraiture as subjects sought to portray themselves as successors to these classical ancestors.

We can trace not only masculine ideals through these forms, but also their anxieties. Uncertainty about role and status translates into uncertainty about ideal form. This can be seen perhaps most clearly in the variety of images produced during the Revolutionary period, when traditional roles, structures, and institutions were swept away and values were in flux. In such ambiguous times, ambiguous bodies flourish. The rise of fragile, vulnerable male bodies typifies this period. A good example is Girodet's *The Sleep of Endymion* (1791, exhibited in the Salon of 1793). The painting was enthusiastically received on its initial showing. Numerous imitations followed, including a sculpture (1819–22) by Canova. The subject matter of the painting derives from the story told in Ovid, Lucian, and Apollodorus about the Moon who was so smitten with the beauty of the shepherd boy Endymion whom she found asleep on Mount Latmos that she condemned him to perpetual slumber so that she could enjoy the pleasure of gazing at and caressing his body for eternity. It is the quintessential story of the vulnerability of male beauty in the face of powerful, unstoppable female desire and has been used to prefigure the love of noble women for men of lower status (Greer 2003: 112–15). These themes are brought to the fore in Girodet's painting, in which we find the soft, girlish figure of the shepherd sprawled in a lush bower. Lost in sleep, he is naked and defenceless as shafts of moonlight play upon his skin. Passive and antiheroic, the figure of Endymion mediates anxieties about contemporary threats to masculinity (Solomon-Godeau 1997: 65–84) at the same time that it challenges traditional masculine paradigms (Davis 1994: 176–84).

There is indeed a darker side to these nudes, for they can also tell a story about improper desire. Despite the protestations of art critics, it was never fully possible to eradicate notions of the erotic from these classical displays. Sexual desire always threatens to emerge from these images. Thus, Correggio's sequence of paintings on the loves of Zeus, which had been proudly displayed in a number of European courts in the sixteenth century, were deemed so obscene in the eighteenth century that they were displayed behind curtains. A similar fate befell the *Tepidarium* (1881) of Alma-Tadema, in which he depicted a nude woman relaxing in a Roman bath. There is a history of scandal that attends classical pieces. The performances of Emma Hamilton (1765–1815) in imitation of classical statuary were pilloried for their decadence by contemporary satirists, who saw in them confirmation of the loose morals of Nelson's mistress (Boardman 2004: 52). Public art seems particularly susceptible. The colossal naked bronze Achilles erected as a memorial to the Duke of Wellington and his men in Hyde Park in 1822 was derided as inappropriate by contemporary broadsheets, and Horatio Greenough's seminude classicizing depiction of George Washington (1841) was so unpopular on its unveiling that it was quickly moved from its intended spot in the Capitol and now lurks as an embarrassment in a corner of the Smithsonian Museum. These classical bodies not only regulate notions of beauty, but contemporary morality as well. They function as a litmus test of purity in which the morals of the viewer and the artists are put under examination.

   Although artistic representation of classicizing male bodies faded away in the nineteenth century, we see a resurgence in the twentieth century. Fascism, for example, attempted to appropriate the classical male body for political purposes. Mussolini regularly depicted himself as a modern Hercules – much to the amusement of other European leaders who privately mocked his "sideshow strongman" performances (Blanshard 2005: xvii; Boardman 2004: 52–3). One of the distinctive features of European fascism was its focus on individual morality. This morality was communicated through a distinctive classicizing aesthetic (Taylor and Van der Will 1991). Onto the classical male form were grafted the virtues of discipline, courage, and self-sacrifice (Mangan 1999). Riefenstahl's *Olympia*, which celebrated the 1936 Olympic games in Berlin, exemplifies this attempt at appropriation. From its opening sequence we see Riefenstahl endeavoring to create a genealogy for Aryan man through stressing the continuity of the Greek past with the German present. Thus, the ruins of classical Greece fade into the bucolic idyll of the athlete's village on the Olympic games site, and Myron's *Discobolus* (the discus thrower) is transformed into the figure of a contemporary German athlete (McFee and Tomlinson 1999). Through such artistic conceits, Reifenstahl was able to communicate the Fascist vision of its new "supermen."

   Liberal democracies were also not adverse to the idea of their soft male populace transforming themselves into hard-bodied superheroes. In particular, one of the most indelible legacies of the classical past can be found in the rippling abdominals and bulging biceps of the modern bodybuilder (Wyke 1997a). The figure conventionally identified as the father of modern bodybuilding is Eugene Sandow (Kasson 2001: 21–76; Blanshard 2005: 151–7). Previously, sideshow strongmen had preferred bulk over definition – they were more fat than muscle. Strongmen may have worn lionskins in imitation of Hercules, but that was where the physical resemblance ended. What distinguished Sandow was the perfection of his muscle definition. His body was so amazing to his audience that Sandow eschewed feats of physical strength in favor of poses and flexing. Throughout his performances and publicity, Sandow constantly alluded to the classical past. He powdered his body so that it looked like a marble statue. The poses he adopted in his act were all derived from classical statuary. Over the course of his show, Sandow appeared as the *Discobolus*, *Apoxyomenos*, *Farnese Hercules* (with club and lion skin props), and *Dying Gaul*. These poses in imitation of statuary would form the basis of the first-ever bodybuilding competition held in the Royal Albert Hall in September 1901. Indeed, some are still used in modern body-building competitions.

Sandow had numerous imitators, many of whom continued his classicizing style either in their stage names ("Charles Atlas") or in their performances. Perhaps one of the most influential of these was Steve Reeves, whose performance as Hercules in the film *Le fatiche di Ercole* (The labours of Hercules, 1957) made him an international star and raised the profile of bodybuilding to new heights (Solomon 2001: 119–22; Wyke 1997a: 63–8). The film enjoyed tremendous success. It was seen by 24 million people and made up to $18,000,000 at the box-office. Reeves's success even created a minigenre of muscle films set in antiquity. Christened "peplum" films by the French critics (after the short tunics worn by the male leads), these films were produced largely in Italy and starred American bodybuilders in the lead roles. Over 170 such films were produced. Again male anxiety seems to be a driving force in the adoption of these classical bodies. To the flabby, disempowered office workers of sixties America, these bronzed heroes became aspirational figures. These films were respon-sible for filling the gyms and introducing the art of bodybuilding into mainstream culture.

While the male body could (with work) be perfected, the fate of the female body was far more precarious. Condemned by classical medical writers as imperfect, defi-cient, malformed, even at times monstrous, the female body was hard to redeem. It is hard to overstate the impact of such writings on the history of medicine in western Europe. The writings of Galen, Hippocrates, and Aristotle were crucial in under-standing the operation of the human body from the medieval period through the Renaissance and into the Enlightenment (Maclean 1980). Even when doctors were being innovative, they still often preferred to invoke classical authority to cloak the novelty of their suggestions.

This central role played by classical texts had a number of important implications for the conception and treatment of women, especially given the strong belief that behavior and temperament had biological origins. Supposed feminine attributes such as physical weakness, irrationality, and uncontrollable appetite were all attributed at various times to bodily causes. According to a traditional reading of Aristotle and Galen (using passages such as *De generatione animalium* [On the generation of animals] 737a27, *Historia animalium* [The history of animals] 608a21–5, and *De usu partium corporis* [On the usefulness of parts of the body] 14.6), women were passive, dominated by cold and moist humors, and driven by a desire to achieve completion through copulation. The origins of this difference lay in the lack of heat during the process of generation. This lack of heat caused a woman's genitals not to form correctly and to remain internal. It also meant that she was, by nature, prey to the dominance of cold and moist humors and unable to manufacture perfect "semen." This prejudice against the female body can be found in a number of writers.

For example, Kaspar Hofmann (1575–1648), in his 1625 commentary on Galen's *De usu partium corporis*, combines passages drawn from Hippocrates and Aristotle as well as Galen to equate the high heat that attends the generation of men with perfection. It is this heat that makes men stronger, larger, healthier, and longer-lived than women. Moreover, this heat also endows a man with a complementary set of moral qualities. Man is more courageous, open, strong-willed, and honest. Women either lack these qualities or have corresponding vices (Maclean 1980).

Admittedly, many of these views were later rejected or fell out of favor, especially with the rise of the "feminist" school of medical practitioners in the late sixteenth century who argued that there was nothing inherently wrong with the female body and that it was a mistake to regard female genitals as flawed versions of the male genitals. Nevertheless, the prejudices set up by these views were never completely eliminated, and their legacy can be seen in the pathologization of female behavior, particularly in relation to diseases such as hysteria (Rousseau 1993) and "green sickness" (King 1996, 2004).

5   Sex and Desire

Integral to the story of gender is the story of sexuality. The protocols that govern intercourse have increasingly played an important part in defining gender roles. Some have even claimed that modern manhood is incomprehensible without an acknowledgment that every facet of masculinity is underpinned by the notion of the "homosexual" (Sedgwick 1990). Gender and sexuality are unified by process. In both cases, society slyly attempts to graft itself onto biology. Intercourse comes to be so much more than just a biomechanical act. It becomes a signifier of identity. This shift from act to identity is normally envisioned as a nineteenth-century phenomenon. However, like most paradigm shifts, there has been a tendency amongst scholars to over-schematize the transition (Halperin 2002: 27–32). The collocation of sex acts and identity is a process whose history stretches back to antiquity. However, these earlier protosexualities were ephemeral affairs that neither dominated the field nor made any claims to exclusivity. The libertine and the pederast may have been identifiable by more than their sexual activities, but these personages did not claim to be the only character types around, or the most essential aspects of the self. What distinguishes the nineteenth-century "turn to sexuality" is the importance of the claims made about sexuality and the reduction of the wide varieties of sexual practice to two overarching categories of heterosexuality and homosexuality. Sex had become the touchstone of normative behavior. It was only in the act of coitus that the true self was revealed.

There had always been a link between antiquity and sex acts. Fired up by Christian polemic, the classical world enjoyed a reputation as a place of moral depravity in which gluttony, drunkenness, and fornication were rife. Sodomy for a long period was described by the euphemism *amor Socraticus* (Socratic love; Dall'Orto 1989). The explicit references to oral sex in Martial made a strong impression on Ben Jonson (Boehrer 1998). Despite the best efforts of Neoplatonic allegorists, the story of the abduction of Ganymede by Zeus was never quite able to slough off its erotic connotations (Saslow 1986). Works such as Karl Forberg's *De figuris veneris* (On depictions of love) (1824) collected together references to all the various sexual acts found in classical sources. This work was a popular one, with English, French, and Italian translations in circulation. Later editions even included pornographic etchings by the French artist Paul Avril. Over the course of 19 plates, Avril offered a trip through classical antiquity that stressed the wide variety of pleasures available. Viewers were treated to such images of sodomy as Hadrian anally penetrating Antinous over the end of a couch, while the Nile flowed in the background and a bare-breasted female attendant gently fanned the sweaty figures. Meanwhile on the island of Lesbos, the poet Sappho enjoyed cunnilingus and frolicking mermaids mimicked her pleasure. On Capri, we find the emperor Tiberius digitally penetrating a young girl, and in another scene an unnamed Pompeian couple engaged in fellatio whilst Vesuvius explodes in the background. The classical world depicted by Avril seems to be frantically exploring every possible combination of coupling. Nineteen plates can barely contain the range of practices.

The queer world of Avril's etchings marks a final flourish. Just as the discourse on sex narrows and solidifies around two sexualities, so the interest in works such as Forberg's diminishes. Attention moved away from cataloguing every species of sexual practices. Now only two seemed to matter – homosexual and heterosexual acts – and the focus on the classical world shifts correspondingly. In particular, there was a new urgent interest shown in the classical past by the first generation of self-identifying homosexuals. One of the key debates in the period surrounds the origins of homosexual behavior. Was homosexuality the product of an aberrant physiology or psychology, or were its origins grounded in nature? In order to naturalize their desire, homosexual apologists were keen to stress an historical continuity of homosexual persons that extended to antiquity. So, for example, John Addington Symonds (1840–93) remarks, "The truth is that ancient Greece offers insuperable difficulties to theorists who treat sexual inversion exclusively from the points of view of neuropathology, tainted heredity, or masturbation" (Blanshard 2000). Perhaps the most famous of these homosexual genealogies is contained in Wilde's famous speech on the "Love that dare not speak its name" given in his 1895 trial, in which Wilde recited a list of famous figures beginning with David and Jonathan and continuing through Plato, Michelangelo, and Shakespeare. It is a fairly conventional list. Every "sexual invert" in London could have listed these names and a dozen more. Edward Carpenter (1844–1929) in *Homogenic Love*, published two months before the Wilde trial, remarks:

> Certainly it is remarkable that some of the world's greatest leaders and artists have been dowered either wholly or in part with the Uranian temperament – as in the cases of Plato, Socrates, Michel Angelo, Shakespeare, Alexander the Great, Julius Caesar, or, among women, Christine of Sweden, Sappho the poetess, and others.

Such rhetorical gestures were even the subject of parody in works such as Mallock's *The New Republic* (1877). A number of undergraduate pamphlets circulated throughout Oxford and Cambridge, each proclaiming the historical continuity of same-sex practice. *Boy Love* and *Boy Worship* (1880) are the most (in)famous, but they merely represent the most extreme examples of discursive practice that circulated through poetry, letters, diary entries, art, and informal conversation. It was not just in the imagined past that homosexuals sought refuge. They often fled to Mediterranean countries to live amongst the classical ruins, setting up enclaves in which they could enjoy the freedom to live alternate lifestyles free from the strictures of their home countries (Aldrich 1993). This homosexual appropriation of the classical past continued well into the late twentieth century. The importance of Sappho to contemporary lesbian identity is well documented (Reynolds 2003; Vanita 1996). Derek Jarman's *Sebastiane* (1976), in turn, updated the story of the Roman martyr for contemporary queer politics (Wyke 1998) and created a figure whose plight only continued to resonate more strongly with the deepening of the AIDS crisis (Kaye 1996).

FURTHER READING

There are numerous introductions to the field of gender studies. The collections by Meade and Wiesner-Hanks (2003) and Essed et al. (2004) provide coverage of the important issues and debates. On the topic of classical exemplars, a translation with facing Latin text of Giovanni Boccaccio's *De claris mulieribus* is available in the I Tatti Renaissance Library series (Brown 2001). On the image of Alexander the Great, see the studies by Aerts et al. (1978), Bunt (1994), Bridges and Bürgel (1996), Cary (1956), Cizek (1995), and Stoneman (1994). For the Hercules myth, the most comprehensive treatment is Galinsky (1972). See also Blanshard (2005), Schultze (1999), and Riley (2004). The use of classical myth in constructing modern masculinity is discussed in Holtsmark (1981). For the use of classical history in a school context, see Toebes (2001). On the rape of Lucretia, see Camino (1995) and Donaldson (1982). On the image of the Amazon, see Blok (1995), Daniels (2000), March and Passman (1994), and Passman (1991). For feminist appropriations of Clytemnestra, see Komar (2003). For other significant uses of myth, see Meagher (1995), Rudd (1994), Solterer (1995), Van Keuren (1998), and Yarnall (1994). The use of Cleopatra is treated in studies by Hamer (1993), Hughes-Hallett (1990), and Wyke (2002: 244–320; cf. 321–90 on the image of Messalina). The way in which issues of gender intersect with race in the figure of Cleopatra is examined by Royster (2003). On Jane Ellen Harrison the most sensitive treatment is Beard (2000). For a general discussion of the notion of women in classical medicine, see King (1993, 1998) and Harrison (1995). For Renaissance medicine, see Dixon (1995), Maclean (1980), and Thompson (1999). A useful collection of essays on hysteria has been assembled by Gilman et al. (1993). On "peplum films," see Chapman (2002). On modern bodybuilding, see Dutton (1995) and Kasson (2001). For political use of the classical body, see Leoussi (1998). On sexuality and antiquity, see Gold et al. (1997), Goldhill (2004), Montague (1994), Paxson and

Gravalee (1998), and Tomlinson (1992). A desire of eroticized antiquity even embraces the Minoans (Lapatin 2002). For a general history of homosexuality and its treatment in early-modern Europe, see Boswell (1980) and Brooten (1997). On Victorian homosexuality and its relationship with Hellenism, see Dowling (1994). Its impact on art is discussed in Barrow (2000).

CHAPTER TWENTY-THREE

Fascism

Katie Fleming

1 Introduction

"Naturally," wrote Speer in the secret diary that he kept in Spandau prison, Hitler "had a passion for antiquity" (Speer 1975: 166). The Führer's notably unsystematic remarks about the ancient world, and indeed the visibility of Greece and/or Rome in the ideologies of European fascism more generally, have become a source of fascination for many.[1] Of course, it would be an uncommon kind of western government, totalitarian or otherwise, that did not, at some point, seek to draw analogies between itself and certain – no doubt carefully selected – features of the classical past, whether democratic, republican, or imperial (Richard 1994; Stray 1998; Winterer 2002; Roberts 1994). In this sense, Nazism and Italian Fascism were hardly innovative. Yet it is tempting, when reflecting on these charged moments in the classical tradition, to linger on the perceived megalomania of the dictators and to isolate their appropriations of the past within an acceptable narrative of tyrannical excess. However, behind the predictable (note Speer's "naturally") prominence of antiquity in the political *imaginaires* of twentieth-century tyrants, lies a far more complex and revealing set of classical appropriations. While it can be said, superficially at least, that Hitler and Mussolini turned to the ancient world for similar ends (namely, political, social, and historical legitimization), the context through and means by which they arrived at them differed in a number of important and instructive ways, belying the tempting classification of a homogenous "fascist" reception of the ancient world. Of particular importance to classical scholars, too, must be the concurrent differences that Nazism and Italian Fascism made to the classical scholarship produced in Germany and Italy during this period (and, critically, its postwar reception). With these distinctions in mind, then, this chapter will be divided into two parts, in which I shall sketch out the role of the ancient world in fascist Italy (1922–43) and Nazi Germany (1933–45), although my discussion of the former regime will be briefer than that of the latter, for reasons that I hope will become clear.

2   *Civis Romanus Sum* – "I Am a Roman Citizen"

Over half a century before Mussolini's Caesarean march on Rome in 1922 (although, in the event, the Duce himself infamously took a sleeping car to Rome), Giuseppe Garibaldi, similarly set on the eternal city, marshaled his forces in the struggle for the reunification of Italy (the Risorgimento) under the banner of the ancient republican tradition (Bondanella 1997; Treves 1962). The general, along with many of his Risorgimento colleagues, invoked the republican trappings of ancient Rome as the symbol by and through which all Italy could be united, with all Italians heirs, figuratively and literally, of antiquity (Bondanella 1987; Giardina and Vauchez 2000). "Rome," Momigliano has observed, "was more than a claim to ancient greatness: it was a promise of unity" (Momigliano 1987: 78).

In the decades following the Risorgimento this (re)turn to Rome remained a central and defining feature of the Italian political and intellectual landscape. Despite Mazzini's insistence on the "universal" and nonimperial nature of the "idea" of Rome, *romanità* (Romanness) nevertheless gave impetus to Italy's efforts to reestablish and expand its empire in the Mediterranean and the Horn of Africa during the late nineteenth and early twentieth centuries (campaigns that sowed the seeds for Mussolini's own imperial ambitions, most notoriously the invasion and conquest of Abyssinia in 1935). Emilio Gentile, for one, has noted that this increasingly conservative concept of *romanità* acquired an almost religious dimension and offered both an alternative to the unifying power of the Roman Catholic Church, which had resisted the reunification of Italy (and the loss of the Papal States) throughout the nineteenth century, and a legitimizing narrative for a new "civilizing" imperial mission (Gentile 1990, 1993). The subsequent rise and – more importantly – success of nationalist *romanità* as political religion and cult in the Fascist regime of 1922–43 had its roots, therefore, in the political consciousness of the recently unified nation-state, and was frequently associated – whether legitimately or not – with the Mazzinian Risorgimento ideal (Chabod 1951: 179–323; Giardina and Vauchez 2000: 117–21). *Romanità* was, then, an integral part of an educated Italian's mindset (Visser 1992).

In this sense, despite its claims to have precipitated a radical "new order" in Italy, Italian Fascism, *qua* intellectual endeavor, inherited and developed, rather than revolutionized, the political terrain (Wyke 1999a; Sternhell 1978). Mussolini himself, in a speech given in 1925 before the national association of war-wounded, argued that Italian Fascism was the continuation of the Mazzinian Risorgimento by means of its extension to the people en masse: where the nineteenth-century liberal intelligentsia had failed in creating a vital and organic third Italian civilization (after Rome and the Renaissance), Fascism would succeed (Susmel 1951–81: 29:439–41; Gentile 1997). While I would not want to insist on its intellectual "qualities," it is clear that, although Italian Fascism indulged in political hooliganism, anti-intellectualism did not amount to a defining feature of the movement as it did in National Socialism. In any case, academics and intellectuals were not only attracted to it, but also central to some of its formative and foundational moments. The myth of Rome was frequently intrinsic to this process (Cagnetta 1976; Canfora 1976, 1980, 1989).

However, as Stone and Aicher, among others, have shown, *romanità* was a malleable and ever-changing phenomenon (Stone 1999; Aicher 2000). For Aicher, at least, its adoption by Fascism signified a "distinctive new phase of the myth of Rome," which, "always present, ... now took center stage" (Aicher 2000: 119). In fact, more than this, it can be argued that in the two decades of Fascist rule in Italy, three distinct stages of *romanità*, correlative to the three main phases of the regime, are visible. Maria Wyke offers a succinct and helpful summary of this trajectory:

> From the establishment of the regime in 1922 to the proclamation of a dictatorship in 1925, ancient Rome was translated into an ideal model for present revolutionary action, for the organization of combat, and for the promotion of Italian unity. *Romanità* then took on fresh authority and a new direction in the long build up to and following the declaration of an Italian empire, which took place in May 1936 after the conclusion of the Ethiopian war. Rome's empire was now persistently mobilized to justify an aggressive foreign policy, imperial expansion, and a claim to new territories in the Mediterranean. Finally, in a climate of increasing racism towards the end of the 1930s, the Romans and their Latin language were utilized to isolate and elaborate the presumed physical, spiritual, and moral perfection of their Italian descendants. (Wyke 1999b: 168)

This use of Rome, as its historical precedents indicate, was not an opportunistic anomaly; rather, *romanità* comes to stand for the apparent paradox at the heart of Italian Fascism itself. For just as Fascism claimed both to bring about national renewal through the rejection of the previous, bourgeois order and also to continue and to reinvigorate the Risorgimento project, so, too, was *romanità* a "flexible" myth, both revolutionary and reactionary. Rome, therefore, not merely offered coherence or continuity for Italian Fascism, but was a critical palingenetic myth that shaped and propelled it (Stone 1999; Griffin 1991: 73–4).

At the epicenter of the use of Rome in the political currency of Italian Fascism and critical to this tripartite development was Benito Mussolini himself, not merely in his enthusiastic endorsement of *romanità* as a central tenet of Fascist ideology, but particularly in the analogies drawn – by the Duce, his supporters, and, indeed, his critics – between the dictator and at first Caesar, and then Augustus (Cagnetta 1976; Wyke 1999b).[2] As Griffin writes, "[a]ll [the] myths of national renewal were subsumed in the leader-cult or *ducismo*. Mussolini was the *dux*, a modern Caesar, the restorer of the Augustan age, the heir of Mazzini and Garibaldi combined, the inaugurator of a new age" (Griffin 1991: 74–5).

It is worth separating the two models of Caesar and Augustus that Griffin here conflates. At the outset of his leadership, Mussolini adopted the persona of Caesar, the vigorous general and dictator who rescued Rome from the corruption of the decaying Republic (Kostof 1978: 284). Luciano Canfora has argued that fascist historiography recognized in the Caesarean regime, and particularly the three years following the death of Caesar, a Roman "revolution," analogous to the fascist revolution with its violent rejection of democracy and suppression of the privileged classes (Canfora 1980: 253–4). Yet this observation also highlights the weakness of the Caesarean exemplar: it was Caesar's *death* that precipitated the so-called "revolution." As such, this paradigm could only be a temporary one for the

Duce. Augustus, therefore, particularly in the wake of Italy's imperial activities of the 1930s, became the more popular model. This found its most complete and extravagant realization in the 1937–8 *Mostra Augustea della Romanità* (The Augustan exhibition of Romanness), an exhibition in Rome that attracted over one million visitors. Although its stated purpose was to celebrate the two-thousandth anniversary of the birthday of Augustus, the event was – unsurprisingly – used to draw explicit parallels between the golden age of the Roman empire and the contemporary fascist regime, with an emphasis on the continuity between past and present.

In retrospect, the vigorous use of Rome in the aesthetics and ideology of Italian Fascism may seem dramatically anomalous. Yet, from the intimate association of *romanità* with Italian nationalism – whether imperial, republican, or monarchic – derives a frequent congruence between Italian Fascism and more traditional forms of political thought. When considering studies on the Roman world produced during the Fascist period, it is thus more difficult to isolate specifically "fascist" scholarship from work that displays a more "generic" nationalistic tenor. Of course, studies that make explicit, for example, the parallels between Mussolini and Caesar in a hagiographical fashion or those that reproduce a recognizably fascist vocabulary might now be easily dismissed, but other scholarship produced at the time can be difficult to categorize (Canfora 1980: 76–103). Furthermore, the various roots of Italian Fascism, from anarchic socialism to nationalism, futurism to cubism, made it – at least initially – acceptable, if not attractive, to a wide variety of figures.

Emblematic of this problem is the *Enciclopedia italiana*, begun in 1925. Much like other encyclopedic works of its kind, it remains the Italian equivalent of the *Encyclopaedia Britannica*; additional appendices are still added today. Nonetheless, this was a project that – initially at least – was intimately associated with Italian Fascism. In 1932, in volume 14 of the encyclopedia, under the subject heading "Fascismo," leading figures of the movement, including Mussolini, endeavored to expound to the world a summary of fascist doctrine. The *Enciclopedia*, then, contained a determined attempt by a stable regime at the formation of a coherent ideology. It is on the most famous entry, "The Doctrine of Fascism," that the attention of historians of fascism has inevitably focused.[3] Rome is, of course, critical to this definition:

> Anti-individualistic, fascist thought is for the state; and for the individual in as much as he coincides with the state, the conscious, and the universal will of man in his historic existence.... Fascism is for the only liberty which can be a serious thing, the liberty of the state and of the individual in the state. Therefore, for the fascist, everything is in the state, and no human or spiritual thing exists, or has any sort of value, outside the state. In this sense fascism is totalitarian, and the fascist state, which is the synthesis and unity of every value, interprets, develops, and strengthens the entire life of the people.... The fascist state is a will to power and empire. The Roman tradition is here a powerful force. According to the doctrine of fascism, empire is not only a territorial or military or mercantile concept, but a spiritual and moral one. One can think of an empire, that is, a nation, which directly or indirectly guides other nations, without the need to conquer a single square kilometre of territory. ("La dottrina del fascismo," Gentile 1932: 14:847–8).

Naturally it is fascinating – although not at all unexpected – to find (the idea of) Rome in this critical and definitive statement of Italian Fascist thought. Less predictable, but not less interesting – for my argument at least – is the fact that amongst the many academic contributors to the *Enciclopedia* were a number of distinguished classicists, including Giorgio Pasquali, Gaetano De Sanctis, and the latter's younger pupil, Arnaldo Momigliano. The biographies of these scholars are proof of the complicated nature of Italian intellectual life in the 1930s: Pasquali was among the signatories of Benedetto Croce's 1925 "anti-fascist manifesto"; De Sanctis, a staunchly Catholic nationalist, refused to take the Fascist oath that was required from all employees of the state; Momigliano swore the oath, but then had to emigrate to England when, in the wake of Italy's increasingly close alliance with Germany, a series of anti-Semitic racial laws were promulgated in 1938. None of these men could be rightly thought of as intellectual collaborators with Italian Fascism: rather their contributions show that scholars from different backgrounds felt able – for whatever reason – to participate in the work of the *Enciclopedia italiana* regardless (or perhaps because) of its political associations. Mariella Cagnetta has discussed the complex political, institutional, and cultural issues at stake in this matter with regard to classical scholarship in her study *Antichità classiche nell'Enciclopedia italiana* (Classical antiquities in the *Enciclopedia italiana* [1990]). The *Enciclopedia* and (for the purposes of this chapter at least) its classical contributors provide a good illustration of the problem facing scholars approaching the relationship between scholarship, Italian Fascism, and the idea of Rome.

3   Classics and the Third Reich

No German could, of course, claim to be a "citizen of Rome" (or indeed of Greece), and Germany had no such smooth relationship with the classical past.[4] The uneasy relationship between Germany and Rome following the Reformation confirmed the eternal city as a contentious exemplar for German intellectuals and statesmen; Greece, therefore, was made to provide an alternative locus of authority. Given the association of Germany with philhellenism, it is worth reiterating that this turn to Greece was, for want of a better expression, a state of mind. Nevertheless, while the "tyranny" (Butler 1935) of Greece over eighteenth- and nineteenth-century German thought may well have been exaggerated, it seems beyond doubt that the Greeks played a formative role in the formation of modern German intellectual consciousness (Cambiano 1988; Schmidt 2001; Christ 1986; Gildenhard and Ruehl 2003; Marchand 1996; Rawson 1969).

Hitler's pronouncements on ancient Greece, by contrast, were not prompted by real or imaginary philosophical, intellectual, or even artistic affinities, but by what he thought of as racial contiguity. Famous remarks, such as his assessment of Sparta, "the clearest race-state in history" (Schmuhl 1992: 152),[5] and his assertion of German lineage, "[w]hen someone asks us about our ancestors, we should always point to the Greeks" (Picker 1976: 85), confirm this racialized "use" of antiquity. The doctrine of racial and national purity, of Aryanism, and its association with the ancient Hellenes were not, however, his own invention:[6] de Gobineau, H. S. Chamberlain, and their successful twentieth-century heir, H. F. K. Günther (nicknamed *Rasse-Günther* [race-Günther], advocate of *Aufnordung* [renordification], *Eugenik* [eugenics], and *Rassenhygiene* [racial hygiene]), had long proposed such racial doctrine (Günther 1925, 1928, 1929). Günther's 1922 volume, an "ethnography" (*Rassenkunde*) of the German people, sold over a quarter of a million copies (Griffin 1995: 124). Alfred Rosenberg, leading ideologue of Nazism and author of the wildly successful *Mythus des 20. Jahrhunderts* (The myth of the twentieth century [1930]), also expounded the superiority of the Nordic race, whose ancestors are to be found in the ancient world. His book, outsold in Germany only by *Mein Kampf* (My struggle) (Bollmus 1970: 25ff.), argues that world history is marked by the key racial struggle between the Aryan race and corrupting Semitic influence (Nova 1986). R. W. Darré, Nazi minister for food and agriculture, coined the Nazi slogan *Blut und Boden* (Blood and soil), and in a series of books argued both for the Nordic "creation" of European culture and the necessity of establishing a new racial aristocracy (*Neuadel*) (Darré 1934, 1935). Greece, then, was seen to offer an exemplary racial model and point of contact; in this respect, Hitler's remarks are consistent with much popular racist discourse of his day.

Contrary, however, to the Winckelmannian tradition in Germany, which privileged and imitated Greek art and architecture, Hitler was, it would seem, more preoccupied with the impressive scale of ancient Roman monuments. He famously envisaged the urban renewal of Berlin – to be renamed "Germania" – along Roman lines. With an Ozymandian eye to posterity, he developed with Albert Speer the concept of the "ruin-value" of major buildings, anticipating the awe with which future generations would behold even the vast remains of the Third Reich. This desire to replicate, or rather to exceed, the imposing structures of imperial power made Rome the more prominent ancient archetype (Losemann 1999; Scobie 1990; Quinn 2000).[7] While Speer characterized Hitler's interest in the visual impact of the Roman model as megalomania, Alex Scobie, in his 1990 study *Hitler's State Architecture: The Impact of Classical Antiquity*, has suggested that Hitler's desire to replicate Roman architecture was a part of a much more coherent programmatic design, and that the new buildings of the Reich were to play an important part in the psychological and communal development and sustenance of the Nazi empire. Certainly Hitler's appropriation of Roman monumentality and his admiration for the vast conquests of the empire coincide exactly with his understanding of the power of *Versammlungsarchitektur* (assembly architecture, architecture in which large numbers of people can be gathered) and his longstanding obsession with the acquisition of *Lebensraum* (living space) for the German nation. Aphoristic though his remarks on Rome, Greece, and Sparta may have been, Adolf Hitler's opinions of antiquity can therefore arguably be aligned with his wider worldview. Antiquity provided a decorative canvas for both his violent anti-Semitism (and more general racism, particularly with regard to Eastern Europe and Russia) and his imperialist vision.

Hitler's relatively infrequent and often esoteric remarks about the ancient world, however, do little to explain why many scholars (whether classical or otherwise) should have followed the racist propaganda of the National Socialist government so enthusiastically. Of course – and this must be stated immediately – the institutional pressures placed on scholars by Nazism were frequently immense, and as the regime became more murderous throughout the 1930s, it would have taken remarkable courage to resist (Losemann 1977; Noakes 1993). That many scholars, however, did not pay mere lip service to the regime is also undeniable. While some of this may be attributed to personal prejudice, flourishing under a climate of hatred and fear, the relationship between race, classics, and the Third Reich can be better understood against a number of intellectual precedents in German philhellenism and classical scholarship. This may provide some way of explaining how classical scholars could have managed to reconcile their work with the ideology of Nazism.

It has long been observed that German philhellenism was often consistent or concomitant with trends of thought that would have alarming twentieth-century consequences (Rawson 1969; Marchand 1996). For instance, the fourth of Johann Gottlieb Fichte's "addresses" (*Reden an die deutsche Nation* [Addresses to the German nation] [1808]), texts central to the philosophy and development of German organic nationalism, makes a case for the peculiar spiritual affinity between Germany and Greece. It is possible, too, as Athena Leoussi's work has shown, to draw a convincing genealogical line between the nineteenth-century philological study of Indo-European languages and the development of Aryan chauvinism and racism in the twentieth century (not least through such figures as de Gobineau and H. S. Chamberlain) (Leoussi 1998). Of particular importance, as Elizabeth Rawson has shown, was the connection of Sparta with the "nordic" Dorians, supposed to be the "true" Greeks (Rawson 1969). More specifically, it has also been proposed that certain expressions of philhellenism (and by extension, classical scholarship) have some inherent connections with anti-Semitism (Glucksmann 1980; Cancik and Cancik-Lindemaier 1991). All too often, the Greeks, or Dorians, were placed in polar opposition, as original and "pure" Europeans, to Semitic languages and people (Hall 1997). Conflated with the idea of the *Urvolk* (the original people, a fantasy of Romanticism), this could become a powerful formula. Matters of race or, more pertinently, racial superiority can therefore be seen to be intrinsic to certain trends in German classical scholarship. Recently Luciano Canfora and Egon Flaig have argued that Ulrich von Wilamowitz-Moellendorff was disposed to such lines of thought, although their theses have been vigorously opposed by Hugh Lloyd-Jones (Canfora 1985; Flaig 2003; Lloyd-Jones 2004).

In the wake of World War I, a number of anxieties about the state of German society and concerns over national identity focused the attention of many on issues of education. Much of this debate revolved around the perceived decline of the classical *Gymnasium* (secondary school) in Germany after 1918 and the sense that "traditional" values were slipping away (Solmsen 1989). Classicists were necessarily involved in this debate. It should be noted at this point that the traditionalist and decidedly antidemocratic position adopted by several classical scholars during the 1920s and 1930s makes it difficult to distinguish between work that is the product of conservative postwar disenchantment and that which coheres more consciously to the catholic doctrines of National Socialism (which could range from left to right). That classical scholars were unable to disassociate their conservative position from the

Party's chauvinistic doctrines is evident from the inadequate response made (or, rather, not made) by many to the new political situation. As Marchand suggests, "[i]f these men bear a measure of responsibility for the failure of the Weimar Republic it lies in their resistance to progressive reform" and in their employment of "the arguments of the new Right to defend the status quo"(Marchand 1996: 304; Lloyd-Jones 1999).

A further complication lies in the fact that many scholars – such as W. F. Otto, author of *Dionysus* (1933) – adopted, on the contrary, a Nietzschean language that was itself appropriated by Nazism (von Blumenthal 1939; Cancik 1995). A conflict of scholarly models became epitomized in the opposition between the *Wissenschaft* (the traditional scholarship) of Wilamowitz and the *Zukunfts-philologie* (the philology of the future) of F. W. Nietzsche. This clash between the historicism associated with Wilamowitz and a more aesthetic appreciation of Greek culture advocated by Nietzsche defined classical scholarship in 1920s and 1930s Germany. Scholars endeavored to return "meaning" to the study of ancient literature in the face of the cultural dislocation provoked by World War I (Solmsen 1989; Caldar, Flashar, and Lindken 1985; Flashar 1995).

Of this matter Werner Jaeger, inventor of and spokesman for the so-called "Third Humanism," is symbolic (Calder 1983; Calder 1992; White 1992).[8] Jaeger is probably best known now amongst nonspecialists for his three-volume work *Paideia* (the first volume was published in 1934). Throughout the 1920s and early 1930s, he put forward the educational, political, and cultural value of ancient Greece as the solution to the perceived crises of the Weimar Republic (Jaeger 1960). While this can be seen as a product of the fusion of the profound sense of postwar anxiety, Wilhelmine antidemocratic sentiment, and inherent academic conservatism and elitism, equally important was Jaeger's desire to find a "third way" between Wilamowitz and Nietzsche. Thus, long before the success of *Paideia*, Jaeger mapped out a new vision of humanism (which shook itself free from the "purely aesthetic" humanism of Goethe and Humboldt), hoping to reinstate the model whereby the cultural and political coincided, a model he saw depicted in ancient Greece.

Jaeger's early lectures single out Plato as the supreme theorist of *paideia/Bildung* (Jaeger 1960: *passim*). But for all their obvious sincerity his appeals appear, in retrospect, rather generic and vague. Just how the literature of ancient Greece and the particular example of Plato were supposed to educate and form German citizens for a truly organic and "whole" political life remains unclear (Kahn 1992). Such was the criticism leveled at Jaeger's work by Bruno Snell in his famous review of *Paideia* (Snell 1966). Snell rightly pointed out that Jaeger's programmatic search for *paideia* throughout Greek literature and his dismissal of German neohumanism left an unappealing political vacuum too easily appropriated by politics of any sort. Indeed, Paul Friedländer, in the marginalia to his copy of *Paideia*, did not hesitate to make these politics clear: *schlecht* (bad), *die Nähe Hitlers!* (the closeness to Hitler!), and *Nazi* are a few of his remarks (Calder and Braun 1996). Rudolf Pfeiffer, too, in a long and fair analysis of the work, made clear his uneasiness with the careless anachronisms of *Paideia*, which made him critical of Jaeger's organic and over-theorizing approach. While recognizing the need for debate on the subject of humanism, he suggested that Jaeger, by reading a modern spirit too invasively into the past, made Greek literature less strange and more "classic" than it is (Pfeiffer 1935).

The relevance of Greece and its relationship to contemporary politics was a central feature of Jaeger's outlook. In 1930, lamenting that the international values of Renaissance humanism had been lost in the pure, narrow scholarship of the nineteenth century, he advocated once again a new – German – humanism:

> The most important supranational task which is placed before humanism in Germany at present is to keep alive internally our bond with old Europe and to forearm ourselves against outright spiritual surrender before eastern powers; if it should succeed in this to insert and to draw up in each soul the common inheritance of antiquity with ever-new employment of its whole strength, then this educational act is at the same time the greatest service which German humanism is able to perform indirectly for the cohesion of the European culture-community. (Jaeger 1960: 185)

Jaeger, therefore, like many others, collapsed the concepts of *Bildung* (education) and *Kultur* (culture) into Greek *paideia* – the source and location of true humanism (Jaeger 1960: 108–9, 202). As such, Jaeger's humanism coincided with more nationalistic appropriations of antiquity. Certainly, Jaeger offered his *paideia* as a means of generating and sustaining the spiritual *Gemeinschaft* (community) of Germany (Näf 1992). The unity of classical culture, Jaeger argued, could be used to unify (or face down) the plurality of cultures in Weimar Germany (Jaeger 1960: 126). While Jaegar's total commitment to *paideia*, or *Bildung*, provides a distinct alternative to the *Volk* (nation) of nationalist and Nazi ideology, nevertheless *Paideia I* exhibits a vocabulary of race that corresponds with the racial lexicon of Nazism.[9] Problematic, too, was Jaeger's willing participation in the *Gleichschaltung* (the bringing into line) of universities that took place following the Nazi seizure of power, when he contributed a short piece, "Die Erziehung des politischen Menschen und die Antike" (The education of political men and antiquity), to Ernst Krieck's nationalist and racist pedagogical journal, *Volk im Werden* (A people in becoming) (Jaeger 1933; cf. White 1992 and Orozco 1995). Although this would seem to have been an exercise in (mere) academic opportunism, an attempt to convince the new powers of the compatibility of his "Third Humanism" (which would offer the perfect educational mold for forming the political community of National Socialism) with Party aims, it also shows how easily "Third Humanism," like so much else in 1930s Germany, could be aligned with Nazism.

In general, it was around Plato, education, and *Bildung* that much of the discussion on humanism centered, but the terms of this debate became critical with the emphasis placed on the formation of "new men" under National Socialism (Demetriou 2002). The year 1933 saw the publication of *Humanistische Bildung im nationalsozialistischen Staate* (Humanism in the National Socialist state), to which a number of leading classical scholars, including Hans Oppermann and Fritz Schachermeyr, contributed (Oppermann 1933; Schachermeyr 1933; Losemann 1977; Christ 1982; Malitz 1998). The tone of the book was decisively against Jaeger's "Third Humanism" (although, naturally, not for the reasons given by Snell or Pfeiffer). Amongst the articles was "Plato als Erzieher zum deutschen Menschen" (Plato as educator for German men), by Adolf Rusch. Although it reflects contemporary interest in Plato, this article does not quite concur with the praise, given by H. F. K. Günther in his (1928) work *Platon als Hüter des Lebens* (Plato as guardian of life), for the ancient author as the founder of the doctrine of racial superiority (despite reading like a shopping-list of ideal characteristics in German youth). It is to the ideology of *völkische Gemeinschaft* (the national community) that Rusch pleads, illustrating Plato's suitability as a reading text for school students, who would learn of the sacrifice of leading intellects to the greater good of the spiritual community.

Also in this volume Gustav Klingenstein, in an article revealingly entitled "Humanistische Bildung als deutsche Waffe" (Humanist education as German weapon), lauds the ability of a classical education to teach heroism and competitive spirit. Importantly, he draws a contrast between Erasmus, the leading light of sixteenth-century cosmopolitan humanism, detractor of religious warfare and, by the end of his life, firm opponent of Martin Luther, and Ulrich von Hutten, the German humanist, patriot, and knight who fought with von Sickingen for Martin Luther against the ecclesiastical princes of southwest Germany.

> Two figures are prominent at the beginning of German humanism, Erasmus and Hutten. At all times, both have had followers in Germany; the first must now stand back, the others are today men of the hour, whose noble ancestor Hutten made his life a struggle for the German way and his humanism a sword. (Klingenstein 1933: 29)

This tension between the international and the fiercely national faces of German classical scholarship and humanism, and the challenge offered to them by the chameleonic politics of National Socialism, are themes encountered again and again in this debate. The rivalry between *German* humanism and its foreign (particularly Italian) counterparts is striking, and reminds the reader of the deep tension felt in the German academy over the perceived importance of such "alien" intellectual trends (Schäfer 1943; Fuhrmann 1984; Visser 2001). Indeed, the Nazi party continued to propose (alongside the enthusiastic embracing of the "Doric" Greeks) a more Bismarckian rejection of Greek cultural models in favor of Germanic ones (Michalski 1998; Niven 2000).

Connected to this was the charge of intellectualism raised against Jaeger's project. Pfister, in an article entitled "Der politische Humanismus" (Political humanism) (thus indicating the direction that discussion on humanism will take), argues that this "so-called" humanism is unable to accomplish the education of Germans as political men. "True" political humanism would draw direct examples – of race, of *Gemeinschaft*, of will and *Weltanschauung* (worldview) – from the ancients (Pfister 1934). Bengl, in 1941, also associates the substance of "Third Humanism" with the benign and (crucially) cosmopolitan humanisms of the past. Genuine, *völkisch*-political humanism turns to antiquity for exemplary confirmation: for instance, the heroic militarism of the *Iliad*, or the racial laws of Solon and Pericles (Bengl 1941). Likewise, in 1942, Vorwahl contrasts explicitly "contemporary" humanism with "political" humanism. His reference to Günther as the most outstanding authority of political humanism lays bare its racialized structure (Vorwahl 1942: 112–13).

Jaeger's "Third Humanism" was, it would seem, rejected almost uniformly by the academic community, both Nazi and non-Nazi (Losemann 1977: 97–108; Näf 1992). Helmut Berve (who in Jaeger's absence would become a [self-appointed] spokesman for political classical scholarship) in a 1934 article, which programmatically encourages the politicization of the study of ancient history, dismisses the new humanism for its lack of vitality (Berve 1993). Yet even his "politicized" scholarship produced uneven results: a 1942 volume, *Das neue Bild der Antike: Hellas* (The new picture of antiquity: Greece), edited by Berve contains a number of articles that conform to the new model, but also several that do not (Berve 1942; Englert 1942; Gadamer 1942; Losemann 1977; Näf 1986; Nippel 1993).

But humanism in general also came under attack from National Socialist educational theorists and philosophers who rejected humanistic *Bildung* in favor of a new *völkische Erziehung* (national education) (Kneller 1942). Although they eschewed traditional elite education, they nonetheless still embraced the exemplary potential of the ancient Greeks. In particular, two ideological pedagogues, Ernst Krieck and Alfred Baeumler, whose educational philosophies were dominant and popular throughout the National Socialist period, embraced both the heroic-soldierly values of ancient Greece and the potential of the totalitarian state in Plato (Baeumler 1939, 1943; Krieck 1933, 1934a, 1934b, 1934c, 1935). In his rectorial address of 1933, Baeumler cast aside the "idealistic-humanist philosophy of *Bildung*" (Baeumler 1943: 136), whose aspirations were too individualistic and purely aesthetic for the purposes of the new state, in favor of the political pedagogy of Plato, whose tripartite division of society would provide both an educational and military ideal, and also mold the development of a Party-elite (Baeumler 1939). National Socialist education must be total, committed to the political and communal development of the *Volk* (nation). Simultaneously, it would also be the organic expression of the *völkisch* will.

Krieck, despite early collaboration with Jaeger (hence Jaeger's publication in *Volk im Werden*), soon disassociated himself from what he saw as academic frivolity. Critically, Jaeger's "humanism," as we have already seen, was not *völkisch* enough, a feature of education Krieck had long called for:

> Provided that we see the collective responsibility placed before the German people to be the production of national-political life-unity (*der völkisch-politischen Lebensganzheit*), by which we mean the appropriate world-view (*Weltanschauung*) and direction of will (*Willensrichtung*), then in the future the national-political (*völkisch-politische*) university must take the place of the obsolete humanistic university. (Krieck 1934a: 81)

Krieck, too, with Plato as a model, described education in symbiosis with the state, as an organ of the will of the people that both produces and sustains itself (Krieck 1935: 96).

National Socialism, then, both crystallized and encouraged a number of long-standing debates. The cultural arguments of the neohumanists and Idealists were transferred from cosmopolitanism to a new framework of cultural vision – the *Volk*. The subsequent vision of humanism and society, abstracted from practice, was embedded in reactionary tradition and was an "anti-modernist, anti-democratic endeavour" (White 1992: 275) and a remote search after *organischer Zusammenhang* (organic connection) and *das Ganze* (unity) (Sontheimer 1968). It was all too easy for already-disenchanted cultural critics to slip into more radicalized and extremist positions. In the end, this language of crisis was one appropriated by the extreme nationalists (Stern 1965; Glaser 1978). Yet ironically, the regime that attracted so many academics was itself trenchantly anti-intellectual (Fuhrmann 1984).

4   Conclusion

As it is well-known, for many years, Italian speakers and journalists used to argue very much about the Roman Empire, comparing and confusing ancient and modern conditions. Thus, the natural reaction of thinking people was a wide-spread distrust of every fact concerning Roman history. But, at the same time, the value of the Roman Empire appeared a problem of the modern moral and political conscience. It was easy to find an able or a prudent answer to the continual questions of one's own pupils about the real value of the Roman Empire and of its most representative figures. It was difficult to give a *true* answer. The same difficulty I found increased when I was asked to write a sketch of the History of the Roman Empire for the Italian Encyclopaedia. The difficulty consisted, obviously enough, in eliminating modern interferences from the question, while at the same time conserving for the question the character of a problem of the modern conscience. What has no value, has no history. Yet the values of history are not matter for polemics, but for plain knowledge. The spontaneous result was that the interpretation of the Roman Empire became more and more a point of evaluation of Pagan Civilisation in its decline and of Christian Civilisation in its dawn. The problem was transplanted into its proper ground: it was the very problem of the foundation of our modern life. I could perceive in my pupils a keener interest and less suspicion. (Momigliano 1996: xx–xxi)

Thus Momigliano, in Cambridge, in 1940. As other chapters in this volume demonstrate, antiquity has long been used to impart value and authority to the modern world. That this use of the ancient world becomes particularly visible – and *seemingly* problematic or anomalous – when made by or under Nazism or fascism is an implication that appears to inform many studies on these matters. Yet this is surely the consequence of our deep historical fascination with and repulsion for the totalitarian regimes of the twentieth century (given their impact on the politics and culture of the postwar era). As I hope to have implied in this chapter, the uses of Rome and Greece in the ideologies of National Socialist Germany or fascist Italy were, on the whole, embedded in specific and longstanding national circumstances. It is undeniable, of course, that the establishment of authoritarian governments bent on molding national culture crystallized and – more importantly – catalyzed certain aspects of these appropriations. But these will be understood, and finally confronted, only when returned to the context of the classical tradition in its entirety.

NOTES

1 See Brunner (1970), answered by Schnur (1970) and Villard (1972). For studies, in English, of the varying appropriations of antiquity in these regimes see Ades et al. (1995); Aicher (2000); Kopff (2000); Kostof (1978); Lane (2001); Lebrecht Schmidt (2001); Losemann (1999); Marchand (1996); Quinn (2000); Rawson (1969); Scobie (1990); Stone (1999); Thomas (2000, 2001b); Visser (1992); Wyke (1997b, 1999a, 1999b); and Ziolkowski (1993). There is, of course, a substantial amount of important work done in German and Italian, of which Losemann (1977) and Canfora (1979, 1980) are seminal. For a comprehensive bibliography see Näf (2001). *Der Neue Pauly* contains a number of relevant entries. For Fascism and Nazism in general, see, e.g., Kershaw (1987, 2000); Mosse (1964, 1980, 1999); Nolte (1966); Griffin (1991, 2003); Weber (1964). More relevant to this article is the critical relationship between Fascism and culture and the nature of the "Fascist aesthetic:" see, e.g., Affron and Antliff (1997); Brenner (1963); Campiglio et al. (2003); Cannistraro (1975); Falasca-Zamponi (1997); Gentile (1993); Golsan (1992); Griffin (1996, 2001); Kemal and Gaskell (2000); Kühnl (1996); Malvano (1988); Millon and Nochlin (1978); Petropoulos (1996); Spotts (2002).

2 Ronald Syme noted the parallels implicitly in his important 1939 study *The Roman Revolution.*

3 Although attributed at the time to Mussolini, this piece was in fact written by the general editor, the neo-idealist philosopher Giovanni Gentile.

4 See, e.g., Canfora (1979) for this debate played on in the reception of Tacitus' *Germania.* My thanks to Chris Whitton for allowing me to read his unpublished 2004 Cambridge MPhil thesis on this subject, "The Reception of Tacitus' *Germania* in the Third Reich."

5 The context for this remark is important. It was made, at the 1929 Nuremberg Party-Day rally, in praise of proactive euthanasia as a means of state-controlled eugenics.

6 Nor indeed was it limited to Germany. See, e.g., Leoussi (1998).

7 See, however, Schäche (1979) for an account of more pluralistic influences, at least in the planning of the Berlin Museum.

8 Jaeger in fact used this term only twice in his writing, although in rather significant places. See Jaeger (1933, 1934). For a contemporary response, see Rüdiger (1970).

9 Calder (1983) cites Gisela Müller, *Die Kulturprogrammatik des dritten Humanismus als Teil imperialistischer Ideologie in Deutschland zwischen erstem Weltkrieg und Faschismus* (The cultural aims and objectives of Third Humanism as a part of imperialist ideology in Germany between the First World War and Fascism), as demonstrating the racist elements of *Paideia I* (particularly its introduction).

CHAPTER TWENTY-FOUR

Psychology

Fabio Stok

1 Introduction

In antiquity psychology, as the science of the *psychē* (Greek for "soul"), was a part of philosophy. Psychological problems (perception, emotions, behavior, etc.) were actually treated by various philosophical schools, which proposed different accounts depending on their different theories about the substance of the psyche (materialist or immaterial), its structure (either unitary or divided into rational and sensitive parts), and so on.

Besides philosophy, psychological topics were also treated by ancient medicine, which was interested in the study of sense-organs, psychopathology, and related issues. The medical approach to psychology differs from the philosophical one in giving priority to the somatic causes of the phenomena in question; by doing so, it assumes an influence of the human body upon psychic life. This approach is present in the Hippocratic treatises: the principal thesis of *De morbo sacro* (On sacred disease) is that epilepsy and mental disorders are caused by humoral pathologies of the brain (3, 3.366 Littré), and in the *Aphorisms* (6.23, 4.568 Littré) we read that fear (*phobos*) and sadness (*dystymia*) are symptoms of melancholia (the disease caused by black bile), so that an organic fluid, the black bile itself, has an influence upon emotions.

Throughout antiquity the philosophical and the medical approach coexisted as different interpreting codes for psychic phenomena, but the boundaries between the two fields were different in different times and places. The Peripatetic school was inclined to acknowledge the influence of the body on the psychic life, as revealed by its interest in physiognomics, the theory that individual characters are recognizable from somatic features (Ps.-Aristotle *Physiognomics* 1, 805a), or by its speculations about the melancholia of poets, statesmen, and so on, according to which they are all affected by black bile (Ps.-Aristotle *Problems* 30, 953a). The Stoic school, on the other hand, made use of medical language to describe the features of the psyche and called the passions "diseases of the soul," to be cured by means of reason and philosophy (e.g., Diogenes Laertius 7.110–16; Cicero, *Tusculan Disputations* 4.11–21). The Stoics were obviously aware that diseases such as melancholia could involve the use of reason (Diogenes Laertius 7.127), but they generally admitted only a limited number of such instances and explained human behavior from the rational and moral perspective. Posidonius, trying to delimit more precisely the boundaries between the two fields, distinguished four types of diseases: diseases of the body, diseases of the soul, diseases that "do not belong to the soul but are physical with mental effects" (like melancholia), and those that "do not belong to the body but are mental with physical effects" (fragment 154 Kidd).

An example of this last type of disease is "love sickness." It is the object of an anecdote that is known in several versions with different protagonists. In one of the versions the famous physician Erasistratos (third century BC) is called to cure the sickness of Antiochos II Soter, son of Seleucus, king of Syria. From pulsation and other physical symptoms, Erasistratos realizes that Antiochos was not suffering from a somatic disease but was in love with Stratonike, his stepmother (Plutarch *Life of Demosthenes* 38).

This anecdote shows that the boundary between diseases of the body and diseases of the soul was well fixed on practical and professional grounds. On theoretical grounds, however, apart from Posidonius' classification, the connection remained unresolved, as shown by Galen's ambiguous position. In his work entitled *Quod animi mores corporis temperamenta sequuntur* (That the faculties of the soul follow the temperaments of the body, 14.767–822 Kühn), he points out the influence exerted by the body upon the soul: the body is not involved in mental disorders only, but it also affects man's character and the whole of his psychic life. In his subsequent work *De animi cuiuslibet affectuum dignotione et curatione* (The diagnosis and cure of the soul's passions and errors, 5.1–57 Kühn), however, Galen adopts both a philosophical point of view and a philosophical language, explaining the passions as diseases of the soul and ascribing to philosophy the function of *paidagōgia* (pedagogy), as in the Stoic tradition (Stok 1996: 2371–5).

The two approaches we have found in antiquity are the roots of the modern mind–body dualism, as Karl Popper demonstrated by pointing out the Hippocratic *De morbo sacro* as its prototype (Eccles and Popper 1977: 161). Moreover, both approaches continued throughout the Middle Ages and into modern times. The philosophical approach was inherited, through late antiquity, by Christian thought, in which the concept of the soul acquired religious and theological implications. In its turn, modern psychology, from Descartes on, also derives from the philosophical tradition. The medical approach, on the other hand, continued in the Galenism of the late Middle Ages and Renaissance.

In modern times, too, the boundaries between medicine and psychology experienced changes and modifications. In the following sections we shall explore some episodes of this history in which the reception of ancient authors or topics demonstrates some importance.

2 Characters and Temperaments

The tendency to classify human behavior in a system of characters (psychological types representing the variety of attitudes and behaviors present in a community) is very old. In Greece and then in Rome, this tendency was supported by comic theater, which presupposes both characters and social and psychological patterns. Theophrastos' typology – which includes 30 characters with specific ethical and psychological features (the careless, the suspicious, the adulator, etc.) – is probably connected to comic theater.

Besides the ethical and psychological typologies, like that of Theophrastos, typologies that involve both psychological and somatic features, presupposing an ancient correlation between the two dimensions, are also found in antiquity. This approach is already present in physiognomics, a practice that had much success throughout antiquity and that claimed to infer the character of people (and sometimes also their future development) from their somatic features. A real typology is that founded on humors (the organic fluids present in the human body). The idea is that different humors are the cause of different characters.

Humoralism is the basis itself of the dominant physiology and pathology of medicine from antiquity to William Harvey (1578–1657). The canonic system was that of the four humors established by Polybos, son-in-law of Hippocrates, in the treatise *De natura hominis* (On the nature of man, ca. 410 BC): blood, phlegm, yellow (or red) bile, and black bile. The same Polybos connected the four humors with the four primary qualities (hot, wet, cold, and dry), with the four seasons, and with the four ages of human life.

Polybos' typology regards physiology and pathology, not psychology. The passage to a psychological humoral typology took place later, at a time not possible to specify precisely. Testimonies come from late antiquity, but the idea that humors influence characters is already present in Aristotle, who says that the courage and intelligence of animals are the product of the quality of their blood (*Parts of animals* 647b); Sextus Empiricus says that humors influence sensorial perception (*Outlines of Pyrrhonism* 1.51); and Galen informs us about the theory that humors influence moral qualities (*Commentary on Hippocrates' On the Nature of Man* 1.38, 15.97 Kühn). Perhaps in *Epistles* 1.18.89–90, Horace already alludes to the psychological humoral typology (Stok 1997: 164–70).

It is also difficult to determine the cultural milieu in which this typology was elaborated. In the medical tradition, the excess of one of the humors was regarded as pathological; the idea of the balance of the humors (*krasis* or *complexio*) excluded the possibility of several physiological states. Galen considers a typology of eight mixtures produced by the prevalence of one of the four primary qualities (hot, wet, etc.), or of two of them, but he includes in the typology also a ninth, well-balanced mixture, the frame of reference for all the others (*On Temperaments* 2.1, 1.572 Kühn).

The persistence in the medical tradition of this unitary concept of the human species is attested, from late antiquity to early modern times, by an ambiguity in the use of the term *melancholicus*, which for physicians denotes a person affected by melancholia, while in the typological system it means one of the four possible temperaments. (The situation is complicated by the pseudo-Aristotelian theory of the melancholia of geniuses, which was very influential in the Renaissance, thanks to Marsilio Ficino and the other humanists.) The humoral typology, on the whole, also remained marginal in medieval and early modern medicine, both of which were characterized by the prevalence of Galenism.

Among late ancient testimonies, the most important is that of the physician Vindicianus, a friend of St. Augustine. He explains the humoral typology in a letter to his nephew Pentadius: the sanguine temperament is characterized by simplicity and a good disposition; the choleric one by anger, shrewdness, and fickleness; the melancholic one by sadness, envy, and shyness; and the phlegmatic one by composure and reflectiveness. In late antiquity this typology is also known to Isidore of Seville (*Etymologies* 4.5.6; 10.30; 10.176) and Bede (*On the Reckoning of Time* 30).

In the Middle Ages the humoral typology reappears at the beginning of the twelfth century in the milieu of the School of Chartres, where it is used by William of Conches (ca. 1080–1154). It is uncertain whether the typology was transmitted directly by texts surviving in the West, like Vindicianus' epistle, or through Arabic medicine and the medical school of Salerno, where, however, Galenic orthodoxy (e.g., in the works of Avicenna and Costantinus Africanus) was dominant. In the school of Salerno the humoral typology appears in the second half of the twelfth century, with the *Flores diaetarum* (Anthology of treatments) ascribed to a John of St. Paul.

After William of Conches the humoral typology was adopted by many masters of Scholasticism. This presence is a bit surprising, considering that the typology is "the single most striking example of the habitual preference in ancient, medieval, and Renaissance medicine for materialist explanations of mental and emotional states" (Siraisi 1990: 106). As early as the time of Bishop Nemesios of Emesa in the fourth and fifth centuries (Temkin 1973: 81–92), Galen himself was opposed because of his position about the nature of the soul – sometimes he was even compared to the materialist Epicurus. But the humoral typology, just because it did not involve problems of the soul, was indeed "moralizable" and capable of being brought into agreement with Christian doctrine: William of Conches, in his *Summa philosophiae* (Summation of philosophy), connects the plurality of temperaments with original sin; Hugo of Fouilloy (ca. 1100–1172/3), in the *De medicina animae* (On the medicine of the soul), locates in the four humors the moral qualities of the soul; and St. Hildegard of Bingen (1098–1179), in the *Causae et curae* (Causes and cures), considers the influence of humors upon sexual behavior and distinguishes between female and male temperaments.

During the Middle Ages the humoral typology also involved astrology: the four temperaments were connected with four of the planets, the melancholic one with Saturn, the phlegmatic one with the Moon, the choleric one with Mars, and the sanguine one with Jupiter. Connections between planets and parts of the body were already known in ancient astrology, but the astrological use of the four humors appears for the first time in Arabic texts of the ninth century and was transmitted to the West through the Latin translation of the *Introductorium maius* (Greater introduction) of Alcabitius.

In the Renaissance humoral typology was well known and influenced literature and art extensively (Klibansky, Panofsky, and Saxl 1964; Filipczak 1997). Musicology, too, was interested in typology; for example, in the theory of Bartolomé Ramos de Pareja (1440–1522), who connected the four humors and their psychological affections with musical tonalities.

Already in the poetry of the late Middle Ages the word "melancholy" acquired the meaning of "mental disposition" or "psychic condition." The original meaning of "disease" was still used mainly by physicians: for example, in the *Anatomy of Melancholy* by Robert Burton (1577–1640), who is, however, acquainted with the new meaning of the term.

Humoral typology was still in use after the fall of Galenism, until the eighteenth century, as a purely psychological typology without real connection with humors. It is used, for example, by Johann Caspar Lavater (1741–1801) in his treatise on physiognomics, the ancient doctrine rediscovered in the Renaissance and divulged with some success in the early modern age.

After Lavater both physiognomic and humoral typology were degraded to pseudosciences, but temperaments remained alive in literary and artistic memory. They still live again in the recent novel of Rupert Thomson, *Divided Kingdom* (2005), where an imaginary organization of government and society is founded upon segregation of the people by four character types based on humors.

3 Medical Psychology

Medieval and early modern medicine inherits from Galenism a certain indifference toward psychology. This indifference persists also after the fall of Galenic humoralism, until the end of the eighteenth century, so that the mainstream approach to mental disorders remained for a long time a predominantly somatic one, from both an etiological and a therapeutic point of view.

Psychopathological nosology continued for a long time to be viewed in ancient terms, focusing on traditional areas such as mania and melancholy, with the addition of some "diseases" entrusted to medical competence during late antiquity and the Middle Ages. Such "diseases" include lycanthropy (the supposed transformation of a human being into a wolf, considered by physicians of this time as a form of melancholia) and *amor hereos* (passionate love), the ancient love sickness that in the anecdote quoted above was considered a disease of the soul but was included by Arnald of Villanova (ca. 1240–1311), for example, among the physical disorders.

Besides Galen, the only ancient physician with whom the Middle Ages were acquainted and who was interested in mental pathology is Rufos of Ephesos (first to second century BC), a supporter of humoralism as well and the author of a treatise on melancholia that was appreciated by Galen himself. There are also ancient physicians, like Cornelius Celsus, Aretaeus of Cappadocia, and Caelius Aurelianus, who followed other medical theories. They give detailed accounts of mental disorders with both pharmaceutical and relational therapeutic prescriptions, but their works were rediscovered only in the Renaissance and influenced only a few authors, whereas the cultural context was still dominated by Galenism. Among the authors of the early modern age interested in the psychological dimension of mental disorders, we should mention, for example, Paolo Zacchia (1584–1659), from Rome, physician of popes and founder of legal medicine, who made use of Celsus and the ancient moral philosophers in the psychopathological part of his *Quaestiones medico-legales* (Medical-legal questions; see Stok 2006).

This situation changed in the Enlightenment, when the French physician Philippe Pinel (1745–1826) elaborated a medical psychology that had great relevance in the history of psychiatry and psychiatric care (he also reformed the Parisian asylums of Bicêtre and Salpêtrière, as illustrated by Michel Foucault in his *History of Insanity in the Age of Reason*). In his *Medico-Philosophical Treatise on Mental Alienation* (1801), Pinel pushed aside the somatic approach hitherto prevailing and highlighted the importance of the passions as causes for mental disorders. From a therapeutical point of view, he elaborated the so-called "moral treatment" – a relational treatment aimed at controlling the behavior, the way of thinking, and the emotions of the patients. As the title of his work suggests, Pinel attempts in this way to give a philosophical foundation to medical discourse. He is obviously thinking of contemporary philosophy (Locke, Condillac, the Ideologues, and others), which was characterized by an approach to psychology that was detached from the problems of the soul.

But Pinel's ideas are also influenced by his classical background (Pigeaud 1994): his theory of the passions as causes of mental disorders comes partially from the Stoic theory of the passions discussed in Cicero's *Tusculan Disputations,* and his moral therapy is like the ancient "medicine of the soul." According to Stoic doctrine, however, philosophy must eradicate the passions; not so for Pinel, who believes that they are to be controlled and disciplined by medicine through application of the moral treatment. Pinel's classicism is also remarkable in his attitude toward the ancient physicians. He is resolutely hostile to Galen, to whose influence he ascribes the difficulties hitherto encountered by medicine in the psychopathological field. On the other hand, he thinks highly of Celsus, Aretaeus, and Caelius Aurelianus.

The second great exponent of French psychiatry was Jean-Etienne-Dominique Esquirol (1772–1840): he, too, used ancient authors, both medical and philosophical. In the essay entitled *The Passions Considered as Causes, Symptoms, and Means of Cure in Cases of Insanity* (1805), he affirms an approach to anger and madness evidently suggested to him by Seneca (*On Anger* 1.2). Like Pinel he praises Celsus, Aretaeus, and Caelius, along with Erasistratos, evidently for his treatment of love sickness. In the anecdote mentioned above, however, Erasistratos recognized the boundary between the medicine of the body and that of the soul, whereas Esquirol enlarged the field of medicine to include love sickness.

Hippocratic aphorism 6.23, on melancholia, is also discussed by Esquirol in his proposal for a new psychopathological denomination, that of lypemania (in an essay contained in his *On Mental Disease Considered in Medical, Hygienic, and Medico-Legal Terms*, 1838). This was a clinical condition that foreshadows today's pathologic depression (Jackson 1986: 152–3) and which has provided the term that has been used by psychiatrists for some decades. Unlike melancholia, use of the term "lypemania," for Esquirol, had the advantage of avoiding the obsolete reference to humoralism (for him this disease was mainly caused by "moral affections"), along with the ambiguity connected with the humoral typology.

Ancient authors probably also influenced the important distinction theorized by Esquirol in 1817 between hallucination (the perception of an object when no object is present) and illusion (the deceptive perception of reality), a distinction already suggested by ancient philosophy and medicine (Cicero *Academics* 1.88–9; Aretaeus 3.6; Caelius Aurelianus *On Acute Diseases* 1.118–19).

In the second half of the nineteenth century, an approach based on the organic and neurological aspects of mental disorders again prevailed in psychiatry. The German psychiatrist Wilhelm Griesinger (1817–68) programmatically declared that "mental diseases are diseases of the brain," a declaration reminiscent of the one we found in the Hippocratic *De morbo sacro*. Psychiatric research, consequently, was giving priority to anatomy and neurophysiology. In Vienna the most influential exponents of this approach were, in the seventies and eighties, the psychiatrist Thedor Meynert (1833–92) and the neuropathologist Ernst von Brücke (1819–92). It was with these teachers that Sigmund Freud (1856–1939) began his scientific career.

4   Psychoanalysis

The term "psychoanalysis" was first used by Freud in 1897 to denote the treatment of hysteria devised with Breuer in the preceding years. In choosing this term, Freud revived the ancient tradition of the "medicine of the soul," as shown by the beginning of a short essay published by him in 1890, "Psychical (or Mental) Treatment." Here he underlines the original meaning of the Greek word *psychē* (soul; German *Seele*) and claims the validity of a treatment made "by means which operate in the first instance and immediately upon the human mind (*Seelische*)," adding that the most important of these means is the word (Standard Edition 7.283).

These statements highlight how far Freud was in these years from the psychiatry of Meynert and from the histological researches on which he had worked in the Viennese Institute directed by Brücke. His withdrawal from medical positivism was begun during his stay in Paris (1885–6), at the clinic for the treatment of nervous maladies at the Salpêtrière directed by J.-M. Charcot: a few years later Freud compared Charcot's "discovery" of hysteria with the liberation of madness from its chains as achieved by Pinel (Standard Edition 3.22). Afterward the Freudian theory, still remaining chiefly a therapeutic practice, deeply influenced humanistic studies and contemporary culture as a whole.

We shall deal in the remainder of this chapter with the presence of classical culture in the works of Freud, and then with the influence of psychoanalysis upon classical studies.

4.1   *Freud and the classical world*

Greek and Latin authors, myths, and topics are present in Freud's works in a variety of ways. We can distinguish three different aspects of this presence. The first, sometimes quite difficult to evaluate, is the influence of Freud's classical learning on the formation of psychoanalysis, from his neuroanatomical inquiries in the eighties to his founding of a new method of psychological research. Second, we must consider Freud's use of classical authors and topics as "precursors" of psycho-analytical concepts, as part of a strategy directed toward underlining not only the novelty of psychoanalysis in the face of contemporary science, but also its con-sonance with the thoughts and topics of antiquity. The third aspect of the classical presence in Freud's work regards the quotations of Greek and especially Latin authors, particularly mottoes and famous phrases. In some cases, as we shall see, the phrases are pertinent to the context, but more often they belong to the rhetorical dimension of Freud's writing (Mahony 1987).

Freud's familiarity with classical texts obviously originated during his school years. His juvenile interest in the ancient world is shown by his self-identification with the Semite Hannibal, as a kind of revenge against the anti-Semitic discriminations suffered by his father. This self-identification is connected by Freud himself with the phobic inhibition that prevented him until 1901 from going to Rome, the city Hannibal never conquered (Standard Edition 4.194–7; Letters to Fliess 285). Besides this "Roman phobia," Freud was also fascinated by the other capital of ancient culture, Athens, where he suffered a sudden state of disorientation on the occasion of his visit to the Acropolis in 1904 (*A Disturbance of Memory on the Acropolis,* Standard Edition 22.239).

In his earlier years Freud had taken a great interest in archaic Greece, stimulated by the archaeological discoveries that brought to light the Mycenaean civilization (Freud's interest in archaic cultures is confirmed by his archaeological collection, which eventually included over 3,000 pieces). In 1899 he read *The History of Greek Culture* by J. Burckhardt, finding in it "unexpected parallels," as he writes in a letter to Fliess, adding that his "predilection for the prehistoric in all its human forms has remained the same" (Letters to Fliess 342). A few months later he says to Fliess that he has read the autobiography of Heinrich Schliemann, the discoverer of Troy (Letters to Fliess 353); at the end of the same year he presents the interpretation of a sexual childhood dream of E., one of his patients, as the discovery of a new Troy, "which had hitherto been deemed a fable" (Letters to Fliess 391–2). A comparison with the discovery of Troy is again advanced in *Moses and Monotheism* (1934–8), once more in connection with the emergence of the unconscious (Standard Edition 23.70), while in *Civilization and Its Discontents* (1930) the archaeological stratifica-tion of Rome is compared to the evolution of the psychic apparatus (Standard Edition 21.69–70).

After his school studies Freud continued to be interested in the classics during his first years at university: in 1874–6 he attended the courses in philosophy offered by Franz Brentano, who introduced him to Theodor Gomperz (1832–1912), professor of philology at the University of Vienna. Gomperz asked Freud to translate the twelfth volume of John Stuart Mill's works, which also contained an essay on Plato. Later Freud had as one of his patients Gomperz's wife, who supported him in his academic career (Letters to Fliess 456). Replying in 1907 to a questionnaire on reading, Freud listed the *Greek Thinkers* by Gomperz (1896–1902) as one of the 10 books that he recommended. On the same occasion he listed the Homeric poems and the tragedies of Sophocles among the 10 best works of world literature (Standard Edition 9.245).

References to classical antiquity are also made frequently by contemporary authors used by Freud: for example, Havelock Ellis (1859–1939) and Friedrich Nietzsche (1844–1900). Beginning in 1897, Ellis published *Studies in the Psychology of Sex*, an encyclopedic compendium of sexual behavior in which he also quotes classical authors. Nietzsche had taken up his academic career as a classical philologist, and in his *Birth of Tragedy* (1872) proposed a theory on the division of personality into Apollonian and Dionysian that provoked hostile reactions by U. von Wilamowitz-Moellendorff (1848–1931) and other philologists. In 1900 Freud told Fliess that he had acquired Nietzsche's works and was hoping to find in them "words for much that remains mute in me" (Letters to Fliess 398); in a letter sent in 1931 to L. Bickel (quoted by Gay 1988: 42n), he claims to have refused the study of Nietzsche but acknowledges that there are similarities between his philosophy and psychoanalysis.

Besides Gomperz, another classical philologist known to Freud was Jakob Bernays (1824–81), professor at Breslau and the uncle of his wife Martha; Bernays' interpretation of Aristotle's catharsis was used by Freud in his *Studies on Hysteria*, a work written in collaboration with Josef Breuer (1842–1925), his senior colleague at the Institute directed by Brücke.

4.2   *Freud, Breuer, and Aristotle's catharsis*

The *Studies on Hysteria* (1895) are considered the first important stage in the elaboration of psychoanalysis, after the initial physiological studies and Freud's experience with Charcot and Hyppolite Bernheim. Freud and Breuer developed Charcot's theories on hysteria, showing that the traumas of children are the cause of this disease and conceiving a hypnotic therapy aimed at making their patients eliminate their neurotic symptoms by reliving their forgotten traumas. In order to differentiate their own therapeutic method from Charcot's hypnosis, Freud and Breuer made use of the Greek concept of catharsis, which Aristotle used in his *Poetics* to describe the psychological reaction of the audience to tragic performances: "through pity (*eleos*) and fear (*phobos*)," Aristotle writes, tragedy "brings relief (*katharsis*) to these and similar emotions" (1449b).

The traditional interpretation, accepted, for example, by Lessing in his *Hamburg Dramaturgy*, gave a moral value to the term *katharsis*, which was understood as a "purification from passions," to be accomplished through a process at the end of which the spectator is a more virtuous person. A different interpretation was proposed in 1858 by Bernays: in his view, Aristotle took the concept from ancient medicine, in which *katharsis* denotes the evacuation of the corrupted humors, so that in the *Poetics* the term would denote the purgation from passions.

Freud and Breuer clearly followed Bernays' interpretation in their use of the concept of catharsis (e.g., Standard Edition 2.9). Perhaps they were also influenced by Gomperz, who kept up a correspondence with Breuer about this issue (he also published in 1896 an edition of Aristotle's *Poetics*). Bernays' works are not quoted in the *Studies*, but they were certainly known to Freud, who in 1932 gave the writer Arnold Zweig a book commemorating Bernays.

4.3   *From* The Interpretation of Dreams *to the Oedipus Complex*

After the publication of the *Studies*, Freud broke with Breuer, discovered the sexual etiology of children's neuroses, and elaborated the free-association technique. These topics are contained in the important work published in 1900, *The Interpretation of Dreams*. In this essay Freud criticizes contemporary research about dreams, which focused on the neurophysiological side of the phenomenon, aiming instead to investigate the meaning of the dream's content. This research had a precedent in the ancient *oneirokritika*, and especially in the work of Artemidorus of Daldis (second century AD). Freud used the partial translation of Artemidorus by F. Kraus (1881), deprecating "the moral indignation which induced the translator to take the liberty of keeping the chapter on sexual dreams from his readers' knowledge" (Standard Edition 5.606 n); later he used the translation of the omitted parts that was published in 1912 by H. Light.

In the first edition of *The Interpretation*, Artemidorus is mentioned as an example of "lay opinion," particularly of a "decoding method" that treats dreams as a kind of cryptography, giving a meaning to every detail of the dreams. Another form of "lay opinion" is the symbolic one, which interprets the whole of the dream (Standard Edition 4.96). To these methods Freud opposes his own "scientific" one, characterized by the use of free association, as he writes in a note added in 1914 (Standard Edition 4.98n).

The quotations of Artemidorus become more frequent starting from the third edition of *The Interpretation* (1911). In the previously cited note from the 1914 edition, Freud presents the work by Artemidorus as the one that "has left us the most complete and painstaking study of dream-interpretation as practiced in the Graeco-Roman world." In another addition (Standard Edition 4.99n) Freud praises the interpretation of the dream of Alexander the Great given by Artemidorus at 4.24: the Satyr (*satyros*) in Alexander's dream is interpreted as an admonishment to take possession of the town of Tyros (*sa Tyros*: i.e., Tyros is yours). Freud also mentions this dream in his *Introductory Lectures on Psychoanalysis* (1915–17), where he says that "this interpretation, which has a sufficient artificial appearance, was undoubtedly the right one" (Standard Edition 15.236).

In *The History of the Psychoanalytical Movement* (1914), Freud writes that "the close connection between psychoanalytic dream-interpretation and the art of dream interpretation as practiced and held in such high esteem in antiquity only became clear to me much later" (Standard Edition 14.19–20). This affirmation suggests that Freud closely examined the work by Artemidorus only after the publication of the first edition of *The Interpretation*, but in fact we can imagine further reasons for explaining why Freud emphasizes the influence of Artemidorus on his own work only at a later moment: first, his growing inclination to quote classical authors as precedents and precursors of his theories; second, the greater relevance attributed by Freud to the "extent and importance of symbolism in dreams" in the preface of the third edition (Standard Edition 4.xxvii), which may have suggested to him that he should pay more attention to the *Oneirokritika*.

There is in fact an unquestionable continuity between Artemidorus and Freud, in spite of their different aims (Artemidorus was mainly interested in the prediction of the future). This is shown by Freud's statement that "dreams do have a meaning," and by his declaration that, in spite of what contemporary science believes, "a scientific procedure for interpreting them is possible" (Standard Edition 4.100). By establishing this continuity, Freud has furthermore achieved a "rediscovery" of Artemidorus, an author disparaged by contemporary philology precisely for his conception of dreams (this undervaluation of Artemidorus is also present in two books used by Freud when writing the *Interpretation*; i.e., *Traum und Traumdeutung im Altertum* [Dream and interpretation of dreams in antiquity] by B. Büchsenschütz [1868] and *Traumdeutung und Zauberei* [Interpretation of dreams and magics] by Gomperz [1866]).

The bibliography of the *Interpretation* includes another classical writer, Aristotle, quoted for the *De divinatione per somnium* (On divination through dream) and the *De somniis* (On dreams). In the first edition of his work Freud seems to assign a limited importance to him: while he concedes that for Aristotle the dream "becomes a subject for psychological study," since it is no longer seen as "sent by the god," nonetheless, in a note later suppressed, he affirms that "insufficient knowledge" and "lack of specialist assistance" prevent him from a deeper consideration of Aristotle's treatise (Standard Edition 4.3n). On the other hand, already in the chapter on the dream as wish-fulfilment, Freud underlines the importance of Aristotle's definition of the dream as "thinking that persists (in so far as we are asleep) in the state of sleep" (Standard Edition 5.549), a paraphrase of *De divinatione per somnium* 462a: "the mental picture (*phantasma*) that arises from the movement of sense-impressions when one is asleep, in so far as this condition exists." The definition is repeatedly quoted by Freud in his later works: in a note added to the *Autobiography* (1935), he writes that Aristotle's old definition "still holds good" (Standard Edition 14.46n).

A third classical author, Vergil, is present in *The Interpretation*: as an epigraph to the entire work, Freud quotes two Vergilian lines: *Flectere si nequeo superos, Acheronta movebo* (If I cannot prevail upon the gods above, then I shall move Hell!). These are words spoken by Juno in book 7 of the *Aeneid* (lines 311–12), when she announces her decision to summon the infernal goddess Allecto.

This motto was later interpreted by the philosopher W. Achelis as a symptom of Freud's desire for revenge on the medical and scientific world, which had him banished. To this "Promethean" interpretation Freud objected (in a letter to the same Achelis in 1927) that he had simply copied the motto from the socialist politician F. Lassalle. But it seems very likely that Freud, in choosing that motto, was assigning it a meaning related to his further work: already in 1896 he was planning to use it for a projected work on hysteria, as we read in a letter to Fliess (Letters to Fliess 205). On this possible meaning of the motto, there are different interpretations: for Damrosch (1986) Freud identified himself with the female goddess Juno, in opposition to the male Jupiter; Heller (1956) and Timpanaro (1984) connected the motto with Freud's "semitical" identification with Hannibal (in the *Aeneid* Juno supplies protection to the Carthaginian Dido); for Starobinski

(1999) and Traverso (2000) the hell evoked by Juno symbolizes the unconscious brought to light by Freud. This last interpretation seems confirmed by the presence of the same Vergilian lines in the work itself, where Freud writes that "during the night, under the sway of an impetus toward the construction of compromises, this suppressed material finds methods and means of forcing its way into consciousness" (Standard Edition 5.608).

In *The Interpretation* Freud refers for the first time to the protagonist of Sophocles's *Oedipus Rex* as a prototype of the sexual desire felt by children for their mothers. This reference was already proposed in a letter to Fliess in 1897 (Letters to Fliess 272), the definition "Oedipus complex" was introduced in 1910 (Standard Edition 11.171), and in *The Interpretation* Freud speaks of the "Oedipus dream" (e.g., Standard Edition 5.398). Sophocles' tragedy was well known to Freud, who translated some lines of it (and some of Vergil's *Aeneid*) in his departure examination from school (as he wrote in 1873 to E. Fluss). In *The Interpretation* the reference to Sophocles is justified by Freud with the consideration that classical antiquity transmits "a legend whose profound and universal power to move can only be understood if the hypothesis I have put forward in regard to the psychology of children has an equally universal validity" (Standard Edition 4.261). Criticizing the traditional interpretation of *Oedipus Rex* as "destiny's tragedy," Freud affirms that

> if *Oedipus Rex* moves a modern audience no less than it did the contemporary Greek one, the explanation can only be that its effect does not lie in the contrast between destiny and human will, but is to be looked for in the particular nature of the material on which that contrast is exemplified.

The same tragedy and its action "with cunning delays" is presented as "a process that can be likened to the work of psychoanalysis" (Standard Edition 4.262).

The hypothesis that myths give testimony to a sort of infancy in the human being later induced Freud to use other mythological figures to represent psychological processes. Narcissus had already been used by Havelock Ellis (1898) to denote narcissism (the sexual satisfaction derived from contemplation of one's own physical endowment). Freud used the term in the *Three Essays on the Theory of Sexuality* (1910) and then in his essay *On Narcissism* (1913). About the symbolic meaning of the head of Medusa, the infantile fear of castration, Freud wrote a short note in 1922 (published posthumously in 1940), where he says that "we have not often attempted to interpret individual mythological themes, but an interpretation suggests itself easily in the case of the horrifying decapitated head of Medusa" (Standard Edition 18.273). Another myth discussed by Freud was that of Prometheus, whose acquisition and control of fire was interpreted as a phallic symbol (Standard Edition 22.187).

4.4   Plato and Empedocles

Freud referred to Plato already in *The Interpretation*, where a note added in 1914 praises the statement that "the best men are those who only *dream* what other men *do* in the waking life" (Standard Edition 4.67): this is a paraphrase of Plato's

Republic 9 571c–d, where Freud's attention was perhaps aroused by one of the dreams mentioned by Plato, the dream "of lying with one's own mother."

A more striking reference to Plato was proposed later by Freud for his theory of the libido, as associated with the Platonic concept of *erōs*. In the *Autobiography* (1924) Freud affirms that he had discovered quite late that his own theory went back "to the very beginnings of medicine" and followed up "a thought of Plato's" (Standard Edition 20.24), adding that he had realized it when he read an article published in 1898 by Havelock Ellis (Standard Edition 20.24).

The reference to Platonic *erōs* was proposed by Freud for the first time in the preface to the fourth edition of the *Three Essays* (1920), where he invites the reader to consider "how closely the enlarged sexuality of psychoanalysis coincides with the Eros of the divine Plato" (Standard Edition 7.134). The reference reappears insistently in the following works, sometimes with other names associated with that of Plato: in the *Group Psychology* (1921), besides Plato, Freud mentions the *Epistle to the Corinthians*, where the apostle Paul praises "love above all else" (Standard Edition 18.91). Again in *Why War?*, in a letter to Albert Einstein (1932), Freud affirms that the sexual instincts are to be understood "exactly in the sense in which Plato uses the word (i.e., *erōs*) in his *Symposium*" (Standard Edition 22.209).

Plato, in this case, is used by Freud in order to legitimate, or ennoble, his own theory on sexuality, which aroused particular hostility among his critics. The comparison between *erōs* and libido in fact seems superficial (there are more considerable analogies between Freud and Plato, explored, for example, by Simon [1973]) and not supported by a serious reading of Plato's works: Freud utilized an article published in 1915 by M. Nachmansohn, who limited himself to looking for precedents of Freudian theory in Plato's *Symposion*.

The only precise reference by Freud to the *Symposion* is that proposed in *Beyond the Pleasure Principle* (1920), where he praises the myth told by Aristophanes (but further rejected by Socrates, who represents Plato's position), for which the sexual genders arose from a primary androgynous being (189d–191b). Freud had already referred to this "poetic fable" in the *Three Essays* (Standard Edition 7.136), without explicit reference to Plato. In this myth Freud was seeing a confirmation of his own theory that sexual instinct is "a need to restore an earlier state of things"; he also points out the probable Babylonian origin of the myth, for which he quotes both an article by K. Ziegler and the opinion expressed by Heinrich Gomperz, son of the philologist (Standard Edition 18.57).

But 18 years later, in *An Outline of Psychoanalysis* (1938), Freud denied the validity of the myth, now qualified as a fancy of "creative writers," because "nothing like it is known to us from the actual history of living substance" (Standard Edition 23.149n). Instead of Plato, the antecedent of the Freudian theory of instincts was now becoming another ancient philosopher, Empedocles, quoted for his theory of the two natural energies, *philia* (love) and *neikos* (discordance), which cause conjunction and separation of the elements, and so the life and death of living beings. In this theory Freud sees an antecedent of his own theory of the instincts, the sexual one and the death instinct, a theory, as Freud observes, which was shocking even for many psychoanalysts.

Empedocles had been rediscovered by Freud the year before in *Analysis Terminable and Interminable* (1937), where he says that he recently "came upon his theory in mind in the writing of one of the great thinkers of ancient Greece" (Standard Edition 23.244). Freud found the fragments of Empedocles included in the *Vorsokratiker* by W. Capelle, published in 1935. He does not exclude the possibility of having been influenced in elaborating his theory by Empedocles himself, whose work he could have read among the many books he read in his youth (in this case, Freud says, he would have suffered from a cryptamnesia).

In the case of Plato, psychoanalytical theory had reached independently, as we have seen, the idea of *erōs*; in the case of Empedocles, eventually Freud preferred to propose himself as the direct heir of ancient wisdom.

4.5   *After Freud*

Freud's interest in classical literature was inherited by several of his followers, who attempted to verify psychoanalytical theories in classical texts. Besides the article quoted by Nachmansohn about Plato's *erōs*, we should mention at least the essays by H. Gomperz (1924) about the personalities of Parmenides and Socrates (the latter was diagnosed as a homosexual, who would have sublimated his love into a passion for teaching), and by A. von Winterstein (1925) on Greek tragedy (his thesis, inspired by Freud's *Totem and Taboo*, is that Greek tragedy has its roots in the Oedipal relationship between father, mother, and son). Several essays on classical topics were published by *Imago*, the review edited since 1913 by O. Rank and H. Sachs to support psychoanalytical research in the humanities.

Much research has been devoted to mythological topics, in order to verify the hypothesis that myths are expressions of the desires of whole communities: for example, K. Abraham wrote *Dreams and Myths* (1909), R. de Saussure (son of the linguist) defined the "Jocasta-complex" (1920), T. Reik wrote on Oedipus and the Sphinx (1920), and S. Bernfeld on Sisyphus (1925) and Tantalus (1931). The debate about the universality of the Oedipus complex involved anthropologists: in 1924 the review *Imago* organized a forum in which the anthropologist B. Malinowski, among others, participated. Anthropological researches founded on psychoanalysis were then conducted by G. Roheim and by G. Devereux (the latter also wrote essays on Euripides' tragedies). C. Lévi-Strauss also put important emphasis on the Oedipus complex in *The Elementary Structures of Kinship* (1947), but in his subsequent works on structural anthropology left Freudian positions behind.

Freud's interest in myth was inherited by Carl Gustav Jung (1875–1961), who in 1911–12 separated himself from psychoanalysis and founded analytical psychology. For Jung myths, fables, and dreams are influenced by archetypes, inherited mental images of the collective unconscious. The idea of "archetype" was suggested to Jung, as he himself wrote, by St. Augustine ("Archetypes of the Collective Unconscious," in *Collected Works* 9.1 p. 4). In his research on myth Jung was collaborating with the historian of religions K. Kerényi, with whom he wrote *Essays in the Science of Mythology* (1941). Research on classical texts was also published later by Jungian scholars (M.-L. von Franz, C. A. Maier, J. Hillmann, and many others).

Among the more recent exponents of psychoanalysis it is possible here to mention only Jacques Lacan (1901–81), whose *Seminary 7* on *The Ethics of Psychoanalysis* (1959–60: Lacan 1992) contains a study of Sophocles' *Antigone* (a text that was also studied by Freud's daughter, Anna, and is now quite popular in gender studies).

4.6   *Psychoanalysis and classical studies*

The application of psychoanalysis to classical studies gave rise to different reactions. Brown (1957) published a programmatic manifesto; Sullivan (1974) edited a collection of studies; and several scholars used Freudian, Jungian, and recently also Lacanian concepts to study classical texts (prevailingly Greek, but also Latin ones). Psychoanalysis, on the other hand, was criticized by many classical philologists: for example, as regards Freud's uses of classical authors. The most controversial matter remains Freud's reading of Sophocles' *Oedipus Rex*: accepted by Van der Sterren (1948), it was refuted in 1972 by Vernant (1988), Bollack (1993), and others. Some scholars attempted to save Freud's interpretation by integrating it with other ideas, Politzer (1974) by drawing on the theories of Bachhofen, Paduano (1994) by making use of the theory of the unconscious elaborated by the psychoanalyst I. Matte Blanco.

A comparison between psychoanalysis and textual philology was made by the philologist S. Timpanaro, who took as starting point the slip made by Freud when he quoted a line by Vergil (*Aeneid* 4.625) in *Psychopathology of the Everyday Life* to demonstrate that several of Freud's slips are explainable as mnemonic errors, similar to those committed by copyists of manuscripts (Timpanaro 1976). Timpanaro's criticisms of the scientific nature of psychoanalysis recall those addressed to Freud by Popper and have been utilized in the epistemological debate on psychoanalysis (Timpanaro's work has been very influential also in the field of textual criticism, as an alternative to Housman's mechanistic approach).

More than through direct application, psychoanalysis has influenced classical studies indirectly, at first through anthropological studies influenced by Freudian experience. Very important in this regard was the work of J. E. Harrison, a student of ancient religion who was interested especially in Freud's *Totem and Taboo* (different from another Cambridge Ritualist scholar, Sir J. Frazer, who refused to read Freud but was largely used by Freud himself in *Totem and Taboo*). The experience of the Cambridge Ritualists was developed by E. R. Dodds (1893–1979) in *The Greeks and the Irrational* (1951); for the later essay *Pagan and Christian in an Age of Anxiety* (1965) Dodds was influenced also by the neo-Freudian E. Fromm.

Psychoanalytical concepts are also present in another essay on the anthropology of the ancient world, *Homo necans: The Anthropology of Ancient Greek Sacrificial Ritual and Myth*, by W. Burkert (1972), who afterward dropped his Freudian inspiration in order to achieve, with his *Creation of the Sacred* (1996), an evolutionist and biological approach to the history of religion.

Other authors who have contributed more recently in various ways to the reception of psychoanalytical culture in classical studies are P. Ricoeur, J. Derrida, and M. Foucault. The latter in 1967 placed Freud, together with Marx and Nietzsche, among the most innovative thinkers of the contemporary age (Foucault 1994:

564–74), but in his later *History of Sexuality* (1976–84), which was largely devoted to classical antiquity, Foucault, too, took an approach very different from the Freudian one (Black 1998).

FURTHER READING

Essays on several topics of psychology in antiquity are collected by Everson (1991), and a comparison with the contemporary mind–body debate is proposed by Ostenfeld (1987). On the ancient treatment of characters, see Ginsberg (1983). On Nemesios of Emesa (and Galen), Debru (2005). On humoral typology in modern times, one should read the classic work by Klibansky, Panofsky, and Saxl (1964) and, on the influence of the humors on modern art, Filipczak (1997). The *Musica practica* (1482) by Ramos de Pareja is available in the Spanish edition by Terni (1983). English translations are available of Pinel (1962) and Esquirol (1965). Besides Pigeaud (1983), the classical influence upon Pinel is mentioned by Lanteri-Laura (1991). On Freud's classical culture, see Tourney (1965) and Mitchell-Boyask (1994). On Freud's archaeological collection, Ransohoff (1975). On Freud and Greek mythology, Downing (1975) and Caldwell (1996). On Freud and H. Ellis, Sulloway (1979): 305–15. On Freud's "Roman phobia," Timpanaro (1984) and Damrosh (1986). Bernays' and Gomperz's intepretations of Aristotle's catharsis are analyzed by Langholf (1990). Differences between Freud and Artemidorus in the interpretation of dreams are clarified by Price (1986). On Freud and Plato, see Simon (1978) and Santas (1988). On the Oedipus complex and Sophocles (besides the essays quoted above), Chase (1979), Bremmer (1987), and Rudnytsky (1987). On Lévi-Strauss (and the Oedipus myth), see Carroll (1978) and Delrieu (1999). On Antigone (and Lacan), Wolman (1965), Butler (2000), and Leonard (2003). Bibliographies and essays on psychoanalysis and classical studies include Glenn (1972, 1976), Caldwell (1974), Will (1966), Lloyd-Jones (1985), and Selden (1990: 171–4). On Dodds (and psychoanalysis), Cambiano (1991). On Derrida, and Foucault (and Lacan), Miller (1999).

CHAPTER TWENTY-FIVE

Modern and Postmodern Art and Architecture

Gail Levin

1   Nietzsche and Freud

Well before the inventions of the postmodernists in the 1960s and 1970s, the classical component in Western culture had already been subjected by others to radical revisions that might have stimulated interest among artists. The old academic vision of the classics had been undermined and new meanings and values anticipated by powerful appropriations. Artists developed a whole range of responses to the classics, from the most immediate and idiosyncratic to those more typical of ideas, which became widely diffused, that were suggested (mediated if not dictated) by the cultural authority of others, proposed elsewhere and solidified into currency as compelling cultural myths – above all by Friedrich Nietzsche and Sigmund Freud, along with disciples of Freud such as Otto Rank and Carl Jung. Another key source of classical influence on artists is *The Golden Bough* (1922) by Sir James G. Frazer.

   Nietzsche himself was a classicist, but too speculative and bold for most scholars. He burst the limits of academic discipline in *The Birth of Tragedy from the Spirit of Music* (1872), which confidently posited a dynamic of Greek culture in terms of opposing tendencies of the human psyche, the Apollonian and Dionysian. The dichotomy proved unforgettable. It was to acquire mythic status in modern culture, all the while remaining controversial and problematic, especially among the classicists of his own time (Silk and Stern 1981: 88–9). Nietzsche's analysis effectively undermined the cultural myth of serenity and rationalism in Greece, proposing instead a vision of conflict between rationalistic optimism and dark forces. Nietzsche dramatized the heroic role of the artist and more generally of creative will as a central and overarching value. His ideas had received a degree of fame in America by 1915, when Willard Huntington Wright wrote in his book *What Nietzsche Taught* that Nietzsche's "adherents have already reached the dimensions of a small army"

(Wright 1915: 10). Wright dedicated his work to H. L. Mencken, his friend and fellow journalist, whom he credited as, "The critic who has given the greatest impetus to the study of Nietzsche in America."

Nietzsche had a strong impact on European modern artists, especially the Italian Giorgio de Chirico (1888–1978), who grew up in Greece and whose early education was more philosophical than visual. In his early writings, de Chirico indicated that he perceived the importance of *revelation* from the philosopher:

> When Nietzsche tells how he came to conceive Zarathustra and says, "I was surprised by Zarathustra," all the enigma of a sudden revelation is contained in this participle "surprised." When (in another case) a revelation is generated by the sight of a composition of object, then the work that is manifested in our thoughts is closely connected with the circumstances that provoked its birth. (De Chirico, quoted in Fagiolo dell'Arco 1982: 11)

De Chirico's *Hector and Andromache* (1917), *The Hall of Apollo* (1920), *The Departure of the Argonauts*, and his *Self-Portrait with the Head of Mercury* attest to his engagement not only with classical themes, but also with classical forms.

Classical influence in the modern age arrived not only through Nietzsche, but also through Freud, who posited a dramatic conflict within the human spirit, although in terms that were destined to have even broader and deeper impact, albeit in simplified and popularized forms. Freud's immense American reception was facilitated by a new climate of public opinion, which had begun to perceive medicine as a field where scientific progress was possible. The influence of Freud began to spread from Europe to America with his lectures at Clark University in Worcester, Massachusetts, in 1909.

Beyond scientific authority, Freud's themes could reach everyone directly, notably his claim that dreams could be interpreted to reveal an unconscious, and that the underlying drive was sexual. In 1911, *Forum Magazine* featured Edward M. Weyer's "New Art of Interpreting Dreams" with emphasis on what it meant for the individual, who now could acquire the "habit of picking the skeletons of his own dreams immediately upon waking in the morning," adding that "The wealth of his own dream life will probably astonish him at first: then he will come to know himself as the proprietor of a busy theatre – owner, spectator, and critic in one" (Hoffman 1959: 50). The metaphors ring ironically in retrospect. The images of inner wealth and flourishing business seem idiotically insouciant, optimistic, in view of the mythic paradigms that Freud had transferred from classical tragedy to the psychic stage, most notoriously the stories of corrupt families symbolized by Electra and Oedipus.

Examples of classical reverberation could be multiplied for visual artists in the theater, fiction, poetry, dance, and music. Freudian readings of classical myth abound in literature. The intellectual fashion in the decades of the 20s and 30s saw the ideas of Freud play a leading part in transforming values. Opposition arose to everything that had been accepted before and during World War I. Among the young, it became fashionable to reject the standardization of society, assert the free life of the pagan, and confess to the psychoanalyst (Hoffman 1959: 60–1). In this cultural climate, the term "Puritan," which had referred to a specific part of earlier American experience, underwent a powerful metaphoric expansion and assimilation to the Freudian per-spective. Puritan became "separated from its historical context and extended to include almost all of the guardians of the nation's morality and business," as one observer remarked, adding paradoxically that it seemed as if the "virtues [not the sins] of the founding fathers had been visited upon their sons.... The nation had fallen victim to a serious moral illness – repression" (Hoffman 1959: 62). With this metaphoric expansion, critics began to reinterpret the very character and history of America in Freudian terms. Whether bold insight or audacious simplification, one paradoxical effect was to facilitate further and powerful reverberations of classical paradigms by American minds.

One reverberation suggested and justified by the expanded idea of puritanism transformed tragedy, a genre that could feed on the concept of a determining and perverse strain in the American character. "The busy theater" of the American psyche, as perceived by Freud's early journalistic herald cited above, became a stage for forbidding psychological drama in which puritanical inhibitions destroyed innate spiritual freedom. As early as 1926, Eugene O'Neill (1888–1953) began work on what would grow into the trilogy *Mourning Becomes Electra* (1931), using no lesser model than the *Oresteia* of Aeschylus (525/4–456 BC). In O'Neill's conception, puritanical meanness, raised to mythic dimensions in three generations of a rich and powerful New England family, becomes a curse even more destructive than the violent pride and hostile fate that destroyed the descendants of Atreus in the Aeschylean trilogy. Beyond the horror and vengefulness, Aeschylus had offered a vision of the hero's redemption in the civic order of Athens, through the establishment of legal institutions. No similar affirmation lightens O'Neill's American scene. After deaths by murder and suicide, O'Neill's version of Electra turns away at the end from the hostile, puritanical society around her to immure herself in isolation with her memories of frustration, violence, and misplaced passions in the family's ancestral mansion, which had been built in Greek revival style.

2   Surrealism, Abstract Expressionism, and Realism

In Europe, the Surrealists, such as André Masson and Matta as well as Picasso, had absorbed Freud and turned to classical mythology. They also admired De Chirico's work with his classical references. Between 1932 and 1934 alone, Masson (1896–1987) painted works reflecting his increasing engagement with Greek myth, includ-ing *The Silenuses* (1932), *Bacchanal* (1933), *Daphne and Apollo* (1933), *Orpheus* (1934), and *The Horses of Diomedes* (1934). Masson did not just take his subject matter from classical mythology, he also paraphrased forms, such as that of a running figure of Apollo from a Greek vase (Lanchner 1976: 137).

The Surrealists singled out the Minotaur, a monster that was half man and half bull, as a being from classical mythology that "corresponded in its duality to the conflicts within the conscious and subconscious minds" (Penrose 1973: 111). Ovid (*Ars amatoria* 2.24) tells how the Cretan Queen Pasiphaë's affair with a white bull resulted in the monster's birth. In 1933, the Surrealists named their new journal *Minotaur*, and

Figure 25.1 *Persephone* by Thomas Hart Benton, ca. 1938. Tempera with oil glazes on canvas, mounted on panel, 72–1/8 × 56–1/16 inches (183.20 × 142.40 cm). The Nelson-Atkins Museum of Art, Kansas City, Missouri. Purchase: acquired through the Yellow Freight Foundation Art Acquisition Fund and the generosity of Mrs. Herbert O. Peet, Richard J. Stern, the Doris Jones Stein Foundation, the Jacob L. and Ella C. Loose Foundation, Mr. and Mrs. Richard M. Levin, and Mr. and Mrs. Marvin Rich, F86-57. Photo by Jamison Miller. © T. H. Benton and R. P. Benton Testamentary Trusts/DACS, London/VAGA, New York 2006

the poets André Breton and Paul Eluard asked Picasso to design their first cover. Picasso chose to explore the Minotaur at length, creating a series of etchings, the Vollard Suite (1933–7), including *The Sculptor's Studio*, in which he shows the sculptor as a bearded Athenian. In his vision, the lustful Minotaur invades the studio and interacts with the nude model, sometimes depicted as a sleeping nymph.

The Surrealists registered despair resulting from World War I and the Great Depression. There was despair enough to go around on both sides of the Atlantic. The once-accepted notion that influence came from European to American art has been modified by studies that document how the American modernists sought to define themselves by their own return to the classical past, as they understood it through the filtering medium of Freud and Nietzsche, above all Nietzsche's *Birth of Tragedy from the Spirit of Music*, which gave such a central role to myth and to the artist (Polcari 1991: 54–5). This picture of a return to Greco-Roman myth via Freud and Nietzsche can be enlarged yet further by recalling how widespread the impact of Freud and Nietzsche had already been in the other arts, penetrating and transforming American consciousness since the century's first decades. The Abstract Expressionists were thus enmeshed in a process of cultural realignments that had been under way in America since before World War I.

In 1914, Walter Lippmann, who had studied with William James at Harvard, inaugurated a long career on the New York intellectual scene by publishing *A Preface to Politics*, which brought the theories of Nietzsche and Freud to bear on American public life (Hoffman 1959: 54). Sexuality, mythic reverberation, and the shock of contemporary intrusion also characterize the painting that became arguably one of the most notorious visual icons of the tumultuous period between the wars: *Persephone* (1939) by Thomas Hart Benton (1889–1975).

Benton's art and life pass through the modernist crisis in their own fashion: Benton begins in the country, then passes through a period of urban and cosmopolitan abstraction in Paris and New York, only to return to his rural regional roots and vivid narrative. He switched from abstraction to representation with the claim that he just "couldn't paint George Washington as a rainbow," yet his realism remains stylized. He conceived of a nude *Persephone*, which he followed eight years later with *Hercules and Achelous* (1947). His *Persephone* mingles classical and popular forms, resembling at once the old master Correggio's version of the myth of Antiope visited by Jupiter and pinup art of the period. Yet some details reinforce the classical reverberation for the informed viewer: thus the grain harvest in the background recalls the goddess of grain and fertility, Demeter, the mother of Persephone; the mule-drawn wagon ironically reinterprets the chariot in which Persephone's uncle, Pluto, carried her off; and the vines of Dionysus creep into the foreground. The curves of the female form merge with the land, leading interpreters to see a new version of the old metaphor that identifies the fecundity of earth and woman. The corollary, which was not uncommon in American art of the time, was that the agricultural exploitation which produced the Great Depression's dust bowl had been a rape (Adams 1989: 289).

Among the students Benton taught in New York during the 1930s was Jackson Pollock (1912–56), who in the 1940s became one of the pioneers of Abstract Expressionism. During the heyday of this "last hurrah" of modernism, artists took a vigorous interest in classical myth. Pollock changed the title of a major abstract painting from *Moby Dick* to *Pasiphae* (ca. 1943) after the curator, James Johnson Sweeney, told him the story of the Cretan queen who fell in love with the white bull sent by Poseidon to her husband, King Minos of Crete. Pollock left two sheets of notes on *Pasiphae*, complete with quotations from Ovid and Dante (O'Connor and Thaw 1978: 1:78).

Pollock, who was in Jungian psychotherapy during 1939–42, stated, "We're all of us influenced by Freud, I guess. I've been a Jungian for a long time" (Polcari 1991: 43). In *Modern Man in Search of a Soul*, Jung's 1933 collection of essays addressed to a general public, he wrote about primitive cultures preserving their systems of secret teaching

> about hidden things…handed on to younger men in the rites of initiation. The mysteries of the Greco-Roman world performed the same office, and the rich mythology of antiquity is a relic of such experiences in the earliest stages of human development. (Jung 1936: 189)

Among Pollock's contemporaries, the choreographer Martha Graham is also known to have undergone Jungian analysis. Interest in both Jung and Freud is well documented by the painter Adolph Gottlieb's comment "Oh, we were all interested. First we discovered Freud, and then Jung" (Polcari 1991: 43). Not surprisingly, the painters Gottlieb, Mark Rothko, William Baziotes, Barnett Newman, and Byron Browne, as well as the sculptor Isamu Noguchi and his occasional collaborator, Martha Graham, all drew upon classical themes, giving mythic titles to works produced in the 1940s.

Noguchi was the son of a Japanese writer and an Irish-American mother, Leonie Gilmour, who taught him as a child about classical myth, which he later related to Japanese mythology. Noguchi met Graham through his mother, who helped with costumes for Graham's dance company. When he designed sets and costumes in 1946 for Graham's *Cave of the Heart*, based on the story of Medea, he called it a "dance of transformation as in the Noh drama." He wrote about his collaboration in 1948 with Igor Stravinsky and George Ballanchine on the ballet *Orpheus*, for which he designed sets and costumes:

> I interpreted "Orpheus" as the story of the artist blinded by his vision (the mask). Even inanimate objects move to his touch – as do the rocks, at the pluck of his lyre. To find his bride or seek his dream or to fulfill his mission, he is drawn by the spirit of darkness to the netherworld.… Here, too, entranced by his art, all obey him; and even Pluto's rock turns to Eurydice in his embrace.… (Ashton 1992: 6)

The following year, Noguchi traveled to Europe, where he visited Pompeii, describing the nearby Villa of the Mysteries as a "beautiful integration of painting and architecture," and Paestum, where he saw the Temple of Poseidon and commented on the "sacred relation of man to nature," and Greece, among other places (Ashton 1992: 82). He sketched an ancient sculpture of Apollo as the shepherd. Noguchi even titled one of his abstract marble sculptures *Kouros* (1944–5) after the archaic Greek male figures stiffly carved in marble. He also continued to choose titles that make reference to the classics, in one case calling a bronze sculpture *Cronos* (1947) after the Titan son of Uranus and Gaia who was the father of Zeus, and in another case, naming a two-part marble sculpture *Euripides* (1966). In order to acquire Greek marble for his sculptures, Noguchi often stopped off in Greece en route to America from Japan.

One of the closest students of classical myth was Rothko (1903–70). His famous radio broadcast of 1943 with his long-time friend Gottlieb shows how Nietzschean and Freudian thinking led to a new interest in myth:

> If our titles recall the known myths of antiquity, we have used them again because they are the eternal symbols upon which we must fall back to express basic psychological ideas. They are the symbols of man's primitive fears and motivations, no matter which land or what time, changing only in detail but never in substance, be they Greek, Aztec, Icelandic, or Egyptian. And modern psychology finds them persisting still in our dreams, our vernacular, and our art for all the changes in the outward conditions of life. (Rothko quoted in Polcari 1991: 118)

In Rothko's case, he may even have taken time out from painting to study myth, in order "to break with what they considered stagnant in the European tradition and with the provincial American past" (Gottlieb's wife, Esther, quoted in Chave 1989: 78). But, as a Jewish immigrant from Latvia, he must also have been responding to the tragic situation of the Jews in Europe during World War II.

Rothko invoked the ancient religious practice of predicting the future course of events in his canvas *The Omen of the Eagle* (1942), where he drew upon Greek literature, specifically Agamemnon, the first play of the *Oresteia* by Aeschylus, in which two eagles sweep down on a pregnant hare and devour its unborn young, an omen of the coming war with Troy and the sacrifice of Iphigenia. Here the image of feet gets adapted from chiton-clad figures in Greek vase painting (Polcari 1991: 123). Rothko also chose themes from Sophocles' Oedipus trilogy, including *Tiresias* (1944), the seer of Thebes, who, though blinded but long-lived and prophetic, suggested metaphorically Rothko's own vision about the future of art as he renounced the tradition of representation.

Rothko's colleague, Gottlieb (1903–74), produced, in addition to other classical subjects, a series of paintings from 1941 to 1945 on the Oedipus myth. In the *Hands of Oedipus* (1943) and the *Eyes of Oedipus* (1945), we can see Gottlieb's concern with vision, recalling that in Sophocles' play, once Oedipus saw the tragic truth behind and beyond appearance and circumstance, he turned against literal sight and destroyed its organs, gouging out his own eyes. This myth may have appealed to Gottlieb for its bearing on his own spiritual and artistic development, as he, a Jew, sought to express his pain at the Holocaust, the human tragedy he had no power to stop, by turning away from representational art toward painting where one no longer sees a literal object. The state of the world may have seemed beyond representation.

Other examples among the Abstract Expressionists who drew upon classical myth include Barnett Newman's *Song of Orpheus* (1944–5), William Baziotes's *Cyclops* (1947), and *Onyx of Electra* (1944) by Matta, a Chilean-born Surrealist who had

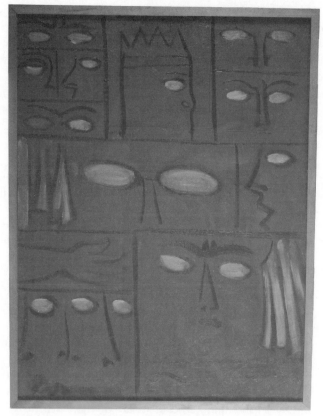

Figure 25.2 *Eyes of Oedipus*, 1941, by Adolph Gottlieb, oil on canvas, 32-1/4" × 25"
(81.9 cm × 63.5 cm), #4104. © Adolph and Esther Gottlieb Foundation/VAGA, New York/
DACS, London

moved from Paris to New York for a time. From the same period, we should also mention an African-American artist, Romare Bearden (1911–88), who showed with many
of the Abstract Expressionists, particularly at the Samuel Kootz Gallery in New York,
where he knew Gottlieb, Baziotes, and Hans Hofmann (who immigrated to the US
from Germany), all of whom used classical references in their work during the 1940s.

   In 1947, Bearden, an avid reader, began a series related to Homer's *Iliad*. Working
in oil, he produced such paintings as *The Walls of Ilium*, where, fascinated by the
tragedy of the city destroyed, he showed flames shooting out from Troy's stone walls.
In 1948, he also produced a series of watercolors inspired by the *Iliad*, where the
walls resemble those in the oil painting. Many of these watercolors focused on two
individuals, as in *The Parting Cup*, where a woman offers a goblet to her departing
warrior. Continuing his engagement with classical myth, Bearden produced in 1977
20 large collage depictions of Homer's *Odyssey*. For this project, he mixed classical
antiquity with the iconography of the African-American experience. He imagines the
treacherous goddess *Circe* as a seductive, black-skinned figure surrounded by bold
colors that suggest a jazz performer.

Figure 25.3 *The Cyclops*, 1977, by Romare H. Bearden collage, 14 ½"×11". © Romare Bearden Foundation/DACS, London/VAGA, New York 2006

A less obvious reference to the classics appears in the work of the American realist Edward Hopper (1882–1967), who called one canvas *Excursion into Philosophy* (1959). In this painting, a sulking nude female lies stiffly on what looks like a hard, cold bed, her buttocks upwards. The man sits abject, an open book by his side. To explain the sense of disassociation and modernist dissonance, Hopper made an enigmatic remark to his dealer, purporting to explain why the male figure in the painting appeared so glum. According to Hopper, who usually spoke with a taciturnity and point worthy of New England, "He's been reading Plato rather late in life." This from a man whose pert and independent-minded wife, the painter Josephine Nivison Hopper, called a group of her female friends "the Euripides gang" and inspired her husband to inscribe a holiday card to her in French, "ma petite Xantippe," comparing her to the wife of Socrates, known for her ill humor and peevish disposition (Levin 1995: 525). Hopper read classical literature, but he was also steeped in Freud and Jung. Both their names appear on books under the arm of a skinny figure with outsized fetal head and huge eyeglasses that Hopper sketched, in what looks like a self-caricature as both an impressionable infant, vulnerable to neuroses, and an adult voracious reader fascinated with the latest fashion for dissecting the human species (Levin 1995: 93).

By contrast to Hopper's stubborn rejection of modernist abstractions are the classical references made by Cy Twombly (born 1928), who moved from the US and settled in Rome in 1957. There Twombly developed a fascination with graffiti, which led him to consider the ancient graffiti in his Roman surroundings. Clearly he both embraced the classical past and struggled to make aspects of its narrative his own. Eventually he incorporated a number of classical literary references into his abstract compositions. Written on his works in Twombly's own graffiti-influenced style, we find these familiar names and many others from classical antiquity: "Ovid" visible on *Untitled* (1960), *Ode to Psyche* (1960), *Venus and Mars* (1962), *Vergil* (1973), *Orpheus* (1975), *Apollo and the Artist* (1975), *Mars and the Artist* (1975), and *Phaedrus* (1977). But then there is also *Aristaeus Mourning the Loss of His Bees* (1973) with its green paint in streaks and the word "Bucolic" scrawled across the top of the composition, although Aristaeus loses his bees in Vergil's *Georgics*, not his pastoral *Bucolics*.

Twombly showed his *Nine Discourses on Commodus* (1963) with the Leo Castelli Gallery in New York in 1964. The title of this series of abstract canvases referred to the degenerate son of Marcus Aurelius, who became emperor in the second century (AD), went mad, and was strangled. Although the paintings are completely unrepresentational, the chaotic and violent application of paint evokes the madness and the violence of the story alluded to by the title.

3   Postmodernism

By the next decade, references to classical traditions show that further dissociation from the tradition of modernism was well underway. There emerged in art and architecture a new historicism that looked back at the classical artistic and architectural tradition, often in an ironic way, in order to subvert convention. Thus, even when parodied, forgotten classical themes became visible once again in the new art. What was being subverted was the long-dominant austerity and inherent elitism of high modernism, where sacrosanct images were usually abstract and "quality" in the visual arts was defined exclusively by the white male creator. Among the innovators, women artists and artists of color appropriated classical themes and forms, carving out their new territories in what came to be called "postmodernism." For them, Greek and Latin classics proved easily recognizable and therefore adaptable in different ways, according to the individual needs of the artist.

Postmodern art was often playful, ironic, eclectic, and parodic. Already in 1962, the French Nouveau Réaliste Yves Klein (1928–62) covered a reproduction of the *Victory of Samothrace* with a coat of his signature deep blue paint, making a contemporary work of art out of the classic enshrined in the Louvre, presented in the guise of a reproduction. The American Pop artist Roy Lichtenstein (1923–97) produced playful appropriations of images from comic books and other aspects of popular culture. Looking to subvert the dominant modernist style of abstract expressionism, Lichtenstein recounted that he had pondered what would be most unacceptable as a subject to paint, choosing comics and advertisements. But he also mined classical tradition, turning to the cliché of Greek architecture in his painting *Temple of Apollo* (1964) and other related images. The image pleased him enough that he reproduced it again as a color lithograph, *Temple*.

Perhaps Lichtenstein never would have turned to the Greek temple if he had known of its appreciation by the leading modernist architect and city planner, the

Figure 25.4 *Temple of Apollo*, 1964, by Roy Lichtenstein, magna and oil on canvas, 94" × 128". Collection of Mr. and Mrs. Robert Brown. © The Estate of Roy Lichtenstein/DACS

Swiss-born Le Corbusier (Charles-Édouard Jeanneret 1887–1965). In his 1923 book, *Towards a New Architecture*, Le Corbusier had warned, "To send architectural students to Rome is to cripple them for life" (Le Corbusier 1986: 173). His book reproduced photographs and sketches of the Pantheon, the forum in Pompeii, the Parthenon, and a Greek temple at Paestum, noting, "The Parthenon is a product of selection applied to an established standard. Already for a century the Greek Temple had been standardized in all its parts" (Le Corbusier 1986: 133). And he exclaimed, "The plastic system of Doric work is so pure that it gives almost the feeling of a natural growth" (Le Corbusier 1986: 209). Appreciating other classical architecture, he recommended Hadrian's Villa, for "One can meditate there on the greatness of Rome. There, they really planned" (Le Corbusier 1986: 157).

A more widespread revival of interest in classical styles and themes in the visual arts and in architecture emerged during the 1970s and 1980s as postmodern art and architecture became the vogue. Postmodernism also successfully challenged traditional cultural values and began to blur distinctions between high and low art. The term "postmodernism" gained currency in a book on architecture by Charles Jencks, who attacked the International style – the style of the European Bauhaus and the dominant tradition of modernism – by arguing for a more eclectic approach. Eclecticism arrived with postmodernism.

By the early 1960s, the architect Philip Johnson had declared that he was bored with the work of the Bauhaus veteran Ludwig Mies van der Rohe, although he still considered the modernist architect "a genius." For his own direction, Johnson rejected "academic revivalism. There are no classic orders or Gothic finials. I try to pick what I like throughout history" (Johnson, quoted in Jencks 1984: 82). Johnson's building for the AT&T Corporate Headquarters (1978–83) in New York earned him unprecedented international attention. It features a Roman-style arch at the entrance, but a broken pediment that tops the building draws more upon the eighteenth-century English furniture-maker Chippendale than on classical Greek or Roman styles.

Perhaps "classic orders" had heretofore seemed too tainted for Johnson because of their association with both Mussolini's Fascist Rome and Nazi architecture, as in the work of Albert Speer, or with Hitler's admiration for classical forms (Jaskot 1996: 622). The Nazi admiration for forms of Greek classicism was a part of a deep German admiration for Greek antiquity and a preference for the classical over the contemporary (Silk and Stern 1981: 4). It has been pointed out that Hitler's views on Greek art and architecture were similar and perhaps indebted to those of the great German scholar and art historian Johann Joachim Winckelmann (1717–68), whose dictum he was known to repeat: "the only way for us to become great . . . lies in the imitation of the Greeks" (Spotts 2002: 20). During the 1930s, Johnson himself had sympathized publicly with, and promoted, fascist ideology and the Third Reich, but by the mid-1950s, he had publicly atoned and had designed a synagogue in suburban New York. Also encouraged by the antimodernist polemics of Robert Venturi, whose *Complexity and Contradiction in Architecture* appeared in 1966, classical grammar crept back into contemporary architecture.

Figure 25.5   Piazza d'Italia, Charles Moore. © Brendan Nee www.picturethecity.com

Classical revivalism in the US included John Paul Getty's museum for antiquities in Malibu, California, designed in the early 1970s by the firm of Langdon & Wilson, with Norman Neuerberg as historical consultant and recreating the Villa of the Papyri at Herculaneum. Architects have both condemned the Getty's *trompe l'oeil* columns, false marble, and "contradictory painted shadows" and praised it as a good replica that functions appropriately for its purpose (Jencks 1984: 82, 94–5). The project served to make prominent the issue of historicism in the early 1970s.

By the late 1970s, there emerged a postmodernist classicism. Architects such as Charles Moore, James Stirling, Hans Hollein, Aldo Rossi, and others incorporated convention, metaphor, ornament, and polychromy to create a "free-style classicism" (Jencks 1984: 147). Moore's *Piazza d'Italia* (1976–9), an open plaza dedicated to the Italian-American Community in New Orleans, Louisiana, exemplifies this new classicism. This project draws upon elements inspired by the Greek Agora and the Roman forum, including classical arches and columns, although there are also echoes of Renaissance and Baroque architecture. But Moore had his Ionic capitals made of spirals of bright stainless steel, the impact of which he enhanced by adding the glow and color of the neon light. Such bold revisions led architect Robert Stern to dub this variant of postmodernism, "ironic classicism."

4 Feminism

During that same decade, at the time of the Women's Movement, feminist art emerged, critiquing modernism and emphasizing content. A number of the leading feminist artists looked to classical culture for material with which to express their political point of view. Their interest coincided with the development of feminist scholarship among classicists and historians, as documented in the bibliography about ancient women published in *Arethusa* in 1973. Classicist Barbara McManus (1997) has surveyed the theoretical and methodological principles developed by pioneering feminist classical scholars, such as Sarah B. Pomeroy, who in *Goddesses, Whores, Wives, Women and Slaves* (1975) sought to recover information about women from skimpy and dispersed evidence filtered through centuries of patriarchal assessment.

Feminist artists such as Judy Chicago (born 1939) imbibed such scholarship, eager to know more about women in ancient times. In researching her major art work *The Dinner Party* (1979), Chicago sought to create a work about the history of women in western culture that would be so monumental and important that it could not, like so much earlier art by women, be erased from memory. She designed a triangular table with 39 ceramic place settings, each on a cloth runner, illustrated by needlework, representing women from myth and history. Working with hundreds of volunteers to research and complete this work, Chicago chose not only these 39 women, but 999 others whose names are represented on the porcelain floor.

Among the 39 place settings are five women from antiquity who reflect the new scholarship in classical studies: Sappho, the Greek poet from Lesbos; the Athenian Aspasia, who was the influential consort of Pericles; Boadaceia, whom, as Tacitus recounts, the Romans fought in the British Isles during the first century AD;

Figure 25.6a Sappho placesetting from *The Dinner Party*. Plate: 14" in diameter, China paint on Porcelain. Runner: 5' × 3'. Mixed media. Collection: The Brooklyn Museum of Art. © Judy Chicago 1979, 2006 / Artists Rights Society (ARS), New York

Hypatia, the Greek upper-class mathematician who lived in the Roman era; and Marcella, a Roman widow who devoted herself to Christianity. In addition, on the "heritage floor" at the center of the triangular table, we find such names as Anyte, Anasandra, Carmenta, Cleobuline, Corinna of Tanagra, Cresilla, Erinna, Helena, Artemisia I, Cleopatra, and Zenobia.

The Dinner Party has had a tremendous impact on its audience, raising consciousness about the significant roles played by women in western civilization. Judy Chicago has written, "Greco-Roman goddesses paled beside their historical antecedents, and the position of Greek women was summed up in this famous remark . . . : 'That

Figure 25.6b Installation view of *The Dinner Party*. Featuring Judith and Sappho place-settings. Photo © Donald Woodman. Collection: The Brooklyn Museum of Art. © Judy Chicago 1979, 2006 / Artists Rights Society (ARS), New York

Figure 25.6c Installation view of *The Dinner Party*. Wing One & Heritage Floor. Photo © Donald Woodman. Collection: The Brooklyn Museum of Art. © Judy Chicago 1979, 2006 / Artists Rights Society (ARS), New York

woman is best who is least spoken of among men, whether for good or evil.'" The comment to which she referred was made by the political leader and statesman Pericles, as reported by Thucydides. Chicago went on to write, "The destruction of the Goddess reflected the gradual erosion of women's political, social, and religious authority.... While Roman women were in a similar legal position to that of their Greek predecessors, in actuality they were far less oppressed" (Chicago 1996: 17).

The lives and contributions of particular women represented in *The Dinner Party* have since inspired entire books. Likewise, Sappho's plate made its way into a recent scholarly book on women, sexuality, and gender in classical art and archaeology. There, Jane McIntosh Synder wrote,

> Who knows, it may be that Judy Chicago comes much closer to the heart of Sappho's poetry, with its sensuous images of trembling bodies, soft beds, purple headbands, roses and honey-lotus, garlands and perfume, and the rosy-fingered moon, than did the Athenian vase-painters, striving to create images that would please the Athenian men who wanted to please their wives with a suitable – and suitably safe – gift. (Snyder 1997: 117–18)

For the debut of *The Dinner Party* at the San Francisco Museum of Modern Art in 1979, a day-long conference called "A Celebration of Women's Heritage" took place and featured a panel discussion about "Women in the Ancient World," with Harrianne Mills, Marilyn Skinner, and Bella Zweig, all classicists by profession. In addition, Amazons and witches were the subject of a talk by Susan Rennie, an author and editor of the feminist journal *Crysalis*.

During the same period, the feminist artist Nancy Spero (born 1926) was also drawing upon images from classical antiquity to explore the imbalance of power between the sexes and between oppressors and victims. By utilizing classical images long associated with the masculine – even the giant phallus – Spero forged new symbols of feminine power by creating a new context for these images. She first became interested in ancient images, especially Roman and Etruscan, while living in Europe and specifically when making a long visit to Italy with her husband, artist Leon Golub, in 1956. Her subsequent use of classical imagery is distinguished by her use of either a frieze or mural arrangement of smaller figures, as in her *Athena-Sky Goddess-Masha Bruskina* (1974–92).

Spero's interest in ancient imagery has been ongoing. She even called her 1994 show at the New York gallery, P. O. W., "Black and Red III," making an allusion to the colors of classical Greek vases, from which she borrowed "dildo dancers." Her references are different from Chicago's use of metaphoric representation of ancient women or from the heroic dimensions of the figures adopted by the feminist sculptor Audrey Flack (born 1931).

Flack was already well established as a photo-realist painter when she gave up painting in the mid-1980s and took up sculpture, the content of which often derives from classical tradition. Already in her paintings, Flack was drawn to images of spirituality, such as a Gothic cathedral, the Madonna, or Buddha. She had also depicted iconic images – from *Isis* (1983) to Marilyn Monroe (1978) to Michelangelo's *David* (1971).

Figure 25.7   *Colossal Head of Medusa*, 1990, by Audrey Flack. Courtesy Meisel Gallery

Thus it was but a small leap to move on to sculpt figures that evoke images from classical antiquity.

Flack's sculptures in the classical tradition include *Diana* (1988), *American Athena* (1989), *Colossal Head of Medusa* (1990), and *Galatea* (1998). For Medusa, Flack sought to reimagine the ancient myth and to question the traditionally negative identity given to this, the most beautiful of three Gorgon sisters. Learning that Medusa had suffered a rape in the temple of Athena, Flack saw in Medusa a metaphor for the rape of the earth.

Modeled and cast in bronze, Flack's forms often have distant classical sources, but these have evolved under the influence of European academic traditions from the eighteenth and nineteenth centuries. Flack endows her figures with an intentional grandeur and often imagines her sculptures positioned in prominent public spaces.

Joyce Kozloff (born 1942), another important feminist, drew upon Greek classical vases in some of her watercolors called "Patterns of Desire," a cross-cultural and witty exploration of eroticism, in which she alternately mixed figures from a Greek red-figure amphora with Chinese imagery on a Chinese-shaped vessel that she called *Smut Dynasty Vase* (1987). Around the same time, she also used imagery from both classical Greek black-figured and red-figured vases on her own "revolutionary tex-tiles," which parody early Soviet designs. By combining the classical with Asian motifs, Kozloff showed the universality of Eros.

Like so many other feminist artists, Eleanor Antin (born 1935) has successfully appropriated classical imagery for her own ends. In her 2001 series *The Last Days of*

Figure 25.8 *Pornament is Crime #4: Smut Dynasty Vase*, 1987, by Joyce Kozloff, 22" × 22". Collection of Terry Stept. Photo: Eeva Inkevi

Figure 25.9 "The Artist's Studio" from *The Last Days of Pompeii*, 2001 by Eleanor Antin. Courtesy Ronald Feldman Fine Arts, New York

Pompeii, she conveys the decadence of Roman life through carefully staged photographs with costumed actors that she directed. Her imagined scenes include an artist's studio complete with nude model, a Roman banquet, and the death of Petronius.

On the wall of Antin's most recent show, "Roman Allegories," held in the spring of 2005 at the Ronald Feldman Gallery in New York, she quoted Pliny the Younger: "That summer, in the first year of the reign of Titus, there appeared a small band of players who met with some success until they disappeared without trace, leaving behind one of their number." The show featured 12 large tableaux, beautifully staged and photographed. Her characters included Columbine, the Lover, the Trickster, an ex-gladiator Strong Man, the Poet, and a little girl, all of whom act out episodes in Roman times, along with a fully costumed Bacchanal and sylvan scenes that are clearly allegorical. The parodic and ironic aspects of Antin's work make it postmodern. Malcolm Bradbury's literary term, "parodic realism," appears appropriate for her work (Rose 1993: 270).

5   Other Works of The Eighties and Nineties

Beyond the appearance of classical referents in the work of these feminist artists, perhaps the most prominent use of the classical by a postmodernist has been in the word pictures of Jean Michel Basquiat (1961–88). Like Twombly, Basquiat was interested in the incorporation of names and words for their graphic power, which he sometimes utilized instead of, or combined with, pictorial images. In 1982, he painted *Speaks for Itself*, a triptych that features the words "NERO, CARTHAGE, PUNIC WARS" and "ROME SACKED BY GOTHS" in block letters on its first panel, alluding to Nero, who fought Hannibal in the second Punic War during the third century BC. Basquiat continued to convey this military theme with gestural brush strokes, violent drips of paint, and bold, red graffiti. He moves forward in time to more violence, when the northern Visigoths sacked Rome in 410 AD. The middle panel treats the fourth century BC, when in "THE BATTLE OF PERSIA" Alexander the Great killed Darius III in the Battle of Gaugamela in Mesopotamia in 331 BC, a date that appears on the right-hand panel. Since Basquiat's own life was cut so short, we cannot know if he would have continued such imagery as Twombly does, but his interest seems to have been more than trivial.

The name "Alexander the Great" also appears across the top of Basquiat's *All Colored Cast (Part II)* of 1982 above the *faux* Roman numerals "MCLMVX XIIVI." Both the image and the name "Alexander the Great" recur in *False*, which is one of the 32 untitled drawings (1982–3) of the Daros Suite in a Swiss Collection. *False*, boldly executed in black and red on a white ground, also features labeled linear drawings of Aphrodite, Pericles, a Greek Soldier, Romulus and Remus, and a "BAR-BARIAN INVADER" who "SEES ROME FOR THE FIRST TIME." Other names, words, and phrases include Plato, Homer, Socrates, "PAX ROMANA," "BRUTUS AS 1ST CONSUL," and "ROME IS SACKED BY GOTHS."

Around the same time as Basquiat's classical references, Francesco Clemente (born 1952), one of a group of Italian painters who in the late 1970s and early 1980s became known as the "Transavanguardia," produced a self-portrait as a nude male striding figure carrying a model of the Pantheon in his arms, which he titled *Perseverance* (1981). Painting in a neo-expressionist, gestural style, Clemente had just come to live in New York from Italy, where he had known Twombly in Rome, after having moved there to study architecture. Clemente described this canvas:

> The first night I slept in the studio in New York, I had a dream where shit was raining from the sky. This painting came after that dream, with the Pantheon sort of protecting me from this rain of shit. What that means, I don't know. One should remember that downtown New York was a city of ruins back then.... It was an archaeological site with the Roman gods still walking around. (Adams 2003)

Since Clemente would collaborate with Basquiat in 1984, it is interesting that he, too, occasionally mined the ancient world for some of his imagery.

Unlike so many of these artists who engage briefly with classical themes, Andrea Eis (born 1952) trained as a classical scholar. When she abandoned scholarship for the visual arts, she kept her passion for classical civilization, finding her themes there. She works in photography and creates installations. For example, she made an installation about the conflict between Antigone and Kreon called *Antigone's Cave, No. 2* (1990), questioning "the conflict of personal and ethical boundaries and governmental

authority." She expressed authority and social order in architecturally controlled
pathways, which she created through a "ritual corridor" made of pairs of fluted
wooden columns, each pair progressively taller, through which the viewer walked.
At the end of the corridor, a sharply lit photograph of a woman's hands twisting in
tension and frustration, scaled much larger than life, confronted the viewer. Eis
created another large-scale installation, *Labyrinth for Theseus and Ariadne* (2000),

Figure 25.10a *Antigone's cave, No. 2* by Andrea Eis. Photo © Andrea Eis

Figure 25.10b   *Antigone's Cave, No. 2* by Andrea Eis Photo © Andrea Eis

in which she "returns the path to Theseus," but "gives Ariadne the final word." This piece involves translucent fabric with a photograph dyed into it; it is both fragile like the past and suggestive of a labyrinth. Her goal is to use articulations of space combined with manipulations of images and texts to create metaphorical connections to the insights of ancient myths. Eis has written, "With our own society's myths becoming increasingly hollow, perhaps exploring the Greek myths can provoke a re-evaluation of what we believe, and why" (Eis 1993: 3).

While interest in the classical never completely disappears, certain periods and particular artists find innovative uses for the familiar forms, names, and characters. As we have seen, even an arch-modernist like Le Corbusier appreciated classical architecture. While we should not expect Alexander the Great to figure in the work of an artist inspired by graffiti such as Basquiat's, we should not be surprised. Nor should the fascination with the classics among feminist artists seem unlikely. For they were not rebelling against Praxiteles or Lysippos, but against the domination of modernist formalism with its suppression of content. For all of the artists who want to draw upon rich cultural traditions, classical forms and literature offer a rich and readily available body of sources.

CHAPTER TWENTY-SIX

Film

Karl Galinsky

1   Introduction and Basic Perspectives

Over the past few decades, film has developed as probably the largest window for the general public on the world of ancient Greece and Rome. This development and others in popular culture should be welcomed by anyone interested in these civilizations because it is another manifestation of the classical tradition's ongoing vitality. And it can be a useful springboard for deepening the public's understanding of these civilizations; an analogous example is the helpful scholarship literary bestsellers about the ancient world, such as Dan Brown's *The Da Vinci Code*, have attracted. In other words, the study of the classical world in cinema is a legitimate, and important, part of classical scholarship today. At this point (late 2006), it can be said that a good start has been made in this new area, but universal acceptance is still lagging. To wit: whenever a new adaptation of a classical subject – most recently, for example, *Gladiator, Troy,* and *Alexander the Great* – appears on the screen, the response of most professional classicists to whom the general public might turn is still to recite a catalogue of "inaccuracies" and engage in a general plaint that the meaning of the original work has been robbed of its grandeur and profundity, with no or little respect for its "authenticity." The underlying assumption seems to be that only documentaries can do ancient subjects justice.

Such notions and others, especially when they are asserted sweepingly in lieu of the consideration of individual merits, are far too limited. Before I proceed, then, it will be useful to lay out the framework of information and perspectives for this chapter.

I will give a condensed, interpretive chronological overview; detailed and good treatments, notably Jon Solomon's (2001), are readily available. Before and after, a few perspectives. One is that the development of the genre, its variegated manifestations, its high points, and its hiatuses can be viewed usefully from the aspect of reception and reception theory – in that regard, once more, film is no different than the reception of classical themes in art, literature, and architecture. Projecting the past, to use the title of Maria Wyke's book (1997b), tells us something not only about the past but also, and sometimes even more, about the present and contemporary milieu of reception. Gladiatorial combat, for instance, was only one of many forms of entertainment in ancient Rome and certainly not the key to Roman civilization; as J. E. Lendon has observed, our fascination with it "tells us more about ourselves" (Lendon 2000: 404). Reception in film is affected by many of the same factors as reception in other cultural genres, such as political and personal agendas (*Spartacus* is a paradigm), contemporary sensibilities (an audience today will not spend three hours and $10 to watch the egomania of the "authentically" Homeric Achilles), and reinvention.

What is authenticity, then? There are parameters, and it would be too facile to resort to reception aesthetics that are blithely relativizing – do with the subject whatever you want, it's all a construct anyway. Mainly, as for authenticity, movies should not be judged by standards different from those we use for Shakespeare's historical plays or Derek Walcott's *Odyssey.* The adaptation of historical material has its limits: we would not condone Caesar killing Brutus, for instance, unless, perhaps, Rosencrantz and Guildenstern would stay alive, too. While it is simply a given that box office films are not PBS or BBC documentaries and should not be expected to behave as such, a continuing characteristic, especially of movies about Rome, is the uneasy negotiation of creative liberties and authentic historical setting. Many movies are trying to have it both ways with the more-than-occasional result of falling between two stools; HBO's series *Rome* (2005) is a good recent example.

The case is different for mythological subjects. We should remind ourselves that myths in antiquity were in constant flux and thrived on retelling, embroidering, and adaptation; the canonization in compendia and textbooks came about only in late antiquity and did not stop literary adaptors in the following centuries from making creative additions (cf. Stanford 1963, and Galinsky 1972 and forthcoming). In fact, "ignorance," as Stanford put it so nicely, "can be the mother of mythopoeia" – Dante's treatment of Ulysses, who sails past the straits of Gibraltar and after three days falls into a very deep pit in hell, is a sterling example (Stanford 1963: 178–82). And would ancient readers really have considered it outlandish that Hercules, one of the most traveled heroes, would wind up in the new world of the Incas (*Hercules Against the Sons of the Sun*, 1964) or in New York (1970)? And that his English had to be dubbed in, as Arnold Schwarzenegger's (a.k.a. Arnold Strong) was, because at the time it was even more heavily accented than it is now? To be sure, such versions are not textbook illustrations. Some are inventive (in various ways: take Ray Harryhausen) and some are a silly mess – just like myths in antiquity. Like these, however, they continue the tradition of creative vitality, for better or for worse.

Benedetto Croce's distinction (1949: 50–65) between the life of the myth and the life of its interpretation is apropos here. Due to the ancient Renaissance allegorizers and Freud, Jung, Campbell, and Lévi-Strauss, we tend to look at myths mostly for their deep meaning rather than consider them for their entertainment value. But, as Geoffrey Kirk (1971: esp. 253ff.) has rightly emphasized, the narrative and entertainment aspects of myth are among its principal functions. The same is true of Homer's epics. No doubt, as Werner Jaeger (1965) articulated this commonplace, they were part of the Greek formation of character (*paideia*), but the *Odyssey* in particular could also be enjoyed as a pure adventure story. Again, this may not be the focus that tenure-minded academics would choose for investigation, but Ovid's *Metamorphoses*, for one, is an outstanding example of reviving myth by enabling different levels of reading and being none too heavy-handed about conveying myth's serious aspects. The emphasis on entertainment, then, of myths and other ancient subjects in film needs to be viewed not as a deviation, but as part of the same panorama of reader, viewer, and general cultural reception that applies to many other areas, including Roman art (Elsner 1995) and opera production.[1]

Since ancient times, the mix of *prodesse* (to be useful) and *delectare* (to entertain; Horace *Art of Poetry* 333) has been a matter of individual choice. The best movies on classical subjects have been successful because of the combination of action/adventure and a compelling human interest story to which a modern audience can relate while enjoying the escape into an ancient setting. It is, in the end, not so much a matter of delivering historical authenticity as of creating resonances, which need not be anachronistic, with both timeless and contemporary themes, sensibilities, and concerns. This was a major reason, to cite two paradigms, for the enormous success of *Ben Hur* (1959) and *Gladiator* (2000). Take the latter: themes of empire, individual integrity versus public corruption, vengeance, struggle against injustice, violence in sports and in battle, dedication to family, thoughts about the next life – to name just a few (extended discussion by Cyrino 2005). It is, of course, the same formula as for historical novels and plays and it underlies, more subtly, even phenomena like classicism in postmodern architecture: witness Charles Moore's rationale for choosing the façades of three churches on the Celian Hill in Rome to embellish some drab campus architecture at the University of California at Irvine (Moore and Attoe 1986: 123–4). And:

> It seems to me (of course) that the fact that our building started life as a copy does not rob it of passion, or of legitimacy, or of authenticity. Our building has a new life for new people in a new place for a new function. It is a safe bet that few, if any, of the inhabitants have ever seen Ponzio's chapels on the Celian Hill, so the new buildings will have to stir up their own connections with the inhabitants' memories. I was delighted to be told (without asking) that, at least for some, they do. (Galinsky 1992: 33–4)

To sum up: the cinematic treatments of Greek and Roman subjects are part of the continuing vitality of the classical tradition. They don't stand in isolation from that tradition; rather, they need to be viewed within its context and with the approaches and criteria we use for other aspects of reception.

2   Chronological Survey

In the history of cinema, "ancient" films were present at creation and have continued to hold their own till the present. While the phenomenon is international, these films did not follow the same cycle of ups and downs in every country – when American studios, for instance, stayed away from the genre after the financial Actium of

Cleopatra (1963), Italy revved up its production of "peplum" movies, right alongside spaghetti westerns and spearheaded by the well-built body of Hercules, while the French, as always, marched to their own drummer, even if his name was Roberto Rossellini (see Solomon 1996: 118). The result has been an almost continuous output in the major western movie-producing countries on subjects connected with ancient Greece and Rome. It is impossible to catalogue this unbroken tradition here, nor can I do justice to all of its aspects, such as the many allusions and references to classical themes in film (cf. Winkler 1991; Solomon 1996) or the similarity between mythological archetypes and the western hero (Winkler 1985). They are important for the whole fabric (and an affinity version like *O Brother Where Art Thou* [2000] possesses more creative sparks than the plodding retelling of the *Odyssey* in the TV movie of the same name [1997]), and I will refer to them occasionally. Because of limitations of space, however, I will concentrate on the movies with actual Greek and Roman subjects, including those biblical ones like Mel Gibson's *The Passion of the Christ* (2004) that have a substantial Roman component. Three periods stand stand out – the silent era, the large-screen boom in the late 1950s and early 1960s, and the recent revival – but there was plenty of activity in between, including television series.

In the earliest cinema, up to 1914, antiquity was a frequent subject. We should not be surprised to find hundreds of titles, especially in France and Italy, since both countries, after all, had strong Roman roots (Asterix came later). In terms of thematics, two phenomena deserve special comment because they turned out to be abiding in subsequent cinematic history, too. One is the plenitude of adaptations of previous literary treatments; there were several versions of *Quo Vadis, Ben Hur*, and *The Last Days of Pompeii*, to name only a few. Here we can work well with reception theory and reader/viewer response criticism: the audience already comes prepared. They know the script, so to speak, and they can fill in the "gap" (Iser 1978) of the missing audio. In fact, it can be argued that the unavailability of sound actually heightens the viewers' involvement as they have to supply the missing dimension (to the amusement of family members, I often watch movies that way on transatlantic flights, although it helps to know the story). Similar considerations apply to the other factor, the concentration on well-known, riveting, dramatic, complex, and flamboyant, if not charismatic, characters of whom there was no shortage in Greece and Rome, whether in history or mythology or the realm shared by both. Accordingly, early cinema was populated, often with repeated incarnations, by the likes of Julius Caesar, Nero, the heroes of the Trojan war, Spartacus, Attila, Cleopatra (and Antony), the Minotaur, Hercules, and a host of biblical characters from Moses to Jesus. These characters' notoriety, for good or bad, made them attractive, and so did the audience's ability to provide the (con)text. For further perspective, we should not forget that the most popular theatrical entertainment in the early Roman empire was the pantomime (Beacham 2005: 167–72), which was the silent (albeit, as with the movies, to musical accompaniment) acting out of highlights from Greek drama and mythology. Similarly, if film had its Egyptomania, so did interior decoration in Augustan Rome after the country's conquest (de Vos 1980); the tradition of putting up obelisks in imperial capitals goes back to that time also.

Some cinematic landmarks stand out, as always. One was Giovanni Pastrone's *Cabiria* (1914), the prototype of future spectacles such as Cecil B. DeMille's. The plot involves what *The New York Times* called "what otherwise would be a purely historical work of limited appeal" (cited from Smith 2004: 40), that is, the Elder Scipio's war against Carthage and, more specifically, his assault on Carthaginian Cirta and on Syracuse. But the panorama is far more sweeping, with tableau after tableau, including Hannibal's march over the Alps, an eruption of Mt. Etna (*The Last Days of Pompeii* [1900]), after all, had featured the eruption of Vesuvius), Archimedes' attempt to incinerate the Roman armada with Hellenistic technology's equivalent of laser rays, the palpitating atmosphere of the temple of Moloch reeking of human sacrifices, and so on. Amidst all this, the human interest story: Roman ingenue winding up in Carthage as a slave; rescued by, and then separated from, a Roman noble undercover officer and his servant Maciste, who is as noble of soul as he is teeming with muscle; placed at the court of the Carthaginian princess Sophonisba, who ultimately commits suicide (no, not by asps); then reunited with her rescuers and riding off with her man (the officer) into the sunset while angels flutter about. The impact of all this on subsequent movies is obvious, and the debate starts here: what should get the upper hand, spectacle or human interest story? It's an abiding issue that has to be decided by every director and, in true reception fashion, will often be answered differently by different critics and viewers; the real successes, of course, strike a good balance. *Cabiria* also was pioneering for its many technical innovations (Solomon 2001: 48): the camera dolly, extensive artificial lighting (welcome to the Forum Shops in Las Vegas), and extensive editing (more than three-quarters of the takes wound up on the cutting room floor). In addition, the enormous budget ($100,000 at the time) set a precedent for later epic ventures like *Ben Hur* (1959) and *Cleopatra* (1963); another prededent was plucking the muscle boy not from acting studios, but from locales like the docks of Genoa or bodybuilding outfits. Finally, besides *Cabiria's* Maciste (Bartolomeo Pagano) continuing the role in several other movies, Italian movies with Maciste *redivivus* in the 1960s were "morphed" into Hercules films by their American distributors.

The other landmark film that exploited the possibilities of the new medium to the epic maximum and became an influential forerunner was D. W. Griffith's *Intolerance* (1916). It was conceived on an epic scale (it ultimately cost $2,000,000) as a tetraptych (the novelty of the endeavor deserves a novel word), juxtaposing and interposing four stories that illustrated the theme: a contemporary melodrama, dealing with the exploitation of factory workers; the massacre of the Huguenots in France; the crucifixion of Christ; and the fall of Babylon to the Persians. The final product, which spiraled out of control and flopped like *Heaven's Gate* (1980), never was shown in its entirety in the theaters; instead, the Babylon segment ultimately was released separately (with a new happy ending) and is the one that "set a standard for scope and detail that helped shape the genre" (Solomon 2001: 234): sumptuous sets, hundreds of extras, authentic looking costumes and buildings, and gripping battle and siege scenes.

But the movie was a precursor in other important ways, too. One was the negotiation of the striving for authenticity with departures from historical facts. The latter

Figure 26.1 Giovanni Pastrone, *Cabiria* (1914): The Temple of Moloch, site of the miraculous rescue of the heroine from human sacrifice. Photo: Kobal Archive

included, most notably, a Persian siege that never occurred but was too good a spectacle to pass up; compare Cleopatra's entrance, in the 1963 movie, into Rome through the Arch of Constantine, undoubtedly one of the truly (or, to turn the usual argument on its head, authentically) unequalled moments in all of film history. At the same time, Griffith thoroughly researched all available resources for history, costume, art, and architecture, and went with the scholars in preferring the accounts from newly found Mesopotamian tablets to the narrative in the book of Daniel. Secondly, it was the orgy scenes (which actually had their basis in Daniel) that captivated Griffith's attention and led him to allocate more resources to the Babylonian part than the passion of the Christ and the suffering of the Huguenots. One later, and perhaps involuntary, parallel was that orgiastic characters like Peter Ustinov's Nero in *Quo Vadis* (1951) and Jay Robinson's over-the-top Caligula in *Demetrius and the Gladiators* (1954) stole the show from the good guys, the Christians, who were virtuous and, therefore, rather dull. A third trend-setting aspect of *Intolerance* was cinematic intertextuality: there were deliberate echoes of *Cabiria* even in some of the set design, just as *Cabiria* had looked back to the volcanic spectacle of the earlier *The Last Days of Pompeii*. Such citations became a staple and are another reception aspect that links classicism in the cinema with classicism in literature and architecture. Two recent examples are Maximus' battle against the chariots in *Gladiator*, which would be unthinkable without *Ben Hur*, and the *testudo* formation of Achilles' Myrmidons as they hit the beach in *Troy* (2004), with their shields interlocked over their heads in imitation of the historically correct usage in just about any film involving the Roman army.

It is interesting to speculate why the tide of Greco-Roman subjects receded with the arrival of sound. Sure, there was ongoing production,[2] but it was eclipsed by a preference for biblical themes and, probably not coincidentally, a marked sermonizing tendency. Besides, there was no need to take up Roman decadence when it could be found in real Hollywood. Still, DeMille turned to an old standby, *Cleopatra* (it had been produced at least nine times previously; see Kleiner 2005: 310) in 1934, even if he had to do so on a reduced budget, as his two immediately preceding movies (both nonhistorical) had not fared well at the box office. *Cleopatra* (with Claudette Colbert in the title role and running for less than two hours) was highly successful, earning several Oscar nominations and winning the award for cinematography. Otherwise, however, the lull continued; among other factors, World War II was as little conducive to ancient warrior epics in film as World War I had been to Griffith's indictment of intolerance.

The pendulum swung back mightily in the 50s and early 60s. Spurred on by blockbusters like DeMille's *Samson and Delilah* (1949) and his colossal *The Ten Commandments* (1956), the major studios vied with one another to fill the big screen. That, literally, was the objective: television had started invading the American living room, and the customers had to be reminded that a small black-and-white screen could not deliver the goods like a huge one in a movie house. It was the time that witnessed the introduction of several large-screen formats, including Cinema-Scope and Panavision, and the concomitant onset of *horror vacui* (a fear of empty spaces): the screen existed not for the exploration of two characters' inner anguish (*Goodbye*, Ingmar Bergman) but had to be filled at all cost. And what better way to do so than with lavish recreations of ancient metropolises and palaces, sweeping vistas of Roman armies and navies, and spectacles in the arena? Lew Wallace's unbeatable combination, which he dreamed up in 1879 in his many spare hours as Governor of the New Mexico Territory, of the Bible and Rome in *Ben Hur* (the subtitle was *A Tale of the Christ*) roared to its grandest success ever under William Wyler's direction in 1959. It set all kinds of records and precedents: most Academy Awards ever (unsurpassed to this day, even if tied by *Titanic* [1999]); most expensive production, the cost of which (over $15,000,000) was eclipsed within a year by revenue from Ben Hur merchandise, including Ben His and Ben Hers towels; and a chariot race for the ages that, aside from being a cinematic milestone that is unlikely to be surpassed, also marked one of the few happy moments in history when Jews and Arabs cheered in unison (against the *pax Romana*, the Roman peace, of course). While not quite as grandiose as *Ben Hur*, other films used the same formula of melding Roman and New Testament themes for success, including the first CinemaScope movie, *The Robe* (1953), with its edifying tale of the conversion and martyrdom of the Roman tribune Gallio (Richard Burton), who wins Christ's garment in a dice game at the foot of the cross. Other ventures that turned out to be less memorable include *Sign of the Pagan* (1954), with Jack Palance defending the Roman empire, and the enjoyable and lavish *Helen of Troy* (1955), during whose filming, history repeated itself as its Troy set in

Cinecittà went up in premature flames (almost half a century later, Wolfgang Petersen's set of *Troy* [2004] in Baja California was wiped out by a hurricane – call it Priam's curse). Undeterred, the Italians produced *The Trojan Horse* (1961), wisely focusing on Aeneas (Steve Reeves), who got away from the inferno; and Victor Mature marched across the Alps and more in *Hannibal* (1960), although "the real stars of the show are the forty-five elephants who comprise the bulk of Hannibal's army. With little effort, they manage to upstage the human performers in the film" (Smith 2004: 118). Enough said.

The second coming of "ancient" movies cut an even wider swath. Hercules, the most adapted and adaptable figure of Greek mythology, was the subject of dozens of films. Many were made in Italy, including the prototype with Steve Reeves (1959), and then conquered America and other markets without much labor. Greece got some attention, as in a Cold War paean to democracy, *The 300 Spartans* (1963), which tellingly strikes that note in the first few frames against the backdrop of the Athenian Acropolis rather than Sparta. But Rome was the preferred venue because one could have it both ways. On the one hand, Rome signified decadence and imperialism (cf. Winkler 2001b: 272–90, and Winkler 2001a), and Crassus (in *Spartacus* [1959]), Caligula, and Nero became its easy icons; so, to an extent, does Messala in *Ben Hur*. The virtuous time was that of the Roman Republic, as it had been for America's founding fathers. But, as Margaret Malamud (2001) has pointed out, a funny thing happened along the way: once the US became an imperial power, empire began to look not all that bad. In fact, its opulence and even excess called for celebration in life, and the new icon became Caesar's Place in Las Vegas, which opened in 1966. It has been expanded several times since, and its adjacent, Roman-themed Forum Shops today are the mall with the highest merchandise revenue per square foot in the entire US. In the same year, 1966, Richard Lester adapted Broadway's *A Funny Thing Happened on the Way to the Forum*, which was true to Plautine comedy by being a musical and a mélange (*contaminatio*) of diverse comedies. It functioned, at least on one level, as a parody of the moralizing heavies of the preceding 13 years, including the chariot race in *Ben Hur* (the movie's context and comic antecedents in cinema are well discussed by Malamud 2001: 191–208).

The grand finale, however, of the period may have cheered the moralizers: like the Roman Empire, *Cleopatra* (1963), which did not sermonize, fell because of its own excess. Call some of it bad planning: whoever was responsible for thinking that English fall weather (in 1961) would be hospitable to a story set in the Mediterranean should have been fired and probably was, and that was only the beginning of multiple personnel changes, relocations, and stupendous cost overruns that forced Twentieth Century Fox to sell some of its properties in Los Angeles to stave off bankruptcy. In the affair of the two protagonists (Burton and Taylor), life began to imitate art (cf. Wyke 1997b: 101–5). A final vignette was that after some $30,000,000 in expenses, there was no money to provide Antony with an army in Egypt and Burton had to face Octavian's legions like the Lone Ranger. *Cleopatra*'s story has been told many times; it is still a stupendous spectacle and ultimately broke even, but no studio would touch a big budget film on Greece or Rome until the next millenium. Fittingly, Anthony Mann's *The Fall of the Roman Empire* (1964) provides the whimper to

Cleopatra's bang. It had already been in production (in Europe) as *Cleopatra* was winding up and, besides Sophia Loren, it featured Stephen Boyd, who had risen from Messala's ashes, while the looks of Alec Guinness's Marcus Aurelius prefigure Richard Harris's in *Gladiator*, as did some of the plot themes (virtuous Republican sympathizers vs. the depraved Commodus – alas, the Republic had been gone for two hundred years and the Empire did not fall for another three hundred). Despite a strong cast, good acting, and one of the best sets of Rome, the movie got caught badly in the downdraft of *Cleopatra* and failed commercially, driving the last nail into a big coffin.

The interregnum, as I observed earlier, was not lacking in ongoing activity. Fittingly, several Greek tragedies were brought to the screen by Michael Cacoyannis, two with Irene Papas playing the protagonist (*Electra* [1962]; *The Trojan Women* [1971]). Idiosyncratic efforts like *Fellini Satyricon* (1969), Pasolini's *Medea* with a stunning Maria Callas (1970), and, regrettably, Bob Guccione's *Caligula* (1979) have some memorable qualities, but they did not reach a mass audience. Ray Harryhausen came closer in *Jason and the Argonauts* (1963) and *Clash of the Titans* (1981); his stop-motion technique (Dynamation) offered some novelty, and so did his campy treatment of the Olympic gods – how else could they be handled in modern film after Lucan had already jettisoned them in his blood-and-guts epic of the first century AD? Television, therefore, became the medium for classical subjects to draw large numbers of viewers, especially through multipart series like Zeffirelli's beautifully filmed *Jesus of Nazareth* (1977) and *Masada* (1981), which combined thoughtful issues, good acting (especially by Peter O'Toole, who seemed happy to put his role as Tiberius in *Caligula* behind him as quickly as possible), and absorbing action. Highbrows could indulge in the eccentricities and misogynism – it's good to keep in mind that some Julio-Claudians actually died of natural causes rather than by Livia's machinations – of the BBC/PBS 13-part series *I, Claudius* (1977–8; see Joshel 2001: 119–61), which reaffirmed once and for all that Romans spoke with a British accent (a divide that had been established in *Spartacus* and *Ben Hur*, where the representatives of the evil empire are played by English actors vs. American freedom fighters and Bravehearts).

The unexpected success of *Titanic* (1997) with its $200 million budget suggested to studios that cinemepics somehow based on history could be a worthwhile venture again. The best and most profitable of the ensuing ancient trio came first: Ridley Scott's *Gladiator* (2000), which won several Oscars, including one for Russell Crowe, was followed in 2004 by the less resounding *Troy* and Oliver Stone's *Alexander*, both of which actually cost more to produce. They all created the climate for the expensively ($100,000,000) produced HBO/BBC 12-part series *Rome* (2005), which excelled in authentic – and, therefore, often dimly lit – settings, but fell short of the brio and zippy dialogue of previous HBO series, such as *The Sopranos* and *Six Feet Under*, which had put the network on the map. *Rome* was soon eclipsed in its time slot by ABC's more inventive *Desperate Housewives*, but the series will return for 12 more parts in 2007, ending where *I, Claudius* begins. And it is more than a coincidence that Mel Gibson's *The Passion of the Christ*, with Romans in a major role and even speaking in Latin, also appeared in 2004.

All in all, this is quite a record for the classical tradition in cinema. It has had a major starring role, far greater than that of the Middle Ages and Renaissance, and it includes some of cinema's greatest names and achievements (see the list in Solomon 2001: 33–4). I will spend the remainder of this chapter not on special effects, but, using the three most recent films as a springboard, on highlighting some pertinent issues for further reflection and debate.

3   Greece, Rome, and Stereotypes

Over time, Rome has held greater appeal than Greece for America. That is one reason for the prevalence of Roman themes in the box office cynosures; another mighty factor was the convergence of Rome and early Christianity. Greek-themed films, while plentiful – witness the several dozen cinematic sons of Hercules (typically enough, he retained his Latin name) and Harryhausen's creations – were mostly the escapist fare of mythology. The same is basically true of the movie versions connected with Troy, including the 1954 Italian production of *Ulysses* with Kirk Douglas (it had its moments, such as Polyphemus' exclamation at his repast, "Uh, those Greeks are tough," a line not found in Homer) and the vivacious 1997 animated version by Disney. Greek historical fare has been few and far between; besides *The 300 Spartans* (a new version, *300*, is currently in production by Warner Brothers), there is the 1956 version of *Alexander the Great* with Richard Burton as Alexander, but Alexander never conquered film like Julius Caesar, Giulio Cesare, or Jules César.

The reasons for this American preference of Rome, which now is playing out in popular culture (cf. Bondanella 1987: 207–52; Joshel, Malamud, and McGuire 2001), are deep-rooted. Nor were they ever static, as Rome offered an infinite palette of identifications with the changing times. Like Rome, America had declared itself free from a monarch it had perceived as bad. The slave-holding, landed aristocracy that shaped the destiny of the early US saw its equivalent in that of Rome and adopted a constitution of checks and balances. America, as noted before, looked in its Roman mirror again when it became an imperial nation and liked what it saw: the *pax Americana* (American peace). An ensuing global phenomenon was that Americaniza-tion, just like Romanization, was a matter not of cultural imperialism but of a culture, and especially popular culture, that people everywhere could readily adopt, and did. The underlying reason, in both the Roman Empire and the world today, is that both Rome and America are fundamentally hybrid cultures due to the many ethnicities, traditions, religions, and so on they incorporate and take inspirations from. Being multicultural, these cultures are inherently cosmopolitan rather than narrowly national and therefore hold worldwide appeal (cf. Galinsky 1992; Appiah 2006; Pells 2006).

The portrayal of Romans in the movies has been evolving in this context. Bad Rome could be imperial Britain; hence the demarcation of accents to which I alluded earlier. But there could also be double coding: while in *Spartacus*, for instance, the slave-holding Roman rulers (who, moreover, are into decadence of the snails and oysters type) are of the British tongue, they were also meant to represent McCarthyist America. Often, of course, stereotypes have come in handy: there is the cruel Roman

Figure 26.2 It's never lonely in the arena: Maximus (Russell Crowe) and friends in Ridley Scott's *Gladiator* (2000). Photo: Kobal Archive

villain like Messala, Caligula, Nero, and Commodus; add to the parade the Roman soldier in the animated Christmas special *The Little Drummer Boy* (1968; revised 1996), who runs the boy's pet lamb over in his chariot (the revival of the animal in the manger becomes Baby Jesus' first miracle), thus leaving an indelible first impression of Roman brutality and Amazing Grace on young minds. And where would *Quo Vadis* go, literally, absent the Roman decadence without which many movies of the genre, including HBO's *Rome*, would be very dull indeed? Besides these staples, however, a few good Romans showed up occasionally, such as the consul Arrius in *Ben Hur*, although they, too, did not aim to transcend stereotypes (Shakespeare's Antony and Brutus, of course, are another matter; for good reason, the 1953 black-and-white version of *Julius Caesar*, with a superb performance by Marlon Brando, was nominated for several Academy Awards). Finally, in the *Life of Brian* (1979), the Romans in the not-so-Holy Land are heartily spoofed along with everything else.

One of the many factors in *Gladiator*'s success was that it stayed away from the orgies and presented a Roman that audiences could cheer for. He was not a stereotype, but he was not too complex, either. As in Shakespeare, it was Roman against Roman, and not Roman against Jew or Thracian slave. Similarly, Commodus is a sadly warped character rather than a caricature. A most interesting example, however, of increasing nuance is the changing portrayal of Pontius Pilate. Among the many criticisms of Mel Gibson's *Passion* was that his characterization of Pilate was altogether too friendly – after all, Pilate had been demonized for centuries, starting with his mention in the Nicene Creed. The departure, however, already came in Zeffirelli's *Jesus of Nazareth*, which cast the undersized and pudgy Rod Steiger as a

Figure 26.3 Roman soldiers just doing their job: with a bloodied Jesus (James Cavaziel) and Joseph of Arimathea (Giacinto Ferro) in Mel Gibson's *The Passion of the Christ* (2004). Photo: Kobal Archive

small and merely human cog in the machinery of history and, more immediately, Roman administration on the margins of the Empire. Steiger's Pilate is a humanly believable, harassed functionary whose plans for a quiet weekend are interrupted by yet one more instance of obduracy of the natives whose mentality exasperates him: "How can you govern such people?" he sighs at one point. True to all four Gospels, Zeffirelli's and Gibson's Pilate is far from hell-bent on crucifying Jesus, but tries to avert it several times. In Gibson's *Passion*, this humane portrayal, along with that of Pilate's wife, establishes some counterpoise to the otherwise relentless masochistic mayhem of the Roman soldiery who reduce Christ to a zombied pulp early on. No chance for character development here, and that may be another reason why Pilate's role absorbed most of that aspect. But while *The Passion* tapped, sickeningly, into the cinematic and literary tradition of Roman brutality, it did so not simply for its own sake but in order to introduce a realistic departure, even if by overcompensation, from the tradition of passion plays and artistic representations that tended to be conspicuously bloodless. A comparandum is the 20 minutes of utter carnage with which Steven Spielberg chose to begin *Saving Private Ryan* (1998). It stood in deliberate contrast to previous versions of the Normandy landing in which John Wayne & Co., while encountering some resistance, had basically stridden ashore and one could start hearing the dominoes fall all the way to Berlin. Reality was different.

What contributes to the greater success of Roman-themed movies with their audiences, then, is both longstanding cultural identification and the greater variety of characters who reinforce this identification with compelling human interest that an audience can relate to; HBO's *Rome* smartly extended the tradition by viewing the events through the eyes of two protagonists that are ordinary people. By comparison, films centering on Greek historical characters are far fewer and held to different standards precisely because they are rarer. The overly critical reception of Oliver Stone's *Alexander* is a case in point, and one of the dominant issues was the narrow construction of "authenticity." Others have taken up this issue well (see my suggestions for further reading, below) and therefore I can limit myself to the obvious comparative perspective: it is not an issue, in my opinion, that would have played a significant role in the assessment of a "Roman" film. Because of the prevalence of Rome in cinema, moviegoers and critics are used to a far longer tradition of creative liberties and, with the exception of the usual academic guild, have stopped beating a dead horse. The rest of the world has learned how to live with Joseph Mankiewicz' classic answer to such concerns. For, when it was pointed out to him that the arch through which his Cleopatra entered Rome was not around at the time, he replied: "Who would know?" Transpositions of this kind, and others, are what we expect to see in movies that are based on history, but clearly are not meant to be documentaries. It is the same creative allowance that characterizes literary and artistic adaptations from early on; a typical example, dating to the middle of the sixth century BC, is a black-figure vase from Etruria that shows Achilles fighting Aeneas (*Iliad* 20) – with the addition of Paris, who is pointing his arrow at Achilles' heel. This "unhistorical" collocation makes excellent sense. And you don't have to be Lessing to see that the artist simply used the distinctive possibilities of the visual medium. Filmmakers today do the same – and should.

Such allowances, however, were not granted to *Alexander* (at the same time, the reception of the movie suffered, in the wake of the US electoral campaign, for being too authentic about Alexander's sexual orientation). That is a pity, because "Stone's 'Alexander' is certainly not a loosely-constructed film: it is the result of fifteen years' thinking and refining" (Fox 2004: 168) and solidly grounded in the historical sources. Its transpositions overwhelmingly are those required by the medium for reasons of space and drama. In the end, the superficiality was not that of the

Figure 26.4 Coming together in Rome: the Sphinx, Constantine's Arch, Cleopatra (Elizabeth Taylor), and hosts in *Cleopatra* (1963). Photo: Kobal Archive

Figure 26.5 Early telescoping technique: Achilles (center) fights against Aeneas (left) while Paris (right) prepares to shoot him in the heel. Pontic amphora, mid-sixth cent. BC. Source: K. Galinsky, *Aeneas, Sicily, and Rome* (Princeton, 1969) Fig. 99

movie, but of many of the critics (cf. Solomon 2005). But there is no point beating those dead horses either. Instead, I want to conclude, on the positive note that befits the entire subject of this chapter, by pointing out, with the example of *Alexander*, the useful and welcome dimension "classical" cinema can add to courses about the ancient world at our colleges and universities – courses that in effect constitute the classical tradition for many people today.

Alexander can be incorporated into a variety of courses, whether Greek civilization, Hellenistic history, Greece and Rome in film, (multi)cultural studies, or even military history. It is an excellent way to acquaint students with the variety of traditions, the conflicting nature of the sources, and the controversies about a character who changed the world and the way he did it. Imagine you wanted to make a movie about Alexander. What do we know about him, and how do we know it? What is the nature of the evidence? Do we have anything written by him? What did he look like, and again, how do we know? What about bisexuality in Greece? Is a psychohistorical approach warranted, given Alexander's relationship with his parents and the relationships of many of our students with theirs? (Many college students are at the end of their teens, and these issues are anything but academic to them.) Was that dimension overdone in *Alexander* with Stone's technique of parallel-cutting? Does Olympias (Angelina Jolie) really have to carry on with all those snakes, evoking a tradition from the Minoan snake goddess to Cleopatra? And finally, after we have looked at some material on all this in the lectures and readings, the big question: if you had three hours for an Alexander movie, how would you do it? What episodes would you select and why? Would you telescope some of the events? How would you convey

Alexander's complexity, or would you? And would you cast him as a *conquistador* or a visionary of the unity of all mankind? Should the movie have a message, and what would be the right balance between action/entertainment and such a message?

I cannot think of a better way to get students involved in exploring these basic issues, and I know from experience that it works. For they can see firsthand not only the relevant information (instead of textbook distillations) but also the way we try to arrive at it. As always, the journey is more rewarding than the arrival (see Cavafy's *Ithaca*, which I regularly use in connection with my teaching of the *Odyssey*). The adaptations of the classical world in the cinema have not been on as long a journey as their counterparts in literature, art, and architecture, but they already have made a tremendous impact. With Cavafy, I can only hope that their journey be long, and I have no doubt that it will.[3]

FURTHER READING

The study of ancient Greece and Rome in film is an incipient field, but several good treatments are available. Solomon (2001) is the second and updated edition of his standard work, first published in 1978. Martin Winkler has been another pioneer; see especially the chapter collections he edited in 1991 and 2001. Wyke (1997b) offers a perceptive case study of some major Hollywood movies. Margaret Malamud is making unique contributions by situating film in the context of America's reception of Rome; see her chapters in Joshel, Malamud, and McGuire (2001). Winkler (2005) offers a variety of perspectives on *Gladiator*; cf. Robin Lane Fox's thorough discussion of Stone's *Alexander* (2004). Monica Cyrino's *Big Screen Rome* (2005) is an excellent treatment of the major Roman cinemepics. The "authenticity" question, really a red herring, is discussed incisively by Winkler (2005: 21–3) and by Solomon in Winkler's forthcoming volume on *Troy* (Blackwell, 2006). Finally, my course website is http://www.utexas.edu/courses/ancientfilmCC304.

NOTES

1   I recall with pleasure Daniel Barenboim's first production as the new music director of the Staatsoper in Berlin in 1993: an outdoor staging of *The Magic Flute* that struck the local critics as far too entertaining at the expense of *Tiefsinn*.
2   Besides DeMille's *Cleopatra*, mention should be made of the reprise (not the last, as it turned out) of *The Last Days of Pompeii* (1935), which featured some superb technical effects, and the problem-plagued *Caesar and Cleopatra* (1945), which was adapted – none too successfully – for the screen by George Bernard Shaw himself.
3   My thanks to Jon Solomon for critiquing an earlier version of this chapter.

Bibliography

Aalto, P. (1980) *Classical Studies in Finland 1828–1918*. Societas Scientiarum Fennica, Helsinki.

Abbott, D. P. (1996) *Rhetoric in the New World: Rhetorical Theory and Practice in Colonial Spanish America*. University of South Carolina Press, Columbia.

Abrams, M. H. (1953) *The Mirror and the Lamp: Romantic Theory and the Critical Tradition*. Oxford University Press, Oxford & New York.

Ackermann, R. (1991) *The Myth and Ritual School: J. G. Frazer and the Cambridge Ritualists*. Garland Publishing, New York.

Acton, H. B. (1938) The Alleged Fascism of Plato. *Philosophy* 13, 302–12.

Adair, D. & Schutz, J. A. (1966) *The Spur of Fame: Dialogues of John Adams and Benjamin Rush, 1805–1813*. Huntington Library, San Marino.

Adam, A. (1974) *Grandeur and Illusion: French Literature and Society 1600–1715*, trans. H. Tint. Penguin Books, Harmondsworth.

Adam, A. (1996) *Histoire de la littérature française du XVIIe siècle*, 3 vols. A. Michel, Paris.

Adam, P. (1992) *The Arts of the Third Reich*. Thames and Hudson, London.

Adams, B. (2003) Francesco Clemente Talks to Brooks Adams – 80s then – Interview. *Artforum*, March, http://64.233.161.104/search?q=cache:tFfXVU4Mpg EJ: www.findarticles.com/p/articles/mi_m0268/is_7_41/ai_98918644+%22 Franusco + Clemente %22+%2B +Pantheon&hl=en.

Adams, B. S. (1965) The Eclogues of Miklós Radnóti. *Slavonic and East European Review* 43:2 (June), 390–9.

Adams, H. (1989) *Thomas Hart Benton, an American Original*. Alfred A. Knopf, New York.

Adams, H. (1999) *The Education of Henry Adams*, ed. I. B. Nadel. Oxford University Press, Oxford.

Adams, J. (1962) *Diary and Autobiography of John Adams*, ed. L. H. Butterfield, 4 vols. Belknap Press, Cambridge, Mass.

Adamska, A. & Moster, M. (eds.) (2004) *The Development of Literate Mentalities in East Central Europe*. Brepols, Turnhout.

Addison, J. (1965) *The Spectator*, ed. D. Bond, 5 vols. Clarendon, Oxford.

Ades, D. et al. (1995) *Art and Power. Europe under the Dictators 1930–45.* Hayward Gallery, London.

Aerts, W. J. et al. (eds.) (1978) *Alexander the Great in the Middle Ages: Ten Studies on the Last Days of Alexander in Literary and Historical Writing.* Alfa Nijmegen, Nijmegen.

Affron, M. & Antliff, M. (1997) An Introduction. In Affron & Antliff (1997): 2–24.

Affron, M. & Antliff, M. (eds.) (1997) *Fascist Visions: Art and Ideology in France and Italy.* Princeton University Press, Princeton.

Agricola, R. (2002) *Letters,* ed. A. van der Laan and F. Akkerman. Arizona Center for Medieval and Renaissance Studies, Tempe.

Aicher, P. (2000) Mussolini's Forum and the Myth of Augustan Rome. *Classical Bulletin* 76, 117–39.

Aili, H. (1995) Sweden. In Jensen (1995): 129–58.

Akkerman, F. & Vanderjagt, A. J. (eds.) (1988) *Rudolphus Agricola Frisius 1444–1485. Proceedings of the International Conference at the University of Groningen 28–30 October 1985.* E. J. Brill, Leiden.

Albrecht, M. von (1988) *Rom: Spiegel Europas. Texte und Themen.* Stauffenburg, Tübingen.

Albrecht, M. von (1994) *Geschichte der römischen Literatur. Von Andronicus bis Boethius. Mit Berücksichtigung ihrer Bedeutung für die Neuzeit,* 2nd edn. Francke, Bern.

Albrecht, M. von (2003) *Literatur als Brücke. Studien zur Rezeptionsgeschichte und Komparatistik.* Olms, Hildesheim.

Aldrich, R. (1993) *The Seduction of the Mediterranean: Writing, Art, and Homosexual Fantasy.* Routledge, London.

Alenius, M. et al. (1991) *Latin og nationalsprog i Norden efter reformationen.* Museum Tusculanum, Copenhagen.

Alessio, G. C., Billanovich, G., & de Angelis, V. (1985) L'alba del Petrarca filologo. Il Virgilio Ambrosiano. *Studi petrarcheschi* 11, 15–82.

Allen, P. S., Allen, H. M., & Garrod, H. W. (eds.) (1906–58) *Opus Epistularum Desiderii Erasmi Roterodami,* 12 vols. Oxford University Press, Oxford.

Allen, W. S. & Brink, C. O. (1980) The Old Order and the New: A Case History. *Lingua* 50, 61–100.

Alpers, S. (2005) *The Vexations of Art: Velázquez and Others.* Yale University Press, New Haven.

Alvar, A. & Fumaroli, M. (1998) *Les Origines du Collège de France (1510–1560): Actes du colloque international* (Paris, December 1995). Collège de France, Paris.

American Classical League (1924) *The Classical Investigation Conducted by the Advisory Committee of the American Classical League....* Princeton University Press, Princeton.

Amo, A. W. (1729) De jure Maurorum in Europa. Dissertation University of Halle.

Amo, A. W. (1734) *De humane mentis Ἀπάθεια.* Officina Scholmachiana, Witttenberg.

Amo, A. W. (1738) *Tractatus de arte sobrie et accurate philosophandi.* Officina Kitleriana, Halle.

Anadón, J. (ed.) (1998) *Garcilaso Inca de la Vega: An American Humanist.* University of Notre Dame Press, Notre Dame.

Anderson, R. D. (2004) *European Universities from the Enlightenment to 1914.* Oxford University Press, Oxford.

Andrés, E. de (1988) *Helenistas españoles del siglo XVII.* FUE, Madrid.

Andrews, J. & Coroleu, A. (eds.) (2007) *Mexico 1680: Cultural and Intellectual Life in the Barroco de Indias.* HiPLAM, Bristol.

Appiah, K. A. (2006) *Cosmopolitanism: Ethics in a World of Strangers.* W. W. Norton, New York.

Arcipreste de Hita (1983), *Libro de buen amor*, ed. A. Blecua. Planeta, Barcelona.

Aristotle (1509) *La philosophia moral del Aristóteles*, trans. C. Viana. Coci, Zaragoza.

Arlen, S. (1990) *The Cambridge Ritualists: An Annotated Bibliography of the Works by and about Jane Ellen Harrison, Gilbert Murray, Francis M. Cornford, and Arthur Bernard Cook*. Scarecrow Press, Metuchen.

Arlt, P. (1988) Antikerezeption in der bildenden Kunst der DDR. Zu den Entwicklungsprozessen der antik-mythologischen Ikonographie in Malerei, Grafik und Plastik von 1945 bis 1985 und der ikonographisch-ikonologischen Methode in der Kunstwissenschaft der DDR. Dissertation Pädagogische Hochschule Erfurt-Mühlhausen.

Armah, A. K. (1968) *The Beautyful Ones Are Not Yet Born*. Houghton Mifflin, Boston.

Armstrong, R. H. (2005) *A Compulsion for Antiquity: Freud and the Ancient World*. Cornell University Press, Ithaca.

Arnold, M. (1965, 1979) *Poems*, ed. Kenneth Allott. Longmans, London.

Artaza, E. (1988) *El "Ars narrandi" en la España del siglo XVI*. Universidad de Deusto, Bilbao.

Artaza, E. (2000) Las retóricas barrocas (1600–1650). Notas introductorias. In Artaza, E. (ed.) *Estudios de filología y retórica en homenaje a Luisa López Grigera*. Deusto, Bilbao, 45–66.

Ascoli, A. R. (2000) Authority. In Lansing, R. (ed.) *The Dante Encyclopedia*. Garland Publishing, New York, 72–5.

Asensio, E. (1974) *Estudios portugueses*. Fundaçâo Calouste Gulbenkian, Paris.

Asensio, E. (2005a) Ciceronianos contra erasmistas en España. Dos momentos (1528–1560). In *De Fray Luis de León a Quevedo y otros estudios sobre retórica, poética y humanismo*. Ediciones Universidad, Salamanca, 229–50.

Asensio, E. (2005b) Un Quevedo incógnito: Las *Silvas*. In *De Fray Luis de León a Quevedo y otros estudios sobre retórica, poética y humanismo*. Ediciones Universidad, Salamanca, 149–88.

Asensio, E. & de Pina Martins, J. V. (1982) *Luis de Camões*. Fundaçâo C. Gulbenkian, Paris.

Ashton, D. (1992) *Noguchi East and West*. Alfred A. Knopf, New York.

Atherton C. (1998) Children, Slaves, Animals and Grammar. In Too, Y. L. & Livingstone, N. (eds.) *Pedagogy and Power: Rhetorics of Classical Learning*. Cambridge University Press, Cambridge, 214–44.

Atkinson, J. B. & Sices, D. (trans.) (1996) *Machiavelli and His Friends: Their Personal Correspondence*. Northern Illinois University Press, De Kalb.

Avenarius, A. (2000) *Die byzantinische Kultur und die Slawen. Zum Problem der Rezeption und Transformation (6. bis 12. Jahrhundert)*. R. Oldenbourg, Vienna.

Axer, J. (1994a) Da Pułaski a Kościuszko. Cicerone nella tradizione repubblicana dei protagonisti polacchi della rivoluzione americana. In *Ciceroniana. Nuova Serie 8. Atti dell'VIII Colloquium Tullianum: New York, 6–9 maggio 1991*. Centro di Studi Ciceroniani, Rome, 53–62.

Axer, J. (1994b) Latin in Poland and East-Central Europe: Continuity and Discontinuity. *European Review* 2:4, 305–9.

Axer, J. (1996 [1997]) The Classical Tradition in Polish Culture: Between Rome and Byzantium. *Eos* (Supp. to 84), 61–8.

Axer, J. (1998) Latein als Sprache der Adelsnation in der polnisch-litauischen Konfederation (16 bis 18 Jahrhundert). Eine These. In Guthmuller, B. (ed.) *Latein und Nationalsprachen in der Renaissance. Vorträge des 37. Wolfenbütteler Symposions in der Herzog August Bibliothek Wolfenbüttel vom 25. bis 28. September 1995.* Harrassowitz Verlag, Wiesbaden, 131–7.

Axer, J. (2002) Neo-Latin Studies and National Identity: The Case of East-Central Europe. *Eos* 89, 331–42.

Axer, J. (ed.) (2004a) *Łacina jako język elit.* OBTA–DiG, Warsaw.

Axer, J. (2004b) Wielogłosowe przesłanie *Pieśni o żubrze* Mikołaja Hussowskiego. In Axer, J. (ed.) *Łacina jako język elit.* OBTA–DiG, Warsaw, 319–27.

Axer, J. (2004c) Latin as the Language of the Elites. Introductory Remarks. In Axer, J. (ed.) *Łacina jako język elit.* OBTA–DiG, Warsaw, 15–22.

Axer, J. (2005) Présentation. Une République aux confins de l'Europe. In Mickiewicz, A. (ed.) *Les Slaves. Cours du Collège de France 1842.* Klincksieck, Paris, v–xxi.

Axer, J. (forthcoming) Polish Philhellenism. In Konstantinou, E. (ed.) Philhellenische Studien, vol. 13. Peter Lang, Frankfurt a.M & New York.

Axer, J. & Kieniewicz, J. (1999) Poland. In Grendler, P. F. (ed.) *Encyclopedia of the Renaissance.* Charles Scribner's Sons, New York, 101–5.

Azim, F. (2001) Post-colonial Theory. In Knellwolf, C. & Norris, C. (eds.) *The Cambridge History of Literary Criticism*, vol. 9, *Twentieth-Century Historical, Philosophical and Psychological Perspectives.* Cambridge University Press, Cambridge, 237–47.

Baeumler, A. (1939) *Politik und Erziehung: Reden und Aufsätze.* Junker & Dünnhaupt, Berlin.

Baeumler, A. (1943) *Männerbund und Wissenschaft.* Junker & Dünnhaupt, Berlin.

Bailyn, B. (1967) *Ideological Origins of the American Revolution.* Belknap Press of Harvard University Press, Cambridge, Mass.

Bakhtin, M. (1968) *Rabelais and His World*, trans. H. Iswolsky. Massachusetts Institute of Technology Press Cambridge, Mass.

Banac, I. & Sysyn, F. (eds.) (1986) *Concepts of Nationhood in Early Modern Eastern Europe.* Ukrainian Research Institute, Harvard University, Cambridge, Mass.

Bannes, J. (1933) *Hitlers Kampf und Platons Staat: Eine Studie über den ideologischen Aufbau der nationalsozialistischen Freiheitsbewegung.* W. de Gruyter, Berlin.

Bar On, B. A. (1994) *Engendering Origins: Critical Feminist Readings in Plato and Aristotle.* State University of New York Press, Albany.

Barajas Durán, R. (2002) Retrato de un siglo. ¿Cómo ser mexicano en el XIX? In *Espejo Mexicano.* Fondo de Cultura Económica, Mexico City, 116–77.

Barbero, A. (2004) *Charlemagne, Father of a Continent*, trans. A. Cameron. University of California Press, Berkeley.

Barkan, E. & Bush R. (eds.) (1995) *Prehistories of the Future: The Primitivist Project and the Culture of Modernism.* Stanford University Press, Stanford.

Barkan, L. (1986) *The Gods Made Flesh: Metamorphosis and the Pursuit of Paganism.* Yale University Press, New Haven.

Barkan, L. (1999) *Unearthing the Past: Archaeology and Aesthetics in the Making of Renaissance Culture.* Yale University Press, New Haven.

Barker, S. (1996) *Excavations and Their Objects: Freud's Collection of Antiquity.* State University of New York Press, Albany.

Baron, H. (1966) *The Crisis of the Early Italian Renaissance: Civic Humanism and Republican Liberty in an Age of Classicism and Tyranny.* Princeton University Press, Princeton.

Barrow, R. (2000) "Mad about the Boy": Mythological Models and Victorian Painting. *Dialogos* 7, 124–42.

Barthes, R. (1990) *S/Z*, trans. R. Miller. Blackwell, Oxford.

Bartók, I. (ed.) (2005) *Companion to the History of the Neo-Latin Studies in Hungary.* Universitas Publishing House, Budapest.

Bassnett, S. & Trivedi, H. (1999) *Post-Colonial Translation: Theory and Practice.* Routledge, London & New York.

Baswell, C. (1995) *Virgil in Medieval England: Figuring the Aeneid from the Twelfth Century to Chaucer.* Cambridge University Press, Cambridge.

Batllori, M. (1987) *Humanismo y Renacimiento. Estudios hispano-europeos.* Ariel, Barcelona.

Baumbach, M. (ed.) (2000) *Tradita et Inventa. Beiträge zur Rezeption der Antike.* Winter, Heidelberg.

Bayoumi, M. & Rubin, A. (eds.) (2001) *The Edward Saïd Reader.* Granta Books, London.

Beacham, R. (2005) The Emperor as Impresario: Producing the Pageantry of Power. In Galinsky, K. (ed.) *The Cambridge Companion to the Age of Augustus.* Cambridge University Press, Cambridge, 151–74.

Beard, M. (2000) *The Invention of Jane Ellen Harrison.* Harvard University Press, Cambridge, Mass.

Beard, M. & Henderson, J. (1995) *Classics: A Very Short Introduction.* Oxford University Press, Oxford & New York.

Beardsley, T. S., Jr. (1970) *Hispano-Classical Translations Printed between 1482 and 1699.* Duquesne University Press, Pittsburgh.

Beaton, R. (1991) *George Seferis.* Bristol Classical Press, Bristol.

Bebbington, D. W. (2004) *The Mind of Gladstone: Religion, Homer and Politics.* Oxford University Press, Oxford.

Becker, Edwin et al. (eds.) (1996) *Sir Lawrence Alma-Tadema.* Van Gogh Museum, Amsterdam.

Bedaux, J. B. (1992) Velázquez's *Fable of Arachne* (*Las Hilanderas*): A Continuing Story. *Simiolus* 21, 296–305.

Beinart, B. (1952) *Roman Law in South African Practice: Inaugural Lecture Delivered Before the University of Cape Town on 6 November 1951.* Oxford University Press, Cape Town.

Bemba, S. [a.k.a. Martial Melinda] (1970) *L'enfer, c'est Orféo.* ORTF, Paris.

Bemba, S. [a.k.a. Martial Melinda] (1984) *Le dernier des Cargonautes.* Harmattan, Paris.

Bemba, S. [a.k.a. Martial Melinda] (1990) *Black Wedding Candles for Blessed Antigone.* In *Theatre and Politics: An International Anthology,* trans. T. Brewster. Ubu Repertory, New York, 1–62.

Bemba, S. [a.k.a. Martial Melinda] (1995) *Noces posthumes de Santigone.* Le bruit des autres, Solignac.

Bene, S. (2006) Latin Historiography in Hungary: Writing and Rewriting Myths of Origin. In *Myth and Reality: Latin Historiography in Hungary 15th – 18th Centuries.* Exhibition in the National Széchényi Library, 7 July – 3 September 2006. National Széchényi Library, Budapest.

Bengl, H. (1941) Die Antike und die Erziehung zum politischen Deutschen. *Die Alten Sprachen* 6, 3–8.

ben-Jochannan, Y. A. A. (1970) *African Origins of the Major "Western Religions."* Black Classic Press, Baltimore.

ben-Jochannan, Y. A. A. (1988) *Africa: Mother of Western Civilization.* Black Classic Press, Baltimore.

Benediktsson, J. (1991) Arngrímur Jónsson – en islandsk humanist omkring år 1600. In Alenius et al. (1991): 93–103.

Benko, S. (1980) Virgil's Fourth *Eclogue* in Christian Interpretation. In Temporini, H. (ed.) *Aufstieg und Niedergang der römischen Welt: Geschichte und Kultur Roms im Spiegel der neueren Forschung.* W. de Gruyter, Berlin, part 2, vol. 31.1, 646–70.

Benson, R. L. & Constable, G. (1984) *Renaissance and Renewal in the Twelfth Century.* Clarendon Press, Oxford.

Benson, R. L. & Constable, G. with Lanham, C. D. (eds.) (1982) *Renaissance and Renewal in the Twelfth Century.* Harvard University Press, Cambridge, Mass.

Bentley, R. (1697) *A Dissertation upon the Epistles of Phalaris.* Printed by J. Leake, for Peter Buck, London.

Bergh, B. & Platen, M. von (trans. and ed.) (1994) *Resan till Världsstaden av Olof Verelius.* Almqvist & Wiksell International, Gothenburg & Stockholm.

Bernal, M. (1987) *Black Athena: The Afroasiatic Roots of Classical Civilization,* vol. 1: *The Fabrication of Ancient Greece 1785–1985.* Rutgers University Press, New Brunswick.

Bernal, M. (1991) *Black Athena: The Afroasiatic Roots of Classical Civilization,* vol. 2: *The Archaeological and Documentary Evidence.* Rutgers University Press, New Brunswick.

Bernardo, A. S. & Levin, S. (eds.) (1990) *The Classics in the Middle Ages.* Center for Medieval and Early Renaissance Studies, Binghamton.

Bernhardt, R. (1983) *Odysseus' Tod – Prometheus' Leben. Antike Mythen in der Literatur der DDR.* Mitteldt. Verlag, Halle & Leipzig.

Berschin, W. (1980) *Griechisch-lateinisches Mittelalter. Von Hieronymus zu Nikolaus von Kues.* Francke, Bern & Munich.

Berschin, W. (1988) *Greek Letters and the Latin Middle Ages from Jerome to Nicholas of Cusa,* trans. J. C. Frakes, rev. edn. Catholic University of America Press, Washington.

Berve, H. (1993) Antike und nationalsozialistischer Staat. In Nippel (1993): 283–99.

Berve, H. (ed.) (1942) *Das neue Bild der Antike,* vol. 1: *Hellas.* Koehler und Amelang, Leipzig.

Bery, A. & Murray, P. (2000) *Comparing Postcolonial Literatures: Dislocations.* St. Martin's Press, London & New York.

Bethell, L. (ed.) (1987) *Colonial Brazil.* Cambridge University Press, Cambridge & New York.

Bhabha, H. (1994) *The Location of Culture.* Routledge, London.

Biermann, V. (2001) The Virtue of a King and the Desire of a Woman? Mythological Representations in the Collection of Queen Christina. In Camille, M. & Rifkin, A. (eds.) *Other Objects of Desire: Collectors and Collecting Queerly.* Blackwell, Oxford, 51–68.

Birnbaum, M. (1986) *Humanists in the Shattered World: Croatian and Hungarian Latinity in the Sixteenth Century.* Ohio State University Press, Columbus.

Black, J. (1998) Taking the Sex out of Sexuality: Foucault's Failed History. In *Rethinking Sexuality: Foucault and Classical Antiquity.* Princeton University Press, Princeton, 42–60.

Black, R. (2001) *Humanism and Education in Medieval and Renaissance Italy: Tradition and Innovation in Latin Schools from the Twelfth to the Fifteenth Century.* Cambridge University Press, Cambridge.

Blackwell, T. (1735) *An Enquiry into the Life and Writings of Homer.* N.p., London.

Blake, W. (1967) *Complete Poetry and Prose,* ed. Geoffrey Keynes, 4th edn. Nonesuch, London.

Blankert, A. (1999) *Hollands classicisme in de zeventiende-eeuwse schilderkunst.* Städelsches Kunstinstitut und Städtische Galerie, Rotterdam.

Blanshard, A. (2000) Hellenic Fantasies: Aesthetics, Desire and Symonds' *A Problem in Greek Ethics. Dialogos* 7, 99–123.

Blanshard, A. (2005) *Hercules: A Heroic Life*. Granta Books, London.

Blok, J. H. (1995) *The Early Amazons: Modern and Ancient Perspectives on a Persistent Myth*. E. J. Brill, Leiden.

Blüher, K. A. (1969) *Seneca in Spanien*. Francke, Munich.

Blüher, K. A. (1983) *Séneca en España, investigaciones sobre la recepción de Séneca en España desde el siglo XIII hasta el siglo XVII*, trans. Juan Conde. Gredos, Madrid.

Blumenberg, H. (1990) *Arbeit und Mythos*. Suhrkamp, Frankfurt a.M.

Blumenthal, A. von (1939) Nietzsche und die klassische Altertumswissenschaft in Deutschland. *Die Welt als Geschichte. Eine Zeitschrift für Universalgeschichte* 5, 156–67.

Blunt, A. (2005) *Borromini*. Belknap Press of Harvard University Press, Cambridge, Mass.

Boardman, J. (2004) Nudity in Art. In Kurtz, D. (ed.) *Reception of Classical Art: An Introduction*. Archaeopress, Oxford, 47–54.

Boas, G. (1973) Primitivism. In Wiener, P. (ed.) *Dictionary of the History of Ideas*. Scribner, New York, 577–98.

Bober, P. & Rubenstein, R. (1986) *Renaissance Artists and Antique Sculpture: A Handbook of Sources*. Oxford University Press, Oxford.

Boehrer, B. T. (1998) Renaissance Classicism and Roman Sexuality: Ben Jonson's Marginalia and the Trope of the *Os impurum*. *International Journal of the Classical Tradition* 4:3, 364–80.

Bogaerts, T. (1969) *De antieke wereld van Louis Couperus*. Polak & Van Gennep, Amsterdam.

Boileau, N. (1708) *Boileau's Lutrin*, trans. J. Ozell. E. Sanger & E. Curll, London.

Boileau, N. (1966) *Oeuvres complètes*. Gallimard, Paris.

Bolaños, A. F. & Verdesio, G. (eds.) (2002) *Colonialism Past and Present: Reading and Writing about Colonial Latin America Today*. State University of New York Press, Albany.

Bolgar, R. R. (1954) *The Classical Heritage and Its Beneficiaries*. Cambridge University Press, Cambridge.

Bollack, J. (1993) Der Menschensohn. Freuds Ödipusmythos. *Psyche* 47, 647–83.

Bollmus, R. (1970) *Das Amt Rosenberg und seine Gegner. Studien zum Machtkampf im nationalsozialistischen Herrschaftssystem*. Deutsche Verlags-Anstalt, Stuttgart.

Bondanella, P. (1987) *The Eternal City: Roman Images in the Modern World*. University of North Carolina Press, Chapel Hill.

Bonfante, L. (1989) Nudity as Costume in Classical Art. *American Journal of Archaeology* 93, 543–70.

Borinski, K. (1914–1924) *Die Antike in Poetik und Kunsttheorie vom Ausgang des klassischen Altertums bis auf Goethe und Wilhelm von Humboldt*. Dieterich, Leipzig.

Borst, A. (1957–63) *Der Turmbau von Babel. Geschichte der Meinungen über Ursprung und Vielfalt der Sprachen und Völker*, 4 vols. Anton Hiersemann Verlag, Stuttgart.

Bosco, L. (2004) *"Das furchtbar-schöne Gorgonenhaupt des Klassischen" (1755–1875)*. Königshausen & Neumann, Würzburg.

Boswell, J. (1980) *Christianity, Social Tolerance, and Homosexuality: Gay People in Western Europe from the Beginning of the Christian Era to the Fourteenth Century*. University of Chicago Press, Chicago & London.

Boswell, J. (1982) *Past Ruined Ilion* ... : *A Bibliography of English and American Literature Based on Greco-Roman Mythology.* Scarecrow Press, Metuchen.

Brading, D. (1991) *The First America: The Spanish Monarchy, Creole Patriots, and the Liberal State 1492–1867.* Cambridge University Press, Cambridge.

Brancaforte, B. (ed.) (1990) *Las Metamorfosis y las Heroidas de Ovidio en la General estoria de Alfonso el Sabio.* Hispanic Seminary of Medieval Studies, Madison.

Brathwaite, K. (1967) *Odale's Choice.* Evans, London.

Brathwaite, K. (1984) *History of the Voice: The Development of Nation Language in Anglophone Caribbean Poetry.* New Beacon Books, London.

Bray, R. (1927) *Formation de la doctrine classique en France.* Hachette, Paris. Rpt. Libraire Nizet, Paris, 1966.

Brejon de Lavergnée, A. et al. (2004) Peter Paul Rubens, *Rubens.* Snoeck Publishers, Ghent.

Bremmer, J. (ed.) (1987) Oedipus and the Greek Oedipus-complex. In *Interpretations of Greek Mythology.* Croom Helm, London, 41–59.

Brenner, H. (1963) *Die Kunstpolitik des Nationalsozialismus.* Rowohlt, Hamburg.

Bridges, M. & Bürgel, J. C. (eds.) (1996) *The Problematics of Power: Eastern and Western Representations of Alexander the Great.* Schweizer Asiatische Studien 22. Peter Lang, Bern, Berlin, & Frankfurt.

Brink, A. P. (1961) *Caesar: 'n Drama.* Nasionale Boekhandel Beperk, Cape Town.

Brink, C. O. (1985) *English Classical Scholarship: Historical Reflections on Bentley, Porson and Houseman.* Oxford University Press, Oxford & New York.

Broch, H. (1983) *The Death of Virgil*, trans. J. S. Untermeyer. North Point Press, San Francisco.

Brock, M. G. & Curthoys, M. C. (eds.) (1998–2000) *The History of the University of Oxford*, vols. 6–7. Oxford University Press, Oxford.

Brockliss, L. W. B. (1997) The European University in an Age of Revolution, 1789–1850. In Brock, M. G. &. Curthoys, M. C. (eds.) *The History of the University of Oxford*, vol. 6: *Nineteenth-Century Oxford, Part I.* Oxford University Press, Oxford, 77–133.

Brooten, B. J. (1997) *Love Between Women: Early Christian Responses to Female Homo-eroticism.* University of Chicago Press, Chicago & London.

Brown, C. (1973) *Mandelstam.* Cambridge University Press, Cambridge.

Brown, J. (1986) *Velázquez: Painter and Courtier.* Yale University Press, New Haven & London.

Brown, N. O. (1957) Psychoanalysis and the Classics. *Classical Journal* 52, 241–5.

Brown, V. (2001) *Giovanni Boccaccio. Famous Women.* Harvard University Press, Cambridge, Mass.

Brunel, P. (ed.) (1999) *Le Mythe d'Orphée aux XIXe and XXe siècle: Actes du colloque de la Sorbonne.* Didier Érudition, Paris.

Brunhölzl F. (1975–92) *Geschichte der lateinischen Literatur des Mittelalters*, 2 vols. Fink, Munich. French trans. H. Rochais, with bibliographical suppl. J.-P. Bouhout, Brepols, Turnhout, 1990–6.

Brunner, T. F. (1970) Adolf Hitler on the Classics. *Classical Journal* 65:6, 260–2.

Bryce, J. B. (1901) *Studies in History and Jurisprudence.* Books for Libraries Press, Freeport.

Budelmann, F. (2005) West-African Adaptations of Greek Tragedy. *Proceedings of the Cambridge Philological Society* 50, 1–28. Rpt. in B. Goff (ed.) *Classics and Colonialism.* Duckworth, London, 2005, 118–46.

Budelmann, F. (forthcoming) *Trojan Women in Yorubaland: Femi Òsòfisan's Women of Owu.* In Hardwick, L. & Gillespie, C. (eds.) *Classics in Post-Colonial Worlds.* Oxford University Press, Oxford.

Bull, M. (2005) *The Mirror of the Gods: How Renaissance Artists Rediscovered the Pagan Gods.* Oxford University Press, Oxford.

Bullen, J. B. (2003) *Byzantium Rediscovered: The Byzantine Revival in Europe and America.* Phaidon, New York.

Bunt, G. H. V. (1994) *Alexander the Great in the Literature of Medieval Britain.* Egbert Forsten, Groningen.

Burckhardt, J. (1958) *The Civilization of the Renaissance in Italy,* 2 vols. Harper and Row, New York.

Burke, E. (1998) *A Philosophical Enquiry into the Origin of Our Ideas of the Sublime and Beautiful,* ed. A. Phillips. Oxford University Press, Oxford & New York.

Burke, P. (1978) *Popular Culture in Early Modern Europe.* New York University Press, New York.

Burke, P. (1988) *The European Renaissance: Centres and Peripheries.* Blackwell, Oxford.

Burke, P. (1999) Erasmus and the Republic of Letters. *European Review* 7:1, 5–17.

Burris, S. (1990) *The Poetry of Resistance: Seamus Heaney and the Pastoral Tradition.* Ohio University Press, Athens.

Bush, D. (1932) *Mythology and the Renaissance Tradition in English Poetry.* University of Minnesota Press, Minneapolis & London.

Bush, D. (1937) *Mythology and the Romantic Tradition in English Poetry.* Harvard University Press, Cambridge, Mass.

Bush, R. (1976) *The Genesis of Ezra Pound's Cantos.* Princeton University Press, Princeton.

Bush, R. (1983) Gathering the Limbs of Osiris: The Subject of Pound's *Homage to Sextus Propertius.* In Hoffman, D. (ed.) *Ezra Pound and William Carlos Williams.* University of Pennsylvania Press, Philadelphia, 61–79.

Butler, E. M. (1935) *The Tyranny of Greece over Germany. A Study of the Influence Exercised by Greek Art and Poetry over the Great German Writers of the Eighteenth, Nineteenth and Twentieth Centuries.* Cambridge University Press, Cambridge.

Butler, G. (1990) *Demea.* David Philip, Cape Town.

Butler, J. (2000) *Antigone's Claim: Kinship Between Life and Death.* Columbia University Press, New York.

Butterfield, L. H. (ed.) (1963–75) *Adams Family Correspondence,* 7 vols. Belknap Press, Cambridge, Mass.

Cagnetta, M. (1976) Il mito di Augusto e la "rivoluzione" fascista. *Quaderni di storia* 3, 139–82.

Cagnetta, M. (1990) *Antichità classiche nell'Enciclopedia italiana.* Laterza, Bari.

Cagnetta, M. & Schiano, C. (1999) Faschismus, trans. B. Lienert. In Landfester (1999): vol. 13, cols. 1084–1105.

Calasso, R. (2001) *La letteratura e gli dèi.* Adelphi, Milan. Eng. trans. T. Parks, *Literature and the Gods,* Knopf, New York, 2001.

Calder, W. M. (1983) Werner Jaeger and Richard Harder: An *Erklärung. Quaderni di storia* 17, 99–121.

Calder, W. M. (ed.) (1991) *The Cambridge Ritualists Reconsidered.* Scholars Press, Atlanta.

Calder, W. M. (ed.) (1992) *Werner Jaeger Reconsidered.* Scholars Press, Atlanta.

Calder, W. M. (1994) Classical Scholarship in the United States: An Introductory Essay. In Briggs, W. W. (ed.) *Biographical Dictionary of North American Classicists.* Greenwood Press, Westport, xi–xxxix.

Calder, W. M. & Braun, M. (1996) "Tell It Hitler! Ecco!" Paul Friedländer on Werner Jaeger's *Paideia. Quaderni di storia* 43, 211–48.

Calder, W. M., Flashar, H., & Lindken, T. (eds.) (1985) *Wilamowitz nach 50 Jahren.* Wissenschaftliche Buchgesellschaft, Darmstadt.

Caldwell, R. S. (1974) Selected Bibliography on Psychoanalysis and Classical Studies. *Arethusa* 7, 115–34.

Caldwell, R. S. (1996) The Psychoanalytic Interpretations of Greek Mythology. In Edmunds, L. (ed.) *Approaches to Greek Mythology.* Johns Hopkins University Press, Baltimore & London, 342–89.

Cambiano, G. (1988) *Il ritorno degli antichi.* Laterza, Rome & Bari.

Cambiano, G. (1991) Eric Dodds entre psychanalyse et parapsychologie. *Revue de histoire de religion* 208, 3–26.

Camino, M. M. (1995) *"The Stage Am I": Raping Lucrece in Early Modern England.* Edwin Mellen Press, Lewiston & Salzburg.

Camões, L. V. de. (1572) *Os Lusíadas.* Antonio Gõçalvez, Lisbon.

Campbell, R. (1930) *Adamastor.* Faber and Faber, London.

Campiglio, P. et al. (2003) *Scultura Lingua Morta: Sculpture from Fascist Italy.* Henry Moore Institute, Leeds.

Cancik, H. (1995). Der Einfluss Friedrich Nietzsche auf klassische Philologen in Deutschland bis 1945. In Flashar (1995): 381–402.

Cancik, H. (1998) *Antik–Modern. Beiträge zur römischen und deutschen Kulturgeschichte.* J. B. Metzler, Stuttgart & Weimar.

Cancik, H. & Cancik-Lindemaier, H. (1991) Philhellénisme et antisémitisme en Allemagne: le cas Nietzsche. In Bourel, D. & Le Rider, J. (eds.) *De Sils-Maria à Jérusalem: Nietzsche et le judaïsme. Les intellectuels juifs et Nietzsche.* Cerf, Paris, 21–46.

Cancik, H., Schneider, H., & Landfester, M. (eds.) (1996–2003) *Der Neue Pauly: Enzyklopädie der Antike,* 16 vols. J. B. Metzler, Stuttgart & Weimar.

Canfora, L. (1976) Classicismo e fascismo. *Quaderni di storia* 3, 15–48.

Canfora, L. (1979) *La Germania di Tacito da Engels al nazismo.* Liguori, Naples.

Canfora, L. (1980) *Ideologie del classicismo.* G. Einaudi, Turin.

Canfora, L. (1985) Wilamowitz: "Politik" in der Wissenschaft. In Calder, Flashar, & Lindken (1985): 56–79.

Canfora, L. (1987) Platon im Staatsdenken der Weimarer Republik. In Funke, H. (ed.) *Utopie und Tradition. Platons Lehre vom Staat in der Moderne.* Königshausen & Neumann, Würzburg, 133–48.

Canfora, L. (1989) *Le vie del classicismo.* Laterza, Rome & Bari.

Cañizares-Esguerra, J. (2001) *How to Write the History of the New World: Histories, Epistemologies, and Identities in the Eighteenth-Century Atlantic World.* Stanford University Press, Stanford.

Cannistraro, P. V. (1975) *La fabbrica del consenso: fascismo e mass media.* Laterza, Rome & Bari.

Capitein, J. E. J. (1742) *Dissertatio politico-theologica de servitute libertati Christianae non contraria.* Samuel Luchtmans et Filius, Leiden.

Cappon, L. J. (1959) *The Adams-Jefferson Letters: The Complete Correspondence between Thomas Jefferson and Abigail and John Adams.* University of North Carolina Press, Chapel Hill.

Cardinal, R. (1996) Primitivism. In Turner, J. (ed.) *The Dictionary of Art*. Grove Dictionaries, New York, 25:582–5.

Cardwell, R. A. & Hamilton, J. (eds.) (1986) *Virgil in a Cultural Tradition*. University of Nottingham Press, Nottingham.

Carne-Ross, D. S. (1979) *Instaurations: Essays in and out of Literature, Pindar to Pound*. University of California Press, Berkeley.

Carne-Ross, D. S. (1985) *Pindar*. Yale University Press, New Haven.

Carnochan W. B. (1993) *The Battleground of Curriculum: Liberal Education and American Experience*. Stanford University Press, Stanford.

Carroll, M. P. (1978) Lévi-Strauss on the Oedipus Myth: A Reconsideration. *American Anthropologist* 80, 805–14.

Cary, G. (1956) *The Medieval Alexander*. Cambridge University Press, Cambridge.

Castillo Didier, M. (2003) Los estudios clásicos en Chile. In Grammatico Amari, Arbea Gavilán & Edwards (2003): 1:261–74.

Castro G. F. (1924) Observaciones sobre las fuentes literarias de "La Celestina". *Rivista de filología española*, supp. 5, Madrid.

Cavanaugh, C. (1995) *Osip Mandelstam and the Modernist Creation of Tradition*. Princeton University Press, Princeton.

Cave, T. (1979) *The Cornucopian Text: Problems of Writing in the French Renaissance*. Clarendon Press, Oxford.

Cervato, D. (1993) *Raterio di Verona e di Liegi. Il terzo periodo del suo episcopato veronese (961–968): scritti e attività*. Segno editrice, Verona.

Césaire, A. (1955) *Discours sur le Colonialism*. English trans. J. Pinkham. Monthly Review Press, Paris, 1972.

Chabod, F. (1951) *Storia della politica estera italiana dal 1870 al 1896*. Laterza, Bari.

Chambers, M. (1992) The Historian as Educator: Jaeger on Thucydides. In Calder (1992): 25–35.

Chance, J. (1994–2000) *Medieval Mythography*, 2 vols. University Press of Florida, Gainesville.

Chang, K. (2004) From Oral Disputation to Written Text: The Transformation of the Dissertation in Early Modern Europe. *History of Universities* 19, 129–87.

Chapman, D. (2002) *Retro Stud: Muscle Movie Posters from around the World*. Collectors Press, Portland.

Chase, C. (1979) Oedipal Textuality: Reading Freud's Reading of Oedipus. *Diacritics* 9, 54–68.

Chave, A. C. (1989) *Mark Rothko Subjects in Abstraction*. Yale University Press, New Haven.

Chicago, J. (1996) *The Dinner Party*. Penguin Books, New York.

Chinard, G. (1933) *Honest John Adams*. Little, Brown, Boston.

Christ, K. (1982) *Römische Geschichte und Wissenschaftsgeschichte*. Wissenschaftliche Buchgesellschaft, Darmstadt.

Christ, K. (1986) Spartaforschung und Spartabild: Eine Einleitung. In Christ, K. (ed.) *Sparta*. Wissenschaftliche Buchgesellschaft, Darmstadt, 1–72.

Cicero (1981) *Ad C. Herennium*, English trans. H. Caplan. Harvard University Press, Cambridge, Mass.

Cicero (2002) *Cicero on the Emotions: Tusculan Disputations 3 and 4*, ed. and trans. Margaret Graver. University of Chicago Press, Chicago.

Cizek, A. (1955) *Le roi et le sage: études sur la légende d'Alexandre de l'Antiquité au Moyen Âge*. Éditions Adosa, Clermont-Ferrand.

Claes, P. (1984) *De mot zit in de mythe: Hugo Claus en de oudheid*. Bezige Bij, Amsterdam. 2nd edn., 1985.

Claes, P. (2000) *De Gulden Tak. Antieke mythe en moderne literatuur*. Bezige Bij, Amsterdam.

Clancey, R. W. (1999) *Wordsworth's Classical Undersong*. St. Martin's Press, New York.

Clark, D. R. & McGuire, J. B. (1989) *W. B. Yeats: The Writing of Sophocles' King Oedipus*. American Philosophical Society, Philadelphia.

Clark, E. & Hatch, D. (1981) *The Golden Bough, The Oaken Cross, The Vergilian Cento of Faltonia Betitia Proba*. Scholars Press, Chico.

Clark, J. P. (1964) *Song of a Goat*. In *Three Plays: Song of a Goat, The Masquerade, The Raft*. Oxford University Press, London, 1–48.

Clarke, M. L. (1959) *Classical Education in Great Britain 1500–1900*. Cambridge University Press, Cambridge.

Clavigero, F. J. (1973) *Rules of the Aztec Language*, trans. A. J. O. Anderson. University of Utah Press, Salt Lake City.

Clavigero, F. J. (2003) *Historia antigua de Mexico: edición y prólogo de R. P. Mariano Cuevas [Edición del original escrito en castellano por el autor]*. Porrúa, Mexico City. Italian orig. Bologna, 1780.

Cleary, M. (2000) Freeing "Incarcerated Souls": Margaret Fuller, Women and Classical Mythology. *New England Classics Journal* 27:2, 59–67.

Clogan, P. M. (ed.) (1968) *The Medieval Achilleid of Statius*. E. J. Brill, Leiden.

Cogswell, J. (1819) On the Means of Education, and the State of Learning, in the United States. *Blackwood's Edinburgh Magazine* 4, 546–649.

Coleman, D. G. (1979) *The Gallo-Roman Muse: Aspects of Roman Literary Tradition in Sixteenth-Century France*. Cambridge University Press, Cambridge.

Collected Works of Erasmus (1974–). University of Toronto Press, Toronto & Buffalo.

Comenius, J. (1970) *Orbis sensualium pictus*. Scolar Press, Aldershot. Facsimile of 1659 Nuremberg edn.

Commager, H. S. (1971) The American Enlightenment and the Ancient World: A Study in Paradox. *Proceedings of the Massachusetts Historical Society* 83, 3–15.

Commager, H. S. (1975) *Jefferson, Nationalism, and the Enlightenment*. G. Braziller, New York, 123–39.

Comparetti, D. (1997) *Vergil in the Middle Ages*, trans. E. F. M. Benecke, with a new introduction by J. Ziolkowski. Princeton University Press, Princeton. Rpt. of 1885 edn.

Conley, T. (forthcoming) *Cicero Hunnicus*: Miklos Oláh's Eloquent Attila. *Rhetorica*.

Connors, J. (1989) Alliance and Enmity in Roman Baroque Urbanism. *Römisches Jahrbuch der Bibliotheca Hertziana* 25, 207–94.

Connors, J. (1990) Ars Tornandi: Baroque Architecture and the Lathe. *Journal of the Warburg and Courtauld Institutes* 53, 217–36.

Conradie, P. J. (1996) Debates Surrounding an Approach to African Tragedy. *South African Theatre Journal* 10:1, 25–34.

Constantine, D. (1989) The Question of Authenticity in Some Early Accounts of Greece. In Clarke, G. W. (ed.) *Rediscovering Hellenism*. Cambridge University Press, Cambridge, 1–31.

Cooper, W. (1993) *The Classical Taste in America 1800–1840*. Abbeville Press, New York.

Cormier, R. J. (1973) *One Heart One Mind: The Rebirth of Virgil's Hero in Medieval French Romance*. Romance Monographs, University of Mississippi, Oxford.

Coroleu, A. (2004) On the Awareness of the Renaissance. In Perini, G. B. (ed.) *Il latino nell'età dell'Umanesimo*, Atti del Convegno, Mantua, October 26–7, 2001. Leo S. Olschki, Florence, 3–15.

Corte, F. della (1988) *Enciclopedia virgiliana*. Istituto de la Enciclopedia Italiana, Rome.

Coulson, F. T. (1991) *The "Vulgate" Commentary on Ovid's Metamorphoses*. Toronto Medieval Latin Texts, Toronto.

Coulson, F. T. & Roy, B. (2000) *Incipitarium Ovidianum: A Finding Guide for Texts in Latin Related to the Study of Ovid in the Middle Ages and Renaissance*. Publications of the Journal of Medieval Latin 3. Brepols, Turnhout.

Cowling, E. (2002) *Picasso: Style and Meaning*. Phaidon, London.

Cribiore, R. (2001) The Grammarians' Choice: The Popularity of Euripides' *Phoenissae* in Hellenistic and Roman Education. In Too, Y. L. (ed.) *Education in Greek and Roman Antiquity*. E. J. Brill, Leiden, 241–59.

Cribiore, R. (2005) *Gymnastics of the Mind: Greek Education in Hellenistic and Roman Egypt*. Princeton University Press, Princeton.

Cripps, C. (2005) Interview with Femi Elufowoju, Jr. *Independent*, May 26, 2005, 49.

Croce, B. (1949) *Varietà di storia letteraria e civile*. Laterza, Bari.

Cronin, M. (1996) *Translating Ireland: Translation, Languages, Cultures*. Cork University Press, Cork.

Crook, J. M. (1972) *The Greek Revival*. J. Murray, London.

Crow, B. & Banfield, C. (1996) *An Introduction to Post-Colonial Theatre*. Cambridge University Press, Cambridge.

Crummell, A. (1992) *Destiny and Race: Selected Writings, 1840–1898*. University of Massachusetts Press, Amherst.

Csobádi, P. et al. (eds.) (1990) *Antike Mythen im Musiktheater des 20. Jahrhunderts*. Müller-Speiser, Anif & Salzburg.

Curran, B. A. (2004) The Sphinx in the City: Egyptian Memories and Urban Spaces in Renaissance Rome (and Viterbo). In Campbell, S. J. & Milner, S. J. (eds.) *Artistic Exchange and Cultural Translation in the Italian Renaissance City*. Cambridge University Press, Cambridge and New York, 294–326.

Curtius, E. R. (1953) *European Literature and the Latin Middle Ages*, trans. W. Trask. Princeton University Press, Princeton. Rpt. 1990.

Cyriac of Ancona (2003) *Later Travels*, ed. and trans. E. W. Bodnar. Harvard University Press, Cambridge, Mass., & London.

Cyrino, M. (2005) *Big Screen Rome*. Blackwell, Oxford.

Cyrino, M. (2005) *Gladiator* and Contemporary American Society. In Winkler (2004): 124–49.

Czapla, R. G. (1998) Zur Topik und Faktur postantiker Romgedichte (Hildebert von Lavardin, Joachim Du Bellay, Andreas Gryphius). Mit einem Exkurs über die Rezeption von Hildeberts *Carmen 36 Scott* in der Frühen Neuzeit. *Daphnis* 27, 141–83.

Dall'Orto, G. (1989) "Socratic Love" as a Disguise for Same-Sex Love in the Italian Renaissance. In Gerard, K. & Hekma, G. (eds.) *The Pursuit of Sodomy: Male Homosexuality in Renaissance and Enlightenment Europe*. Haworth Press, New York, 33–66.

D'Amico, J. (1983) *Renaissance Humanism in Papal Rome: Humanists and Churchmen on the Eve of the Reformation*. Johns Hopkins University Press, Baltimore & London.

D'Amico, J. (1988) *Theory and Practice in Renaissance Textual Criticism: Beatus Rhenanus Between Conjecture and History*. University of California Press, Berkeley, Los Angeles, & London.

Damrosch, D. (1986) The Politics of Ethics: Freud and Rome. In Smith, J. H. & Kerrigan, W. (eds.) *Pragmatism's Freud: The Moral Disposition of Psychoanalysis.* Johns Hopkins University Press, Baltimore & London, 103–25.

Daniels, L. (2000) *Wonder Woman: The Life and Times of the Amazon Princess.* Chronicle Books, San Francisco.

Danto, A. C. (1965) *Analytical Philosophy of History.* Cambridge University Press, Cambridge.

Darré, R. W. (1934) *Das Bauerntum als Lebensquell der nordischen Rasse.* J. F. Lehmann, Munich.

Darré, R. W. (1935) *Neuadel aus Blut und Boden.* J. F. Lehmann, Munich.

Davenport, G. (1987) *Every Force Evolves a Form.* North Point Press, San Francisco.

Davidson, P. (1995) *Ezra Pound and Roman Poetry: A Preliminary Survey.* Rodopi, Amsterdam.

Davie, D. (1986) Virgil's Presence in Ezra Pound and Others. In Cardwell & Hamilton (1986): 135–46.

Davies, A. M. (1998) *Nineteenth-Century Linguistics.* Longman, London.

Davies, N. (1982) *God's Playground: A History of Poland*, 2 vols. Columbia University Press, New York.

Davies, P. (2005) Myth and Maternalism in the Work of Johann Jakob Bachofen. *German Studies Review* 28:3 (October), 501–18.

Davis, G. (1997a) *Aimé Césaire.* Cambridge University Press, Cambridge.

Davis, G. (ed.) (1997b) The Poetics of Derek Walcott: Intertextual Perspectives. *South Atlantic Quarterly* 96:2 (spring), 227–8.

Davis, W. (1994) The Renunciation of Reaction in Girodet's *Sleep of Endymion.* In Bryson, N. et al. (eds.) *Visual Culture: Images and Interpretations.* University Press of New England, Hanover, 168–202.

De Cordoba, F. M. (1964) *Compendio de la fortuna.* BAE, Madrid.

De Rynck, P. & Welkenhuysen, A. (1997) *De Oudheid in het Nederlands. Repertorium en bibliografische gids voor vertalingen van Griekse en Latijnse auteurs en geschriften.* Baarn, Amsterdam.

De Vos, M. & De Vos, A. (1980) *L'egittomania in pitture e mosaici romano-campani della prima età imperiale.* E. J. Brill, Leiden.

Deane, S. (intr. and ed.) (1991–2002) *The Field Day Anthology of Irish Writing.* Field Day Publications, Northern Ireland.

Debru, A. (2005) Christianisme et Galénisme: le mouvement volontaire chez Némésius d'Émèse. In Boudon-Millot, V. & Pouderon, B. (eds.) *Les Pères de l'Église face à la science médicale de leur temps.* Beauchesne, Paris, 89–103.

Deck, A. F. (1976) *Francisco Javier Alegre: A Study in Mexican Literary Criticism.* Sources and Studies for the History of the Americas 13. Jesuit Historical Institute, Rome & Tucson.

Deck, A. F. (1998) *Selections from Peter Martyr: De Orbe Novo.* Brepols, Turnhout.

Deck, A. F. (1999a) Peter Martyr's Account of the First Contacts with Mexico. *Viator* 30, 397–421.

Deck, A. F. (1999b) Fracastoro's Beautiful Idea. In Haskell & Hardie (1999): 105–24.

Decreus, F. (forthcoming) The Same Kind of Smile: About the Use and Abuse of Theory in Defining the Relations between Classics and Post-Colonialism. In Hardwick & Gillespie (forthcoming).

Decreus, F. & Kolk, M. (eds.) (2004) *Rereading Classics in East and West: Post-colonial Perspectives on the Tragic.* Documenta 22.4. University of Ghent, Ghent.

Delaura, D. (1969) *Hebrew and Hellene in Victorian England: Newman, Arnold and Pater.* University of Texas Press, Austin & London.

Delrieu, A. (1999) *Lévi-Strauss lecteur de Freud: le droit, l'incest, le père et l'échange des femmes.* Anthropos, Paris.

Demandt, A. (1979). Alte Geschichte an der Berliner Universität 1810–1960. In Arenhövel, W. (ed.) *Berlin und die Antike.* Wasmuth, Berlin, 2:69–97.

Demerson, G. (1983) *Dorat en son temps: culture classique et présence au monde.* Adosa, Clermont-Ferrand.

Demetriou, K. N. (2002) A "Legend" in Crisis: The Debate over Plato's Politics, 1930–1960. *Polis* 19, 61–92.

Demetrius (1982) *On Style,* trans. W. R. Roberts. In Aristotle, *Poetics,* "Longinus," *On the Sublime,* and Demetreius.... Harvard University Press, Cambridge, Mass. & London, 294–487.

Derolez A. (1995) The Place of the Latin Classics in the Late Medieval Library Catalogues of Germany and the Southern Low Countries. In Leonardi, C. & Munk Olsen, B. (eds.) *The Classical Tradition in the Middle Ages and in the Renaissance.* Centro Italiano di Studi sull'Alto Medioevo, Spoleto, 33–46.

Derolez, A. et al. (1966–2001) *Corpus Catalogorum Belgii. The Medieval Booklists of the Southern Low Countries,* 4 vols. Paleis der Academiën, Brussels.

Deyermond, A. D. (1961) *The Petrarchan Sources of "La Celestina."* Oxford University Press, London.

Deyermond, A. D. (1971) *The Middle Ages.* Benn, London.

Di Camillo, O. (1989) Humanism in Spain. In Rabil, A. Jr. (ed.) *Renaissance Humanism. Foundation, Forms and Legacy.* University of Pennsylvania Press, Philadelphia, 2:55–108.

Dillon, J. & Wilmer, S. (eds.) (2005) *Rebel Women.* Methuen, London.

Diop, C. A. (1955) *Nations nègres et culture.* Présence Africaine, Paris.

Diop, C. A. (1967). *Antériorité des civilizations nègres: mythe ou vérité historique.* Présence Africaine, Paris.

Diop, C. A. (1981). *Civilisation ou barbarie: anthropologie sans complaisance.* Présence Africaine, Paris.

Dixon, L. (1995) *Perilous Chastity: Women and Illness in Pre-enlightenment Art and Medicine.* Cornell University Press, Ithaca & London.

Djisenu, J. (forthcoming) Cross-Cultural Bonds between Ancient Greece and Africa; Implications for Contemporary Staging Practices. In Hardwick & Gillespie (forthcoming).

Dobson, A. (1902) *Collected Poems,* 5th edn. Kegan Paul, London.

Dodds, E. R. (1951) *The Greeks and the Irrational.* University of California Press, Berkeley & London.

Dodds, E. R. (1959) *Plato's Gorgias.* Oxford University Press, Oxford.

Dolbeau, F. (1979) Un nouveau catalogue des manuscrits de Lobbes aux XIe et XIIe siècles. *Recherches augustiniennes* 13, 3–36 and 14, 191–248.

Dominik, W. J. (1999) Afrika. In Landfester et al. (1999–2003): 13:22–6.

Dominik, W. J. (2003) Süd Afrika. In Landfester et al. (1999–2003): 15.3:342–6.

Dominik, W. J. (2006) Writing Power and Politics in Classically Derived Afrikaans Drama. In Hilton, J. L. & Gosling, M. A. (eds.) *Alma Parens Originalis? The Reception of Classical Ideas in Africa, Europe, Cuba and the United States.* Peter Lang, Frankfurt, 93–113.

Donaldson, I. (1982) *The Rapes of Lucretia: A Myth and Its Transformations.* Clarendon Press, Oxford.

Doumas, C. (1991) The Discovery of Early Cycladic Civilization. In Renfrew, C. (ed.) *The Cycladic Spirit*. Harry N. Abrams, New York, 25–30.

Dowling, L. (1994) *Hellenism and Homosexuality in Victorian Oxford*. Cornell University Press, Ithaca & London.

Downing, C. (1975) Sigmund Freud and the Greek Mythological Tradition. *Journal of the American Academy of Religion* 43, 9–68.

Draak, M. (1957) Construe Marks in Hiberno-Latin Manuscripts. *Mededelingen der Koninklijke Nederlandse Akademie van Wetenschappen*, Afd. Letterkunde, n.s. 20 (no. 10), 261–82.

Dronke, P. (1974) *Fabula: Explorations into the Uses of Myth in Medieval Platonism*. Mittellateinische Studien und Texte 9. E. J. Brill, Leiden.

Dryden, J. (1956–2000) *Works*, ed. H. T. Swedenberg et al., 20 vols. University of California Press, Berkeley.

Dryden, J. (1962a) *Of Dramatic Poesy and Other Critical Essays*, ed. G. Watson, 2 vols. Dent, London.

Dryden, J. (1962b) *Poems and Fables of John Dryden*, ed. James Kinsley. Oxford University Press, London.

Du Bellay, J. (1904) *La Deffence et illustration de la langue francoyse*, ed. H. Chamard. Albert Fontemoing, Paris.

Dunn, P. N. (1975) *Fernando de Rojas* [*La Celestina*]. Twayne, New York.

Dutton, K. R. (1995) *The Perfectible Body: The Western Ideal of Physical Development*. Cassell, London.

Dyer, R. (1997) *White*. Routledge, London & New York.

Dzielska, M. (1995) *Hypatia of Alexandria*, trans. F. Lyra. Harvard University Press, Cambridge, Mass.

Easterling, P. (ed.) (1997) *The Cambridge Companion to Greek Tragedy*. Cambridge University Press, Cambridge.

Eaton, C. (1964a) *The Freedom of Thought Struggle in the Old South*. Harper and Row, New York.

Eaton, C. (1964b) *The Mind of the Old South*. Louisiana State University Press, Baton Rouge.

Eaton, C. & O'Brien, M. (2004) *Conjectures of Order: Intellectual Life in the American South 1810–1860*. University of North Carolina Press, Chapel Hill.

Eatough, G. (1984) *Fracastoro's Syphilis: Introduction, Text, Translations, and Notes*. Francis Cairns, Liverpool.

Eatough, G. (1998) *Selections from Peter Martyr: De Orbe Novo*. Brepols, Turnhout.

Eatough, G. (1999a) Peter Martyr's Account of the First Contacts with Mexico. *Viator* 30, 397–421.

Eatough, G. (1999b) Fracastoro's Beautiful Idea. In Haskell & Hardie (1999): 105–24.

Eccles, J. C. & Popper, K. R. (1977) *The Self and Its Brain*. Springer, Berlin, Heidelberg, London, & New York.

Eco, U. (1993) *La ricerca della lingua perfetta nella cultura europea*. Laterza, Bari & Rome. English version issued contemporaneously by Blackwell, Oxford.

Edmunds, L. (2001) *Intertextuality and the Reading of Roman Poetry*. Johns Hopkins University Press, Baltimore & London.

Edwards, C. (ed.) (1999) *Roman Presences: Receptions of Rome in European Culture, 1789–1945*. Cambridge University Press, Cambridge.

Ehrenberg, V. (1946) *Aspects of the Ancient World: Essays and Reviews*. Oxford University Press, Oxford.

Eichmann Oehrli, A. (2003) El latín en Charcas–Bolivia (1580–1825). In Grammatico Amari, Arbea Gavilán & Edwards (2003): 1:179–217.

Eis, A. (1993) *Ancient Finds*. Eleusinian Publications, Royal Oak.

Eisenstein, E. L. (1979) *The Printing Press as an Agent of Change: Communications and Cultural Transformations in Early-Modern Europe*, 2 vols. Cambridge University Press, Cambridge.

Ekrem, I. (1995) Norway. In Jensen (1995): 66–95.

Eliot, T. S. (1920) *The Sacred Wood: Essays on Poetry and Criticism*. Methuen, London.

Eliot, T. S. (1975) *Selected Prose*, ed. F. Kermode. Harcourt, Brace, Jovanovich, New York.

Elliott, D. (1988) *Musa Americana: The Classics in the New World*. Catalogue of an exhibition at the John Carter Brown Library. John Carter Brown Library, Providence.

Elsner, J. (1995) *Art and the Roman Viewer*. Cambridge University Press, New York.

Emerson, R. W. (1888) Historic Notes of Life and Letters in New England. In *Emerson's Complete Works*. Houghton, Mifflin, Boston, 10:312–16.

Englert, L. (1942) Die Gymnastik und Agonistik der Griechen als politische Leibeserziehung. In Berve (1942): 218–36.

Erskine-Hill, H. (1983) *The Augustan Idea in English Literature*. Edward Arnold, London.

Esquirol, J. E. D. (1965) *Mental Maladies*. Hafner, New York.

Essed, P. et al. (2004) *A Companion to Gender Studies*. Blackwell, Oxford.

Estienne, H. (1565) *Traicté de la conformité du langage François auec le Grec*. H. Estienne, Geneva.

Etienne, R. & Etienne, F. (1992) *The Search for Ancient Greece*. Harry N. Abrams, New York.

Ettinghausen, H. (1972) *Francisco de Quevedo and the Neostoic Movement*. Oxford University Press, Oxford.

Everson, S. (ed.) (1991) *Psychology*. Cambridge University Press, Cambridge.

Faber, R. & Kytzler, B. (eds.) (1992) *Antike heute*. Königshausen & Neumann, Würzburg.

Fagiolo dell'Arco, M. (1982) De Chirico in Paris, 1911–1915. In *De Chirico*. Museum of Modern Art, New York.

Fagunwa, D. O. (1938) *Ogboju Ode Ninu Igbo Irunmale*. Nelson, Apapa.

Fagunwa, D. O. (1949) *Ireke-onibudo: Pelu Opolopo Alayeo*. Nelson, Apapa.

Faisant, C. (1998) *Mort et résurrection de la Pléiade*, ed. J. Rieu et al. Champion, Paris.

Falasca-Zamponi, S. (1997) *Fascist Spectacle: The Aesthetics of Power in Mussolini's Italy*. University of California Press, Berkeley.

Farrell, A. P. (1938) *The Jesuit Code of Liberal Education: Development and Scope of the Ratio Studiorum*. Bruce, Milwaukee.

Faulhaber, C. (1973) Retóricas clásicas y medievales en bibliotecas castellanas. Artes Gráficas Soler, Valencia.

Fazza, M. (1978) Nazionalsocialismo e storia antica. *Studi romani* 26, 145–60.

Feder, L. (1971) *Ancient Myth in Modern Poetry*. Princeton University Press, Princeton.

Feder, L. (1985) Pound and Ovid. In Bornstein, G. (ed.) *Ezra Pound among the Poets*. University of Chicago Press, Chicago, 13–34.

Ferrero, G. (1914) *Ancient Rome and Modern America: A Comparative Study of Morals and Manners*. Putnam's, New York.

Ferruolo, S. C. (1985) *The Schools of Paris and Their Critics, 1100–1215*. Stanford University Press, Stanford.

Ficino, M. (2001–6) *Platonic Theology*, ed. J. Hankins, trans. M. J. B. Allen, 6 vols. Harvard University Press, Cambridge, Mass. & London.

Fiesoli, G. (2004) Percorsi di classici nel medioevo: il Lucrezio Bobiense. Raterio lettore di Plauto e Catullo. *Medioevo e Rinascimento* 18 n.s. 15, 1–37.

Filipczak, Z. K. (1997) *Hot Dry Men, Cold Wet Women: The Theory of the Humours in Western Art 1575–1700*. American Federation of Arts, New York.

Findlen, P. (1999) Academies. In Grendler, P. (ed.) *Encyclopedia of the Renaissance*, 6 vols. Charles Scribner's Sons, New York, 1:4–6.

Findlen, P. (ed.) (2004) *Athanasius Kircher: The Last Man Who Knew Everything*. Routledge, New York & London.

Finley, M. I. (1981) *The Legacy of Greece: A New Appraisal*. Clarendon Press, Oxford.

Fischer, S. R. (2003) *A History of Reading*. Reaktion Books, London.

Fiszman, S. (ed.) (1988) *The Polish Renaissance in Its European Context*. Indiana University Press, Bloomington & Indianapolis.

Flaig, E. (2003) Towards *"Rassenhygiene"*: Wilamowitz and the German New Right. In Gildenhard & Ruehl (2003): 105–28.

Flam, J. (ed.) (2003) *Primitivism and Twentieth-Century Art: A Documentary History*. University of California Press, Berkeley.

Flashar, H. (1991) *Inszenierung der Antike. Das griechische Drama auf der Bühne der Neuzeit 1585–1990*. Beck, Munich.

Flashar, H. (ed.) (1995) *Altertumswissenschaft in den 20er Jahren: Neue Fragen und Impulse*. F. Steiner, Stuttgart.

Fleishman, M. (1990) Workshop Theatre as Oppositional Form. *South African Theatre Journal* 4:1, 88–118.

Fleishman, M. & Reznek, J. (dir.) (1994a) *Medea*. Unpublished text.

Fleishman, M. & Reznek, J. (dir.) (1994b). *Medea*. Video.

Fleishman, M. & Reznek, J. (dir.) (1998a). *In the City of Paradise*. Unpublished text.

Fleishman, M. & Reznek, J. (dir.) (1998b. *In the City of Paradise*. Video.

Florman, L. (2000) *Myth and Metamorphosis: Picasso's Classical Prints of the 1930s*. Massachusetts Institute of Technology Press, Cambridge, Mass.

Foerster, D. (1947) *Homer in English Criticism: The Historical Approach in the Eighteenth Century*. Yale University Press, New Haven.

Forcione, A. K. (1970) *Cervantes, Aristotle, and the "Persiles."* Princeton University Press, Princeton.

Ford, P. (2001) George Buchanan et Montaigne. *Montaigne Studies* 13, 45–63.

Forrest, M. St. J. (1996) *Modernising the Classics: A Study in Curriculum Development*. Exeter University Press, Exeter.

Foster, R. F. (2003) *W. B. Yeats: A Life*. Oxford University Press, Oxford.

Fothergill-Payne, L. (1988) *Seneca and "Celestina"*. Cambridge University Press, Cambridge.

Foucault, M. (1994) *Dit et écrits*, ed. D. Defert & F. Ewalt. Gallimard, Paris.

Fowler, D. (2000) *Roman Constructions*. Oxford University Press, Oxford.

Fowler, R. (1983) "On Not Knowing Greek": The Classics and the Woman of Letters. *Classical Journal* 78, 337–49.

Fowler, R. L. (ed.) (2004) *The Cambridge Companion to Homer*. Cambridge University Press, Cambridge.

Fox, R. L. (2004) *The Making of* Alexander. R. & L., Oxford.

Fraker, C. F. (1996) *The Scope of History: Studies in the Historiography of Alfonso el Sabio*. University of Michigan Press, Ann Arbor.

France, P. (ed.) (1995) *The New Oxford Companion to Literature in French*. Clarendon Press, Oxford.

France, P. (ed.) (2000) *The Oxford Guide to Literature in English Translation*. Oxford University Press, Oxford.

Franklin, B. (1905–7) Observations Relative to the Intentions of the Original Founders of the Academy in Philadelphia, June 1789. In Smyth, A. H. (ed.) *The Writings of Benjamin Franklin*. Macmillan, New York, 10:9–31.

Fransen, H. (1987) Classicism, Baroque, Rococo and Neoclassicism at the Cape. An Investigation into Stylistic Modes in the Architecture and Applied Arts at the Cape of Good Hope: 1652–1820. Dissertation, University of Natal.

Frappier, J. (1982) *Chrétien de Troyes: The Man and His Work*, trans. R. Cormier. Ohio University Press, Ohio & Athens.

Fraunce, A. (1588) *The Arcadian Rhetoric*. Scolar Press, London.

Frazer, J. G. (1922) *The Golden Bough: A Study in Magic and Religion*. Macmillan, London.

Freedberg, D. (2003) *The Eye of the Lynx: Galileo, His Friends, and the Origins of Modern Natural History*. University of Chicago Press, Chicago.

Freeman, E. A. (1872) *The Unity of History*. Rede Lecture. Macmillan, London.

Freeman, M. A. (1979) *The Poetics of Translatio studii and Conjointure: Chrétien de Troyes's Cligès*. French Forum, Lexington.

Frégault, G. & Hamel, R. (1996) *Histoire de la littérature française du XVIIe siècle*, 3 vols. A. Michel, Paris.

Freiert, W. K. (1990) Martha Graham's "Clytemnestra." In MacEwen, S. (ed.) *Views of Clytemnestra, Ancient and Modern*. Edwin Mellen Press, Lewiston, Queenstown & Lampeter, 84–90.

Frenzel, E. (1992) *Stoffe der Weltliteratur. Ein Lexikon dichtungsgeschichtlicher Längsschnitte*. Stuttgart, Kröner.

Fresco, M. F. (1978) *Klassieke motieven in de moderne Nederlandse letterkunde*. Nederlands Klassiek Verbond, Amersfoort.

Freud, S. (1953–74) *The Standard Edition of the Complete Psychological Works*, ed. J. Strachey et al. The Hogarth Press, London.

Freud, S. (1985) *The Complete Letters of Sigmund Freud to Wilhelm Fliess, 1887–1904*, ed. J. M. Masson. Belknap Press of Harvard University Press, Cambridge, Mass.

Friedländer, P. (1928) *Platon. Eidos. Paideia. dialogos*. W. de Gruyter, Berlin & Leipzig.

Friedländer, P. (1958) *Plato*, trans. H. Meyerhoff. Pantheon Books, New York.

Friel, B. (1981) *Translation*. In *Selected Plays*. Faber, London.

Friese, W. (1989) *"... Am Ende der Welt". Zur skandinavischen Literatur der frühen Neuzeit*. Literaturverlag Norden Mark Reinhardt, Leverkusen.

Friis-Jensen, K. (1987) *Saxo Grammaticus as Latin Poet: Studies in the Verse Passages of the Gesta Danorum*. L'Erma di Bretschneider, Rome.

Fugard, A. (1977) *Dimetos*. In *Dimetos and Two Early Plays*. Oxford University Press, Oxford, 1–53.

Fugard, A. (1978) *Orestes*. In Gray (1978): 81–93.

Fugard, A. (1993) The Island. In *Township Plays*. Oxford University Press, Oxford, 194–227.

Fugard, A., Kani, J., & Ntshona, W. (1973) *The Island*. In Fugard, A. (1973) *Statements: Three Plays*. Oxford University Press, Oxford, 45–77.

Fuhrmann, M. (1984) Die humanistische Bildungstradition im Dritten Reich. *Humanistische Bildung* 8, 139–61.

Fumaroli, M. (2002) *L'Âge de l'éloquence: rhétorique et "res literaria" de la Renaissance au seuil de l'époque moderne.* Droz, Geneva.

Fumaroli, M. (ed.) (1998) *Les Origines du Collège de France (1510–1560): actes du colloque international* (Paris, décembre 1995). Collège de France, Paris.

Gadamer, H.-G. (1942) Platos Staat der Erziehung. In Berve (1942): 317–33.

Gadamer, H.-G. (1943) Review of Grassi, E. (ed.) *Geistige Überlieferung. Gnomon* 19, 1–8.

Gadamer, H.-G. (1989) *Truth and Method*, trans. J. Weinsheimer & D. G. Marshall, 2nd edn. Sheed and Ward, London.

Gaisser, J. (1993) *Catullus and His Renaissance Readers.* Clarendon Press, Oxford.

Gaisser, J. (1994) The Roman Odes at School: The Rise of the Imperial Horace. *Classical World* 87, 443–56.

Galenus (1821–33) *Claudius Opera Omnia*, ed. C. G. Kühn, Leipzig. Rpt. Olms, Hildesheim, 1964–5.

Galinsky, K. (1969) *Aeneas, Sicily, and Rome.* Princeton University Press, Princeton.

Galinsky, K. (1972) *The Herakles Theme: The Adaptations of the Hero in Literature from Homer to the Twentieth Century.* Blackwell, Oxford.

Galinsky, K. (1992). *Classical and Modern Interactions.* University of Texas Press, Austin.

Galinsky, K. (forthcoming) Hercules. In Grafton, A., Most, G., & Settis, S. (eds.) *The Classical Tradition.* Harvard University Press, Cambridge, Mass.

Gallagher, L. (1991) *Medusa's Gaze: Casuistry and Conscience in the Renaissance.* Stanford University Press, Stanford.

Gallego Morell, A. (1972) *Garcilaso de la Vega y sus comentaristas. Obras completas del poeta. Acompañadas de los textos íntegros de los comentarios de el Brocense, Fernando de Herrera, Tamayo de Vargas y Azara.* Gredos, Madrid.

Gamwell, L. & Wells, R. (eds.) (1989) *Sigmund Freud and Art: His Personal Collection of Antiquities.* State University of New York Press, Binghamton.

García, G. (1980) *Origen de los indios de el nuevo mundo e indios occidentales.* Fondo de Cultura Económica, Mexico City. Facsimile of 1729 Madrid edn.

García Berrio, A. (1977–80) *Formación de la teoría literaria moderna.* Vol. 1, Planeta, Madrid, 1977; vol. 2, Universidad de Murcia, Murcia, 1980.

Garcilaso de la Vega, El Inca (1966) *Royal Commentaries of the Incas and General History of Perú*, trans. with intro. H. V. Livermore, 2 vols. University of Texas Press, Austin & London.

Garin, E. (1965) *Italian Humanism: Philosophy and Civic Life in the Renaissance*, trans. P. Munz. Harper & Row, New York.

Garrido Camacho, P. (1999) *El tema del reconocimiento en el teatro español del siglo XVI. La teoría de la anagnórisis.* Tamesis, London.

Gay, P. (1966–9) *The Enlightenment: An Interpretation*, 2 vols. Alfred A. Knopf, New York.

Gay, P. (1988) *Freud: A Life for Our Time.* Naton, New York & London.

Géfin, L. K. (1999) The Virgilian Intertext in Miklós Radnóti's Eclogues. In Gömöri, G. & Wilmer, C. (eds.) *The Life and Letters of Miklós Radnóti: Essays.* East European Monographs, Boulder, 91–106.

Gellner, E. (1983) *Nations and Nationalism.* Blackwell, Oxford.

Gentilcore, R. M. (1995) Ann Eliza Bleecker's Wilderness Pastoral: Reading Vergil in Colonial America. *International Journal of the Classical Tradition* 1:4, 86–98.

Gentile, E. (1990) Fascism as a Political Religion. *Journal of Contemporary History* 25, 229–51.

Gentile, E. (1993) *Il culto del littorio. La sacralizzazione della politica nell'Italia fascista.* Laterza, Rome & Bari.

Gentile, E. (1997) The Myth of National Regeneration in Italy: From Modernist Avant-Garde to Fascism. In Affron & Antliff (1997): 25–45.

Gentile, G. (ed.) (1932) *Enciclopedia italiana di scienze, lettere ed arti*, vol. 14. Istituto Giovanni Treccani, Rome.

George, E. (1986) *The Poetry of Miklós Radnóti: A Comparative Study.* Karz-Cohl Publishing, New York.

George, E. (1998) Latin and Spanish: Roman Culture and Hispanic America. In LaFleur, R. A. (ed.) *Latin for the 21st Century: From Concept to Classroom.* Scott Foresman–Addison Wesley, Reading, 227–36.

Gerritsen, W. P. & van Melle, A. G. (eds.) (1998) *A Dictionary of Medieval Heroes: Characters in Medieval Narrative Traditions and Their Afterlife in Literature, Theatre and the Visual Arts*, trans. T. Guest. Boydell and Brewer, New York.

Giardina, A. & Vauchez, A. (2000) *Il mito di Roma. Da Carlo Magno a Mussolini.* Laterza, Rome & Bari.

Gibbs, J. (forthcoming) Antigone and Her African Sisters: West African Versions of a Greek Original. In Hardwick & Gillespie (forthcoming).

Gieselbusch, H. et al. (1933) *Humanistische Bildung im Nationalsozialistischen Staate. Neue Wege zur Antike.* B. G. Teubner, Leipzig & Berlin.

Gil, J. (1988) Virgilio en Spagna. Studi filologici ed edizioni. In Della Corte (1988): 4:953b–956a.

Gil, J. (2004) Marcial en España. *Humanitas* 56, 225–326.

Gil, L. (1981) *Panorama social del humanismo español (1500–1800).* Alhambra, Madrid.

Gil, L. (1984) Terencio en España: del Medievo a la Ilustración. In *Estudios de humanismo y tradición clásica.* Editorial de la Universidad Complutense, Madrid.

Gilbert, H. & Tompkins, J. (1996) *Post-colonial Drama: Theory, Practice, Politics.* Routledge, London & New York.

Gildenhard, I. & Ruehl, M. (eds.) (2003) *Out of Arcadia: Classics and Politics in Germany in the Age of Burckhardt, Nietzsche, and Wilamowitz.* Institute of Classical Studies, University of London, London.

Gilliam, B. (1991) *Richard Strauss's Elektra.* Clarendon Press, Oxford.

Gilman, S. et al. (eds.) (1993) *Hysteria beyond Freud.* University of California Press, Berkeley & Los Angeles.

Gilroy, P. (1993) *The Black Atlantic.* Verso, London & New York.

Ginsberg, W. (1983) *The Cast of Character. The Representation of Personality in Ancient and Medieval Literature.* University of Toronto Press, Toronto.

Girot, J. (2002) *Pindare avant Ronsard: de l'émergence du grec … la publication des "Quatre Premiers Livres des Odes" de Ronsard.* Droz, Geneva.

Glaser, H. (1978), *The Cultural Roots of National Socialism*, trans. E. A. Menze. Croom Helm, London.

Glauche, G. (1970) *Schullektüre im Mittelalter.* Arbeo-Gesellschaft, Munich.

Glauser, J. & Sabel, B. (eds.) *Skandinavische Literaturen der frühen Neuzeit.* A. Francke Verlag, Tübingen & Basel.

Glenn, J. (1972) Psychoanalytical Writings on Greek and Latin Authors 1911–1960. *Classical World* 66, 129–45.

Glenn, J. (1976) Psychoanalytical Writings on Classical Mythology and Religion 1909–1960. *Classical World* 70, 225–47.

Glucksmann, A. (1980) *The Master Thinkers*, trans. B. Pearce. Harvester Press, Brighton, Sussex.

Goff, B. (ed.) (2005) *Classics and Colonialism*. Duckworth, London.

Goff, B. (forthcoming) Antigone's Boat: The Colonial and the Postcolonial in *Tegonni: An African Antigone* by Femi Òsòfisan. In Hardwick & Gillespie (forthcoming).

Goffen, R. (1997) *Titian's Women*. Yale University Press, New Haven & London.

Gold, B. et al. (eds.) (1997) *Sex and Gender in Medieval and Renaissance Texts: The Latin Tradition*. State University of New York Press, Albany.

Goldhill, S. (2002) *Who Needs Greek? Contests in the Cultural History of Hellenism*. Cambridge University Press, Cambridge.

Goldhill, S. (2004) *Love, Sex, and Tragedy: How the Ancient World Shapes our Lives.* John Murray, London.

Goleniščev-Kutuzov, I. N. (1989) *Il Rinascimento italiano e le letterature slave dei secoli XV et XVI*, ed. S. Graciotti & J. Kresalkova. Vita e Pensiero, Milan.

Golsan, R. J. (1992) *Fascism, Aesthetics, Culture*. University Press of New England, Hanover.

Gomperz, H. (1924) Psychologische Beobachtungen an griechischen Philosophen. *Imago* 10, 1–92.

Gordon, D. J. (1962) *W. B. Yeats: Images of a Poet*. Manchester University Press, Manchester.

Gossman, L. (2000) *Basel in the Age of Burckhardt*. University of Chicago Press, Chicago.

Gössmann, E. (1974) *Antiqui und Moderni im Mittelalter: Eine geschichtliche Standort-bestimmung*. F. Schöningh, Munich.

Graciotti, S. (1998–9) Le due Slavie: problemi di terminologia e problemi di idee. *Ricerche slavistiche* 45–6, 5–83.

Grafton, A. (1983) Polyhistor into *Philolog*: Notes on the Transformation of German Classical Scholarship, 1780–1850. *History of Universities* 3, 153–92.

Grafton, A. (1988) The Availability of Ancient Works. In Schmitt (1983): 767–91.

Grafton, A. (1990) *Forgers and Critics: Creativity and Duplicity in Western Scholarship*. Princeton University Press, Princeton.

Grafton, A. (1991) *Defenders of the Text: The Traditions of Scholarship in an Age of Science, 1450–1800*. Harvard University Press, Cambridge, Mass. & London.

Grafton, A. (1992) The Renaissance. In Jenkyns, R. (ed.) *The Legacy of Rome: A New Appraisal*. Oxford University Press, Oxford, 97–123.

Grafton, A. (1993). *Rome Reborn: The Vatican Library and Renaissance Culture*. Library of Congress, Washington.

Grafton, A. (1997) *Commerce with the Classics: Ancient Books and Renaissance Readers*. University of Michigan Press, Ann Arbor.

Grafton, A. (2000) *Leon Battista Alberti: Master Builder of the Italian Renaissance*. Hill and Wang, New York.

Grafton, A. & Jardine, L. (1986) *From Humanism to the Humanities: Education and the Liberal Arts in Fifteenth- and Sixteenth-Century Europe*. Harvard University Press, Cambridge, Mass.

Grafton, A. with Shelford, A. & Siraisi, N. (1992) *New Worlds, Ancient Texts: The Power of Tradition and the Shock of Discovery.* Harvard University Press, Cambridge, Mass. & London.

Grammatico Amari, G., Arbea Gavilán, A., & Edwards, L. M. (eds.) (2003) *América Latina y lo clásico*, 2 vols. Sociedad Chilena de Estudios Clásicos, Santiago de Chile.

Graver, B. (2005) classical Inheritances. In N. Roe (ed.) *Romanticism: An Oxford Guide.* Oxford University Press, Oxford & New York, 38–48.

Graver, M. (forthcoming) *Stoicism and Emotion.* University of Chicago Press, Chicago.

Gray, S. (ed.) (1978) *Theatre One: New South African Drama.* Ad. Donker, Johannesburg.

Green, O. H. (1963) *Spain and the Western Tradition*, 4 vols. University of Wisconsin Press, Madison.

Green, R. (1995) Proba's Cento: Its Date, Purpose and Reception. *Classical Quarterly* 45, 551–63.

Greenblatt, S. (1980) *Renaissance Self-Fashioning, From More to Shakespeare.* University of Chicago Press, Chicago.

Greenblatt, S. (1991) *Marvelous Possessions: The Wonder of the New World.* University of Chicago Press, Chicago.

Greene, T. M. (1982) *The Light in Troy: Imitation and Discovery in Renaissance Poetry.* Yale University Press, New Haven & London.

Greenwood, E. (2004) Classics and the Atlantic Triangle: Caribbean Readings of Greece and Rome via Africa. *Forum of Modern Language Studies* 11:4, 365–76.

Greenwood, E. (2005) We Speak Latin in Trinidad: Uses of the Classics in Caribbean Literature. In Goff (2005): 65–91.

Greer, G. (2003) *The Boy.* Thames and Hudson, London.

Gregorius, Master (1987) *The Marvels of Rome,* trans. J. Osborne. Mediaeval Sources in Translation 31. Pontifical Institute of Mediaeval Studies, Toronto.

Gregory, E. (1997) *H. D. and Hellenism: Classic Lines.* Cambridge University Press, Cambridge.

Greig, D. (1971) *A Guide to Architecture in South Africa.* Howard Timmins, Cape Town.

Grendler, P. (1989) *Schooling in Renaissance Italy: Literacy and Learning, 1300–1600.* Johns Hopkins University Press, Baltimore & London.

Grendler, P. (ed.) (1999) *Encyclopedia of the Renaissance*, 6 vols. Charles Scribner's Sons, New York.

Griffin, R. (1991) *The Nature of Fascism.* Pinter, London.

Griffin, R. (ed.) (1995) *Fascism.* Oxford University Press, Oxford.

Griffin, R. (1996). Staging the Nation's Rebirth: The Politics and Aesthetics of Performance in the Context of Fascist Studies. In Berghaus, G. (ed.) *Fascism and Theatre: Comparative Studies on the Aesthetics and Politics of Performance in Europe, 1925–1945.* Oxford University Press, Oxford, 11–29.

Griffin, R. (2001) Notes towards the Definition of Fascist Culture: The Prospects for Synergy between Marxist and Liberal Heuristic. *Renaissance and Modern Studies* 42, 95–115.

Griffin, R. (2003) The Palingenetic Core of Generic Fascist Ideology. In Campi, A. (ed.) *Che cos'è il fascismo? Interpretazioni e prospettive di ricerche.* Ideazione, Rome, 97–122.

Groom, Nick. (1999) *The Making of Percy's Reliques.* Oxford University Press, Oxford & New York.

Grund, G. (ed. and trans.) (2005) *Humanist Comedies*. Harvard University Press, Cambridge, Mass. & London.

Gruzinski, S. (2002) *The Meztizo Mind: The Intellectual Dynamics of Colonization and Globalization*. Routledge, London.

Gugelberger, G. M. (1991) Decolonizing the Canon: Considerations of Third World Literature. *New Literary History* 22, 505–24.

Günther, H. F. K. (1922) *Rassenkunde des deutschen Volkes*. J. H. Lehmann, Munich.

Günther, H. F. K. (1925) *Kleine Rassenkunde Europas*. J. H. Lehmann, Munich.

Günther, H. F. K. (1928) *Platon als Hüter des Lebens*. J. H. Lehmann, Munich.

Günther, H. F. K. (1929) *Rassenkunde Europas. Mit besonderer Berücksichtigung der Rassengeschichte der Hauptvölker indogermanischer Sprache*. J. H. Lehmann, Munich.

Haase, W. and Reinhold, M. (eds.) (1993) *The Classical Tradition and the Americas*, vol. 1, part 1 (no more published). W. de Gruyter, Berlin & New York.

Habermehl, P. & Seidensticker, B. (1999) Deutschland V. 20. Jahrhundert (ab 1918). In Landfester (1999): vol. 13, cols. 817–28.

Hagen, B. von (1933) Wege zu einem Humanismus im Dritten Reich. In Gieselbusch et al. (1933): 17–22.

Hagendahl, H. (1958) *Latin Fathers and the Classics: A Study on the Apologists, Jerome and Other Christian Writers*. Almqvist and Wiksell, Stockholm.

Hagendahl, H. (1967) *Augustine and the Latin Classics*, 2 vols. Almqvist and Wiksell, Stockholm.

Halecki, O. (1950) *The Limits and Divisions of European History*. Sheed and Ward, London & New York.

Hall, E. (1999) Medea and British Legislation before the First World War. *Greece and Rome* 46:1, 42–77.

Hall, E. (2004) Towards a Theory of Performance Reception. *Arion* 12:1 (spring/summer), 51–89.

Hall, E. & Macintosh, F. (2005) *Greek Tragedy and the British Theatre 1660–1914*. Oxford University Press, Oxford.

Hall, E., Macintosh, F., & Taplin, O. (eds.) (2000) *Medea in Performance 1500–2000*. Oxford University Press, Oxford.

Hall, E., Macintosh, M., & Wrigley, A. (eds.) (2004) *Dionysus since 69*. Oxford University Press, Oxford.

Hall, J. M. (1997) *Ethnic Identity in Greek Antiquity*. Cambridge University Press, Cambridge.

Hall, M. B. (ed.) (2005) *Rome*. Cambridge University Press, Cambridge.

Hall, S. (1990) Cultural Identity and Diaspora. In Rutherford, J. (ed.) *Identity, Community, Culture, Difference*. Lawrence and Wishart, London, 222–37.

Halliwell, S. (1998) *Aristotle's Poetics*, 2nd edn. Duckworth, London.

Halperin, D. M. (2002) *How to Do the History of Homosexuality*. University of Chicago Press, Chicago.

Hamburger, K. (1962) *Von Sophokles zu Sartre. Griechische Dramenfiguren antik und modern*. Kohlhammer, Stuttgart.

Hamer, M. (1993) *Signs of Cleopatra: History, Politics, Representation*. Routledge, London.

Hamilton, D. (1989) *Towards a Theory of Schooling*. Falmer Press, London.

Hammond F. (1994) *Music and Spectacle in Baroque Rome: Barberini Patronage under Urban VIII*. Yale University Press, New Haven & London.

Hankins, J. (1990) *Plato in the Italian Renaissance*, 2 vols. Columbia Studies in the Classical Tradition 17. E. J. Brill, Leiden.

Hardwick, L. (1992) Convergence and Divergence in Reading Homer. In Emlyn-Jones, C., Hardwick, L., & Purkis, J. (eds.) *Homer: Readings and Images*. Duckworth in association with the Open University, London, 227–48.

Hardwick, L. (1995) Classical Distances. In *One World Many Voices*. International Council for Distance Education, Norway, 1:283–6.

Hardwick, L. (1997a) Reception as Simile: The Poetics of Reversal in Homer and Derek Walcott. *International Journal of the Classical Tradition* 3:3, 326–38.

Hardwick, L. (1997b) Women and Classical Scholarship in the 19th Century. *CA News* 17, 2–4.

Hardwick, L. (2000a) *Translating Words, Translating Cultures*. Duckworth, London.

Hardwick, L. (2000b) Theatres of the Mind: Greek Tragedy in Women's Writings in English in the Nineteenth Century. In Easterling, P., Ireland, S., Lowe, N., & Macintosh, F. (eds.) *Theatre Ancient and Modern*. Open University, Milton Keynes, 68–81.

Hardwick, L. (2001) Who Owns the Plays? Issues in the Translation and Performance of Greek Drama on the Modern Stage. *Eirene* 37 (Theatralia special edition), 23–39.

Hardwick, L. (2002) Classical Texts in Post-Colonial Literatures: Consolation, Redress and New Beginnings in the Work of Derek Walcott and Seamus Heaney. *International Journal of the Classical Tradition* 9:2, 236–56.

Hardwick, L. (2003a) *Reception Studies*. Classical Association New Surveys in the Classics 33. Oxford University Press, Oxford.

Hardwick, L. (2003b) Classical Drama in Modern Scotland: The Democratic Stage. In Hardwick & Gillespie (2003): 1–13.

Hardwick, L. (2004a) Greek Drama and Anti-Colonialism: Decolonising Classics. In Hall, Macintosh, & Wrigley (2004): 219–42.

Hardwick, L. (2004b) Shards and Suckers: Contemporary Receptions of Homer. In Fowler (2004): 344–62.

Hardwick, L. (2004c) Sophocles' *Oedipus* and Conflicts of Identity: Post-colonial Contexts. In Decreus & Kolk (2004): 376–86.

Hardwick, L. (2005a) Refiguring Classical Texts: Aspects of the Post-colonial Condition. In Goff (2005): 107–17.

Hardwick, L. (2005b) Staging *Agamemnon*: The Languages of Translation. In Macintosh et al. (2005): 207–21.

Hardwick, L. (2005c) The Praxis of What Is "European" in Modern Performances of Greek Drama: The Multi-lingual Turn. *Parodos* 6, 6–8.

Hardwick, L. (2006a) Remodelling Reception: Greek Drama as Diasporic Performance. In Martindale, C. & Thomas, R. (eds.) *Classics and the Uses of Reception*. Blackwell, Oxford.

Hardwick, L. (2006b) Murmurs in the Cathedral: The Impact of Translations from Greek Poetry and Drama on Modern Work in English by Michael Longley and Seamus Heaney. *Yearbook of English Studies* 36:1, 204–15.

Hardwick, L. (2006c) Contests and Continuities in Classical Traditions: African Migrations in Greek Drama. In Hilton, J. L. & Gosling, A. (eds.) *Alma Parens Originalis? The Receptions of Classical Literature and Thought in South Africa, Cuba and Europe*. Peter Lang, Bern.

Hardwick, L., Easterling, P. E., Ireland, S., Macintosh, F., & Lowe, N. (eds.) (2000) *Theatre: Ancient and Modern. Selected Proceedings of a Two-day International Conference Hosted by the Department of Classical Studies, Faculty of Arts, The Open University, Milton Keynes, 5th and 6th January 1999*. Open University, Milton Keynes.

Hardwick, L. & Gillespie, C. (eds.) (2003) *The Role of Greek Drama and Poetry in Crossing and Redefining Cultural Boundaries.* Open University, Milton Keynes.

Hardwick, L. & Gillespie, C. (eds.) (forthcoming) *Classics in Post-Colonial Worlds.* Oxford University Press, Oxford.

Harris, E. (1982) *Velazquez.* Phaidon, Oxford.

Harris, W. (2003) *The Mask of the Beggar.* Faber and Faber, London.

Harrison, N. (2003) *Postcolonial Criticism: History, Theory and the Work of Fiction.* Cambridge University Press, Cambridge.

Harrison, S. (forthcoming) Virgilian Contexts. In Hardwick, L. & Stray, C. A. (eds.) *A Companion to Classical Receptions.* Blackwell, Oxford.

Harrison, S. J. (ed.) (2001) *Texts, Ideas, and the Classics: Scholarship, Theory, and Classical Literature.* Oxford University Press, Oxford.

Harrison, T. (1998) *Prometheus.* Faber and Faber, London.

Harrison, V. E. F. (1995) The Allegorization of Gender: Plato and Philo on Spiritual Childbearing. In Wimbush, V. L. & Valantasis, R. (eds.) *Asceticism.* Oxford University Press, New York & Oxford, 520–34.

Haskell, F. (1980) *Patrons and Painters: A Study in the Relations between Italian Art and Society in the Age of the Baroque*, revised and enlarged edn. Yale University Press, New Haven & London.

Haskell, F. & Penny, N. (1981) *Taste and the Antique: The Lure of Classical Sculpture, 1500–1900.* Yale University Press, New Haven.

Haskell, Y. A. (2003) *Loyola's Bees: Ideology and Industry in Jesuit Latin Didactic Poetry.* Oxford University Press for The British Academy, Oxford.

Haskell, Y. A. & Hardie, P. R. (eds.) (1999) *Poets and Teachers: Latin Didactic Poetry and the Didactic Authority of the Latin Poet from the Renaissance to the Present.* Levante, Bari.

Haskell, Y. A. & Ruys, J. (eds.) (2009) *Latin and Alterity.* Medieval and Renaissance Texts and Studies, Tempe, Arizona 2007.

Haskins, C. H. (1927) *Renaissance of the Twelfth Century.* Harvard University Press, Cambridge, Mass.

Haubold, J. (forthcoming) Modes of Resonance: Tradition Reception. In Graziosi, B. & Greenwood, E. (eds.) *Homer in the Twentieth Century: Between World Literature and the Western Canon.* Oxford University Press, Oxford.

Haubold, J. & Budelmann, F. (forthcoming) Reception and Tradition. In Hardwick, L. & Stray, C. A. (eds.) *A Companion to Classical Receptions.* Blackwell, Oxford.

Haynes, K. (2003) *English Literature and Ancient Languages.* Oxford University Press, Oxford.

Heaney, S. (1975) *North.* Faber and Faber, London.

Heaney, S. (1987) *The Haw Lantern.* Farrar, Straus, and Giroux, London

Heaney, S. (1990) *The Cure at Troy: A Version of Sophocles' Philoctetes.* Faber in association with Field Day, London.

Heaney, S. (1995) *The Redress of Poetry.* Farrar, Straus, and Giroux, London.

Heaney, S. (1996) *The Spirit Level.* Farrar, Straus, and Giroux, London.

Heaney, S. (1998) *Opened Ground: Poems 1966–1996.* Faber and Faber, London.

Heaney, S. (2001) *Electric Light.* Faber, London.

Heaney, S. (2003) Eclogues *In Extremis:* On the Staying Power of Pastoral. *Proceedings of the Royal Irish Academy* 103c:1, 1–12.

Heaney, S. (2004) *The Burial at Thebes: Sophocles'* Antigone. Farrar, Straus, and Giroux, London.

Heesakkers, Chris L. (2000) "Krassende klanken kastijden kleri-kale kruinen": editie en vertaling met inleiding en annotatie van Janus Dousa's *Sacri calvitii encomium*. In von Martels, Z., Steenbakkers, P., & Vanderjagt, A. (eds.) *Limae labor et mora. Opstellen voor Fokke Akkerman ter gelegenheid van zijn zeventigste verjaardag*. Damon, Leende, 94–108.

Heidegger, M. (1984) *Early Greek Thinking: The Dawn of Western Philosophy*, trans. D. Krell & F. Capuzzi. Harper & Row, San Francisco.

Heidegger, M. (2000) *Introduction to Metaphysics*, trans. G. Fried & R. Polt. Yale University Press, New Haven.

Heidegger, M. (2002) *Off the Beaten Track*, trans. J. Young & K. Haynes. Cambridge University Press, Cambridge.

Helander, H. (2003) *Gustavides*: Latin Epic Literature in Honour of Gustavus Adolphus. In Merisalo & Sarasti-Wilenius (2003): 112–25.

Helander, H. (2004) *Neo-Latin Literature in Sweden in the Period 1620–1720: Stylistics, Vocabulary and Characteristic Ideas*. Uppsala University, Uppsala.

Heller, P. (1956) Zur Biographie Freud. *Merkur* 10, 1233–9.

Hemmy, G. (1767) *De promontorio Bonae Spei*. Dietericus Antonius Harmsen, Hamburg.

Hemmy, G. (1770) *De testimoniis Aethiopum, Chinensium aliorumque paganorum in India Orientali*. Elia Luzac, Leiden.

Henríquez Ureña, P. (1945) *Literary Currents in Hispanic America*. Harvard University Press, Cambridge, Mass.

Herrera Zapién, T. (2000), *Historia del humanismo mexicano: sus textos y contextos neolatinos en cinco siglos*. UNAM, Mexico City.

Hexter, R. J. (1986) *Ovid and Medieval Schooling: Studies in Medieval School Commentaries on Ovid's Ars amatoria, Epistulae ex Ponto, and Epistulae Heroidum*. Arbeo-Gesellschaft, Munich.

Hexter, R. J. (1987) *Latinitas* in the Middle Ages: Horizons and Perspectives. *Helios* 14, 69–92.

Hexter, R. (1989) The *Allegari* of Pierre Bersuire: Interpretation and the *Reductorium morale*. *Allegorica* 10, 49–82.

Higgins, A. (2000) *Constructing the Criollo Archive: Subjects of Knowledge in the Biblioteca Mexicana and the Rusticatio Mexicana*. Purdue University Press, West Lafayette.

Highet, G. (1949) *The Classical Tradition: Greek and Roman Influences on Western Literature*. Oxford University Press, London & New York.

Highet, G. (1967) *The Classical Tradition: Greek and Roman Influences on Western Literature*. Oxford University Press, London.

Highet, G. (1970) *The Classical Tradition: Greek and Roman Influences on Western Literature*. Oxford University Press, New York.

Highet, G. (1971) *The Classical Tradition: Greek and Roman Influences on Western Literature*. Oxford University Press, New York & London.

Hildebrandt, K. (1933) *Platon, der Kampf des Geistes um die Macht*. G. Bondi, Berlin.

Hillebrecht, F. (1997) *Skandinavien – die Heimat der Goten? Der Götizismus als Gerüst eines nordisch-schwedischen Identitätsbewusstseins*. Humboldt-Universität, Berlin.

Hippocrates (1839–61) *Oeuvres complètes*, ed. É. Littré. J. B. Baillière, Paris. Rpt. Hackert, Amsterdam, 1961–2.

Hoberman, R. (1997) *Gendering Classicism: The Ancient World in Twentieth-century Women's Historical Fiction*. State University of New York Press, Albany.

Hobsbawm, E. (1994) *Age of Extremes: The Short Twentieth Century, 1914–1991.* Michael Joseph, London.

Hoernlé, R. F. A. (1938) Would Plato have Approved of the Nationalist Socialist State? *Philosophy* 13, 166–82.

Hoffman, F. J. (1959) *Freudianism and the Literary Mind.* Grove Press, New York.

Hofmann, H. (1993) *"Adveniat tandem Typhis qui detegat orbes."* Columbus in Neo-Latin Epic Poetry (16th–18th Centuries). In Haase & Reinhold (1994): 420–656.

Hofmann, H. (ed.) (1999) *Antike Mythen in der europäischen Tradition.* Attempto, Tübingen.

Hofmann, H. (ed.) (2004) *Troia: Von Homer bis heute.* Attempto, Tübingen.

Holmes, G. F. (1850) Observations on a Passage of Aristotle Relative to Slavery. *Southern Literary Messenger* 16, 193–205.

Holtermann, M. (1999) Deutschland IV. 19. Jahrhundert, bis 1918. In Landfester (1999): vol. 13, cols. 806–17.

Holtsmark, E. B. (1981) *Tarzan and Tradition: Classical Myth in Popular Culture.* Greenwood Press, Westport & London.

Holub, R. C. (1984) *Reception Theory: A Critical Introduction.* Methuen, London & New York.

Holub, R. C. (1995) Reception Theory: School of Constance. In Selden, R. (ed.) *The Cambridge History of Literary Criticism*, vol. 8: *From Formalism to Poststructuralism.* Cambridge University Press, Cambridge, 319–46.

Hopkins, D. (2000) Classical Translation and Imitation. In Womersley, D. (ed.) *A Companion to Literature from Milton to Blake.* Blackwell, Oxford, 76–93.

Horsfall, N. M. (1990) E. Fraenkel. In Briggs, W. W. & Calder, W. M. III (eds.) *Classical Scholarship: A Biographical Encyclopedia.* Garland, New York, 61–7.

Howarth, W. D. (1982) *Molière: A Playwright and His Audience.* Cambridge University Press, Cambridge.

Hsia, F. (2004) Athanasius Kircher's China Illustrata: An Apologia Pro Vita Sua. In Findlen (2004): 383–404.

Hughes-Hallett, L. (1990) *Cleopatra: Histories, Dreams and Distortions.* Bloomsbury, London.

Hugo, V. (1968) *Cromwell*, ed. A. Ubersfeld. Garnier-Flammarion, Paris.

Humphreys, S. C. (ed.) (1997) *Cultures of Scholarship.* University of Michigan Press, Ann Arbor.

Hunger, H. (1988) *Lexikon der griechischen und römischen Mythologie mit Hinweisen auf das Fortwirken antiker Stoffe und Motive in der bildenden Kunst, Literatur und Musik des Abendlandes bis zur Gegenwart.* Hollinek, Vienna.

Hutson, L. (1999) The Housewife and the Humanists. In Hutson, L. (ed.) *Feminism and Renaissance Studies.* Oxford University Press, Oxford, 82–106.

Hyatte, R. (1994) *The Arts of Friendship: The Idealization of Friendship in Medieval and Early Renaissance Literature.* E. J. Brill, Leiden.

IJsewijn, J. (1975) The Coming of Humanism to the Low Countries. In Oberman, H. & Brady, T. Jr. (eds.) *Itinerarium Italicum: The Profile of the Italian Renaissance in the Mirror of Its European Transformations … Dedicated to P. O. Kristeller.* E. J. Brill, Leiden, 193–301.

IJsewijn, J. (1988) Humanism in the Low Countries. In Rabil (1988): 2:156–215.

IJsewijn, J. (1990) *Companion to Neo-Latin Studies*, Part 1: *History and Diffusion of Neo-Latin Literature*, 2nd edn. Leuven University Press, Leuven.

IJsewijn, J. (1993) Latin and the Low Countries. In Hermans, T. & Salverda, R. (eds.) *From Revolt to Riches: Culture and History of the Low Countries 1500–1700, International and Interdisciplinary Perspectives.* Crossways 2. Centre for Low Countries Studies, London, 9–29.

IJsewijn, J. & Sacré, D. (1997) *Companion to Neo-Latin Studies*, Part 2: *Literary, Linguistic, Philological and Editorial Questions*, 2nd edn. Leuven University Press, Leuven.

IJsewijn, J., Tournoy, G. et al. (eds.) (1992–5) Litterae ad Craneveldium Balduinianae. A Preliminary Edition [Parts 1–4]. *Humanistica Lovaniensia* 41, 1–85; 42, 2–51; 43, 15–68; 44, 1–78.

Innes, M. (1997) The Classical Tradition in the Carolingian Renaissance: Ninth-century Encounters with Suetonius. *International Journal of the Classical Tradition* 3:3, 265–82.

International Journal of the Classical Tradition, New Brunswick, 1 (1994/1995) sqq.

Irele, F. A. (2001) *The African Imagination, Literature in Africa and the Black Diaspora.* Oxford University Press, Oxford.

Irele, F. A. & Gikandi, S. (eds.) (2004) *The Cambridge History of African and Caribbean Literature.* Cambridge University Press, Cambridge.

Irigaray, L. (1985) Is the Subject of Science Sexed? *Cultural Critique* 1, 73–88.

Irigaray, L. (1993) *An Ethics of Sexual Difference,* trans. C. Burke. Cornell University Press, Ithaca.

Irwin, M. E. (2004) D'Arcy Wentworth Thompson (the elder). In Todd, R. B. (ed.) *Dictionary of British Classicists,* 3 vols. Thoemmes Continuum, Bristol, 3:962–3.

Isaievych, Y. (2002) Anti-culture's War against Culture: Ukrainian Translators of Classical Literature as Victims of Political Repression. *Eos* 89, 343–51.

Iser, W. (1978) *The Implied Reader: Patterns of Communication in Prose Fiction from Bunyan to Beckett.* Johns Hopkins University Press, Baltimore.

Iser, W. (1980) *The Act of Reading: A Theory of Aesthetic Response.* Johns Hopkins University Press, Baltimore & London.

Iser, W. (1995) Enfoldings in Paterian Discourse: Modes of Translatability. In Shaffer, E. S. (ed.) *Walter Pater and the Culture of the Fin-de-siècle, Comparative Criticism* 17, 41–60.

Iser, W. (2006) *How to Do Theory.* Blackwell, Malden & Oxford.

Issa, I. (1959) *Grandes eaux noires.* Alternance, Paris.

Jacks, P. (1993) *The Antiquarian and the Myth of Antiquity: The Origins of Rome in Renaissance Thought.* Cambridge University Press, Cambridge.

Jackson, S. W. (1986) *Melancholia and Depression.* Yale University Press, New Haven & London.

Jacobus, J. (1962) *Philip Johnson.* George Braziller, New York.

Jaeger, C. S. (1994) *The Envy of Angels: Cathedral Schools and Social Ideals in Medieval Europe, 950–1200.* University of Pennsylvania Press, Philadelphia.

Jaeger, W. (1933) Die Erziehung des politischen Menschen und die Antike. *Volk im Werden* 1, 43–9.

Jaeger, W. (1934) *Paideia: Die Formung des griechischen Menschen*, vol. 1. W. de Gruyter, Berlin & Leipzig.

Jaeger, W. (1944) *Paideia: Die Formung des griechischen Menschen*, vol. 2. W. de Gruyter, Berlin.

Jaeger, W. (1947) *Paideia. Die Formung des griechischen Menschen*, vol. 3. W. de Gruyter, Berlin.

Jaeger, W. (1960) *Humanistische Reden und Vorträge: Zweite erweiterte Auflage.* W. de Gruyter, Berlin.

Jaeger, W. (1965) *Paideia: The Ideals of Greek Culture*, 2nd edn. Oxford University Press.

Jardine, L. (1993) *Erasmus, Man of Letters*. Princeton University Press, Princeton.

Jaskot, P. B. (1996) Anti-Semitic Policy in Albert Speer's Plans for the Rebuilding of Berlin. *Art Bulletin* 78:4, 622–33.

Jauss, H. R. (1982) *Toward an Aesthetic of Reception*, trans. T. Bahti. Harvester Press, Brighton.

Jebb, R. C. (1907) *Translations into Greek and Latin Verse*, 2nd edn. Cambridge University Press, Cambridge.

Jebb, R. C. (trans.) (2004a) *Sophocles: Plays, Antigone*. Bristol Classical Press, London. Rpt. of 1898 edn.

Jebb, R. C. (trans.) (2004b) *Sophocles: Plays, Philoctetes*, intro. F. Budelmann. Bristol Classical Press, London. Rpt. of 1898 edn.

Jefferson, T. (1907) *The Writings of Thomas Jefferson*, 20 vols. Thomas Jefferson Memorial Association of the United States, Washington.

Jencks, C. A. (1977) *The Language of Post-Modern Architecture*. Rizzoli, New York. Rev. edn. 1984.

Jenkyns, R. (1980) *The Victorians and Ancient Greece*. Blackwell, Oxford.

Jenkyns, R. (1991) *Dignity and Decadence: Victorian Art and the Classical Inheritance*. Harper Collins, London.

Jenkyns, R. (ed.) (1992) *The Legacy of Rome*. Oxford University Press, Oxford.

Jensen, M. S. (ed.) (1995) *A History of Nordic Neo-Latin Literature*. Odense University Press, Odense.

Jensen, M. S. (2004) Latinsk renæssancepoesi i Danmark. In Pade, M. & Jensen, M. S. (eds.) *Renæssancen: Dansk – europæisk – globalt*. Museum Tusculanum Press, Copenhagen, 147–60.

Jeyifo, B. (ed.) (2001) *Conversations with Wole Soyinka*. University Press of Mississippi, Jackson.

Jeyifo, B. (ed.) (2002) *Modern African Drama*. W. W. Norton, New York & London.

Johnson, J. W. (1967) *The Formation of English Neo-Classical Thought*. Princeton University Press, Princeton.

Johnson, S. (1905) *Lives of the English Poets*, ed. G. B. Hill, 3 vols. Clarendon Press, Oxford.

Johnson, S. (1958–) *Works*, ed. J. Middendorf et al., 16 vols. Yale University Press, New Haven.

Johnston, K. (1998) *The Hidden Wordsworth: Poet, Lover, Rebel, Spy*. Norton, New York.

Jondorf, G. (1990) *French Renaissance Tragedy: The Dramatic Word*. Cambridge University Press, Cambridge.

Jones, H. M. (1952) *O Strange New World. American Culture: The Formative Years*. Viking Press, New York.

Jones, H. M. (1968) *The Literature of Virginia in the Seventeenth Century*, 2nd edn. University Press of Virginia, Charlottesville.

Jones, H. M. (1974) *Revolution and Romanticism*. Harvard University Press, Cambridge, Mass.

Jones, J. W., Jr. (1986) The Allegorical Traditions of the *Aeneid*. In Bernard, J. D. (ed.) *Vergil at 2000: Commemorative Essays on the Poet and His Influence*. AMS Ars poetica 3. AMS Press, New York, 107–32.

Jones, R. O. (1971a) *The Golden Age: Prose and Poetry*. Benn, London.

Jones, R. O. (1971b) *A Literary History of Spain*. Benn, London.

Joshel, S., Malamud, M., & McGuire, D. (eds.) (2001) *Imperial Projections. Ancient Rome in Modern Popular Culture.* Johns Hopkins University Press, Baltimore.

Joyce, J. (1986) *Ulysses: The Corrected Text*, ed. H. W. Gabler. Random House, New York.

Juana Inés de la Cruz, Sor (1997) *Poems, Protest and a Dream: Selected Writings, Sor Juana Inés de la Cruz*, trans. with notes M. Sayers Peden, intro. I. Stavans. Penguin Books, Harmondsworth.

Jung, C. G. (1936) *Modern Man in Search of a Soul.* Harcourt, Brace, New York.

Jung, C. G. (1953–79) *The Collected Works.* Princeton University Press, New York.

Kahn, C. H. (1992) Werner Jaeger's Portrayal of Plato. In Calder (1992): 69–81.

Kaimowitz, J. H. (1990) Translation of the Apologetical Essay Appended to the *Alexandriad* of Francisco Javier Alegre. In *Dieciocho* 13:1–2, 135–48.

Kajanto, I. (1989–90) *Humanism in a Christian Society*, vol. 1: *The Attitude to Classical Mythology and Religion in Finland 1640–1713*, vol. 2: *Classical Moral Philosophy and Oratory in Finland 1640–1713.* Suomalainen Tiedeakatemia, Helsinki.

Kajanto, I. (1993) *Christina Heroina: Mythological and Historical Exemplification in the Latin Panegyrics of Christina, Queen of Sweden.* Suomalainen Tiedakatemia, Helsinki.

Kajanto, I. (1995) Finland. In Jensen (1995): 159–200.

Kallendorf, C. (1989) *In Praise of Aeneas: Virgil and Epideictic Rhetoric in the Early Italian Renaissance.* University Press of New England, Hanover & London.

Kallendorf, C. (1995) From Virgil to Vida: The *Poeta Theologus* in Italian Renaissance Commentary. *Journal of the History of Ideas* 56, 41–62.

Kallendorf, C. (1999a) Historicizing the "Harvard School": Pessimistic Readings of the *Aeneid* in Italian Renaissance Scholarship. *Harvard Studies in Classical Philology* 99, 391–403.

Kallendorf, C. (1999b) *Virgil and the Myth of Venice: Books and Readers in the Italian Renaissance.* Clarendon Press, Oxford.

Kallendorf, C. (ed.) (2002) *Humanist Educational Treatises.* Harvard University Press, Cambridge, Mass. & London.

Kallendorf, C. (2003) Representing the Other: Ercilla's *La Araucana*, Virgil's *Aeneid*, and the New World Encounter. *Comparative Literature Studies* 40:4, 394–414.

Kallendorf, C. & Kallendorf, H. (2000) Conversations with the Dead: Quevedo and Statius, Annotation and Imitation. *Journal of the Warburg and Courtauld Institutes* 63, 131–68.

Kaminski, T. (1996) Rehabilitating "Augustanism": On the Roots of "Polite Letters" in England. *Eighteenth-Century Life* 20 (November), 49–65.

Kaminski, T. (1997) "Opposition Augustanism" and Pope's *Epistle to Augustus. Studies in Eighteenth Century Culture* 26, 71–86.

Kasson, J. F. (2001) *Houdini, Tarzan and the Perfect Man: The White Male Body and the Challenge of Modernity in America.* Hill and Wang, New York.

Kaster R. A. (1988) *Guardians of Language: The Grammarian and Society in Late Antiquity.* University of California Press, Berkeley.

Kaye, R. A. (1996) Losing His Religion: Saint Sebastian as Contemporary Gay Martyr. In Horne, P. & Lewis, R. (eds.) *Outlooks: Lesbian and Gay Sexualities and Visual Cultures.* Routledge, London, 86–105.

Keeley, E. (1976) *Cavafy's Alexandria: Study of a Myth in Progress.* Harvard University Press, Cambridge.

Kemal, S. & Gaskell, I. (eds.) (2000) *Politics and Aesthetics in the Arts.* Cambridge University Press, Cambridge.

Kennedy, G. (1984) Afterword: An Essay on Classics in America since the Yale Report. In Reinhold (1984): 325–51.

Kennedy, G. A. (1994) Shifting Visions of Classical Paradigms: The "Same" and the "Other." *International Journal of the Classical Tradition* 1:1 (summer), 7–16.

Kennedy, R. G. (1990) *Greek Revival America*. Tabori & Chang, New York.

Kenner, H. (1969) Homer's Sticks and Stones. *James Joyce Quarterly* 6:4 (summer), 285–98.

Kenney, E. J. (2006) "A Little of It Sticks": The Englishman's Horace. In Burnett, C. (ed.) *Britannia Latina*. Oxford University Press, Oxford, 178–93.

Kerber, L. (1997) *Towards an Intellectual History of Women*. University of North Carolina Press, Chapel Hill.

Kermode, F. (2004) *Pleasure and Change: The Aesthetics of Canon*. Oxford University Press, Oxford.

Kershaw, I. (1987) *The Hitler Myth: Image and Reality in the Third Reich*. Oxford University Press, Oxford.

Kershaw, I. (2000) *The Nazi Dictatorship: Problems and Perspectives of Interpretation*. Arnold, London.

Kerson, A. (1988) Enlightened Thought in Diego José Abad's *De Deo, Deoque Homine heroica*. In Revard, S. P., Rädle, F., & Di Cesare, M. (eds.) *Acta Conventus Neo-Latini Guelpherbytani: Proceedings of the Sixth International Congress of Neo-Latin Studies*. MRTS, Binghamton, 617–23.

Kerson, A. (1991) Diego José Abad, *Dissertatio Ludicro-Seria*: Edition, Translation and Notes. *Humanistica Lovaniensia* 40, 357–422.

Kessler, E. & Kuhn, H. C. (eds.) (2003) *Germania latina – Latinitas teutonica: Politik, Wissenschaft, humanistische Kultur vom späten Mittelalter bis in unsere Zeit*, 1–2. Wilhelm Fink Verlag, Munich.

Kestner, J. A. (1989) *Mythology and Misogyny: The Social Discourse of Nineteenth-Century British Classical-Subject Painting*. University of Wisconsin Press, Madison.

Keynes, G. (ed.) (1967) *Poetry and Prose of William Blake*, 4th edn. Nonesuch Press, London.

Kiberd, D. (1995) *Inventing Ireland*. Jonathan Cape, London.

Kiberd, D. (1998) Romantic Ireland's Dead and Gone. *Times Literary Supplement*, June 12, 1998, 12–14.

Kieniewicz, J. (ed.) (2001) *Terra marique: The Cultural Intercourse between the European Centre and Periphery in Modern Time*. OBTA, Warsaw, 11–87.

King, B. (2000) *Derek Walcott: A Caribbean Life*. Oxford University Press, Oxford.

King, D. (2005) *Finding Atlantis: A True Story of Genius, Madness, and an Extraordinary Quest for a Lost World*. Harmony Books, New York.

King, H. (1993) Once upon a Text: Hysteria from Hippocrates. In Gilman, S. et al. (eds.) *Hysteria Beyond Freud*. University of California Press, Berkeley & Los Angeles, 3–90.

King, H. (1996) Green Sickness: Hippocrates, Galen and the Origins of the "Disease of the Virgins." *International Journal of the Classical Tradition* 2:3, 372–87.

King, H. (1998) *Hippocrates' Woman: Reading the Female Body in Ancient Greece*. Routledge, London & New York.

King, H. (2004) *The Disease of Virgins: Green Sickness, Chlorosis and the Problems of Puberty*. Routledge, London & New York.

King, K. C. (1987) *Achilles: Paradigms of the War Hero from Homer to the Middle Ages*. University of California Press, Berkeley & Los Angeles.

Kinney, D. (1990) Mirabilia urbis Romae. In Bernardo, A. & Levin, S. (eds.) *The Classics in the Middle Ages*. MRTS, Binghamton, 207–21.

Kinsella, T. (ed.) (1986) *The New Oxford Book of Irish Verse*. Oxford University Press, Oxford.

Kipling, R. (1899) *Stalky & Co*. Macmillan, London.

Kirby, J. T. (2000) *Secret of the Muses Retold: Classical Influence on Italian Authors of the Twentieth Century*. University of Chicago Press, Chicago & London.

Kirk, G. (1971) *Myth: Its Meaning and Functions in Ancient and Other Cultures*. Cambridge University Press, Cambridge.

Klaniczay, G. & Werner, J. (eds.) (2005) Working paper in *Multiple Antiquities – Multiple Modernities*. Project of Collegium Budapest, Budapest.

Kleiner, D. E. E. (2005) *Cleopatra and Rome*. Harvard University Press, Cambridge, Mass.

Klibansky, R., Panofsky E., & Saxl, F. (1964) *Saturn and Melancholy: Studies in the History of Natural Philosophy, Religion and Art*. Nelson & Sons, London.

Klingenstein, G. (1933) Humanistische Bildung als deutsche Waffe. In Gieselbusch et al. (1933): 23–35.

Kłoczowski, J. (ed.) (2004) *Histoire de l'Europe du Centre-Est*, 2 vols. Presses universitaires de France, Paris.

Kneller, G. F. (1942) *The Educational Philosophy of National Socialism*. Yale University Press, New Haven.

Knellwolf, C. & Norris, C. (2001) *The Cambridge History of Literary Criticism*, vol. 9: *Twentieth-Century Historical, Philosophical and Psychological Perspectives*. Cambridge University Press, Cambridge.

Kohut, K. (1973) *Las teorías literarias en España y Portugal durante los siglos XV y XVI*. CSIC, Madrid.

Kolesnik, W. B. (1962) *Mental Discipline in Modern Education*. University of Wisconsin Press, Madison.

Kolsky, S. D. (2003) *The Genealogy of Women: Studies in Boccaccio's De mulieribus claris*. Peter Lang, New York.

Komar, K. L. (2003) *Reclaiming Klytemnestra: Revenge or Reconciliation*. University of Illinois Press, Urbana.

Koneczny, F. (1962) *On the Plurality of Civilisations*. Polonica Publications, London.

Koninklijke Nederlandse Akademie van Wetenschappen (1984) *The World of Hugo Grotius (1583–1645)*. Holland University Press, Amsterdam.

Kopff, E. C. (2000) Italian Fascism and the Roman Empire. *Classical Bulletin* 76, 109–15.

Kostof, S. (1978) The Emperor and the Duce: The Planning of the Piazzale Augusto Imperatore in Rome. In Millon & Nochlin (1978): 270–325.

Kragelund, P. (1999) *Abildgaard: Kunstneren mellem oprørerne*. Museum Tusculanum Press, Copenhagen.

Krasser, H. & Schmidt, E. A. (eds.) (1996) *Zeitgenosse Horaz: Der Dichter und seine Leser seit zwei Jahrtausenden*. Narr, Tübingen.

Kraye, J. (ed.) (1996) *The Cambridge Companion to Renaissance Humanism*. Cambridge University Press, Cambridge.

Krieck, E. (1933) *Musische Erziehung*. Armanen, Leipzig.

Krieck, E. (1934a) *Wissenschaft, Weltanschauung, Hochschulreform*. Armanen, Leipzig.

Krieck, E. (1934b) *Völkischer Gesamtstaat und Nationale Erziehung.* Bündischer Verlag, Heidelberg.

Krieck, E. (1934c) *Die deutsche Staatsidee.* Armanen, Leipzig.

Krieck, E. (1935) *Nationalpolitische Erziehung.* Armanen, Leipzig.

Kristeller, P. O. et al. (eds.) (1960–) *Catalogus translationum et commentariorum: Medieval and Renaissance Latin Translations and Commentaries, Annotated Lists and Guides,* 8 vols. to date. Catholic University of America Press, Washington.

Kühnl, R. (1996) The Cultural Politics of Fascist Governments. In Berghaus, G. (ed.) *Fascism and Theatre: Comparative Studies on the Aesthetics and Politics of Performance in Europe, 1925–1945.* Berghahn, Providence, 30–8.

Kumaniecki, K. (1957) *Cyceron i jego wspótczésni.* Czytelnik, Warsaw. Italian version: *Cicerone e la crisi della repubblica romana.* Centro di Studi Ciceroniani, Rome, 1972.

Kunze, M. (ed.) (2004) *Ost-westlicher Ikarus: Ein Mythos im geteilten Deutschland. Eine Ausstellung des Winckelmann-Museums Stendal. [Catalogue].* Gulde Druck, Tübingen.

Kuper, A. (1988) *The Invention of Primitive Society: Transformations of an Illusion.* Routledge, London.

Kurtz, D. (2000) *The Reception of Classical Art in Britain: An Oxford Story of Plaster Casts from the Antique.* Archaeopress, London.

Labarre, J. (1989) Belgique. In *La filologia greca e latina nel secolo XX. Atti del Convegno Internazionale, Roma ... 17–21 settembre 1984,* 3 vols. Giardini, Pisa, 2:763–88.

Lacan, J. (1992) *The Ethics of Psychoanalysis,* trans. D. Porter. W. W. Norton, New York.

Lacoue-Labarthe, P. (1987) *La fiction du politique.* C. Bourgois, Paris.

Ladendorf, H. (1953) *Antikenstudium und Antikenkopie. Vorarbeiten zu einer Darstellung ihrer Bedeutung in der mittelalterlichen und neueren Zeit.* Akademie-Verlag, Berlin.

Laird, A. (2002) Juan Luis de la Cerda and the Predicament of Commentary. In Gibson, R. K. & Kraus, C. S. (eds.) *The Classical Commentary.* E. J. Brill, Leiden, 171–204.

Laird, A. (2003) La *Alexandriada* de Francisco Xavier Alegre: *Arcanis sua sensa figuris. Nova Tellus* 21:2, 165–76.

Laird, A. (2004) Selenopolitanus: Diego José Abad, Latin, and Mexican Identity. *Studi Umanistici Piceni* 24, 231–7.

Laird, A. (2006a) *The Epic of America: An Introduction to Rafael Landívar and the Rusticatio Mexicana.* Duckworth, London.

Laird, A. (2006b) Renaissance Emblems and Aztec Glyphs: Italian Humanism and Mexico 1520–1579. *Studi Umanistici Piceni* 26, 227–39.

Laird, A. (2007) The Virgin of Guadalupe and the Birth of the Mexican Epic: Bernardo Ceinos de Riofrío's *Centonicum virgilianum monimentum* (1680). In Andrews & Coroleu (2007): 199–220.

Laird, A. (2009) Latin in Cuauhtémoc's Shadow: Classical humanism and the Politics of Language in Mexico after the Conquest. In Haskell & Ruys (2009): 169–99.

Lanchner, C. (1976) Masson: Origins and Development. In *André Masson.* Museum of Modern Art, New York.

Landau, P. (2005) The Importance of Classical Canon Law in Scandinavia in the 12th and 13th Centuries. In Tamm, D. & Vogt, H. (eds.) *How Nordic Are the Nordic Medieval Laws?* University of Copenhagen Press, Copenhagen.

Landfester, M. (1988) *Humanismus und Gesellschaft im 19. Jahrhundert. Untersuchungen zur politischen und gesellschaftlichen Bedeutung der humanistischen Bildung in Deutschland.* Wissenschaftliche Buchgesellschaft, Darmstadt.

Landfester, M. (1995) Die Naumberger Tagung, "Das Problem des Klassischen und die Antike" (1930). Der Klassikbegriff Werner Jaegers: seine Voraussetzung und seine Wirkung. In Flashar (1995): 11–40.

Landfester, M. et al. (ed.) (1999–2003) *Der Neue Pauly: Enzyklopädie der Antike*, vols. 13–15: *Rezeptions- und Wissenschaftsgeschichte*. J. B. Metzler, Stuttgart & Weimar.

Landi, S. (1996) *Il Sant'Alessio*, Les Arts Florissants, William Christie, director, Elektra/Wea. CD.

Landi, S. (2003) *Homo Fugit velut Umbra*, L'Arpeggiata, Christina Pluhar, director; Marco Beasley, tenor, Alpha Productions. CD.

Lane, M. (2001) *Plato's Progeny: How Plato and Socrates Still Capture the Modern Mind*. Duckworth, London.

Langdon, H. (2000) *Caravaggio: A Life*. Westview Press, New York.

Lange-Churión, P. & Mendieta, E. (eds.) (2001) *Latin American and Postmodernity*. Humanity Books, Amherst, N.Y.

Langholf, V. (1990) Die "kathartische Method": Klassische Philologie, literarische Tradition und Wissenschaftstheorie in der Frühgeschichte der Psychoanalyse. *Medical-Historical Journal* 25, 5–39.

Langosch, K. (1990a) *Europas Latein des Mittelalters. Wesen und Wirkung. Essays und Quellen*. Wissenschaftliche Buchgesellschaft, Darsmtadt.

Langosch, K. (1990b) *Mittellatein und Europa: Führung in die Hauptliteratur des Mittelalters*. Wissenschaftliche Buchgesellschaft, Darmstadt.

Lanteri-Laura, G. (1991) L'Antique et les racines philosophiques de la psychiatrie moderne. *L'Évolution psychiatrique* 56, 533–43.

Lapatin, K. (2002) *Mysteries of the Snake Goddess: Art, Desire, and the Forging of History*. Houghton Mifflin, Boston & New York.

Lapesa, R. (1980) *Historia de la lengua española*. Gredos, Madrid.

Latino, J. (1573) *Epigrammatum liber, deque Sanctissimi Pii Quinti Romanae Ecclesiae Pontificis Summi rebus, Austrias carmen*. Hugo de Mena, Granada.

Law, V. A. (2003) *The History of Linguistics in Europe: From Plato to 1600*. Cambridge University Press, Cambridge.

Lazarus, N. (1999) *Nationalism and Cultural Practice in the Postcolonial World*. Cambridge University Press, Cambridge.

Le Corbusier (1931) *Towards a New Architecture*. Dover Publications, New York. Trans. from the 13th French edn. by Frederick Etchells, 1931, rpt. 1986.

Le Goff, J. (1988) *Medieval Civilization*. Blackwell, Oxford & New York.

Le Goff, J. (1993) *Intellectuals in the Middle Ages*, trans. T. L. Fagan. Blackwell, Cambridge, Mass.

Lebrecht Schmidt, P. (2001) Latin Studies in Germany, 1933–1945: Institutional Conditions, Political Pressures, Scholarly Consequences. In Harrison (2001): 285–300.

Lecky, W. E. H. (1897) *History of European Morals from Augustus to Charlemagne*, 2 vols. Longmans, London.

Lecoy, F. (1938) *Recherches sur le "Libro de Buen Amor" de Juan Ruiz Arcipreste de Hita*. Droz, Paris.

Lefkowitz, M. & Rogers, G. (eds.) (1996) *Black Athena Revisited*. University of North Carolina Press, Chapel Hill & London.

Legaré, H. S. (1828) Classical Learning. *Southern Review* 1:1 (February 1828), 1–49.

Lehmann, P. (1927) *Pseudo-antike Literatur des Mittelalters*. B. G. Teubner, Leipzig.

Leloup, J. (1986). *Gueido*. Editions CLE, Yaoundé.

Lendon, J. E. (2000) Gladiators, review article in *Classical Journal* 95:4, 399–406.

León, L. de (1986) *Poesía*, ed. J. F. Alcina. Cátedra, Madrid.

León, L. de (1992) *Obras propias y traducciones latinas, griegas y italianas. Con la parafrasi de algunos Salmos y Capítulos de Iob*, [. . .] dadas a la impresión don Francisco de Quevedo. Villegas, Madrid. Facsimile edn. Universidad de Salamanca, Salamanca.

León Portilla, M. (2002) *Bernardino de Sahagún: First Anthropologist*. University of Oklahoma Press, Norman.

Leonard, I. (1983) *Baroque Times in Old Mexico*. University of Michigan Press, Ann Arbor. Rpt. of 1959 edn.

Leonard, I. (1992) *Books of the Brave: Being an Account of Books and of Men in the Spanish Conquest and Settlement of the Sixteenth-Century New World*, new intro. R. Adorno. University of California Press, Berkeley & Los Angeles. Rpt. of 1949 Harvard University Press edn.

Leonard, M. (2003) Antigone, the Political, and the Ethics of Psychoanalysis. *Proceedings of the Cambridge Philological Association* 49, 130–54.

Leonardi, C. & Munk Olsen, B. (1995) *The Classical Tradition in the Middle Ages and Renaissance*. Centro Italiano di Studi sull'Alto Medioevo, Spoleto.

Leoussi, A. S. (1998) *Nationalism and Classicism: The Classical Body as National Symbol in Nineteenth-Century England and France*. Macmillan, London.

Leroux, E. (1959) *Hilaria*. Culemborg, Cape Town.

Lessenich, R. (2002) Philhellenismus. In Landfester (2002): vol. 15.2, cols. 231–7.

Lessing, G. E. (1962) *Laocoön*, trans. E. A. McCormick. Bobbs-Merrill, Indianapolis.

Létoublon, F. & Volpilhac-Auger, C. (eds.) (1999) *Homère en France après la querelle (1715–1900)*, Actes du Colloque de Grenoble (October 23–5, 1995). Champion, Paris.

Levin, G. (1995) *Edward Hopper: An Intimate Biography*. Alfred A. Knopf, New York.

Levine, J. (1991) *The Battle of the Books*. Cornell University Press, Ithaca.

Lewcock, R. (1963) *Early Nineteenth Century Architecture in South Africa. A Study of the Interaction of Two Cultures: 1795–1837*. A. A. Balkema, Amsterdam.

Licht, T. (2005) *Untersuchungen zum biographischen Werk Sigeberts von Gembloux*. Winter, Heidelberg.

Lida de Malkiel, M. R. (1950) *Juan de Mena, poeta del prerrenacimiento español*. FCE, Mexico City.

Lida de Malkiel, M. R. (1962) *La originalidad artística de La Celestina*. EUDEBA, Buenos Aires.

Lida de Malkiel, M. R. (1974) *Dido en la literatura española*. Tamesis Books, London.

Lida de Malkiel, M. R. (1975) *La tradición clásica en España*. Ariel, Barcelona.

Liestøl, A. & Sanness Johnsen, I. (1980–90) *Bryggen i Bergen*, vol. 6.1 of Knirk, J. E. (ed.) *Norges innskrifter med de yngre rune*. Norsk historisk Kjeldeskrift-Institutt, Oslo.

Lindberg, B. (1987) *Humanism och vetenskap: Den klassiska filologien i Sverige från 1800-talets början till andra världskriget*. Almqvist & Wiksell International, Stockholm.

Lindberg, B. (1993) *Europa och latinet*. Natur och Kulturs Förlag, Stockholm.

Lippmann, W. (1969) *A Preface to Politics*. University of Michigan Press, Ann Arbor. Rpt. of New York, 1914 edn.

Liversidge, M. & Edwards, C. (eds.) (1996) *British Artists and Rome in the Nineteenth Century*. Bristol City Museum and Art Gallery, Bristol.

Livingstone, D. (1978) *The Sea My Winding Sheet*. In S. Gray (ed.) *Theatre One: New South African Drama*. Ad. Donker, Johannesburg, 95–122.

Llewellyn, N. (1993) Illustrating Ovid. In Martindale (1993): 151–66.

Lloyd-Jones, H. (1982) *Blood for the Ghosts: Classical Influences in the Nineteenth and Twentieth Centuries.* Duckworth, London.

Lloyd-Jones, H. (1985) Psychoanalysis and the Study of the Ancient World. In Horden, P. (ed.) *Freud and the Humanities.* Duckworth, London, 152–80.

Lloyd-Jones, H. (1986) Review of Calder, W. M., Flashar, H., & Lindken, T. (eds.) *Wilamowitz nach 50. Jahren. Classical Review* 36, 400–1.

Lloyd-Jones, H. (1999) A Disapproving Voice. *International Journal of the Classical Tradition* 5, 456–66.

Lloyd-Jones, H. (2004) Review of Gildenhard, I. & Ruehl, M. (eds.) *Out of Arcadia: Classics and Politics in Germany in the Age of Burckhardt, Nietzsche and Wilamowitz. Bryn Mawr Classical Review* 2004.02.43.

Logan, A. M. & Plomp, M. C. (2005) *Peter Paul Rubens: The Drawings.* Metropolitan Museum of Art, New York.

Lohmann Villena, G. (1945) *El arte drámatico en Lima durante el virreinato.* Estades, Madrid.

Lopes, J. (1928) *Jardim das Hespérides, Sonetos do livro Hesperitanas.* J. Rodrigues, Lisbon.

López Grigera, L. (1983) Introduction to the Study of Rhetoric in Sixteenth-Century Spain. *Dispositio* 8 (nos. 22–3), 1–18.

López Grigera, L. (1988) Notas sobre las amistades italianas de Garcilaso: un nuevo manuscrito de Pietro Bembo. In López Grigera, L. & Redondo, A. (eds.) *Homenaje a Eugenio Asensio.* Gredos, Madrid, 291–309.

López Grigera, L. (1998) *Anotaciones de Quevedo a la "Retórica" de Aristóteles.* Gráficas Cervantes, Salamanca.

López Grigera, L. (2003) La prosa de Quevedo y los sistemas elocutivos de su época. In Roncero, V. (ed.) *Quevedo y la crítica a fines del siglo XX (1975–2000).* EUNSA, Pamplona, 2:119–43.

López Grigera, L. (2005) "Por la estafeta he sabido/ que me han apologizado." Otra lectura de la polémica en torno a las *Soledades.* In Piñero Ramírez, P. M. (ed.) *Dejar hablar a los textos. Homenaje a Francisco Márquez Villanueva.* University of Seville, Seville, 2:949–60.

Lorch, M. de P. (1985) *A Defense of Life: Lorenzo Valla's Theory of Pleasure.* Wilhelm Fink Verlag, Munich.

Losemann, V. (1977) *Nationalsozialismus und Antike: Studien zur Entwicklung des Faches Alte Geschichte 1933–1945.* Hoffmann & Campe, Hamburg.

Losemann, V. (1999) The Nazi Concept of Rome. In Edwards (1999): 221–35.

Lotman, Y. M. (1984) The Decembrist in Everyday life. In Shukman, A. (ed.) *The Semiotics of Russian Culture.* Michigan Slavic Publications, Ann Arbor, 71–124.

Ludwig, W. (1997) Die neuzeitliche lateinische Literatur seit der Renaissance. In Graf, F. (ed.) *Einleitung in die lateinische Philologie.* Teubner, Stuttgart & Leipzig, 323–56.

Ludwig, W. (2004–5) *Miscella Neolatina. Ausgewälte Aufsätze zur neulateinischen Literatur aus den Jahren 1989–2004,* 3 vols. Olms, Hildesheim.

Lupher, D. A. (2003) *Romans in a New World: Classical Models in Sixteenth-Century Spanish America.* University of Michigan Press, Ann Arbor.

Lyne, G. M. (1934) *Balbus: A Latin Reading-Book for Junior Forms.* Arnold, London.

MacCormack, S. (1998a) The Incas and Rome. In Anadón (1998), 8–31.

MacCormack, S. (1998b) *The Shadows of Poetry: Vergil in the Mind of Augustine.* University of California Press, Berkeley.

MacDougall, H. A. (1982) *Racial Myth in English History: Trojans, Teutons, and Anglo-Saxons.* University Press of New England, Hanover.

Macintosh, F. (1994) *Dying Acts: Death in Ancient Greek and Modern Irish Tragic Drama.* Cork University Press, Cork.

Macintosh, F. (1997) Tragedy in Performance: Nineteenth and Twentieth-Century Productions. In Easterling (1997): 284–323.

Macintosh, F. (2000a) Introduction: The Performer in Performance. In Hall, Macintosh, & Taplin (2000): 1– 31.

Macintosh, F. (2000b) Medea Transposed: Burlesque and Gender on the Mid-Victorian Stage. In Hall, Macintosh, & Taplin (2000): 75–99.

Macintosh, F. (2001) Oedipus in Africa. *Omnibus* 42, 8–9.

Macintosh, F., Michelakis, P., Hall, E., & Taplin, O. (2005), *Agamemnon in Performance, 458 BC – 2002 AD.* Oxford University Press, Oxford.

MacKendrick, P. (1992) *The Mute Stones Speak: The Story of Archaeology in Italy,* 2nd edn. W. W. Norton, New York & London.

Mackinnon, L. (2001) Rev. of Seamus Heaney, *Electric Light. Daily Telegraph,* March 31, 2001, Arts and Books section, p. 5.

Maclean, I. (1980) *The Renaissance Notion of the Woman: A Study in the Fortunes of Scholasticism and Medical Science in European Intellectual Life.* Cambridge University Press, Cambridge.

Mączak, A., Samsonowicz, H., & Burke, P. (1985) *East-Central Europe in Transition: From the Fourteenth to the Seventeenth Century.* Cambridge University Press, Cambridge.

Magnuson, T. (1981) *Rome in the Age of Bernini: From the Election of Sixtus V to the Death of Urban VIII.* Kungliga vitterhets, historie och antikvitets akademiens handlingar. Humanities Press, Atlantic Highland.

Magnússon, S. A. (1989) A Bird's-Eye View of Icelandic Culture. In Freeman, J. (ed.) *Landscapes from a High Latitude: Icelandic Art 1909–1989.* Lund Humphries, London, 15–19.

Mahony, P. J. (1987) *Freud as a Writer.* Yale University Press, New Haven & London.

Malamud, M. (2001) Brooklyn-on-the-Tiber. Roman Comedy on Broadway and in Film. In Joshel, Malamud, & McGuire (2001): 191–208.

Malherbe, D. F. (1943) Demetrios. In *Die meul dreun: En ander Toneelwerk.* Nasionale Pers Beperk, Cape Town, 93–165.

Malitz, J. (1998) Römertum im "Dritten Reich": Hans Oppermann. In Kneissl, P. & Losemann, V. (eds.) *Imperium Romanum: Studien zu Geschichte und Rezeption. Festschrift für Karl Christ zum 75. Geburtstag.* F. Steiner, Stuttgart, 519–43.

Malvano, L. (1988) *Fascismo e politica dell'immagine.* Bollati Boringhieri, Turin.

Mandela, N. (1994) *Long Walk to Freedom.* Abacus, London.

Mandelstam, O. (1979) *Critical Prose and Letters,* trans. J. G. Harris & C. Link. Ardis Publishers, Ann Arbor.

Mandelstam, O. (1986) *The Noise of Time: The Prose of Osip Mandelstam,* trans. C. Brown. North Point Press, San Francisco.

Mangan, J. A. (1999) Icon of Monumental Brutality: Art and the Aryan Man. In Mangan, J. A. (ed.) *Shaping the Superman: Fascist Body as Political Icon.* Frank Cass, London, 128–52.

Manganaro, M. (1994) Anthropological Theory and Criticism. In Groden, M. & Kreisworth, M. (eds.) *The Johns Hopkins Guide to Literary Theory & Criticism.* Johns Hopkins University Press, Baltimore, 26–30.

Manitius, M. (1911–31) *Geschichte der lateinischen Literatur des Mittelalters*, 3 vols. C. H. Beck, Munich.

Mann, J. (1987) *Ysengrimus: Text with Translation, Commentary and Introduction.* Brill, Leiden.

Mann Phillips, M. (1970) *Erasmus and the Classics.* In Dorey, T. A. (ed.) *Erasmus.* Routledge and Kegan Paul, London, 1–30.

Map, W. (1983) *Courtier's Trifles*, ed. and trans. M. R. James. Clarendon Press, Oxford.

Marasso, A. (1947) *Cervantes.* Academia Argentina de Letras, Buenos Aires.

March, K. & Passman, K. (1993) The Amazon Myth and Latin America. In Haase & Reinhold (1994): 285–338.

Marchand, S. (1996) *Down from Olympus: Archaeology and Philhellenism in Germany, 1750–1970.* Princeton University Press, Princeton.

Marden, C. C. (1976) *Libro de Apollonio: An Old Spanish Poem.* Kraus Reprints, Milwood.

Marder, T. A. (1998) *Bernini and the Art of Architecture.* Abbeville Press, New York.

Marenbon, J. (1987) *Later Medieval Philosophy (1150–1350): An Introduction.* Routledge and Kegan Paul, London.

Maritz, J. (1996) Some Thoughts on the Classical Allusions in the Work of M. B. Zimunya. *Akroterion* 41, 151–60.

Markley, A. A. (2004) *Stateliest Measures: Tennyson and the Literature of Greece and Rome.* University of Toronto Press, Toronto.

Marrou, H. I. (1956) *A History of Education in Antiquity.* Sheed and Ward, London.

Marsh, D. (1980) *The Quattrocento Dialogue: Classical Tradition and Humanist Innovation.* Harvard University Press, Cambridge, Mass. & London.

Martí, J. (2002) *Selected Writings.* Penguin Books, Harmondsworth & New York.

Martin, H. J. (1996) *The French Book.* Johns Hopkins University Press, Baltimore.

Martin, J. (1984) John of Salisbury as Classical Scholar. In Wilks, M. J. (ed.) *The World of John of Salisbury.* Published for the Ecclesiastical History Society by Basil Blackwell, Oxford, 179–201.

Martin, J. M. (1982) Classicism and Style in Latin Literature. In Benson & Constable (1982): 537–68.

Martindale, C. (ed.) (1988) *Ovid Renewed: Ovidian Influences on Literature and Art from the Middle Ages to the Twentieth Century.* Cambridge University Press, Cambridge.

Martindale, C. (1993) *Redeeming the Text: Latin Poetry and the Hermeneutics of Reception.* Cambridge University Press, Cambridge.

Martindale, C. (1995–6) Ruins of Time: T. S. Eliot and the Presence of the Past. *Arion* (3rd ser.) 3:2/3 (fall/winter), 102–40.

Martindale, C. (2000) Shakespeare's Ovid, Ovid's Shakespeare: A Methodological Postscript. In Taylor, A. B. (ed.) *Shakespeare's Ovid: The Metamorphoses in the Plays and Poems.* Cambridge University Press, Cambridge, 198–215.

Martindale, C. (2005) *Latin Poetry and the Judgement of Taste: An Essay in Aesthetics.* Oxford University Press, Oxford.

Martindale, C. & Hopkins, D. (eds.) (1993) *Horace Made New: Horatian Influences on British Writing from the Renaissance to the Twentieth Century.* Cambridge University Press, Cambridge.

Martindale, C. & Thomas, R. F. (eds.) (2006) *Classics and the Uses of Reception.* Blackwell, Malden & Oxford.

Martinez, R. L. (1995) Dante and the Two Canons: Statius in Virgil's Footsteps (*Purgatorio* 21–30). *Comparative Literature Studies* 32, 151–75.

Martins, J. V. de Pina & Asensio, E. (1982) *Luis de Camões. El humanismo en su obra poética. Los Lusiadas y las Rimas en la poesía española (1560–1640)*. Fondaçao Calouste Gulbenkian, Paris.

Mason, H. A. (1988) Is Martial a Classic? *Cambridge Quarterly* 17, 297–368.

Mason, P. (1993) Classical Ethnography and Its Influence on the European Perception of the Peoples of the New World. In Haase & Reinhold (1993): 135–72.

Mateo Gómez, I. (1979) *Temas profanos en la escultura gótica española. Las sillerías de coro*. Instituto Diego Velásquez, Madrid.

Mather, C. (1977) *Magnalia Christi Americana. Books I and II*. Ed. K. B. Murdock, with the assistance of E. W. Miller. Belknap Press, Cambridge, Mass.

Maurens, J. (1966) *La Tragèdie sans tragique: le neo-stoïcisme dans l'oeuvre de Pierre Corneille*. A. Colin, Paris.

Maurer, W. R. (1982) *Gerhart Hauptmann*. Twayne Publishers, Boston.

Mayer, M. (ed.) (2005) *Basquiat*. Brooklyn Museum of Art, Brooklyn.

Mazza, M. (1978) Nazionalsocialismo e storia antica. *Studi romani* 26, 145–60.

McCarthy, G. (1999) Karl Marx and Classical Antiquity: A Bibliographic Introduction. *Helios* 26:2, 165–73.

McDonald, M. (1992), *Ancient Sun, Modern Light: Greek Drama on the Modern Stage*. Columbia University Press, New York.

McDonald, M. (2000) Black Dionysus: Greek Tragedy from Africa. In Hardwick, Easterling, Ireland, Macintosh, & Lowe (2000): 95–108.

McDonald, M. and Walton, J. M. (2002), *Amid our Troubles: Irish Versions of Greek Tragedy*. Methuen, London.

McFarland, T. (1981) *Romanticism and the Forms of Ruin: Wordsworth, Coleridge, and Modalities of Fragmentation*. Princeton University Press, Princeton.

McFee, G. & Tomlinson, A. (1999) Riefenstahl's *Olympia*: Ideology and Aesthetics in the Shaping of the Aryan Athletic Body. In Mangan, J. A. (ed.) *Shaping the Superman: Fascist Body as Political Icon*. Frank Cass, London, 86–106.

McLane, M. (2001) Ballads and Bards: British Romantic Orality. *Modern Philology* 98, 423–43.

McManus, B. (1997) *Classics and Feminism: Gendering the Classics*. Twayne, New York.

McNeal, R. A. (ed.) (1993) *Nicholas Biddle in Greece: The Journals and Letters of 1806*. Pennsylvania State University Press, University Park.

Meade, T. A. & Wiesner-Hanks, M. E. (2003) *A Companion to Gender History*. Blackwell, Oxford.

Meagher, R. E. (1995) *Helen: Myth, Legend, and the Culture of Misogyny*. Continuum, New York.

Medcalf, S. (1988) T. S. Eliot's *Metamorphoses*: Ovid and *The Waste Land*. In Martindale, C. (ed.) *Ovid Renewed: Ovidian Influences on Literature and Art from the Middle Ages to the Twentieth Century*. Cambridge, Cambridge University Press, 233–46.

Medcalf, S. (1993) Horace's Kipling. In Martindale & Hopkins (1993): 217–39.

Menéndez Pelayo, M. (1950–3) *Bibliografía hispano-latina clásica*, 10 vols. CSIC, Madrid.

Menéndez Pelayo, M. (1952–3) *Biblioteca de traductores españoles*, 4 vols. CSIC, Madrid.

Menéndez Pelayo, M. (1962) *Historia de las ideas estéticas en España*. CSIC, Madrid.

Merisalo O. & Sarasti-Wilenius, R. (eds.) (1994) *Mare Balticum Mare Nostrum. Latin in the Countries of the Baltic Sea (1500–1800)*. Gummerus Kirjapaino Oy, Jyväskylä.

Merisalo O. & Sarasti-Wilenius, R. (eds.) (2003) *Erudition and Eloquence: The Use of Latin in the Countries of the Baltic Sea (1500–1800).* Gummerus Kirjapaino Oy, Saarijärvi.

Merrill, L. (1992) *A Pot of Paint: Aesthetics on Trial in Whistler v Ruskin.* Smithsonian Institution Press, Washington & London.

Merton, R. K. (1965) *On the Shoulders of Giants: A Shandean Postscript.* Free Press, New York.

Meyer, D. (ed.) (1994) *Playing out the Empire:* Ben Hur *and Other Toga Plays and Films, 1883–1908. A Critical Anthology.* Clarendon, Oxford.

Mezzabotta, M. (2000) Ancient Greek Drama in the New South Africa. In Hardwick, Easterling, Ireland, Macintosh, & Lowe (2000): 246–68.

Michael, I. (1970) *The Treatment of Classical Material in the "Libro de Alexandre."* Manchester University Press, Manchester.

Michalski, S. (1998), *Public Monuments: Art in Political Bondage 1870–1997.* Reaktion Books, London.

Michel, A. (1986) Scaliger entre Aristote et Virgile. In Cubelier de Beynac, J. & Magnien, M. (eds.) *Acta Scaligeriana: actes du Colloque international organisé pour le cinquième centenaire de la naissance de Jules-César Scaliger* (Agen, septembre 14–16, 1984). Société Académique d'Agen, Agen.

Middlekauff, R. (1963) *Ancients and Axioms: Secondary Education in Eighteenth-Century New England.* Yale University Press, New Haven.

Miller, P. A. (1999) The Classical Roots of Post-Structuralism: Lacan, Derrida, Foucault. *International Journal of the Classical Tradition* 5, 204–25.

Miller, P. N. (2000) *Peiresc's Europe: Learning and Virtue in the Seventeenth Century.* Yale University Press, New Haven & London.

Millon, H. A. & Nochlin, L. (eds.) (1978) *Art and Architecture in the Service of Politics.* Massachusetts Institute of Technology Press, Cambridge, Mass.

Minnis, A. J. (1988) *Medieval Theory of Authorship: Scholastic Literary Attitudes in the Later Middle Ages*, 2nd edn. Aldershot: Scolar Press.

Minnis, A. J. & Scott, A. B. (eds.) (1991) *Medieval Literary Theory and Criticism, c.1100–c.1375: The Commentary Tradition*, 2nd edn. Clarendon Press, Oxford.

Miranda Cancela, E. (2003) *La tradición helénica en Cuba.* Editorial Arte y Literatura, Havana.

Mitchell, L. (1980) *Holland House.* Duckworth, London.

Mitchell-Boyask, R. N. (1994) Freud's Reading of Classical Literature and Classical Philology. In Gilman, S. L. et al. (ed.) *Reading Freud's Reading.* New York University Press, New York, 23–46.

Mittig, H.-E. (2001) Nationalsozialismus. In Landfester et al. (2001): vol. 15.1, cols. 723–67.

Moatti, C. (1993) *The Search for Ancient Rome*, trans. A. Zielonka. Harry N. Abrams, New York.

Modzelewski, K. (forthcoming) *L'Europe des barbares.* Flammarion, Paris.

Moir, D. & Wilson, E. M. (1971) *The Golden Age: Drama, 1492–1700.* Benn, London.

Mokhtar, G. (ed.) (1980) *Histoire générale de l'Afrique*, vol. 2: *Afrique ancienne.* Jeune Afrique-Stock-UNESCO, Paris.

Momigliano, A. (1982) *New Paths of Classicism in the Nineteenth Century.* History and Theory: Studies in the Philosophy of History Beiheft 21. Wesleyan University Press, Middletown.

Momigliano, A. (1987) Classical Scholarship for a Classical Country: The Case of Italy in the Nineteenth and Twentieth Centuries. In *Ottavo contribuito alla storia degli studi classici e del mondo antico*. Laterza, Rome & Bari, 73–89.

Momigliano, A. (1996) *Pace e libertà nel mondo antico. Lezioni a Cambridge, gennaio-marzo 1940*, ed. R. Di Donato. La Nuova Italia, Florence.

Mommsen, T. E. (1942) Petrarch's Conception of the "Dark Ages." *Speculum* 17, 226–42.

Monfasani, J. (1992) Episodes of Anti-Quintilianism in the Italian Renaissance: Quarrels on the Orator as a *Vir bonus* and Rhetoric as the *Scientia bene dicendi*. *Rhetorica* 10, 119–38.

Montagu, J. (1993) *Roman Baroque Sculpture: The Industry of Art*. Yale University Press, New Haven & London.

Montague, H. W. (1994) From Interlude in Aracady to Daphnis and Chloe: Two Thousand Years of Erotic Fantasy. In Tatum, J. (ed.) *The Search for the Ancient Novel*. Johns Hopkins University Press, Baltimore & London, 391–401.

Moore, C. & Attoe, W. (eds.) (1986) *Ah Mediterranean! Twentieth Century Classicism in America*. Rizzoli, New York.

Morawski, K. (1911). *Proza w epoce cyceroński ej. M. Tullius Cicero: życie i dzieła*. Akademia Umiejętności, Kraków.

Morford, M. (1991) *Stoics and Neostoics: Rubens and the Circle of Lipsius*. Princeton University Press, Princeton.

Morgan, T. (1998) *Literate Education in the Hellenistic and Roman Worlds*. Cambridge University Press, Cambridge & New York.

Morreale, M. (1988) [Virgilio en Spagna] Letteratura Castigliana. In Della Corte (1988): 4:956a–972a.

Morreale, M. (2002) El nuevo mundo en las "notaciones" de Juan de Guzmán a su version de las *Geórgicas* (1586). *Bulletin hispanique* 2 (December), 577–626.

Morrissey, J. (2005) *The Genius in the Design: Bernini, Borromini, and the Rivalry That Transformed Rome*. William Morrow, New York.

Moss, A. (1982) *Ovid in Renaissance France: A Survey of the Latin Editions of Ovid and Commentaries Printed in France before 1600*. Warburg Institute Surveys 8. Warburg Institute, London.

Moss, A. (1996) *Printed Commonplace-Books and the Structuring of Renaissance Thought*. Oxford University Press, Oxford.

Mosse, G. (1964) *The Crisis of German Ideology: Intellectual Origins of the Third Reich*. Macmillan, London.

Mosse, G. (1966) *Nazi Culture: Intellectual, Cultural, and Social Life in the Third Reich*. W. H. Allen, London.

Mosse, G. (1980) *Masses and Man: Nationalist and Fascist Perspectives of Reality*. H. Fertig, New York.

Mosse, G. (1999) *The Fascist Revolution*. H. Fertig, New York.

Most, G. (1997) One Hundred Years of Fractiousness: Disciplining Polemics in Nineteenth-century German Classical Scholarship. *Transactions of the American Philological Association* 127, 349–61.

Mouchel C. (1990) *Cicéron et Sénèque dans la rhétorique de la Renaissance*. Hitzeroth, Marburg.

Mouchel, C. (1996) *Juste Lipse (1547–1606) en son temps. Actes du colloque de Strasbourg, 1994*. Colloques, congrès et conférences sur la Renaissance 6. H. Champion, Paris.

Mulroy, D. (2003) *The War against Grammar*. Boynton/Cook, Portsmouth.

Munich, A. (1989) *Andromeda's Chains: Gender and Interpretation in Victorian Literature and Art*. Columbia University Press, New York.

Munk Olsen, B. (1982–9) *L'Étude des auteurs classiques latins au XIe et XIIe siècles*, 3 vols. Études des Centre national de la recherche scientifique, Paris.

Munk Olsen, B. (1991) *I classici nel canone scolastico altomedievale*. Quaderni di cultura mediolatina 1. Centro Italiano di Studi sull'Alto Medioevo, Spoleto.

Munk Olsen, B. & Friis-Jensen, K. (1997) *Medieval and Renaissance Scholarship*. E. J. Brill, Leiden.

Munk Olsen, B. with Leonardi C. (1995) *The Classical Tradition in the Middle Ages and Renaissance*. Centro Italiano di Studi sull'Alto Medioevo, Spoleto.

Murata, M. (ed.) (1997) *Strunk's Source Readings in Baroque Music*, vol. 4: *The Baroque Era*. R. S. Means, Kingston.

Murray, D. (1992) Elektra. In Sadie, S. (ed.) *The New Grove Dictionary of Opera*. Macmillan, London, 2:32–5.

Nader, H. (1979) *The Mendoza Family in the Spanish Renaissance, 1350–1550*. Rutgers University Press, New Brunswick.

Näf, B. (1986) *Von Perikles zu Hitler: Die athenische Demokratie und die deutsche Althistorie bis 1945*. P. Lang, Bern.

Näf, B. (1992) Werner Jaegers *Paideia*: Entstehung, kulturpolitische Absichten und Rezeption. In Calder (1992): 125–46.

Näf, B. (ed.) (2001) *Antike und Altertumswissenschaft in der Zeit von Faschismus und Nationalsozialismus. Kolloquium Universität Zürich 14.–17. Oktober 1998*. Edition Cicero, Mandelbachtel and Cambridge.

Narducci, E. (2004) Appunti sulla fortuna del *De officiis* nelle lettere italiane (de Baldassar Castiglione a Carlo Emilio Gadda). In E. Narducci (ed.) *Cicerone tra antichi e moderni. Atti del IV Symposium Ciceronianum Arpinas*. Felice Le Monnier, Florence, 38–55.

Nellen, H. J. M. (1985) *Hugo de Groot (1583–1645): De loopbaan van een geleerd staatsman*. Heureka, Weesp.

Neruda, P. (1971) El mensajero. In *Don Alonso de Ercilla, inventor de Chile*. Pomaire, Santiago de Chile, 9–12.

Ngugi wa Thiong'o (1986), *Decolonising the Mind*. Heinemann, Oxford, Nairobi, Portsmouth.

Niederehe, H.-J. (1987) *Alfonso X el Sabio y la lingüística de su tiempo*. SGEL, Madrid.

Nietzsche, F. (1956) *The Birth of Tragedy and the Genealogy of Morals*. Doubleday Anchor, New York. Originally pub. in 1872 as *The Birth of Tragedy, Out of the Spirit of Music* (*Die Geburt der Tragödie aus dem Geiste der Musik*). Reissued in 1886 with the title *The Birth of Tragedy, Or: Hellenism and Pessimism* (*Die Geburt der Tragödie, Oder: Griechentum und Pessimismus*).

Niklaus, R. (1970). *A Literary History of France: The Eighteenth Century*. Ernest Benn, London.

Nippel, W. (ed.) (1993) *Über das Studium der alten Geschichte*. Deutscher Taschenbuch, Munich.

Nisard, J. M. N. D. (1834) *Études de moeurs et de critique sur les poètes latins de la décadence*, 3 vols. Louis Hauman, Brussels.

Nivardus (1987) *Ysengrimus: Text with Translation, Commentary and Introduction*, ed. J. Mann. E. J. Brill, Leiden & New York.

Niven, W. (2000) The Birth of Nazi Drama? *Thing*-plays. In London, J. (ed.) *Theatre under the Nazis*. Manchester University Press, Manchester, 54–95.

Noakes, J. (1993) The Ivory Tower under Siege: German Universities in the Third Reich. *Journal of European Studies* 23, 371–407.

Nolan, B. (1992) *Chaucer and the Tradition of the Roman Antique.* Cambridge Studies in Medieval Literature 15. Cambridge University Press, Cambridge.

Nolte, E. (1966) *Three Faces of Fascism: Action Française, Italian Fascism, and National Socialism,* trans. L. Vennewitz. Holt Rinehart & Winston, New York.

Norberg, D. (2004) *An Introduction to the Study of Medieval Latin Versification,* trans. G. C. Roti & J. Skubly, ed. J. M. Ziolkowski. Catholic University of America Press, Washington.

Norton, G. P. (ed.) (1999) *The Cambridge History of Literary Criticism,* vol. 3: *The Renaissance.* Cambridge University Press, Cambridge.

Nova, F. (1986) *Alfred Rosenberg, Nazi Theorist of the Holocaust.* Hippocrene Books, New York.

Nuñez, C. Fragale Pate (2003) A tradiçao clássica no Brasil. In Grammatico Amari, Arbea Gavilán, & Edwards (2003): 1:217–57.

Obenga, T. (1995) *A Lost Tradition: African Philosophy in World History.* Source Editions, Philadelphia.

O'Connor, F. V. & Thaw, E. V. (1978) *Jackson Pollock: A Catalogue Raisonné of Paintings, Drawings, and Other Works.* Yale University Press, New Haven.

O'Daly, G. (2004) S*unt etiam Musis sua ludicra*: Vergil in Ausonius. In Reese, R. (ed.) *"Romane memento": Vergil in the Fourth Century.* Duckworth, London, 141–54.

Oestreich, G. & Mout, N. (1989) *Antiker Geist und moderner Staat bei Justus Lipsius (1547–1606): Der Neustoizismus als politische Bewegung.* Schriftenreihe der Historischen Kommission bei der Bayerischen Akademie der Wissenschaften 38. Vandenhoek & Ruprecht, Göttingen.

Ogilvie, R. M. (1964) *Latin and Greek: A History of the Influence of the Classics on English Life from 1600 to 1918.* Routledge & Kegan Paul, London.

Okenfuss, M. J. (1995) *The Rise and Fall of Latin Humanism in Early-Modern Russia*: *Pagan Authors, Ukrainians, and the Resiliency of Muscovy.* E. J. Brill, Leiden.

Okpewho, I. (1991) Soyinka, Euripides and the Anxiety of Empire. *Research in African Literatures* 30:4, 32–55.

O'Neill, E. (1931) *Mourning Becomes Electra: A Trilogy.* Horace Liveright, New York.

Ong, W. J. (1959) Latin Language Study as a Renaissance Puberty Rite. *Studies in Philology* 56, 103–24.

Ong, W. J. (1982) *Orality and Literacy: The Technologizing of the Word.* Methuen, New York.

Opperman, D. J. (1945) *Heilige beeste.* Nasionale Pers Beperk, Cape Town.

Opperman, D. J. (1956) *Vergelegen.* Nasionale Boekhandel Beperk, Cape Town.

Opperman, D. J. (1960) *Periandros van Korinthe.* Nasionale Boekhandel Beperk, Cape Town.

Oppermann, H. (1933) Der erzieherische Wert des lateinische Unterrichts. In Gieselbusch et al. (1933): 50–8.

Orme, N. (1973) *English Schools in the Middle Ages.* Methuen, New York.

Ormond, L. (1975) *Lord Leighton.* Yale University Press, New Haven.

Orozco, T. (1995) *Platonische Gewalt: Gadamers politische Hermeneutik der NS-Zeit.* Argument-Verlag, Hamburg.

Osborne, J. (trans.) (1987) Master Gregorius, *The Marvels of Rome.* Mediaeval Sources in Translation 31. Pontifical Institute of Mediaeval Studies, Toronto.

Òsòfisan, F. (1998) The Revolution as Muse. Drama as Surreptitious Insurrection in a Post-colonial, Military State. In Boon, R. & Plastow, J. (eds.) *Theatre Matters: Performance and Culture on the World Stage*. Cambridge University Press, Cambridge, 11–35.

Òsòfisan, F. (1999a) Theater and the Rites of "Post-Négritude" Remembering. *Research in African Literatures* 30:1 (spring), 1–11.

Òsòfisan, F. (1999b) Tegonni: An African Antigone, in *Recent Outings: Comprising Tegonni: An African Antigone, and Many Colours Make the Thunder King*. Opon Ifa Readers, Ibadan, 5–141.

Òsòfisan, F. (2004) *Women of Owu*. Performance directed by C. Mike at The Theatre, Chipping Norton, February 2, 2004.

Osorio Romero, I. (1990) *La enseñanza de latín a los indios*. UNAM, Mexico City.

Ostenfeld, E. (1987) *Ancient Greek Psychology and the Modern Mind–Body Debate*. Aarhus University Press, Aarhus.

Ozsváth, Z. (2000) *In the Footsteps of Orpheus: The Life and Times of Miklós Radnóti*. Indiana University Press, Bloomington.

Paduano, G. (1994) *Lunga storia di Edipo re*. Einaudi, Turin.

Passman, K. M. (1991) The Classical Amazon in Contemporary Cinema. *Bucknell Review* 35:1, 81–105.

Patsalidis, S. & Sakellaridou, E. (eds.) (1999) *(Dis)Placing Classical Greek Theatre*. University Studio Press, Thessaloniki.

Paulin, T. (1985), *The Riot Act: A Version of Sophocles' Antigone*. Faber and Faber, London.

Paxson, J. J. & Gravalee, C. A. (eds.) (1998) *Desiring Discourse: The Literature of Love, Ovid through Chaucer*. Susquehanna University Press, Selinsgrove.

Paz, O. (1988) *Sor Juana, or the Traps of Faith*. Harvard University Press, Cambridge, Mass.

Peacock, S. J. (1988) *Jane Ellen Harrison: The Mask and the Self*. Yale University Press, New Haven.

Pells, R. (2006) *From Modernism to the Movies: The Globalization of American Culture in the 20th Century*. Yale University Press, New Haven.

Penrose, R. (1973) Beauty and the Monster. In Penrose, R., Golding, J., & Kahnweiler, D. H. (eds.) *Picasso in Retrospect*. Harper and Row, New York.

Perrault, C. (1964) *Parallèle des anciens et des modernes*, ed. H. R. Jauss. Eidos, Munich.

Petrarca, F. (1975) *De otio religioso*. In A. Bufano (ed.) *Opere latine*. Unione Tipografico-Editrice Torinese, Turin, 1:567–809.

Petropoulos, J. (1996) *Art as Politics in the Third Reich*. University of North Carolina, Chapel Hill.

Pétursson, S. (1995) Iceland. In Jensen (1995): 96–128.

Pfeiffer, R. (1935) Review of Werner Jaeger, *Paideia: Die Formung des griechischen Menschen*, I. *Deutsche Literaturzeitung* 56, 2126–34, 2169–78, 2213–19.

Pfeiffer, R. (1976) *History of Classical Scholarship 1300–1850*. Clarendon Press, Oxford.

Pfister, F. (1934) Der politische Humanismus. *Bayerische Blätter für das Gymnasial-Schulwesen* 70, 65–77.

Phillippo, S. (2003) *Silent Witness: Racine's Non-Verbal Annotations of Euripides*. Legenda, Oxford.

Phillips, H. (1980) *The Theatre and Its Critics in Seventeenth-Century France*. Oxford University Press, Oxford.

Picchio, R. (1984) Guidelines for a Comparative Study of the Language Question Among the Slavs. In Picchio, R. & Goldblatt, H. (eds.) *Aspects of the Slavic Language Question*. Yale Concilium on International and Area Studies, New Haven, 1:1–42.

Picker, H. (1976) *Hitlers Tischgespräche im Führerhauptquartier: Mit bisher unbekannten Selbstzeugnissen Adolf Hitlers*. Seewald, Stuttgart.

Picone, M. (ed.) (1984) *L'enciclopedismo medievale*. Longo Editore, Ravenna.

Pigeaud, J. (1994) L'Antiquité et les débuts de la psychiatrie française. In Postel, J. & Quetel, C. (eds.) *Nouvelle histoire de la psychiatrie*. Dunod, Paris, 129–46. Originally pub. in 1983 by Privat, Toulouse.

Pineda, V. (1994) *La imitación como arte literario en el siglo XVI español, con una edición y traducción del diálogo "De Imitatione" de Sebastián Fox Morcillo*. Diputación provincial, Seville.

Pinel, P. (1962). *A Treatise on Insanity*, trans. P. F. Cranefield. Hafner, New York.

Piotrovksy, M. et al. (2005) *Peter Paul Rubens: A Touch of Brilliance*. Prestel, New York.

Platt, L. (1998) *Joyce and the Anglo-Irish: A Study of Joyce and the Literary Revival*. Rodopi, Amsterdam.

Pocock, J. G. A. (1975) *The Macchiavellian Moment: Florentine Political Thought and the Atlantic Republican Tradition*. Princeton University Press, Princeton.

Polcari, S. (1991) *Abstract Expressionism and the Modern Experience*. Cambridge University Press, Cambridge & New York.

Politzer, H. (1974) *Hatte Ödipus einen Ödipuscomplex?* Piper, Munich.

Pomeroy, S. B. (1973) Selected Bibliography on Women in Antiquity. *Arethusa* 6, 125–52.

Pomeroy, S. B. (1975) *Goddesses, Whores, Wives, Woman and Slaves*. Shocken, New York.

Pomeroy, S. B. with Kraemer, R. S. & Kampen, N. (1984) Selected Bibliography on Women in Antiquity, Part II, 1973–81. In Peradotto, J. & Sullivan, J. P. (eds.) *Women in the Ancient World*. The *Arethusa* Papers. State University of New York Press, Albany.

Pope, A. (1965) *Poems*, ed. J. Butt. Methuen, London.

Pope, A. (1967) *Iliad of Homer*, ed. M. Mack, 2 vols. Methuen, London.

Porter, R. & Teich, M. (eds.) (1994) *The Renaissance in National Context*. Cambridge University Press, Cambridge.

Posidonius (1972–99) *The Fragments*, ed. L. Edelstein and I. G. Kidd. Cambridge University Press, Cambridge.

Potolsky, M. et al. (2004) *Forms and / of Decadence. New Literary History* 35:4, v–xi.

Potts, A. (1994) *Flesh and the Ideal: Winckelmann and the Origins of Art History*. Yale University Press, New Haven.

Pound, E. (1971) *Selected Letters of Ezra Pound, 1907–1941*, ed. D. D. Paige. New Directions, New York.

Prettejohn, E. (2006) Reception and Ancient Art: The Case of the *Venus de Milo*. In Martindale & Thomas (2006): 151–66.

Price, S. R. F. (1986) The Future of Dreams: From Artemidorus. *Past and Present* 113, 3–37. Rpt. in Osborne R. (ed.) *Studies in Ancient Greek and Roman Society*. Cambridge University Press, Cambridge, 226–59.

Prins, Y. (1999a) Greek Maenads, Victorian Spinsters. In Dellamore, R. (ed.) *Victorian Sexual Dissidence*. University of Chicago Press, Chicago, 42–82.

Prins, Y. (1999b) *Victorian Sappho*. Princeton University Press, Princeton.

Programme Notes (1991) Production of S. Heaney's *The Cure at Troy*, Tricycle Theatre, Kilburn, London.

Prost, A. (1986) *Histoire de l'enseignement en France, 1800–1967*, 6th edn. Armand Colin, Paris.

Putnam, M. C. J. & Ziolkowski, J. M. (forthcoming) *The Virgilian Tradition to 1500*. Yale University Press, New Haven.

Pym, A. (2000) *Negotiating the Frontier: Translators and Intercultures in Hispanic History.* St. Jerome Publishing, Manchester.

Quayson, A. (2002) *Strategic Transformations in Nigerian Writing.* Indiana University Press, Bloomington.

Quinn, J. T. (2000) The Ancient Rome of Adolf Hitler. *Classical Bulletin* 76, 141–56.

Quint, D. (1993) *Epic and Empire: Politics and Generic Form from Virgil to Milton.* Princeton University Press, Princeton.

Raabyemagle, H. & Smidt, C. M. (eds.) (1998) *Classicism in Copenhagen: Architecture in the Age of C. F. Hansen*, trans. J. Lundskær-Nielsen, photographs by Jens Lindhe. Gyldendals Forlag, Copenhagen.

Rabelais, F. (1994) *Œuvres complètes*, ed. Mireille Huchon, with the assistance of François Moreau. Bibliothèque de la Pléiade. Gallimard, Paris.

Rabil, A., Jr. (ed.) (1988) *Renaissance Humanism: Foundations, Forms and Legacy*, 3 vols. University of Pennsylvania Press, Philadelphia.

Raby, F. J. E. (1957) *A History of Secular Latin Poetry in the Middle Ages*, 2 vols. Clarendon Press, Oxford. 2nd edn., rpt. 1967.

Rahe, P. (1992) *Republics Ancient and Modern: Classical Republicanism and the American Revolution.* University of North Carolina Press, Chapel Hill.

Ramazani, J. (1997) The Wound of History: Walcott's *Omeros* and the Post-colonial Poetics of Affliction. *Proceedings of the Modern Literature Association* 112:3, 405–15.

Ransohoff, A. (1975) Sigmund Freud, Collector of Antiquities, Student of Archaeology. *Archaeology* 28, 102–11.

Rapacka, J. (2004) Funkcje łaciny w regionalnych i ogólnonarodowych systemach kultury chorwackiej. In Axer (2004): 375–92.

Rawson, E. (1969) *The Spartan Tradition in European Thought.* Oxford University Press, Oxford.

Rebuck, G. (2004) Word Power. *Guardian* review, March 13, 2004, 34–5.

Reed, R. (1975) *The Nature and Making of Parchment.* Elmete, Leeds.

Reeve, M. D. (2001) Reception / History of Scholarship: Introduction. In Harrison (2001): 245–51.

Reeves, G. (1989) *T. S. Eliot: A Virgilian Poet.* St. Martin's Press, New York.

Rehm, R. (2002) *The Play of Space: Spatial Transformation in Greek Tragedy.* Princeton University Press, Princeton.

Rehm, R. (2003) *Radical Greek Theatre: Greek Tragedy and the Modern World.* Duckworth, London.

Rehm, W. (1968) *Griechentum und Goethezeit: Geschichte eines Glaubens*, 4th edn. Francke, Bern & Munich.

Reinhold, M. (1984) *Classica Americana, The Greek and Roman Heritage in the United States.* Wayne State University Press, Detroit.

Reynolds, L. D. (ed.) (1983) *Texts and Transmission: A Survey of the Latin Classics.* Clarendon Press, Oxford.

Reynolds, L. D. & Wilson, N. G. (1991) *Scribes and Scholars: A Guide to the Transmission of Greek and Latin Literature*, 3rd edn. Clarendon Press, Oxford.

Reynolds, M. (2003) *The Sappho History.* Palgrave Macmillan, New York.

Reynolds, S. (1996) *Medieval Reading: Grammar, Rhetoric and the Classical Text.* Cambridge University Press, Cambridge.

Richard, C. J. (1994) *The Founders and the Classics: Greece, Rome, and the American Enlightenment.* Harvard University Press, Cambridge, Mass.

Richards, D. (2000) Canvas of Blood: Okigbo's African Modernism. In Bery and Murray (2000): 229–39.

Richards, S. (1995) In the Border Country: Greek Tragedy and Contemporary Irish Drama. In Barfoot, C. C. and van der Doel, R. (eds.) *Ritual Remembering: History, Myth and Politics and Anglo-Irish Drama.* Rodopi, Amsterdam, 191–200.

Riché, P. (1976) *Education and Culture in the Barbarian West, Sixth through Eighth Centuries,* trans. J. J. Contreni. University of South Carolina Press, Columbia.

Riché, P. (1989) *Ecoles et enseignement dans le Haut Moyen Age: fin du Ve siècle – milieu du XIe siècle,* 2nd edn. Picard, Paris.

Ricks, D. (1989) *The Shade of Homer: A Study in Modern Greek Poetry.* Cambridge University Press, Cambridge.

Rico Verdú, J. (1973) *La retórica española de los siglos XVI y XVII.* CSIC, Madrid.

Ridley, R. T. (1992) *The Eagle and the Spade: Archaeology in Rome during the Napoleonic Era.* Cambridge University Press, Cambridge.

Riedel, V. (1996) *Literarische Antikerezeption: Aufsätze und Vorträge.* Jenaer Studien 2. Bussert & Partner, Jena.

Riedel, V. (2000) *Antikerezeption in der deutschen Literatur vom Renaissance-Humanismus bis zur Gegenwart: Eine Einführung.* J. B. Metzler, Stuttgart & Weimar.

Riedel, V. (2002) *"Der Beste der Griechen"–"Achill das Vieh". Aufsätze und Vorträge zur literarischen Antikerezeption II.* Jenaer Studien 5. Bussert & Stadeler, Jena.

Riley, K. (2004) Heracles as Dr. Strangelove and GI Joe. In Hall, Macintosh, & Wrigley (2004): 113–41.

Riou, Y.-F. (1991) Chronologie et provenance des manuscrits latins neumés. *Revue d'histoire des textes* 21, 77–113.

Rivas Sacconi, J. M. (1993) *El latín en Colombia: bosquejo histórico del humanismo colombiano.* Instituto Caro y Cuerva, Bogotá. Rpt. of 1949 edn.

Roberts, J. T. (1994) *Athens on Trial: The Antidemocratic Tradition in Western Thought.* Princeton University Press, Princeton.

Robertson, J. M. (1989) *Patriotism and Empire.* Richards, London.

Robinson, A. (2002) *The Life and Work of Jane Ellen Harrison.* Oxford University Press, Oxford.

Rojas F. de (1991) *Comedia o tragicomedia de Calisto y Melibea,* 2nd edn. Editorial Castalia, Madrid.

Rojas, F. de (2002) *Celestina comentada,* ed. L. Fothergill-Payne, E. F. Rivera, & P. Fothergill-Payne, with the collaboration of I. Corfis, M. García, & F. Plazolles. Textos recuperados 20. Ediciones Universidad de Salamanca, Salamanca.

Ronnick, M. V. (2004) *The Autobiography of William Sanders Scarborough: An American Journey from Slavery to Scholarship.* Wayne State University Press, Detroit.

Rooney, P. (1994) Recent Work in Feminist Discussions of Reason. *American Philosophical Quarterly* 31:1, 1–21.

Rose, M. A. (1993) *Parody: Ancient, Modern, and Post-modern.* Cambridge University Press, Cambridge & New York.

Rossi, A. (1998) *El primer renacimiento florentino. Ideas y presagios del descubrimiento de América.* UNAM, Mexico City.

Rossi, G. C. (1988) [Virgilio en] Portogallo. In della Corte (1988): 4:225a–227a.

Rothe, A. (1965) *Quevedo und Seneca*. Droz, Geneva & Paris.

Rotimi, O. (1971) *The Gods Are Not to Blame*. Oxford University Press, Oxford.

Rousseau, G. S. (1993) "A Strange Pathology": Hysteria in the Early Modern World, 1500–1800. In Gilman, S. et al. (eds.) *Hysteria Beyond Freud*. University of California Press, Berkeley & Los Angeles, 91–224.

Rousseau, J.-J. (1964) *The First and Second Discourses*, trans. R. and J. Masters. St. Martins, New York.

Rowland, B., Jr. (1963) *The Classical Tradition in Western Art*. Harvard University Press, Cambridge, Mass.

Rowland, I. D. (2004) *The Scarith of Scornello: A Tale of Renaissance Forgery*. University of Chicago Press, Chicago.

Royds, T. F. (1918) *Virgil and Isaiah: A Study of the Pollio*. Basil Blackwell, Oxford.

Royster, F. T. (2003) *Becoming Cleopatra: The Shifting Image of an Icon*. Palgrave Macmillan, New York.

Rubens, P. P., Woodall, J., et al. (2004) *Peter Paul Rubens: A Touch of Brilliance*. Prestel, Munich & London.

Rubin, W. (ed.) (1984) *"Primitivism" in 20th Century Art: An Affinity of the Tribal and the Modern*, 2 vols. Museum of Modern Art, New York.

Rudd, N. (1994) Chaucer and Virgil. Two Portraits of Dido. In *The Classical Tradition in Operation*. Robson Classical Lectures. University of Toronto Press, Toronto, Buffalo, & London, 3–31.

Rüdiger, H. (1970) Der Dritte Humanismus. In Oppermann, H. (ed.) *Humanismus*. Wissenschaftlicher Buchgesellschaft, Darmstadt, 206–23.

Rudnytsky, P. (1987) *Freud and Oedipus*. Columbia University Press, New York.

Rumens, C. (1987) *Selected Poems*. Chatto & Windus, London.

Russell, P. E. (ed.) (1991) *Comedia o tragicomedia de Calisto y Melibea*. Castalia, Madrid.

Rutter, C. (ed.) (1995) *Tony Harrison: Permanently Bard: Selected Poetry*. Bloodaxe Books, Newcastle upon Tyne.

Ryan, J. (1999) *Rilke, Modernism and Poetic Tradition*. Cambridge University Press, Cambridge.

Ryder, M. R. (1990) *Willa Cather and Classical Myth: The Search for a New Parnassus*. Edwin Mellen Press, Lewiston.

Rymer, T. (1956) *Critical Works*, ed. C. Zimansky. Yale University Press, New Haven.

Saïd, E. (1988a) Intellectual Exile: Expatriates and Marginals [1993]. In Bayoumi & Rubin (2001): 368–81.

Saïd, E. (1988b) Yeats and Decolonisation. In Bayoumi & Rubin (2001): 291–313.

Saïd, E. (1993), *Culture and Imperialism*. Chatto & Windus, London.

Saint Clair, W. (1967) *Lord Elgin and the Marbles*. Oxford University Press, London.

Sandy, G. (ed.) (2002) *The Classical Heritage in France*. E. J. Brill, Leiden, Boston, & Cologne.

Sandys, E. (1921) *A History of Classical Scholarship*, 3rd edn., 3 vols. Cambridge University Press, Cambridge.

Santas, G. (1988) *Plato and Freud: Two Theories of Love*. Blackwell, Oxford & New York.

Saslow, J. M. (1986) *Ganymede in the Renaissance: Homosexuality in Art and Society*. Yale University Press, New Haven.

Scaglione, A. (1990) The Classics in Medieval Education. In Bernardo & Levin (1989): 343–62.

Scaliger, J. C. (1561) *Poetices libri septem*. A. Vincent & J. Crespin, Lyon & Geneva.

Schachermeyr, F. (1933) Die nordische Führerpersönlichkeit im Altertum. In Gieselbusch et al. (1933): 36–43.

Schäche, W. (1979) Nationalsozialistische Architektur und Antikenrezeption. In Arenhövel, W. (ed.) *Berlin und die Antike Band II.* Deutsches Archäologisches Institut, Berlin, 558–71.

Schadewaldt, W. (1970) *Hellas und Hesperien Gesammelte Schriften zur Antike und zur neueren Literatur,* 2nd edn. Artemis, Zurich & Stuttgart.

Schäfer, W. (1943) *Wider die Humanisten.* Langen Müller, Munich.

Schama, S. (1995) *Landscape and Memory.* Vintage Books, New York.

Schmidt, D. J. (2001) *On Germans and Other Greeks: Tragedy and the Ethical Life.* Indiana University, Bloomington.

Schmitt, C. B. (1983) *Aristotle and the Renaissance.* Harvard University Press, Cambridge, Mass.

Schmitt, C. B. & Skinner, Q. (eds.) (1988) *The Cambridge History of Renaissance Philosophy.* Cambridge University Press, Cambridge.

Schmuhl, H.-W. (1992) *Rassenhygiene, Nationalsozialismus, Euthanasie.* Vandenhoeck & Ruprecht, Göttingen.

Schnapp, A. (1996) *The Discovery of the Past: The Origins of Archaeology.* British Museum Press, London.

Schnur, H. C. (1970) Dubious *Dicta? Classical Journal* 66, 70–1.

Schnur, R. (ed.) (forthcoming) *Acta Conventus Neo-Latini Bonnensis: Proceedings of the Twelfth International Congress of Neo-Latin Studies.* Arizona Center for Medieval and Renaissance Studies, Tempe.

Schoeman, K. (1984) *'n Ander land.* Human & Rousseau, Cape Town.

Schultze, C. E. (1999) Manliness and the Myth of Hercules in Charlotte M. Yonge's My Young Alcides. *International Journal of the Classical Tradition* 5:3, 383–414.

Schwartzman, M. (1990) *Romare Bearden His Life and Art.* Harry N. Abrams, New York.

Scobie, A. (1990) *Hitler's State Architecture: The Impact of Classical Antiquity.* Pennsylvania State University Press, University Park.

Scott, J. (2005) *Electra after Freud: Myth and Culture.* Cornell University Press, Ithaca.

Scott, J. B. (1991) *Images of Nepotism: The Painted Ceilings of Palazzo Barberini.* Princeton University Press, Princeton.

Screech, M. A. (1998) *Montaigne's Annotated Copy of Lucretius: A Transcription and Study of the Manuscript, Notes and Pen-marks.* Librairie Droz, Geneva.

Searle's Supreme Court Reports, Cape of Good Hope (S. Afr.) (1850–67), 5 vols. J. C. Juta, Cape Town.

Sebök, M. (ed.) (2005). *Republic of Letters, Humanism, Humanities.* Workshop Series No. 15 (Budapest November 25–28, 1999). Collegium Budapest, Budapest.

Sedgwick, E. K. (1990) *Epistemology of the Closet.* University of California Press, Berkeley.

Segal, C. (1989) *Orpheus: The Myth of the Poet.* Johns Hopkins University Press, Baltimore.

Segers, R. T. (1979) An Interview with Hans Robert Jauss. *New Literary History* 11, 83–95.

Seidel, M. (1976) *Epic Geography: James Joyce's Ulysses.* Princeton University Press, Princeton.

Seidensticker, B. (2003) *"Erinnern wird sich wohl noch mancher an uns ..." Studien zur Antikerezeption nach 1945.* Buchner, Bamberg.

Seidensticker, B. & Vöhler, M. (eds.) (2000) *Mythen in nachmythischer Zeit: Die Antike in der deutschsprachigen Literatur der Gegenwart.* W. de Gruyter, Berlin & New York.

Seidensticker, B. & Vöhler, M. (eds.) (2001) *Urgeschichten der Moderne: Die Antike im 20. Jahrhundert*. J. B. Metzler, Stuttgart & Weimar.

Selaiha, N. (2002) Antigone in Palestine. *Al Ahram Weekly*, no. 585, May 9–15, 2002, 16.

Selden, D. L. (1990) Classics and Contemporary Criticism. *Arion* 1, 155–78.

Seneca (1502) *Las epístolas de Séneca*. Pedro Haggenback, Toledo.

Seneca (1510) *Los cinco libros de Seneca*, trans. Alonso de Cartagena. N.p., Toledo.

Senghor, L. (1945) *Chants d'ombre*. Seuil, Paris.

Senghor, L. (1979) *Elégies majeures*. Seuil, Paris.

Ševčenko, I. (1984) The Many Worlds of Peter Mohyla. *Harvard Ukrainian Studies* 8:1–2, 9–44.

Ševčenko, I. (1991) *Byzantium and the Slavs in Letters and Culture*. Harvard Ukrainian Research Institute, Cambridge, Mass., & Istituto Universitario Orientale, Naples.

Ševčenko, I. (1996) *Ukraine between East and West: Essays on Cultural History (to the Early 1700's)*. Canadian Institute of Ukrainian Studies Press, Edmonton & Toronto.

Seznec, J. (1953) *The Survival of the Pagan Gods: The Mythological Tradition and Its Place in Renaissance Humanism and Art*, trans. B. F. Sessions. Princeton University Press, Princeton.

Shankman, S. (ed.) (1996) *The Iliad of Homer Translated by Alexander Pope*. Penguin Books, London.

Shetelig, H. (1949) *Classical Impulses in Scandinavian Art from the Migration Period to the Viking Age*. H. Aschehougs Forlag, Oslo.

Shields, J. C. (2001) *American Aeneas: Classical Origins of the American Self*. University of Tennessee Press, Knoxville.

Silk, M. E. &. Stern, J. P. (1981) *Nietzsche On Tragedy*. Cambridge University Press, Cambridge & New York.

Silk, M. S. (ed.) (1996) *Tragedy and the Tragic: Greek Theatre and Beyond*. Oxford University Press, Oxford.

Silk, M. S. (2005) Walter Headlam: Scholarship, Poetry, Poetics. In Stray, C. A. (ed), *The Owl of Minerva* (*Proceedings of the Cambridge Philological Society*) sup. vol. 28, 69–87.

Simon, B. (1973) Plato and Freud: The Mind in Conflict and the Mind in Dialogue. *Psychoanalytical Quarterly* 42, 91–122.

Simon, B. (1978) Mind and Madness in Ancient Greece: The Classical Roots of Modern Psychiatry. Cornell University Press, Ithaca & London.

Simpson, M. (forthcoming) The Curse of the Canon: Ola Rotimi's *The Gods Are Not to Blame*. In Hardwick & Gillespie (forthcoming).

Siraisi, N. G. (1990) *Medieval & Early Renaissance Medicine*. University of Chicago Press, Chicago & London.

Skard, S. (1980) *Classical Tradition in Norway: An Introduction with Bibliography*. Tromsø, Universitetsförlaget, Oslo, Bergen.

Skolimowska, A. (ed.) (2004) *Ioannes Dantiscus' Latin Letters, 1537*. Corpus Epistularum Ioannis Dantisci, ed. J. Axer with collaboration of A. Skolimowska, part 1: Ioannis Dantisci Epistulae Latinae, vol. 1. OBTA–PAU, Warsaw & Cracow.

Skovgaard-Petersen, K. (1991) Danish Neo-Latin Epic as Anti-Swedish Propaganda. In Dalzell, A., Fantazzi, C., & Schoeck, R. J. (eds.) (1991) *Acta Conventus Neo-Latini Torontonensis*. MRTS, Binghamton, 721–7.

Skovgaard-Petersen, K. (1993) The Literary Feud between Denmark and Sweden in the 16th and 17th Centuries and the Development of Danish Historical Scholarship. In Brink, J. R. & Gentrup, W. F. (eds.) (1993) *Renaissance Culture in Context, Theory and Practice*. Scolar Press, Aldershot, 114–20.

Skovgaard-Petersen, K. (2002) *Historiography at the Court of Christian IV (1588–1648): Studies in the Latin Histories of Denmark by Johannes Pontanus and Johannes Meursius.* Museum Tusculanum Press, Copenhagen.

Skovgaard-Petersen, K. & Zeeberg, P. (1997–) Running Bibliographies of Studies in Nordic Neo-Latin. *Symbolae Osloenses*, beginning from vol. 72.

Smit, B. (1974) *Bacchus in die Boland*. Perskor, Doornfontein.

Smith, G. A. (2004) *Epic Films*, 2nd ed. McFarland Publishers, Jefferson & London.

Smith, P. J. (1970) *The Tenth Muse: A Historical Study of the Opera Libretto*. Alfred A. Knopf, New York.

Smith, S. L. (1995) *The Power of Women: A Topos in Medieval Art and Literature*. University of Pennsylvania Press, Philadelphia.

Smith, W. (1850) Letter to John Murray, November 10, 1850. John Murray Archive, London.

Snell, B. (1966) Review of W. Jaeger *Paideia*. In *Gesammelte Schriften*. Vandenhoeck & Ruprecht, Göttingen, 32–54.

Snyder, J. M. (1997) Sappho in Attic Vase Painting. In Koloski-Ostrow, A. O. & Lyons, C. L. (eds.) *Naked Truths: Women, Sexuality, and Gender in Classical Art and Archaeology*. Routledge, London & New York.

Snyders, G. (1964) *La Pédagogie en France aux XVIIe et XVIIIe siècles*. Presses universitaires de France, Paris.

Solmsen, F. (1989) Classical Scholarship in Berlin Between the Wars. *Greek, Roman, and Byzantine Studies* 30, 117–40.

Solomon, B. M. (1985) *In the Company of Educated Women: A History of Women and Higher Education in America*. Yale University Press, New Haven.

Solomon, J. (1996) In the Wake of *Cleopatra*: The Ancient World in the Cinema since 1963. *Classical Journal* 91:2, 113–40.

Solomon, J. (2001) *The Ancient World in the Cinema*. Yale University Press, New Haven.

Solomon, J. (2005). Model of a Lesser God, review of Oliver Stone's *Alexander*. *Arion* 13.1, 149–60.

Solomon-Godeau, A. (1997) *Male Trouble: A Crisis in Representation*. Thames and Hudson, London & New York.

Solterer, H. (1995) *The Master and Minerva: Disputing Women in French Medieval Culture*. University of California Press, Berkeley, Los Angeles, & London.

Sontheimer, K. (1968) *Antidemokratisches Denken in der Weimarer Republik*. Nymphenburger Verlagshandlung, Munich.

Southern, R. W. (1995–2000) *Scholastic Humanism and the Unification of Europe*, 2 vols. Blackwell, Cambridge, Mass.

Soyinka, W. (1967) *Idanre and Other Poems*. Methuen, London.

Soyinka, W. (1972) *A Shuttle in the Crypt*. Rex Collings, London.

Soyinka, W. (1973) *The Bacchae of Euripides: A Communion Rite*. Methuen, London.

Soyinka, W. (1976) *Myth, Literature and the African World*. Cambridge University Press, Cambridge.

Soyinka, W. (1999) *The Burden of Memory: The Muse of Forgiveness*. Oxford University Press, Oxford.

Sparisci Lovicelli, L. (2003) Tradición clásica en Costa Rica: la retórica clásica en la oratoria costarricense. In Grammatico Amari, Arbea Gavilán, & Edwards (2003), 1:275–87.

Speer, A. (1975) *Spandauer Tagebücher*. Propyläen, Frankfurt.

Spelman, E. (1983) Aristotle and the Politicization of the Soul. In Harding, S. & Hintikka, M. (eds.) *Discovering Reality: Feminist Perspectives on Epistemology, Metaphysics, Methodology, and the Philosophy of Science*. D. Riedel, Boston, 17–30.

Spencer, D. (1996) Alexander the Great and the Popular (Anti-)hero. In Hardwick, L. & Ireland, S. (eds.) *The Reception of Classical Texts and Images: Selected Proceedings of the January Conference 1996 Held at The Open University, Milton Keynes*. Open University Press, Milton Keynes, 174–95.

Spencer, T. (1954) *Fair Greece Sad Relic: Literary Philhellenism from Shakespeare to Byron*. Weidenfeld and Nicolson, London.

Spotts, F. (2002) *Hitler and the Power of Aesthetics*. Overlook Press, Woodstock.

Springborg, P. (1991) Nætter på Island. In Alenius & al. (1991): 157–71.

Stack, F. (1985) *Pope and Horace: Studies in Imitation*. Cambridge University Press, Cambridge.

Stanford, W. B. (1963) *The Ulysses Theme*. Blackwell, Oxford.

Stanford, W. B. (1964) *The Ulysses Theme: Studies in the Adaptability of a Traditional Hero*, 2nd edn. Barnes and Noble, New York.

Stanford, W. B. (1976), *Ireland and the Classical Tradition*. Allen Figgis, Dublin and Rowman & Littlefield, Totowa.

Starobinski, J. (1999) Acheronta movebo. Nachdenken über das Motto der Traumdeutung. In *Hundert Jahre "Traumdeutung" von Sigmund Freud: Drei Essays*. Fischer, Frankfurt a.M., 7–34.

Stechow, W. (1968) *Rubens and the Classical Tradition*. Harvard University Press, Cambridge, Mass.

Stein, L. K. (2002) Three Paintings, a Double Lyre, Opera, and Eliche's Venus: Velázquez and Music at the Royal Court in Madrid. In Stratton-Pruitt, S. L. (ed.) *The Cambridge Companion to Velázquez*. Cambridge University Press, Cambridge, 170–93.

Steiner, G. (1984) *Antigones*. Clarendon Press, Oxford.

Steinmeyer, E. (forthcoming) Mark Fleishman et al: In the City of Paradise (1998). In Hardwick & Gillespie (forthcoming).

Stern, F. (1965) *The Politics of Cultural Despair: A Study in the Rise of the Germanic Ideology*. University of California, Berkeley.

Sternhell, Z. (1978) *La Droite révolutionnaire 1855–1914: les origines françaises du fascisme*. Éditions de Seuil, Paris.

Sterren van den, H. A. (1948) *De lotgevallen van Koning Oedipus*. Scheltema & Holkena, Amsterdam. French trans. PUF, Paris, 1976.

Stevens, M. (2005) Form Follows Fascism. *New York Times*, January 31, 2005.

Stevenson, R. A. M. (1899) *Velasquez*. George Bell & Sons, London.

Stinger, C. L. (1985) *The Renaissance in Rome*. Indiana University Press, Bloomington.

Stok, F. (1996) Follia e malattie mentali nella medicina dell'età romana. In Haase, W. (ed.) *Aufstieg und Niedergang der römischen Welt: Geschichte und Kultur Roms im Spiegel der neueren Forschung*. W. de Gruyter, Berlin & New York, part 2, vol. 37.3, 2281–410.

Stok, F. (1997) *Natura corporis*. Costituzioni e temperamenti in Celso e nella cultura dell'età imperiale. In Sconocchia, S. & Toneatto, L. (eds.) *Lingue tecniche del greco e del latini II*. Pàtron, Bologna, 151–70.

Stok, F. (forthcoming) Paolo Zacchia e il lessico della psicopatologia. In Schnur (forthcoming).

Stone, M. (1997) The State as Patron: Making Official Culture in Fascist Italy. In Affron & Antliff (1997): 205–38.

Stone, M. (1999). A Flexible Rome: Fascism and the Cult of *Romanità*. In Edwards (1999): 205–20.

Stoneman, R. (1994) *Legends of Alexander*. Dent, London.

Stratton-Pruitt, Suzanne L. (ed.) (2003) *Velázquez's Las Meninas*. Masterpieces of Western Painting. Cambridge University Press, Cambridge.

Strauss, W. A. (1971) *Descent and Return: The Orphic Theme in Modern Literature*. Harvard University Press, Cambridge, Mass.

Stray, C. A. (1992) *The Living Word. W. H. D. Rouse and the Crisis of Classics in Edwardian England*. Bristol Classical Press / Duckworth, Bristol & London.

Stray, C. A. (1994) The Smell of Latin Grammar: Contrary Imaginings in English Classrooms. *Bulletin of the John Rylands Library* 76, 201–22.

Stray, C. A. (1996) Primers, Publishing and Politics: The Classical Textbooks of Benjamin Hall Kennedy. *Papers of the Bibliographical Society of America* 90, 451–74.

Stray, C. A. (1998) *Classics Transformed: Schools, Universities, and Society in England 1830–1960*. Oxford University Press, Oxford.

Stray, C. A. (2001) Curriculum and Style in the Collegiate University: Classics in Nineteenth-Century Oxbridge. *History of Universities* 16, 183–218.

Stray, C. A. (2002a) A Parochial Anomaly? The Classical Tripos 1822–1900. In Smith, J. & Stray, C. (eds.) *Teaching and Learning in 19th-Century Cambridge*. Boydell Press, Woodbridge, 31–44.

Stray, C. A. (2002b) A Pedagogic Palace: The Feinaiglian Institution and Its Textbooks. *Long Room* (Dublin) 47, 14–25.

Stray, C. A. (2005) Oral to Written Examinations: Cambridge, Oxford and Dublin 1700–1914. *History of Universities* 20:2, 76–130.

Stray, C. A. (forthcoming) Paper Wraps Stone: The Beginnings of Educational Lithography. *Journal of the Printing Historical Society* n.s. 9.

Sullivan, J. P. (1964) *Ezra Pound and Sextus Propertius*. University of Texas Press, Austin.

Sullivan, J. P. (ed.) (1974) *Arethusa* 7.1, special issue on *Psychoanalysis and the Classics*.

Sulloway, F. J. (1979) *Freud, Biologist of the Mind*. Burnett Books, London.

Susmel, E. & D. (eds.) (1951–81) *Opera omnia di Benito Mussolini*, 44 vols. La Fenice, Florence.

Sutherland, E. (1967) *Edufa*. Longman, London.

Swift, J. (1958) *A Tale of a Tub [and] The Battle of the Books*, ed. A. Guthkelch, 2nd edn. Clarendon Press, Oxford.

Syme, R. (1939) *The Roman Revolution*. Clarendon, Oxford.

Sysyn, F. E. (1986) *Between Poland and the Ukraine: The Dilemma of Adam Kysil*. Harvard University Press, Cambridge, Mass.

Szörenyi, L. (1999) *Arcades ambo: relazioni italo-ungheresi e cultura neo-latina*. Rubettino Editore, Soveria Mannelli.

Szücs, J. (1983) The Three Historical Regions of Europe. *Acta Historica Academiae Scientiarum Hungaricae* 29, 131–84.

Szücs, J. (1985) *Les trois Europes*. L'Harmattan, Paris.

Taine, H. (1957) *Taine's Notes on England*, trans. E. Hyams. Thames & Hudson, London.

Talib, I. S. (2002) *The Language of Postcolonial Literatures*. Routledge, London.

Tanner, M. (1993) *The Last Descendant of Aeneas: The Hapsburgs and the Mythic Image of the Emperor*. Yale University Press, New Haven & London.

Taplin, O. (1977) *The Stagecraft of Aeschylus*. Oxford University Press, Oxford.

Taplin, O. (1978) *Greek Tragedy in Action*. Methuen, London.

Taplin, O. (2002) Contemporary Poetry and Classics. In Wiseman (2002): 1–19.

Taruskin, R. (1992) Igor Stravinsky. In *The New Grove Dictionary of Opera*, ed. S. Sadie. Macmillan, London, 4:575–80.

Taylor, A.-M. (2001) *Young Charles Sumner and the Legacy of the American Enlightenment, 1811–1851*. University of Massachusetts Press, Amherst.

Taylor, B. & Van der Will, W. (eds.) (1991) *The Nazification of Art: Art, Design, Music, Architecture and Film in the Third Reich*. Winchester School of Art Press, Winchester.

Tazbir, J. (2001) *La culture polonaise des XVIe et XVIIe siècles dans le contexte européen*. Unione Internazionale degli Istituti di Archeologia, Storia e Storia dell'Arte, Rome.

Temkin, O. (1973) *Galenism: Rise and Decline of a Medical Philosophy*. Cornell University Press, Ithaca & London.

Tengström, E. (1973) *Latinet i Sverige. Om bruket av latin bland klerker och scholares, diplomater och poeter, lärdomsfolk och vältalere*. Bonniers Förlag, Lund.

Terni, C. (1983) *Música práctica de Bartolomé Ramos de Pareja*. Joyas Bibliográficas, Madrid.

Terras, V. (1966) Classical Motifs in the Poetry of Osip Mandel'štam'. *Slavic and East European Journal* 10:3, 251–67.

The Poem of the Cid: A New Critical Edition of the Spanish Text (1975), intro. and notes Ian Michael, trans. Rita Hamilton and Janet Perry. Manchester University Press, Manchester.

Thirlwall, C. (1845–52) *The History of Greece* (1835–44), 2nd edn., 8 vols. Longman, London.

Thisted, K. (2001) The Impact of Writing on Stories Collected from Nineteenth-Century Inuit Traditions. In Helldén, J. et al. (eds.) *Inclinate Aurem: Oral Perspectives on Early European Verbal Culture*. Odense University Press, Odense, 167–210.

Thomas, R. (2000) Goebbels' Georgics. *Classical Bulletin* 76, 157–68.

Thomas, R. (2001a) *Virgil and the Augustan Reception*. Cambridge University Press, Cambridge.

Thomas, R. (2001b) The Georgics of Resistance: From Virgil to Heaney. *Vergilius* 47, 117–47.

Thompson, C. (1985) *El poeta y el místico*. Trad. Castellana, El Escorial.

Thompson, D. A. W. (1864) *Day-dreams of a Schoolmaster*. A. & C. Black, Edinburgh.

Thompson, L. (1999) *The Wandering Womb: A Cultural History of Outrageous Beliefs about Women*. Prometheus Books, Amherst, N.Y.

Thomson, J. A. K. (1948) *The Classical Background of English Literature*. G. Allen & Unwin, London.

Thomson J. A. K. (1951) *Classical Influences on English Poetry*. Allen & Unwin, London.

Thomson J. A. K. (1956) *Classical Influences on English Prose*. G. Allen & Unwin, London.

Thorndike, S. (1936) Gilbert Murray and Some Actors. In Fisher, H. A. L. et al. (eds.) *Essays in Honour of Gilbert Murray*. George Allen & Unwin, London, 69–77.

Ticknor, G. (1876) *Life, Letters and Journals of George Ticknor*. J. R. Osgood, Boston.

Timpanaro, S. (1976) *The Freudian Slip: Psychoanalysis and Textual Criticism*. New Left Books, London.

Timpanaro, S. (1984) Freud's "Roman Phobia." *New Left Review* 147 (September–October), 4–31.

Todd R. B. (ed.) (2004) *Dictionary of British Classicists*, 3 vols. Thoemmes Continuum, Bristol.

Todorov, T. (1984) *The Conquest of America: The Question of the Other*. Harper and Row, New York.

Toebes, J. (2001) Virtue and Civilisation – Antiquity in Nineteenth-century Dutch School Books. *Tijdschrift voor geschiedenis* 114:2, 515–37.

Tomlinson, C. (1992) *Eros English'd: Classical Erotic Poetry in Translation from Golding to Hardy*. Bristol Classical Press, London.

Tomlinson, C. (2003) *Metamorphoses: Poetry and Translation*. Carcanet, Manchester.

Too, Y. L. (ed.) (2001) *Education in Greek and Roman Antiquity*. E. J. Brill, Leiden.

Tourney, G. (1965) Freud and the Greeks. A Study on the Influence of Classical Greek Mythology and Philosophy upon the Development of Freudian Thought. *Journal of the History of Behavioural Sciences* 1, 67–85.

Tournoy, G. (1998) "Ad ultimas inscitiae lineas imus". Justus Lipsius and Isaac Casaubon in the Changing World of Classical Scholarship. *Bulletin van het Belgisch Historisch Instituut te Rome* 68, 191–208. (Also in Laureys, M. et al. [1998] *The World of Justus Lipsius: A Contribution towards His Intellectual Biography*. . . . Institut historique belge de Rome, Rome.)

Tournoy, G. (2001) Gli umanisti italiani nell'Università di Lovanio nel Quattrocento. In Secchi Tarugi Rotondi, L. (ed.) *Rapporti e scambi tra umanesimo italiano ed umanesimo europeo*. Nuovi Orizzonti, Milan, 39–50.

Trapp, J. B. (1971) The Conformity of Greek and the Vernacular. In Bolgar, R. R. (ed.) *Classical Influences on European Culture AD 500–1500*. Cambridge University Press, Cambridge, 239–44.

Traverso, P. (2000) *"Psyche è una parola greca. . . ."* Compagnia dei Librai, Genoa. German trans.: Psyche ist ein griechisches Wort. . . . In *Rezeption und Wirkung der Antike im Werk von Sigmund Freud*. Suhrkamp, Franhfurt a.M., 2003.

Trevelyan, H. (1941) *Goethe and the Greeks*. Cambridge University Press, Cambridge.

Treves, P. (1962) *L'idea di Roma e la cultura italiana del secolo XIX*. R. Ricciardi, Milan & Naples.

Trillitzsch, W. (1981) *Der deutsche Renaissancehumanismus: Abriß und Auswahl*. Reclams Universal-Bibliothek 900. Reclam, Leipzig.

Trilse, C. (1979) *Antike und Theater heute: Betrachtungen über Mythologie und Realismus, Tradition und Gegenwart, Funktion und Methode, Stücke und Inszenierungen*, 2nd edn. Literatur und Gesellschaft. Akademie-Verlag, Berlin.

Trinkaus, C. (1995) *In Our Image and Likeness: Humanity and Divinity in Italian Humanist Thought*, 2 vols. University of Notre Dame Press, Notre Dame. Rpt. of University of Chicago, Chicago, 1970 edn.

Trivedi, H. & Mukherjee, M. (eds.) (1996) *Interrogating Post-colonialism: Theory, Text and Context*. Indian Institute of Advanced Study, Shimla.

Trumpener, K. (1997) *Bardic Nationalism: The Romantic Novel and the British Empire*. Princeton University Press, Princeton.

Turner, F. (1981) *The Greek Heritage in Victorian Britain*. Yale University Press, New Haven and London.

Twiddy, I. (2006) Seamus Heaney's Versions of Pastoral. *Essays in Criticism* 56:1, 50–71.

Ulčinaitė, E. (1996) *Baroque Literature in Lithuania*. Baltos Lankos, Vilnius.

Ulčinaitė, E. (2003) Classical Education and Specific Features of Lithuanian Literature in the Sixteenth and Seventeenth Centuries. In Merisalo & Sarasti-Wilenius (2003): 208–17.

Ulčinaitė, E. & Jovaišas, A. (2003) *Lietuvių; literatūros istorija XIII–XVIII amžiai*. Lietuvių; literatūros ir tautosakos institutas, Vilnius.

Ullman, B. L. (1963) *Ancient Writing and Its Influence*. Our Debt to Greece and Rome Series. Cooper Square Publishers, New York. Rpt. of Longmans, Green, New York, 1932 edn.

Ullman, B. L. (1973) Renaissance: The Word and the Underlying Concept. In *Studies in the Italian Renaissance*, 2nd. edn. Storia e Letteratura, Raccolta di Studi e Testi 51. Edizioni di Storia e Letteratura, Rome, 11–25.

Upton, C.-A. (ed.) (2000), *Moving Target: Theatre Translation and Cultural Relocation*. St. Jerome Publishing, Manchester & Northampton.

Urzidil, J. (1964) *Amerika und die Antike*. Artemis, Zurich.

Valkonen, M. (1994) *The Golden Age: Finnish Art 1850–1907*, trans. M. Wynne-Ellis Porvoo. Werner Söderström Osakeyhtiö, Helsinki & Juva.

Vallicrosa, J. M. M. (1977) Latinismos semánticos en la poesía de Fray Luis de León. In *Prosistas y poetas de ayer y hoy*. Gredos, Madrid, 110–28.

Van Anrooij, W. (1997) *De Negen Besten in de Nederlanden (1300–1700)*. Amsterdam University Press, Amsterdam.

Van Wyk Louw, N. P. (1956) *Germanicus*. Tafelberg-Uitgewers, Cape Town.

Van Wyk Louw, N. P. (1957) *Asterion: Libretto vir 'n radiofoniese opera*. Human and Rousseau, Cape Town.

Van Wyk Louw, N. P. (1962) *Tristia en ander verse, voorspele en vlugte, 1950–1957*. Human and Rousseau, Cape Town.

Vance, N. (1997) *The Victorians and Ancient Rome*. Blackwell, Oxford.

Vance, W. L. (1989) *America's Rome*. Yale University Press, New Haven.

Van der Paardt, R. (1982) *Antieke motieven in de moderne Nederlandse letterkunde: een eigentijdse Odyssee*. Arbeiderspers / Wetenshappelijke Uitgeverij, Amsterdam.

Van der Paardt, R. (1991) *Mythe en metamorfose: antieke motieven in de moderne literatuur*. Arbeiderspers / Wetenshappelijke Uitgeverij, Amsterdam.

Vanita, R. (1996) *Sappho and the Virgin Mary: Same-Sex Love and the English Literary Imagination*. Columbia University Press, New York.

Van Keuren, F. (ed.) (1998) *Myth, Sexuality and Power: Images of Jupiter in Western Art*. Art and Archaeology Publications, Collège, Erasme, Louvain-La-Neuve.

Van Zyl Smit, B. (2003) The Reception of Greek Tragedy in South Africa. *Eirene* 39, 234–53.

Velásquez Guttiérez, M. E. (1998) *Juan Correa*. Círculo de Arte, Mexico City.

Velghe, D. (1995) Domien Cracco: de ratione docendi. In *Gezelliana*. Nederlandsche Boekhandel, Antwerpen, 78–97.

Venturi, R. (1966) *Complexity and Contradiction in Architecture*. Museum of Modern Art, New York.

Vernant, J. P. (1988) Oedipus Without the Complex. In Vernant, J. P. & Vidal-Naquet, P. *Myth and Tragedy in Ancient Greece*. Zone Books, New York, 85–112.

Vickery, J. B. (1973) *The Literary Impact of The Golden Bough*. Princeton University Press, Princeton.

Vico, G. B. (2001) *New Science*, trans. D. Marsh, 2nd edn. Penguin Books, London.

Vidal, J. L. (1988) [Virgilio en Spagna] Letteratura Catalana. In della Corte (1988): 4:972a–75a.

Villanueva, F. M. (2004) *El concepto cultural alfonsí*, revised and enlarged edn. Bellaterra, Barcelona.

Villard, P. (1972) Antiquité et *Weltanschauung* hitlérienne. *Revue d'histoire de la deux-ième guerre mondiale* 22, 1–18.

Villena, E. de (1979) *La primera versión castellana de "La Eneida" de Virgilio*, ed. R. Santiago Lacuesta. Boletín de la Real Academia Española, Anejo XXXVIII, Madrid.

Villena, E. de (1989) Traducción y glosas de la *Eneida*, ed. Pedro M. Catedra, 3 vols. Biblioteca española del siglo XV, Salamanca.

Virgil, P. (1555) *Los doze libros de la Eneida*, trans. Gregorio Hernández de Velasco. Juan de Ayala, Toledo.

Virgil, P. (1600) *Las obras*, trans. Diego López. Francisco Fernandez e Cordova, Valladolid.

Visser, R. (1992) Fascist Doctrine and the Cult of the Romanità. *Journal of Contemporary History* 27, 5–23.

Visser, R. (2001) Da Atene a Roma, da Roma a Berlino. L'Istituto di Studi Romani, il culto fascista della romanità e la "difesa dell'umanesimo" di Giuseppe Bottai (1936–1943). In Näf (2001): 111–24.

Vives Coll, A. (1959) *Luciano de Samosata en España (1500–1700)*. Sever-Cuesta, Valladolid.

Vocht, H. de (1951–5) *History of the Foundation and the Rise of the Collegium Trilingue Lovaniense*, 4 vols. Humanistica Lovaniensia 10–13. Librairie universitaire, Louvain.

Völher, M. & Seidensticker, B. (eds.) (2005) *Mythenkorrekturen. Zu einer paradoxalen Form der Mythenrezeption*. De Gruyter, Berlin & New York.

Vorwahl, H. (1942) Politischer und gegenwärtiger Humanismus. *Die alten Sprachen* 7, 112–16.

Vos, M. de (1980) *L'egittomania in pitture e mosaici romano-campani della prima età imperiale*. E. J. Brill, Leiden.

Vratovič, V. (1993) *Croatian Latinity and the Mediterranean Constant*. Most / Bridge, Zagreb & Dubrovnik.

Waddy, P. (1990) *Seventeenth-Century Roman Palaces: Use and the Art of the Plan*. Massachusetts Institute Press, Cambridge, Mass.

Walcott, D. (1986) *Collected Poems 1948–1984*. Farrar, Straus, and Giroux, New York.

Walcott, D. (1988) *The Arkansas Testament*. Faber, London.

Walcott, D. (1990) *Omeros*. Faber, London.

Walcott, D. (1993a) *The Odyssey: A Stage Version*. Farrar, Straus, and Giroux, London.

Walcott, D. (1993b) *The Antilles: Fragments of Epic Memory. The Nobel Lecture*. Farrar, Straus, and Giroux, New York.

Walcott, D. (1998) *What the Twilight Says*. Farrar, Straus, and Giroux, London.

Walder, D. (1993), Introduction to Fugard, A. *Township Plays*. Oxford University Press, Oxford, ix–xxxiv.

Walicki, A. (1989) *The Enlightenment and the Birth of Modern Nationhood: Polish Political Thought From the "Noble Republicanism" to Tadeusz Kościuszko*. University of Notre Dame Press, Notre Dame.

Walicki, A. (1994) *Poland between East and West: The Controversies over Self-Definition and Modernization in Partitioned Poland*. Ukrainian Research Institute–Harvard University, Cambridge, Mass.

Walker, D. P. (1972) *The Ancient Theology: Studies in Christian Platonism from the Fifteenth to the Eighteenth Century*. Cornell University Press, Ithaca.

Walsh, S. (1993) *Stravinsky: Oedipus Rex*. Cambridge University Press, Cambridge.

Walton, J. M. (1987) *Living Greek Theatre: A Handbook of Classical Performance and Modern Production*. Greenwood Press, New York.

Walton, J. M. (2002), Hit or Myth: The Greeks and Irish Drama. In McDonald & Walton (2002): 3–36.

Walton, J. M. (forthcoming) *Found in Translation: Greek Drama in English.* Cambridge University Press, Cambridge.

Wandycz, P. S. (2001) *The Price of Freedom: A History of East Central Europe from the Middle Ages to the Present,* 2nd edn. Routledge, London & New York.

Waquet, F. (2001) *Latin or the Empire of a Sign,* trans. J. Howe. Verso, London & New York.

Waswo, R. (1995) Our Ancestors, the Trojans: Inventing Cultural Identity in the Middle Ages. *Exemplaria* 7, 269–90.

Waszink, J. H. (1989) Netherlands. In *La filologia greca e latina nel secolo XX. Atti del Convegno Internazionale, Roma ... 17–21 settembre 1984,* 3 vols. Giardini, Pisa, 1:37–47.

Webb, T. (1993) Romantic Hellenism. In Curran, S. (ed.) *The Cambridge Companion to British Romanticism.* Cambridge University Press, Cambridge, 177–95.

Weber, E. (1964) *Varieties of Fascism: Doctrines of Revolution in the Twentieth Century.* Princeton University Press, Princeton.

Weinberg, B. (1961) *A History of Literary Criticism in the Italian Renaissance,* 2 vols. Chicago, University of Chicago Press, 1961.

Weinbrot, H. D. (1969) *The Formal Strain: Studies in Augustan Imitation and Satire.* University of Chicago Press, Chicago.

Weinbrot, H. D. (1978) *Augustus Caesar in "Augustan" England: The Decline of a Classical Norm.* Princeton University Press, Princeton.

Weiss, R. (1973) *The Renaissance Discovery of Classical Antiquity,* 2nd edn. Basil Blackwell, Oxford. Rpt. of 1973 edn.

Welch, R. (1993) *Changing States: Transformations in Modern Irish Writing.* Routledge, London.

Wellek, R. (1963) The Concept of Romanticism in Literary History. In *Concepts in Criticism.* Yale University Press, New Haven, 128–98.

West, A. F. (1917) *Value of the Classics.* Princeton University Press, Princeton.

West, M. L. (1997), *The East Face of Helicon: West Asiatic Elements in Greek Poetry and Myth.* Oxford University Press, Oxford.

Wetmore, K. J. Jr. (2002) *The Athenian Sun in an African Sky: Modern African Adaptations of Classical Greek Tragedy.* McFarland, Jefferson & London.

Wetmore, K. J. Jr. (2003), *Black Dionysus: Greek Tragedy and African American Theatre.* McFarland, Jefferson & London.

Wheeler, M. (1979) *The Art of Allusion.* Macmillan, London.

Whewell, W. (1838) *On the Principles of English University Education.* J. W. Parker, London.

White, D. O. (1992) Werner Jaeger's "Third Humanism" and the Crisis of Conservative Cultural Politics in Weimar Germany. In Calder (1992): 267–88.

White, N. (2002) *Individual and Conflict in Greek Ethics.* Oxford University Press, Oxford.

Whitfield, J. H. (1971) Momus and the Nature of Humanism. In Bolgar, R. R. (ed.) *Classical Influences on European Culture 1500–1900.* Cambridge University Press, Cambridge, 177–81.

Wiesen, D. S. (1976) The Contribution of Antiquity to American Racial Thought. In Eadie, J. W. (ed.) *Classical Traditions in Early America.* Center for the Coordination of Ancient and Modern Studies, University of Michigan, Ann Arbor, 191–212.

Wiesen, D. S. (1980) Herodotus and the Modern Debate over Race and Slavery. *Ancient World* 3:1, 3–16.

Wiles, D. (2000) *Greek Theatre Performance: An Introduction*. Cambridge University Press, Cambridge.

Wiles, D. (2003) *A Short History of Western Performance Space*. Cambridge University Press, Cambridge.

Wiles, D. (2004), The Use of Masks in Modern Performances of Greek Drama. In Hall, Macintosh, & Wrigley (2004): 245–64.

Wilkins, E. H. (1961) *Life of Petrarch*. University of Chicago Press, Chicago.

Will, F. (1966) Psychoanalysis and the Study of Ancient Greek Literature. In *Literature Inside Out: Ten Speculative Essays*. Press of Western Reserve University, Cleveland, 39–53.

Willans, G. & Searle, R. (1958) *Down with Skool!* Max Parrish, London.

Williams, R. (2005) *Why Study the Past? The Quest for the Historical Church*. Darton, Longman and Todd, London.

Williams, T. (2001) Truth and Representation: The Confrontation of History and Mythology in *Omeros*. *Callaloo* 24:1, 276–86.

Wills, G. (1984) *Cincinnatus: George Washington and the Enlightenment; Images of Power in Early America*. Doubleday, Garden City.

Wills, G. (1992) *Lincoln at Gettysburg: The Words That Remade America*. Simon and Schuster, New York.

Wilmer, S. (1999) Seamus Heaney and the Tragedy of Stasis. In Patsalidis and Sakellaridou (1999): 221–31.

Wilmer, S. (2003) Irish Medeas: Revenge or Redemption? (an Irish Solution to an International Problem). *Eirene* 39, 254–63.

Wilmer, S. (forthcoming) Finding a Post-colonial Voice for Antigone: Seamus Heaney's Burial at Thebes. In Hardwick & Gillespie (forthcoming).

Wilson, N. (1992) *From Byzantium to Italy: Greek Studies in the Italian Renaissance*. Johns Hopkins University Press, Baltimore.

Wiltshire, S. F. (1992) *Greece, Rome and the Bill of Rights*. University of Oklahoma Press, Norman.

Winckelmann, J. (1987) *Reflections on the Imitation of Greek Works in Painting and Sculpture*, trans. E. Heyer and R. Norton. Open Court, La Salle.

Winkler, M. (1985) Classical Mythology and the Western Film. *Comparative Literature Studies* 22, 516–40.

Winkler, M. (1991) *Classics and Cinema*. Bucknell University Press, Lewisburg.

Winkler, M. (2001a) *Classical Myth and Culture in the Cinema*. Oxford University Press, New York.

Winkler, M. (2001b) The Roman Empire in Cinema after 1945. In Joshel, S., Malamud, M., & McGuire, D. (eds.) *Imperial Projections: Ancient Rome in Modern Popular Culture*. Johns Hopkins University Press, Baltimore, 50–74.

Winkler, M. (ed.) (2004) *Gladiator: Film and History*. Blackwell, Oxford.

Winterer, C. (2002) *The Culture of Classicism: Ancient Greece and Rome in American Intellectual Life 1780–1910*. Johns Hopkins University Press, Baltimore.

Winterstein, A. (1925) *Der Ursprung der Tragödie: Ein psychoanalytischer Beitrag zur Geschichte des griechischen Theaters*. Inst. Psychoan. Verlag, Vienna.

Wise, J. (1905). *The Law of Nature in Government*. Old South Leaflets, General Series, vol. 7, no. 165. Directors of Old South Work, Boston.

Wise, J. (1956) A Vindication of the Government of New-England Churches (1717). In Miller, P. (ed.) *The American Puritans: Their Prose and Poetry.* Columbia University Press, New York, 121–37.

Wiseman, T. P. (ed.) (2002) *Classics in Progress; Essays on Ancient Greece and Rome.* Oxford University Press, Oxford.

Wish, H. (1949) Aristotle, Plato, and the Mason-Dixon Line. *Journal of the History of Ideas* 10, 254–66.

Witke, C. (1990) Rome as "Region of Difference" in the Poetry of Hildebert of Lavardin. In Bernardo & Levin (1990): 403–11.

Witt, C. (1998) Form, Normativity and Gender in Aristotle: A Feminist Perspective. In Freeland, C. (ed.) *Feminist Interpretations of Aristotle.* Pennsylvania State University Press, University Park, 118–37.

Witt, R. G. (2000) *"In the Footsteps of the Ancients": The Origins of Humanism from Lovato to Bruni.* E. J. Brill, Leiden.

Wittkower, R. (1999) *Art and Architecture in Italy 1600–1750*, vol. 1: *Early Baroque*, vol. 2: *High Baroque*, rev. J. Connors and J. Montagu. Pelican History of Art. Yale University Press, New Haven.

Wohlleben, J. (1990) *Die Sonne Homers: Zehn Kapitel deutscher Homer-Begeisterung. Von Winckelmann bis Schliemann.* Kleine Vandenhoeck-Reihe 1554. Vandenhoeck & Ruprecht, Göttingen.

Wolf, F. A. (1985) *Prolegomena to Homer 1795*, ed. and trans. A. Grafton, G. W. Most, & J. E. G. Zetzel. Princeton University Press, Princeton.

Wolman, B. (1965) The Antigone Principle. *American Imago* 22, 186–210.

Womersley, D. (ed.) (2000) *A Companion to Literature from Milton to Blake.* Blackwell, Oxford, 76–93.

Wood, C. (1983) *Olympian Dreamers: Victorian Classical Painting 1860–1914.* Constable, London.

Wood, G. S. (1969) *The Creation of the American Republic 1776–1787.* University of North Carolina Press, Chapel Hill.

Wood, R. (1775) *An Essay on the Original Genius and Writings of Homer: with a Comparative View of the Ancient and Present State of the Troade.* Printed by H. Hughes for T. Payne and P. Elmsley, London.

Woodward, C. (2001) *In Ruins.* Chatto and Windus, London.

Wordsworth, W. (1979) *The Prelude 1799, 1805, 1850*, ed. J. Wordsworth, M. H. Abrams, & S. Gill. W. W. Norton, New York.

Wordsworth, W. (1983) *Poems, in Two Volumes, and Other Poems, 1800–1807*, ed. J. Curtis. Cornell University Press, Ithaca.

Wordsworth, W. (1989) *Shorter Poems, 1807–1820*, ed. C. H. Ketcham. Cornell University Press, Ithaca.

Wordsworth, W. (1992) *Lyrical Ballads, and Other Poems*, eds. J. Butler and K. Green. Cornell University Press, Ithaca.

Wordsworth, W. (1998) *Translations of Chaucer and Virgil*, ed. B. Graver. Cornell University Press, Ithaca.

Wotton, W. (1694) *Reflections upon Ancient and Modern Learning.* J. Leake for Peter Buck, London.

Wright, W. H. (1915) *What Nietzsche Taught.* B. W. Huebsch, New York.

Wyke, M. (1997a) Herculean Muscle! The Classicizing Rhetoric of Bodybuilding. *Arion* 4:3, 51–79.

Wyke, M. (1997b) *Projecting the Past: Ancient Rome, Cinema, and History.* Routledge, London & New York.

Wyke, M. (1998) Playing Roman Soldiers: The Martyred Body, Derek Jarman's *Sebastiane*, and the Representation of Male Homosexuality. In Wyke, M. (ed.) *Parchments of Gender: Deciphering the Bodies of Antiquity.* Clarendon Press, Oxford, 243–66.

Wyke, M. (1999a) Screening Ancient Rome in the New Italy. In Edwards (1999): 88–204.

Wyke, M. (1999b) Sawdust Caesar: Mussolini, Julius Caesar, and the Drama of Dictatorship. In Wyke & Biddiss (1999): 167–86.

Wyke, M. (2002) *The Roman Mistress: Ancient and Modern Representations.* Oxford University Press, Oxford.

Wyke, M. & Biddiss, M. (eds.) (1999) *The Uses and Abuses of Antiquity.* Peter Lang, Bern.

Yakovenko (Jakovenko), N. (1995) Szlachcic łaciński czy latynizujący (uwagi o polsko-języcznym poemacie z Wołynia z 1585 roku). In *Między Slavia Latina i Slavia Orthodoxa.* OBTA, Warsaw, 55–9.

[Yale Report] (1829) Original Papers in Relation to a Course of Liberal Education. *American Journal of Science and Arts* 15 (1829): 297–351.

Yarnall, J. (1994) *Transformations of Circe: The History of an Enchantress.* University of Illinois Press, Urbana & Chicago.

Yarrow, P. J. (1967) *A Literary History of France: The Seventeenth Century.* Ernest Benn, London.

Yates, F. A. (1977) *Astraea: The Imperial Theme in the Sixteenth Century.* Penguin Books, Harmondsworth.

Young, J. (1997) *Heidegger, Philosophy, Nazism.* Cambridge University Press, Cambridge.

Young, J. (2002) *Heidegger's Later Philosophy.* Cambridge University Press, Cambridge.

Yourcenar, M. (1980) *With Open Eyes,* trans. A. Goldhammer. Beacon Press, Boston.

Yourcenar, M. (1985) *The Dark Brain of Piranesi and Other Essays,* trans. R. Howard. Farrar, Straus, and Giroux, New York.

Yourgrau, T. (1993) *The Song of Jacob Zulu.* Arcade, New York.

Zavala, S. (1965) *Recuerdo de Vasco de Quiroga.* Porrúa, Mexico City.

Zeeberg, P. (1994) *Tycho Brahes "Urania Titani" – et digt om Sophie Brahe.* Museum Tusculanum Press, Copenhagen.

Zeitler, R. (1990) *Skandinavische Kunst um 1900.* E. A. Seemann Verlag, Leipzig.

Zimmermann, A. & Vuillemin-Diem, G. (eds.) (1974) *Antiqui und Moderni: Traditionsbewusstsein und Fortschrittsbewusstsein im späten Mittelalter.* Miscellanea mediaevalia 9. W. de Gruyter, Berlin & New York.

Zimunya, M. B. (1982a) *Thought Tracks.* Longman, Harlow.

Zimunya, M. B. (1982b) *Kingfisher, Jikinya and Other Poems.* Longman Zimbabwe, Harare.

Zimunya, M. B. (1985) *Country Dawns and City Lights,* Longman Zimbabwe, Harare.

Ziolkowski, J. M. (1985) *Alan of Lille's Grammar of Sex: The Meaning of Grammar to a Twelfth-Century Intellectual.* Speculum Anniversary Monographs 10. Medieval Academy of America, Boston.

Ziolkowski, J. M. (1991) Cultural Diglossia and the Nature of Medieval Latin Literature. In Harris, J. (ed.) *The Ballad and Oral Literature.* Harvard English Studies 16. Harvard University Press, Cambridge, Mass., 193–213.

Ziolkowski, J. M. (1992) A Fairy Tale from before Fairy Tales: Egbert of Liège's "De puella a lupellis servata" and the Medieval Background of "Little Red Riding Hood." *Speculum* 67, 549–75.

Ziolkowski, J. M. (1993) *Talking Animals: Medieval Latin Beast Poetry 750–1150.* University of Pennsylvania Press, Philadelphia.

Ziolkowski, J. M. (2001) The Highest Form of Compliment: *Imitatio* in Medieval Latin Culture. In Marenbon, J. (ed.) *Poetry and Philosophy in the Middle Ages.* Mitellatei-nische Studien und Texte 29. E. J. Brill, Leiden, 293–307.

Ziolkowski, J. M. (forthcoming a). *Fairy Tales from Before Fairy Tales: The Medieval Latin Past of Wonderful Lies.* University of Michigan Press, Ann Arbor.

Ziolkowski, J. M. (forthcoming b) *Nota Bene: Reading Classics and Writing Songs in the Early Middle Ages.* Brepols, Turnhout.

Ziolkowski, T. (1993) *Virgil and the Moderns.* Princeton University Press, Princeton.

Ziolkowski, T. (2005) *Ovid and the Moderns.* Cornell University Press, Ithaca.

Index